FreeBSD Handbook

FreeBSD Handbook

Revision: 51391
2018-01-18 14:30:59 by mat.
Copyright © 1995, 1996, 1997, 1998, 1999, 2000, 2001, 2002, 2003, 2004, 2005, 2006, 2007, 2008, 2009, 2010, 2011, 2012, 2013, 2014, 2015, 2016, 2017 The FreeBSD Documentation Project

Abstract

Welcome to FreeBSD! This handbook covers the installation and day to day use of *FreeBSD 11.1-RELEASE* and *FreeBSD 10.4-RELEASE*. This book is the result of ongoing work by many individuals. Some sections might be outdated. Those interested in helping to update and expand this document should send email to the FreeBSD documentation project mailing list.

The latest version of this book is available from the FreeBSD web site. Previous versions can be obtained from https://docs.FreeBSD.org/doc/ . The book can be downloaded in a variety of formats and compression options from the FreeBSD FTP server or one of the numerous mirror sites. Printed copies can be purchased at the FreeBSD Mall. Searches can be performed on the handbook and other documents on the search page.

Table of Contents

List of Figures

List of Tables

List of Examples

Preface

Intended Audience

The FreeBSD newcomer will find that the first section of this book guides the user through the FreeBSD installation process and gently introduces the concepts and conventions that underpin UNIX®. Working through this section requires little more than the desire to explore, and the ability to take on board new concepts as they are introduced.

Once you have traveled this far, the second, far larger, section of the Handbook is a comprehensive reference to all manner of topics of interest to FreeBSD system administrators. Some of these chapters may recommend that you do some prior reading, and this is noted in the synopsis at the beginning of each chapter.

For a list of additional sources of information, please see Appendix B, *Bibliography*.

Changes from the Third Edition

The current online version of the Handbook represents the cumulative effort of many hundreds of contributors over the past 10 years. The following are some of the significant changes since the two volume third edition was published in 2004:

- Chapter 24, *DTrace* has been added with information about the powerful DTrace performance analysis tool.

- Chapter 20, *Other File Systems* has been added with information about non-native file systems in FreeBSD, such as ZFS from Sun™.

- Chapter 16, *Security Event Auditing* has been added to cover the new auditing capabilities in FreeBSD and explain its use.

- Chapter 21, *Virtualization* has been added with information about installing FreeBSD on virtualization software.

- Chapter 2, *Installing FreeBSD* has been added to cover installation of FreeBSD using the new installation utility, bsdinstall.

Changes from the Second Edition (2004)

The third edition was the culmination of over two years of work by the dedicated members of the FreeBSD Documentation Project. The printed edition grew to such a size that it was necessary to publish as two separate volumes. The following are the major changes in this new edition:

- Chapter 11, *Configuration and Tuning* has been expanded with new information about the ACPI power and resource management, the cron system utility, and more kernel tuning options.

- Chapter 13, *Security* has been expanded with new information about virtual private networks (VPNs), file system access control lists (ACLs), and security advisories.

- Chapter 15, *Mandatory Access Control* is a new chapter with this edition. It explains what MAC is and how this mechanism can be used to secure a FreeBSD system.

- Chapter 17, *Storage* has been expanded with new information about USB storage devices, file system snapshots, file system quotas, file and network backed filesystems, and encrypted disk partitions.

- A troubleshooting section has been added to Chapter 26, *PPP*.

- Chapter 27, *Electronic Mail* has been expanded with new information about using alternative transport agents, SMTP authentication, UUCP, fetchmail, procmail, and other advanced topics.

- Chapter 28, *Network Servers* is all new with this edition. This chapter includes information about setting up the Apache HTTP Server, ftpd, and setting up a server for Microsoft® Windows® clients with Samba. Some sections from Chapter 30, *Advanced Networking* were moved here to improve the presentation.

- Chapter 30, *Advanced Networking* has been expanded with new information about using Bluetooth® devices with FreeBSD, setting up wireless networks, and Asynchronous Transfer Mode (ATM) networking.

- A glossary has been added to provide a central location for the definitions of technical terms used throughout the book.

- A number of aesthetic improvements have been made to the tables and figures throughout the book.

Changes from the First Edition (2001)

The second edition was the culmination of over two years of work by the dedicated members of the FreeBSD Documentation Project. The following were the major changes in this edition:

- A complete Index has been added.

- All ASCII figures have been replaced by graphical diagrams.

- A standard synopsis has been added to each chapter to give a quick summary of what information the chapter contains, and what the reader is expected to know.

- The content has been logically reorganized into three parts: "Getting Started", "System Administration", and "Appendices".

- Chapter 3, *FreeBSD Basics* has been expanded to contain additional information about processes, daemons, and signals.

- Chapter 4, *Installing Applications: Packages and Ports* has been expanded to contain additional information about binary package management.

- Chapter 5, *The X Window System* has been completely rewritten with an emphasis on using modern desktop technologies such as KDE and GNOME on XFree86™ 4.X.

- Chapter 12, *The FreeBSD Booting Process* has been expanded.

- Chapter 17, *Storage* has been written from what used to be two separate chapters on "Disks" and "Backups". We feel that the topics are easier to comprehend when presented as a single chapter. A section on RAID (both hardware and software) has also been added.

- Chapter 25, *Serial Communications* has been completely reorganized and updated for FreeBSD 4.X/5.X.

- Chapter 26, *PPP* has been substantially updated.

- Many new sections have been added to Chapter 30, *Advanced Networking*.

- Chapter 27, *Electronic Mail* has been expanded to include more information about configuring sendmail.

- Chapter 10, *Linux® Binary Compatibility* has been expanded to include information about installing Oracle® and SAP® R/3®.

- The following new topics are covered in this second edition:

- Chapter 11, *Configuration and Tuning*.

- Chapter 7, *Multimedia*.

Organization of This Book

This book is split into five logically distinct sections. The first section, *Getting Started*, covers the installation and basic usage of FreeBSD. It is expected that the reader will follow these chapters in sequence, possibly skipping chapters covering familiar topics. The second section, *Common Tasks*, covers some frequently used features of Free-BSD. This section, and all subsequent sections, can be read out of order. Each chapter begins with a succinct synopsis that describes what the chapter covers and what the reader is expected to already know. This is meant to allow the casual reader to skip around to find chapters of interest. The third section, *System Administration*, covers administration topics. The fourth section, *Network Communication*, covers networking and server topics. The fifth section contains appendices of reference information.

Chapter 1, Introduction
> Introduces FreeBSD to a new user. It describes the history of the FreeBSD Project, its goals and development model.

Chapter 2, Installing FreeBSD
> Walks a user through the entire installation process of FreeBSD 9.*x* and later using bsdinstall.

Chapter 3, FreeBSD Basics
> Covers the basic commands and functionality of the FreeBSD operating system. If you are familiar with Linux® or another flavor of UNIX® then you can probably skip this chapter.

Chapter 4, Installing Applications: Packages and Ports
> Covers the installation of third-party software with both FreeBSD's innovative "Ports Collection" and standard binary packages.

Chapter 5, The X Window System
> Describes the X Window System in general and using X11 on FreeBSD in particular. Also describes common desktop environments such as KDE and GNOME.

Chapter 6, Desktop Applications
> Lists some common desktop applications, such as web browsers and productivity suites, and describes how to install them on FreeBSD.

Chapter 7, Multimedia
> Shows how to set up sound and video playback support for your system. Also describes some sample audio and video applications.

Chapter 8, Configuring the FreeBSD Kernel
> Explains why you might need to configure a new kernel and provides detailed instructions for configuring, building, and installing a custom kernel.

Chapter 9, Printing
> Describes managing printers on FreeBSD, including information about banner pages, printer accounting, and initial setup.

Chapter 10, Linux® Binary Compatibility
> Describes the Linux® compatibility features of FreeBSD. Also provides detailed installation instructions for many popular Linux® applications such as Oracle® and Mathematica®.

Chapter 11, Configuration and Tuning
> Describes the parameters available for system administrators to tune a FreeBSD system for optimum performance. Also describes the various configuration files used in FreeBSD and where to find them.

Chapter 12, The FreeBSD Booting Process

Describes the FreeBSD boot process and explains how to control this process with configuration options.

Chapter 13, Security

Describes many different tools available to help keep your FreeBSD system secure, including Kerberos, IPsec and OpenSSH.

Chapter 14, Jails

Describes the jails framework, and the improvements of jails over the traditional chroot support of FreeBSD.

Chapter 15, Mandatory Access Control

Explains what Mandatory Access Control (MAC) is and how this mechanism can be used to secure a FreeBSD system.

Chapter 16, Security Event Auditing

Describes what FreeBSD Event Auditing is, how it can be installed, configured, and how audit trails can be inspected or monitored.

Chapter 17, Storage

Describes how to manage storage media and filesystems with FreeBSD. This includes physical disks, RAID arrays, optical and tape media, memory-backed disks, and network filesystems.

Chapter 18, GEOM: Modular Disk Transformation Framework

Describes what the GEOM framework in FreeBSD is and how to configure various supported RAID levels.

Chapter 20, Other File Systems

Examines support of non-native file systems in FreeBSD, like the Z File System from Sun™ .

Chapter 21, Virtualization

Describes what virtualization systems offer, and how they can be used with FreeBSD.

Chapter 22, Localization - i18n/L10n Usage and Setup

Describes how to use FreeBSD in languages other than English. Covers both system and application level localization.

Chapter 23, Updating and Upgrading FreeBSD

Explains the differences between FreeBSD-STABLE, FreeBSD-CURRENT, and FreeBSD releases. Describes which users would benefit from tracking a development system and outlines that process. Covers the methods users may take to update their system to the latest security release.

Chapter 24, DTrace

Describes how to configure and use the DTrace tool from Sun™ in FreeBSD. Dynamic tracing can help locate performance issues, by performing real time system analysis.

Chapter 25, Serial Communications

Explains how to connect terminals and modems to your FreeBSD system for both dial in and dial out connections.

Chapter 26, PPP

Describes how to use PPP to connect to remote systems with FreeBSD.

Chapter 27, Electronic Mail

Explains the different components of an email server and dives into simple configuration topics for the most popular mail server software: sendmail.

Chapter 28, Network Servers

Provides detailed instructions and example configuration files to set up your FreeBSD machine as a network filesystem server, domain name server, network information system server, or time synchronization server.

Chapter 29, Firewalls

Explains the philosophy behind software-based firewalls and provides detailed information about the configuration of the different firewalls available for FreeBSD.

Chapter 30, Advanced Networking
> Describes many networking topics, including sharing an Internet connection with other computers on your LAN, advanced routing topics, wireless networking, Bluetooth®, ATM, IPv6, and much more.

Appendix A, Obtaining FreeBSD
> Lists different sources for obtaining FreeBSD media on CDROM or DVD as well as different sites on the Internet that allow you to download and install FreeBSD.

Appendix B, Bibliography
> This book touches on many different subjects that may leave you hungry for a more detailed explanation. The bibliography lists many excellent books that are referenced in the text.

Appendix C, Resources on the Internet
> Describes the many forums available for FreeBSD users to post questions and engage in technical conversations about FreeBSD.

Appendix D, OpenPGP Keys
> Lists the PGP fingerprints of several FreeBSD Developers.

Conventions used in this book

To provide a consistent and easy to read text, several conventions are followed throughout the book.

Typographic Conventions

Italic
> An *italic* font is used for filenames, URLs, emphasized text, and the first usage of technical terms.

Monospace
> A monospaced font is used for error messages, commands, environment variables, names of ports, hostnames, user names, group names, device names, variables, and code fragments.

Bold
> A bold font is used for applications, commands, and keys.

User Input

Keys are shown in bold to stand out from other text. Key combinations that are meant to be typed simultaneously are shown with `+' between the keys, such as:

Ctrl+Alt+Del

Meaning the user should type the Ctrl, Alt, and Del keys at the same time.

Keys that are meant to be typed in sequence will be separated with commas, for example:

Ctrl+X, Ctrl+S

Would mean that the user is expected to type the Ctrl and X keys simultaneously and then to type the Ctrl and S keys simultaneously.

Examples

Examples starting with C:\> indicate a MS-DOS® command. Unless otherwise noted, these commands may be executed from a "Command Prompt" window in a modern Microsoft® Windows® environment.

```
E:\> tools\fdimage floppies\kern.flp A:
```

Examples starting with # indicate a command that must be invoked as the superuser in FreeBSD. You can login as root to type the command, or login as your normal account and use su(1) to gain superuser privileges.

```
# dd if=kern.flp of=/dev/fd0
```

Examples starting with % indicate a command that should be invoked from a normal user account. Unless otherwise noted, C-shell syntax is used for setting environment variables and other shell commands.

```
% top
```

Acknowledgments

The book you are holding represents the efforts of many hundreds of people around the world. Whether they sent in fixes for typos, or submitted complete chapters, all the contributions have been useful.

Several companies have supported the development of this document by paying authors to work on it full-time, paying for publication, etc. In particular, BSDi (subsequently acquired by Wind River Systems) paid members of the FreeBSD Documentation Project to work on improving this book full time leading up to the publication of the first printed edition in March 2000 (ISBN 1-57176-241-8). Wind River Systems then paid several additional authors to make a number of improvements to the print-output infrastructure and to add additional chapters to the text. This work culminated in the publication of the second printed edition in November 2001 (ISBN 1-57176-303-1). In 2003-2004, FreeBSD Mall, Inc, paid several contributors to improve the Handbook in preparation for the third printed edition.

Part I. Getting Started

This part of the handbook is for users and administrators who are new to FreeBSD. These chapters:

- Introduce FreeBSD.

- Guide readers through the installation process.

- Teach UNIX® basics and fundamentals.

- Show how to install the wealth of third party applications available for FreeBSD.

- Introduce X, the UNIX® windowing system, and detail how to configure a desktop environment that makes users more productive.

The number of forward references in the text have been kept to a minimum so that this section can be read from front to back with minimal page flipping.

Table of Contents

Chapter 1. Introduction

Restructured, reorganized, and parts rewritten by Jim Mock.

1.1. Synopsis

Thank you for your interest in FreeBSD! The following chapter covers various aspects of the FreeBSD Project, such as its history, goals, development model, and so on.

After reading this chapter, you will know:

- How FreeBSD relates to other computer operating systems.

- The history of the FreeBSD Project.

- The goals of the FreeBSD Project.

- The basics of the FreeBSD open-source development model.

- And of course: where the name "FreeBSD" comes from.

1.2. Welcome to FreeBSD!

FreeBSD is a 4.4BSD-Lite based operating system for Intel (x86 and Itanium®), AMD64, ARM®, and Sun UltraS-PARC® computers. Ports to other architectures are also under way. You can also read about the history of FreeBSD, or the current release. If you are interested in contributing something to the Project (code, hardware, funding), see the Contributing to FreeBSD article.

1.2.1. What Can FreeBSD Do?

FreeBSD has many noteworthy features. Some of these are:

- *Preemptive multitasking* with dynamic priority adjustment to ensure smooth and fair sharing of the computer between applications and users, even under the heaviest of loads.

- *Multi-user facilities* which allow many people to use a FreeBSD system simultaneously for a variety of things. This means, for example, that system peripherals such as printers and tape drives are properly shared between all users on the system or the network and that individual resource limits can be placed on users or groups of users, protecting critical system resources from over-use.

- Strong *TCP/IP networking* with support for industry standards such as SCTP, DHCP, NFS, NIS, PPP, SLIP, IPsec, and IPv6. This means that your FreeBSD machine can interoperate easily with other systems as well as act as an enterprise server, providing vital functions such as NFS (remote file access) and email services or putting your organization on the Internet with WWW, FTP, routing and firewall (security) services.

- *Memory protection* ensures that applications (or users) cannot interfere with each other. One application crashing will not affect others in any way.

- The industry standard *X Window System* (X11R7) can provide a graphical user interface (GUI) on any machine and comes with full sources.

- *Binary compatibility* with many programs built for Linux, SCO, SVR4, BSDI and NetBSD.

- Thousands of *ready-to-run* applications are available from the FreeBSD *ports* and *packages* collection. Why search the net when you can find it all right here?

- Thousands of additional and *easy-to-port* applications are available on the Internet. FreeBSD is source code compatible with most popular commercial UNIX® systems and thus most applications require few, if any, changes to compile.

- Demand paged *virtual memory* and "merged VM/buffer cache" design efficiently satisfies applications with large appetites for memory while still maintaining interactive response to other users.

- *SMP* support for machines with multiple CPUs.

- A full complement of *C* and *C++* development tools. Many additional languages for advanced research and development are also available in the ports and packages collection.

- *Source code* for the entire system means you have the greatest degree of control over your environment. Why be locked into a proprietary solution at the mercy of your vendor when you can have a truly open system?

- Extensive *online documentation.*

- *And many more!*

FreeBSD is based on the 4.4BSD-Lite release from Computer Systems Research Group (CSRG) at the University of California at Berkeley, and carries on the distinguished tradition of BSD systems development. In addition to the fine work provided by CSRG, the FreeBSD Project has put in many thousands of hours in fine tuning the system for maximum performance and reliability in real-life load situations. FreeBSD offers performance and reliability on par with commercial offerings, combined with many cutting-edge features not available anywhere else.

The applications to which FreeBSD can be put are truly limited only by your own imagination. From software development to factory automation, inventory control to azimuth correction of remote satellite antennae; if it can be done with a commercial UNIX® product then it is more than likely that you can do it with FreeBSD too! FreeBSD also benefits significantly from literally thousands of high quality applications developed by research centers and universities around the world, often available at little to no cost. Commercial applications are also available and appearing in greater numbers every day.

Because the source code for FreeBSD itself is generally available, the system can also be customized to an almost unheard of degree for special applications or projects, and in ways not generally possible with operating systems from most major commercial vendors. Here is just a sampling of some of the applications in which people are currently using FreeBSD:

- *Internet Services:* The robust TCP/IP networking built into FreeBSD makes it an ideal platform for a variety of Internet services such as:

  - World Wide Web servers (standard or secure [SSL])

  - IPv4 and IPv6 routing

  - Firewalls and NAT ("IP masquerading") gateways

  - FTP servers

  - Electronic Mail servers

  - And more...

- *Education:* Are you a student of computer science or a related engineering field? There is no better way of learning about operating systems, computer architecture and networking than the hands on, under the hood experience that FreeBSD can provide. A number of freely available CAD, mathematical and graphic design packages also make it highly useful to those whose primary interest in a computer is to get *other* work done!

- *Research:* With source code for the entire system available, FreeBSD is an excellent platform for research in operating systems as well as other branches of computer science. FreeBSD's freely available nature also makes it possible for remote groups to collaborate on ideas or shared development without having to worry about special licensing agreements or limitations on what may be discussed in open forums.

- *Networking:* Need a new router? A name server (DNS)? A firewall to keep people out of your internal network? FreeBSD can easily turn that unused PC sitting in the corner into an advanced router with sophisticated packet-filtering capabilities.

- *Embedded:* FreeBSD makes an excellent platform to build embedded systems upon. With support for the ARM®, MIPS® and PowerPC® platforms, coupled with a robust network stack, cutting edge features and the permissive BSD license FreeBSD makes an excellent foundation for building embedded routers, firewalls, and other devices.

- *Desktop:* FreeBSD makes a fine choice for an inexpensive desktop solution using the freely available X11 server. FreeBSD offers a choice from many open-source desktop environments, including the standard GNOME and KDE graphical user interfaces. FreeBSD can even boot "diskless" from a central server, making individual workstations even cheaper and easier to administer.

- *Software Development:* The basic FreeBSD system comes with a full complement of development tools including a full C/C++ compiler and debugger suite. Support for many other languages are also available through the ports and packages collection.

FreeBSD is available to download free of charge, or can be obtained on either CD-ROM or DVD. Please see Appendix A, *Obtaining FreeBSD* for more information about obtaining FreeBSD.

1.2.2. Who Uses FreeBSD?

FreeBSD's advanced features, proven security, predictable release cycle, and permissive license have led to its use as a platform for building many commercial and open source appliances, devices, and products. Many of the world's largest IT companies use FreeBSD:

- Apache - The Apache Software Foundation runs most of its public facing infrastructure, including possibly one of the largest SVN repositories in the world with over 1.4 million commits, on FreeBSD.

- Apple - OS X borrows heavily from FreeBSD for the network stack, virtual file system, and many userland components. Apple iOS also contains elements borrowed from FreeBSD.

- Cisco - IronPort network security and anti-spam appliances run a modified FreeBSD kernel.

- Citrix - The NetScaler line of security appliances provide layer 4-7 load balancing, content caching, application firewall, secure VPN, and mobile cloud network access, along with the power of a FreeBSD shell.

- Dell KACE - The KACE system management appliances run FreeBSD because of its reliability, scalability, and the community that supports its continued development.

- Experts Exchange - All public facing web servers are powered by FreeBSD and they make extensive use of jails to isolate development and testing environments without the overhead of virtualization.

- Isilon - Isilon's enterprise storage appliances are based on FreeBSD. The extremely liberal FreeBSD license allowed Isilon to integrate their intellectual property throughout the kernel and focus on building their product instead of an operating system.

- iXsystems - The TrueNAS line of unified storage appliances is based on FreeBSD. In addition to their commercial products, iXsystems also manages development of the open source projects TrueOS and FreeNAS.

- Juniper - The JunOS operating system that powers all Juniper networking gear (including routers, switches, security, and networking appliances) is based on FreeBSD. Juniper is one of many vendors that showcases the symbiotic relationship between the project and vendors of commercial products. Improvements generated at Juniper are upstreamed into FreeBSD to reduce the complexity of integrating new features from FreeBSD back into JunOS in the future.

- McAfee - SecurOS, the basis of McAfee enterprise firewall products including Sidewinder is based on FreeBSD.

- NetApp - The Data ONTAP GX line of storage appliances are based on FreeBSD. In addition, NetApp has contributed back many features, including the new BSD licensed hypervisor, bhyve.

- Netflix - The OpenConnect appliance that Netflix uses to stream movies to its customers is based on FreeBSD. Netflix has made extensive contributions to the codebase and works to maintain a zero delta from mainline FreeBSD. Netflix OpenConnect appliances are responsible for delivering more than 32% of all Internet traffic in North America.

- Sandvine - Sandvine uses FreeBSD as the basis of their high performance real-time network processing platforms that make up their intelligent network policy control products.

- Sony - The PlayStation 4 gaming console runs a modified version of FreeBSD.

- Sophos - The Sophos Email Appliance product is based on a hardened FreeBSD and scans inbound mail for spam and viruses, while also monitoring outbound mail for malware as well as the accidental loss of sensitive information.

- Spectra Logic - The nTier line of archive grade storage appliances run FreeBSD and OpenZFS.

- Stormshield - Stormshield Network Security appliances are based on a hardened version of FreeBSD. The BSD license allows them to integrate their own intellectual property with the system while returning a great deal of interesting development to the community.

- The Weather Channel - The IntelliStar appliance that is installed at each local cable provider's headend and is responsible for injecting local weather forecasts into the cable TV network's programming runs FreeBSD.

- Verisign - Verisign is responsible for operating the .com and .net root domain registries as well as the accompanying DNS infrastructure. They rely on a number of different network operating systems including FreeBSD to ensure there is no common point of failure in their infrastructure.

- Voxer - Voxer powers their mobile voice messaging platform with ZFS on FreeBSD. Voxer switched from a Solaris derivative to FreeBSD because of its superior documentation, larger and more active community, and more developer friendly environment. In addition to critical features like ZFS and DTrace, FreeBSD also offers TRIM support for ZFS.

- WhatsApp - When WhatsApp needed a platform that would be able to handle more than 1 million concurrent TCP connections per server, they chose FreeBSD. They then proceeded to scale past 2.5 million connections per server.

- Wheel Systems - The FUDO security appliance allows enterprises to monitor, control, record, and audit contractors and administrators who work on their systems. Based on all of the best security features of FreeBSD including ZFS, GELI, Capsicum, HAST, and auditdistd.

FreeBSD has also spawned a number of related open source projects:

- BSD Router - A FreeBSD based replacement for large enterprise routers designed to run on standard PC hardware.

- FreeNAS - A customized FreeBSD designed to be used as a network file server appliance. Provides a python based web interface to simplify the management of both the UFS and ZFS file systems. Includes support for NFS, SMB/CIFS, AFP, FTP, and iSCSI. Includes an extensible plugin system based on FreeBSD jails.

- GhostBSD - A desktop oriented distribution of FreeBSD bundled with the Gnome desktop environment.

- mfsBSD - A toolkit for building a FreeBSD system image that runs entirely from memory.

- NAS4Free - A file server distribution based on FreeBSD with a PHP powered web interface.

- OPNSense - OPNsense is an open source, easy-to-use and easy-to-build FreeBSD based firewall and routing platform. OPNsense includes most of the features available in expensive commercial firewalls, and more in many cases. It brings the rich feature set of commercial offerings with the benefits of open and verifiable sources.

- TrueOS - A customized version of FreeBSD geared towards desktop users with graphical utilities to exposing the power of FreeBSD to all users. Designed to ease the transition of Windows and OS X users.

- pfSense - A firewall distribution based on FreeBSD with a huge array of features and extensive IPv6 support.

- ZRouter - An open source alternative firmware for embedded devices based on FreeBSD. Designed to replace the proprietary firmware on off-the-shelf routers.

FreeBSD is also used to power some of the biggest sites on the Internet, including:

- Yahoo!

- Yandex

- Rambler

- Sina

- Pair Networks

- Sony Japan

- Netcraft

- Netflix

- NetEase

- Weathernews

- TELEHOUSE America

and many more. Wikipedia also maintains a list of products based on FreeBSD.

1.3. About the FreeBSD Project

The following section provides some background information on the project, including a brief history, project goals, and the development model of the project.

1.3.1. A Brief History of FreeBSD

The FreeBSD Project had its genesis in the early part of 1993, partially as an outgrowth of the Unofficial 386BSD-Patchkit by the patchkit's last 3 coordinators: Nate Williams, Rod Grimes and Jordan Hubbard.

The original goal was to produce an intermediate snapshot of 386BSD in order to fix a number of problems with it that the patchkit mechanism just was not capable of solving. The early working title for the project was 386BSD 0.5 or 386BSD Interim in reference of that fact.

386BSD was Bill Jolitz's operating system, which had been up to that point suffering rather severely from almost a year's worth of neglect. As the patchkit swelled ever more uncomfortably with each passing day, they decided to assist Bill by providing this interim "cleanup" snapshot. Those plans came to a rude halt when Bill Jolitz suddenly decided to withdraw his sanction from the project without any clear indication of what would be done instead.

The trio thought that the goal remained worthwhile, even without Bill's support, and so they adopted the name "FreeBSD" coined by David Greenman. The initial objectives were set after consulting with the system's current users and, once it became clear that the project was on the road to perhaps even becoming a reality, Jordan contacted Walnut Creek CDROM with an eye toward improving FreeBSD's distribution channels for those many unfortunates without easy access to the Internet. Walnut Creek CDROM not only supported the idea of distributing FreeBSD on CD but also went so far as to provide the project with a machine to work on and a fast Internet connection. Without Walnut Creek CDROM's almost unprecedented degree of faith in what was, at the time, a completely unknown project, it is quite unlikely that FreeBSD would have gotten as far, as fast, as it has today.

The first CD-ROM (and general net-wide) distribution was FreeBSD 1.0, released in December of 1993. This was based on the 4.3BSD-Lite ("Net/2") tape from U.C. Berkeley, with many components also provided by 386BSD and the Free Software Foundation. It was a fairly reasonable success for a first offering, and they followed it with the highly successful FreeBSD 1.1 release in May of 1994.

Around this time, some rather unexpected storm clouds formed on the horizon as Novell and U.C. Berkeley settled their long-running lawsuit over the legal status of the Berkeley Net/2 tape. A condition of that settlement was U.C. Berkeley's concession that large parts of Net/2 were "encumbered" code and the property of Novell, who had in turn acquired it from AT&T some time previously. What Berkeley got in return was Novell's "blessing" that the 4.4BSD-Lite release, when it was finally released, would be declared unencumbered and all existing Net/2 users would be strongly encouraged to switch. This included FreeBSD, and the project was given until the end of July 1994 to stop shipping its own Net/2 based product. Under the terms of that agreement, the project was allowed one last release before the deadline, that release being FreeBSD 1.1.5.1.

FreeBSD then set about the arduous task of literally re-inventing itself from a completely new and rather incomplete set of 4.4BSD-Lite bits. The "Lite" releases were light in part because Berkeley's CSRG had removed large chunks of code required for actually constructing a bootable running system (due to various legal requirements) and the fact that the Intel port of 4.4 was highly incomplete. It took the project until November of 1994 to make this transition, and in December it released FreeBSD 2.0 to the world. Despite being still more than a little rough around the edges, the release was a significant success and was followed by the more robust and easier to install FreeBSD 2.0.5 release in June of 1995.

Since that time, FreeBSD has made a series of releases each time improving the stability, speed, and feature set of the previous version.

For now, long-term development projects continue to take place in the 10.X-CURRENT (trunk) branch, and snapshot releases of 10.X are continually made available from the snapshot server as work progresses.

1.3.2. FreeBSD Project Goals

Contributed by Jordan Hubbard.

The goals of the FreeBSD Project are to provide software that may be used for any purpose and without strings attached. Many of us have a significant investment in the code (and project) and would certainly not mind a little financial compensation now and then, but we are definitely not prepared to insist on it. We believe that our first and foremost "mission" is to provide code to any and all comers, and for whatever purpose, so that the code gets the widest possible use and provides the widest possible benefit. This is, I believe, one of the most fundamental goals of Free Software and one that we enthusiastically support.

That code in our source tree which falls under the GNU General Public License (GPL) or Library General Public License (LGPL) comes with slightly more strings attached, though at least on the side of enforced access rather than the usual opposite. Due to the additional complexities that can evolve in the commercial use of GPL software we do, however, prefer software submitted under the more relaxed BSD copyright when it is a reasonable option to do so.

1.3.3. The FreeBSD Development Model

Contributed by Satoshi Asami.

The development of FreeBSD is a very open and flexible process, being literally built from the contributions of thousands of people around the world, as can be seen from our list of contributors. FreeBSD's development infrastructure allow these thousands of contributors to collaborate over the Internet. We are constantly on the lookout for new developers and ideas, and those interested in becoming more closely involved with the project need simply contact us at the FreeBSD technical discussions mailing list. The FreeBSD announcements mailing list is also available to those wishing to make other FreeBSD users aware of major areas of work.

Useful things to know about the FreeBSD Project and its development process, whether working independently or in close cooperation:

The SVN repositories

For several years, the central source tree for FreeBSD was maintained by CVS (Concurrent Versions System), a freely available source code control tool. In June 2008, the Project switched to using SVN (Subversion). The switch was deemed necessary, as the technical limitations imposed by CVS were becoming obvious due to the rapid expansion of the source tree and the amount of history already stored. The Documentation Project and Ports Collection repositories also moved from CVS to SVN in May 2012 and July 2012, respectively. Please refer to the Synchronizing your source tree section for more information on obtaining the FreeBSD src/ repository and Using the Ports Collection for details on obtaining the FreeBSD Ports Collection.

The committers list

The *committers* are the people who have *write* access to the Subversion tree, and are authorized to make modifications to the FreeBSD source (the term "committer" comes from commit, the source control command which is used to bring new changes into the repository). Anyone can submit a bug to the Bug Database. Before submitting a bug report, the FreeBSD mailing lists, IRC channels, or forums can be used to help verify that an issue is actually a bug.

The FreeBSD core team

The *FreeBSD core team* would be equivalent to the board of directors if the FreeBSD Project were a company. The primary task of the core team is to make sure the project, as a whole, is in good shape and is heading in the right directions. Inviting dedicated and responsible developers to join our group of committers is one of the functions of the core team, as is the recruitment of new core team members as others move on. The current core team was elected from a pool of committer candidates in July 2014. Elections are held every 2 years.

Note

Like most developers, most members of the core team are also volunteers when it comes to FreeBSD development and do not benefit from the project financially, so "commitment" should also not be misconstrued as meaning "guaranteed support." The "board of directors" analogy above is not very accurate, and it may be more suitable to say that these are the people who gave up their lives in favor of FreeBSD against their better judgement!

Outside contributors

Last, but definitely not least, the largest group of developers are the users themselves who provide feedback and bug fixes to us on an almost constant basis. The primary way of keeping in touch with FreeBSD's more non-centralized development is to subscribe to the FreeBSD technical discussions mailing list where such things are discussed. See Appendix C, *Resources on the Internet* for more information about the various FreeBSD mailing lists.

The FreeBSD Contributors List is a long and growing one, so why not join it by contributing something back to FreeBSD today?

Providing code is not the only way of contributing to the project; for a more complete list of things that need doing, please refer to the FreeBSD Project web site.

In summary, our development model is organized as a loose set of concentric circles. The centralized model is designed for the convenience of the *users* of FreeBSD, who are provided with an easy way of tracking one central code base, not to keep potential contributors out! Our desire is to present a stable operating system with a large set of coherent application programs that the users can easily install and use — this model works very well in accomplishing that.

All we ask of those who would join us as FreeBSD developers is some of the same dedication its current people have to its continued success!

1.3.4. Third Party Programs

In addition to the base distributions, FreeBSD offers a ported software collection with thousands of commonly sought-after programs. At the time of this writing, there were over 24,000 ports! The list of ports ranges from http servers, to games, languages, editors, and almost everything in between. The entire Ports Collection requires approximately 500 MB. To compile a port, you simply change to the directory of the program you wish to install, type `make install`, and let the system do the rest. The full original distribution for each port you build is retrieved dynamically so you need only enough disk space to build the ports you want. Almost every port is also provided as a pre-compiled "package", which can be installed with a simple command (`pkg install`) by those who do not wish to compile their own ports from source. More information on packages and ports can be found in Chapter 4, *Installing Applications: Packages and Ports*.

1.3.5. Additional Documentation

All supported FreeBSD versions provide an option in the installer to install additional documentation under `/usr/local/share/doc/freebsd` during the initial system setup. Documentation may also be installed at any later time using packages as described in Section 23.3.2, "Updating Documentation from Ports". You may view the locally installed manuals with any HTML capable browser using the following URLs:

The FreeBSD Handbook
    `/usr/local/share/doc/freebsd/handbook/index.html`

The FreeBSD FAQ
    `/usr/local/share/doc/freebsd/faq/index.html`

You can also view the master (and most frequently updated) copies at `https://www.FreeBSD.org/` .

Chapter 2. Installing FreeBSD

Restructured, reorganized, and parts rewritten by Jim Mock.
Updated for bsdinstall by Gavin Atkinson and Warren Block.
Updated for root-on-ZFS by Allan Jude.

2.1. Synopsis

Beginning with FreeBSD 9.0-RELEASE, FreeBSD provides an easy to use, text-based installation program named bsdinstall. This chapter describes how to install FreeBSD using bsdinstall.

In general, the installation instructions in this chapter are written for the i386™ and AMD64 architectures. Where applicable, instructions specific to other platforms will be listed. There may be minor differences between the installer and what is shown here, so use this chapter as a general guide rather than as a set of literal instructions.

> Note
>
> Users who prefer to install FreeBSD using a graphical installer may be interested in pc-sysinstall, the installer used by the TrueOS Project. It can be used to install either a graphical desktop (TrueOS) or a command line version of FreeBSD. Refer to the TrueOS Users Handbook for details (https://www.trueos.org/handbook/trueos.html).

After reading this chapter, you will know:

- The minimum hardware requirements and FreeBSD supported architectures.

- How to create the FreeBSD installation media.

- How to start bsdinstall.

- The questions bsdinstall will ask, what they mean, and how to answer them.

- How to troubleshoot a failed installation.

- How to access a live version of FreeBSD before committing to an installation.

Before reading this chapter, you should:

- Read the supported hardware list that shipped with the version of FreeBSD to be installed and verify that the system's hardware is supported.

2.2. Minimum Hardware Requirements

The hardware requirements to install FreeBSD vary by architecture. Hardware architectures and devices supported by a FreeBSD release are listed on the FreeBSD Release Information page. The FreeBSD download page also has recommendations for choosing the correct image for different architectures.

A FreeBSD installation requires a minimum of 96 MB of RAM and 1.5 GB of free hard drive space. However, such small amounts of memory and disk space are really only suitable for custom applications like embedded appliances. General-purpose desktop systems need more resources. 2-4 GB RAM and at least 8 GB hard drive space is a good starting point.

These are the processor requirements for each architecture:

amd64

> This is the most common desktop and laptop processor type, used in most modern systems. Intel® calls it Intel64. Other manufacturers sometimes call it x86-64.
>
> Examples of amd64 compatible processors include: AMD Athlon™ 64, AMD Opteron™, multi-core Intel® Xeon™, and Intel® Core™ 2 and later processors.

i386

> Older desktops and laptops often use this 32-bit, x86 architecture.
>
> Almost all i386-compatible processors with a floating point unit are supported. All Intel® processors 486 or higher are supported.
>
> FreeBSD will take advantage of Physical Address Extensions (PAE) support on CPUs with this feature. A kernel with the PAE feature enabled will detect memory above 4 GB and allow it to be used by the system. However, using PAE places constraints on device drivers and other features of FreeBSD. Refer to pae(4) for details.

ia64

> Currently supported processors are the Itanium® and the Itanium® 2. Supported chipsets include the HP zx1, Intel® 460GX, and Intel® E8870. Both Uniprocessor (UP) and Symmetric Multi-processor (SMP) configurations are supported.

pc98

> NEC PC-9801/9821 series with almost all i386-compatible processors, including 80486, Pentium®, Pentium® Pro, and Pentium® II, are all supported. All i386-compatible processors by AMD, Cyrix, IBM, and IDT are also supported. EPSON PC-386/486/586 series, which are compatible with NEC PC-9801 series, are supported. The NEC FC-9801/9821 and NEC SV-98 series should be supported.
>
> High-resolution mode is not supported. NEC PC-98XA/XL/RL/XL^2, and NEC PC-H98 series are supported in normal (PC-9801 compatible) mode only. The SMP-related features of FreeBSD are not supported. The New Extend Standard Architecture (NESA) bus used in the PC-H98, SV-H98, and FC-H98 series, is not supported.

powerpc

> All New World ROM Apple® Mac® systems with built-in USB are supported. SMP is supported on machines with multiple CPUs.
>
> A 32-bit kernel can only use the first 2 GB of RAM.

sparc64

> Systems supported by FreeBSD/sparc64 are listed at the FreeBSD/sparc64 Project.
>
> SMP is supported on all systems with more than 1 processor. A dedicated disk is required as it is not possible to share a disk with another operating system at this time.

2.3. Pre-Installation Tasks

Once it has been determined that the system meets the minimum hardware requirements for installing FreeBSD, the installation file should be downloaded and the installation media prepared. Before doing this, check that the system is ready for an installation by verifying the items in this checklist:

1. Back Up Important Data

    Before installing any operating system, *always* backup all important data first. Do not store the backup on the system being installed. Instead, save the data to a removable disk such as a USB drive, another system on the network, or an online backup service. Test the backup before starting the installation to make sure it contains all of the needed files. Once the installer formats the system's disk, all data stored on that disk will be lost.

2.   Decide Where to Install FreeBSD

If FreeBSD will be the only operating system installed, this step can be skipped. But if FreeBSD will share the disk with another operating system, decide which disk or partition will be used for FreeBSD.

In the i386 and amd64 architectures, disks can be divided into multiple partitions using one of two partitioning schemes. A traditional *Master Boot Record* (MBR) holds a partition table defining up to four *primary partitions*. For historical reasons, FreeBSD calls these primary partition *slices*. One of these primary partitions can be made into an *extended partition* containing multiple *logical partitions*. The *GUID Partition Table* (GPT) is a newer and simpler method of partitioning a disk. Common GPT implementations allow up to 128 partitions per disk, eliminating the need for logical partitions.

Warning

Some older operating systems, like Windows® XP, are not compatible with the GPT partition scheme. If FreeBSD will be sharing a disk with such an operating system, MBR partitioning is required.

The FreeBSD boot loader requires either a primary or GPT partition. If all of the primary or GPT partitions are already in use, one must be freed for FreeBSD. To create a partition without deleting existing data, use a partition resizing tool to shrink an existing partition and create a new partition using the freed space.

A variety of free and commercial partition resizing tools are listed at http://en.wikipedia.org/wiki/List_of_disk_partitioning_software. GParted Live (http://gparted.sourceforge.net/livecd.php) is a free live CD which includes the GParted partition editor. GParted is also included with many other Linux live CD distributions.

Warning

When used properly, disk shrinking utilities can safely create space for creating a new partition. Since the possibility of selecting the wrong partition exists, always backup any important data and verify the integrity of the backup before modifying disk partitions.

Disk partitions containing different operating systems make it possible to install multiple operating systems on one computer. An alternative is to use virtualization (Chapter 21, *Virtualization*) which allows multiple operating systems to run at the same time without modifying any disk partitions.

3.   Collect Network Information

Some FreeBSD installation methods require a network connection in order to download the installation files. After any installation, the installer will offer to setup the system's network interfaces.

If the network has a DHCP server, it can be used to provide automatic network configuration. If DHCP is not available, the following network information for the system must be obtained from the local network administrator or Internet service provider:

1. IP address

2. Subnet mask

3. IP address of default gateway

4. Domain name of the network

5. IP addresses of the network's DNS servers

4. Check for FreeBSD Errata

Although the FreeBSD Project strives to ensure that each release of FreeBSD is as stable as possible, bugs occasionally creep into the process. On very rare occasions those bugs affect the installation process. As these problems are discovered and fixed, they are noted in the FreeBSD Errata (https://www.freebsd.org/releases/11.1R/errata.html) on the FreeBSD web site. Check the errata before installing to make sure that there are no problems that might affect the installation.

Information and errata for all the releases can be found on the release information section of the FreeBSD web site (https://www.freebsd.org/releases/index.html).

2.3.1. Prepare the Installation Media

The FreeBSD installer is not an application that can be run from within another operating system. Instead, download a FreeBSD installation file, burn it to the media associated with its file type and size (CD, DVD, or USB), and boot the system to install from the inserted media.

FreeBSD installation files are available at www.freebsd.org/where.html#download. Each installation file's name includes the release version of FreeBSD, the architecture, and the type of file. For example, to install FreeBSD 10.2 on an amd64 system from a DVD, download `FreeBSD-10.2-RELEASE-amd64-dvd1.iso`, burn this file to a DVD, and boot the system with the DVD inserted.

Installation files are available in several formats. The formats vary depending on computer architecture and media type.

Additional installation files are included for computers that boot with UEFI (Unified Extensible Firmware Interface). The names of these files include the string `uefi`.

File types:

- `-bootonly.iso`: This is the smallest installation file as it only contains the installer. A working Internet connection is required during installation as the installer will download the files it needs to complete the FreeBSD installation. This file should be burned to a CD using a CD burning application.

- `-disc1.iso`: This file contains all of the files needed to install FreeBSD, its source, and the Ports Collection. It should be burned to a CD using a CD burning application.

- `-dvd1.iso`: This file contains all of the files needed to install FreeBSD, its source, and the Ports Collection. It also contains a set of popular binary packages for installing a window manager and some applications so that a complete system can be installed from media without requiring a connection to the Internet. This file should be burned to a DVD using a DVD burning application.

- `-memstick.img`: This file contains all of the files needed to install FreeBSD, its source, and the Ports Collection. It should be burned to a USB stick using the instructions below.

- `-mini-memstick.img`: Like `-bootonly.iso`, does not include installation files, but downloads them as needed. A working internet connection is required during installation. Write this file to a USB stick as shown in Section 2.3.1.1, "Writing an Image File to USB".

After downloading the image file, download `CHECKSUM.SHA256` from the same directory. Calculate a *checksum* for the image file. FreeBSD provides sha256(1) for this, used as `sha256 imagefilename`. Other operating systems have similar programs.

Compare the calculated checksum with the one shown in `CHECKSUM.SHA256`. The checksums must match exactly. If the checksums do not match, the image file is corrupt and must be downloaded again.

2.3.1.1. Writing an Image File to USB

The *.img file is an *image* of the complete contents of a memory stick. It *cannot* be copied to the target device as a file. Several applications are available for writing the *.img to a USB stick. This section describes two of these utilities.

Important

Before proceeding, back up any important data on the USB stick. This procedure will erase the existing data on the stick.

Procedure 2.1. Using dd to Write the Image

Warning

This example uses /dev/da0 as the target device where the image will be written. Be *very careful* that the correct device is used as this command will destroy the existing data on the specified target device.

- The dd(1) command-line utility is available on BSD, Linux®, and Mac OS® systems. To burn the image using dd, insert the USB stick and determine its device name. Then, specify the name of the downloaded installation file and the device name for the USB stick. This example burns the amd64 installation image to the first USB device on an existing FreeBSD system.

```
# dd if=FreeBSD-10.2-RELEASE-amd64-memstick.img    of=/dev/da0 bs=1M conv=sync
```

If this command fails, verify that the USB stick is not mounted and that the device name is for the disk, not a partition. Some operating systems might require this command to be run with sudo(8). Systems like Linux® might buffer writes. To force all writes to complete, use sync(8).

Procedure 2.2. Using Windows® to Write the Image

Warning

Be sure to give the correct drive letter as the existing data on the specified drive will be overwritten and destroyed.

1. Obtaining Image Writer for Windows®

   Image Writer for Windows® is a free application that can correctly write an image file to a memory stick. Download it from https://sourceforge.net/projects/win32diskimager/ and extract it into a folder.

2. Writing the Image with Image Writer

   Double-click the Win32DiskImager icon to start the program. Verify that the drive letter shown under Device is the drive with the memory stick. Click the folder icon and select the image to be written to the memory stick. Click [Save] to accept the image file name. Verify that everything is correct, and that no folders on the memory stick are open in other windows. When everything is ready, click [Write] to write the image file to the memory stick.

You are now ready to start installing FreeBSD.

2.4. Starting the Installation

> Important
>
> By default, the installation will not make any changes to the disk(s) before the following message:
>
> ```
> Your changes will now be written to disk.  If you
> have chosen to overwrite existing data, it will
> be PERMANENTLY ERASED. Are you sure you want to
> commit your changes?
> ```
>
> The install can be exited at any time prior to this warning. If there is a concern that something is incorrectly configured, just turn the computer off before this point and no changes will be made to the system's disks.

This section describes how to boot the system from the installation media which was prepared using the instructions in Section 2.3.1, "Prepare the Installation Media". When using a bootable USB stick, plug in the USB stick before turning on the computer. When booting from CD or DVD, turn on the computer and insert the media at the first opportunity. How to configure the system to boot from the inserted media depends upon the architecture.

2.4.1. Booting on i386™ and amd64

These architectures provide a BIOS menu for selecting the boot device. Depending upon the installation media being used, select the CD/DVD or USB device as the first boot device. Most systems also provide a key for selecting the boot device during startup without having to enter the BIOS. Typically, the key is either F10, F11, F12, or Escape.

If the computer loads the existing operating system instead of the FreeBSD installer, then either:

1. The installation media was not inserted early enough in the boot process. Leave the media inserted and try restarting the computer.

2. The BIOS changes were incorrect or not saved. Double-check that the right boot device is selected as the first boot device.

3. This system is too old to support booting from the chosen media. In this case, the Plop Boot Manager (http://www.plop.at/en/bootmanagers.html) can be used to boot the system from the selected media.

2.4.2. Booting on PowerPC®

On most machines, holding C on the keyboard during boot will boot from the CD. Otherwise, hold Command+Option+O+F, or Windows+Alt+O+F on non-Apple® keyboards. At the 0 > prompt, enter

```
boot cd:,\ppc\loader cd:0
```

2.4.3. Booting on SPARC64®

Most SPARC64® systems are set up to boot automatically from disk. To install FreeBSD from a CD requires a break into the PROM.

To do this, reboot the system and wait until the boot message appears. The message depends on the model, but should look something like this:

```
Sun Blade 100 (UltraSPARC-IIe), Keyboard Present
Copyright 1998-2001 Sun Microsystems, Inc.  All rights reserved.
OpenBoot 4.2, 128 MB memory installed, Serial #51090132.
Ethernet address 0:3:ba:b:92:d4, Host ID: 830b92d4.
```

If the system proceeds to boot from disk at this point, press L1+A or Stop+A on the keyboard, or send a **BREAK** over the serial console. When using tip or cu, ~# will issue a BREAK. The PROM prompt will be ok on systems with one CPU and ok {0} on SMP systems, where the digit indicates the number of the active CPU.

At this point, place the CD into the drive and type boot cdrom from the PROM prompt.

2.4.4. FreeBSD Boot Menu

Once the system boots from the installation media, a menu similar to the following will be displayed:

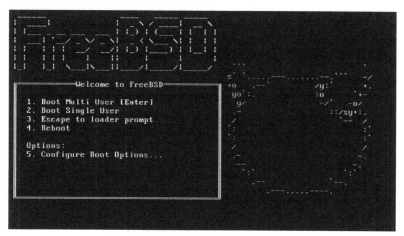

Figure 2.1. FreeBSD Boot Loader Menu

By default, the menu will wait ten seconds for user input before booting into the FreeBSD installer or, if FreeBSD is already installed, before booting into FreeBSD. To pause the boot timer in order to review the selections, press Space. To select an option, press its highlighted number, character, or key. The following options are available.

- Boot Multi User : This will continue the FreeBSD boot process. If the boot timer has been paused, press 1, upper- or lower-case B, or Enter.

- Boot Single User : This mode can be used to fix an existing FreeBSD installation as described in Section 12.2.4.1, "Single-User Mode". Press 2 or the upper- or lower-case S to enter this mode.

- Escape to loader prompt : This will boot the system into a repair prompt that contains a limited number of low-level commands. This prompt is described in Section 12.2.3, "Stage Three". Press 3 or Esc to boot into this prompt.

- Reboot: Reboots the system.

- Configure Boot Options: Opens the menu shown in, and described under, Figure 2.2, "FreeBSD Boot Options Menu".

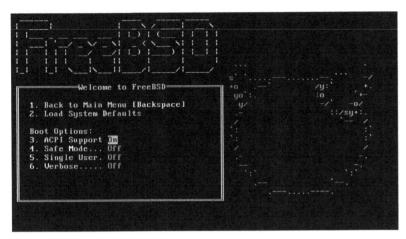

Figure 2.2. FreeBSD Boot Options Menu

The boot options menu is divided into two sections. The first section can be used to either return to the main boot menu or to reset any toggled options back to their defaults.

The next section is used to toggle the available options to On or Off by pressing the option's highlighted number or character. The system will always boot using the settings for these options until they are modified. Several options can be toggled using this menu:

- ACPI Support: If the system hangs during boot, try toggling this option to Off.

- Safe Mode: If the system still hangs during boot even with ACPI Support set to Off, try setting this option to On.

- Single User: Toggle this option to On to fix an existing FreeBSD installation as described in Section 12.2.4.1, "Single-User Mode". Once the problem is fixed, set it back to Off.

- Verbose: Toggle this option to On to see more detailed messages during the boot process. This can be useful when troubleshooting a piece of hardware.

After making the needed selections, press 1 or Backspace to return to the main boot menu, then press Enter to continue booting into FreeBSD. A series of boot messages will appear as FreeBSD carries out its hardware device probes and loads the installation program. Once the boot is complete, the welcome menu shown in Figure 2.3, "Welcome Menu" will be displayed.

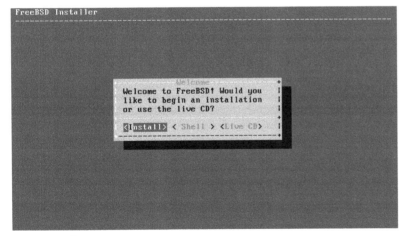

Figure 2.3. Welcome Menu

Press Enter to select the default of [Install] to enter the installer. The rest of this chapter describes how to use this installer. Otherwise, use the right or left arrows or the colorized letter to select the desired menu item. The

[Shell] can be used to access a FreeBSD shell in order to use command line utilities to prepare the disks before installation. The [Live CD] option can be used to try out FreeBSD before installing it. The live version is described in Section 2.10, "Using the Live CD".

Tip

To review the boot messages, including the hardware device probe, press the upper- or lower-case S and then Enter to access a shell. At the shell prompt, type more /var/run/dmesg.boot and use the space bar to scroll through the messages. When finished, type exit to return to the welcome menu.

2.5. Using bsdinstall

This section shows the order of the bsdinstall menus and the type of information that will be asked before the system is installed. Use the arrow keys to highlight a menu option, then Space to select or deselect that menu item. When finished, press Enter to save the selection and move onto the next screen.

2.5.1. Selecting the Keymap Menu

Depending on the system console being used, bsdinstall may initially display the menu shown in Figure 2.4, "Keymap Selection".

Figure 2.4. Keymap Selection

To configure the keyboard layout, press Enter with [YES] selected, which will display the menu shown in Figure 2.5, "Selecting Keyboard Menu". To instead use the default layout, use the arrow key to select [NO] and press Enter to skip this menu screen.

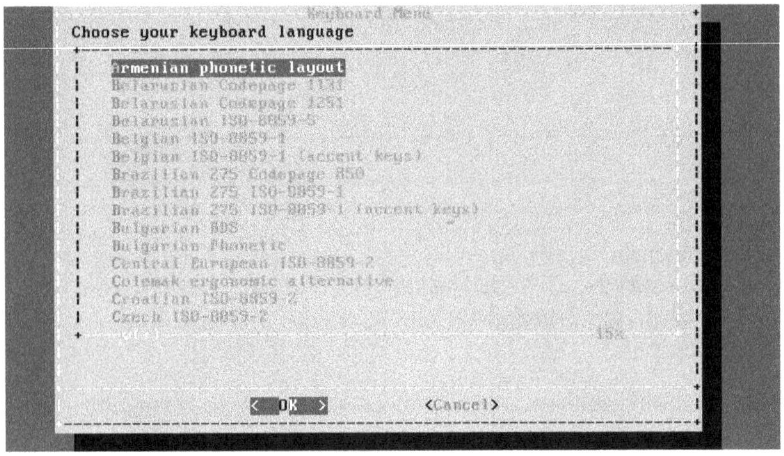

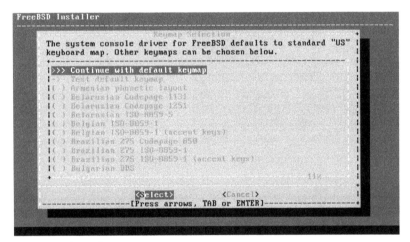

Figure 2.5. Selecting Keyboard Menu

When configuring the keyboard layout, use the up and down arrows to select the keymap that most closely represents the mapping of the keyboard attached to the system. Press Enter to save the selection.

Note

Pressing Esc will exit this menu and use the default keymap. If the choice of keymap is not clear, United States of America ISO-8859-1 is also a safe option.

In FreeBSD 10.0-RELEASE and later, this menu has been enhanced. The full selection of keymaps is shown, with the default preselected. In addition, when selecting a different keymap, a dialog is displayed that allows the user to try the keymap and ensure it is correct before proceeding.

Figure 2.6. Enhanced Keymap Menu

2.5.2. Setting the Hostname

The next bsdinstall menu is used to set the hostname for the newly installed system.

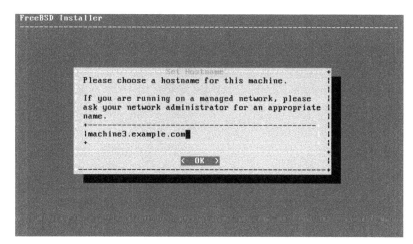

Figure 2.7. Setting the Hostname

Type in a hostname that is unique for the network. It should be a fully-qualified hostname, such as machine3.example.com.

2.5.3. Selecting Components to Install

Next, bsdinstall will prompt to select optional components to install.

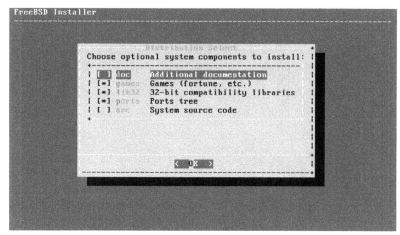

Figure 2.8. Selecting Components to Install

Deciding which components to install will depend largely on the intended use of the system and the amount of disk space available. The FreeBSD kernel and userland, collectively known as the *base system*, are always installed. Depending on the architecture, some of these components may not appear:

- doc - Additional documentation, mostly of historical interest, to install into /usr/share/doc . The documentation provided by the FreeBSD Documentation Project may be installed later using the instructions in Section 23.3, "Updating the Documentation Set".

- games - Several traditional BSD games, including fortune, rot13, and others.

- lib32 - Compatibility libraries for running 32-bit applications on a 64-bit version of FreeBSD.

- ports - The FreeBSD Ports Collection is a collection of files which automates the downloading, compiling and installation of third-party software packages. Chapter 4, *Installing Applications: Packages and Ports* discusses how to use the Ports Collection.

Warning

The installation program does not check for adequate disk space. Select this option only if sufficient hard disk space is available. The FreeBSD Ports Collection takes up about 500 MB of disk space.

- src - The complete FreeBSD source code for both the kernel and the userland. Although not required for the majority of applications, it may be required to build device drivers, kernel modules, or some applications from the Ports Collection. It is also used for developing FreeBSD itself. The full source tree requires 1 GB of disk space and recompiling the entire FreeBSD system requires an additional 5 GB of space.

2.5.4. Installing from the Network

The menu shown in Figure 2.9, "Installing from the Network" only appears when installing from a -bootonly.iso CD as this installation media does not hold copies of the installation files. Since the installation files must be retrieved over a network connection, this menu indicates that the network interface must be first configured.

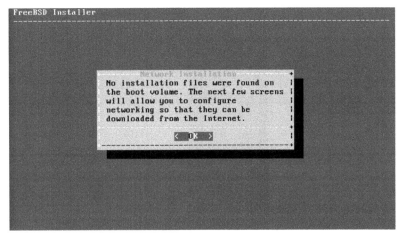

Figure 2.9. Installing from the Network

To configure the network connection, press Enter and follow the instructions in Section 2.8.2, "Configuring Network Interfaces". Once the interface is configured, select a mirror site that is located in the same region of the world as the computer on which FreeBSD is being installed. Files can be retrieved more quickly when the mirror is close to the target computer, reducing installation time.

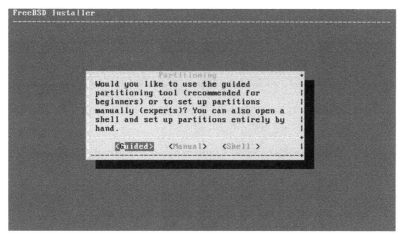

Figure 2.10. Choosing a Mirror

Installation will then continue as if the installation files were located on the local installation media.

2.6. Allocating Disk Space

The next menu is used to determine the method for allocating disk space. The options available in the menu depend upon the version of FreeBSD being installed.

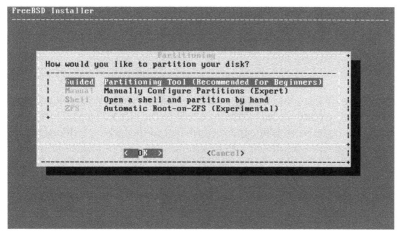

Figure 2.11. Partitioning Choices on FreeBSD 9.x

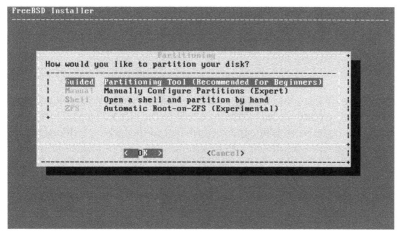

Figure 2.12. Partitioning Choices on FreeBSD 10.x and Higher

Guided partitioning automatically sets up the disk partitions, Manual partitioning allows advanced users to create customized partitions from menu options, and Shell opens a shell prompt where advanced users can create customized partitions using command-line utilities like gpart(8), fdisk(8), and bsdlabel(8). ZFS partitioning, only available in FreeBSD 10 and later, creates an optionally encrypted root-on-ZFS system with support for *boot environments*.

This section describes what to consider when laying out the disk partitions. It then demonstrates how to use the different partitioning methods.

2.6.1. Designing the Partition Layout

When laying out file systems, remember that hard drives transfer data faster from the outer tracks to the inner. Thus, smaller and heavier-accessed file systems should be closer to the outside of the drive, while larger partitions like /usr should be placed toward the inner parts of the disk. It is a good idea to create partitions in an order similar to: /, swap, /var, and /usr.

The size of the /var partition reflects the intended machine's usage. This partition is used to hold mailboxes, log files, and printer spools. Mailboxes and log files can grow to unexpected sizes depending on the number of users and how long log files are kept. On average, most users rarely need more than about a gigabyte of free disk space in /var.

Note

Sometimes, a lot of disk space is required in /var/tmp. When new software is installed, the packaging tools extract a temporary copy of the packages under /var/tmp. Large software packages, like Firefox, Apache OpenOffice or LibreOffice may be tricky to install if there is not enough disk space under /var/tmp.

The /usr partition holds many of the files which support the system, including the FreeBSD Ports Collection and system source code. At least 2 gigabytes of space is recommended for this partition.

When selecting partition sizes, keep the space requirements in mind. Running out of space in one partition while barely using another can be a hassle.

As a rule of thumb, the swap partition should be about double the size of physical memory (RAM). Systems with minimal RAM may perform better with more swap. Configuring too little swap can lead to inefficiencies in the VM page scanning code and might create issues later if more memory is added.

On larger systems with multiple SCSI disks or multiple IDE disks operating on different controllers, it is recommended that swap be configured on each drive, up to four drives. The swap partitions should be approximately the same size. The kernel can handle arbitrary sizes but internal data structures scale to 4 times the largest swap partition. Keeping the swap partitions near the same size will allow the kernel to optimally stripe swap space across disks. Large swap sizes are fine, even if swap is not used much. It might be easier to recover from a runaway program before being forced to reboot.

By properly partitioning a system, fragmentation introduced in the smaller write heavy partitions will not bleed over into the mostly read partitions. Keeping the write loaded partitions closer to the disk's edge will increase I/O performance in the partitions where it occurs the most. While I/O performance in the larger partitions may be needed, shifting them more toward the edge of the disk will not lead to a significant performance improvement over moving /var to the edge.

2.6.2. Guided Partitioning

When this method is selected, a menu will display the available disk(s). If multiple disks are connected, choose the one where FreeBSD is to be installed.

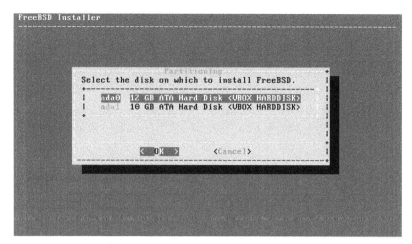

Figure 2.13. Selecting from Multiple Disks

Once the disk is selected, the next menu prompts to install to either the entire disk or to create a partition using free space. If [Entire Disk] is chosen, a general partition layout filling the whole disk is automatically created. Selecting [Partition] creates a partition layout from the unused space on the disk.

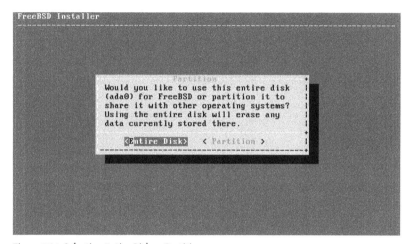

Figure 2.14. Selecting Entire Disk or Partition

After the partition layout has been created, review it to ensure it meets the needs of the installation. Selecting [Revert] will reset the partitions to their original values and pressing [Auto] will recreate the automatic FreeBSD partitions. Partitions can also be manually created, modified, or deleted. When the partitioning is correct, select [Finish] to continue with the installation.

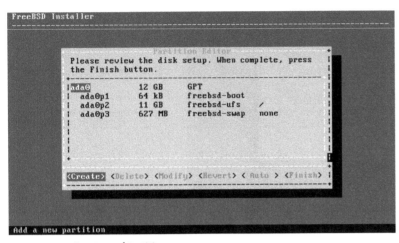

Figure 2.15. Review Created Partitions

2.6.3. Manual Partitioning

Selecting this method opens the partition editor:

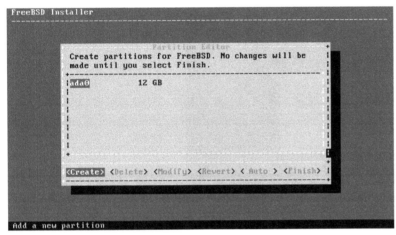

Figure 2.16. Manually Create Partitions

Highlight the installation drive (ada0 in this example) and select [Create] to display a menu of available partition schemes:

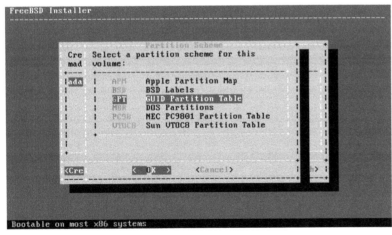

Figure 2.17. Manually Create Partitions

GPT is usually the most appropriate choice for amd64 computers. Older computers that are not compatible with GPT should use MBR. The other partition schemes are generally used for uncommon or older computers.

Table 2.1. Partitioning Schemes

Abbreviation	Description
APM	Apple Partition Map, used by PowerPC®.
BSD	BSD label without an MBR, sometimes called *dangerously dedicated mode* as non-BSD disk utilities may not recognize it.
GPT	GUID Partition Table (http://en.wikipedia.org/wiki/GUID_Partition_Table).
MBR	Master Boot Record (http://en.wikipedia.org/wiki/Master_boot_record).
PC98	MBR variant used by NEC PC-98 computers (http://en.wikipedia.org/wiki/Pc9801).
VTOC8	Volume Table Of Contents used by Sun SPARC64 and UltraSPARC computers.

After the partitioning scheme has been selected and created, select [Create] again to create the partitions.

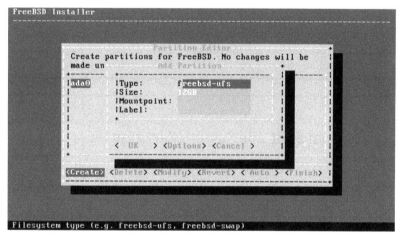

Figure 2.18. Manually Create Partitions

A standard FreeBSD GPT installation uses at least three partitions:

- freebsd-boot - Holds the FreeBSD boot code.

- freebsd-ufs - A FreeBSD UFS file system.

- freebsd-swap - FreeBSD swap space.

Another partition type worth noting is freebsd-zfs, used for partitions that will contain a FreeBSD ZFS file system (Chapter 19, *The Z File System (ZFS)*). Refer to gpart(8) for descriptions of the available GPT partition types.

Multiple file system partitions can be created and some people prefer a traditional layout with separate partitions for /, /var, /tmp, and /usr. See Example 2.1, "Creating Traditional Split File System Partitions" for an example.

The Size may be entered with common abbreviations: *K* for kilobytes, *M* for megabytes, or *G* for gigabytes.

Tip

Proper sector alignment provides the best performance, and making partition sizes even multiples of 4K bytes helps to ensure alignment on drives with either 512-byte or 4K-byte sectors. Generally, using partition sizes that are even multiples of 1M or 1G is the easiest way to make sure every partition starts at an even multiple of 4K. There is one exception: the *freebsd-boot* partition should be no larger than 512K due to current boot code limitations.

A `Mountpoint` is needed if the partition will contain a file system. If only a single UFS partition will be created, the mountpoint should be `/`.

The `Label` is a name by which the partition will be known. Drive names or numbers can change if the drive is connected to a different controller or port, but the partition label does not change. Referring to labels instead of drive names and partition numbers in files like `/etc/fstab` makes the system more tolerant to hardware changes. GPT labels appear in `/dev/gpt/` when a disk is attached. Other partitioning schemes have different label capabilities and their labels appear in different directories in `/dev/`.

Tip

Use a unique label on every partition to avoid conflicts from identical labels. A few letters from the computer's name, use, or location can be added to the label. For instance, use `lab-root` or `rootfslab` for the UFS root partition on the computer named `lab`.

Example 2.1. Creating Traditional Split File System Partitions

For a traditional partition layout where the `/`, `/var`, `/tmp`, and `/usr` directories are separate file systems on their own partitions, create a GPT partitioning scheme, then create the partitions as shown. Partition sizes shown are typical for a 20G target disk. If more space is available on the target disk, larger swap or `/var` partitions may be useful. Labels shown here are prefixed with ex for "example", but readers should use other unique label values as described above.

By default, FreeBSD's `gptboot` expects the first UFS partition to be the `/` partition.

Partition Type	Size	Mountpoint	Label
freebsd-boot	512K		
freebsd-ufs	2G	/	exrootfs
freebsd-swap	4G		exswap
freebsd-ufs	2G	/var	exvarfs
freebsd-ufs	1G	/tmp	extmpfs
freebsd-ufs	accept the default (remainder of the disk)	/usr	exusrfs

After the custom partitions have been created, select [Finish] to continue with the installation.

2.6.4. Root-on-ZFS Automatic Partitioning

Support for automatic creation of root-on-ZFS installations was added in FreeBSD 10.0-RELEASE. This partitioning mode only works with whole disks and will erase the contents of the entire disk. The installer will automatically create partitions aligned to 4k boundaries and force ZFS to use 4k sectors. This is safe even with 512 byte sector disks, and has the added benefit of ensuring that pools created on 512 byte disks will be able to have 4k sector disks added in the future, either as additional storage space or as replacements for failed disks. The installer can also optionally employ GELI disk encryption as described in Section 17.12.2, "Disk Encryption with geli". If encryption is enabled, a 2 GB unencrypted boot pool containing the /boot directory is created. It holds the kernel and other files necessary to boot the system. A swap partition of a user selectable size is also created, and all remaining space is used for the ZFS pool.

The main ZFS configuration menu offers a number of options to control the creation of the pool.

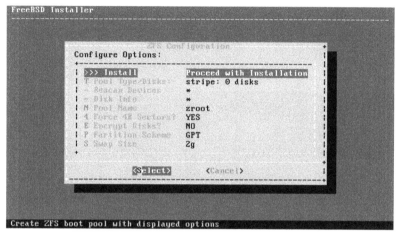

Figure 2.19. ZFS Partitioning Menu

Select T to configure the Pool Type and the disk(s) that will constitute the pool. The automatic ZFS installer currently only supports the creation of a single top level vdev, except in stripe mode. To create more complex pools, use the instructions in Section 2.6.5, "Shell Mode Partitioning" to create the pool. The installer supports the creation of various pool types, including stripe (not recommended, no redundancy), mirror (best performance, least usable space), and RAID-Z 1, 2, and 3 (with the capability to withstand the concurrent failure of 1, 2, and 3 disks, respectively). While selecting the pool type, a tooltip is displayed across the bottom of the screen with advice about the number of required disks, and in the case of RAID-Z, the optimal number of disks for each configuration.

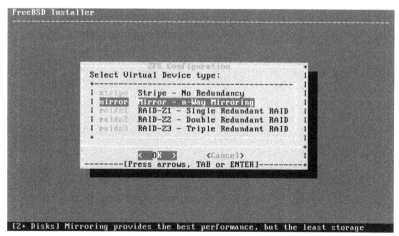

Figure 2.20. ZFS Pool Type

Once a Pool Type has been selected, a list of available disks is displayed, and the user is prompted to select one or more disks to make up the pool. The configuration is then validated, to ensure enough disks are selected. If not, select <Change Selection> to return to the list of disks, or <Cancel> to change the pool type.

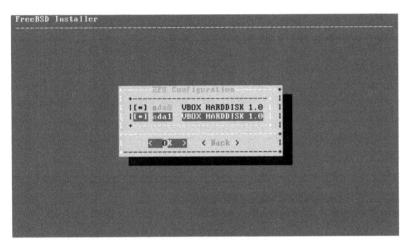

Figure 2.21. Disk Selection

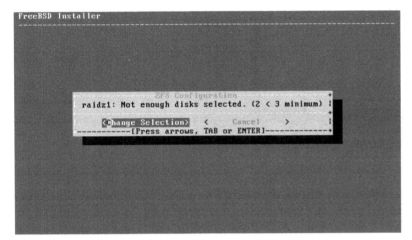

Figure 2.22. Invalid Selection

If one or more disks are missing from the list, or if disks were attached after the installer was started, select - Rescan Devices to repopulate the list of available disks. To avoid accidentally erasing the wrong disk, the - Disk Info menu can be used to inspect each disk, including its partition table and various other information such as the device model number and serial number, if available.

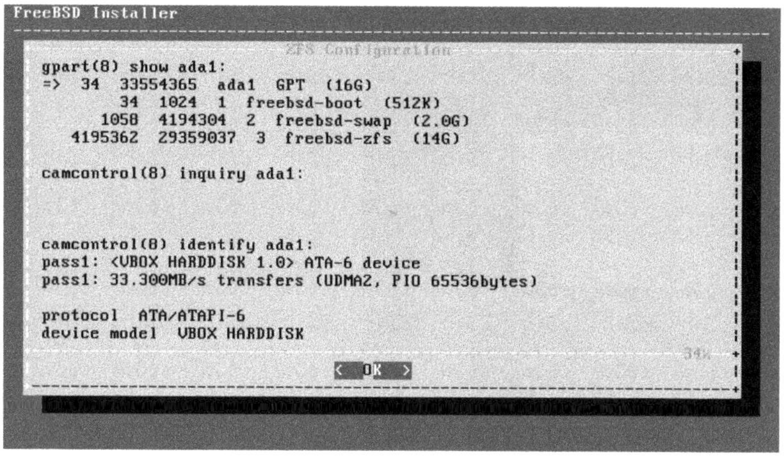

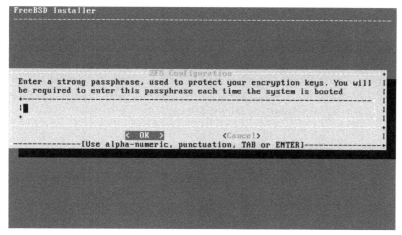

Figure 2.23. Analyzing a Disk

The main ZFS configuration menu also allows the user to enter a pool name, disable forcing 4k sectors, enable or disable encryption, switch between GPT (recommended) and MBR partition table types, and select the amount of swap space. Once all options have been set to the desired values, select the >>> Install option at the top of the menu.

If GELI disk encryption was enabled, the installer will prompt twice for the passphrase to be used to encrypt the disks.

Figure 2.24. Disk Encryption Password

The installer then offers a last chance to cancel before the contents of the selected drives are destroyed to create the ZFS pool.

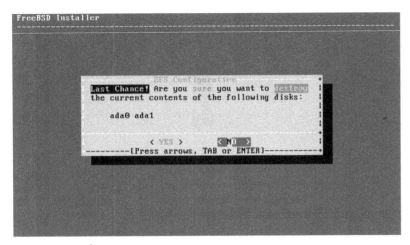

Figure 2.25. Last Chance

The installation then proceeds normally.

2.6.5. Shell Mode Partitioning

When creating advanced installations, the bsdinstall partitioning menus may not provide the level of flexibility required. Advanced users can select the Shell option from the partitioning menu in order to manually partition the drives, create the file system(s), populate /tmp/bsdinstall_etc/fstab , and mount the file systems under /mnt. Once this is done, type exit to return to bsdinstall and continue the installation.

2.7. Committing to the Installation

Once the disks are configured, the next menu provides the last chance to make changes before the selected hard drive(s) are formatted. If changes need to be made, select [Back] to return to the main partitioning menu. [Revert & Exit] will exit the installer without making any changes to the hard drive.

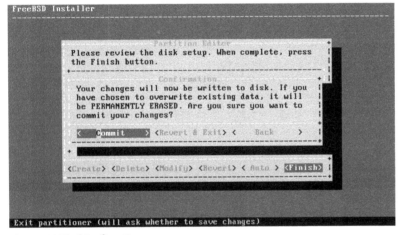

Figure 2.26. Final Confirmation

To instead start the actual installation, select [Commit] and press Enter.

Installation time will vary depending on the distributions chosen, installation media, and speed of the computer. A series of messages will indicate the progress.

First, the installer formats the selected disk(s) and initializes the partitions. Next, in the case of a bootonly media, it downloads the selected components:

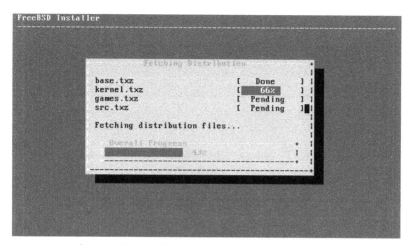

Figure 2.27. Fetching Distribution Files

Next, the integrity of the distribution files is verified to ensure they have not been corrupted during download or misread from the installation media:

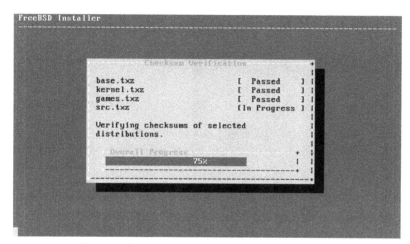

Figure 2.28. Verifying Distribution Files

Finally, the verified distribution files are extracted to the disk:

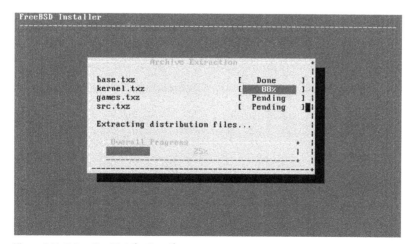

Figure 2.29. Extracting Distribution Files

Once all requested distribution files have been extracted, bsdinstall displays the first post-installation configuration screen. The available post-configuration options are described in the next section.

2.8. Post-Installation

Once FreeBSD is installed, bsdinstall will prompt to configure several options before booting into the newly installed system. This section describes these configuration options.

Tip

Once the system has booted, bsdconfig provides a menu-driven method for configuring the system using these and additional options.

2.8.1. Setting the root Password

First, the root password must be set. While entering the password, the characters being typed are not displayed on the screen. After the password has been entered, it must be entered again. This helps prevent typing errors.

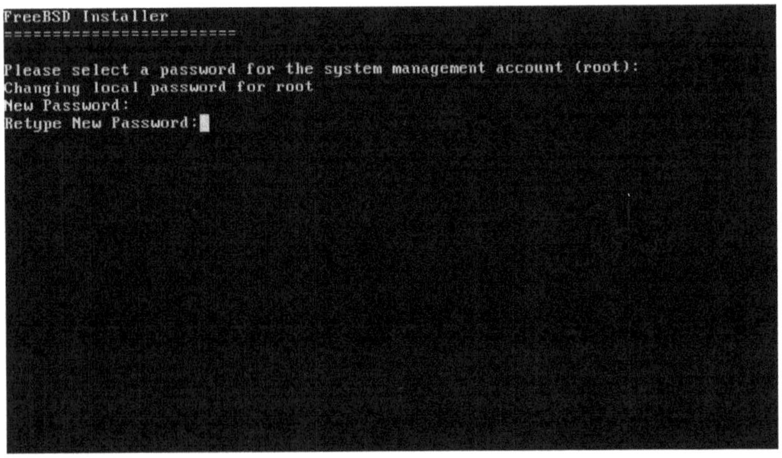

```
FreeBSD Installer
=========================

Please select a password for the system management account (root):
Changing local password for root
New Password:
Retype New Password:
```

Figure 2.30. Setting the root Password

2.8.2. Configuring Network Interfaces

Next, a list of the network interfaces found on the computer is shown. Select the interface to configure.

Note

The network configuration menus will be skipped if the network was previously configured as part of a *bootonly* installation.

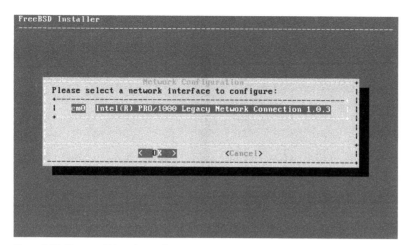

Figure 2.31. Choose a Network Interface

If an Ethernet interface is selected, the installer will skip ahead to the menu shown in Figure 2.35, "Choose IPv4 Networking". If a wireless network interface is chosen, the system will instead scan for wireless access points:

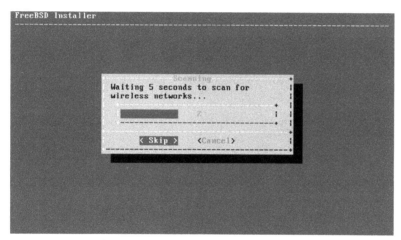

Figure 2.32. Scanning for Wireless Access Points

Wireless networks are identified by a Service Set Identifier (SSID), a short, unique name given to each network. SSIDs found during the scan are listed, followed by a description of the encryption types available for that network. If the desired SSID does not appear in the list, select [Rescan] to scan again. If the desired network still does not appear, check for problems with antenna connections or try moving the computer closer to the access point. Rescan after each change is made.

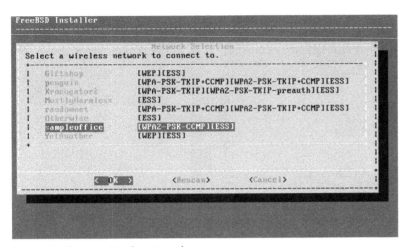

Figure 2.33. Choosing a Wireless Network

Next, enter the encryption information for connecting to the selected wireless network. WPA2 encryption is strongly recommended as older encryption types, like WEP, offer little security. If the network uses WPA2, input the password, also known as the Pre-Shared Key (PSK). For security reasons, the characters typed into the input box are displayed as asterisks.

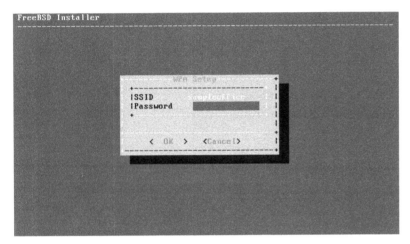

Figure 2.34. WPA2 Setup

Next, choose whether or not an IPv4 address should be configured on the Ethernet or wireless interface:

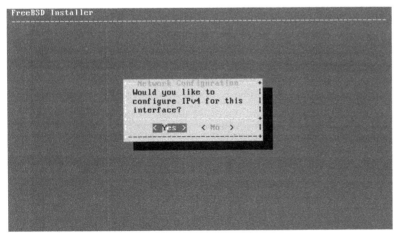

Figure 2.35. Choose IPv4 Networking

There are two methods of IPv4 configuration. DHCP will automatically configure the network interface correctly and should be used if the network provides a DHCP server. Otherwise, the addressing information needs to be input manually as a static configuration.

Note

Do not enter random network information as it will not work. If a DHCP server is not available, obtain the information listed in Required Network Information from the network administrator or Internet service provider.

If a DHCP server is available, select [Yes] in the next menu to automatically configure the network interface. The installer will appear to pause for a minute or so as it finds the DHCP server and obtains the addressing information for the system.

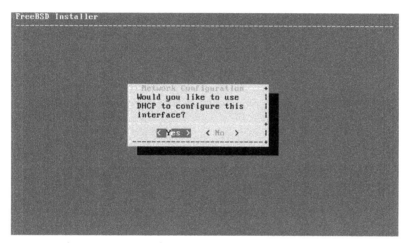

Figure 2.36. Choose IPv4 DHCP Configuration

If a DHCP server is not available, select [No] and input the following addressing information in this menu:

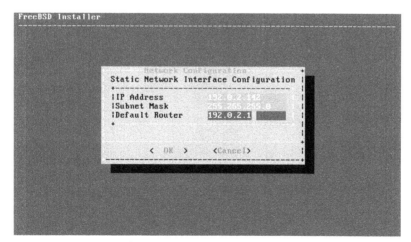

Figure 2.37. IPv4 Static Configuration

- IP Address - The IPv4 address assigned to this computer. The address must be unique and not already in use by another piece of equipment on the local network.

- Subnet Mask - The subnet mask for the network.

- `Default Router` - The IP address of the network's default gateway.

The next screen will ask if the interface should be configured for IPv6. If IPv6 is available and desired, choose [Yes] to select it.

Figure 2.38. Choose IPv6 Networking

IPv6 also has two methods of configuration. StateLess Address AutoConfiguration (SLAAC) will automatically request the correct configuration information from a local router. Refer to http://tools.ietf.org/html/rfc4862 for more information. Static configuration requires manual entry of network information.

If an IPv6 router is available, select [Yes] in the next menu to automatically configure the network interface. The installer will appear to pause for a minute or so as it finds the router and obtains the addressing information for the system.

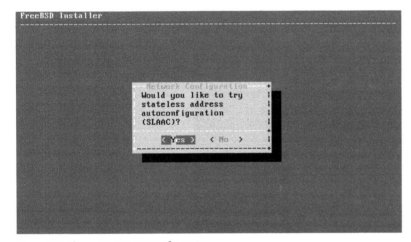

Figure 2.39. Choose IPv6 SLAAC Configuration

If an IPv6 router is not available, select [No] and input the following addressing information in this menu:

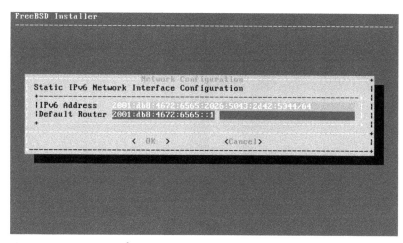

Figure 2.40. IPv6 Static Configuration

- **IPv6 Address** - The IPv6 address assigned to this computer. The address must be unique and not already in use by another piece of equipment on the local network.

- **Default Router** - The IPv6 address of the network's default gateway.

The last network configuration menu is used to configure the Domain Name System (DNS) resolver, which converts hostnames to and from network addresses. If DHCP or SLAAC was used to autoconfigure the network interface, the Resolver Configuration values may already be filled in. Otherwise, enter the local network's domain name in the Search field. DNS #1 and DNS #2 are the IPv4 and/or IPv6 addresses of the DNS servers. At least one DNS server is required.

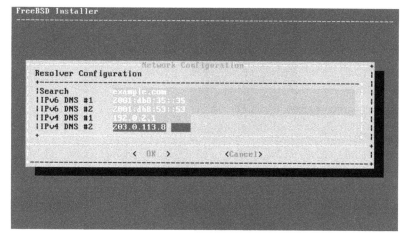

Figure 2.41. DNS Configuration

2.8.3. Setting the Time Zone

The next menu asks if the system clock uses UTC or local time. When in doubt, select [No] to choose the more commonly-used local time.

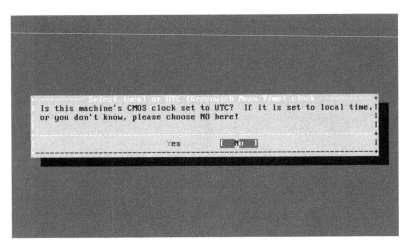

Figure 2.42. Select Local or UTC Clock

The next series of menus are used to determine the correct local time by selecting the geographic region, country, and time zone. Setting the time zone allows the system to automatically correct for regional time changes, such as daylight savings time, and perform other time zone related functions properly.

The example shown here is for a machine located in the Eastern time zone of the United States. The selections will vary according to the geographical location.

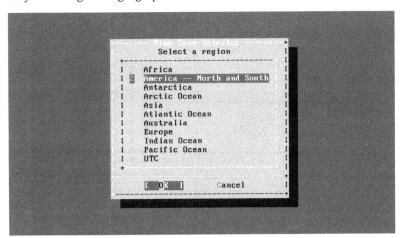

Figure 2.43. Select a Region

The appropriate region is selected using the arrow keys and then pressing Enter.

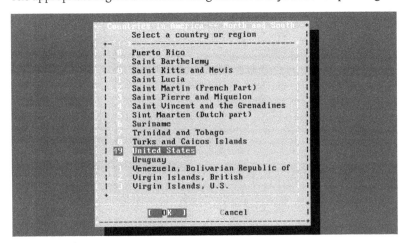

Figure 2.44. Select a Country

Select the appropriate country using the arrow keys and press Enter.

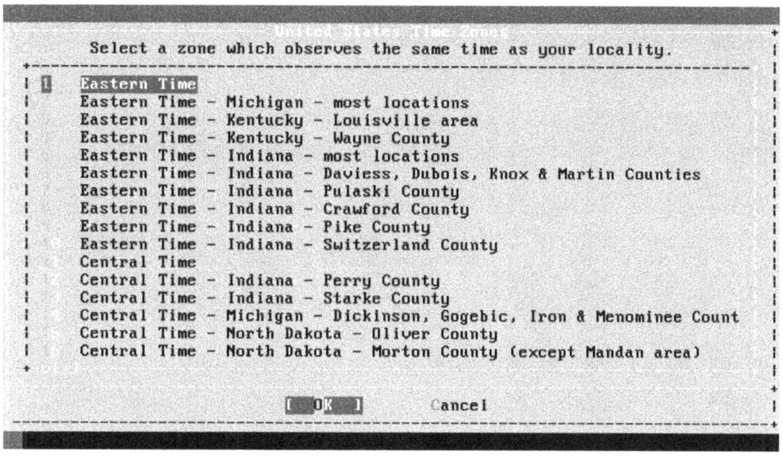

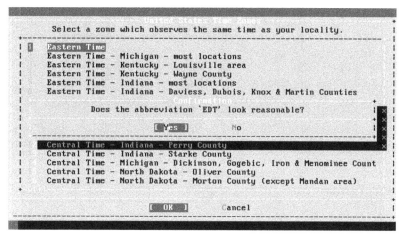

Figure 2.45. Select a Time Zone

The appropriate time zone is selected using the arrow keys and pressing Enter.

Figure 2.46. Confirm Time Zone

Confirm the abbreviation for the time zone is correct. If it is, press Enter to continue with the post-installation configuration.

2.8.4. Enabling Services

The next menu is used to configure which system services will be started whenever the system boots. All of these services are optional. Only start the services that are needed for the system to function.

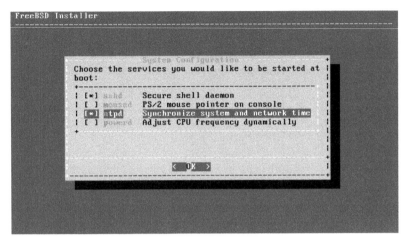

Figure 2.47. Selecting Additional Services to Enable

Here is a summary of the services which can be enabled in this menu:

- sshd - The Secure Shell (SSH) daemon is used to remotely access a system over an encrypted connection. Only enable this service if the system should be available for remote logins.

- moused - Enable this service if the mouse will be used from the command-line system console.

- ntpd - The Network Time Protocol (NTP) daemon for automatic clock synchronization. Enable this service if there is a Windows®, Kerberos, or LDAP server on the network.

- powerd - System power control utility for power control and energy saving.

2.8.5. Enabling Crash Dumps

The next menu is used to configure whether or not crash dumps should be enabled. Enabling crash dumps can be useful in debugging issues with the system, so users are encouraged to enable crash dumps.

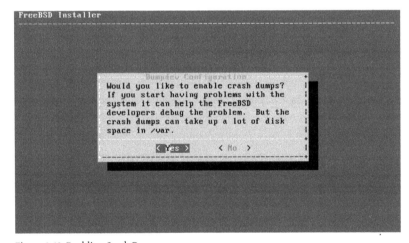

Figure 2.48. Enabling Crash Dumps

2.8.6. Add Users

The next menu prompts to create at least one user account. It is recommended to login to the system using a user account rather than as root. When logged in as root, there are essentially no limits or protection on what can be done. Logging in as a normal user is safer and more secure.

Select [Yes] to add new users.

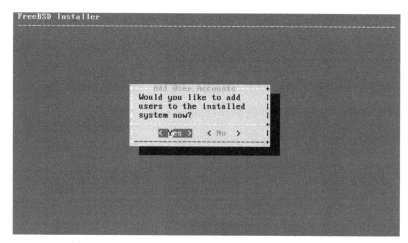

Figure 2.49. Add User Accounts

Follow the prompts and input the requested information for the user account. The example shown in Figure 2.50, "Enter User Information" creates the `asample` user account.

```
FreeBSD Installer
=========================
Add Users

Username: asample
Full name: Arthur Sample
Uid (Leave empty for default):
Login group [asample]:
Login group is asample. Invite asample into other groups? []: wheel
Login class [default]:
Shell (sh csh tcsh nologin) [sh]: csh
Home directory [/home/asample]:
Home directory permissions (Leave empty for default):
Use password-based authentication? [yes]:
Use an empty password? (yes/no) [no]:
Use a random password? (yes/no) [no]:
Enter password:
Enter password again:
Lock out the account after creation? [no]: █
```

Figure 2.50. Enter User Information

Here is a summary of the information to input:

- `Username` - The name the user will enter to log in. A common convention is to use the first letter of the first name combined with the last name, as long as each username is unique for the system. The username is case sensitive and should not contain any spaces.

- `Full name` - The user's full name. This can contain spaces and is used as a description for the user account.

- `Uid` - User ID. Typically, this is left blank so the system will assign a value.

- `Login group` - The user's group. Typically this is left blank to accept the default.

- `Invite user into other groups?` - Additional groups to which the user will be added as a member. If the user needs administrative access, type `wheel` here.

- `Login class` - Typically left blank for the default.

- `Shell` - Type in one of the listed values to set the interactive shell for the user. Refer to Section 3.9, "Shells" for more information about shells.

- `Home directory` - The user's home directory. The default is usually correct.

- `Home directory permissions` - Permissions on the user's home directory. The default is usually correct.

- Use password-based authentication? - Typically yes so that the user is prompted to input their password at login.

- Use an empty password? - Typically no as it is insecure to have a blank password.

- Use a random password? - Typically no so that the user can set their own password in the next prompt.

- Enter password - The password for this user. Characters typed will not show on the screen.

- Enter password again - The password must be typed again for verification.

- Lock out the account after creation? - Typically no so that the user can login.

After entering everything, a summary is shown for review. If a mistake was made, enter no and try again. If everything is correct, enter yes to create the new user.

```
Login group [asample]:
Login group is asample. Invite asample into other groups? []: wheel
Login class [default]:
Shell (sh csh tcsh nologin) [sh]: csh
Home directory [/home/asample]:
Home directory permissions (Leave empty for default):
Use password-based authentication? [yes]:
Use an empty password? (yes/no) [no]:
Use a random password? (yes/no) [no]:
Enter password:
Enter password again:
Lock out the account after creation? [no]:
Username    : asample
Password    : *****
Full Name   : Arthur Sample
Uid         : 1001
Class       :
Groups      : asample wheel
Home        : /home/asample
Home Mode   :
Shell       : /bin/csh
Locked      : no
OK? (yes/no): yes
adduser: INFO: Successfully added (asample) to the user database.
Add another user? (yes/no):
```

Figure 2.51. Exit User and Group Management

If there are more users to add, answer the Add another user? question with yes. Enter no to finish adding users and continue the installation.

For more information on adding users and user management, see Section 3.3, "Users and Basic Account Management".

2.8.7. Final Configuration

After everything has been installed and configured, a final chance is provided to modify settings.

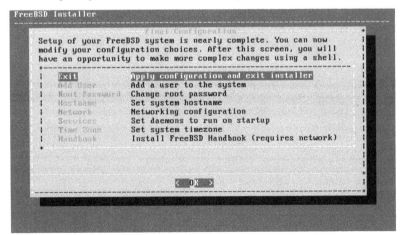

Figure 2.52. Final Configuration

Use this menu to make any changes or do any additional configuration before completing the installation.

- **Add User** - Described in Section 2.8.6, "Add Users".

- **Root Password** - Described in Section 2.8.1, "Setting the root Password".

- **Hostname** - Described in Section 2.5.2, "Setting the Hostname".

- **Network** - Described in Section 2.8.2, "Configuring Network Interfaces".

- **Services** - Described in Section 2.8.4, "Enabling Services".

- **Time Zone** - Described in Section 2.8.3, "Setting the Time Zone".

- **Handbook** - Download and install the FreeBSD Handbook.

After any final configuration is complete, select Exit.

Figure 2.53. Manual Configuration

bsdinstall will prompt if there are any additional configuration that needs to be done before rebooting into the new system. Select [Yes] to exit to a shell within the new system or [No] to proceed to the last step of the installation.

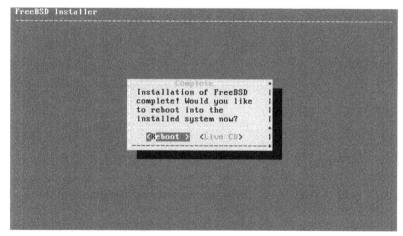

Figure 2.54. Complete the Installation

If further configuration or special setup is needed, select [Live CD] to boot the install media into Live CD mode.

If the installation is complete, select [Reboot] to reboot the computer and start the new FreeBSD system. Do not forget to remove the FreeBSD install media or the computer may boot from it again.

As FreeBSD boots, informational messages are displayed. After the system finishes booting, a login prompt is displayed. At the login: prompt, enter the username added during the installation. Avoid logging in as root. Refer to Section 3.3.1.3, "The Superuser Account" for instructions on how to become the superuser when administrative access is needed.

The messages that appeared during boot can be reviewed by pressing Scroll-Lock to turn on the scroll-back buffer. The PgUp, PgDn, and arrow keys can be used to scroll back through the messages. When finished, press Scroll-Lock again to unlock the display and return to the console. To review these messages once the system has been up for some time, type less /var/run/dmesg.boot from a command prompt. Press q to return to the command line after viewing.

If sshd was enabled in Figure 2.47, "Selecting Additional Services to Enable", the first boot may be a bit slower as the system will generate the RSA and DSA keys. Subsequent boots will be faster. The fingerprints of the keys will be displayed, as seen in this example:

```
Generating public/private rsa1 key pair.
Your identification has been saved in /etc/ssh/ssh_host_key.
Your public key has been saved in /etc/ssh/ssh_host_key.pub.
The key fingerprint is:
10:a0:f5:af:93:ae:a3:1a:b2:bb:3c:35:d9:5a:b3:f3 root@machine3.example.com
The key's randomart image is:
+--[RSA1 1024]----+
|      o..        |
|    o . .        |
|   .   o         |
|        o        |
|     o  S        |
|    + + o        |
|o . + *          |
|0+ ..+ .         |
|==o..o+E         |
+-----------------+
Generating public/private dsa key pair.
Your identification has been saved in /etc/ssh/ssh_host_dsa_key.
Your public key has been saved in /etc/ssh/ssh_host_dsa_key.pub.
The key fingerprint is:
7e:1c:ce:dc:8a:3a:18:13:5b:34:b5:cf:d9:d1:47:b2 root@machine3.example.com
The key's randomart image is:
+--[ DSA 1024]----+
|      ..     . . |
|     o .    . + |
|    . ...    . E .|
|    .. o o . . |
|     + S = .    |
|     + . = o     |
|      + . * .    |
|     .. o .      |
|      .o. .      |
+-----------------+
Starting sshd.
```

Refer to Section 13.8, "OpenSSH" for more information about fingerprints and SSH.

FreeBSD does not install a graphical environment by default. Refer to Chapter 5, *The X Window System* for more information about installing and configuring a graphical window manager.

Proper shutdown of a FreeBSD computer helps protect data and hardware from damage. *Do not turn off the power before the system has been properly shut down!* If the user is a member of the wheel group, become the superuser by typing su at the command line and entering the root password. Then, type shutdown -p now and the system will shut down cleanly, and if the hardware supports it, turn itself off.

2.9. Troubleshooting

This section covers basic installation troubleshooting, such as common problems people have reported.

Check the Hardware Notes (https://www.freebsd.org/releases/index.html) document for the version of FreeBSD to make sure the hardware is supported. If the hardware is supported and lock-ups or other problems occur, build a custom kernel using the instructions in Chapter 8, *Configuring the FreeBSD Kernel* to add support for devices which are not present in the GENERIC kernel. The default kernel assumes that most hardware devices are in their factory default configuration in terms of IRQs, I/O addresses, and DMA channels. If the hardware has been reconfigured, a custom kernel configuration file can tell FreeBSD where to find things.

> ### Note
>
> Some installation problems can be avoided or alleviated by updating the firmware on various hardware components, most notably the motherboard. Motherboard firmware is usually referred to as the BIOS. Most motherboard and computer manufacturers have a website for upgrades and upgrade information.
>
> Manufacturers generally advise against upgrading the motherboard BIOS unless there is a good reason for doing so, like a critical update. The upgrade process *can* go wrong, leaving the BIOS incomplete and the computer inoperative.

If the system hangs while probing hardware during boot, or it behaves strangely during install, ACPI may be the culprit. FreeBSD makes extensive use of the system ACPI service on the i386, amd64, and ia64 platforms to aid in system configuration if it is detected during boot. Unfortunately, some bugs still exist in both the ACPI driver and within system motherboards and BIOS firmware. ACPI can be disabled by setting the `hint.acpi.0.disabled` hint in the third stage boot loader:

```
set hint.acpi.0.disabled="1"
```

This is reset each time the system is booted, so it is necessary to add `hint.acpi.0.disabled="1"` to the file `/boot/loader.conf`. More information about the boot loader can be found in Section 12.1, "Synopsis".

2.10. Using the Live CD

The welcome menu of bsdinstall, shown in Figure 2.3, "Welcome Menu", provides a [Live CD] option. This is useful for those who are still wondering whether FreeBSD is the right operating system for them and want to test some of the features before installing.

The following points should be noted before using the [Live CD]:

• To gain access to the system, authentication is required. The username is root and the password is blank.

• As the system runs directly from the installation media, performance will be significantly slower than that of a system installed on a hard disk.

• This option only provides a command prompt and not a graphical interface.

Chapter 3. FreeBSD Basics

3.1. Synopsis

This chapter covers the basic commands and functionality of the FreeBSD operating system. Much of this material is relevant for any UNIX®-like operating system. New FreeBSD users are encouraged to read through this chapter carefully.

After reading this chapter, you will know:

- How to use and configure virtual consoles.

- How to create and manage users and groups on FreeBSD.

- How UNIX® file permissions and FreeBSD file flags work.

- The default FreeBSD file system layout.

- The FreeBSD disk organization.

- How to mount and unmount file systems.

- What processes, daemons, and signals are.

- What a shell is, and how to change the default login environment.

- How to use basic text editors.

- What devices and device nodes are.

- How to read manual pages for more information.

3.2. Virtual Consoles and Terminals

Unless FreeBSD has been configured to automatically start a graphical environment during startup, the system will boot into a command line login prompt, as seen in this example:

```
FreeBSD/amd64 (pc3.example.org) (ttyv0)

login:
```

The first line contains some information about the system. The amd64 indicates that the system in this example is running a 64-bit version of FreeBSD. The hostname is pc3.example.org, and ttyv0 indicates that this is the "system console". The second line is the login prompt.

Since FreeBSD is a multiuser system, it needs some way to distinguish between different users. This is accomplished by requiring every user to log into the system before gaining access to the programs on the system. Every user has a unique name "username" and a personal "password".

To log into the system console, type the username that was configured during system installation, as described in Section 2.8.6, "Add Users", and press Enter. Then enter the password associated with the username and press Enter. The password is *not echoed* for security reasons.

Once the correct password is input, the message of the day (MOTD) will be displayed followed by a command prompt. Depending upon the shell that was selected when the user was created, this prompt will be a #, $, or % character. The prompt indicates that the user is now logged into the FreeBSD system console and ready to try the available commands.

3.2.1. Virtual Consoles

While the system console can be used to interact with the system, a user working from the command line at the keyboard of a FreeBSD system will typically instead log into a virtual console. This is because system messages are configured by default to display on the system console. These messages will appear over the command or file that the user is working on, making it difficult to concentrate on the work at hand.

By default, FreeBSD is configured to provide several virtual consoles for inputting commands. Each virtual console has its own login prompt and shell and it is easy to switch between virtual consoles. This essentially provides the command line equivalent of having several windows open at the same time in a graphical environment.

The key combinations Alt+F1 through Alt+F8 have been reserved by FreeBSD for switching between virtual consoles. Use Alt+F1 to switch to the system console (ttyv0), Alt+F2 to access the first virtual console (ttyv1), Alt+F3 to access the second virtual console (ttyv2), and so on.

When switching from one console to the next, FreeBSD manages the screen output. The result is an illusion of having multiple virtual screens and keyboards that can be used to type commands for FreeBSD to run. The programs that are launched in one virtual console do not stop running when the user switches to a different virtual console.

Refer to kbdcontrol(1), vidcontrol(1), atkbd(4), syscons(4), and vt(4) for a more technical description of the FreeBSD console and its keyboard drivers.

In FreeBSD, the number of available virtual consoles is configured in this section of /etc/ttys :

```
# name    getty                        type  status comments
#
ttyv0   "/usr/libexec/getty Pc"        xterm  on  secure
# Virtual terminals
ttyv1   "/usr/libexec/getty Pc"        xterm  on  secure
ttyv2   "/usr/libexec/getty Pc"        xterm  on  secure
ttyv3   "/usr/libexec/getty Pc"        xterm  on  secure
ttyv4   "/usr/libexec/getty Pc"        xterm  on  secure
ttyv5   "/usr/libexec/getty Pc"        xterm  on  secure
ttyv6   "/usr/libexec/getty Pc"        xterm  on  secure
ttyv7   "/usr/libexec/getty Pc"        xterm  on  secure
ttyv8   "/usr/X11R6/bin/xdm -nodaemon" xterm  off secure
```

To disable a virtual console, put a comment symbol (#) at the beginning of the line representing that virtual console. For example, to reduce the number of available virtual consoles from eight to four, put a # in front of the last four lines representing virtual consoles ttyv5 through ttyv8. *Do not* comment out the line for the system console ttyv0. Note that the last virtual console (ttyv8) is used to access the graphical environment if Xorg has been installed and configured as described in Chapter 5, *The X Window System*.

For a detailed description of every column in this file and the available options for the virtual consoles, refer to ttys(5).

3.2.2. Single User Mode

The FreeBSD boot menu provides an option labelled as "Boot Single User". If this option is selected, the system will boot into a special mode known as "single user mode". This mode is typically used to repair a system that will not boot or to reset the root password when it is not known. While in single user mode, networking and other virtual consoles are not available. However, full root access to the system is available, and by default, the root password is not needed. For these reasons, physical access to the keyboard is needed to boot into this mode and determining who has physical access to the keyboard is something to consider when securing a FreeBSD system.

The settings which control single user mode are found in this section of /etc/ttys :

```
# name  getty                      type   status   comments
#
# If console is marked "insecure", then init will ask for the root password
# when going to single-user mode.
```

```
console none                                    unknown  off  secure
```

By default, the status is set to secure. This assumes that who has physical access to the keyboard is either not important or it is controlled by a physical security policy. If this setting is changed to insecure, the assumption is that the environment itself is insecure because anyone can access the keyboard. When this line is changed to insecure, FreeBSD will prompt for the root password when a user selects to boot into single user mode.

Note

Be careful when changing this setting to insecure! If the root password is forgotten, booting into single user mode is still possible, but may be difficult for someone who is not familiar with the FreeBSD booting process.

3.2.3. Changing Console Video Modes

The FreeBSD console default video mode may be adjusted to 1024x768, 1280x1024, or any other size supported by the graphics chip and monitor. To use a different video mode load the VESA module:

```
# kldload vesa
```

To determine which video modes are supported by the hardware, use vidcontrol(1). To get a list of supported video modes issue the following:

```
# vidcontrol -i mode
```

The output of this command lists the video modes that are supported by the hardware. To select a new video mode, specify the mode using vidcontrol(1) as the root user:

```
# vidcontrol MODE_279
```

If the new video mode is acceptable, it can be permanently set on boot by adding it to /etc/rc.conf :

```
allscreens_flags="MODE_279"
```

3.3. Users and Basic Account Management

FreeBSD allows multiple users to use the computer at the same time. While only one user can sit in front of the screen and use the keyboard at any one time, any number of users can log in to the system through the network. To use the system, each user should have their own user account.

This chapter describes:

• The different types of user accounts on a FreeBSD system.

• How to add, remove, and modify user accounts.

• How to set limits to control the resources that users and groups are allowed to access.

• How to create groups and add users as members of a group.

3.3.1. Account Types

Since all access to the FreeBSD system is achieved using accounts and all processes are run by users, user and account management is important.

There are three main types of accounts: system accounts, user accounts, and the superuser account.

3.3.1.1. System Accounts

System accounts are used to run services such as DNS, mail, and web servers. The reason for this is security; if all services ran as the superuser, they could act without restriction.

Examples of system accounts are daemon, operator, bind, news, and www.

nobody is the generic unprivileged system account. However, the more services that use nobody, the more files and processes that user will become associated with, and hence the more privileged that user becomes.

3.3.1.2. User Accounts

User accounts are assigned to real people and are used to log in and use the system. Every person accessing the system should have a unique user account. This allows the administrator to find out who is doing what and prevents users from clobbering the settings of other users.

Each user can set up their own environment to accommodate their use of the system, by configuring their default shell, editor, key bindings, and language settings.

Every user account on a FreeBSD system has certain information associated with it:

User name
: The user name is typed at the login: prompt. Each user must have a unique user name. There are a number of rules for creating valid user names which are documented in passwd(5). It is recommended to use user names that consist of eight or fewer, all lower case characters in order to maintain backwards compatibility with applications.

Password
: Each account has an associated password.

User ID (UID)
: The User ID (UID) is a number used to uniquely identify the user to the FreeBSD system. Commands that allow a user name to be specified will first convert it to the UID. It is recommended to use a UID less than 65535, since higher values may cause compatibility issues with some software.

Group ID (GID)
: The Group ID (GID) is a number used to uniquely identify the primary group that the user belongs to. Groups are a mechanism for controlling access to resources based on a user's GID rather than their UID. This can significantly reduce the size of some configuration files and allows users to be members of more than one group. It is recommended to use a GID of 65535 or lower as higher GIDs may break some software.

Login class
: Login classes are an extension to the group mechanism that provide additional flexibility when tailoring the system to different users. Login classes are discussed further in Section 13.13.1, "Configuring Login Classes".

Password change time
: By default, passwords do not expire. However, password expiration can be enabled on a per-user basis, forcing some or all users to change their passwords after a certain amount of time has elapsed.

Account expiration time
: By default, FreeBSD does not expire accounts. When creating accounts that need a limited lifespan, such as student accounts in a school, specify the account expiry date using pw(8). After the expiry time has elapsed, the account cannot be used to log in to the system, although the account's directories and files will remain.

User's full name
: The user name uniquely identifies the account to FreeBSD, but does not necessarily reflect the user's real name. Similar to a comment, this information can contain spaces, uppercase characters, and be more than 8 characters long.

Home directory

The home directory is the full path to a directory on the system. This is the user's starting directory when the user logs in. A common convention is to put all user home directories under */home/username* or */usr/home/username*. Each user stores their personal files and subdirectories in their own home directory.

User shell

The shell provides the user's default environment for interacting with the system. There are many different kinds of shells and experienced users will have their own preferences, which can be reflected in their account settings.

3.3.1.3. The Superuser Account

The superuser account, usually called root, is used to manage the system with no limitations on privileges. For this reason, it should not be used for day-to-day tasks like sending and receiving mail, general exploration of the system, or programming.

The superuser, unlike other user accounts, can operate without limits, and misuse of the superuser account may result in spectacular disasters. User accounts are unable to destroy the operating system by mistake, so it is recommended to login as a user account and to only become the superuser when a command requires extra privilege.

Always double and triple-check any commands issued as the superuser, since an extra space or missing character can mean irreparable data loss.

There are several ways to gain superuser privilege. While one can log in as root, this is highly discouraged.

Instead, use su(1) to become the superuser. If - is specified when running this command, the user will also inherit the root user's environment. The user running this command must be in the wheel group or else the command will fail. The user must also know the password for the root user account.

In this example, the user only becomes superuser in order to run make install as this step requires superuser privilege. Once the command completes, the user types exit to leave the superuser account and return to the privilege of their user account.

Example 3.1. Install a Program As the Superuser

```
% configure
% make
% su -
Password:
# make install
# exit
%
```

The built-in su(1) framework works well for single systems or small networks with just one system administrator. An alternative is to install the security/sudo package or port. This software provides activity logging and allows the administrator to configure which users can run which commands as the superuser.

3.3.2. Managing Accounts

FreeBSD provides a variety of different commands to manage user accounts. The most common commands are summarized in Table 3.1, "Utilities for Managing User Accounts", followed by some examples of their usage. See the manual page for each utility for more details and usage examples.

Table 3.1. Utilities for Managing User Accounts

Command	Summary
adduser(8)	The recommended command-line application for adding new users.
rmuser(8)	The recommended command-line application for removing users.
chpass(1)	A flexible tool for changing user database information.
passwd(1)	The command-line tool to change user passwords.
pw(8)	A powerful and flexible tool for modifying all aspects of user accounts.

3.3.2.1. adduser

The recommended program for adding new users is adduser(8). When a new user is added, this program automatically updates /etc/passwd and /etc/group . It also creates a home directory for the new user, copies in the default configuration files from /usr/share/skel , and can optionally mail the new user a welcome message. This utility must be run as the superuser.

The adduser(8) utility is interactive and walks through the steps for creating a new user account. As seen in Example 3.2, "Adding a User on FreeBSD", either input the required information or press Return to accept the default value shown in square brackets. In this example, the user has been invited into the wheel group, allowing them to become the superuser with su(1). When finished, the utility will prompt to either create another user or to exit.

Example 3.2. Adding a User on FreeBSD

```
# adduser
Username: jru
Full name: J. Random User
Uid (Leave empty for default):
Login group [jru]:
Login group is jru. Invite jru into other groups? []: wheel
Login class [default]:
Shell (sh csh tcsh zsh nologin) [sh]: zsh
Home directory [/home/jru]:
Home directory permissions (Leave empty for default):
Use password-based authentication? [yes]:
Use an empty password? (yes/no) [no]:
Use a random password? (yes/no) [no]:
Enter password:
Enter password again:
Lock out the account after creation? [no]:
Username   : jru
Password   : ****
Full Name  : J. Random User
Uid        : 1001
Class      :
Groups     : jru wheel
Home       : /home/jru
Shell      : /usr/local/bin/zsh
Locked     : no
OK? (yes/no): yes
adduser: INFO: Successfully added (jru) to the user database.
Add another user? (yes/no): no
Goodbye!
#
```

Note

Since the password is not echoed when typed, be careful to not mistype the password when creating the user account.

3.3.2.2. rmuser

To completely remove a user from the system, run rmuser(8) as the superuser. This command performs the following steps:

1. Removes the user's crontab(1) entry, if one exists.

2. Removes any at(1) jobs belonging to the user.

3. Kills all processes owned by the user.

4. Removes the user from the system's local password file.

5. Optionally removes the user's home directory, if it is owned by the user.

6. Removes the incoming mail files belonging to the user from /var/mail .

7. Removes all files owned by the user from temporary file storage areas such as /tmp.

8. Finally, removes the username from all groups to which it belongs in /etc/group . If a group becomes empty and the group name is the same as the username, the group is removed. This complements the per-user unique groups created by adduser(8).

rmuser(8) cannot be used to remove superuser accounts since that is almost always an indication of massive destruction.

By default, an interactive mode is used, as shown in the following example.

Example 3.3. rmuser Interactive Account Removal

```
# rmuser jru
Matching password entry:
jru:*:1001:1001::0:0:J. Random User:/home/jru:/usr/local/bin/zsh
Is this the entry you wish to remove? y
Remove user's home directory (/home/jru)? y
Removing user (jru): mailspool home passwd.
#
```

3.3.2.3. chpass

Any user can use chpass(1) to change their default shell and personal information associated with their user account. The superuser can use this utility to change additional account information for any user.

When passed no options, aside from an optional username, chpass(1) displays an editor containing user information. When the user exits from the editor, the user database is updated with the new information.

Note

This utility will prompt for the user's password when exiting the editor, unless the utility is run as the superuser.

In Example 3.4, "Using chpass as Superuser", the superuser has typed chpass jru and is now viewing the fields that can be changed for this user. If jru runs this command instead, only the last six fields will be displayed and available for editing. This is shown in Example 3.5, "Using chpass as Regular User".

Example 3.4. Using chpass as Superuser

```
#Changing user database information for jru.
Login: jru
Password: *
Uid [#]: 1001
Gid [# or name]: 1001
Change [month day year]:
Expire [month day year]:
Class:
Home directory: /home/jru
Shell: /usr/local/bin/zsh
Full Name: J. Random User
Office Location:
Office Phone:
Home Phone:
Other information:
```

Example 3.5. Using chpass as Regular User

```
#Changing user database information for jru.
Shell: /usr/local/bin/zsh
Full Name: J. Random User
Office Location:
Office Phone:
Home Phone:
Other information:
```

Note

The commands chfn(1) and chsh(1) are links to chpass(1), as are ypchpass(1), ypchfn(1), and ypchsh(1). Since NIS support is automatic, specifying the yp before the command is not necessary. How to configure NIS is covered in Chapter 28, *Network Servers*.

3.3.2.4. passwd

Any user can easily change their password using passwd(1). To prevent accidental or unauthorized changes, this command will prompt for the user's original password before a new password can be set:

Example 3.6. Changing Your Password

```
% passwd
Changing local password for jru.
Old password:
New password:
Retype new password:
passwd: updating the database...
passwd: done
```

The superuser can change any user's password by specifying the username when running passwd(1). When this utility is run as the superuser, it will not prompt for the user's current password. This allows the password to be changed when a user cannot remember the original password.

Example 3.7. Changing Another User's Password as the Superuser

```
# passwd jru
Changing local password for jru.
New password:
Retype new password:
passwd: updating the database...
passwd: done
```

Note

As with chpass(1), yppasswd(1) is a link to passwd(1), so NIS works with either command.

3.3.2.5. pw

The pw(8) utility can create, remove, modify, and display users and groups. It functions as a front end to the system user and group files. pw(8) has a very powerful set of command line options that make it suitable for use in shell scripts, but new users may find it more complicated than the other commands presented in this section.

3.3.3. Managing Groups

A group is a list of users. A group is identified by its group name and GID. In FreeBSD, the kernel uses the UID of a process, and the list of groups it belongs to, to determine what the process is allowed to do. Most of the time, the GID of a user or process usually means the first group in the list.

The group name to GID mapping is listed in /etc/group . This is a plain text file with four colon-delimited fields. The first field is the group name, the second is the encrypted password, the third the GID, and the fourth the comma-delimited list of members. For a more complete description of the syntax, refer to group(5).

The superuser can modify /etc/group using a text editor. Alternatively, pw(8) can be used to add and edit groups. For example, to add a group called teamtwo and then confirm that it exists:

Example 3.8. Adding a Group Using pw(8)

```
# pw groupadd teamtwo
# pw groupshow teamtwo
teamtwo:*:1100:
```

In this example, 1100 is the GID of teamtwo. Right now, teamtwo has no members. This command will add jru as a member of teamtwo.

Example 3.9. Adding User Accounts to a New Group Using pw(8)

```
# pw groupmod teamtwo -M jru
# pw groupshow teamtwo
teamtwo:*:1100:jru
```

The argument to -M is a comma-delimited list of users to be added to a new (empty) group or to replace the members of an existing group. To the user, this group membership is different from (and in addition to) the user's primary group listed in the password file. This means that the user will not show up as a member when using groupshow with pw(8), but will show up when the information is queried via id(1) or a similar tool. When pw(8) is used to add a user to a group, it only manipulates /etc/group and does not attempt to read additional data from /etc/passwd.

Example 3.10. Adding a New Member to a Group Using pw(8)

```
# pw groupmod teamtwo -m db
# pw groupshow teamtwo
teamtwo:*:1100:jru,db
```

In this example, the argument to -m is a comma-delimited list of users who are to be added to the group. Unlike the previous example, these users are appended to the group and do not replace existing users in the group.

Example 3.11. Using id(1) to Determine Group Membership

```
% id jru
uid=1001(jru) gid=1001(jru) groups=1001(jru), 1100(teamtwo)
```

In this example, jru is a member of the groups jru and teamtwo.

For more information about this command and the format of /etc/group , refer to pw(8) and group(5).

3.4. Permissions

In FreeBSD, every file and directory has an associated set of permissions and several utilities are available for viewing and modifying these permissions. Understanding how permissions work is necessary to make sure that users are able to access the files that they need and are unable to improperly access the files used by the operating system or owned by other users.

This section discusses the traditional UNIX® permissions used in FreeBSD. For finer grained file system access control, refer to Section 13.9, "Access Control Lists".

In UNIX®, basic permissions are assigned using three types of access: read, write, and execute. These access types are used to determine file access to the file's owner, group, and others (everyone else). The read, write, and execute permissions can be represented as the letters r, w, and x. They can also be represented as binary numbers as each permission is either on or off (0). When represented as a number, the order is always read as rwx, where r has an on value of 4, w has an on value of 2 and x has an on value of 1.

Table 4.1 summarizes the possible numeric and alphabetic possibilities. When reading the "Directory Listing" column, a - is used to represent a permission that is set to off.

Table 3.2. UNIX® Permissions

Value	Permission	Directory Listing
0	No read, no write, no execute	- - -
1	No read, no write, execute	- -x
2	No read, write, no execute	-w-
3	No read, write, execute	-wx
4	Read, no write, no execute	r--
5	Read, no write, execute	r-x
6	Read, write, no execute	rw-
7	Read, write, execute	rwx

Use the -l argument to ls(1) to view a long directory listing that includes a column of information about a file's permissions for the owner, group, and everyone else. For example, a ls -l in an arbitrary directory may show:

```
% ls -l
total 530
-rw-r--r--  1 root  wheel      512 Sep  5 12:31 myfile
-rw-r--r--  1 root  wheel      512 Sep  5 12:31 otherfile
-rw-r--r--  1 root  wheel     7680 Sep  5 12:31 email.txt
```

The first (leftmost) character in the first column indicates whether this file is a regular file, a directory, a special character device, a socket, or any other special pseudo-file device. In this example, the - indicates a regular file. The next three characters, rw- in this example, give the permissions for the owner of the file. The next three characters, r--, give the permissions for the group that the file belongs to. The final three characters, r--, give the permissions for the rest of the world. A dash means that the permission is turned off. In this example, the permissions are set so the owner can read and write to the file, the group can read the file, and the rest of the world can only read the file. According to the table above, the permissions for this file would be 644, where each digit represents the three parts of the file's permission.

How does the system control permissions on devices? FreeBSD treats most hardware devices as a file that programs can open, read, and write data to. These special device files are stored in /dev/.

Directories are also treated as files. They have read, write, and execute permissions. The executable bit for a directory has a slightly different meaning than that of files. When a directory is marked executable, it means it is possible to change into that directory using cd(1). This also means that it is possible to access the files within that directory, subject to the permissions on the files themselves.

In order to perform a directory listing, the read permission must be set on the directory. In order to delete a file that one knows the name of, it is necessary to have write *and* execute permissions to the directory containing the file.

There are more permission bits, but they are primarily used in special circumstances such as setuid binaries and sticky directories. For more information on file permissions and how to set them, refer to chmod(1).

3.4.1. Symbolic Permissions

Contributed by Tom Rhodes.

Symbolic permissions use characters instead of octal values to assign permissions to files or directories. Symbolic permissions use the syntax of (who) (action) (permissions), where the following values are available:

Option	Letter	Represents
(who)	u	User
(who)	g	Group owner
(who)	o	Other
(who)	a	All ("world")
(action)	+	Adding permissions
(action)	-	Removing permissions
(action)	=	Explicitly set permissions
(permissions)	r	Read
(permissions)	w	Write
(permissions)	x	Execute
(permissions)	t	Sticky bit
(permissions)	s	Set UID or GID

These values are used with chmod(1), but with letters instead of numbers. For example, the following command would block other users from accessing *FILE*:

```
% chmod go= FILE
```

A comma separated list can be provided when more than one set of changes to a file must be made. For example, the following command removes the group and "world" write permission on *FILE*, and adds the execute permissions for everyone:

```
% chmod go-w,a+x  FILE
```

3.4.2. FreeBSD File Flags

Contributed by Tom Rhodes.

In addition to file permissions, FreeBSD supports the use of "file flags". These flags add an additional level of security and control over files, but not directories. With file flags, even root can be prevented from removing or altering files.

File flags are modified using chflags(1). For example, to enable the system undeletable flag on the file file1, issue the following command:

```
# chflags sunlink file1
```

To disable the system undeletable flag, put a "no" in front of the sunlink:

```
# chflags nosunlink file1
```

To view the flags of a file, use -lo with ls(1):

```
# ls -lo file1
```

```
-rw-r--r--  1 trhodes  trhodes  sunlnk 0 Mar  1 05:54 file1
```

Several file flags may only be added or removed by the root user. In other cases, the file owner may set its file flags. Refer to chflags(1) and chflags(2) for more information.

3.4.3. The `setuid`, `setgid`, and `sticky` Permissions

Contributed by Tom Rhodes.

Other than the permissions already discussed, there are three other specific settings that all administrators should know about. They are the `setuid`, `setgid`, and `sticky` permissions.

These settings are important for some UNIX® operations as they provide functionality not normally granted to normal users. To understand them, the difference between the real user ID and effective user ID must be noted.

The real user ID is the UID who owns or starts the process. The effective UID is the user ID the process runs as. As an example, passwd(1) runs with the real user ID when a user changes their password. However, in order to update the password database, the command runs as the effective ID of the root user. This allows users to change their passwords without seeing a Permission Denied error.

The setuid permission may be set by prefixing a permission set with the number four (4) as shown in the following example:

```
# chmod 4755 suidexample.sh
```

The permissions on *suidexample.sh* now look like the following:

```
-rwsr-xr-x  1 trhodes  trhodes    63 Aug 29 06:36 suidexample.sh
```

Note that a `s` is now part of the permission set designated for the file owner, replacing the executable bit. This allows utilities which need elevated permissions, such as passwd(1).

 Note

The `nosuid` mount(8) option will cause such binaries to silently fail without alerting the user. That option is not completely reliable as a `nosuid` wrapper may be able to circumvent it.

To view this in real time, open two terminals. On one, type `passwd` as a normal user. While it waits for a new password, check the process table and look at the user information for passwd(1):

In terminal A:

```
Changing local password for trhodes
Old Password:
```

In terminal B:

```
# ps aux | grep passwd
```

```
trhodes  5232  0.0  0.2  3420  1608   0  R+   2:10AM  0:00.00 grep passwd
root     5211  0.0  0.2  3620  1724   2  I+   2:09AM  0:00.01 passwd
```

Although passwd(1) is run as a normal user, it is using the effective UID of root.

The `setgid` permission performs the same function as the `setuid` permission; except that it alters the group settings. When an application or utility executes with this setting, it will be granted the permissions based on the group that owns the file, not the user who started the process.

To set the `setgid` permission on a file, provide chmod(1) with a leading two (2):

```
# chmod 2755 sgidexample.sh
```

In the following listing, notice that the s is now in the field designated for the group permission settings:

```
-rwxr-sr-x   1 trhodes   trhodes    44 Aug 31 01:49 sgidexample.sh
```

> **Note**
>
> In these examples, even though the shell script in question is an executable file, it will not run with a different EUID or effective user ID. This is because shell scripts may not access the setuid(2) system calls.

The setuid and setgid permission bits may lower system security, by allowing for elevated permissions. The third special permission, the sticky bit, can strengthen the security of a system.

When the sticky bit is set on a directory, it allows file deletion only by the file owner. This is useful to prevent file deletion in public directories, such as /tmp, by users who do not own the file. To utilize this permission, prefix the permission set with a one (1):

```
# chmod 1777 /tmp
```

The sticky bit permission will display as a t at the very end of the permission set:

```
# ls -al / | grep tmp
```

```
drwxrwxrwt  10 root   wheel      512 Aug 31 01:49 tmp
```

3.5. Directory Structure

The FreeBSD directory hierarchy is fundamental to obtaining an overall understanding of the system. The most important directory is root or, "/". This directory is the first one mounted at boot time and it contains the base system necessary to prepare the operating system for multi-user operation. The root directory also contains mount points for other file systems that are mounted during the transition to multi-user operation.

A mount point is a directory where additional file systems can be grafted onto a parent file system (usually the root file system). This is further described in Section 3.6, "Disk Organization". Standard mount points include / usr/, /var/, /tmp/, /mnt/, and /cdrom/. These directories are usually referenced to entries in /etc/fstab. This file is a table of various file systems and mount points and is read by the system. Most of the file systems in /etc/ fstab are mounted automatically at boot time from the script rc(8) unless their entry includes noauto. Details can be found in Section 3.7.1, "The fstab File".

A complete description of the file system hierarchy is available in hier(7). The following table provides a brief overview of the most common directories.

Directory	Description
/	Root directory of the file system.
/bin/	User utilities fundamental to both single-user and multi-user environments.
/boot/	Programs and configuration files used during operating system bootstrap.
/boot/defaults/	Default boot configuration files. Refer to loader.conf(5) for details.
/dev/	Device nodes. Refer to intro(4) for details.

Directory	Description
/etc/	System configuration files and scripts.
/etc/defaults/	Default system configuration files. Refer to rc(8) for details.
/etc/mail/	Configuration files for mail transport agents such as sendmail(8).
/etc/periodic/	Scripts that run daily, weekly, and monthly, via cron(8). Refer to periodic(8) for details.
/etc/ppp/	ppp(8) configuration files.
/mnt/	Empty directory commonly used by system administrators as a temporary mount point.
/proc/	Process file system. Refer to procfs(5), mount_procfs(8) for details.
/rescue/	Statically linked programs for emergency recovery as described in rescue(8).
/root/	Home directory for the root account.
/sbin/	System programs and administration utilities fundamental to both single-user and multi-user environments.
/tmp/	Temporary files which are usually *not* preserved across a system reboot. A memory-based file system is often mounted at /tmp. This can be automated using the tmpmfs-related variables of rc.conf(5) or with an entry in /etc/fstab ; refer to mdmfs(8) for details.
/usr/	The majority of user utilities and applications.
/usr/bin/	Common utilities, programming tools, and applications.
/usr/include/	Standard C include files.
/usr/lib/	Archive libraries.
/usr/libdata/	Miscellaneous utility data files.
/usr/libexec/	System daemons and system utilities executed by other programs.
/usr/local/	Local executables and libraries. Also used as the default destination for the FreeBSD ports framework. Within /usr/local, the general layout sketched out by hier(7) for /usr should be used. Exceptions are the man directory, which is directly under /usr/local rather than under /usr/local/share , and the ports documentation is in share/doc/ *port*.
/usr/obj/	Architecture-specific target tree produced by building the /usr/src tree.
/usr/ports/	The FreeBSD Ports Collection (optional).
/usr/sbin/	System daemons and system utilities executed by users.
/usr/share/	Architecture-independent files.
/usr/src/	BSD and/or local source files.
/var/	Multi-purpose log, temporary, transient, and spool files. A memory-based file system is sometimes mounted at

Directory	Description
	/var. This can be automated using the varmfs-related variables in rc.conf(5) or with an entry in /etc/fstab ; refer to mdmfs(8) for details.
/var/log/	Miscellaneous system log files.
/var/mail/	User mailbox files.
/var/spool/	Miscellaneous printer and mail system spooling directories.
/var/tmp/	Temporary files which are usually preserved across a system reboot, unless /var is a memory-based file system.
/var/yp/	NIS maps.

3.6. Disk Organization

The smallest unit of organization that FreeBSD uses to find files is the filename. Filenames are case-sensitive, which means that readme.txt and README.TXT are two separate files. FreeBSD does not use the extension of a file to determine whether the file is a program, document, or some other form of data.

Files are stored in directories. A directory may contain no files, or it may contain many hundreds of files. A directory can also contain other directories, allowing a hierarchy of directories within one another in order to organize data.

Files and directories are referenced by giving the file or directory name, followed by a forward slash, /, followed by any other directory names that are necessary. For example, if the directory foo contains a directory bar which contains the file readme.txt , the full name, or *path*, to the file is foo/bar/readme.txt . Note that this is different from Windows® which uses \ to separate file and directory names. FreeBSD does not use drive letters, or other drive names in the path. For example, one would not type c:\foo\bar\readme.txt on FreeBSD.

Directories and files are stored in a file system. Each file system contains exactly one directory at the very top level, called the *root directory* for that file system. This root directory can contain other directories. One file system is designated the *root file system* or /. Every other file system is *mounted* under the root file system. No matter how many disks are on the FreeBSD system, every directory appears to be part of the same disk.

Consider three file systems, called A, B, and C. Each file system has one root directory, which contains two other directories, called A1, A2 (and likewise B1, B2 and C1, C2).

Call A the root file system. If ls(1) is used to view the contents of this directory, it will show two subdirectories, A1 and A2. The directory tree looks like this:

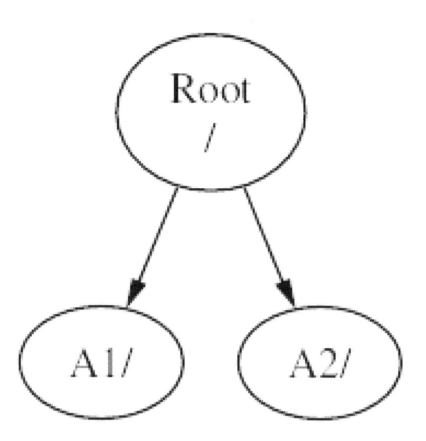

A file system must be mounted on to a directory in another file system. When mounting file system B on to the directory A1, the root directory of B replaces A1, and the directories in B appear accordingly:

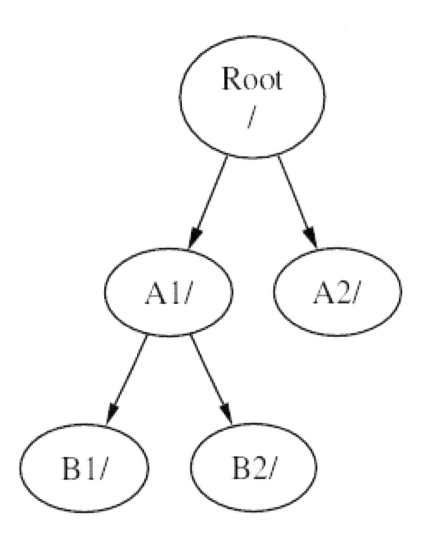

Any files that are in the **B1** or **B2** directories can be reached with the path /A1/B1 or /A1/B2 as necessary. Any files that were in /A1 have been temporarily hidden. They will reappear if **B** is *unmounted* from **A**.

If **B** had been mounted on **A2** then the diagram would look like this:

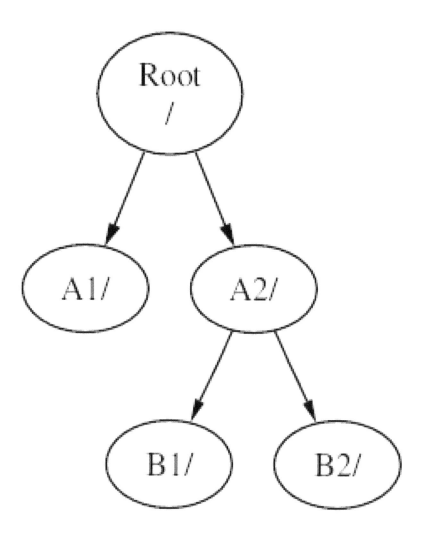

and the paths would be /A2/B1 and /A2/B2 respectively.

File systems can be mounted on top of one another. Continuing the last example, the C file system could be mounted on top of the B1 directory in the B file system, leading to this arrangement:

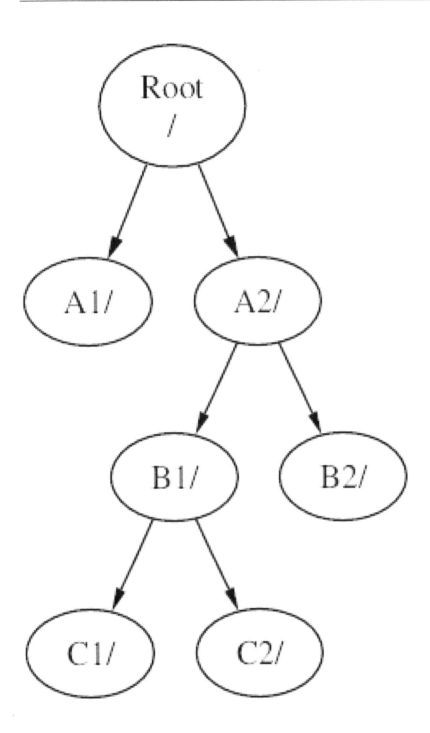

Or C could be mounted directly on to the A file system, under the A1 directory:

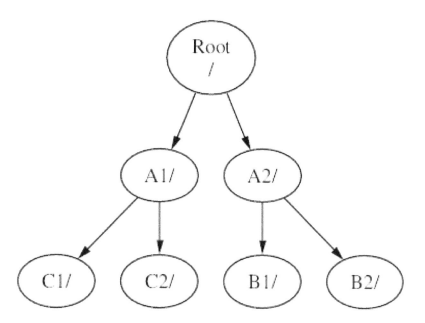

It is entirely possible to have one large root file system, and not need to create any others. There are some drawbacks to this approach, and one advantage.

- Different file systems can have different *mount options*. For example, the root file system can be mounted read-only, making it impossible for users to inadvertently delete or edit a critical file. Separating user-writable file systems, such as /home, from other file systems allows them to be mounted *nosuid*. This option prevents the *suid/guid* bits on executables stored on the file system from taking effect, possibly improving security.

- FreeBSD automatically optimizes the layout of files on a file system, depending on how the file system is being used. So a file system that contains many small files that are written frequently will have a different optimization to one that contains fewer, larger files. By having one big file system this optimization breaks down.

- FreeBSD's file systems are robust if power is lost. However, a power loss at a critical point could still damage the structure of the file system. By splitting data over multiple file systems it is more likely that the system will still come up, making it easier to restore from backup as necessary.

- File systems are a fixed size. If you create a file system when you install FreeBSD and give it a specific size, you may later discover that you need to make the partition bigger. This is not easily accomplished without backing up, recreating the file system with the new size, and then restoring the backed up data.

 Important

FreeBSD features the growfs(8) command, which makes it possible to increase the size of file system on the fly, removing this limitation.

File systems are contained in partitions. This does not have the same meaning as the common usage of the term partition (for example, MS-DOS® partition), because of FreeBSD's UNIX® heritage. Each partition is identified by a letter from a through to h. Each partition can contain only one file system, which means that file systems are often described by either their typical mount point in the file system hierarchy, or the letter of the partition they are contained in.

FreeBSD also uses disk space for *swap space* to provide *virtual memory*. This allows your computer to behave as though it has much more memory than it actually does. When FreeBSD runs out of memory, it moves some of the data that is not currently being used to the swap space, and moves it back in (moving something else out) when it needs it.

Some partitions have certain conventions associated with them.

Partition	Convention
a	Normally contains the root file system.
b	Normally contains swap space.
c	Normally the same size as the enclosing slice. This allows utilities that need to work on the entire slice, such as a bad block scanner, to work on the c partition. A file system would not normally be created on this partition.
d	Partition d used to have a special meaning associated with it, although that is now gone and d may work as any normal partition.

Disks in FreeBSD are divided into slices, referred to in Windows® as partitions, which are numbered from 1 to 4. These are then divided into partitions, which contain file systems, and are labeled using letters.

Slice numbers follow the device name, prefixed with an s, starting at 1. So "da0s1" is the first slice on the first SCSI drive. There can only be four physical slices on a disk, but there can be logical slices inside physical slices of the appropriate type. These extended slices are numbered starting at 5, so "ada0s5" is the first extended slice on the first SATA disk. These devices are used by file systems that expect to occupy a slice.

Slices, "dangerously dedicated" physical drives, and other drives contain *partitions*, which are represented as letters from a to h. This letter is appended to the device name, so "da0a" is the a partition on the first da drive, which is "dangerously dedicated". "ada1s3e" is the fifth partition in the third slice of the second SATA disk drive.

Finally, each disk on the system is identified. A disk name starts with a code that indicates the type of disk, and then a number, indicating which disk it is. Unlike slices, disk numbering starts at 0. Common codes are listed in Table 3.3, "Disk Device Names".

When referring to a partition, include the disk name, s, the slice number, and then the partition letter. Examples are shown in Example 3.12, "Sample Disk, Slice, and Partition Names".

Example 3.13, "Conceptual Model of a Disk" shows a conceptual model of a disk layout.

When installing FreeBSD, configure the disk slices, create partitions within the slice to be used for FreeBSD, create a file system or swap space in each partition, and decide where each file system will be mounted.

Table 3.3. Disk Device Names

Drive Type	Drive Device Name
SATA and IDE hard drives	ada or ad
SCSI hard drives and USB storage devices	da
SATA and IDE CD-ROM drives	cd or acd
SCSI CD-ROM drives	cd
Floppy drives	fd
Assorted non-standard CD-ROM drives	mcd for Mitsumi CD-ROM and scd for Sony CD-ROM devices

Drive Type	Drive Device Name
SCSI tape drives	sa
IDE tape drives	ast
RAID drives	Examples include aacd for Adaptec® AdvancedRAID, mlxd and mlyd for Mylex®, amrd for AMI MegaRAID®, idad for Compaq Smart RAID, twed for 3ware® RAID.

Example 3.12. Sample Disk, Slice, and Partition Names

Name	Meaning
ada0s1a	The first partition (a) on the first slice (s1) on the first SATA disk (ada0).
da1s2e	The fifth partition (e) on the second slice (s2) on the second SCSI disk (da1).

Example 3.13. Conceptual Model of a Disk

This diagram shows FreeBSD's view of the first SATA disk attached to the system. Assume that the disk is 250 GB in size, and contains an 80 GB slice and a 170 GB slice (MS-DOS® partitions). The first slice contains a Windows® NTFS file system, C:, and the second slice contains a FreeBSD installation. This example FreeBSD installation has four data partitions and a swap partition.

The four partitions each hold a file system. Partition a is used for the root file system, d for /var/, e for /tmp/, and f for /usr/. Partition letter c refers to the entire slice, and so is not used for ordinary partitions.

3.7. Mounting and Unmounting File Systems

The file system is best visualized as a tree, rooted, as it were, at /. /dev, /usr, and the other directories in the root directory are branches, which may have their own branches, such as /usr/local, and so on.

There are various reasons to house some of these directories on separate file systems. /var contains the directories log/, spool/, and various types of temporary files, and as such, may get filled up. Filling up the root file system is not a good idea, so splitting /var from / is often favorable.

Another common reason to contain certain directory trees on other file systems is if they are to be housed on separate physical disks, or are separate virtual disks, such as Network File System mounts, described in Section 28.3, "Network File System (NFS)", or CDROM drives.

3.7.1. The fstab File

During the boot process (Chapter 12, *The FreeBSD Booting Process*), file systems listed in /etc/fstab are automatically mounted except for the entries containing noauto. This file contains entries in the following format:

```
device          /mount-point  fstype     options      dumpfreq    passno
```

device
> An existing device name as explained in Table 3.3, "Disk Device Names".

mount-point
> An existing directory on which to mount the file system.

fstype
> The file system type to pass to mount(8). The default FreeBSD file system is ufs.

options
> Either rw for read-write file systems, or ro for read-only file systems, followed by any other options that may be needed. A common option is noauto for file systems not normally mounted during the boot sequence. Other options are listed in mount(8).

dumpfreq
> Used by dump(8) to determine which file systems require dumping. If the field is missing, a value of zero is assumed.

passno
> Determines the order in which file systems should be checked. File systems that should be skipped should have their passno set to zero. The root file system needs to be checked before everything else and should have its passno set to one. The other file systems should be set to values greater than one. If more than one file system has the same passno, fsck(8) will attempt to check file systems in parallel if possible.

Refer to fstab(5) for more information on the format of /etc/fstab and its options.

3.7.2. Using mount(8)

File systems are mounted using mount(8). The most basic syntax is as follows:

```
# mount device mountpoint
```

This command provides many options which are described in mount(8). The most commonly used options include:

-a
> Mount all the file systems listed in /etc/fstab , except those marked as "noauto", excluded by the -t flag, or those that are already mounted.

-d
> Do everything except for the actual mount system call. This option is useful in conjunction with the -v flag to determine what mount(8) is actually trying to do.

-f
> Force the mount of an unclean file system (dangerous), or the revocation of write access when downgrading a file system's mount status from read-write to read-only.

-r
> Mount the file system read-only. This is identical to using -o ro.

-t fstype
> Mount the specified file system type or mount only file systems of the given type, if -a is included. "ufs" is the default file system type.

-u

> Update mount options on the file system.

-v

> Be verbose.

-w

> Mount the file system read-write.

The following options can be passed to -o as a comma-separated list:

nosuid

> Do not interpret setuid or setgid flags on the file system. This is also a useful security option.

3.7.3. Using umount(8)

To unmount a file system use umount(8). This command takes one parameter which can be a mountpoint, device name, -a or -A.

All forms take -f to force unmounting, and -v for verbosity. Be warned that -f is not generally a good idea as it might crash the computer or damage data on the file system.

To unmount all mounted file systems, or just the file system types listed after -t, use -a or -A. Note that -A does not attempt to unmount the root file system.

3.8. Processes and Daemons

FreeBSD is a multi-tasking operating system. Each program running at any one time is called a *process*. Every running command starts at least one new process and there are a number of system processes that are run by FreeBSD.

Each process is uniquely identified by a number called a *process ID* (PID). Similar to files, each process has one owner and group, and the owner and group permissions are used to determine which files and devices the process can open. Most processes also have a parent process that started them. For example, the shell is a process, and any command started in the shell is a process which has the shell as its parent process. The exception is a special process called init(8) which is always the first process to start at boot time and which always has a PID of 1.

Some programs are not designed to be run with continuous user input and disconnect from the terminal at the first opportunity. For example, a web server responds to web requests, rather than user input. Mail servers are another example of this type of application. These types of programs are known as *daemons*. The term daemon comes from Greek mythology and represents an entity that is neither good nor evil, and which invisibly performs useful tasks. This is why the BSD mascot is the cheerful-looking daemon with sneakers and a pitchfork.

There is a convention to name programs that normally run as daemons with a trailing "d". For example, BIND is the Berkeley Internet Name Domain, but the actual program that executes is named. The Apache web server program is httpd and the line printer spooling daemon is lpd. This is only a naming convention. For example, the main mail daemon for the Sendmail application is sendmail, and not maild.

3.8.1. Viewing Processes

To see the processes running on the system, use ps(1) or top(1). To display a static list of the currently running processes, their PIDs, how much memory they are using, and the command they were started with, use ps(1). To display all the running processes and update the display every few seconds in order to interactively see what the computer is doing, use top(1).

By default, ps(1) only shows the commands that are running and owned by the user. For example:

```
% ps
```

```
PID TT  STAT    TIME COMMAND
8203  0  Ss   0:00.59 /bin/csh
8895  0  R+   0:00.00 ps
```

The output from ps(1) is organized into a number of columns. The PID column displays the process ID. PIDs are assigned starting at 1, go up to 99999, then wrap around back to the beginning. However, a PID is not reassigned if it is already in use. The TT column shows the tty the program is running on and STAT shows the program's state. TIME is the amount of time the program has been running on the CPU. This is usually not the elapsed time since the program was started, as most programs spend a lot of time waiting for things to happen before they need to spend time on the CPU. Finally, COMMAND is the command that was used to start the program.

A number of different options are available to change the information that is displayed. One of the most useful sets is auxww, where a displays information about all the running processes of all users, u displays the username and memory usage of the process' owner, x displays information about daemon processes, and ww causes ps(1) to display the full command line for each process, rather than truncating it once it gets too long to fit on the screen.

The output from top(1) is similar:

```
% top
last pid:  9609;  load averages:  0.56,  0.45,  0.36              up 0+00:20:03  10:21:46
107 processes: 2 running, 104 sleeping, 1 zombie
CPU:  6.2% user,  0.1% nice,  8.2% system,  0.4% interrupt, 85.1% idle
Mem: 541M Active, 450M Inact, 1333M Wired, 4064K Cache, 1498M Free
ARC: 992M Total, 377M MFU, 589M MRU, 250K Anon, 5280K Header, 21M Other
Swap: 2048M Total, 2048M Free

  PID USERNAME    THR PRI NICE    SIZE    RES STATE   C   TIME   WCPU COMMAND
  557 root          1 -21  r31    136M 42296K select  0   2:20  9.96% Xorg
 8198 dru           2  52    0    449M 82736K select  3   0:08  5.96% kdeinit4
 8311 dru          27  30    0   1150M   187M uwait   1   1:37  0.98% firefox
  431 root          1  20    0  14268K  1728K select  0   0:06  0.98% moused
 9551 dru           1  21    0  16600K  2660K CPU3    3   0:01  0.98% top
 2357 dru           4  37    0    718M   141M select  0   0:21  0.00% kdeinit4
 8705 dru           4  35    0    480M    98M select  2   0:20  0.00% kdeinit4
 8076 dru           6  20    0    552M   113M uwait   0   0:12  0.00% soffice.bin
 2623 root          1  30   10  12088K  1636K select  3   0:09  0.00% powerd
 2338 dru           1  20    0    440M 84532K select  1   0:06  0.00% kwin
 1427 dru           5  22    0    605M 86412K select  1   0:05  0.00% kdeinit4
```

The output is split into two sections. The header (the first five or six lines) shows the PID of the last process to run, the system load averages (which are a measure of how busy the system is), the system uptime (time since the last reboot) and the current time. The other figures in the header relate to how many processes are running, how much memory and swap space has been used, and how much time the system is spending in different CPU states. If the ZFS file system module has been loaded, an ARC line indicates how much data was read from the memory cache instead of from disk.

Below the header is a series of columns containing similar information to the output from ps(1), such as the PID, username, amount of CPU time, and the command that started the process. By default, top(1) also displays the amount of memory space taken by the process. This is split into two columns: one for total size and one for resident size. Total size is how much memory the application has needed and the resident size is how much it is actually using now.

top(1) automatically updates the display every two seconds. A different interval can be specified with -s.

3.8.2. Killing Processes

One way to communicate with any running process or daemon is to send a *signal* using kill(1). There are a number of different signals; some have a specific meaning while others are described in the application's documentation. A user can only send a signal to a process they own and sending a signal to someone else's process will result in a permission denied error. The exception is the root user, who can send signals to anyone's processes.

The operating system can also send a signal to a process. If an application is badly written and tries to access memory that it is not supposed to, FreeBSD will send the process the "Segmentation Violation" signal (SIGSEGV). If an application has been written to use the alarm(3) system call to be alerted after a period of time has elapsed, it will be sent the "Alarm" signal (SIGALRM).

Two signals can be used to stop a process: SIGTERM and SIGKILL. SIGTERM is the polite way to kill a process as the process can read the signal, close any log files it may have open, and attempt to finish what it is doing before shutting down. In some cases, a process may ignore SIGTERM if it is in the middle of some task that cannot be interrupted.

SIGKILL cannot be ignored by a process. Sending a SIGKILL to a process will usually stop that process there and then. [1].

Other commonly used signals are SIGHUP, SIGUSR1, and SIGUSR2. Since these are general purpose signals, different applications will respond differently.

For example, after changing a web server's configuration file, the web server needs to be told to re-read its configuration. Restarting httpd would result in a brief outage period on the web server. Instead, send the daemon the SIGHUP signal. Be aware that different daemons will have different behavior, so refer to the documentation for the daemon to determine if SIGHUP will achieve the desired results.

Procedure 3.1. Sending a Signal to a Process

This example shows how to send a signal to inetd(8). The inetd(8) configuration file is /etc/inetd.conf, and inetd(8) will re-read this configuration file when it is sent a SIGHUP.

1. Find the PID of the process to send the signal to using pgrep(1). In this example, the PID for inetd(8) is 198:

    ```
    % pgrep -l inetd
    198   inetd -wW
    ```

2. Use kill(1) to send the signal. Because inetd(8) is owned by root, use su(1) to become root first.

    ```
    % su
    Password:
    # /bin/kill -s HUP 198
    ```

Like most UNIX® commands, kill(1) will not print any output if it is successful. If a signal is sent to a process not owned by that user, the message kill: *PID*: Operation not permitted will be displayed. Mistyping the PID will either send the signal to the wrong process, which could have negative results, or send the signal to a PID that is not currently in use, resulting in the error kill: *PID*: No such process.

Why Use /bin/kill?

Many shells provide kill as a built in command, meaning that the shell will send the signal directly, rather than running /bin/kill. Be aware that different shells have a different syntax for specifying the name of the signal to send. Rather than try to learn all of them, it can be simpler to specify /bin/kill.

When sending other signals, substitute TERM or KILL with the name of the signal.

---

[1]There are a few tasks that cannot be interrupted. For example, if the process is trying to read from a file that is on another computer on the network, and the other computer is unavailable, the process is said to be "uninterruptible". Eventually the process will time out, typically after two minutes. As soon as this time out occurs the process will be killed.

Important

Killing a random process on the system is a bad idea. In particular, init(8), PID 1, is special. Running /bin/kill -s KILL 1 is a quick, and unrecommended, way to shutdown the system. *Always* double check the arguments to kill(1) *before* pressing Return.

3.9. Shells

A *shell* provides a command line interface for interacting with the operating system. A shell receives commands from the input channel and executes them. Many shells provide built in functions to help with everyday tasks such as file management, file globbing, command line editing, command macros, and environment variables. FreeBSD comes with several shells, including the Bourne shell (sh(1)) and the extended C shell (tcsh(1)). Other shells are available from the FreeBSD Ports Collection, such as zsh and bash.

The shell that is used is really a matter of taste. A C programmer might feel more comfortable with a C-like shell such as tcsh(1). A Linux® user might prefer bash. Each shell has unique properties that may or may not work with a user's preferred working environment, which is why there is a choice of which shell to use.

One common shell feature is filename completion. After a user types the first few letters of a command or filename and presses Tab, the shell completes the rest of the command or filename. Consider two files called foobar and football. To delete foobar, the user might type rm foo and press Tab to complete the filename.

But the shell only shows rm foo. It was unable to complete the filename because both foobar and football start with foo. Some shells sound a beep or show all the choices if more than one name matches. The user must then type more characters to identify the desired filename. Typing a t and pressing Tab again is enough to let the shell determine which filename is desired and fill in the rest.

Another feature of the shell is the use of environment variables. Environment variables are a variable/key pair stored in the shell's environment. This environment can be read by any program invoked by the shell, and thus contains a lot of program configuration. Table 3.4, "Common Environment Variables" provides a list of common environment variables and their meanings. Note that the names of environment variables are always in uppercase.

Table 3.4. Common Environment Variables

Variable	Description
USER	Current logged in user's name.
PATH	Colon-separated list of directories to search for binaries.
DISPLAY	Network name of the Xorg display to connect to, if available.
SHELL	The current shell.
TERM	The name of the user's type of terminal. Used to determine the capabilities of the terminal.
TERMCAP	Database entry of the terminal escape codes to perform various terminal functions.
OSTYPE	Type of operating system.
MACHTYPE	The system's CPU architecture.
EDITOR	The user's preferred text editor.

Variable	Description
PAGER	The user's preferred utility for viewing text one page at a time.
MANPATH	Colon-separated list of directories to search for manual pages.

How to set an environment variable differs between shells. In tcsh(1) and csh(1), use `setenv` to set environment variables. In sh(1) and bash, use `export` to set the current environment variables. This example sets the default EDITOR to /usr/local/bin/emacs for the tcsh(1) shell:

```
% setenv EDITOR /usr/local/bin/emacs
```

The equivalent command for bash would be:

```
% export EDITOR="/usr/local/bin/emacs"
```

To expand an environment variable in order to see its current setting, type a $ character in front of its name on the command line. For example, echo $TERM displays the current $TERM setting.

Shells treat special characters, known as meta-characters, as special representations of data. The most common meta-character is *, which represents any number of characters in a filename. Meta-characters can be used to perform filename globbing. For example, echo * is equivalent to ls because the shell takes all the files that match * and echo lists them on the command line.

To prevent the shell from interpreting a special character, escape it from the shell by starting it with a backslash (\). For example, echo $TERM prints the terminal setting whereas echo \$TERM literally prints the string $TERM.

3.9.1. Changing the Shell

The easiest way to permanently change the default shell is to use chsh. Running this command will open the editor that is configured in the **EDITOR** environment variable, which by default is set to vi(1). Change the Shell: line to the full path of the new shell.

Alternately, use chsh -s which will set the specified shell without opening an editor. For example, to change the shell to bash:

```
% chsh -s /usr/local/bin/bash
```

Note

The new shell *must* be present in /etc/shells . If the shell was installed from the FreeBSD Ports Collection as described in Chapter 4, *Installing Applications: Packages and Ports*, it should be automatically added to this file. If it is missing, add it using this command, replacing the path with the path of the shell:

```
# echo /usr/local/bin/bash  >> /etc/shells
```

Then, rerun chsh(1).

3.9.2. Advanced Shell Techniques

Written by Tom Rhodes.

The UNIX® shell is not just a command interpreter, it acts as a powerful tool which allows users to execute commands, redirect their output, redirect their input and chain commands together to improve the final command output. When this functionality is mixed with built in commands, the user is provided with an environment that can maximize efficiency.

Shell redirection is the action of sending the output or the input of a command into another command or into a file. To capture the output of the ls(1) command, for example, into a file, redirect the output:

```
% ls > directory_listing.txt
```

The directory contents will now be listed in `directory_listing.txt`. Some commands can be used to read input, such as sort(1). To sort this listing, redirect the input:

```
% sort < directory_listing.txt
```

The input will be sorted and placed on the screen. To redirect that input into another file, one could redirect the output of sort(1) by mixing the direction:

```
% sort < directory_listing.txt > sorted.txt
```

In all of the previous examples, the commands are performing redirection using file descriptors. Every UNIX® system has file descriptors, which include standard input (stdin), standard output (stdout), and standard error (stderr). Each one has a purpose, where input could be a keyboard or a mouse, something that provides input. Output could be a screen or paper in a printer. And error would be anything that is used for diagnostic or error messages. All three are considered I/O based file descriptors and sometimes considered streams.

Through the use of these descriptors, the shell allows output and input to be passed around through various commands and redirected to or from a file. Another method of redirection is the pipe operator.

The UNIX® pipe operator, "|" allows the output of one command to be directly passed or directed to another program. Basically, a pipe allows the standard output of a command to be passed as standard input to another command, for example:

```
% cat directory_listing.txt | sort | less
```

In that example, the contents of `directory_listing.txt` will be sorted and the output passed to less(1). This allows the user to scroll through the output at their own pace and prevent it from scrolling off the screen.

3.10. Text Editors

Most FreeBSD configuration is done by editing text files. Because of this, it is a good idea to become familiar with a text editor. FreeBSD comes with a few as part of the base system, and many more are available in the Ports Collection.

A simple editor to learn is ee(1), which stands for easy editor. To start this editor, type ee *filename* where *filename* is the name of the file to be edited. Once inside the editor, all of the commands for manipulating the editor's functions are listed at the top of the display. The caret (^) represents Ctrl, so ^e expands to Ctrl+e. To leave ee(1), press Esc, then choose the "leave editor" option from the main menu. The editor will prompt to save any changes if the file has been modified.

FreeBSD also comes with more powerful text editors, such as vi(1), as part of the base system. Other editors, like editors/emacs and editors/vim, are part of the FreeBSD Ports Collection. These editors offer more functionality at the expense of being more complicated to learn. Learning a more powerful editor such as vim or Emacs can save more time in the long run.

Many applications which modify files or require typed input will automatically open a text editor. To change the default editor, set the EDITOR environment variable as described in Section 3.9, "Shells".

3.11. Devices and Device Nodes

A device is a term used mostly for hardware-related activities in a system, including disks, printers, graphics cards, and keyboards. When FreeBSD boots, the majority of the boot messages refer to devices being detected. A copy of the boot messages are saved to `/var/run/dmesg.boot` .

Each device has a device name and number. For example, adsa0 is the first SATA hard drive, while kbd0 represents the keyboard.

Most devices in FreeBSD must be accessed through special files called device nodes, which are located in /dev.

3.12. Manual Pages

The most comprehensive documentation on FreeBSD is in the form of manual pages. Nearly every program on the system comes with a short reference manual explaining the basic operation and available arguments. These manuals can be viewed using man:

```
% man command
```

where *command* is the name of the command to learn about. For example, to learn more about ls(1), type:

```
% man ls
```

Manual pages are divided into sections which represent the type of topic. In FreeBSD, the following sections are available:

1. User commands.

2. System calls and error numbers.

3. Functions in the C libraries.

4. Device drivers.

5. File formats.

6. Games and other diversions.

7. Miscellaneous information.

8. System maintenance and operation commands.

9. System kernel interfaces.

In some cases, the same topic may appear in more than one section of the online manual. For example, there is a chmod user command and a chmod() system call. To tell man(1) which section to display, specify the section number:

```
% man 1 chmod
```

This will display the manual page for the user command chmod(1). References to a particular section of the online manual are traditionally placed in parenthesis in written documentation, so chmod(1) refers to the user command and chmod(2) refers to the system call.

If the name of the manual page is unknown, use man -k to search for keywords in the manual page descriptions:

```
% man -k mail
```

This command displays a list of commands that have the keyword "mail" in their descriptions. This is equivalent to using apropos(1).

To read the descriptions for all of the commands in /usr/bin, type:

```
% cd /usr/bin
% man -f * | more
```

or

```
% cd /usr/bin
% whatis * |more
```

3.12.1. GNU Info Files

FreeBSD includes several applications and utilities produced by the Free Software Foundation (FSF). In addition to manual pages, these programs may include hypertext documents called info files. These can be viewed using info(1) or, if editors/emacs is installed, the info mode of emacs.

To use info(1), type:

```
% info
```

For a brief introduction, type h. For a quick command reference, type ?.

Chapter 4. Installing Applications: Packages and Ports

4.1. Synopsis

FreeBSD is bundled with a rich collection of system tools as part of the base system. In addition, FreeBSD provides two complementary technologies for installing third-party software: the FreeBSD Ports Collection, for installing from source, and packages, for installing from pre-built binaries. Either method may be used to install software from local media or from the network.

After reading this chapter, you will know:

• The difference between binary packages and ports.

• How to find third-party software that has been ported to FreeBSD.

• How to manage binary packages using pkg.

• How to build third-party software from source using the Ports Collection.

• How to find the files installed with the application for post-installation configuration.

• What to do if a software installation fails.

4.2. Overview of Software Installation

The typical steps for installing third-party software on a UNIX® system include:

1. Find and download the software, which might be distributed in source code format or as a binary.

2. Unpack the software from its distribution format. This is typically a tarball compressed with a program such as compress(1), gzip(1), bzip2(1) or xz(1).

3. Locate the documentation in `INSTALL`, `README` or some file in a `doc/` subdirectory and read up on how to install the software.

4. If the software was distributed in source format, compile it. This may involve editing a `Makefile` or running a `configure` script.

5. Test and install the software.

A FreeBSD *port* is a collection of files designed to automate the process of compiling an application from source code. The files that comprise a port contain all the necessary information to automatically download, extract, patch, compile, and install the application.

If the software has not already been adapted and tested on FreeBSD, the source code might need editing in order for it to install and run properly.

However, over 24,000 third-party applications have already been ported to FreeBSD. When feasible, these applications are made available for download as pre-compiled *packages*.

Packages can be manipulated with the FreeBSD package management commands.

Both packages and ports understand dependencies. If a package or port is used to install an application and a dependent library is not already installed, the library will automatically be installed first.

A FreeBSD package contains pre-compiled copies of all the commands for an application, as well as any configuration files and documentation. A package can be manipulated with the pkg(8) commands, such as pkg install.

While the two technologies are similar, packages and ports each have their own strengths. Select the technology that meets your requirements for installing a particular application.

- A compressed package tarball is typically smaller than the compressed tarball containing the source code for the application.

- Packages do not require compilation time. For large applications, such as Mozilla, KDE, or GNOME, this can be important on a slow system.

- Packages do not require any understanding of the process involved in compiling software on FreeBSD.

- Packages are normally compiled with conservative options because they have to run on the maximum number of systems. By compiling from the port, one can change the compilation options.

- Some applications have compile-time options relating to which features are installed. For example, Apache can be configured with a wide variety of different built-in options.

  In some cases, multiple packages will exist for the same application to specify certain settings. For example, Ghostscript is available as a ghostscript package and a ghostscript-nox11 package, depending on whether or not Xorg is installed. Creating multiple packages rapidly becomes impossible if an application has more than one or two different compile-time options.

- The licensing conditions of some software forbid binary distribution. Such software must be distributed as source code which must be compiled by the end-user.

- Some people do not trust binary distributions or prefer to read through source code in order to look for potential problems.

- Source code is needed in order to apply custom patches.

To keep track of updated ports, subscribe to the FreeBSD ports mailing list and the FreeBSD ports bugs mailing list.

Warning

Before installing any application, check https://vuxml.freebsd.org/ for security issues related to the application or type pkg audit -F to check all installed applications for known vulnerabilities.

The remainder of this chapter explains how to use packages and ports to install and manage third-party software on FreeBSD.

4.3. Finding Software

FreeBSD's list of available applications is growing all the time. There are a number of ways to find software to install:

- The FreeBSD web site maintains an up-to-date searchable list of all the available applications, at https://www.FreeBSD.org/ports/. The ports can be searched by application name or by software category.

- Dan Langille maintains FreshPorts.org which provides a comprehensive search utility and also tracks changes to the applications in the Ports Collection. Registered users can create a customized watch list in order to receive an automated email when their watched ports are updated.

- If finding a particular application becomes challenging, try searching a site like SourceForge.net or GitHub.com then check back at the FreeBSD site to see if the application has been ported.

- To search the binary package repository for an application:

```
# pkg search subversion
git-subversion-1.9.2
java-subversion-1.8.8_2
p5-subversion-1.8.8_2
py27-hgsubversion-1.6
py27-subversion-1.8.8_2
ruby-subversion-1.8.8_2
subversion-1.8.8_2
subversion-book-4515
subversion-static-1.8.8_2
subversion16-1.6.23_4
subversion17-1.7.16_2
```

Package names include the version number and, in the case of ports based on python, the version number of the version of python the package was built with. Some ports also have multiple versions available. In the case of Subversion, there are different versions available, as well as different compile options. In this case, the statically linked version of Subversion. When indicating which package to install, it is best to specify the application by the port origin, which is the path in the ports tree. Repeat the pkg search with -o to list the origin of each package:

```
# pkg search -o subversion
devel/git-subversion
java/java-subversion
devel/p5-subversion
devel/py-hgsubversion
devel/py-subversion
devel/ruby-subversion
devel/subversion16
devel/subversion17
devel/subversion
devel/subversion-book
devel/subversion-static
```

Searching by shell globs, regular expressions, exact match, by description, or any other field in the repository database is also supported by pkg search. After installing ports-mgmt/pkg or ports-mgmt/pkg-devel, see pkg-search(8) for more details.

- If the Ports Collection is already installed, there are several methods to query the local version of the ports tree. To find out which category a port is in, type whereis *file*, where *file* is the program to be installed:

```
# whereis lsof
lsof: /usr/ports/sysutils/lsof
```

Alternately, an echo(1) statement can be used:

```
# echo /usr/ports/*/*lsof*
/usr/ports/sysutils/lsof
```

Note that this will also return any matched files downloaded into the /usr/ports/distfiles directory.

- Another way to find software is by using the Ports Collection's built-in search mechanism. To use the search feature, cd to /usr/ports then run make search name=program-name where *program-name* is the name of the software. For example, to search for lsof:

```
# cd /usr/ports
# make search name=lsof
Port:   lsof-4.88.d,8
Path:   /usr/ports/sysutils/lsof
```

```
Info:    Lists information about open files (similar to fstat(1))
Maint:   ler@lerctr.org
Index:   sysutils
B-deps:
R-deps:
```

Tip

The built-in search mechanism uses a file of index information. If a message indicates that the INDEX is required, run make fetchindex to download the current index file. With the INDEX present, make search will be able to perform the requested search.

The "Path:" line indicates where to find the port.

To receive less information, use the quicksearch feature:

```
# cd /usr/ports
# make quicksearch name=lsof
Port:    lsof-4.88.d,8
Path:    /usr/ports/sysutils/lsof
Info:    Lists information about open files (similar to fstat(1))
```

For more in-depth searching, use make search key=*string* or make quicksearch key=*string*, where *string* is some text to search for. The text can be in comments, descriptions, or dependencies in order to find ports which relate to a particular subject when the name of the program is unknown.

When using search or quicksearch, the search string is case-insensitive. Searching for "LSOF" will yield the same results as searching for "lsof".

4.4. Using pkg for Binary Package Management

pkg is the next generation replacement for the traditional FreeBSD package management tools, offering many features that make dealing with binary packages faster and easier.

For sites wishing to only use prebuilt binary packages from the FreeBSD mirrors, managing packages with pkg can be sufficient.

However, for those sites building from source or using their own repositories, a separate port management tool will be needed.

Since pkg only works with binary packages, it is not a replacement for such tools. Those tools can be used to install software from both binary packages and the Ports Collection, while pkg installs only binary packages.

4.4.1. Getting Started with pkg

FreeBSD includes a bootstrap utility which can be used to download and install pkg and its manual pages. This utility is designed to work with versions of FreeBSD starting with 10.*X*.

Note

Not all FreeBSD versions and architectures support this bootstrap process. The current list is at https://pkg.freebsd.org/. For other cases, pkg must instead be installed from the Ports Collection or as a binary package.

To bootstrap the system, run:

```
# /usr/sbin/pkg
```

You must have a working Internet connection for the bootstrap process to succeed.

Otherwise, to install the port, run:

```
# cd /usr/ports/ports-mgmt/pkg
# make
# make install clean
```

When upgrading an existing system that originally used the older pkg_* tools, the database must be converted to the new format, so that the new tools are aware of the already installed packages. Once pkg has been installed, the package database must be converted from the traditional format to the new format by running this command:

```
# pkg2ng
```

Note

This step is not required for new installations that do not yet have any third-party software installed.

Important

This step is not reversible. Once the package database has been converted to the pkg format, the traditional pkg_* tools should no longer be used.

Note

The package database conversion may emit errors as the contents are converted to the new version. Generally, these errors can be safely ignored. However, a list of software that was not successfully converted is shown after pkg2ng finishes. These applications must be manually reinstalled.

To ensure that the Ports Collection registers new software with pkg instead of the traditional packages database, FreeBSD versions earlier than 10.X require this line in /etc/make.conf :

```
WITH_PKGNG= yes
```

By default, pkg uses the binary packages from the FreeBSD package mirrors (the *repository*). For information about building a custom package repository, see Section 4.6, "Building Packages with Poudriere".

Additional pkg configuration options are described in pkg.conf(5).

Usage information for pkg is available in the pkg(8) manual page or by running pkg without additional arguments.

Each pkg command argument is documented in a command-specific manual page. To read the manual page for pkg install, for example, run either of these commands:

```
# pkg help install
```

```
# man pkg-install
```

The rest of this section demonstrates common binary package management tasks which can be performed using pkg. Each demonstrated command provides many switches to customize its use. Refer to a command's help or man page for details and more examples.

4.4.2. Obtaining Information About Installed Packages

Information about the packages installed on a system can be viewed by running pkg info which, when run without any switches, will list the package version for either all installed packages or the specified package.

For example, to see which version of pkg is installed, run:

```
# pkg info pkg
pkg-1.1.4_1
```

4.4.3. Installing and Removing Packages

To install a binary package use the following command, where *packagename* is the name of the package to install:

```
# pkg install packagename
```

This command uses repository data to determine which version of the software to install and if it has any unin-stalled dependencies. For example, to install curl:

```
# pkg install curl
Updating repository catalogue
/usr/local/tmp/All/curl-7.31.0_1.txz          100% of 1181 kB 1380 kBps 00m01s

/usr/local/tmp/All/ca_root_nss-3.15.1_1.txz  100% of  288 kB 1700 kBps 00m00s

Updating repository catalogue
The following 2 packages will be installed:

        Installing ca_root_nss: 3.15.1_1
        Installing curl: 7.31.0_1

The installation will require 3 MB more space

0 B to be downloaded

Proceed with installing packages [y/N]: y
Checking integrity... done
[1/2] Installing ca_root_nss-3.15.1_1... done
[2/2] Installing curl-7.31.0_1... done
Cleaning up cache files...Done
```

The new package and any additional packages that were installed as dependencies can be seen in the installed packages list:

```
# pkg info
ca_root_nss-3.15.1_1 The root certificate bundle from the Mozilla Project
curl-7.31.0_1 Non-interactive tool to get files from FTP, GOPHER, HTTP(S) servers
```

```
pkg-1.1.4_6 New generation package manager
```

Packages that are no longer needed can be removed with pkg delete . For example:

```
# pkg delete curl
The following packages will be deleted:

 curl-7.31.0_1

The deletion will free 3 MB

Proceed with deleting packages [y/N]: y
[1/1] Deleting curl-7.31.0_1... done
```

4.4.4. Upgrading Installed Packages

Installed packages can be upgraded to their latest versions by running:

```
# pkg upgrade
```

This command will compare the installed versions with those available in the repository catalogue and upgrade them from the repository.

4.4.5. Auditing Installed Packages

Software vulnerabilities are regularly discovered in third-party applications. To address this, pkg includes a built-in auditing mechanism. To determine if there are any known vulnerabilities for the software installed on the system, run:

```
# pkg audit -F
```

4.4.6. Automatically Removing Leaf Dependencies

Removing a package may leave behind dependencies which are no longer required. Unneeded packages that were installed as dependencies can be automatically detected and removed using:

```
# pkg autoremove
Packages to be autoremoved:
 ca_root_nss-3.15.1_1

The autoremoval will free 723 kB

Proceed with autoremoval of packages [y/N]: y
Deinstalling ca_root_nss-3.15.1_1... done
```

4.4.7. Restoring the Package Database

Unlike the traditional package management system, pkg includes its own package database backup mechanism. This functionality is enabled by default.

 Tip

To disable the periodic script from backing up the package database, set daily_backup_p-kgdb_enable="NO" in periodic.conf(5).

To restore the contents of a previous package database backup, run the following command replacing /path/to/pkg.sql with the location of the backup:

```
# pkg backup -r /path/to/pkg.sql
```

Note

If restoring a backup taken by the periodic script, it must be decompressed prior to being restored.

To run a manual backup of the pkg database, run the following command, replacing */path/to/pkg.sql* with a suitable file name and location:

```
# pkg backup -d /path/to/pkg.sql
```

4.4.8. Removing Stale Packages

By default, pkg stores binary packages in a cache directory defined by `PKG_CACHEDIR` in pkg.conf(5). Only copies of the latest installed packages are kept. Older versions of pkg kept all previous packages. To remove these outdated binary packages, run:

```
# pkg clean
```

The entire cache may be cleared by running:

```
# pkg clean -a
```

4.4.9. Modifying Package Metadata

Software within the FreeBSD Ports Collection can undergo major version number changes. To address this, pkg has a built-in command to update package origins. This can be useful, for example, if lang/php5 is renamed to lang/php53 so that lang/php5 can now represent version 5.4.

To change the package origin for the above example, run:

```
# pkg set -o lang/php5:lang/php53
```

As another example, to update lang/ruby18 to lang/ruby19, run:

```
# pkg set -o lang/ruby18:lang/ruby19
```

As a final example, to change the origin of the libglut shared libraries from graphics/libglut to graphics/freeglut, run:

```
# pkg set -o graphics/libglut:graphics/freeglut
```

Note

When changing package origins, it is important to reinstall packages that are dependent on the package with the modified origin. To force a reinstallation of dependent packages, run:

```
# pkg install -Rf graphics/freeglut
```

4.5. Using the Ports Collection

The Ports Collection is a set of Makefiles, patches, and description files. Each set of these files is used to compile and install an individual application on FreeBSD, and is called a *port*.

By default, the Ports Collection itself is stored as a subdirectory of /usr/ports .

Before an application can be compiled using a port, the Ports Collection must first be installed. If it was not installed during the installation of FreeBSD, use one of the following methods to install it:

Procedure 4.1. Portsnap Method

The base system of FreeBSD includes Portsnap. This is a fast and user-friendly tool for retrieving the Ports Collection and is the recommended choice for most users. This utility connects to a FreeBSD site, verifies the secure key, and downloads a new copy of the Ports Collection. The key is used to verify the integrity of all downloaded files.

1. To download a compressed snapshot of the Ports Collection into /var/db/portsnap :

    ```
    # portsnap fetch
    ```

2. When running Portsnap for the first time, extract the snapshot into /usr/ports :

    ```
    # portsnap extract
    ```

3. After the first use of Portsnap has been completed as shown above, /usr/ports can be updated as needed by running:

    ```
    # portsnap fetch
    # portsnap update
    ```

    When using fetch, the extract or the update operation may be run consecutively, like so:

    ```
    # portsnap fetch update
    ```

Procedure 4.2. Subversion Method

If more control over the ports tree is needed or if local changes need to be maintained, Subversion can be used to obtain the Ports Collection. Refer to the Subversion Primer for a detailed description of Subversion.

1. Subversion must be installed before it can be used to check out the ports tree. If a copy of the ports tree is already present, install Subversion like this:

    ```
    # cd /usr/ports/devel/subversion
    # make install clean
    ```

    If the ports tree is not available, or pkg is being used to manage packages, Subversion can be installed as a package:

    ```
    # pkg install subversion
    ```

2. Check out a copy of the ports tree:

    ```
    # svn checkout https://svn.FreeBSD.org/ports/head /usr/ports
    ```

3. As needed, update /usr/ports after the initial Subversion checkout:

    ```
    # svn update /usr/ports
    ```

The Ports Collection contains directories for software categories. Inside each category are subdirectories for individual applications. Each application subdirectory contains a set of files that tells FreeBSD how to compile and install that program, called a *ports skeleton*. Each port skeleton includes these files and directories:

- Makefile: contains statements that specify how the application should be compiled and where its components should be installed.

- distinfo: contains the names and checksums of the files that must be downloaded to build the port.

- `files/`: this directory contains any patches needed for the program to compile and install on FreeBSD. This directory may also contain other files used to build the port.

- `pkg-descr`: provides a more detailed description of the program.

- `pkg-plist`: a list of all the files that will be installed by the port. It also tells the ports system which files to remove upon deinstallation.

Some ports include `pkg-message` or other files to handle special situations. For more details on these files, and on ports in general, refer to the FreeBSD Porter's Handbook.

The port does not include the actual source code, also known as a `distfile`. The extract portion of building a port will automatically save the downloaded source to `/usr/ports/distfiles`.

4.5.1. Installing Ports

This section provides basic instructions on using the Ports Collection to install or remove software. The detailed description of available `make` targets and environment variables is available in ports(7).

> ## Warning
>
> Before compiling any port, be sure to update the Ports Collection as described in the previous section. Since the installation of any third-party software can introduce security vulnerabilities, it is recommended to first check https://vuxml.freebsd.org/ for known security issues related to the port. Alternately, run `pkg audit -F` before installing a new port. This command can be configured to automatically perform a security audit and an update of the vulnerability database during the daily security system check. For more information, refer to pkg-audit(8) and periodic(8).

Using the Ports Collection assumes a working Internet connection. It also requires superuser privilege.

To compile and install the port, change to the directory of the port to be installed, then type `make install` at the prompt. Messages will indicate the progress:

```
# cd /usr/ports/sysutils/lsof
# make install
>> lsof_4.88D.freebsd.tar.gz doesn't seem to exist in /usr/ports/distfiles/.
>> Attempting to fetch from ftp://lsof.itap.purdue.edu/pub/tools/unix/lsof/.
===> Extracting for lsof-4.88
...
[extraction output snipped]
...
>> Checksum OK for lsof_4.88D.freebsd.tar.gz.
===> Patching for lsof-4.88.d,8
===> Applying FreeBSD patches for lsof-4.88.d,8
===> Configuring for lsof-4.88.d,8
...
[configure output snipped]
...
===> Building for lsof-4.88.d,8
...
[compilation output snipped]
...

===> Installing for lsof-4.88.d,8
...
[installation output snipped]
...
```

```
===>    Generating temporary packing list
===>    Compressing manual pages for lsof-4.88.d,8
===>    Registering installation for lsof-4.88.d,8
===>  SECURITY NOTE:
      This port has installed the following binaries which execute with
      increased privileges.
/usr/local/sbin/lsof
#
```

Since `lsof` is a program that runs with increased privileges, a security warning is displayed as it is installed. Once the installation is complete, the prompt will be returned.

Some shells keep a cache of the commands that are available in the directories listed in the `PATH` environment variable, to speed up lookup operations for the executable file of these commands. Users of the `tcsh` shell should type `rehash` so that a newly installed command can be used without specifying its full path. Use `hash -r` instead for the `sh` shell. Refer to the documentation for the shell for more information.

During installation, a working subdirectory is created which contains all the temporary files used during compilation. Removing this directory saves disk space and minimizes the chance of problems later when upgrading to the newer version of the port:

```
# make clean
===>  Cleaning for lsof-88.d,8
#
```

Note

To save this extra step, instead use `make install clean` when compiling the port.

4.5.1.1. Customizing Ports Installation

Some ports provide build options which can be used to enable or disable application components, provide security options, or allow for other customizations. Examples include www/firefox, security/gpgme, and mail/sylpheed-claws. If the port depends upon other ports which have configurable options, it may pause several times for user interaction as the default behavior is to prompt the user to select options from a menu. To avoid this and do all of the configuration in one batch, run `make config-recursive` within the port skeleton. Then, run `make install [clean]` to compile and install the port.

Tip

When using `config-recursive`, the list of ports to configure are gathered by the `all-depends-list` target. It is recommended to run `make config-recursive` until all dependent ports options have been defined, and ports options screens no longer appear, to be certain that all dependency options have been configured.

There are several ways to revisit a port's build options menu in order to add, remove, or change these options after a port has been built. One method is to `cd` into the directory containing the port and type `make config`. Another option is to use `make showconfig`. Another option is to execute `make rmconfig` which will remove all selected options and allow you to start over. All of these options, and others, are explained in great detail in ports(7).

The ports system uses fetch(1) to download the source files, which supports various environment variables. The `FTP_PASSIVE_MODE`, `FTP_PROXY`, and `FTP_PASSWORD` variables may need to be set if the FreeBSD system is behind a firewall or FTP/HTTP proxy. See fetch(3) for the complete list of supported variables.

For users who cannot be connected to the Internet all the time, make fetch can be run within /usr/ports , to fetch all distfiles, or within a category, such as /usr/ports/net , or within the specific port skeleton. Note that if a port has any dependencies, running this command in a category or ports skeleton will *not* fetch the distfiles of ports from another category. Instead, use make fetch-recursive to also fetch the distfiles for all the dependencies of a port.

In rare cases, such as when an organization has a local distfiles repository, the MASTER_SITES variable can be used to override the download locations specified in the Makefile. When using, specify the alternate location:

```
# cd /usr/ports/ directory
# make MASTER_SITE_OVERRIDE= \
ftp://ftp.organization.org/pub/FreeBSD/ports/distfiles/    fetch
```

The WRKDIRPREFIX and PREFIX variables can override the default working and target directories. For example:

```
# make WRKDIRPREFIX=/usr/home/example/ports install
```

will compile the port in /usr/home/example/ports and install everything under /usr/local .

```
# make PREFIX=/usr/home/example/local install
```

will compile the port in /usr/ports and install it in /usr/home/example/local . And:

```
# make WRKDIRPREFIX=../ports PREFIX=../local install
```

will combine the two.

These can also be set as environmental variables. Refer to the manual page for your shell for instructions on how to set an environmental variable.

4.5.2. Removing Installed Ports

Installed ports can be uninstalled using pkg delete . Examples for using this command can be found in the pkg-delete(8) manual page.

Alternately, make deinstall can be run in the port's directory:

```
# cd /usr/ports/sysutils/lsof
make deinstall
===>   Deinstalling for sysutils/lsof
===>    Deinstalling
Deinstallation has been requested for the following 1 packages:

 lsof-4.88.d,8

The deinstallation will free 229 kB
[1/1] Deleting lsof-4.88.d,8... done
```

It is recommended to read the messages as the port is uninstalled. If the port has any applications that depend upon it, this information will be displayed but the uninstallation will proceed. In such cases, it may be better to reinstall the application in order to prevent broken dependencies.

4.5.3. Upgrading Ports

Over time, newer versions of software become available in the Ports Collection. This section describes how to determine which software can be upgraded and how to perform the upgrade.

To determine if newer versions of installed ports are available, ensure that the latest version of the ports tree is installed, using the updating command described in either Procedure 4.1, "Portsnap Method" or Procedure 4.2, "Subversion Method". On FreeBSD 10 and later, or if the system has been converted to pkg, the following command will list the installed ports which are out of date:

```
# pkg version -l "<"
```

For FreeBSD 9.X and lower, the following command will list the installed ports that are out of date:

```
# pkg_version -l "<"
```

 Important

Before attempting an upgrade, read /usr/ports/UPDATING from the top of the file to the date closest to the last time ports were upgraded or the system was installed. This file describes various issues and additional steps users may encounter and need to perform when updating a port, including such things as file format changes, changes in locations of configuration files, or any incompatibilities with previous versions. Make note of any instructions which match any of the ports that need upgrading and follow these instructions when performing the upgrade.

4.5.3.1. Tools To Upgrade And Manage Ports

The Ports Collection contains several utilities to perform the actual upgrade. Each has its strengths and weaknesses.

Historically, most installations used either Portmaster or Portupgrade. Synth is a newer alternative.

 Note

The choice of which tool is best for a particular system is up to the system administrator. It is recommended practice to back up your data before using any of these tools.

4.5.3.2. Upgrading Ports Using Portmaster

ports-mgmt/portmaster is a very small utility for upgrading installed ports. It is designed to use the tools installed with the FreeBSD base system without depending on other ports or databases. To install this utility as a port:

```
# cd /usr/ports/ports-mgmt/portmaster
# make install clean
```

Portmaster defines four categories of ports:

- Root port: has no dependencies and is not a dependency of any other ports.

- Trunk port: has no dependencies, but other ports depend upon it.

- Branch port: has dependencies and other ports depend upon it.

- Leaf port: has dependencies but no other ports depend upon it.

To list these categories and search for updates:

```
# portmaster -L
===>>> Root ports (No dependencies, not depended on)
===>>> ispell-3.2.06_18
===>>> screen-4.0.3
        ===>>> New version available: screen-4.0.3_1
===>>> tcpflow-0.21_1
===>>> 7 root ports
...
```

```
===>>> Branch ports (Have dependencies, are depended on)
===>>> apache22-2.2.3
       ===>>> New version available: apache22-2.2.8
...
===>>> Leaf ports (Have dependencies, not depended on)
===>>> automake-1.9.6_2
===>>> bash-3.1.17
       ===>>> New version available: bash-3.2.33
...
===>>> 32 leaf ports

===>>> 137 total installed ports
       ===>>> 83 have new versions available
```

This command is used to upgrade all outdated ports:

```
# portmaster -a
```

Note

By default, Portmaster makes a backup package before deleting the existing port. If the installation of the new version is successful, Portmaster deletes the backup. Using -b instructs Portmaster not to automatically delete the backup. Adding -i starts Portmaster in interactive mode, prompting for confirmation before upgrading each port. Many other options are available. Read through the manual page for portmaster(8) for details regarding their usage.

If errors are encountered during the upgrade process, add -f to upgrade and rebuild all ports:

```
# portmaster -af
```

Portmaster can also be used to install new ports on the system, upgrading all dependencies before building and installing the new port. To use this function, specify the location of the port in the Ports Collection:

```
# portmaster  shells/bash
```

More information about ports-mgmt/portmaster may be found in its pkg-descr.

4.5.3.3. Upgrading Ports Using Portupgrade

ports-mgmt/portupgrade is another utility that can be used to upgrade ports. It installs a suite of applications which can be used to manage ports. However, it is dependent upon Ruby. To install the port:

```
# cd /usr/ports/ports-mgmt/portupgrade
# make install clean
```

Before performing an upgrade using this utility, it is recommended to scan the list of installed ports using pkgdb -F and to fix all the inconsistencies it reports.

To upgrade all the outdated ports installed on the system, use portupgrade -a. Alternately, include -i to be asked for confirmation of every individual upgrade:

```
# portupgrade -ai
```

To upgrade only a specified application instead of all available ports, use portupgrade *pkgname*. It is very important to include -R to first upgrade all the ports required by the given application:

```
# portupgrade -R firefox
```

If -P is included, Portupgrade searches for available packages in the local directories listed in PKG_PATH. If none are available locally, it then fetches packages from a remote site. If packages can not be found locally or fetched remotely, Portupgrade will use ports. To avoid using ports entirely, specify -PP. This last set of options tells Portupgrade to abort if no packages are available:

```
# portupgrade -PP gnome3
```

To just fetch the port distfiles, or packages, if -P is specified, without building or installing anything, use -F. For further information on all of the available switches, refer to the manual page for portupgrade.

More information about ports-mgmt/portupgrade may be found in its pkg-descr.

4.5.4. Ports and Disk Space

Using the Ports Collection will use up disk space over time. After building and installing a port, running make clean within the ports skeleton will clean up the temporary work directory. If Portmaster is used to install a port, it will automatically remove this directory unless -K is specified. If Portupgrade is installed, this command will remove all work directories found within the local copy of the Ports Collection:

```
# portsclean -C
```

In addition, outdated source distribution files accumulate in /usr/ports/distfiles over time. To use Portupgrade to delete all the distfiles that are no longer referenced by any ports:

```
# portsclean -D
```

Portupgrade can remove all distfiles not referenced by any port currently installed on the system:

```
# portsclean -DD
```

If Portmaster is installed, use:

```
# portmaster --clean-distfiles
```

By default, this command is interactive and prompts the user to confirm if a distfile should be deleted.

In addition to these commands, ports-mgmt/pkg_cutleaves automates the task of removing installed ports that are no longer needed.

4.6. Building Packages with Poudriere

Poudriere is a BSD-licensed utility for creating and testing FreeBSD packages. It uses FreeBSD jails to set up isolated compilation environments. These jails can be used to build packages for versions of FreeBSD that are different from the system on which it is installed, and also to build packages for i386 if the host is an amd64 system. Once the packages are built, they are in a layout identical to the official mirrors. These packages are usable by pkg(8) and other package management tools.

Poudriere is installed using the ports-mgmt/poudriere package or port. The installation includes a sample configuration file /usr/local/etc/poudriere.conf.sample . Copy this file to /usr/local/etc/poudriere.conf . Edit the copied file to suit the local configuration.

While ZFS is not required on the system running poudriere, it is beneficial. When ZFS is used, ZPOOL must be specified in /usr/local/etc/poudriere.conf and FREEBSD_HOST should be set to a nearby mirror. Defining CCACHE_DIR enables the use of devel/ccache to cache compilation and reduce build times for frequently-compiled code. It may be convenient to put poudriere datasets in an isolated tree mounted at /poudriere . Defaults for the other configuration values are adequate.

The number of processor cores detected is used to define how many builds will run in parallel. Supply enough virtual memory, either with RAM or swap space. If virtual memory runs out, the compilation jails will stop and be torn down, resulting in weird error messages.

4.6.1. Initialize Jails and Port Trees

After configuration, initialize poudriere so that it installs a jail with the required FreeBSD tree and a ports tree. Specify a name for the jail using -j and the FreeBSD version with -v. On systems running FreeBSD/amd64, the architecture can be set with -a to either i386 or amd64. The default is the architecture shown by uname.

```
# poudriere jail -c -j  10amd64  -v 10.0-RELEASE
====>> Creating 10amd64 fs... done
====>> Fetching base.txz for FreeBSD 10.0-RELEASE amd64
/poudriere/jails/10amd64/fromftp/base.txz      100% of   59 MB 1470 kBps 00m42s
====>> Extracting base.txz... done
====>> Fetching src.txz for FreeBSD 10.0-RELEASE amd64
/poudriere/jails/10amd64/fromftp/src.txz       100% of  107 MB 1476 kBps 01m14s
====>> Extracting src.txz... done
====>> Fetching games.txz for FreeBSD 10.0-RELEASE amd64
/poudriere/jails/10amd64/fromftp/games.txz     100% of  865 kB  734 kBps 00m01s
====>> Extracting games.txz... done
====>> Fetching lib32.txz for FreeBSD 10.0-RELEASE amd64
/poudriere/jails/10amd64/fromftp/lib32.txz     100% of   14 MB 1316 kBps 00m12s
====>> Extracting lib32.txz... done
====>> Cleaning up... done
====>> Jail 10amd64 10.0-RELEASE amd64 is ready to be used
```

```
# poudriere ports -c -p  local
====>> Creating local fs... done
====>> Extracting portstree "local"...
Looking up portsnap.FreeBSD.org mirrors... 7 mirrors found.
Fetching public key from ec2-eu-west-1.portsnap.freebsd.org... done.
Fetching snapshot tag from ec2-eu-west-1.portsnap.freebsd.org... done.
Fetching snapshot metadata... done.
Fetching snapshot generated at Tue Feb 11 01:07:15 CET 2014:
94a3431f0ce567f6452ffde4fd3d7d3c6e1da143efec76100% of   69 MB 1246 kBps 00m57s
Extracting snapshot... done.
Verifying snapshot integrity... done.
Fetching snapshot tag from ec2-eu-west-1.portsnap.freebsd.org... done.
Fetching snapshot metadata... done.
Updating from Tue Feb 11 01:07:15 CET 2014 to Tue Feb 11 16:05:20 CET 2014.
Fetching 4 metadata patches... done.
Applying metadata patches... done.
Fetching 0 metadata files... done.
Fetching 48 patches.
(48/48) 100.00%  done.
done.
Applying patches...
done.
Fetching 1 new ports or files... done.
/poudriere/ports/tester/CHANGES
/poudriere/ports/tester/COPYRIGHT

[...-]

Building new INDEX files... done.
```

On a single computer, poudriere can build ports with multiple configurations, in multiple jails, and from different port trees. Custom configurations for these combinations are called *sets*. See the CUSTOMIZATION section of poudriere(8) for details after ports-mgmt/poudriere or ports-mgmt/poudriere-devel is installed.

The basic configuration shown here puts a single jail-, port-, and set-specific make.conf in /usr/local/etc/poudriere.d . The filename in this example is created by combining the jail name, port name, and set name: *10amd64-local-workstation* -make.conf . The system make.conf and this new file are combined at build time to create the make.conf used by the build jail.

Packages to be built are entered in *10amd64-local-workstation* -pkglist :

```
editors/emacs
```

```
devel/git
ports-mgmt/pkg
...
```

Options and dependencies for the specified ports are configured:

```
# poudriere options -j  10amd64 -p local -z workstation -f 10amd64-local-workstation-pkglist
```

Finally, packages are built and a package repository is created:

```
# poudriere bulk -j  10amd64 -p local -z workstation -f 10amd64-local-workstation-pkglist
```

While running, pressing Ctrl+t displays the current state of the build. Poudriere also builds files in /poudriere/ logs/bulk/ *jailname* that can be used with a web server to display build information.

After completion, the new packages are now available for installation from the poudriere repository.

For more information on using poudriere, see poudriere(8) and the main web site, https://github.com/freebsd/poudriere/wiki.

4.6.2. Configuring pkg Clients to Use a Poudriere Repository

While it is possible to use both a custom repository along side of the official repository, sometimes it is useful to disable the official repository. This is done by creating a configuration file that overrides and disables the official configuration file. Create /usr/local/etc/pkg/repos/FreeBSD.conf that contains the following:

```
FreeBSD: {
 enabled: no
}
```

Usually it is easiest to serve a poudriere repository to the client machines via HTTP. Set up a webserver to serve up the package directory, for instance: /usr/local/poudriere/data/packages/ *10amd64*, where *10amd64* is the name of the build.

If the URL to the package repository is: http://pkg.example.com/10amd64 , then the repository configuration file in /usr/local/etc/pkg/repos/custom.conf would look like:

```
custom: {
 url: "http://pkg.example.com/10amd64  ",
 enabled: yes,
}
```

4.7. Post-Installation Considerations

Regardless of whether the software was installed from a binary package or port, most third-party applications require some level of configuration after installation. The following commands and locations can be used to help determine what was installed with the application.

- Most applications install at least one default configuration file in /usr/local/etc . In cases where an application has a large number of configuration files, a subdirectory will be created to hold them. Often, sample configuration files are installed which end with a suffix such as .sample. The configuration files should be reviewed and possibly edited to meet the system's needs. To edit a sample file, first copy it without the .sample extension.

- Applications which provide documentation will install it into /usr/local/share/doc and many applications also install manual pages. This documentation should be consulted before continuing.

- Some applications run services which must be added to /etc/rc.conf before starting the application. These applications usually install a startup script in /usr/local/etc/rc.d . See Starting Services for more information.

Note

By design, applications do not run their startup script upon installation, nor do they run their stop script upon deinstallation or upgrade. This decision is left to the individual system administrator.

- Users of csh(1) should run rehash to rebuild the known binary list in the shells PATH.

- Use pkg info to determine which files, man pages, and binaries were installed with the application.

4.8. Dealing with Broken Ports

When a port does not build or install, try the following:

1. Search to see if there is a fix pending for the port in the Problem Report database. If so, implementing the proposed fix may fix the issue.

2. Ask the maintainer of the port for help. Type make maintainer in the ports skeleton or read the port's Makefile to find the maintainer's email address. Remember to include the $FreeBSD: line from the port's Makefile and the output leading up to the error in the email to the maintainer.

Note

Some ports are not maintained by an individual but instead by a group maintainer represented by a mailing list. Many, but not all, of these addresses look like <freebsd-list name@FreeBSD.org>. Please take this into account when sending an email.

In particular, ports maintained by <ports@FreeBSD.org> are not maintained by a specific individual. Instead, any fixes and support come from the general community who subscribe to that mailing list. More volunteers are always needed!

If there is no response to the email, use Bugzilla to submit a bug report using the instructions in Writing FreeBSD Problem Reports.

3. Fix it! The Porter's Handbook includes detailed information on the ports infrastructure so that you can fix the occasional broken port or even submit your own!

4. Install the package instead of the port using the instructions in Section 4.4, "Using pkg for Binary Package Management".

Chapter 5. The X Window System

5.1. Synopsis

An installation of FreeBSD using bsdinstall does not automatically install a graphical user interface. This chapter describes how to install and configure Xorg, which provides the open source X Window System used to provide a graphical environment. It then describes how to find and install a desktop environment or window manager.

 Note

Users who prefer an installation method that automatically configures the Xorg and offers a choice of window managers during installation should refer to the http://www.trueos.org/ website.

For more information on the video hardware that Xorg supports, refer to the x.org website.

After reading this chapter, you will know:

- The various components of the X Window System, and how they interoperate.

- How to install and configure Xorg.

- How to install and configure several window managers and desktop environments.

- How to use TrueType® fonts in Xorg.

- How to set up your system for graphical logins (XDM).

Before reading this chapter, you should:

- Know how to install additional third-party software as described in Chapter 4, *Installing Applications: Packages and Ports*.

5.2. Terminology

While it is not necessary to understand all of the details of the various components in the X Window System and how they interact, some basic knowledge of these components can be useful.

X server
> X was designed from the beginning to be network-centric, and adopts a "client-server" model. In this model, the "X server" runs on the computer that has the keyboard, monitor, and mouse attached. The server's responsibility includes tasks such as managing the display, handling input from the keyboard and mouse, and handling input or output from other devices such as a tablet or a video projector. This confuses some people, because the X terminology is exactly backward to what they expect. They expect the "X server" to be the big powerful machine down the hall, and the "X client" to be the machine on their desk.

X client
> Each X application, such as XTerm or Firefox, is a "client". A client sends messages to the server such as "Please draw a window at these coordinates", and the server sends back messages such as "The user just clicked on the OK button".

> In a home or small office environment, the X server and the X clients commonly run on the same computer. It is also possible to run the X server on a less powerful computer and to run the X applications on a more

powerful system. In this scenario, the communication between the X client and server takes place over the network.

window manager

X does not dictate what windows should look like on-screen, how to move them around with the mouse, which keystrokes should be used to move between windows, what the title bars on each window should look like, whether or not they have close buttons on them, and so on. Instead, X delegates this responsibility to a separate window manager application. There are dozens of window managers available. Each window manager provides a different look and feel: some support virtual desktops, some allow customized keystrokes to manage the desktop, some have a "Start" button, and some are themeable, allowing a complete change of the desktop's look-and-feel. Window managers are available in the x11-wm category of the Ports Collection.

Each window manager uses a different configuration mechanism. Some expect configuration file written by hand while others provide graphical tools for most configuration tasks.

desktop environment

KDE and GNOME are considered to be desktop environments as they include an entire suite of applications for performing common desktop tasks. These may include office suites, web browsers, and games.

focus policy

The window manager is responsible for the mouse focus policy. This policy provides some means for choosing which window is actively receiving keystrokes and it should also visibly indicate which window is currently active.

One focus policy is called "click-to-focus". In this model, a window becomes active upon receiving a mouse click. In the "focus-follows-mouse" policy, the window that is under the mouse pointer has focus and the focus is changed by pointing at another window. If the mouse is over the root window, then this window is focused. In the "sloppy-focus" model, if the mouse is moved over the root window, the most recently used window still has the focus. With sloppy-focus, focus is only changed when the cursor enters a new window, and not when exiting the current window. In the "click-to-focus" policy, the active window is selected by mouse click. The window may then be raised and appear in front of all other windows. All keystrokes will now be directed to this window, even if the cursor is moved to another window.

Different window managers support different focus models. All of them support click-to-focus, and the majority of them also support other policies. Consult the documentation for the window manager to determine which focus models are available.

widgets

Widget is a term for all of the items in the user interface that can be clicked or manipulated in some way. This includes buttons, check boxes, radio buttons, icons, and lists. A widget toolkit is a set of widgets used to create graphical applications. There are several popular widget toolkits, including Qt, used by KDE, and GTK+, used by GNOME. As a result, applications will have a different look and feel, depending upon which widget toolkit was used to create the application.

5.3. Installing Xorg

On FreeBSD, Xorg can be installed as a package or port.

The binary package can be installed quickly but with fewer options for customization:

```
# pkg install xorg
```

To build and install from the Ports Collection:

```
# cd /usr/ports/x11/xorg
# make install clean
```

Either of these installations results in the complete Xorg system being installed. Binary packages are the best option for most users.

A smaller version of the X system suitable for experienced users is available in x11/xorg-minimal. Most of the documents, libraries, and applications will not be installed. Some applications require these additional components to function.

5.4. Xorg Configuration

Warren Block

5.4.1. Quick Start

Xorg supports most common video cards, keyboards, and pointing devices.

> Tip
>
> Video cards, monitors, and input devices are automatically detected and do not require any manual configuration. Do not create xorg.conf or run a -configure step unless automatic configuration fails.

1. If Xorg has been used on this computer before, move or remove any existing configuration files:

    ```
    # mv /etc/X11/xorg.conf ~/xorg.conf.etc
    # mv /usr/local/etc/X11/xorg.conf ~/xorg.conf.localetc
    ```

2. Add the user who will run Xorg to the video or wheel group to enable 3D acceleration when available. To add user *jru* to whichever group is available:

    ```
    # pw groupmod video -m jru || pw groupmod wheel -m jru
    ```

3. The TWM window manager is included by default. It is started when Xorg starts:

    ```
    % startx
    ```

4. On some older versions of FreeBSD, the system console must be set to vt(4) before switching back to the text console will work properly. See Section 5.4.3, "Kernel Mode Setting (KMS)".

5.4.2. User Group for Accelerated Video

Access to /dev/dri is needed to allow 3D acceleration on video cards. It is usually simplest to add the user who will be running X to either the video or wheel group. Here, pw(8) is used to add user *slurms* to the video group, or to the wheel group if there is no video group:

```
# pw groupmod video -m slurms || pw groupmod wheel -m slurms
```

5.4.3. Kernel Mode Setting (KMS)

When the computer switches from displaying the console to a higher screen resolution for X, it must set the video output *mode*. Recent versions of Xorg use a system inside the kernel to do these mode changes more efficiently. Older versions of FreeBSD use sc(4), which is not aware of the KMS system. The end result is that after closing X, the system console is blank, even though it is still working. The newer vt(4) console avoids this problem.

Add this line to /boot/loader.conf to enable vt(4):

```
kern.vty=vt
```

5.4.4. Configuration Files

Manual configuration is usually not necessary. Please do not manually create configuration files unless autoconfiguration does not work.

5.4.4.1. Directory

Xorg looks in several directories for configuration files. `/usr/local/etc/X11/` is the recommended directory for these files on FreeBSD. Using this directory helps keep application files separate from operating system files.

Storing configuration files in the legacy `/etc/X11/` still works. However, this mixes application files with the base FreeBSD files and is not recommended.

5.4.4.2. Single or Multiple Files

It is easier to use multiple files that each configure a specific setting than the traditional single `xorg.conf`. These files are stored in the `xorg.conf.d/` subdirectory of the main configuration file directory. The full path is typically `/usr/local/etc/X11/xorg.conf.d/`.

Examples of these files are shown later in this section.

The traditional single `xorg.conf` still works, but is neither as clear nor as flexible as multiple files in the `xorg.conf.d/` subdirectory.

5.4.5. Video Cards

Intel®
> 3D acceleration is supported on most Intel® graphics up to Ivy Bridge (HD Graphics 2500, 4000, and P4000), including Iron Lake (HD Graphics) and Sandy Bridge (HD Graphics 2000).
>
> Driver name: `intel`
>
> For reference, see https://en.wikipedia.org/wiki/List_of_Intel_graphics_processing_units.

AMD® Radeon
> 2D and 3D acceleration is supported on Radeon cards up to and including the HD6000 series.
>
> Driver name: `radeon`
>
> For reference, see https://en.wikipedia.org/wiki/List_of_AMD_graphics_processing_units.

NVIDIA
> Several NVIDIA drivers are available in the x11 category of the Ports Collection. Install the driver that matches the video card.
>
> For reference, see https://en.wikipedia.org/wiki/List_of_Nvidia_graphics_processing_units.

Hybrid Combination Graphics
> Some notebook computers add additional graphics processing units to those built into the chipset or processor. *Optimus* combines Intel® and NVIDIA hardware. *Switchable Graphics* or *Hybrid Graphics* are a combination of an Intel® or AMD® processor and an AMD® Radeon GPU.
>
> Implementations of these hybrid graphics systems vary, and Xorg on FreeBSD is not able to drive all versions of them.
>
> Some computers provide a BIOS option to disable one of the graphics adapters or select a *discrete* mode which can be used with one of the standard video card drivers. For example, it is sometimes possible to disable the NVIDIA GPU in an Optimus system. The Intel® video can then be used with an Intel® driver.
>
> BIOS settings depend on the model of computer. In some situations, both GPUs can be left enabled, but creating a configuration file that only uses the main GPU in the `Device` section is enough to make such a system functional.

Other Video Cards

Drivers for some less-common video cards can be found in the x11-drivers directory of the Ports Collection.

Cards that are not supported by a specific driver might still be usable with the x11-drivers/xf86-video-vesa driver. This driver is installed by x11/xorg. It can also be installed manually as x11-drivers/xf86-video-vesa. Xorg attempts to use this driver when a specific driver is not found for the video card.

x11-drivers/xf86-video-scfb is a similar nonspecialized video driver that works on many UEFI and ARM® computers.

Setting the Video Driver in a File

To set the Intel® driver in a configuration file:

Example 5.1. Select Intel® Video Driver in a File

`/usr/local/etc/X11/xorg.conf.d/driver-intel.conf`

```
Section "Device"
 Identifier "Card0"
 Driver     "intel"
 # BusID    "PCI:1:0:0"
EndSection
```

If more than one video card is present, the BusID identifier can be uncommented and set to select the desired card. A list of video card bus IDs can be displayed with `pciconf -lv | grep -B3 display`.

To set the Radeon driver in a configuration file:

Example 5.2. Select Radeon Video Driver in a File

`/usr/local/etc/X11/xorg.conf.d/driver-radeon.conf`

```
Section "Device"
 Identifier "Card0"
 Driver     "radeon"
EndSection
```

To set the VESA driver in a configuration file:

Example 5.3. Select VESA Video Driver in a File

`/usr/local/etc/X11/xorg.conf.d/driver-vesa.conf`

```
Section "Device"
 Identifier "Card0"
 Driver     "vesa"
EndSection
```

To set the scfb driver for use with a UEFI or ARM® computer:

Example 5.4. Select scfb Video Driver in a File

/usr/local/etc/X11/xorg.conf.d/driver-scfb.conf

```
Section "Device"
 Identifier "Card0"
 Driver     "scfb"
EndSection
```

5.4.6. Monitors

Almost all monitors support the Extended Display Identification Data standard (EDID). Xorg uses EDID to communicate with the monitor and detect the supported resolutions and refresh rates. Then it selects the most appropriate combination of settings to use with that monitor.

Other resolutions supported by the monitor can be chosen by setting the desired resolution in configuration files, or after the X server has been started with xrandr(1).

Using xrandr(1)

Run xrandr(1) without any parameters to see a list of video outputs and detected monitor modes:

```
% xrandr
Screen 0: minimum 320 x 200, current 3000 x 1920, maximum 8192 x 8192
DVI-0 connected primary 1920x1200+1080+0 (normal left inverted right x axis y axis) ↻
495mm x 310mm
   1920x1200     59.95*+
   1600x1200     60.00
   1280x1024     85.02    75.02    60.02
   1280x960      60.00
   1152x864      75.00
   1024x768      85.00    75.08    70.07    60.00
   832x624       74.55
   800x600       75.00    60.32
   640x480       75.00    60.00
   720x400       70.08
DisplayPort-0 disconnected (normal left inverted right x axis y axis)
HDMI-0 disconnected (normal left inverted right x axis y axis)
```

This shows that the DVI-0 output is being used to display a screen resolution of 1920x1200 pixels at a refresh rate of about 60 Hz. Monitors are not attached to the DisplayPort-0 and HDMI-0 connectors.

Any of the other display modes can be selected with xrandr(1). For example, to switch to 1280x1024 at 60 Hz:

```
% xrandr --mode 1280x1024 --rate 60
```

A common task is using the external video output on a notebook computer for a video projector.

The type and quantity of output connectors varies between devices, and the name given to each output varies from driver to driver. What one driver calls HDMI-1, another might call HDMI1. So the first step is to run xrandr(1) to list all the available outputs:

```
% xrandr
Screen 0: minimum 320 x 200, current 1366 x 768, maximum 8192 x 8192
LVDS1 connected 1366x768+0+0 (normal left inverted right x axis y axis) 344mm x 193mm
   1366x768      60.04*+
   1024x768      60.00
   800x600       60.32    56.25
```

```
    640x480       59.94
VGA1 connected (normal left inverted right x axis y axis)
   1280x1024     60.02 +  75.02
   1280x960      60.00
   1152x864      75.00
   1024x768      75.08    70.07    60.00
   832x624       74.55
   800x600       72.19    75.00    60.32    56.25
   640x480       75.00    72.81    66.67    60.00
   720x400       70.08
HDMI1 disconnected (normal left inverted right x axis y axis)
DP1 disconnected (normal left inverted right x axis y axis)
```

Four outputs were found: the built-in panel LVDS1, and external VGA1, HDMI1, and DP1 connectors.

The projector has been connected to the VGA1 output. xrandr(1) is now used to set that output to the native resolution of the projector and add the additional space to the right side of the desktop:

```
% xrandr --output VGA1 --auto --right-of LVDS1
```

--auto chooses the resolution and refresh rate detected by EDID. If the resolution is not correctly detected, a fixed value can be given with --mode instead of the --auto statement. For example, most projectors can be used with a 1024x768 resolution, which is set with --mode 1024x768 .

xrandr(1) is often run from .xinitrc to set the appropriate mode when X starts.

Setting Monitor Resolution in a File
To set a screen resolution of 1024x768 in a configuration file:

Example 5.5. Set Screen Resolution in a File

/usr/local/etc/X11/xorg.conf.d/screen-resolution.conf

```
Section "Screen"
 Identifier "Screen0"
 Device     "Card0"
 SubSection "Display"
 Modes      "1024x768"
 EndSubSection
EndSection
```

The few monitors that do not have EDID can be configured by setting HorizSync and VertRefresh to the range of frequencies supported by the monitor.

Example 5.6. Manually Setting Monitor Frequencies

/usr/local/etc/X11/xorg.conf.d/monitor0-freq.conf

```
Section "Monitor"
 Identifier   "Monitor0"
 HorizSync    30-83   # kHz
 VertRefresh  50-76   # Hz
EndSection
```

5.4.7. Input Devices

5.4.7.1. Keyboards

Keyboard Layout

The standardized location of keys on a keyboard is called a *layout*. Layouts and other adjustable parameters are listed in xkeyboard-config(7).

A United States layout is the default. To select an alternate layout, set the XkbLayout and XkbVariant options in an InputClass. This will be applied to all input devices that match the class.

This example selects a French keyboard layout with the oss variant.

Example 5.7. Setting a Keyboard Layout

/usr/local/etc/X11/xorg.conf.d/keyboard-fr-oss.conf

```
Section "InputClass"
 Identifier "KeyboardDefaults"
 Driver   "keyboard"
 MatchIsKeyboard "on"
 Option  "XkbLayout" "fr"
 Option  "XkbVariant" "oss"
EndSection
```

Example 5.8. Setting Multiple Keyboard Layouts

Set United States, Spanish, and Ukrainian keyboard layouts. Cycle through these layouts by pressing Alt+Shift. x11/xxkb or x11/sbxkb can be used for improved layout switching control and current layout indicators.

/usr/local/etc/X11/xorg.conf.d/kbd-layout-multi.conf

```
Section "InputClass"
 Identifier "All Keyboards"
 MatchIsKeyboard "yes"
 Option  "XkbLayout" "us, es, ua"
EndSection
```

Closing Xorg From the Keyboard

X can be closed with a combination of keys. By default, that key combination is not set because it conflicts with keyboard commands for some applications. Enabling this option requires changes to the keyboard InputDevice section:

Example 5.9. Enabling Keyboard Exit from X

/usr/local/etc/X11/xorg.conf.d/keyboard-zap.conf

```
Section "InputClass"
 Identifier "KeyboardDefaults"
 Driver   "keyboard"
```

```
    MatchIsKeyboard "on"
    Option   "XkbOptions" "terminate:ctrl_alt_bksp"
EndSection
```

5.4.7.2. Mice and Pointing Devices

Many mouse parameters can be adjusted with configuration options. See mousedrv(4) for a full list.

Mouse Buttons

The number of buttons on a mouse can be set in the mouse `InputDevice` section of `xorg.conf`. To set the number of buttons to 7:

Example 5.10. Setting the Number of Mouse Buttons

`/usr/local/etc/X11/xorg.conf.d/mouse0-buttons.conf`

```
Section "InputDevice"
  Identifier  "Mouse0"
  Option      "Buttons" "7"
EndSection
```

5.4.8. Manual Configuration

In some cases, Xorg autoconfiguration does not work with particular hardware, or a different configuration is desired. For these cases, a custom configuration file can be created.

Warning

Do not create manual configuration files unless required. Unnecessary manual configuration can prevent proper operation.

A configuration file can be generated by Xorg based on the detected hardware. This file is often a useful starting point for custom configurations.

Generating an `xorg.conf`:

```
# Xorg -configure
```

The configuration file is saved to `/root/xorg.conf.new`. Make any changes desired, then test that file with:

```
# Xorg -config /root/xorg.conf.new
```

After the new configuration has been adjusted and tested, it can be split into smaller files in the normal location, `/usr/local/etc/X11/xorg.conf.d/`.

5.5. Using Fonts in Xorg

5.5.1. Type1 Fonts

The default fonts that ship with Xorg are less than ideal for typical desktop publishing applications. Large presentation fonts show up jagged and unprofessional looking, and small fonts are almost completely unintelligible.

However, there are several free, high quality Type1 (PostScript®) fonts available which can be readily used with Xorg. For instance, the URW font collection (x11-fonts/urwfonts) includes high quality versions of standard type1 fonts (Times Roman®, Helvetica®, Palatino® and others). The Freefonts collection (x11-fonts/freefonts) includes many more fonts, but most of them are intended for use in graphics software such as the Gimp, and are not complete enough to serve as screen fonts. In addition, Xorg can be configured to use TrueType® fonts with a minimum of effort. For more details on this, see the X(7) manual page or Section 5.5.2, "TrueType® Fonts".

To install the above Type1 font collections from binary packages, run the following commands:

```
# pkg install urwfonts
```

Alternatively, to build from the Ports Collection, run the following commands:

```
# cd /usr/ports/x11-fonts/urwfonts
# make install clean
```

And likewise with the freefont or other collections. To have the X server detect these fonts, add an appropriate line to the X server configuration file (/etc/X11/xorg.conf), which reads:

```
FontPath "/usr/local/share/fonts/urwfonts/"
```

Alternatively, at the command line in the X session run:

```
% xset fp+ /usr/local/share/fonts/urwfonts
% xset fp rehash
```

This will work but will be lost when the X session is closed, unless it is added to the startup file (~/.xinitrc for a normal startx session, or ~/.xsession when logging in through a graphical login manager like XDM). A third way is to use the new /usr/local/etc/fonts/local.conf as demonstrated in Section 5.5.3, "Anti-Aliased Fonts".

5.5.2. TrueType® Fonts

Xorg has built in support for rendering TrueType® fonts. There are two different modules that can enable this functionality. The freetype module is used in this example because it is more consistent with the other font rendering back-ends. To enable the freetype module just add the following line to the "Module" section of /etc/X11/xorg.conf .

```
Load  "freetype"
```

Now make a directory for the TrueType® fonts (for example, /usr/local/share/fonts/TrueType) and copy all of the TrueType® fonts into this directory. Keep in mind that TrueType® fonts cannot be directly taken from an Apple® Mac®; they must be in UNIX®/MS-DOS®/Windows® format for use by Xorg. Once the files have been copied into this directory, use mkfontdir to create a fonts.dir , so that the X font renderer knows that these new files have been installed. mkfontdir can be installed as a package:

```
# pkg install mkfontdir
```

Then create an index of X font files in a directory:

```
# cd /usr/local/share/fonts/TrueType
# mkfontdir
```

Now add the TrueType® directory to the font path. This is just the same as described in Section 5.5.1, "Type1 Fonts":

```
% xset fp+ /usr/local/share/fonts/TrueType
% xset fp rehash
```

or add a FontPath line to xorg.conf .

Now Gimp, Apache OpenOffice, and all of the other X applications should now recognize the installed TrueType® fonts. Extremely small fonts (as with text in a high resolution display on a web page) and extremely large fonts (within StarOffice™) will look much better now.

5.5.3. Anti-Aliased Fonts

All fonts in Xorg that are found in /usr/local/share/fonts/ and ~/.fonts/ are automatically made available for anti-aliasing to Xft-aware applications. Most recent applications are Xft-aware, including KDE, GNOME, and Firefox.

To control which fonts are anti-aliased, or to configure anti-aliasing properties, create (or edit, if it already exists) the file /usr/local/etc/fonts/local.conf . Several advanced features of the Xft font system can be tuned using this file; this section describes only some simple possibilities. For more details, please see fonts-conf(5).

This file must be in XML format. Pay careful attention to case, and make sure all tags are properly closed. The file begins with the usual XML header followed by a DOCTYPE definition, and then the <fontconfig> tag:

```
<?xml version="1.0"?>
    <!DOCTYPE fontconfig SYSTEM "fonts.dtd">
    <fontconfig>
```

As previously stated, all fonts in /usr/local/share/fonts/ as well as ~/.fonts/ are already made available to Xft-aware applications. To add another directory outside of these two directory trees, add a line like this to /usr/local/etc/fonts/local.conf :

```
<dir>/path/to/my/fonts</dir>
```

After adding new fonts, and especially new font directories, rebuild the font caches:

```
# fc-cache -f
```

Anti-aliasing makes borders slightly fuzzy, which makes very small text more readable and removes "staircases" from large text, but can cause eyestrain if applied to normal text. To exclude font sizes smaller than 14 point from anti-aliasing, include these lines:

```
    <match target="font">
    <test name="size" compare="less">
  <double>14</double>
    </test>
    <edit name="antialias" mode="assign">
  <bool>false</bool>
    </edit>
</match>
<match target="font">
    <test name="pixelsize" compare="less" qual="any">
  <double>14</double>
    </test>
    <edit mode="assign" name="antialias">
  <bool>false</bool>
    </edit>
</match>
```

Spacing for some monospaced fonts might also be inappropriate with anti-aliasing. This seems to be an issue with KDE, in particular. One possible fix is to force the spacing for such fonts to be 100. Add these lines:

```
<match target="pattern" name="family">
    <test qual="any" name="family">
        <string>fixed</string>
    </test>
    <edit name="family" mode="assign">
        <string>mono</string>
    </edit>
</match>
<match target="pattern" name="family">
    <test qual="any" name="family">
```

```
<string>console</string>
    </test>
    <edit name="family" mode="assign">
<string>mono</string>
    </edit>
</match>
```

(this aliases the other common names for fixed fonts as "mono"), and then add:

```
        <match target="pattern" name="family">
    <test qual="any" name="family">
<string>mono</string>
    </test>
    <edit name="spacing" mode="assign">
<int>100</int>
    </edit>
</match>
```

Certain fonts, such as Helvetica, may have a problem when anti-aliased. Usually this manifests itself as a font that seems cut in half vertically. At worst, it may cause applications to crash. To avoid this, consider adding the following to local.conf:

```
        <match target="pattern" name="family">
    <test qual="any" name="family">
<string>Helvetica</string>
    </test>
    <edit name="family" mode="assign">
<string>sans-serif</string>
    </edit>
</match>
```

After editing local.conf, make certain to end the file with the </fontconfig> tag. Not doing this will cause changes to be ignored.

Users can add personalized settings by creating their own ~/.config/fontconfig/fonts.conf . This file uses the same XML format described above.

One last point: with an LCD screen, sub-pixel sampling may be desired. This basically treats the (horizontally separated) red, green and blue components separately to improve the horizontal resolution; the results can be dramatic. To enable this, add the line somewhere in local.conf:

```
<match target="font">
    <test qual="all" name="rgba">
<const>unknown</const>
    </test>
    <edit name="rgba" mode="assign">
<const>rgb</const>
    </edit>
</match>
```

Note

Depending on the sort of display, rgb may need to be changed to bgr, vrgb or vbgr: experiment and see which works best.

5.6. The X Display Manager

Contributed by Seth Kingsley.

Xorg provides an X Display Manager, XDM, which can be used for login session management. XDM provides a graphical interface for choosing which display server to connect to and for entering authorization information such as a login and password combination.

This section demonstrates how to configure the X Display Manager on FreeBSD. Some desktop environments provide their own graphical login manager. Refer to Section 5.7.1, "GNOME" for instructions on how to configure the GNOME Display Manager and Section 5.7.2, "KDE" for instructions on how to configure the KDE Display Manager.

5.6.1. Configuring XDM

To install XDM, use the x11/xdm package or port. Once installed, XDM can be configured to run when the machine boots up by editing this entry in /etc/ttys :

```
ttyv8   "/usr/local/bin/xdm -nodaemon"  xterm   off secure
```

Change the off to on and save the edit. The ttyv8 in this entry indicates that XDM will run on the ninth virtual terminal.

The XDM configuration directory is located in /usr/local/lib/X11/xdm . This directory contains several files used to change the behavior and appearance of XDM, as well as a few scripts and programs used to set up the desktop when XDM is running. Table 5.1, "XDM Configuration Files" summarizes the function of each of these files. The exact syntax and usage of these files is described in xdm(1).

Table 5.1. XDM Configuration Files

File	Description
Xaccess	The protocol for connecting to XDM is called the X Display Manager Connection Protocol (XDMCP) This file is a client authorization ruleset for controlling XDMCP connections from remote machines. By default, this file does not allow any remote clients to connect.
Xresources	This file controls the look and feel of the XDM display chooser and login screens. The default configuration is a simple rectangular login window with the hostname of the machine displayed at the top in a large font and "Login:" and "Password:" prompts below. The format of this file is identical to the app-defaults file described in the Xorg documentation.
Xservers	The list of local and remote displays the chooser should provide as login choices.
Xsession	Default session script for logins which is run by XDM after a user has logged in. Normally each user will have a customized session script in ~/.xsession that overrides this script
Xsetup_*	Script to automatically launch applications before displaying the chooser or login interfaces. There is a script for each display being used, named Xsetup_*, where * is the local display number. Typically these scripts run one or two programs in the background such as xconsole.
xdm-config	Global configuration for all displays running on this machine.
xdm-errors	Contains errors generated by the server program. If a display that XDM is trying to start hangs, look at this file for error messages. These messages are also written to the user's ~/.xsession-errors on a per-session basis.

File	Description
xdm-pid	The running process ID of XDM.

5.6.2. Configuring Remote Access

By default, only users on the same system can login using XDM. To enable users on other systems to connect to the display server, edit the access control rules and enable the connection listener.

To configure XDM to listen for any remote connection, comment out the `DisplayManager.requestPort` line in `/usr/local/lib/X11/xdm/xdm-config` by putting a ! in front of it:

```
! SECURITY: do not listen for XDMCP or Chooser requests
! Comment out this line if you want to manage X terminals with xdm
DisplayManager.requestPort:    0
```

Save the edits and restart XDM. To restrict remote access, look at the example entries in `/usr/local/lib/X11/xdm/Xaccess` and refer to xdm(1) for further information.

5.7. Desktop Environments

Contributed by Valentino Vaschetto.

This section describes how to install three popular desktop environments on a FreeBSD system. A desktop environment can range from a simple window manager to a complete suite of desktop applications. Over a hundred desktop environments are available in the x11-wm category of the Ports Collection.

5.7.1. GNOME

GNOME is a user-friendly desktop environment. It includes a panel for starting applications and displaying status, a desktop, a set of tools and applications, and a set of conventions that make it easy for applications to cooperate and be consistent with each other. More information regarding GNOME on FreeBSD can be found at https://www.Free-BSD.org/gnome. That web site contains additional documentation about installing, configuring, and managing GNOME on FreeBSD.

This desktop environment can be installed from a package:

```
# pkg install gnome3
```

To instead build GNOME from ports, use the following command. GNOME is a large application and will take some time to compile, even on a fast computer.

```
# cd /usr/ports/x11/gnome3
# make install clean
```

GNOME requires /proc to be mounted. Add this line to `/etc/fstab` to mount this file system automatically during system startup:

```
proc            /proc        procfs  rw  0   0
```

GNOME uses D-Bus and HAL for a message bus and hardware abstraction. These applications are automatically installed as dependencies of GNOME. Enable them in `/etc/rc.conf` so they will be started when the system boots:

```
dbus_enable="YES"
hald_enable="YES"
```

After installation, configure Xorg to start GNOME. The easiest way to do this is to enable the GNOME Display Manager, GDM, which is installed as part of the GNOME package or port. It can be enabled by adding this line to `/etc/rc.conf`:

```
gdm_enable="YES"
```

It is often desirable to also start all GNOME services. To achieve this, add a second line to /etc/rc.conf :

```
gnome_enable="YES"
```

GDM will start automatically when the system boots.

A second method for starting GNOME is to type startx from the command-line after configuring ~/.xinitrc. If this file already exists, replace the line that starts the current window manager with one that starts /usr/ local/bin/gnome-session . If this file does not exist, create it with this command:

```
% echo "exec /usr/local/bin/gnome-session" > ~/.xinitrc
```

A third method is to use XDM as the display manager. In this case, create an executable ~/.xsession:

```
% echo "#!/bin/sh" > ~/.xsession
% echo "exec /usr/local/bin/gnome-session" >> ~/.xsession
% chmod +x ~/.xsession
```

5.7.2. KDE

KDE is another easy-to-use desktop environment. This desktop provides a suite of applications with a consistent look and feel, a standardized menu and toolbars, keybindings, color-schemes, internationalization, and a centralized, dialog-driven desktop configuration. More information on KDE can be found at http://www.kde.org/. For FreeBSD-specific information, consult http://freebsd.kde.org.

To install the KDE package, type:

```
# pkg install x11/kde4
```

To instead build the KDE port, use the following command. Installing the port will provide a menu for selecting which components to install. KDE is a large application and will take some time to compile, even on a fast computer.

```
# cd /usr/ports/x11/kde4
# make install clean
```

KDE requires /proc to be mounted. Add this line to /etc/fstab to mount this file system automatically during system startup:

```
proc            /proc          procfs  rw  0   0
```

KDE uses D-Bus and HAL for a message bus and hardware abstraction. These applications are automatically installed as dependencies of KDE. Enable them in /etc/rc.conf so they will be started when the system boots:

```
dbus_enable="YES"
hald_enable="YES"
```

The installation of KDE includes the KDE Display Manager, KDM. To enable this display manager, add this line to /etc/rc.conf :

```
kdm4_enable="YES"
```

A second method for launching KDE is to type startx from the command line. For this to work, the following line is needed in ~/.xinitrc:

```
exec /usr/local/bin/startkde
```

A third method for starting KDE is through XDM. To do so, create an executable ~/.xsession as follows:

```
% echo "#!/bin/sh" > ~/.xsession
% echo "exec /usr/local/bin/startkde" >> ~/.xsession
% chmod +x ~/.xsession
```

Once KDE is started, refer to its built-in help system for more information on how to use its various menus and applications.

5.7.3. Xfce

Xfce is a desktop environment based on the GTK+ toolkit used by GNOME. However, it is more lightweight and provides a simple, efficient, easy-to-use desktop. It is fully configurable, has a main panel with menus, applets, and application launchers, provides a file manager and sound manager, and is themeable. Since it is fast, light, and efficient, it is ideal for older or slower machines with memory limitations. More information on Xfce can be found at http://www.xfce.org.

To install the Xfce package:

```
# pkg install xfce
```

Alternatively, to build the port:

```
# cd /usr/ports/x11-wm/xfce4
# make install clean
```

Unlike GNOME or KDE, Xfce does not provide its own login manager. In order to start Xfce from the command line by typing startx, first add its entry to ~/.xinitrc:

```
% echo "exec /usr/local/bin/startxfce4 --with-ck-launch" > ~/.xinitrc
```

An alternate method is to use XDM. To configure this method, create an executable ~/.xsession:

```
% echo "#!/bin/sh" > ~/.xsession
% echo "exec /usr/local/bin/startxfce4 --with-ck-launch" >> ~/.xsession
% chmod +x ~/.xsession
```

5.8. Installing Compiz Fusion

One way to make using a desktop computer more pleasant is with nice 3D effects.

Installing the Compiz Fusion package is easy, but configuring it requires a few steps that are not described in the port's documentation.

5.8.1. Setting up the FreeBSD nVidia Driver

Desktop effects can cause quite a load on the graphics card. For an nVidia-based graphics card, the proprietary driver is required for good performance. Users of other graphics cards can skip this section and continue with the xorg.conf configuration.

To determine which nVidia driver is needed see the FAQ question on the subject.

Having determined the correct driver to use for your card, installation is as simple as installing any other package.

For example, to install the latest driver:

```
# pkg install x11/nvidia-driver
```

The driver will create a kernel module, which needs to be loaded at system startup. Add the following line to /boot/loader.conf :

```
nvidia_load="YES"
```

> **Note**
>
> To immediately load the kernel module into the running kernel by issuing a command like kldload nvidia, however it has been noted that the some versions of Xorg will not function

> properly if the driver is not loaded at boot time. After editing /boot/loader.conf , a reboot
> is recommended.

With the kernel module loaded, you normally only need to change a single line in xorg.conf to enable the proprietary driver:

Find the following line in /etc/X11/xorg.conf :

```
Driver        "nv"
```

and change it to:

```
Driver        "nvidia"
```

Start the GUI as usual, and you should be greeted by the nVidia splash. Everything should work as usual.

5.8.2. Configuring xorg.conf for Desktop Effects

To enable Compiz Fusion, /etc/X11/xorg.conf   needs to be modified:

Add the following section to enable composite effects:

```
Section "Extensions"
    Option          "Composite" "Enable"
EndSection
```

Locate the "Screen" section which should look similar to the one below:

```
Section "Screen"
    Identifier      "Screen0"
    Device          "Card0"
    Monitor         "Monitor0"
    ...
```

and add the following two lines (after "Monitor" will do):

```
DefaultDepth    24
Option          "AddARGBGLXVisuals" "True"
```

Locate the "Subsection" that refers to the screen resolution that you wish to use. For example, if you wish to use 1280x1024, locate the section that follows. If the desired resolution does not appear in any subsection, you may add the relevant entry by hand:

```
SubSection      "Display"
    Viewport    0 0
    Modes       "1280x1024"
EndSubSection
```

A color depth of 24 bits is needed for desktop composition, change the above subsection to:

```
SubSection      "Display"
    Viewport    0 0
    Depth       24
    Modes       "1280x1024"
EndSubSection
```

Finally, confirm that the "glx" and "extmod" modules are loaded in the "Module" section:

```
Section "Module"
    Load            "extmod"
    Load            "glx"
    ...
```

The preceding can be done automatically with x11/nvidia-xconfig by running (as root):

```
# nvidia-xconfig --add-argb-glx-visuals
# nvidia-xconfig --composite
# nvidia-xconfig --depth=24
```

5.8.3. Installing and Configuring Compiz Fusion

Installing Compiz Fusion is as simple as any other package:

```
# pkg install x11-wm/compiz-fusion
```

When the installation is finished, start your graphic desktop and at a terminal, enter the following commands (as a normal user):

```
% compiz --replace --sm-disable --ignore-desktop-hints ccp &
% emerald --replace &
```

Your screen will flicker for a few seconds, as your window manager (e.g. Metacity if you are using GNOME) is replaced by Compiz Fusion. Emerald takes care of the window decorations (i.e. close, minimize, maximize buttons, title bars and so on).

You may convert this to a trivial script and have it run at startup automatically (e.g. by adding to "Sessions" in a GNOME desktop):

```
#! /bin/sh
compiz --replace --sm-disable --ignore-desktop-hints ccp &
emerald --replace &
```

Save this in your home directory as, for example, `start-compiz` and make it executable:

```
% chmod +x ~/start-compiz
```

Then use the GUI to add it to Startup Programs (located in System, Preferences, Sessions on a GNOME desktop).

To actually select all the desired effects and their settings, execute (again as a normal user) the Compiz Config Settings Manager:

```
% ccsm
```

Note

In GNOME, this can also be found in the System, Preferences menu.

If you have selected "gconf support" during the build, you will also be able to view these settings using `gconf-editor` under `apps/compiz`.

5.9. Troubleshooting

If the mouse does not work, you will need to first configure it before proceeding. In recent Xorg versions, the `InputDevice` sections in `xorg.conf` are ignored in favor of the autodetected devices. To restore the old behavior, add the following line to the `ServerLayout` or `ServerFlags` section of this file:

```
Option "AutoAddDevices" "false"
```

Input devices may then be configured as in previous versions, along with any other options needed (e.g., keyboard layout switching).

Note

As previously explained the hald daemon will, by default, automatically detect your keyboard. There are chances that your keyboard layout or model will not be correct, desktop environments like GNOME, KDE or Xfce provide tools to configure the keyboard. However, it is possible to set the keyboard properties directly either with the help of the setxkbmap(1) utility or with a hald's configuration rule.

For example if, one wants to use a PC 102 keys keyboard coming with a french layout, we have to create a keyboard configuration file for hald called x11-input.fdi and saved in the /usr/local/etc/hal/fdi/policy directory. This file should contain the following lines:

```xml
<?xml version="1.0" encoding="iso-8859-1"?>
<deviceinfo version="0.2">
  <device>
    <match key="info.capabilities" contains="input.keyboard">
    <merge key="input.x11_options.XkbModel" type="string">pc102</merge>
    <merge key="input.x11_options.XkbLayout" type="string">fr</merge>
    </match>
  </device>
</deviceinfo>
```

If this file already exists, just copy and add to your file the lines regarding the keyboard configuration.

You will have to reboot your machine to force hald to read this file.

It is possible to do the same configuration from an X terminal or a script with this command line:

```
% setxkbmap -model pc102 -layout fr
```

/usr/local/share/X11/xkb/rules/base.lst lists the various keyboard, layouts and options available.

The xorg.conf.new configuration file may now be tuned to taste. Open the file in a text editor such as emacs(1) or ee(1). If the monitor is an older or unusual model that does not support autodetection of sync frequencies, those settings can be added to xorg.conf.new under the "Monitor" section:

```
Section "Monitor"
  Identifier   "Monitor0"
  VendorName   "Monitor Vendor"
  ModelName    "Monitor Model"
  HorizSync    30-107
  VertRefresh  48-120
EndSection
```

Most monitors support sync frequency autodetection, making manual entry of these values unnecessary. For the few monitors that do not support autodetection, avoid potential damage by only entering values provided by the manufacturer.

X allows DPMS (Energy Star) features to be used with capable monitors. The xset(1) program controls the timeouts and can force standby, suspend, or off modes. If you wish to enable DPMS features for your monitor, you must add the following line to the monitor section:

```
Option       "DPMS"
```

While the xorg.conf.new configuration file is still open in an editor, select the default resolution and color depth desired. This is defined in the "Screen" section:

```
Section "Screen"
 Identifier "Screen0"
 Device     "Card0"
 Monitor    "Monitor0"
 DefaultDepth 24
 SubSection "Display"
  Viewport  0 0
  Depth     24
  Modes     "1024x768"
 EndSubSection
EndSection
```

The DefaultDepth keyword describes the color depth to run at by default. This can be overridden with the -depth command line switch to Xorg(1). The Modes keyword describes the resolution to run at for the given color depth. Note that only VESA standard modes are supported as defined by the target system's graphics hardware. In the example above, the default color depth is twenty-four bits per pixel. At this color depth, the accepted resolution is 1024 by 768 pixels.

Finally, write the configuration file and test it using the test mode given above.

Note

One of the tools available to assist you during troubleshooting process are the Xorg log files, which contain information on each device that the Xorg server attaches to. Xorg log file names are in the format of /var/log/Xorg.0.log . The exact name of the log can vary from Xorg.0.log to Xorg.8.log and so forth.

If all is well, the configuration file needs to be installed in a common location where Xorg(1) can find it. This is typically /etc/X11/xorg.conf or /usr/local/etc/X11/xorg.conf .

```
# cp xorg.conf.new /etc/X11/xorg.conf
```

The Xorg configuration process is now complete. Xorg may be now started with the startx(1) utility. The Xorg server may also be started with the use of xdm(1).

5.9.1. Configuration with Intel® i810 Graphics Chipsets

Configuration with Intel® i810 integrated chipsets requires the agpgart AGP programming interface for Xorg to drive the card. See the agp(4) driver manual page for more information.

This will allow configuration of the hardware as any other graphics board. Note on systems without the agp(4) driver compiled in the kernel, trying to load the module with kldload(8) will not work. This driver has to be in the kernel at boot time through being compiled in or using /boot/loader.conf .

5.9.2. Adding a Widescreen Flatpanel to the Mix

This section assumes a bit of advanced configuration knowledge. If attempts to use the standard configuration tools above have not resulted in a working configuration, there is information enough in the log files to be of use in getting the setup working. Use of a text editor will be necessary.

Current widescreen (WSXGA, WSXGA+, WUXGA, WXGA, WXGA+, et.al.) formats support 16:10 and 10:9 formats or aspect ratios that can be problematic. Examples of some common screen resolutions for 16:10 aspect ratios are:

• 2560x1600

- 1920x1200

- 1680x1050

- 1440x900

- 1280x800

At some point, it will be as easy as adding one of these resolutions as a possible `Mode` in the `Section "Screen"` as such:

```
Section "Screen"
Identifier "Screen0"
Device     "Card0"
Monitor    "Monitor0"
DefaultDepth 24
SubSection "Display"
 Viewport  0 0
 Depth     24
 Modes     "1680x1050"
EndSubSection
EndSection
```

Xorg is smart enough to pull the resolution information from the widescreen via I2C/DDC information so it knows what the monitor can handle as far as frequencies and resolutions.

If those `ModeLines` do not exist in the drivers, one might need to give Xorg a little hint. Using `/var/log/Xorg.0.log` one can extract enough information to manually create a `ModeLine` that will work. Simply look for information resembling this:

```
(II) MGA(0): Supported additional Video Mode:
(II) MGA(0): clock: 146.2 MHz   Image Size:  433 x 271 mm
(II) MGA(0): h_active: 1680  h_sync: 1784  h_sync_end 1960 h_blank_end 2240 h_border: 0
(II) MGA(0): v_active: 1050  v_sync: 1053  v_sync_end 1059 v_blanking: 1089 v_border: 0
(II) MGA(0): Ranges: V min: 48  V max: 85 Hz, H min: 30  H max: 94 kHz, PixClock max ↺
170 MHz
```

This information is called EDID information. Creating a `ModeLine` from this is just a matter of putting the numbers in the correct order:

```
ModeLine <name> <clock> <4 horiz. timings> <4 vert. timings>
```

So that the `ModeLine` in `Section "Monitor"` for this example would look like this:

```
Section "Monitor"
Identifier      "Monitor1"
VendorName      "Bigname"
ModelName       "BestModel"
ModeLine        "1680x1050" 146.2 1680 1784 1960 2240 1050 1053 1059 1089
Option          "DPMS"
EndSection
```

Now having completed these simple editing steps, X should start on your new widescreen monitor.

5.9.3. Troubleshooting Compiz Fusion

Q: I have installed Compiz Fusion, and after running the commands you mention, my windows are left without title bars and buttons. What is wrong?

A: You are probably missing a setting in `/etc/X11/xorg.conf` . Review this file carefully and check especially the `DefaultDepth` and `AddARGBGLXVisuals` directives.

Q: When I run the command to start Compiz Fusion, the X server crashes and I am back at the console. What is wrong?

A: If you check `/var/log/Xorg.0.log` , you will probably find error messages during the X startup. The most
common would be:

```
(EE) NVIDIA(0):       Failed to initialize the GLX module; please check in your X
(EE) NVIDIA(0):       log file that the GLX module has been loaded in your X
(EE) NVIDIA(0):       server, and that the module is the NVIDIA GLX module.  If
(EE) NVIDIA(0):       you continue to encounter problems, Please try
(EE) NVIDIA(0):       reinstalling the NVIDIA driver.
```

This is usually the case when you upgrade Xorg. You will need to reinstall the x11/nvidia-driver package
so glx is built again.

Part II. Common Tasks

Now that the basics have been covered, this part of the book discusses some frequently used features of FreeBSD. These chapters:

- Introduce popular and useful desktop applications: browsers, productivity tools, document viewers, and more.

- Introduce a number of multimedia tools available for FreeBSD.

- Explain the process of building a customized FreeBSD kernel to enable extra functionality.

- Describe the print system in detail, both for desktop and network-connected printer setups.

- Show how to run Linux applications on the FreeBSD system.

Some of these chapters recommend prior reading, and this is noted in the synopsis at the beginning of each chapter.

Table of Contents

Chapter 6. Desktop Applications

6.1. Synopsis

While FreeBSD is popular as a server for its performance and stability, it is also suited for day-to-day use as a desktop. With over 24,000 applications available as FreeBSD packages or ports, it is easy to build a customized desktop that runs a wide variety of desktop applications. This chapter demonstrates how to install numerous desktop applications, including web browsers, productivity software, document viewers, and financial software.

> **Note**
>
> Users who prefer to install a pre-built desktop version of FreeBSD rather than configuring one from scratch should refer to the trueos.org website.

Readers of this chapter should know how to:

- Install additional software using packages or ports as described in Chapter 4, *Installing Applications: Packages and Ports*.

- Install X and a window manager as described in Chapter 5, *The X Window System*.

For information on how to configure a multimedia environment, refer to Chapter 7, *Multimedia*.

6.2. Browsers

FreeBSD does not come with a pre-installed web browser. Instead, the www category of the Ports Collection contains many browsers which can be installed as a package or compiled from the Ports Collection.

The KDE and GNOME desktop environments include their own HTML browser. Refer to Section 5.7, "Desktop Environments" for more information on how to set up these complete desktops.

Some lightweight browsers include www/dillo2, www/links, and www/w3m.

This section demonstrates how to install the following popular web browsers and indicates if the application is resource-heavy, takes time to compile from ports, or has any major dependencies.

Application Name	Resources Needed	Installation from Ports	Notes
Firefox	medium	heavy	FreeBSD, Linux®, and localized versions are available
Opera	light	light	FreeBSD and Linux® versions are available
Konqueror	medium	heavy	Requires KDE libraries
Chromium	medium	heavy	Requires Gtk+

6.2.1. Firefox

Firefox is an open source browser that is fully ported to FreeBSD. It features a standards-compliant HTML display engine, tabbed browsing, popup blocking, extensions, improved security, and more. Firefox is based on the Mozilla codebase.

To install the package of the latest release version of Firefox, type:

```
# pkg install firefox
```

To instead install Firefox Extended Support Release (ESR) version, use:

```
# pkg install firefox-esr
```

Localized versions are available in www/firefox-i18n and www/firefox-esr-i18n.

The Ports Collection can instead be used to compile the desired version of Firefox from source code. This example builds www/firefox, where firefox can be replaced with the ESR or localized version to install.

```
# cd /usr/ports/www/firefox
# make install clean
```

6.2.2. Opera

Opera is a full-featured and standards-compliant browser which is still lightweight and fast. It comes with a built-in mail and news reader, an IRC client, an RSS/Atom feeds reader, and more. It is available as a native FreeBSD version and as a version that runs under Linux® emulation.

This command installs the package of the FreeBSD version of Opera. Replace opera with linux-opera to instead install the Linux® version.

```
# pkg install opera
```

Alternately, install either version through the Ports Collection. This example compiles the native version:

```
# cd /usr/ports/www/opera
# make install clean
```

To install the Linux® version, substitute linux-opera in place of opera.

To install Adobe® Flash® plugin support, first compile the www/linux-flashplayer port. Licensing restrictions prevent making a package available. Then install www/opera-linuxplugins. This example compiles both applications from ports:

```
# cd /usr/ports/www/linux-flashplayer
# make install clean
# cd /usr/ports/www/opera-linuxplugins
# make install clean
```

Once installed, check the presence of the plugin by starting the browser, entering opera:plugins in the location bar and pressing Enter. A list should appear with all the currently available plugins.

To add the Java™ plugin, follow install java/icedtea-web.

6.2.3. Konqueror

Konqueror is more than a web browser as it is also a file manager and a multimedia viewer. It is included in the x11/kde4-baseapps package or port.

Konqueror supports WebKit as well as its own KHTML. WebKit is a rendering engine used by many modern browsers including Chromium. To use WebKit with Konqueror on FreeBSD, install the www/kwebkitpart package or port. This example installs the package:

```
# pkg install kwebkitpart
```

To install from the Ports Collection:

```
# cd /usr/ports/www/kwebkitpart
# make install clean
```

To enable WebKit within Konqueror, click "Settings", "Configure Konqueror". In the "General" settings page, click the drop-down menu next to "Default web browser engine" and change "KHTML" to "WebKit".

Konqueror also supports Flash®. A "How To" guide for getting Flash® support on Konqueror is available at http://freebsd.kde.org/howtos/konqueror-flash.php .

6.2.4. Chromium

Chromium is an open source browser project that aims to build a safer, faster, and more stable web browsing experience. Chromium features tabbed browsing, popup blocking, extensions, and much more. Chromium is the open source project upon which the Google Chrome web browser is based.

Chromium can be installed as a package by typing:

```
# pkg install chromium
```

Alternatively, Chromium can be compiled from source using the Ports Collection:

```
# cd /usr/ports/www/chromium
# make install clean
```

Note

The executable for Chromium is /usr/local/bin/chrome , not /usr/local/bin/chromium .

6.3. Productivity

When it comes to productivity, users often look for an office suite or an easy-to-use word processor. While some desktop environments like KDE provide an office suite, there is no default productivity package. Several office suites and graphical word processors are available for FreeBSD, regardless of the installed window manager.

This section demonstrates how to install the following popular productivity software and indicates if the application is resource-heavy, takes time to compile from ports, or has any major dependencies.

Application Name	Resources Needed	Installation from Ports	Major Dependencies
Calligra	light	heavy	KDE
AbiWord	light	light	Gtk+ or GNOME
The Gimp	light	heavy	Gtk+
Apache OpenOffice	heavy	huge	JDK™ and Mozilla
LibreOffice	somewhat heavy	huge	Gtk+, or KDE/ GNOME, or JDK™

6.3.1. Calligra

The KDE desktop environment includes an office suite which can be installed separately from KDE. Calligra includes standard components that can be found in other office suites. Words is the word processor, Sheets is the spreadsheet program, Stage manages slide presentations, and Karbon is used to draw graphical documents.

In FreeBSD, editors/calligra can be installed as a package or a port. To install the package:

```
# pkg install calligra
```

If the package is not available, use the Ports Collection instead:

```
# cd /usr/ports/editors/calligra
# make install clean
```

6.3.2. AbiWord

AbiWord is a free word processing program similar in look and feel to Microsoft® Word. It is fast, contains many features, and is user-friendly.

AbiWord can import or export many file formats, including some proprietary ones like Microsoft® .rtf.

To install the AbiWord package:

```
# pkg install abiword
```

If the package is not available, it can be compiled from the Ports Collection:

```
# cd /usr/ports/editors/abiword
# make install clean
```

6.3.3. The GIMP

For image authoring or picture retouching, The GIMP provides a sophisticated image manipulation program. It can be used as a simple paint program or as a quality photo retouching suite. It supports a large number of plugins and features a scripting interface. The GIMP can read and write a wide range of file formats and supports interfaces with scanners and tablets.

To install the package:

```
# pkg install gimp
```

Alternately, use the Ports Collection:

```
# cd /usr/ports/graphics/gimp
# make install clean
```

The graphics category (freebsd.org/ports/graphics.html) of the Ports Collection contains several GIMP-related plugins, help files, and user manuals.

6.3.4. Apache OpenOffice

Apache OpenOffice is an open source office suite which is developed under the wing of the Apache Software Foundation's Incubator. It includes all of the applications found in a complete office productivity suite: a word processor, spreadsheet, presentation manager, and drawing program. Its user interface is similar to other office suites, and it can import and export in various popular file formats. It is available in a number of different languages and internationalization has been extended to interfaces, spell checkers, and dictionaries.

The word processor of Apache OpenOffice uses a native XML file format for increased portability and flexibility. The spreadsheet program features a macro language which can be interfaced with external databases. Apache OpenOffice is stable and runs natively on Windows®, Solaris™, Linux®, FreeBSD, and Mac OS® X. More information about Apache OpenOffice can be found at openoffice.org. For FreeBSD specific information refer to porting.openoffice.org/freebsd/.

To install the Apache OpenOffice package:

```
# pkg install apache-openoffice
```

Once the package is installed, type the following command to launch Apache OpenOffice:

```
% openoffice- X.Y.Z
```

where *X.Y.Z* is the version number of the installed version of Apache OpenOffice. The first time Apache OpenOffice launches, some questions will be asked and a .openoffice.org folder will be created in the user's home directory.

If the desired Apache OpenOffice package is not available, compiling the port is still an option. However, this requires a lot of disk space and a fairly long time to compile:

```
# cd /usr/ports/editors/openoffice-4
# make install clean
```

 Note

To build a localized version, replace the previous command with:

```
# make LOCALIZED_LANG= your_language  install clean
```

Replace *your_language* with the correct language ISO-code. A list of supported language codes is available in files/Makefile.localized, located in the port's directory.

6.3.5. LibreOffice

LibreOffice is a free software office suite developed by documentfoundation.org. It is compatible with other major office suites and available on a variety of platforms. It is a rebranded fork of Apache OpenOffice and includes applications found in a complete office productivity suite: a word processor, spreadsheet, presentation manager, drawing program, database management program, and a tool for creating and editing mathematical formulæ. It is available in a number of different languages and internationalization has been extended to interfaces, spell checkers, and dictionaries.

The word processor of LibreOffice uses a native XML file format for increased portability and flexibility. The spreadsheet program features a macro language which can be interfaced with external databases. LibreOffice is stable and runs natively on Windows®, Linux®, FreeBSD, and Mac OS® X. More information about LibreOffice can be found at libreoffice.org.

To install the English version of the LibreOffice package:

```
# pkg install libreoffice
```

The editors category (freebsd.org/ports/editors.html) of the Ports Collection contains several localizations for LibreOffice. When installing a localized package, replace libreoffice with the name of the localized package.

Once the package is installed, type the following command to run LibreOffice:

```
% libreoffice
```

During the first launch, some questions will be asked and a .libreoffice folder will be created in the user's home directory.

If the desired LibreOffice package is not available, compiling the port is still an option. However, this requires a lot of disk space and a fairly long time to compile. This example compiles the English version:

```
# cd /usr/ports/editors/libreoffice
# make install clean
```

Note

To build a localized version, cd into the port directory of the desired language. Supported languages can be found in the editors category (freebsd.org/ports/editors.html) of the Ports Collection.

6.4. Document Viewers

Some new document formats have gained popularity since the advent of UNIX® and the viewers they require may not be available in the base system. This section demonstrates how to install the following document viewers:

Application Name	Resources Needed	Installation from Ports	Major Dependencies
Xpdf	light	light	FreeType
gv	light	light	Xaw3d
Geeqie	light	light	Gtk+ or GNOME
ePDFView	light	light	Gtk+
Okular	light	heavy	KDE

6.4.1. Xpdf

For users that prefer a small FreeBSD PDF viewer, Xpdf provides a light-weight and efficient viewer which requires few resources. It uses the standard X fonts and does not require any additional toolkits.

To install the Xpdf package:

```
# pkg install xpdf
```

If the package is not available, use the Ports Collection:

```
# cd /usr/ports/graphics/xpdf
# make install clean
```

Once the installation is complete, launch xpdf and use the right mouse button to activate the menu.

6.4.2. gv

gv is a PostScript® and PDF viewer. It is based on ghostview, but has a nicer look as it is based on the Xaw3d widget toolkit. gv has many configurable features, such as orientation, paper size, scale, and anti-aliasing. Almost any operation can be performed with either the keyboard or the mouse.

To install gv as a package:

```
# pkg install gv
```

If a package is unavailable, use the Ports Collection:

```
# cd /usr/ports/print/gv
# make install clean
```

6.4.3. Geeqie

Geeqie is a fork from the unmaintained GQView project, in an effort to move development forward and integrate the existing patches. Geeqie is an image manager which supports viewing a file with a single click, launching an external editor, and thumbnail previews. It also features a slideshow mode and some basic file operations, making it easy to manage image collections and to find duplicate files. Geeqie supports full screen viewing and internationalization.

To install the Geeqie package:

```
# pkg install geeqie
```

If the package is not available, use the Ports Collection:

```
# cd /usr/ports/graphics/geeqie
# make install clean
```

6.4.4. ePDFView

ePDFView is a lightweight PDF document viewer that only uses the Gtk+ and Poppler libraries. It is currently under development, but already opens most PDF files (even encrypted), save copies of documents, and has support for printing using CUPS.

To install ePDFView as a package:

```
# pkg install epdfview
```

If a package is unavailable, use the Ports Collection:

```
# cd /usr/ports/graphics/epdfview
# make install clean
```

6.4.5. Okular

Okular is a universal document viewer based on KPDF for KDE. It can open many document formats, including PDF, PostScript®, DjVu, CHM, XPS, and ePub.

To install Okular as a package:

```
# pkg install okular
```

If a package is unavailable, use the Ports Collection:

```
# cd /usr/ports/graphics/okular
# make install clean
```

6.5. Finance

For managing personal finances on a FreeBSD desktop, some powerful and easy-to-use applications can be installed. Some are compatible with widespread file formats, such as the formats used by Quicken and Excel.

This section covers these programs:

Application Name	Resources Needed	Installation from Ports	Major Dependencies
GnuCash	light	heavy	GNOME
Gnumeric	light	heavy	GNOME
KMyMoney	light	heavy	KDE

6.5.1. GnuCash

GnuCash is part of the GNOME effort to provide user-friendly, yet powerful, applications to end-users. GnuCash can be used to keep track of income and expenses, bank accounts, and stocks. It features an intuitive interface while remaining professional.

GnuCash provides a smart register, a hierarchical system of accounts, and many keyboard accelerators and auto-completion methods. It can split a single transaction into several more detailed pieces. GnuCash can import and merge Quicken QIF files. It also handles most international date and currency formats.

To install the GnuCash package:

```
# pkg install gnucash
```

If the package is not available, use the Ports Collection:

```
# cd /usr/ports/finance/gnucash
# make install clean
```

6.5.2. Gnumeric

Gnumeric is a spreadsheet program developed by the GNOME community. It features convenient automatic guessing of user input according to the cell format with an autofill system for many sequences. It can import files in a number of popular formats, including Excel, Lotus 1-2-3, and Quattro Pro. It has a large number of built-in functions and allows all of the usual cell formats such as number, currency, date, time, and much more.

To install Gnumeric as a package:

```
# pkg install gnumeric
```

If the package is not available, use the Ports Collection:

```
# cd /usr/ports/math/gnumeric
# make install clean
```

6.5.3. KMyMoney

KMyMoney is a personal finance application created by the KDE community. KMyMoney aims to provide the important features found in commercial personal finance manager applications. It also highlights ease-of-use and proper double-entry accounting among its features. KMyMoney imports from standard Quicken QIF files, tracks investments, handles multiple currencies, and provides a wealth of reports.

To install KMyMoney as a package:

```
# pkg install kmymoney-kde4
```

If the package is not available, use the Ports Collection:

```
# cd /usr/ports/finance/kmymoney-kde4
# make install clean
```

Chapter 7. Multimedia

Edited by Ross Lippert.

7.1. Synopsis

FreeBSD supports a wide variety of sound cards, allowing users to enjoy high fidelity output from a FreeBSD system. This includes the ability to record and play back audio in the MPEG Audio Layer 3 (MP3), Waveform Audio File (WAV), Ogg Vorbis, and other formats. The FreeBSD Ports Collection contains many applications for editing recorded audio, adding sound effects, and controlling attached MIDI devices.

FreeBSD also supports the playback of video files and DVDs. The FreeBSD Ports Collection contains applications to encode, convert, and playback various video media.

This chapter describes how to configure sound cards, video playback, TV tuner cards, and scanners on FreeBSD. It also describes some of the applications which are available for using these devices.

After reading this chapter, you will know how to:

- Configure a sound card on FreeBSD.

- Troubleshoot the sound setup.

- Playback and encode MP3s and other audio.

- Prepare a FreeBSD system for video playback.

- Play DVDs, .mpg, and .avi files.

- Rip CD and DVD content into files.

- Configure a TV card.

- Install and setup MythTV on FreeBSD

- Configure an image scanner.

Before reading this chapter, you should:

- Know how to install applications as described in Chapter 4, *Installing Applications: Packages and Ports*.

7.2. Setting Up the Sound Card

Contributed by Moses Moore.
Enhanced by Marc Fonvieille.

Before beginning the configuration, determine the model of the sound card and the chip it uses. FreeBSD supports a wide variety of sound cards. Check the supported audio devices list of the Hardware Notes to see if the card is supported and which FreeBSD driver it uses.

In order to use the sound device, its device driver must be loaded. The easiest way is to load a kernel module for the sound card with kldload(8). This example loads the driver for a built-in audio chipset based on the Intel specification:

```
# kldload snd_hda
```

To automate the loading of this driver at boot time, add the driver to /boot/loader.conf . The line for this driver is:

```
snd_hda_load="YES"
```

Other available sound modules are listed in /boot/defaults/loader.conf . When unsure which driver to use, load the snd_driver module:

```
# kldload snd_driver
```

This is a metadriver which loads all of the most common sound drivers and can be used to speed up the search for the correct driver. It is also possible to load all sound drivers by adding the metadriver to /boot/loader.conf .

To determine which driver was selected for the sound card after loading the snd_driver metadriver, type cat / dev/sndstat .

7.2.1. Configuring a Custom Kernel with Sound Support

This section is for users who prefer to statically compile in support for the sound card in a custom kernel. For more information about recompiling a kernel, refer to Chapter 8, *Configuring the FreeBSD Kernel*.

When using a custom kernel to provide sound support, make sure that the audio framework driver exists in the custom kernel configuration file:

```
device sound
```

Next, add support for the sound card. To continue the example of the built-in audio chipset based on the Intel specification from the previous section, use the following line in the custom kernel configuration file:

```
device snd_hda
```

Be sure to read the manual page of the driver for the device name to use for the driver.

Non-PnP ISA sound cards may require the IRQ and I/O port settings of the card to be added to /boot/device.hints . During the boot process, loader(8) reads this file and passes the settings to the kernel. For example, an old Creative SoundBlaster® 16 ISA non-PnP card will use the snd_sbc(4) driver in conjunction with snd_sb16. For this card, the following lines must be added to the kernel configuration file:

```
device snd_sbc
device snd_sb16
```

If the card uses the 0x220 I/O port and IRQ 5, these lines must also be added to /boot/device.hints :

```
hint.sbc.0.at="isa"
hint.sbc.0.port="0x220"
hint.sbc.0.irq="5"
hint.sbc.0.drq="1"
hint.sbc.0.flags="0x15"
```

The syntax used in /boot/device.hints is described in sound(4) and the manual page for the driver of the sound card.

The settings shown above are the defaults. In some cases, the IRQ or other settings may need to be changed to match the card. Refer to snd_sbc(4) for more information about this card.

7.2.2. Testing Sound

After loading the required module or rebooting into the custom kernel, the sound card should be detected. To confirm, run dmesg | grep pcm . This example is from a system with a built-in Conexant CX20590 chipset:

```
pcm0: <NVIDIA (0x001c) (HDMI/DP 8ch)> at nid 5 on hdaa0
pcm1: <NVIDIA (0x001c) (HDMI/DP 8ch)> at nid 6 on hdaa0
pcm2: <Conexant CX20590 (Analog 2.0+HP/2.0)> at nid 31,25 and 35,27 on hdaa1
```

The status of the sound card may also be checked using this command:

```
# cat /dev/sndstat
FreeBSD Audio Driver (newpcm: 64bit 2009061500/amd64)
Installed devices:
pcm0: <NVIDIA (0x001c) (HDMI/DP 8ch)> (play)
pcm1: <NVIDIA (0x001c) (HDMI/DP 8ch)> (play)
pcm2: <Conexant CX20590 (Analog 2.0+HP/2.0)> (play/rec) default
```

The output will vary depending upon the sound card. If no pcm devices are listed, double-check that the correct device driver was loaded or compiled into the kernel. The next section lists some common problems and their solutions.

If all goes well, the sound card should now work in FreeBSD. If the CD or DVD drive is properly connected to the sound card, one can insert an audio CD in the drive and play it with cdcontrol(1):

```
% cdcontrol -f /dev/acd0 play 1
```

Warning

Audio CDs have specialized encodings which means that they should not be mounted using mount(8).

Various applications, such as audio/workman, provide a friendlier interface. The audio/mpg123 port can be installed to listen to MP3 audio files.

Another quick way to test the card is to send data to /dev/dsp :

```
% cat filename > /dev/dsp
```

where filename can be any type of file. This command should produce some noise, confirming that the sound card is working.

Note

The /dev/dsp* device nodes will be created automatically as needed. When not in use, they do not exist and will not appear in the output of ls(1).

7.2.3. Troubleshooting Sound

Table 7.1, "Common Error Messages" lists some common error messages and their solutions:

Table 7.1. Common Error Messages

Error	Solution
sb_dspwr(XX) timed out	The I/O port is not set correctly.
bad irq XX	The IRQ is set incorrectly. Make sure that the set IRQ and the sound IRQ are the same.
xxx: gus pcm not attached, out of memory	There is not enough available memory to use the device.
xxx: can't open /dev/dsp!	Type fstat | grep dsp to check if another application is holding the device open. Noteworthy troublemakers are esound and KDE's sound support.

Modern graphics cards often come with their own sound driver for use with HDMI. This sound device is sometimes enumerated before the sound card meaning that the sound card will not be used as the default playback device. To check if this is the case, run dmesg and look for pcm. The output looks something like this:

```
...
hdac0: HDA Driver Revision: 20100226_0142
hdac1: HDA Driver Revision: 20100226_0142
hdac0: HDA Codec #0: NVidia (Unknown)
hdac0: HDA Codec #1: NVidia (Unknown)
hdac0: HDA Codec #2: NVidia (Unknown)
hdac0: HDA Codec #3: NVidia (Unknown)
pcm0: <HDA NVidia (Unknown) PCM #0 DisplayPort> at cad 0 nid 1 on hdac0
pcm1: <HDA NVidia (Unknown) PCM #0 DisplayPort> at cad 1 nid 1 on hdac0
pcm2: <HDA NVidia (Unknown) PCM #0 DisplayPort> at cad 2 nid 1 on hdac0
pcm3: <HDA NVidia (Unknown) PCM #0 DisplayPort> at cad 3 nid 1 on hdac0
hdac1: HDA Codec #2: Realtek ALC889
pcm4: <HDA Realtek ALC889 PCM #0 Analog> at cad 2 nid 1 on hdac1
pcm5: <HDA Realtek ALC889 PCM #1 Analog> at cad 2 nid 1 on hdac1
pcm6: <HDA Realtek ALC889 PCM #2 Digital> at cad 2 nid 1 on hdac1
pcm7: <HDA Realtek ALC889 PCM #3 Digital> at cad 2 nid 1 on hdac1
...
```

In this example, the graphics card (NVidia) has been enumerated before the sound card (Realtek ALC889). To use the sound card as the default playback device, change hw.snd.default_unit to the unit that should be used for playback:

```
# sysctl hw.snd.default_unit= n
```

where n is the number of the sound device to use. In this example, it should be 4. Make this change permanent by adding the following line to /etc/sysctl.conf :

```
hw.snd.default_unit=4
```

7.2.4. Utilizing Multiple Sound Sources

Contributed by Munish Chopra.

It is often desirable to have multiple sources of sound that are able to play simultaneously. FreeBSD uses "Virtual Sound Channels" to multiplex the sound card's playback by mixing sound in the kernel.

Three sysctl(8) knobs are available for configuring virtual channels:

```
# sysctl dev.pcm.0.play.vchans=4
# sysctl dev.pcm.0.rec.vchans=4
# sysctl hw.snd.maxautovchans=4
```

This example allocates four virtual channels, which is a practical number for everyday use. Both de-v.pcm.0.play.vchans=4 and dev.pcm.0.rec.vchans=4 are configurable after a device has been attached and represent the number of virtual channels pcm0 has for playback and recording. Since the pcm module can be loaded independently of the hardware drivers, hw.snd.maxautovchans indicates how many virtual channels will be given to an audio device when it is attached. Refer to pcm(4) for more information.

> **Note**
>
> The number of virtual channels for a device cannot be changed while it is in use. First, close any programs using the device, such as music players or sound daemons.

The correct pcm device will automatically be allocated transparently to a program that requests /dev/dsp0 .

7.2.5. Setting Default Values for Mixer Channels

Contributed by Josef El-Rayes.

The default values for the different mixer channels are hardcoded in the source code of the pcm(4) driver. While sound card mixer levels can be changed using mixer(8) or third-party applications and daemons, this is not a permanent solution. To instead set default mixer values at the driver level, define the appropriate values in /boot/ device.hints, as seen in this example:

```
hint.pcm.0.vol="50"
```

This will set the volume channel to a default value of 50 when the pcm(4) module is loaded.

7.3. MP3 Audio

Contributed by Chern Lee.

This section describes some MP3 players available for FreeBSD, how to rip audio CD tracks, and how to encode and decode MP3s.

7.3.1. MP3 Players

A popular graphical MP3 player is XMMS. It supports Winamp skins and additional plugins. The interface is intuitive, with a playlist, graphic equalizer, and more. Those familiar with Winamp will find XMMS simple to use. On FreeBSD, XMMS can be installed from the multimedia/xmms port or package.

The audio/mpg123 package or port provides an alternative, command-line MP3 player. Once installed, specify the MP3 file to play on the command line. If the system has multiple audio devices, the sound device can also be specified:

```
# mpg123 -a /dev/dsp1.0 Foobar-GreatestHits.mp3
High Performance MPEG 1.0/2.0/2.5 Audio Player for Layers 1, 2 and 3
        version 1.18.1; written and copyright by Michael Hipp and others
        free software (LGPL) without any warranty but with best wishes

Playing MPEG stream from Foobar-GreatestHits.mp3 ...
MPEG 1.0 layer III, 128 kbit/s, 44100 Hz joint-stereo
```

Additional MP3 players are available in the FreeBSD Ports Collection.

7.3.2. Ripping CD Audio Tracks

Before encoding a CD or CD track to MP3, the audio data on the CD must be ripped to the hard drive. This is done by copying the raw CD Digital Audio (CDDA) data to WAV files.

The cdda2wav tool, which is installed with the sysutils/cdrtools suite, can be used to rip audio information from CDs.

With the audio CD in the drive, the following command can be issued as root to rip an entire CD into individual, per track, WAV files:

```
# cdda2wav -D 0,1,0 -B
```

In this example, the -D 0,1,0 indicates the SCSI device 0,1,0 containing the CD to rip. Use cdrecord -scanbus to determine the correct device parameters for the system.

To rip individual tracks, use -t to specify the track:

```
# cdda2wav -D 0,1,0 -t 7
```

To rip a range of tracks, such as track one to seven, specify a range:

```
# cdda2wav -D 0,1,0 -t 1+7
```

To rip from an ATAPI (IDE) CDROM drive, specify the device name in place of the SCSI unit numbers. For example, to rip track 7 from an IDE drive:

```
# cdda2wav -D /dev/acd0 -t 7
```

Alternately, dd can be used to extract audio tracks on ATAPI drives, as described in Section 17.5.5, "Duplicating Audio CDs".

7.3.3. Encoding and Decoding MP3s

Lame is a popular MP3 encoder which can be installed from the audio/lame port. Due to patent issues, a package is not available.

The following command will convert the ripped WAV file *audio01.wav* to *audio01.mp3*:

```
# lame -h -b 128 --tt "Foo Song Title " --ta "FooBar Artist " --tl "FooBar Album " \
--ty "2014" --tc "Ripped and encoded by Foo " --tg "Genre" audio01.wav audio01.mp3
```

The specified 128 kbits is a standard MP3 bitrate while the 160 and 192 bitrates provide higher quality. The higher the bitrate, the larger the size of the resulting MP3. The -h turns on the "higher quality but a little slower" mode. The options beginning with --t indicate ID3 tags, which usually contain song information, to be embedded within the MP3 file. Additional encoding options can be found in the lame manual page.

In order to burn an audio CD from MP3s, they must first be converted to a non-compressed file format. XMMS can be used to convert to the WAV format, while mpg123 can be used to convert to the raw Pulse-Code Modulation (PCM) audio data format.

To convert audio01.mp3 using mpg123, specify the name of the PCM file:

```
# mpg123 -s audio01.mp3 > audio01.pcm
```

To use XMMS to convert a MP3 to WAV format, use these steps:

Procedure 7.1. Converting to WAV Format in XMMS

1.   Launch XMMS.

2.   Right-click the window to bring up the XMMS menu.

3.   Select Preferences under Options.

4.   Change the Output Plugin to "Disk Writer Plugin".

5.   Press Configure.

6.   Enter or browse to a directory to write the uncompressed files to.

7.   Load the MP3 file into XMMS as usual, with volume at 100% and EQ settings turned off.

8.   Press Play. The XMMS will appear as if it is playing the MP3, but no music will be heard. It is actually playing the MP3 to a file.

9.   When finished, be sure to set the default Output Plugin back to what it was before in order to listen to MP3s again.

Both the WAV and PCM formats can be used with cdrecord. When using WAV files, there will be a small tick sound at the beginning of each track. This sound is the header of the WAV file. The audio/sox port or package can be used to remove the header:

```
% sox -t wav -r 44100 -s -w -c 2  track.wav track.raw
```

Refer to Section 17.5, "Creating and Using CD Media" for more information on using a CD burner in FreeBSD.

7.4. Video Playback

Contributed by Ross Lippert.

Before configuring video playback, determine the model and chipset of the video card. While Xorg supports a wide variety of video cards, not all provide good playback performance. To obtain a list of extensions supported by the Xorg server using the card, run xdpyinfo while Xorg is running.

It is a good idea to have a short MPEG test file for evaluating various players and options. Since some DVD applications look for DVD media in /dev/dvd by default, or have this device name hardcoded in them, it might be useful to make a symbolic link to the proper device:

```
# ln -sf /dev/cd0 /dev/dvd
```

Due to the nature of devfs(5), manually created links will not persist after a system reboot. In order to recreate the symbolic link automatically when the system boots, add the following line to /etc/devfs.conf:

```
link cd0 dvd
```

DVD decryption invokes certain functions that require write permission to the DVD device.

To enhance the shared memory Xorg interface, it is recommended to increase the values of these sysctl(8) variables:

```
kern.ipc.shmmax=67108864
kern.ipc.shmall=32768
```

7.4.1. Determining Video Capabilities

There are several possible ways to display video under Xorg and what works is largely hardware dependent. Each method described below will have varying quality across different hardware.

Common video interfaces include:

1. Xorg: normal output using shared memory.

2. XVideo: an extension to the Xorg interface which allows video to be directly displayed in drawable objects through a special acceleration. This extension provides good quality playback even on low-end machines. The next section describes how to determine if this extension is running.

3. SDL: the Simple Directmedia Layer is a porting layer for many operating systems, allowing cross-platform applications to be developed which make efficient use of sound and graphics. SDL provides a low-level abstraction to the hardware which can sometimes be more efficient than the Xorg interface. On FreeBSD, SDL can be installed using the devel/sdl20 package or port.

4. DGA: the Direct Graphics Access is an Xorg extension which allows a program to bypass the Xorg server and directly alter the framebuffer. Because it relies on a low level memory mapping, programs using it must be run as root. The DGA extension can be tested and benchmarked using dga(1). When dga is running, it changes the colors of the display whenever a key is pressed. To quit, press q.

5. SVGAlib: a low level console graphics layer.

7.4.1.1. XVideo

To check whether this extension is running, use `xvinfo`:

```
% xvinfo
```

XVideo is supported for the card if the result is similar to:

```
X-Video Extension version 2.2
  screen #0
  Adaptor #0: "Savage Streams Engine"
    number of ports: 1
    port base: 43
    operations supported: PutImage
    supported visuals:
      depth 16, visualID 0x22
      depth 16, visualID 0x23
    number of attributes: 5
      "XV_COLORKEY" (range 0 to 16777215)
              client settable attribute
              client gettable attribute (current value is 2110)
      "XV_BRIGHTNESS" (range -128 to 127)
              client settable attribute
              client gettable attribute (current value is 0)
      "XV_CONTRAST" (range 0 to 255)
              client settable attribute
              client gettable attribute (current value is 128)
      "XV_SATURATION" (range 0 to 255)
              client settable attribute
              client gettable attribute (current value is 128)
      "XV_HUE" (range -180 to 180)
              client settable attribute
              client gettable attribute (current value is 0)
    maximum XvImage size: 1024 x 1024
    Number of image formats: 7
      id: 0x32595559 (YUY2)
        guid: 59555932-0000-0010-8000-00aa00389b71
        bits per pixel: 16
        number of planes: 1
        type: YUV (packed)
      id: 0x32315659 (YV12)
        guid: 59563132-0000-0010-8000-00aa00389b71
        bits per pixel: 12
        number of planes: 3
        type: YUV (planar)
      id: 0x30323449 (I420)
        guid: 49343230-0000-0010-8000-00aa00389b71
        bits per pixel: 12
        number of planes: 3
        type: YUV (planar)
      id: 0x36315652 (RV16)
        guid: 52563135-0000-0000-0000-000000000000
        bits per pixel: 16
        number of planes: 1
        type: RGB (packed)
        depth: 0
        red, green, blue masks: 0x1f, 0x3e0, 0x7c00
      id: 0x35315652 (RV15)
        guid: 52563136-0000-0000-0000-000000000000
        bits per pixel: 16
        number of planes: 1
        type: RGB (packed)
        depth: 0
        red, green, blue masks: 0x1f, 0x7e0, 0xf800
      id: 0x31313259 (Y211)
        guid: 59323131-0000-0010-8000-00aa00389b71
```

```
        bits per pixel: 6
        number of planes: 3
        type: YUV (packed)
   id: 0x0
        guid: 00000000-0000-0000-0000-000000000000 ˜
        bits per pixel: 0
        number of planes: 0
        type: RGB (packed)
        depth: 1
        red, green, blue masks: 0x0, 0x0, 0x0
```

The formats listed, such as YUV2 and YUV12, are not present with every implementation of XVideo and their absence may hinder some players.

If the result instead looks like:

```
X-Video Extension version 2.2
screen #0
no adaptors present
```

XVideo is probably not supported for the card. This means that it will be more difficult for the display to meet the computational demands of rendering video, depending on the video card and processor.

7.4.2. Ports and Packages Dealing with Video

This section introduces some of the software available from the FreeBSD Ports Collection which can be used for video playback.

7.4.2.1. MPlayer and MEncoder

MPlayer is a command-line video player with an optional graphical interface which aims to provide speed and flexibility. Other graphical front-ends to MPlayer are available from the FreeBSD Ports Collection.

MPlayer can be installed using the multimedia/mplayer package or port. Several compile options are available and a variety of hardware checks occur during the build process. For these reasons, some users prefer to build the port rather than install the package.

When compiling the port, the menu options should be reviewed to determine the type of support to compile into the port. If an option is not selected, MPlayer will not be able to display that type of video format. Use the arrow keys and spacebar to select the required formats. When finished, press Enter to continue the port compile and installation.

By default, the package or port will build the mplayer command line utility and the gmplayer graphical utility. To encode videos, compile the multimedia/mencoder port. Due to licensing restrictions, a package is not available for MEncoder.

The first time MPlayer is run, it will create ~/.mplayer in the user's home directory. This subdirectory contains default versions of the user-specific configuration files.

This section describes only a few common uses. Refer to mplayer(1) for a complete description of its numerous options.

To play the file *testfile.avi*, specify the video interfaces with -vo, as seen in the following examples:

```
% mplayer -vo xv testfile.avi
```

```
% mplayer -vo sdl testfile.avi
```

```
% mplayer -vo x11 testfile.avi
```

```
# mplayer -vo dga testfile.avi
```

```
# mplayer -vo 'sdl:dga' testfile.avi
```

It is worth trying all of these options, as their relative performance depends on many factors and will vary significantly with hardware.

To play a DVD, replace *testfile.avi* with dvd://*N* -dvd-device *DEVICE*, where *N* is the title number to play and *DEVICE* is the device node for the DVD. For example, to play title 3 from /dev/dvd :

```
# mplayer -vo xv dvd://3 -dvd-device /dev/dvd
```

> ## Note
>
> The default DVD device can be defined during the build of the MPlayer port by including the WITH_DVD_DEVICE=/path/to/desired/device option. By default, the device is /dev/cd0. More details can be found in the port's Makefile.options.

To stop, pause, advance, and so on, use a keybinding. To see the list of keybindings, run mplayer -h or read mplayer(1).

Additional playback options include -fs -zoom, which engages fullscreen mode, and -framedrop, which helps performance.

Each user can add commonly used options to their ~/.mplayer/config like so:

```
vo=xv
fs=yes
zoom=yes
```

mplayer can be used to rip a DVD title to a .vob. To dump the second title from a DVD:

```
# mplayer -dumpstream -dumpfile out.vob dvd://2 -dvd-device /dev/dvd
```

The output file, out.vob, will be in MPEG format.

Anyone wishing to obtain a high level of expertise with UNIX® video should consult mplayerhq.hu/DOCS as it is technically informative. This documentation should be considered as required reading before submitting any bug reports.

Before using mencoder, it is a good idea to become familiar with the options described at mplayerhq.hu/DOCS/HTML/en/mencoder.html. There are innumerable ways to improve quality, lower bitrate, and change formats, and some of these options may make the difference between good or bad performance. Improper combinations of command line options can yield output files that are unplayable even by mplayer.

Here is an example of a simple copy:

```
% mencoder input.avi -oac copy -ovc copy -o output.avi
```

To rip to a file, use -dumpfile with mplayer.

To convert *input.avi* to the MPEG4 codec with MPEG3 audio encoding, first install the audio/lame port. Due to licensing restrictions, a package is not available. Once installed, type:

```
% mencoder input.avi -oac mp3lame -lameopts br=192 \
  -ovc lavc -lavcopts vcodec=mpeg4:vhq -o output.avi
```

This will produce output playable by applications such as mplayer and xine.

input.avi can be replaced with dvd://1 -dvd-device /dev/dvd and run as root to re-encode a DVD title directly. Since it may take a few tries to get the desired result, it is recommended to instead dump the title to a file and to work on the file.

7.4.2.2. The xine Video Player

xine is a video player with a reusable base library and a modular executable which can be extended with plugins. It can be installed using the multimedia/xine package or port.

In practice, xine requires either a fast CPU with a fast video card, or support for the XVideo extension. The xine video player performs best on XVideo interfaces.

By default, the xine player starts a graphical user interface. The menus can then be used to open a specific file.

Alternatively, xine may be invoked from the command line by specifying the name of the file to play:

```
% xine -g -p mymovie.avi
```

Refer to xine-project.org/faq for more information and troubleshooting tips.

7.4.2.3. The Transcode Utilities

Transcode provides a suite of tools for re-encoding video and audio files. Transcode can be used to merge video files or repair broken files using command line tools with stdin/stdout stream interfaces.

In FreeBSD, Transcode can be installed using the multimedia/transcode package or port. Many users prefer to compile the port as it provides a menu of compile options for specifying the support and codecs to compile in. If an option is not selected, Transcode will not be able to encode that format. Use the arrow keys and spacebar to select the required formats. When finished, press Enter to continue the port compile and installation.

This example demonstrates how to convert a DivX file into a PAL MPEG-1 file (PAL VCD):

```
% transcode -i input.avi -V --export_prof vcd-pal -o output_vcd
% mplex -f 1 -o output_vcd.mpg output_vcd.m1v output_vcd.mpa
```

The resulting MPEG file, *output_vcd.mpg*, is ready to be played with MPlayer. The file can be burned on a CD media to create a video CD using a utility such as multimedia/vcdimager or sysutils/cdrdao.

In addition to the manual page for `transcode` , refer to transcoding.org/cgi-bin/transcode for further information and examples.

7.5. TV Cards

Original contribution by Josef El-Rayes.
Enhanced and adapted by Marc Fonvieille.

TV cards can be used to watch broadcast or cable TV on a computer. Most cards accept composite video via an RCA or S-video input and some cards include a FM radio tuner.

FreeBSD provides support for PCI-based TV cards using a Brooktree Bt848/849/878/879 video capture chip with the bktr(4) driver. This driver supports most Pinnacle PCTV video cards. Before purchasing a TV card, consult bktr(4) for a list of supported tuners.

7.5.1. Loading the Driver

In order to use the card, the bktr(4) driver must be loaded. To automate this at boot time, add the following line to /boot/loader.conf :

```
bktr_load="YES"
```

Alternatively, one can statically compile support for the TV card into a custom kernel. In that case, add the following lines to the custom kernel configuration file:

```
device  bktr
```

```
device iicbus
device iicbb
device smbus
```

These additional devices are necessary as the card components are interconnected via an I2C bus. Then, build and install a new kernel.

To test that the tuner is correctly detected, reboot the system. The TV card should appear in the boot messages, as seen in this example:

```
bktr0: <BrookTree 848A> mem 0xd7000000-0xd7000fff irq 10 at device 10.0 on pci0
iicbb0: <I2C bit-banging driver> on bti2c0
iicbus0: <Philips I2C bus> on iicbb0 master-only
iicbus1: <Philips I2C bus> on iicbb0 master-only
smbus0: <System Management Bus> on bti2c0
bktr0: Pinnacle/Miro TV, Philips SECAM tuner.
```

The messages will differ according to the hardware. If necessary, it is possible to override some of the detected parameters using sysctl(8) or custom kernel configuration options. For example, to force the tuner to a Philips SECAM tuner, add the following line to a custom kernel configuration file:

```
options OVERRIDE_TUNER=6
```

or, use sysctl(8):

```
# sysctl hw.bt848.tuner=6
```

Refer to bktr(4) for a description of the available sysctl(8) parameters and kernel options.

7.5.2. Useful Applications

To use the TV card, install one of the following applications:

- multimedia/fxtv provides TV-in-a-window and image/audio/video capture capabilities.

- multimedia/xawtv is another TV application with similar features.

- audio/xmradio provides an application for using the FM radio tuner of a TV card.

More applications are available in the FreeBSD Ports Collection.

7.5.3. Troubleshooting

If any problems are encountered with the TV card, check that the video capture chip and the tuner are supported by bktr(4) and that the right configuration options were used. For more support or to ask questions about supported TV cards, refer to the freebsd-multimedia mailing list.

7.6. MythTV

MythTV is a popular, open source Personal Video Recorder (PVR) application. This section demonstrates how to install and setup MythTV on FreeBSD. Refer to mythtv.org/wiki for more information on how to use MythTV.

MythTV requires a frontend and a backend. These components can either be installed on the same system or on different machines.

The frontend can be installed on FreeBSD using the multimedia/mythtv-frontend package or port. Xorg must also be installed and configured as described in Chapter 5, *The X Window System*. Ideally, this system has a video card that supports X-Video Motion Compensation (XvMC) and, optionally, a Linux Infrared Remote Control (LIRC)-compatible remote.

To install both the backend and the frontend on FreeBSD, use the multimedia/mythtv package or port. A MySQL™ database server is also required and should automatically be installed as a dependency. Optionally, this system should have a tuner card and sufficient storage to hold recorded data.

7.6.1. Hardware

MythTV uses Video for Linux (V4L) to access video input devices such as encoders and tuners. In FreeBSD, MythTV works best with USB DVB-S/C/T cards as they are well supported by the multimedia/webcamd package or port which provides a V4L userland application. Any Digital Video Broadcasting (DVB) card supported by webcamd should work with MythTV. A list of known working cards can be found at wiki.freebsd.org/WebcamCompat. Drivers are also available for Hauppauge cards in the multimedia/pvr250 and multimedia/pvrxxx ports, but they provide a non-standard driver interface that does not work with versions of MythTV greater than 0.23. Due to licensing restrictions, no packages are available and these two ports must be compiled.

The wiki.freebsd.org/HTPC page contains a list of all available DVB drivers.

7.6.2. Setting up the MythTV Backend

To install MythTV using binary packages:

```
# pkg install mythtv
```

Alternatively, to install from the Ports Collection:

```
# cd /usr/ports/multimedia/mythtv
# make install
```

Once installed, set up the MythTV database:

```
# mysql -uroot -p < /usr/local/share/mythtv/database/mc.sql
```

Then, configure the backend:

```
# mythtv-setup
```

Finally, start the backend:

```
# echo 'mythbackend_enable="YES"' >> /etc/rc.conf
# service mythbackend start
```

7.7. Image Scanners

Written by Marc Fonvieille.

In FreeBSD, access to image scanners is provided by SANE (Scanner Access Now Easy), which is available in the FreeBSD Ports Collection. SANE will also use some FreeBSD device drivers to provide access to the scanner hardware.

FreeBSD supports both SCSI and USB scanners. Depending upon the scanner interface, different device drivers are required. Be sure the scanner is supported by SANE prior to performing any configuration. Refer to http://www.sane-project.org/sane-supported-devices.html for more information about supported scanners.

This chapter describes how to determine if the scanner has been detected by FreeBSD. It then provides an overview of how to configure and use SANE on a FreeBSD system.

7.7.1. Checking the Scanner

The GENERIC kernel includes the device drivers needed to support USB scanners. Users with a custom kernel should ensure that the following lines are present in the custom kernel configuration file:

```
device usb
device uhci
device ohci
device ehci
```

To determine if the USB scanner is detected, plug it in and use dmesg to determine whether the scanner appears in the system message buffer. If it does, it should display a message similar to this:

```
ugen0.2: <EPSON> at usbus0
```

In this example, an EPSON Perfection® 1650 USB scanner was detected on /dev/ugen0.2 .

If the scanner uses a SCSI interface, it is important to know which SCSI controller board it will use. Depending upon the SCSI chipset, a custom kernel configuration file may be needed. The GENERIC kernel supports the most common SCSI controllers. Refer to /usr/src/sys/conf/NOTES to determine the correct line to add to a custom kernel configuration file. In addition to the SCSI adapter driver, the following lines are needed in a custom kernel configuration file:

```
device scbus
device pass
```

Verify that the device is displayed in the system message buffer:

```
pass2 at aic0 bus 0 target 2 lun 0
pass2: <AGFA SNAPSCAN 600 1.10> Fixed Scanner SCSI-2 device
pass2: 3.300MB/s transfers
```

If the scanner was not powered-on at system boot, it is still possible to manually force detection by performing a SCSI bus scan with camcontrol:

```
# camcontrol rescan all
Re-scan of bus 0 was successful
Re-scan of bus 1 was successful
Re-scan of bus 2 was successful
Re-scan of bus 3 was successful
```

The scanner should now appear in the SCSI devices list:

```
# camcontrol devlist
<IBM DDRS-34560 S97B>              at scbus0 target 5 lun 0 (pass0,da0)
<IBM DDRS-34560 S97B>              at scbus0 target 6 lun 0 (pass1,da1)
<AGFA SNAPSCAN 600 1.10>           at scbus1 target 2 lun 0 (pass3)
<PHILIPS CDD3610 CD-R/RW 1.00>     at scbus2 target 0 lun 0 (pass2,cd0)
```

Refer to scsi(4) and camcontrol(8) for more details about SCSI devices on FreeBSD.

7.7.2. SANE Configuration

The SANE system is split in two parts: the backends (graphics/sane-backends) and the frontends (graphics/sane-frontends or graphics/xsane). The backends provide access to the scanner. Refer to http://www.sane-project.org/sane-supported-devices.html to determine which backend supports the scanner. The frontends provide the graphical scanning interface. graphics/sane-frontends installs xscanimage while graphics/xsane installs xsane.

To install the two parts from binary packages:

```
# pkg install xsane sane-frontends
```

Alternatively, to install from the Ports Collection

```
# cd /usr/ports/graphics/sane-frontends
# make install clean
# cd /usr/ports/graphics/xsane
```

```
# make install clean
```

After installing the graphics/sane-backends port or package, use `sane-find-scanner` to check the scanner detection by the SANE system:

```
# sane-find-scanner -q
found SCSI scanner "AGFA SNAPSCAN 600 1.10" at /dev/pass3
```

The output should show the interface type of the scanner and the device node used to attach the scanner to the system. The vendor and the product model may or may not appear.

 Note

Some USB scanners require firmware to be loaded. Refer to sane-find-scanner(1) and sane(7) for details.

Next, check if the scanner will be identified by a scanning frontend. The SANE backends include `scanimage` which can be used to list the devices and perform an image acquisition. Use `-L` to list the scanner devices. The first example is for a SCSI scanner and the second is for a USB scanner:

```
# scanimage -L
device `snapscan:/dev/pass3' is a AGFA SNAPSCAN 600 flatbed scanner
# scanimage -L
device 'epson2:libusb:/dev/usb:/dev/ugen0.2' is a Epson GT-8200 flatbed scanner
```

In this second example, `'epson2:libusb:/dev/usb:/dev/ugen0.2'` is the backend name (epson2) and `/dev/ugen0.2` is the device node used by the scanner.

If `scanimage` is unable to identify the scanner, this message will appear:

```
# scanimage -L

No scanners were identified. If you were expecting something different,
check that the scanner is plugged in, turned on and detected by the
sane-find-scanner tool (if appropriate). Please read the documentation
which came with this software (README, FAQ, manpages).
```

If this happens, edit the backend configuration file in `/usr/local/etc/sane.d/` and define the scanner device used. For example, if the undetected scanner model is an EPSON Perfection® 1650 and it uses the epson2 backend, edit `/usr/local/etc/sane.d/epson2.conf`. When editing, add a line specifying the interface and the device node used. In this case, add the following line:

```
usb /dev/ugen0.2
```

Save the edits and verify that the scanner is identified with the right backend name and the device node:

```
# scanimage -L
device 'epson2:libusb:/dev/usb:/dev/ugen0.2' is a Epson GT-8200 flatbed scanner
```

Once `scanimage -L` sees the scanner, the configuration is complete and the scanner is now ready to use.

While `scanimage` can be used to perform an image acquisition from the command line, it is often preferable to use a graphical interface to perform image scanning. The graphics/sane-frontends package or port installs a simple but efficient graphical interface, xscanimage.

Alternately, xsane, which is installed with the graphics/xsane package or port, is another popular graphical scanning frontend. It offers advanced features such as various scanning modes, color correction, and batch scans. Both of these applications are usable as a GIMP plugin.

7.7.3. Scanner Permissions

In order to have access to the scanner, a user needs read and write permissions to the device node used by the scanner. In the previous example, the USB scanner uses the device node /dev/ugen0.2 which is really a symlink to the real device node /dev/usb/0.2.0 . The symlink and the device node are owned, respectively, by the wheel and operator groups. While adding the user to these groups will allow access to the scanner, it is considered insecure to add a user to wheel. A better solution is to create a group and make the scanner device accessible to members of this group.

This example creates a group called *usb*:

```
# pw groupadd usb
```

Then, make the /dev/ugen0.2 symlink and the /dev/usb/0.2.0 device node accessible to the usb group with write permissions of 0660 or 0664 by adding the following lines to /etc/devfs.rules :

```
[system=5]
add path ugen0.2 mode 0660 group usb
add path usb/0.2.0 mode 0666 group usb
```

Finally, add the users to *usb* in order to allow access to the scanner:

```
# pw groupmod usb -m joe
```

For more details refer to pw(8).

Chapter 8. Configuring the FreeBSD Kernel

8.1. Synopsis

The kernel is the core of the FreeBSD operating system. It is responsible for managing memory, enforcing security controls, networking, disk access, and much more. While much of FreeBSD is dynamically configurable, it is still occasionally necessary to configure and compile a custom kernel.

After reading this chapter, you will know:

- When to build a custom kernel.

- How to take a hardware inventory.

- How to customize a kernel configuration file.

- How to use the kernel configuration file to create and build a new kernel.

- How to install the new kernel.

- How to troubleshoot if things go wrong.

All of the commands listed in the examples in this chapter should be executed as root.

8.2. Why Build a Custom Kernel?

Traditionally, FreeBSD used a monolithic kernel. The kernel was one large program, supported a fixed list of devices, and in order to change the kernel's behavior, one had to compile and then reboot into a new kernel.

Today, most of the functionality in the FreeBSD kernel is contained in modules which can be dynamically loaded and unloaded from the kernel as necessary. This allows the running kernel to adapt immediately to new hardware and for new functionality to be brought into the kernel. This is known as a modular kernel.

Occasionally, it is still necessary to perform static kernel configuration. Sometimes the needed functionality is so tied to the kernel that it can not be made dynamically loadable. Some security environments prevent the loading and unloading of kernel modules and require that only needed functionality is statically compiled into the kernel.

Building a custom kernel is often a rite of passage for advanced BSD users. This process, while time consuming, can provide benefits to the FreeBSD system. Unlike the GENERIC kernel, which must support a wide range of hardware, a custom kernel can be stripped down to only provide support for that computer's hardware. This has a number of benefits, such as:

- Faster boot time. Since the kernel will only probe the hardware on the system, the time it takes the system to boot can decrease.

- Lower memory usage. A custom kernel often uses less memory than the GENERIC kernel by omitting unused features and device drivers. This is important because the kernel code remains resident in physical memory at all times, preventing that memory from being used by applications. For this reason, a custom kernel is useful on a system with a small amount of RAM.

- Additional hardware support. A custom kernel can add support for devices which are not present in the GENERIC kernel.

Before building a custom kernel, consider the reason for doing so. If there is a need for specific hardware support, it may already exist as a module.

Kernel modules exist in /boot/kernel and may be dynamically loaded into the running kernel using kldload(8). Most kernel drivers have a loadable module and manual page. For example, the ath(4) wireless Ethernet driver has the following information in its manual page:

```
Alternatively, to load the driver as a module at boot time, place the
following line in loader.conf(5):

    if_ath_load="YES"
```

Adding if_ath_load="YES" to /boot/loader.conf will load this module dynamically at boot time.

In some cases, there is no associated module in /boot/kernel. This is mostly true for certain subsystems.

8.3. Finding the System Hardware

Before editing the kernel configuration file, it is recommended to perform an inventory of the machine's hardware. On a dual-boot system, the inventory can be created from the other operating system. For example, Microsoft®'s Device Manager contains information about installed devices.

Note

Some versions of Microsoft® Windows® have a System icon which can be used to access Device Manager.

If FreeBSD is the only installed operating system, use dmesg(8) to determine the hardware that was found and listed during the boot probe. Most device drivers on FreeBSD have a manual page which lists the hardware supported by that driver. For example, the following lines indicate that the psm(4) driver found a mouse:

```
psm0: <PS/2 Mouse> irq 12 on atkbdc0
psm0: [GIANT-LOCKED]
psm0: [ITHREAD]
psm0: model Generic PS/2 mouse, device ID 0
```

Since this hardware exists, this driver should not be removed from a custom kernel configuration file.

If the output of dmesg does not display the results of the boot probe output, instead read the contents of /var/run/dmesg.boot.

Another tool for finding hardware is pciconf(8), which provides more verbose output. For example:

```
% pciconf -lv
ath0@pci0:3:0:0:        class=0x020000 card=0x058a1014 chip=0x1014168c rev=0x01 hdr=0x00
    vendor     = 'Atheros Communications Inc.'
    device     = 'AR5212 Atheros AR5212 802.11abg wireless'
    class      = network
    subclass   = ethernet
```

This output shows that the ath driver located a wireless Ethernet device.

The -k flag of man(1) can be used to provide useful information. For example, it can be used to display a list of manual pages which contain a particular device brand or name:

```
# man -k Atheros
ath(4)                    - Atheros IEEE 802.11 wireless network driver
ath_hal(4)                - Atheros Hardware Access Layer (HAL)
```

Once the hardware inventory list is created, refer to it to ensure that drivers for installed hardware are not removed as the custom kernel configuration is edited.

8.4. The Configuration File

In order to create a custom kernel configuration file and build a custom kernel, the full FreeBSD source tree must first be installed.

If /usr/src/ does not exist or it is empty, source has not been installed. Source can be installed using Subversion and the instructions in Section A.3, "Using Subversion".

Once source is installed, review the contents of /usr/src/sys . This directory contains a number of subdirectories, including those which represent the following supported architectures: amd64, i386, ia64, pc98, powerpc, and sparc64 . Everything inside a particular architecture's directory deals with that architecture only and the rest of the code is machine independent code common to all platforms. Each supported architecture has a conf subdirectory which contains the GENERIC kernel configuration file for that architecture.

Do not make edits to GENERIC. Instead, copy the file to a different name and make edits to the copy. The convention is to use a name with all capital letters. When maintaining multiple FreeBSD machines with different hardware, it is a good idea to name it after the machine's hostname. This example creates a copy, named MYKERNEL, of the GENERIC configuration file for the amd64 architecture:

```
# cd /usr/src/sys/ amd64 /conf
# cp GENERIC MYKERNEL
```

MYKERNEL can now be customized with any ASCII text editor. The default editor is vi, though an easier editor for beginners, called ee, is also installed with FreeBSD.

The format of the kernel configuration file is simple. Each line contains a keyword that represents a device or subsystem, an argument, and a brief description. Any text after a # is considered a comment and ignored. To remove kernel support for a device or subsystem, put a # at the beginning of the line representing that device or subsystem. Do not add or remove a # for any line that you do not understand.

Warning

It is easy to remove support for a device or option and end up with a broken kernel. For example, if the ata(4) driver is removed from the kernel configuration file, a system using ATA disk drivers may not boot. When in doubt, just leave support in the kernel.

In addition to the brief descriptions provided in this file, additional descriptions are contained in NOTES, which can be found in the same directory as GENERIC for that architecture. For architecture independent options, refer to /usr/src/sys/conf/NOTES .

Tip

When finished customizing the kernel configuration file, save a backup copy to a location outside of /usr/src .

Alternately, keep the kernel configuration file elsewhere and create a symbolic link to the file:

```
# cd /usr/src/sys/amd64/conf
# mkdir /root/kernels
# cp GENERIC /root/kernels/MYKERNEL
```

```
# ln -s /root/kernels/MYKERNEL
```

An include directive is available for use in configuration files. This allows another configuration file to be included in the current one, making it easy to maintain small changes relative to an existing file. If only a small number of additional options or drivers are required, this allows a delta to be maintained with respect to GENERIC, as seen in this example:

```
include GENERIC
ident MYKERNEL

options         IPFIREWALL
options         DUMMYNET
options         IPFIREWALL_DEFAULT_TO_ACCEPT
options         IPDIVERT
```

Using this method, the local configuration file expresses local differences from a GENERIC kernel. As upgrades are performed, new features added to GENERIC will also be added to the local kernel unless they are specifically prevented using nooptions or nodevice. A comprehensive list of configuration directives and their descriptions may be found in config(5).

Note

To build a file which contains all available options, run the following command as root:

```
# cd /usr/src/sys/ arch/conf && make LINT
```

8.5. Building and Installing a Custom Kernel

Once the edits to the custom configuration file have been saved, the source code for the kernel can be compiled using the following steps:

Procedure 8.1. Building a Kernel

1. Change to this directory:

    ```
    # cd /usr/src
    ```

2. Compile the new kernel by specifying the name of the custom kernel configuration file:

    ```
    # make buildkernel KERNCONF= MYKERNEL
    ```

3. Install the new kernel associated with the specified kernel configuration file. This command will copy the new kernel to /boot/kernel/kernel and save the old kernel to /boot/kernel.old/kernel :

    ```
    # make installkernel KERNCONF= MYKERNEL
    ```

4. Shutdown the system and reboot into the new kernel. If something goes wrong, refer to The kernel does not boot.

By default, when a custom kernel is compiled, all kernel modules are rebuilt. To update a kernel faster or to build only custom modules, edit /etc/make.conf before starting to build the kernel.

For example, this variable specifies the list of modules to build instead of using the default of building all modules:

```
MODULES_OVERRIDE = linux acpi
```

Alternately, this variable lists which modules to exclude from the build process:

```
WITHOUT_MODULES = linux acpi sound
```

Additional variables are available. Refer to make.conf(5) for details.

8.6. If Something Goes Wrong

There are four categories of trouble that can occur when building a custom kernel:

config fails
> If config fails, it will print the line number that is incorrect. As an example, for the following message, make sure that line 17 is typed correctly by comparing it to GENERIC or NOTES:
>
> ```
> config: line 17: syntax error
> ```

make fails
> If make fails, it is usually due to an error in the kernel configuration file which is not severe enough for config to catch. Review the configuration, and if the problem is not apparent, send an email to the FreeBSD general questions mailing list which contains the kernel configuration file.

The kernel does not boot
> If the new kernel does not boot or fails to recognize devices, do not panic! Fortunately, FreeBSD has an excellent mechanism for recovering from incompatible kernels. Simply choose the kernel to boot from at the FreeBSD boot loader. This can be accessed when the system boot menu appears by selecting the "Escape to a loader prompt" option. At the prompt, type boot *kernel.old*, or the name of any other kernel that is known to boot properly.
>
> After booting with a good kernel, check over the configuration file and try to build it again. One helpful resource is /var/log/messages which records the kernel messages from every successful boot. Also, dmesg(8) will print the kernel messages from the current boot.

Note

When troubleshooting a kernel, make sure to keep a copy of GENERIC, or some other kernel that is known to work, as a different name that will not get erased on the next build. This is important because every time a new kernel is installed, kernel.old is overwritten with the last installed kernel, which may or may not be bootable. As soon as possible, move the working kernel by renaming the directory containing the good kernel:

```
# mv /boot/kernel  /boot/kernel.bad
# mv /boot/kernel.good  /boot/kernel
```

The kernel works, but ps(1) does not
> If the kernel version differs from the one that the system utilities have been built with, for example, a kernel built from -CURRENT sources is installed on a -RELEASE system, many system status commands like ps(1) and vmstat(8) will not work. To fix this, recompile and install a world built with the same version of the source tree as the kernel. It is never a good idea to use a different version of the kernel than the rest of the operating system.

Chapter 9. Printing

Originally contributed by Warren Block.

Putting information on paper is a vital function, despite many attempts to eliminate it. Printing has two basic components. The data must be delivered to the printer, and must be in a form that the printer can understand.

9.1. Quick Start

Basic printing can be set up quickly. The printer must be capable of printing plain ASCII text. For printing to other types of files, see Section 9.5.3, "Filters".

1. Create a directory to store files while they are being printed:

    ```
    # mkdir -p /var/spool/lpd/lp
    # chown daemon:daemon /var/spool/lpd/lp
    # chmod 770 /var/spool/lpd/lp
    ```

2. As root, create /etc/printcap with these contents:

    ```
    lp:\
     :lp=/dev/unlpt0:\     ❶
     :sh:\
     :mx#0:\
     :sd=/var/spool/lpd/lp:\
     :lf=/var/log/lpd-errs:
    ```

    ❶   This line is for a printer connected to a USB port.

        For a printer connected to a parallel or "printer" port, use:

        ```
        :lp=/dev/lpt0:\
        ```

        For a printer connected directly to a network, use:

        ```
        :lp=:rm=network-printer-name:rp=raw:\
        ```

        Replace *network-printer-name* with the DNS host name of the network printer.

3. Enable lpd by editing /etc/rc.conf, adding this line:

    ```
    lpd_enable="YES"
    ```

    Start the service:

    ```
    # service lpd start
    Starting lpd.
    ```

4. Print a test:

    ```
    # printf "1. This printer can print.\n2. This is the second line.\n" | lpr
    ```

>
> **Tip**
>
> If both lines do not start at the left border, but "stairstep" instead, see Section 9.5.3.1, "Preventing Stairstepping on Plain Text Printers".

Text files can now be printed with `lpr`. Give the filename on the command line, or pipe output directly into `lpr`.

```
% lpr textfile.txt
% ls -lh | lpr
```

9.2. Printer Connections

Printers are connected to computer systems in a variety of ways. Small desktop printers are usually connected directly to a computer's USB port. Older printers are connected to a parallel or "printer" port. Some printers are directly connected to a network, making it easy for multiple computers to share them. A few printers use a rare serial port connection.

FreeBSD can communicate with all of these types of printers.

USB
> USB printers can be connected to any available USB port on the computer.
>
> When FreeBSD detects a USB printer, two device entries are created: `/dev/ulpt0` and `/dev/unlpt0`. Data sent to either device will be relayed to the printer. After each print job, `ulpt0` resets the USB port. Resetting the port can cause problems with some printers, so the `unlpt0` device is usually used instead. `unlpt0` does not reset the USB port at all.

Parallel (IEEE-1284)
> The parallel port device is `/dev/lpt0`. This device appears whether a printer is attached or not, it is not autodetected.
>
> Vendors have largely moved away from these "legacy" ports, and many computers no longer have them. Adapters can be used to connect a parallel printer to a USB port. With such an adapter, the printer can be treated as if it were actually a USB printer. Devices called *print servers* can also be used to connect parallel printers directly to a network.

Serial (RS-232)
> Serial ports are another legacy port, rarely used for printers except in certain niche applications. Cables, connectors, and required wiring vary widely.
>
> For serial ports built into a motherboard, the serial device name is `/dev/cuau0` or `/dev/cuau1`. Serial USB adapters can also be used, and these will appear as `/dev/cuaU 0`.
>
> Several communication parameters must be known to communicate with a serial printer. The most important are *baud rate* or BPS (Bits Per Second) and *parity*. Values vary, but typical serial printers use a baud rate of 9600 and no parity.

Network
> Network printers are connected directly to the local computer network.
>
> The DNS hostname of the printer must be known. If the printer is assigned a dynamic address by DHCP, DNS should be dynamically updated so that the host name always has the correct IP address. Network printers are often given static IP addresses to avoid this problem.
>
> Most network printers understand print jobs sent with the LPD protocol. A print queue name can also be specified. Some printers process data differently depending on which queue is used. For example, a `raw` queue prints the data unchanged, while the `text` queue adds carriage returns to plain text.
>
> Many network printers can also print data sent directly to port 9100.

9.2.1. Summary

Wired network connections are usually the easiest to set up and give the fastest printing. For direct connection to the computer, USB is preferred for speed and simplicity. Parallel connections work but have limitations on cable length and speed. Serial connections are more difficult to configure. Cable wiring differs between models, and communication parameters like baud rate and parity bits must add to the complexity. Fortunately, serial printers are rare.

9.3. Common Page Description Languages

Data sent to a printer must be in a language that the printer can understand. These languages are called Page Description Languages, or PDLs.

ASCII

Plain ASCII text is the simplest way to send data to a printer. Characters correspond one to one with what will be printed: an A in the data prints an A on the page. Very little formatting is available. There is no way to select a font or proportional spacing. The forced simplicity of plain ASCII means that text can be printed straight from the computer with little or no encoding or translation. The printed output corresponds directly with what was sent.

Some inexpensive printers cannot print plain ASCII text. This makes them more difficult to set up, but it is usually still possible.

PostScript®

PostScript® is almost the opposite of ASCII. Rather than simple text, a PostScript® program is a set of instructions that draw the final document. Different fonts and graphics can be used. However, this power comes at a price. The program that draws the page must be written. Usually this program is generated by application software, so the process is invisible to the user.

Inexpensive printers sometimes leave out PostScript® compatibility as a cost-saving measure.

PCL (Printer Command Language)

PCL is an extension of ASCII, adding escape sequences for formatting, font selection, and printing graphics. Many printers provide PCL5 support. Some support the newer PCL6 or PCLXL. These later versions are supersets of PCL5 and can provide faster printing.

Host-Based

Manufacturers can reduce the cost of a printer by giving it a simple processor and very little memory. These printers are not capable of printing plain text. Instead, bitmaps of text and graphics are drawn by a driver on the host computer and then sent to the printer. These are called *host-based* printers.

Communication between the driver and a host-based printer is often through proprietary or undocumented protocols, making them functional only on the most common operating systems.

9.3.1. Converting PostScript® to Other PDLs

Many applications from the Ports Collection and FreeBSD utilities produce PostScript® output. This table shows the utilities available to convert that into other common PDLs:

Table 9.1. Output PDLs

Output PDL	Generated By	Notes
PCL or PCL5	print/ghostscript9	-sDEVICE=ljet4 for monochrome, -sDEVICE=cljet5 for color
PCLXL or PCL6	print/ghostscript9	-sDEVICE=pxlmono for monochrome, -sDEVICE=pxlcolor for color

Output PDL	Generated By	Notes
ESC/P2	print/ghostscript9	-sDEVICE=uniprint
XQX	print/foo2zjs	

9.3.2. Summary

For the easiest printing, choose a printer that supports PostScript®. Printers that support PCL are the next preferred. With print/ghostscript, these printers can be used as if they understood PostScript® natively. Printers that support PostScript® or PCL directly almost always support direct printing of plain ASCII text files also.

Line-based printers like typical inkjets usually do not support PostScript® or PCL. They often can print plain ASCII text files. print/ghostscript supports the PDLs used by some of these printers. However, printing an entire graphic-based page on these printers is often very slow due to the large amount of data to be transferred and printed.

Host-based printers are often more difficult to set up. Some cannot be used at all because of proprietary PDLs. Avoid these printers when possible.

Descriptions of many PDLs can be found at http://www.undocprint.org/formats/page_description_languages. The particular PDL used by various models of printers can be found at http://www.openprinting.org/printers.

9.4. Direct Printing

For occasional printing, files can be sent directly to a printer device without any setup. For example, a file called sample.txt can be sent to a USB printer:

```
# cp sample.txt /dev/unlpt0
```

Direct printing to network printers depends on the abilities of the printer, but most accept print jobs on port 9100, and nc(1) can be used with them. To print the same file to a printer with the DNS hostname of *netlaser*:

```
# nc netlaser 9100 < sample.txt
```

9.5. LPD (Line Printer Daemon)

Printing a file in the background is called *spooling*. A spooler allows the user to continue with other programs on the computer without waiting for the printer to slowly complete the print job.

FreeBSD includes a spooler called lpd(8). Print jobs are submitted with lpr(1).

9.5.1. Initial Setup

A directory for storing print jobs is created, ownership is set, and the permissions are set to prevent other users from viewing the contents of those files:

```
# mkdir -p /var/spool/lpd/lp
# chown daemon:daemon /var/spool/lpd/lp
# chmod 770 /var/spool/lpd/lp
```

Printers are defined in /etc/printcap. An entry for each printer includes details like a name, the port where it is attached, and various other settings. Create /etc/printcap with these contents:

```
lp:\        ❶
  :lp=/dev/unlpt0:\ ❷
  :sh:\     ❸
  :mx#0:\   ❹
  :sd=/var/spool/lpd/lp:\ ❺
```

```
:lf=/var/log/lpd-errs: ❻
```

❶ The name of this printer. lpr(1) sends print jobs to the lp printer unless another printer is specified with -P, so the default printer should be named lp.

❷ The device where the printer is connected. Replace this line with the appropriate one for the connection type shown here.

Connection Type	Device Entry in **/etc/printcap**
USB	`:lp=/dev/unlpt0:\` This is the *non-resetting* USB printer device. If problems are experienced, use ulpt0 instead, which resets the USB port on each use.
Parallel	`:lp=/dev/lpt0:\`

Network	For a printer supporting the LPD protocol:
	
	 `:lp=:rm=network-printer-name :rp=raw:\`
	
	 For printers supporting port 9100 printing:
	
	 `:lp=9100@network-printer-name :\`
	
	 For both types, replace *network-printer-name* with the DNS host name of the network printer.

Serial	`:lp=/dev/cuau0:br=9600:pa=none:\` These values are for a typical serial printer connected to a motherboard serial port. The baud rate is 9600, and no parity is used.

❸ Suppress the printing of a header page at the start of a print job.

❹ Do not limit the maximum size of a print job.

❺ The path to the spooling directory for this printer. Each printer uses its own spooling directory.

❻ The log file where errors on this printer will be reported.

After creating /etc/printcap, use chkprintcap(8) to test it for errors:

```
# chkprintcap
```

Fix any reported problems before continuing.

Enable lpd(8) in /etc/rc.conf :

```
lpd_enable="YES"
```

Start the service:

```
# service lpd start
```

9.5.2. Printing with lpr(1)

Documents are sent to the printer with lpr. A file to be printed can be named on the command line or piped into lpr. These two commands are equivalent, sending the contents of doc.txt to the default printer:

```
% lpr doc.txt
% cat doc.txt | lpr
```

Printers can be selected with -P. To print to a printer called *laser*:

```
% lpr -Plaser doc.txt
```

9.5.3. Filters

The examples shown so far have sent the contents of a text file directly to the printer. As long as the printer understands the content of those files, output will be printed correctly.

Some printers are not capable of printing plain text, and the input file might not even be plain text.

Filters allow files to be translated or processed. The typical use is to translate one type of input, like plain text, into a form that the printer can understand, like PostScript® or PCL. Filters can also be used to provide additional features, like adding page numbers or highlighting source code to make it easier to read.

The filters discussed here are *input filters* or *text filters*. These filters convert the incoming file into different forms. Use su(1) to become root before creating the files.

Filters are specified in /etc/printcap with the if= identifier. To use /usr/local/libexec/lf2crlf as a filter, modify /etc/printcap like this:

```
lp:\
  :lp=/dev/unlpt0:\
  :sh:\
  :mx#0:\
  :sd=/var/spool/lpd/lp:\
  :if=/usr/local/libexec/lf2crlf:\    ❶
  :lf=/var/log/lpd-errs:
```

❶   if= identifies the *input filter* that will be used on incoming text.

Tip

The backslash *line continuation* characters at the end of the lines in printcap entries reveal that an entry for a printer is really just one long line with entries delimited by colon characters. An earlier example can be rewritten as a single less-readable line:

```
lp:lp=/dev/unlpt0:sh:mx#0:sd=/var/spool/lpd/lp:if=/usr/local/libexec/
lf2crlf:lf=/var/log/lpd-errs:
```

9.5.3.1. Preventing Stairstepping on Plain Text Printers

Typical FreeBSD text files contain only a single line feed character at the end of each line. These lines will "stairstep" on a standard printer:

```
A printed file looks
                    like the steps of a staircase
                                          scattered by the wind
```

A filter can convert the newline characters into carriage returns and newlines. The carriage returns make the printer return to the left after each line. Create /usr/local/libexec/lf2crlf with these contents:

```
#!/bin/sh
CR=$'\r'
/usr/bin/sed -e "s/$/${CR}/g"
```

Set the permissions and make it executable:

```
# chmod 555 /usr/local/libexec/lf2crlf
```

Modify /etc/printcap to use the new filter:

```
:if=/usr/local/libexec/lf2crlf:\
```

Test the filter by printing the same plain text file. The carriage returns will cause each line to start at the left side of the page.

9.5.3.2. Fancy Plain Text on PostScript® Printers with print/enscript

GNU Enscript converts plain text files into nicely-formatted PostScript® for printing on PostScript® printers. It adds page numbers, wraps long lines, and provides numerous other features to make printed text files easier to read. Depending on the local paper size, install either print/enscript-letter or print/enscript-a4 from the Ports Collection.

Create /usr/local/libexec/enscript with these contents:

```
#!/bin/sh
/usr/local/bin/enscript -o -
```

Set the permissions and make it executable:

```
# chmod 555 /usr/local/libexec/enscript
```

Modify /etc/printcap to use the new filter:

```
:if=/usr/local/libexec/enscript:\
```

Test the filter by printing a plain text file.

9.5.3.3. Printing PostScript® to PCL Printers

Many programs produce PostScript® documents. However, inexpensive printers often only understand plain text or PCL. This filter converts PostScript® files to PCL before sending them to the printer.

Install the Ghostscript PostScript® interpreter, print/ghostscript9, from the Ports Collection.

Create /usr/local/libexec/ps2pcl with these contents:

```
#!/bin/sh
/usr/local/bin/gs -dSAFER -dNOPAUSE -dBATCH -q -sDEVICE=ljet4 -sOutputFile=- -
```

Set the permissions and make it executable:

```
# chmod 555 /usr/local/libexec/ps2pcl
```

PostScript® input sent to this script will be rendered and converted to PCL before being sent on to the printer.

Modify /etc/printcap to use this new input filter:

```
:if=/usr/local/libexec/ps2pcl:\
```

Test the filter by sending a small PostScript® program to it:

```
% printf "%%\!PS \n /Helvetica findfont 18 scalefont setfont \
72 432 moveto (PostScript printing successful.) show showpage \004" | lpr
```

9.5.3.4. Smart Filters

A filter that detects the type of input and automatically converts it to the correct format for the printer can be very convenient. The first two characters of a PostScript® file are usually %!. A filter can detect those two characters. PostScript® files can be sent on to a PostScript® printer unchanged. Text files can be converted to PostScript® with Enscript as shown earlier. Create /usr/local/libexec/psif with these contents:

```
#!/bin/sh
#
#   psif - Print PostScript or plain text on a PostScript printer
```

```
#
IFS="" read -r first_line
first_two_chars=`expr "$first_line" : '\(..\)'`

case "$first_two_chars" in
%!)
    # %! : PostScript job, print it.
    echo "$first_line" && cat && exit 0
    exit 2
    -;;
*)
    # otherwise, format with enscript
    ( echo "$first_line"; cat ) | /usr/local/bin/enscript -o - && exit 0
    exit 2
    -;;
esac
```

Set the permissions and make it executable:

```
# chmod 555 /usr/local/libexec/psif
```

Modify /etc/printcap to use this new input filter:

```
:if=/usr/local/libexec/psif:\
```

Test the filter by printing PostScript® and plain text files.

9.5.3.5. Other Smart Filters

Writing a filter that detects many different types of input and formats them correctly is challenging. print/apsfilter from the Ports Collection is a smart "magic" filter that detects dozens of file types and automatically converts them to the PDL understood by the printer. See http://www.apsfilter.org for more details.

9.5.4. Multiple Queues

The entries in /etc/printcap are really definitions of *queues*. There can be more than one queue for a single printer. When combined with filters, multiple queues provide users more control over how their jobs are printed.

As an example, consider a networked PostScript® laser printer in an office. Most users want to print plain text, but a few advanced users want to be able to print PostScript® files directly. Two entries can be created for the same printer in /etc/printcap:

```
textprinter:\
 :lp=9100@officelaser:\
 :sh:\
 :mx#0:\
 :sd=/var/spool/lpd/textprinter:\
 :if=/usr/local/libexec/enscript:\
 :lf=/var/log/lpd-errs:

psprinter:\
 :lp=9100@officelaser:\
 :sh:\
 :mx#0:\
 :sd=/var/spool/lpd/psprinter:\
 :lf=/var/log/lpd-errs:
```

Documents sent to textprinter will be formatted by the /usr/local/libexec/enscript filter shown in an earlier example. Advanced users can print PostScript® files on psprinter, where no filtering is done.

This multiple queue technique can be used to provide direct access to all kinds of printer features. A printer with a duplexer could use two queues, one for ordinary single-sided printing, and one with a filter that sends the command sequence to enable double-sided printing and then sends the incoming file.

9.5.5. Monitoring and Controlling Printing

Several utilities are available to monitor print jobs and check and control printer operation.

9.5.5.1. lpq(1)

lpq(1) shows the status of a user's print jobs. Print jobs from other users are not shown.

Show the current user's pending jobs on a single printer:

```
% lpq -P lp
Rank   Owner    Job  Files                          Total Size
1st    jsmith   0    (standard input)               12792 bytes
```

Show the current user's pending jobs on all printers:

```
% lpq -a
lp:
Rank   Owner    Job  Files                          Total Size
1st    jsmith   1    (standard input)               27320 bytes

laser:
Rank   Owner    Job  Files                          Total Size
1st    jsmith   287  (standard input)               22443 bytes
```

9.5.5.2. lprm(1)

lprm(1) is used to remove print jobs. Normal users are only allowed to remove their own jobs. root can remove any or all jobs.

Remove all pending jobs from a printer:

```
# lprm -P lp -
dfA002smithy dequeued
cfA002smithy dequeued
dfA003smithy dequeued
cfA003smithy dequeued
dfA004smithy dequeued
cfA004smithy dequeued
```

Remove a single job from a printer. lpq(1) is used to find the job number.

```
% lpq
Rank   Owner    Job  Files                          Total Size
1st    jsmith   5    (standard input)               12188 bytes
% lprm -P lp 5
dfA005smithy dequeued
cfA005smithy dequeued
```

9.5.5.3. lpc(8)

lpc(8) is used to check and modify printer status. lpc is followed by a command and an optional printer name. all can be used instead of a specific printer name, and the command will be applied to all printers. Normal users can view status with lpc(8). Only class="username">root can use commands which modify printer status.

Show the status of all printers:

```
% lpc status all
lp:
 queuing is enabled
 printing is enabled
 1 entry in spool area
 printer idle
laser:
```

```
queuing is enabled
printing is enabled
1 entry in spool area
waiting for laser to come up
```

Prevent a printer from accepting new jobs, then begin accepting new jobs again:

```
# lpc disable lp
lp:
 queuing disabled
# lpc enable lp
lp:
 queuing enabled
```

Stop printing, but continue to accept new jobs. Then begin printing again:

```
# lpc stop lp
lp:
 printing disabled
# lpc start lp
lp:
 printing enabled
 daemon started
```

Restart a printer after some error condition:

```
# lpc restart lp
lp:
 no daemon to abort
 printing enabled
 daemon restarted
```

Turn the print queue off and disable printing, with a message to explain the problem to users:

```
# lpc down lp Repair parts will arrive on Monday
lp:
 printer and queuing disabled
 status message is now: Repair parts will arrive on Monday
```

Re-enable a printer that is down:

```
# lpc up lp
lp:
 printing enabled
 daemon started
```

See lpc(8) for more commands and options.

9.5.6. Shared Printers

Printers are often shared by multiple users in businesses and schools. Additional features are provided to make sharing printers more convenient.

9.5.6.1. Aliases

The printer name is set in the first line of the entry in /etc/printcap. Additional names, or *aliases*, can be added after that name. Aliases are separated from the name and each other by vertical bars:

```
lp|repairsprinter |salesprinter :\
```

Aliases can be used in place of the printer name. For example, users in the Sales department print to their printer with

```
% lpr -Psalesprinter sales-report.txt
```

Users in the Repairs department print to *their* printer with

```
% lpr -Prepairsprinter  repairs-report.txt
```

All of the documents print on that single printer. When the Sales department grows enough to need their own printer, the alias can be removed from the shared printer entry and used as the name of a new printer. Users in both departments continue to use the same commands, but the Sales documents are sent to the new printer.

9.5.6.2. Header Pages

It can be difficult for users to locate their documents in the stack of pages produced by a busy shared printer. *Header pages* were created to solve this problem. A header page with the user name and document name is printed before each print job. These pages are also sometimes called *banner* or *separator* pages.

Enabling header pages differs depending on whether the printer is connected directly to the computer with a USB, parallel, or serial cable, or is connected remotely over a network.

Header pages on directly-connected printers are enabled by removing the :sh:\ (Suppress Header) line from the entry in /etc/printcap. These header pages only use line feed characters for new lines. Some printers will need the /usr/share/examples/printing/hpif filter to prevent stairstepped text. The filter configures PCL printers to print both carriage returns and line feeds when a line feed is received.

Header pages for network printers must be configured on the printer itself. Header page entries in /etc/printcap are ignored. Settings are usually available from the printer front panel or a configuration web page accessible with a web browser.

9.5.7. References

Example files: /usr/share/examples/printing/ .

The *4.3BSD Line Printer Spooler Manual*, /usr/share/doc/smm/07.lpd/paper.ascii.gz .

Manual pages: printcap(5), lpd(8), lpr(1), lpc(8), lprm(1), lpq(1).

9.6. Other Printing Systems

Several other printing systems are available in addition to the built-in lpd(8). These systems offer support for other protocols or additional features.

9.6.1. CUPS (Common UNIX® Printing System)

CUPS is a popular printing system available on many operating systems. Using CUPS on FreeBSD is documented in a separate article:https://www.FreeBSD.org/doc/en_US.ISO8859-1/articles/cups

9.6.2. HPLIP

Hewlett Packard provides a printing system that supports many of their inkjet and laser printers. The port is print/hplip. The main web page is at http://hplipopensource.com/hplip-web/index.html. The port handles all the installation details on FreeBSD. Configuration information is shown at http://hplipopensource.com/hplip-web/install/manual/hp_setup.html.

9.6.3. LPRng

LPRng was developed as an enhanced alternative to lpd(8). The port is sysutils/LPRng. For details and documentation, see http://www.lprng.com/.

Chapter 10. Linux® Binary Compatibility

Restructured and parts updated by Jim Mock.
Originally contributed by Brian N. Handy and Rich Murphey.

10.1. Synopsis

FreeBSD provides binary compatibility with Linux®, allowing users to install and run most Linux® binaries on a FreeBSD system without having to first modify the binary. It has even been reported that, in some situations, Linux® binaries perform better on FreeBSD than they do on Linux®.

However, some Linux®-specific operating system features are not supported under FreeBSD. For example, Linux® binaries will not work on FreeBSD if they overly use i386™ specific calls, such as enabling virtual 8086 mode.

>
>
> Note
>
> Support for 64-bit binary compatibility with Linux® was added in FreeBSD 10.3.

After reading this chapter, you will know:

- How to enable Linux® binary compatibility on a FreeBSD system.

- How to install additional Linux® shared libraries.

- How to install Linux® applications on a FreeBSD system.

- The implementation details of Linux® compatibility in FreeBSD.

Before reading this chapter, you should:

- Know how to install additional third-party software.

10.2. Configuring Linux® Binary Compatibility

By default, Linux® libraries are not installed and Linux® binary compatibility is not enabled. Linux® libraries can either be installed manually or from the FreeBSD Ports Collection.

Before attempting to build the port, load the Linux® kernel module, otherwise the build will fail:

```
# kldload linux
```

For 64-bit compatibility:

```
# kldload linux64
```

To verify that the module is loaded:

```
% kldstat
    Id Refs Address    Size     Name
```

```
1   2 0xc0100000 16bdb8   kernel
7   1 0xc24db000 d000     linux.ko
```

The emulators/linux_base-c6 package or port is the easiest way to install a base set of Linux® libraries and binaries on a FreeBSD system. To install the port:

```
# pkg install emulators/linux_base-c6
```

For Linux® compatibility to be enabled at boot time, add this line to /etc/rc.conf :

```
linux_enable="YES"
```

On 64-bit machines, /etc/rc.d/abi will automatically load the module for 64-bit emulation.

Since the Linux binary compatibility layer has gained support for running both 32- and 64-bit Linux binaries (on 64-bit x86 hosts), it is no longer possible to link the emulation functionality statically into a custom kernel.

10.2.1. Installing Additional Libraries Manually

If a Linux® application complains about missing shared libraries after configuring Linux® binary compatibility, determine which shared libraries the Linux® binary needs and install them manually.

From a Linux® system, ldd can be used to determine which shared libraries the application needs. For example, to check which shared libraries linuxdoom needs, run this command from a Linux® system that has Doom installed:

```
% ldd linuxdoom
libXt.so.3 (DLL Jump 3.1) => /usr/X11/lib/libXt.so.3.1.0
libX11.so.3 (DLL Jump 3.1) => /usr/X11/lib/libX11.so.3.1.0
libc.so.4 (DLL Jump 4.5pl26) => /lib/libc.so.4.6.29
```

Then, copy all the files in the last column of the output from the Linux® system into /compat/linux on the Free-BSD system. Once copied, create symbolic links to the names in the first column. This example will result in the following files on the FreeBSD system:

```
/compat/linux/usr/X11/lib/libXt.so.3.1.0
/compat/linux/usr/X11/lib/libXt.so.3 -> libXt.so.3.1.0
/compat/linux/usr/X11/lib/libX11.so.3.1.0
/compat/linux/usr/X11/lib/libX11.so.3 -> libX11.so.3.1.0
/compat/linux/lib/libc.so.4.6.29
/compat/linux/lib/libc.so.4 -> libc.so.4.6.29
```

If a Linux® shared library already exists with a matching major revision number to the first column of the ldd output, it does not need to be copied to the file named in the last column, as the existing library should work. It is advisable to copy the shared library if it is a newer version, though. The old one can be removed, as long as the symbolic link points to the new one.

For example, these libraries already exist on the FreeBSD system:

```
/compat/linux/lib/libc.so.4.6.27
/compat/linux/lib/libc.so.4 -> libc.so.4.6.27
```

and ldd indicates that a binary requires a later version:

```
libc.so.4 (DLL Jump 4.5pl26) -> libc.so.4.6.29
```

Since the existing library is only one or two versions out of date in the last digit, the program should still work with the slightly older version. However, it is safe to replace the existing libc.so with the newer version:

```
/compat/linux/lib/libc.so.4.6.29
/compat/linux/lib/libc.so.4 -> libc.so.4.6.29
```

Generally, one will need to look for the shared libraries that Linux® binaries depend on only the first few times that a Linux® program is installed on FreeBSD. After a while, there will be a sufficient set of Linux® shared libraries on the system to be able to run newly installed Linux® binaries without any extra work.

10.2.2. Installing Linux® ELF Binaries

ELF binaries sometimes require an extra step. When an unbranded ELF binary is executed, it will generate an error message:

```
% ./my-linux-elf-binary
ELF binary type not known
Abort
```

To help the FreeBSD kernel distinguish between a FreeBSD ELF binary and a Linux® binary, use brandelf(1):

```
% brandelf -t Linux my-linux-elf-binary
```

Since the GNU toolchain places the appropriate branding information into ELF binaries automatically, this step is usually not necessary.

10.2.3. Installing a Linux® RPM Based Application

To install a Linux® RPM-based application, first install the archivers/rpm4 package or port. Once installed, root can use this command to install a .rpm:

```
# cd /compat/linux
# rpm2cpio < /path/to/linux.archive.rpm | cpio -id
```

If necessary, brandelf the installed ELF binaries. Note that this will prevent a clean uninstall.

10.2.4. Configuring the Hostname Resolver

If DNS does not work or this error appears:

```
resolv+: "bind" is an invalid keyword resolv+:
"hosts" is an invalid keyword
```

configure /compat/linux/etc/host.conf as follows:

```
order hosts, bind
multi on
```

This specifies that /etc/hosts is searched first and DNS is searched second. When /compat/linux/etc/host.conf does not exist, Linux® applications use /etc/host.conf and complain about the incompatible Free-BSD syntax. Remove bind if a name server is not configured using /etc/resolv.conf .

10.3. Advanced Topics

This section describes how Linux® binary compatibility works and is based on an email written to Free-BSD chat mailing list by Terry Lambert <tlambert@primenet.com> (Message ID: <199906020108.SAA07001@us-r09.primenet.com>).

FreeBSD has an abstraction called an "execution class loader". This is a wedge into the execve(2) system call.

Historically, the UNIX® loader examined the magic number (generally the first 4 or 8 bytes of the file) to see if it was a binary known to the system, and if so, invoked the binary loader.

If it was not the binary type for the system, the execve(2) call returned a failure, and the shell attempted to start executing it as shell commands. The assumption was a default of "whatever the current shell is".

Later, a hack was made for sh(1) to examine the first two characters, and if they were :\n, it invoked the csh(1) shell instead.

FreeBSD has a list of loaders, instead of a single loader, with a fallback to the #! loader for running shell interpreters or shell scripts.

For the Linux® ABI support, FreeBSD sees the magic number as an ELF binary. The ELF loader looks for a specialized *brand*, which is a comment section in the ELF image, and which is not present on SVR4/Solaris™ ELF binaries.

For Linux® binaries to function, they must be *branded* as type Linux using brandelf(1):

```
# brandelf -t Linux file
```

When the ELF loader sees the Linux brand, the loader replaces a pointer in the proc structure. All system calls are indexed through this pointer. In addition, the process is flagged for special handling of the trap vector for the signal trampoline code, and several other (minor) fix-ups that are handled by the Linux® kernel module.

The Linux® system call vector contains, among other things, a list of sysent[] entries whose addresses reside in the kernel module.

When a system call is called by the Linux® binary, the trap code dereferences the system call function pointer off the proc structure, and gets the Linux®, not the FreeBSD, system call entry points.

Linux® mode dynamically *reroots* lookups. This is, in effect, equivalent to the union option to file system mounts. First, an attempt is made to lookup the file in /compat/linux/*original-path*. If that fails, the lookup is done in /*original-path*. This makes sure that binaries that require other binaries can run. For example, the Linux® toolchain can all run under Linux® ABI support. It also means that the Linux® binaries can load and execute FreeBSD binaries, if there are no corresponding Linux® binaries present, and that a uname(1) command can be placed in the /compat/linux directory tree to ensure that the Linux® binaries cannot tell they are not running on Linux®.

In effect, there is a Linux® kernel in the FreeBSD kernel. The various underlying functions that implement all of the services provided by the kernel are identical to both the FreeBSD system call table entries, and the Linux® system call table entries: file system operations, virtual memory operations, signal delivery, and System V IPC. The only difference is that FreeBSD binaries get the FreeBSD *glue* functions, and Linux® binaries get the Linux® *glue* functions. The FreeBSD *glue* functions are statically linked into the kernel, and the Linux® *glue* functions can be statically linked, or they can be accessed via a kernel module.

Technically, this is not really emulation, it is an ABI implementation. It is sometimes called "Linux® emulation" because the implementation was done at a time when there was no other word to describe what was going on. Saying that FreeBSD ran Linux® binaries was not true, since the code was not compiled in.

Part III. System Administration

The remaining chapters cover all aspects of FreeBSD system administration. Each chapter starts by describing what will be learned as a result of reading the chapter, and also details what the reader is expected to know before tackling the material.

These chapters are designed to be read as the information is needed. They do not need to be read in any particular order, nor must all of them be read before beginning to use FreeBSD.

Table of Contents

Chapter 11. Configuration and Tuning

Written by Chern Lee.
Based on a tutorial written by Mike Smith.
Also based on tuning(7) written by Matt Dillon.

11.1. Synopsis

One of the important aspects of FreeBSD is proper system configuration. This chapter explains much of the FreeBSD configuration process, including some of the parameters which can be set to tune a FreeBSD system.

After reading this chapter, you will know:

- The basics of rc.conf configuration and /usr/local/etc/rc.d startup scripts.

- How to configure and test a network card.

- How to configure virtual hosts on network devices.

- How to use the various configuration files in /etc.

- How to tune FreeBSD using sysctl(8) variables.

- How to tune disk performance and modify kernel limitations.

Before reading this chapter, you should:

- Understand UNIX® and FreeBSD basics (Chapter 3, *FreeBSD Basics*).

- Be familiar with the basics of kernel configuration and compilation (Chapter 8, *Configuring the FreeBSD Kernel*).

11.2. Starting Services

Contributed by Tom Rhodes.

Many users install third party software on FreeBSD from the Ports Collection and require the installed services to be started upon system initialization. Services, such as mail/postfix or www/apache22 are just two of the many software packages which may be started during system initialization. This section explains the procedures available for starting third party software.

In FreeBSD, most included services, such as cron(8), are started through the system startup scripts.

11.2.1. Extended Application Configuration

Now that FreeBSD includes rc.d, configuration of application startup is easier and provides more features. Using the key words discussed in Section 11.4, "Managing Services in FreeBSD", applications can be set to start after certain other services and extra flags can be passed through /etc/rc.conf in place of hard coded flags in the startup script. A basic script may look similar to the following:

```
#!/bin/sh
#
# PROVIDE: utility
# REQUIRE: DAEMON
# KEYWORD: shutdown

. /etc/rc.subr
```

```
name=utility
rcvar=utility_enable

command="/usr/local/sbin/utility"

load_rc_config $name

#
# DO NOT CHANGE THESE DEFAULT VALUES HERE
# SET THEM IN THE /etc/rc.conf FILE
#
utility_enable=${utility_enable-"NO"}
pidfile=${utility_pidfile-"/var/run/utility.pid"}

run_rc_command "$1"
```

This script will ensure that the provided utility will be started after the DAEMON pseudo-service. It also provides a method for setting and tracking the process ID (PID).

This application could then have the following line placed in /etc/rc.conf :

```
utility_enable="YES"
```

This method allows for easier manipulation of command line arguments, inclusion of the default functions provided in /etc/rc.subr , compatibility with rcorder(8), and provides for easier configuration via rc.conf .

11.2.2. Using Services to Start Services

Other services can be started using inetd(8). Working with inetd(8) and its configuration is described in depth in Section 28.2, "The inetd Super-Server".

In some cases, it may make more sense to use cron(8) to start system services. This approach has a number of advantages as cron(8) runs these processes as the owner of the crontab(5). This allows regular users to start and maintain their own applications.

The @reboot feature of cron(8), may be used in place of the time specification. This causes the job to run when cron(8) is started, normally during system initialization.

11.3. Configuring cron(8)

Contributed by Tom Rhodes.

One of the most useful utilities in FreeBSD is cron. This utility runs in the background and regularly checks /etc/crontab for tasks to execute and searches /var/cron/tabs for custom crontab files. These files are used to schedule tasks which cron runs at the specified times. Each entry in a crontab defines a task to run and is known as a *cron job*.

Two different types of configuration files are used: the system crontab, which should not be modified, and user crontabs, which can be created and edited as needed. The format used by these files is documented in crontab(5). The format of the system crontab, /etc/crontab includes a who column which does not exist in user crontabs. In the system crontab, cron runs the command as the user specified in this column. In a user crontab, all commands run as the user who created the crontab.

User crontabs allow individual users to schedule their own tasks. The root user can also have a user crontab which can be used to schedule tasks that do not exist in the system crontab.

Here is a sample entry from the system crontab, /etc/crontab :

```
# /etc/crontab - root's crontab for FreeBSD
#
```

```
# $FreeBSD$
# ❶
SHELL=/bin/sh
PATH=/etc:/bin:/sbin:/usr/bin:/usr/sbin ❷
#
#minute hour mday month wday who command ❸
#
*/5 * * * * root /usr/libexec/atrun ❹
```

❶ Lines that begin with the # character are comments. A comment can be placed in the file as a reminder of what and why a desired action is performed. Comments cannot be on the same line as a command or else they will be interpreted as part of the command; they must be on a new line. Blank lines are ignored.

❷ The equals (=) character is used to define any environment settings. In this example, it is used to define the SHELL and PATH. If the SHELL is omitted, cron will use the default Bourne shell. If the PATH is omitted, the full path must be given to the command or script to run.

❸ This line defines the seven fields used in a system crontab: minute, hour, mday, month, wday, who, and command. The minute field is the time in minutes when the specified command will be run, the hour is the hour when the specified command will be run, the mday is the day of the month, month is the month, and wday is the day of the week. These fields must be numeric values, representing the twenty-four hour clock, or a *, representing all values for that field. The who field only exists in the system crontab and specifies which user the command should be run as. The last field is the command to be executed.

❹ This entry defines the values for this cron job. The */5, followed by several more * characters, specifies that /usr/libexec/atrun is invoked by root every five minutes of every hour, of every day and day of the week, of every month.

Commands can include any number of switches. However, commands which extend to multiple lines need to be broken with the backslash "\" continuation character.

11.3.1. Creating a User Crontab

To create a user crontab, invoke crontab in editor mode:

```
% crontab -e
```

This will open the user's crontab using the default text editor. The first time a user runs this command, it will open an empty file. Once a user creates a crontab, this command will open that file for editing.

It is useful to add these lines to the top of the crontab file in order to set the environment variables and to remember the meanings of the fields in the crontab:

```
SHELL=/bin/sh
PATH=/etc:/bin:/sbin:/usr/bin:/usr/sbin
# Order of crontab fields
# minute hour mday month wday command
```

Then add a line for each command or script to run, specifying the time to run the command. This example runs the specified custom Bourne shell script every day at two in the afternoon. Since the path to the script is not specified in PATH, the full path to the script is given:

```
0 14 * * * /usr/home/dru/bin/mycustomscript.sh
```

Tip

Before using a custom script, make sure it is executable and test it with the limited set of environment variables set by cron. To replicate the environment that would be used to run the above cron entry, use:

```
env -i SHELL=/bin/sh PATH=/etc:/bin:/sbin:/usr/bin:/usr/sbin HOME=/
home/dru LOGNAME=dru /usr/home/dru/bin/mycustomscript.sh
```

> The environment set by cron is discussed in crontab(5). Checking that scripts operate correctly in a cron environment is especially important if they include any commands that delete files using wildcards.

When finished editing the crontab, save the file. It will automatically be installed and cron will read the crontab and run its cron jobs at their specified times. To list the cron jobs in a crontab, use this command:

```
% crontab -l
0 14 * * * /usr/home/dru/bin/mycustomscript.sh
```

To remove all of the cron jobs in a user crontab:

```
% crontab -r
remove crontab for dru? y
```

11.4. Managing Services in FreeBSD

Contributed by Tom Rhodes.

FreeBSD uses the rc(8) system of startup scripts during system initialization and for managing services. The scripts listed in /etc/rc.d provide basic services which can be controlled with the start, stop, and restart options to service(8). For instance, sshd(8) can be restarted with the following command:

```
# service sshd restart
```

This procedure can be used to start services on a running system. Services will be started automatically at boot time as specified in rc.conf(5). For example, to enable natd(8) at system startup, add the following line to /etc/rc.conf :

```
natd_enable="YES"
```

If a natd_enable="NO" line is already present, change the NO to YES. The rc(8) scripts will automatically load any dependent services during the next boot, as described below.

Since the rc(8) system is primarily intended to start and stop services at system startup and shutdown time, the start, stop and restart options will only perform their action if the appropriate /etc/rc.conf variable is set. For instance, sshd restart will only work if sshd_enable is set to YES in /etc/rc.conf . To start, stop or restart a service regardless of the settings in /etc/rc.conf , these commands should be prefixed with "one". For instance, to restart sshd(8) regardless of the current /etc/rc.conf setting, execute the following command:

```
# service sshd onerestart
```

To check if a service is enabled in /etc/rc.conf , run the appropriate rc(8) script with rcvar. This example checks to see if sshd(8) is enabled in /etc/rc.conf :

```
# service sshd rcvar
# sshd
#
sshd_enable="YES"
#   (default: "")
```

Note

The # sshd line is output from the above command, not a root console.

To determine whether or not a service is running, use status. For instance, to verify that sshd(8) is running:

```
# service sshd status
sshd is running as pid 433.
```

In some cases, it is also possible to reload a service. This attempts to send a signal to an individual service, forcing the service to reload its configuration files. In most cases, this means sending the service a SIGHUP signal. Support for this feature is not included for every service.

The rc(8) system is used for network services and it also contributes to most of the system initialization. For instance, when the /etc/rc.d/bgfsck script is executed, it prints out the following message:

```
Starting background file system checks in 60 seconds.
```

This script is used for background file system checks, which occur only during system initialization.

Many system services depend on other services to function properly. For example, yp(8) and other RPC-based services may fail to start until after the rpcbind(8) service has started. To resolve this issue, information about dependencies and other meta-data is included in the comments at the top of each startup script. The rcorder(8) program is used to parse these comments during system initialization to determine the order in which system services should be invoked to satisfy the dependencies.

The following key word must be included in all startup scripts as it is required by rc.subr(8) to "enable" the startup script:

- PROVIDE: Specifies the services this file provides.

The following key words may be included at the top of each startup script. They are not strictly necessary, but are useful as hints to rcorder(8):

- REQUIRE: Lists services which are required for this service. The script containing this key word will run *after* the specified services.

- BEFORE: Lists services which depend on this service. The script containing this key word will run *before* the specified services.

By carefully setting these keywords for each startup script, an administrator has a fine-grained level of control of the startup order of the scripts, without the need for "runlevels" used by some UNIX® operating systems.

Additional information can be found in rc(8) and rc.subr(8). Refer to this article for instructions on how to create custom rc(8) scripts.

11.4.1. Managing System-Specific Configuration

The principal location for system configuration information is /etc/rc.conf. This file contains a wide range of configuration information and it is read at system startup to configure the system. It provides the configuration information for the rc* files.

The entries in /etc/rc.conf override the default settings in /etc/defaults/rc.conf. The file containing the default settings should not be edited. Instead, all system-specific changes should be made to /etc/rc.conf.

A number of strategies may be applied in clustered applications to separate site-wide configuration from system-specific configuration in order to reduce administration overhead. The recommended approach is to place system-specific configuration into /etc/rc.conf.local. For example, these entries in /etc/rc.conf apply to all systems:

```
sshd_enable="YES"
keyrate="fast"
defaultrouter="10.1.1.254"
```

Whereas these entries in /etc/rc.conf.local apply to this system only:

```
hostname="node1.example.org"
ifconfig_fxp0="inet 10.1.1.1/8"
```

Distribute /etc/rc.conf to every system using an application such as rsync or puppet, while /etc/rc.conf.local remains unique.

Upgrading the system will not overwrite /etc/rc.conf , so system configuration information will not be lost.

 Tip

Both /etc/rc.conf and /etc/rc.conf.local are parsed by sh(1). This allows system operators to create complex configuration scenarios. Refer to rc.conf(5) for further information on this topic.

11.5. Setting Up Network Interface Cards

Contributed by Marc Fonvieille.

Adding and configuring a network interface card (NIC) is a common task for any FreeBSD administrator.

11.5.1. Locating the Correct Driver

First, determine the model of the NIC and the chip it uses. FreeBSD supports a wide variety of NICs. Check the Hardware Compatibility List for the FreeBSD release to see if the NIC is supported.

If the NIC is supported, determine the name of the FreeBSD driver for the NIC. Refer to /usr/src/sys/conf/ NOTES and /usr/src/sys/ arch/conf/NOTES for the list of NIC drivers with some information about the supported chipsets. When in doubt, read the manual page of the driver as it will provide more information about the supported hardware and any known limitations of the driver.

The drivers for common NICs are already present in the GENERIC kernel, meaning the NIC should be probed during boot. The system's boot messages can be viewed by typing more /var/run/dmesg.boot and using the spacebar to scroll through the text. In this example, two Ethernet NICs using the dc(4) driver are present on the system:

```
dc0: <82c169 PNIC 10/100BaseTX> port 0xa000-0xa0ff mem 0xd3800000-0xd38
000ff irq 15 at device 11.0 on pci0
miibus0: <MII bus> on dc0
bmtphy0: <BCM5201 10/100baseTX PHY> PHY 1 on miibus0
bmtphy0:  10baseT, 10baseT-FDX, 100baseTX, 100baseTX-FDX, auto
dc0: Ethernet address: 00:a0:cc:da:da:da
dc0: [ITHREAD]
dc1: <82c169 PNIC 10/100BaseTX> port 0x9800-0x98ff mem 0xd3000000-0xd30
000ff irq 11 at device 12.0 on pci0
miibus1: <MII bus> on dc1
bmtphy1: <BCM5201 10/100baseTX PHY> PHY 1 on miibus1
bmtphy1:  10baseT, 10baseT-FDX, 100baseTX, 100baseTX-FDX, auto
dc1: Ethernet address: 00:a0:cc:da:da:db
dc1: [ITHREAD]
```

If the driver for the NIC is not present in GENERIC, but a driver is available, the driver will need to be loaded before the NIC can be configured and used. This may be accomplished in one of two ways:

- The easiest way is to load a kernel module for the NIC using kldload(8). To also automatically load the driver at boot time, add the appropriate line to /boot/loader.conf . Not all NIC drivers are available as modules.

- Alternatively, statically compile support for the NIC into a custom kernel. Refer to /usr/src/sys/conf/NOTES , /usr/src/sys/ arch/conf/NOTES and the manual page of the driver to determine which line to add to the custom kernel configuration file. For more information about recompiling the kernel, refer to Chapter 8, *Configuring the FreeBSD Kernel*. If the NIC was detected at boot, the kernel does not need to be recompiled.

11.5.1.1. Using Windows® NDIS Drivers

Unfortunately, there are still many vendors that do not provide schematics for their drivers to the open source community because they regard such information as trade secrets. Consequently, the developers of FreeBSD and other operating systems are left with two choices: develop the drivers by a long and pain-staking process of reverse engineering or using the existing driver binaries available for Microsoft® Windows® platforms.

FreeBSD provides "native" support for the Network Driver Interface Specification (NDIS). It includes ndisgen(8) which can be used to convert a Windows® XP driver into a format that can be used on FreeBSD. Because the ndis(4) driver uses a Windows® XP binary, it only runs on i386™ and amd64 systems. PCI, CardBus, PCMCIA, and USB devices are supported.

To use ndisgen(8), three things are needed:

1. FreeBSD kernel sources.

2. A Windows® XP driver binary with a .SYS extension.

3. A Windows® XP driver configuration file with a .INF extension.

Download the .SYS and .INF files for the specific NIC. Generally, these can be found on the driver CD or at the vendor's website. The following examples use W32DRIVER.SYS and W32DRIVER.INF .

The driver bit width must match the version of FreeBSD. For FreeBSD/i386, use a Windows® 32-bit driver. For FreeBSD/amd64, a Windows® 64-bit driver is needed.

The next step is to compile the driver binary into a loadable kernel module. As root, use ndisgen(8):

```
# ndisgen /path/to/W32DRIVER.INF /path/to/W32DRIVER.SYS
```

This command is interactive and prompts for any extra information it requires. A new kernel module will be generated in the current directory. Use kldload(8) to load the new module:

```
# kldload ./W32DRIVER_SYS.ko
```

In addition to the generated kernel module, the ndis.ko and if_ndis.ko modules must be loaded. This should happen automatically when any module that depends on ndis(4) is loaded. If not, load them manually, using the following commands:

```
# kldload ndis
# kldload if_ndis
```

The first command loads the ndis(4) miniport driver wrapper and the second loads the generated NIC driver.

Check dmesg(8) to see if there were any load errors. If all went well, the output should be similar to the following:

```
ndis0: <Wireless-G PCI Adapter> mem 0xf4100000-0xf4101fff irq 3 at device 8.0 on pci1
ndis0: NDIS API version: 5.0
ndis0: Ethernet address: 0a:b1:2c:d3:4e:f5
ndis0: 11b rates: 1Mbps 2Mbps 5.5Mbps 11Mbps
ndis0: 11g rates: 6Mbps 9Mbps 12Mbps 18Mbps 36Mbps 48Mbps 54Mbps
```

From here, ndis0 can be configured like any other NIC.

To configure the system to load the ndis(4) modules at boot time, copy the generated module, W32DRIVER_SYS.ko , to /boot/modules . Then, add the following line to /boot/loader.conf :

```
W32DRIVER_SYS_load="YES"
```

11.5.2. Configuring the Network Card

Once the right driver is loaded for the NIC, the card needs to be configured. It may have been configured at installation time by bsdinstall(8).

To display the NIC configuration, enter the following command:

```
% ifconfig
dc0: flags=8843<UP,BROADCAST,RUNNING,SIMPLEX,MULTICAST> metric 0 mtu 1500
        options=80008<VLAN_MTU,LINKSTATE>
        ether 00:a0:cc:da:da:da
        inet 192.168.1.3 netmask 0xffffff00 broadcast 192.168.1.255
        media: Ethernet autoselect (100baseTX <full-duplex>)
        status: active
dc1: flags=8802<UP,BROADCAST,RUNNING,SIMPLEX,MULTICAST> metric 0 mtu 1500
        options=80008<VLAN_MTU,LINKSTATE>
        ether 00:a0:cc:da:da:db
        inet 10.0.0.1 netmask 0xffffff00 broadcast 10.0.0.255
        media: Ethernet 10baseT/UTP
        status: no carrier
lo0: flags=8049<UP,LOOPBACK,RUNNING,MULTICAST> metric 0 mtu 16384
        options=3<RXCSUM,TXCSUM>
        inet6 fe80::1%lo0 prefixlen 64 scopeid 0x4
        inet6 ::1 prefixlen 128
        inet 127.0.0.1 netmask 0xff000000
        nd6 options=3<PERFORMNUD,ACCEPT_RTADV>
```

In this example, the following devices were displayed:

- dc0: The first Ethernet interface.

- dc1: The second Ethernet interface.

- lo0: The loopback device.

FreeBSD uses the driver name followed by the order in which the card is detected at boot to name the NIC. For example, sis2 is the third NIC on the system using the sis(4) driver.

In this example, dc0 is up and running. The key indicators are:

1. UP means that the card is configured and ready.

2. The card has an Internet (inet) address, 192.168.1.3 .

3. It has a valid subnet mask (netmask), where 0xffffff00 is the same as 255.255.255.0 .

4. It has a valid broadcast address, 192.168.1.255 .

5. The MAC address of the card (ether) is 00:a0:cc:da:da:da.

6. The physical media selection is on autoselection mode (media: Ethernet autoselect (100baseTX <full-duplex>)). In this example, dc1 is configured to run with 10baseT/UTP media. For more information on available media types for a driver, refer to its manual page.

7. The status of the link (status) is active, indicating that the carrier signal is detected. For dc1, the status: no carrier status is normal when an Ethernet cable is not plugged into the card.

If the ifconfig(8) output had shown something similar to:

```
dc0: flags=8843<BROADCAST,SIMPLEX,MULTICAST> metric 0 mtu 1500
 options=80008<VLAN_MTU,LINKSTATE>
 ether 00:a0:cc:da:da:da
 media: Ethernet autoselect (100baseTX <full-duplex>)
 status: active
```

it would indicate the card has not been configured.

The card must be configured as root. The NIC configuration can be performed from the command line with ifconfig(8) but will not persist after a reboot unless the configuration is also added to /etc/rc.conf . If a DHCP server is present on the LAN, just add this line:

```
ifconfig_dc0="DHCP"
```

Replace *dc0* with the correct value for the system.

The line added, then, follow the instructions given in Section 11.5.3, "Testing and Troubleshooting".

Note

If the network was configured during installation, some entries for the NIC(s) may be already present. Double check /etc/rc.conf before adding any lines.

In the case, there is no DHCP server, the NIC(s) have to be configured manually. Add a line for each NIC present on the system, as seen in this example:

```
ifconfig_dc0="inet 192.168.1.3 netmask 255.255.255.0"
ifconfig_dc1="inet 10.0.0.1 netmask 255.255.255.0 media 10baseT/UTP"
```

Replace dc0 and dc1 and the IP address information with the correct values for the system. Refer to the man page for the driver, ifconfig(8), and rc.conf(5) for more details about the allowed options and the syntax of /etc/rc.conf.

If the network is not using DNS, edit /etc/hosts to add the names and IP addresses of the hosts on the LAN, if they are not already there. For more information, refer to hosts(5) and to /usr/share/examples/etc/hosts .

Note

If there is no DHCP server and access to the Internet is needed, manually configure the default gateway and the nameserver:

```
# echo 'defaultrouter=" your_default_router "' >> /etc/rc.conf
# echo 'nameserver your_DNS_server ' >> /etc/resolv.conf
```

11.5.3. Testing and Troubleshooting

Once the necessary changes to /etc/rc.conf are saved, a reboot can be used to test the network configuration and to verify that the system restarts without any configuration errors. Alternatively, apply the settings to the networking system with this command:

```
# service netif restart
```

Note

If a default gateway has been set in /etc/rc.conf , also issue this command:

```
# service routing restart
```

Once the networking system has been relaunched, test the NICs.

11.5.3.1. Testing the Ethernet Card

To verify that an Ethernet card is configured correctly, ping(8) the interface itself, and then ping(8) another machine on the LAN:

```
% ping -c5 192.168.1.3
PING 192.168.1.3 (192.168.1.3): 56 data bytes
64 bytes from 192.168.1.3: icmp_seq=0 ttl=64 time=0.082 ms
64 bytes from 192.168.1.3: icmp_seq=1 ttl=64 time=0.074 ms
64 bytes from 192.168.1.3: icmp_seq=2 ttl=64 time=0.076 ms
64 bytes from 192.168.1.3: icmp_seq=3 ttl=64 time=0.108 ms
64 bytes from 192.168.1.3: icmp_seq=4 ttl=64 time=0.076 ms

--- 192.168.1.3 ping statistics ---
5 packets transmitted, 5 packets received, 0% packet loss
round-trip min/avg/max/stddev = 0.074/0.083/0.108/0.013 ms

% ping -c5 192.168.1.2
PING 192.168.1.2 (192.168.1.2): 56 data bytes
64 bytes from 192.168.1.2: icmp_seq=0 ttl=64 time=0.726 ms
64 bytes from 192.168.1.2: icmp_seq=1 ttl=64 time=0.766 ms
64 bytes from 192.168.1.2: icmp_seq=2 ttl=64 time=0.700 ms
64 bytes from 192.168.1.2: icmp_seq=3 ttl=64 time=0.747 ms
64 bytes from 192.168.1.2: icmp_seq=4 ttl=64 time=0.704 ms

--- 192.168.1.2 ping statistics ---
5 packets transmitted, 5 packets received, 0% packet loss
round-trip min/avg/max/stddev = 0.700/0.729/0.766/0.025 ms
```

To test network resolution, use the host name instead of the IP address. If there is no DNS server on the network, /etc/hosts must first be configured. To this purpose, edit /etc/hosts to add the names and IP addresses of the hosts on the LAN, if they are not already there. For more information, refer to hosts(5) and to /usr/share/examples/etc/hosts .

11.5.3.2. Troubleshooting

When troubleshooting hardware and software configurations, check the simple things first. Is the network cable plugged in? Are the network services properly configured? Is the firewall configured correctly? Is the NIC supported by FreeBSD? Before sending a bug report, always check the Hardware Notes, update the version of FreeBSD to the latest STABLE version, check the mailing list archives, and search the Internet.

If the card works, yet performance is poor, read through tuning(7). Also, check the network configuration as incorrect network settings can cause slow connections.

Some users experience one or two device timeout messages, which is normal for some cards. If they continue, or are bothersome, determine if the device is conflicting with another device. Double check the cable connections. Consider trying another card.

To resolve watchdog timeout errors, first check the network cable. Many cards require a PCI slot which supports bus mastering. On some old motherboards, only one PCI slot allows it, usually slot 0. Check the NIC and the motherboard documentation to determine if that may be the problem.

No route to host messages occur if the system is unable to route a packet to the destination host. This can happen if no default route is specified or if a cable is unplugged. Check the output of netstat -rn and make sure there is a valid route to the host. If there is not, read Section 30.2, "Gateways and Routes".

ping: sendto: Permission denied error messages are often caused by a misconfigured firewall. If a firewall is enabled on FreeBSD but no rules have been defined, the default policy is to deny all traffic, even ping(8). Refer to Chapter 29, Firewalls for more information.

Sometimes performance of the card is poor or below average. In these cases, try setting the media selection mode from autoselect to the correct media selection. While this works for most hardware, it may or may not resolve the issue. Again, check all the network settings, and refer to tuning(7).

11.6. Virtual Hosts

A common use of FreeBSD is virtual site hosting, where one server appears to the network as many servers. This is achieved by assigning multiple network addresses to a single interface.

A given network interface has one "real" address, and may have any number of "alias" addresses. These aliases are normally added by placing alias entries in /etc/rc.conf , as seen in this example:

```
ifconfig_fxp0_alias0="inet xxx.xxx.xxx.xxx netmask xxx.xxx.xxx.xxx"
```

Alias entries must start with alias 0 using a sequential number such as alias0 , alias1 , and so on. The configuration process will stop at the first missing number.

The calculation of alias netmasks is important. For a given interface, there must be one address which correctly represents the network's netmask. Any other addresses which fall within this network must have a netmask of all 1s, expressed as either 255.255.255.255 or 0xffffffff .

For example, consider the case where the fxp0 interface is connected to two networks: 10.1.1.0 with a netmask of 255.255.255.0 and 202.0.75.16 with a netmask of 255.255.255.240 . The system is to be configured to appear in the ranges 10.1.1.1 through 10.1.1.5 and 202.0.75.17 through 202.0.75.20 . Only the first address in a given network range should have a real netmask. All the rest (10.1.1.2 through 10.1.1.5 and 202.0.75.18 through 202.0.75.20) must be configured with a netmask of 255.255.255.255 .

The following /etc/rc.conf entries configure the adapter correctly for this scenario:

```
ifconfig_fxp0="inet 10.1.1.1 netmask 255.255.255.0"
ifconfig_fxp0_alias0="inet 10.1.1.2 netmask 255.255.255.255"
ifconfig_fxp0_alias1="inet 10.1.1.3 netmask 255.255.255.255"
ifconfig_fxp0_alias2="inet 10.1.1.4 netmask 255.255.255.255"
ifconfig_fxp0_alias3="inet 10.1.1.5 netmask 255.255.255.255"
ifconfig_fxp0_alias4="inet 202.0.75.17 netmask 255.255.255.240"
ifconfig_fxp0_alias5="inet 202.0.75.18 netmask 255.255.255.255"
ifconfig_fxp0_alias6="inet 202.0.75.19 netmask 255.255.255.255"
ifconfig_fxp0_alias7="inet 202.0.75.20 netmask 255.255.255.255"
```

A simpler way to express this is with a space-separated list of IP address ranges. The first address will be given the indicated subnet mask and the additional addresses will have a subnet mask of 255.255.255.255 .

```
ifconfig_fxp0_aliases="inet 10.1.1.1-5/24 inet 202.0.75.17-20/28"
```

11.7. Configuring System Logging

Contributed by Niclas Zeising.

Generating and reading system logs is an important aspect of system administration. The information in system logs can be used to detect hardware and software issues as well as application and system configuration errors. This information also plays an important role in security auditing and incident response. Most system daemons and applications will generate log entries.

FreeBSD provides a system logger, syslogd, to manage logging. By default, syslogd is started when the system boots. This is controlled by the variable syslogd_enable in /etc/rc.conf . There are numerous application arguments that can be set using syslogd_flags in /etc/rc.conf . Refer to syslogd(8) for more information on the available arguments.

This section describes how to configure the FreeBSD system logger for both local and remote logging and how to perform log rotation and log management.

11.7.1. Configuring Local Logging

The configuration file, /etc/syslog.conf , controls what syslogd does with log entries as they are received. There are several parameters to control the handling of incoming events. The *facility* describes which subsystem generated the message, such as the kernel or a daemon, and the *level* describes the severity of the event that occurred. This makes it possible to configure if and where a log message is logged, depending on the facility and level. It is also possible to take action depending on the application that sent the message, and in the case of remote logging, the hostname of the machine generating the logging event.

This configuration file contains one line per action, where the syntax for each line is a selector field followed by an action field. The syntax of the selector field is *facility.level* which will match log messages from *facility* at level *level* or higher. It is also possible to add an optional comparison flag before the level to specify more precisely what is logged. Multiple selector fields can be used for the same action, and are separated with a semicolon (;). Using * will match everything. The action field denotes where to send the log message, such as to a file or remote log host. As an example, here is the default syslog.conf from FreeBSD:

```
# $FreeBSD$
#
#       Spaces ARE valid field separators in this file. However,
#       other *nix-like systems still insist on using tabs as field
#       separators. If you are sharing this file between systems, you
#       may want to use only tabs as field separators here.
#       Consult the syslog.conf(5) manpage.
*.err;kern.warning;auth.notice;mail.crit                /dev/console
*.notice;authpriv.none;kern.debug;lpr.info;mail.crit;news.err    /var/log/messages
security.*                                              /var/log/security
auth.info;authpriv.info                                 /var/log/auth.log
mail.info                                               /var/log/maillog
lpr.info                                                /var/log/lpd-errs
ftp.info                                                /var/log/xferlog
cron.*                                                  /var/log/cron
!-devd
*.=debug                                                /var/log/debug.log
*.emerg                                                 *
# uncomment this to log all writes to /dev/console to /var/log/console.log
#console.info                                           /var/log/console.log
# uncomment this to enable logging of all log messages to /var/log/all.log
# touch /var/log/all.log and chmod it to mode 600 before it will work
#*.*                                                    /var/log/all.log
# uncomment this to enable logging to a remote loghost named loghost
#*.*                                                    @loghost
# uncomment these if you're running inn
# news.crit                                             /var/log/news/news.crit
# news.err                                              /var/log/news/news.err
# news.notice                                           /var/log/news/news.notice
# Uncomment this if you wish to see messages produced by devd
# !devd
# *.>=info
!ppp
*.*                                                     /var/log/ppp.log
!*
```

In this example:

- Line 8 matches all messages with a level of err or higher, as well as kern.warning, auth.notice and mail.crit, and sends these log messages to the console (/dev/console).

- Line 12 matches all messages from the mail facility at level info or above and logs the messages to /var/log/maillog.

- Line 17 uses a comparison flag (=) to only match messages at level debug and logs them to /var/log/debug.log.

- Line 33 is an example usage of a program specification. This makes the rules following it only valid for the specified program. In this case, only the messages generated by ppp are logged to /var/log/ppp.log.

The available levels, in order from most to least critical are emerg, alert, crit, err, warning, notice, info, and debug.

The facilities, in no particular order, are auth, authpriv, console, cron, daemon, ftp, kern, lpr, mail, mark, news, security, syslog, user, uucp, and local0 through local7. Be aware that other operating systems might have different facilities.

To log everything of level notice and higher to /var/log/daemon.log , add the following entry:

```
daemon.notice                                    /var/log/daemon.log
```

For more information about the different levels and facilities, refer to syslog(3) and syslogd(8). For more information about /etc/syslog.conf , its syntax, and more advanced usage examples, see syslog.conf(5).

11.7.2. Log Management and Rotation

Log files can grow quickly, taking up disk space and making it more difficult to locate useful information. Log management attempts to mitigate this. In FreeBSD, newsyslog is used to manage log files. This built-in program periodically rotates and compresses log files, and optionally creates missing log files and signals programs when log files are moved. The log files may be generated by syslogd or by any other program which generates log files. While newsyslog is normally run from cron(8), it is not a system daemon. In the default configuration, it runs every hour.

To know which actions to take, newsyslog reads its configuration file, /etc/newsyslog.conf . This file contains one line for each log file that newsyslog manages. Each line states the file owner, permissions, when to rotate that file, optional flags that affect log rotation, such as compression, and programs to signal when the log is rotated. Here is the default configuration in FreeBSD:

```
# configuration file for newsyslog
# $FreeBSD$
#
# Entries which do not specify the '/pid_file' field will cause the
# syslogd process to be signalled when that log file is rotated.  This
# action is only appropriate for log files which are written to by the
# syslogd process (ie, files listed in /etc/syslog.conf).  If there
# is no process which needs to be signalled when a given log file is
# rotated, then the entry for that file should include the 'N' flag.
#
# The 'flags' field is one or more of the letters: BCDGJNUXZ or a '-'.
#
# Note: some sites will want to select more restrictive protections than the
# defaults.  In particular, it may be desirable to switch many of the 644
# entries to 640 or 600.  For example, some sites will consider the
# contents of maillog, messages, and lpd-errs to be confidential.  In the
# future, these defaults may change to more conservative ones.
#
# logfilename            [owner:group]    mode count size when  flags [/pid_file] [sig_num]
/var/log/all.log                          600  7     *    @T00  J
/var/log/amd.log                          644  7     100  *     J
/var/log/auth.log                         600  7     100  @0101T JC
/var/log/console.log                      600  5     100  *     J
/var/log/cron                             600  3     100  *     JC
/var/log/daily.log                        640  7     *    @T00  JN
/var/log/debug.log                        600  7     100  *     JC
/var/log/kerberos.log                     600  7     100  *     J
/var/log/lpd-errs                         644  7     100  *     JC
/var/log/maillog                          640  7     *    @T00  JC
/var/log/messages                         644  5     100  @0101T JC
/var/log/monthly.log                      640  12    *    $M1D0 JN
/var/log/pflog                            600  3     100  *     JB   /var/run/pflogd.pid
/var/log/ppp.log         root:network     640  3     100  *     JC
/var/log/devd.log                         644  3     100  *     JC
/var/log/security                         600  10    100  *     JC
/var/log/sendmail.st                      640  10    *    168   B
/var/log/utx.log                          644  3     *    @01T05 B
/var/log/weekly.log                       640  5     1    $W6D0 JN
/var/log/xferlog                          600  7     100  *     JC
```

Each line starts with the name of the log to be rotated, optionally followed by an owner and group for both rotated and newly created files. The mode field sets the permissions on the log file and count denotes how many rotated log files should be kept. The size and when fields tell newsyslog when to rotate the file. A log file is rotated when either its size is larger than the size field or when the time in the when field has passed. An asterisk (*) means that this field is ignored. The *flags* field gives further instructions, such as how to compress the rotated file or to create the log file if it is missing. The last two fields are optional and specify the name of the Process ID (PID) file of a process and a signal number to send to that process when the file is rotated.

For more information on all fields, valid flags, and how to specify the rotation time, refer to newsyslog.conf(5). Since newsyslog is run from cron(8), it cannot rotate files more often than it is scheduled to run from cron(8).

11.7.3. Configuring Remote Logging

Contributed by Tom Rhodes.

Monitoring the log files of multiple hosts can become unwieldy as the number of systems increases. Configuring centralized logging can reduce some of the administrative burden of log file administration.

In FreeBSD, centralized log file aggregation, merging, and rotation can be configured using syslogd and newsyslog. This section demonstrates an example configuration, where host A, named logserv.example.com, will collect logging information for the local network. Host B, named logclient.example.com, will be configured to pass logging information to the logging server.

11.7.3.1. Log Server Configuration

A log server is a system that has been configured to accept logging information from other hosts. Before configuring a log server, check the following:

- If there is a firewall between the logging server and any logging clients, ensure that the firewall ruleset allows UDP port 514 for both the clients and the server.

- The logging server and all client machines must have forward and reverse entries in the local DNS. If the network does not have a DNS server, create entries in each system's /etc/hosts . Proper name resolution is required so that log entries are not rejected by the logging server.

On the log server, edit /etc/syslog.conf to specify the name of the client to receive log entries from, the logging facility to be used, and the name of the log to store the host's log entries. This example adds the hostname of B, logs all facilities, and stores the log entries in /var/log/logclient.log .

Example 11.1. Sample Log Server Configuration

```
+logclient.example.com
*.*        /var/log/logclient.log
```

When adding multiple log clients, add a similar two-line entry for each client. More information about the available facilities may be found in syslog.conf(5).

Next, configure /etc/rc.conf :

```
syslogd_enable="YES"
syslogd_flags="-a logclient.example.com -v -v"
```

The first entry starts syslogd at system boot. The second entry allows log entries from the specified client. The -v -v increases the verbosity of logged messages. This is useful for tweaking facilities as administrators are able to see what type of messages are being logged under each facility.

Multiple `-a` options may be specified to allow logging from multiple clients. IP addresses and whole netblocks may also be specified. Refer to syslogd(8) for a full list of possible options.

Finally, create the log file:

```
# touch /var/log/logclient.log
```

At this point, syslogd should be restarted and verified:

```
# service syslogd restart
# pgrep syslog
```

If a PID is returned, the server restarted successfully, and client configuration can begin. If the server did not restart, consult `/var/log/messages` for the error.

11.7.3.2. Log Client Configuration

A logging client sends log entries to a logging server on the network. The client also keeps a local copy of its own logs.

Once a logging server has been configured, edit `/etc/rc.conf` on the logging client:

```
syslogd_enable="YES"
syslogd_flags="-s -v -v"
```

The first entry enables syslogd on boot up. The second entry prevents logs from being accepted by this client from other hosts (`-s`) and increases the verbosity of logged messages.

Next, define the logging server in the client's `/etc/syslog.conf`. In this example, all logged facilities are sent to a remote system, denoted by the @ symbol, with the specified hostname:

```
*.*    @logserv.example.com
```

After saving the edit, restart syslogd for the changes to take effect:

```
# service syslogd restart
```

To test that log messages are being sent across the network, use logger(1) on the client to send a message to syslogd:

```
# logger "Test message from logclient "
```

This message should now exist both in `/var/log/messages` on the client and `/var/log/logclient.log` on the log server.

11.7.3.3. Debugging Log Servers

If no messages are being received on the log server, the cause is most likely a network connectivity issue, a hostname resolution issue, or a typo in a configuration file. To isolate the cause, ensure that both the logging server and the logging client are able to ping each other using the hostname specified in their `/etc/rc.conf`. If this fails, check the network cabling, the firewall ruleset, and the hostname entries in the DNS server or `/etc/hosts` on both the logging server and clients. Repeat until the ping is successful from both hosts.

If the ping succeeds on both hosts but log messages are still not being received, temporarily increase logging verbosity to narrow down the configuration issue. In the following example, `/var/log/logclient.log` on the logging server is empty and `/var/log/messages` on the logging client does not indicate a reason for the failure. To increase debugging output, edit the `syslogd_flags` entry on the logging server and issue a restart:

```
syslogd_flags="-d -a logclient.example.com -v -v"
```

```
# service syslogd restart
```

Debugging data similar to the following will flash on the console immediately after the restart:

```
logmsg: pri 56, flags 4, from logserv.example.com, msg syslogd: restart
syslogd: restarted
logmsg: pri 6, flags 4, from logserv.example.com, msg syslogd: kernel boot file is /boot/
kernel/kernel
Logging to FILE /var/log/messages
syslogd: kernel boot file is /boot/kernel/kernel
cvthname(192.168.1.10)
validate: dgram from IP 192.168.1.10, port 514, name logclient.example.com;
rejected in rule 0 due to name mismatch.
```

In this example, the log messages are being rejected due to a typo which results in a hostname mismatch. The client's hostname should be logclient, not logclien. Fix the typo, issue a restart, and verify the results:

```
# service syslogd restart
logmsg: pri 56, flags 4, from logserv.example.com, msg syslogd: restart
syslogd: restarted
logmsg: pri 6, flags 4, from logserv.example.com, msg syslogd: kernel boot file is /boot/
kernel/kernel
syslogd: kernel boot file is /boot/kernel/kernel
logmsg: pri 166, flags 17, from logserv.example.com,
msg Dec 10 20:55:02 <syslog.err> logserv.example.com syslogd: exiting on signal 2
cvthname(192.168.1.10)
validate: dgram from IP 192.168.1.10, port 514, name logclient.example.com;
accepted in rule 0.
logmsg: pri 15, flags 0, from logclient.example.com, msg Dec 11 02:01:28 trhodes: Test ↵
message 2
Logging to FILE /var/log/logclient.log
Logging to FILE /var/log/messages
```

At this point, the messages are being properly received and placed in the correct file.

11.7.3.4. Security Considerations

As with any network service, security requirements should be considered before implementing a logging server. Log files may contain sensitive data about services enabled on the local host, user accounts, and configuration data. Network data sent from the client to the server will not be encrypted or password protected. If a need for encryption exists, consider using security/stunnel, which will transmit the logging data over an encrypted tunnel.

Local security is also an issue. Log files are not encrypted during use or after log rotation. Local users may access log files to gain additional insight into system configuration. Setting proper permissions on log files is critical. The built-in log rotator, newsyslog, supports setting permissions on newly created and rotated log files. Setting log files to mode 600 should prevent unwanted access by local users. Refer to newsyslog.conf(5) for additional information.

11.8. Configuration Files

11.8.1. /etc Layout

There are a number of directories in which configuration information is kept. These include:

/etc	Generic system-specific configuration information.
/etc/defaults	Default versions of system configuration files.
/etc/mail	Extra sendmail(8) configuration and other MTA configuration files.
/etc/ppp	Configuration for both user- and kernel-ppp programs.
/usr/local/etc	Configuration files for installed applications. May contain per-application subdirectories.
/usr/local/etc/rc.d	rc(8) scripts for installed applications.
/var/db	Automatically generated system-specific database files, such as the package database and the locate(1) database.

11.8.2. Hostnames

11.8.2.1. `/etc/resolv.conf`

How a FreeBSD system accesses the Internet Domain Name System (DNS) is controlled by resolv.conf(5).

The most common entries to /etc/resolv.conf are:

nameserver	The IP address of a name server the resolver should query. The servers are queried in the order listed with a maximum of three.
search	Search list for hostname lookup. This is normally determined by the domain of the local hostname.
domain	The local domain name.

A typical /etc/resolv.conf looks like this:

```
search example.com
nameserver 147.11.1.11
nameserver 147.11.100.30
```

> **Note**
>
> Only one of the search and domain options should be used.

When using DHCP, dhclient(8) usually rewrites /etc/resolv.conf with information received from the DHCP server.

11.8.2.2. `/etc/hosts`

/etc/hosts is a simple text database which works in conjunction with DNS and NIS to provide host name to IP address mappings. Entries for local computers connected via a LAN can be added to this file for simplistic naming purposes instead of setting up a named(8) server. Additionally, /etc/hosts can be used to provide a local record of Internet names, reducing the need to query external DNS servers for commonly accessed names.

```
# $FreeBSD$
#
#
# Host Database
#
# This file should contain the addresses and aliases for local hosts that
# share this file.  Replace 'my.domain' below with the domainname of your
# machine.
#
# In the presence of the domain name service or NIS, this file may
# not be consulted at all; see /etc/nsswitch.conf for the resolution order.
#
#
::1    localhost localhost.my.domain
127.0.0.1  localhost localhost.my.domain
#
# Imaginary network.
#10.0.0.2  myname.my.domain myname
#10.0.0.3  myfriend.my.domain myfriend
#
# According to RFC 1918, you can use the following IP networks for
# private nets which will never be connected to the Internet:
#
```

```
# 10.0.0.0 -   10.255.255.255
# 172.16.0.0 -  172.31.255.255
# 192.168.0.0 -  192.168.255.255
#
# In case you want to be able to connect to the Internet, you need
# real official assigned numbers.  Do not try to invent your own network
# numbers but instead get one from your network provider (if any) or
# from your regional registry (ARIN, APNIC, LACNIC, RIPE NCC, or AfriNIC.)
#
```

The format of /etc/hosts is as follows:

```
[Internet address] [official hostname] [alias1] [alias2] ...
```

For example:

```
10.0.0.1 myRealHostname.example.com myRealHostname foobar1 foobar2
```

Consult hosts(5) for more information.

11.9. Tuning with sysctl(8)

sysctl(8) is used to make changes to a running FreeBSD system. This includes many advanced options of the TCP/IP stack and virtual memory system that can dramatically improve performance for an experienced system administrator. Over five hundred system variables can be read and set using sysctl(8).

At its core, sysctl(8) serves two functions: to read and to modify system settings.

To view all readable variables:

```
% sysctl -a
```

To read a particular variable, specify its name:

```
% sysctl kern.maxproc
kern.maxproc: 1044
```

To set a particular variable, use the *variable=value* syntax:

```
# sysctl kern.maxfiles=5000
kern.maxfiles: 2088 -> 5000
```

Settings of sysctl variables are usually either strings, numbers, or booleans, where a boolean is 1 for yes or 0 for no.

To automatically set some variables each time the machine boots, add them to /etc/sysctl.conf . For more information, refer to sysctl.conf(5) and Section 11.9.1, "sysctl.conf".

11.9.1. sysctl.conf

The configuration file for sysctl(8), /etc/sysctl.conf , looks much like /etc/rc.conf . Values are set in a variable=value form. The specified values are set after the system goes into multi-user mode. Not all variables are settable in this mode.

For example, to turn off logging of fatal signal exits and prevent users from seeing processes started by other users, the following tunables can be set in /etc/sysctl.conf :

```
# Do not log fatal signal exits (e.g., sig 11)
kern.logsigexit=0
```

```
# Prevent users from seeing information about processes that
# are being run under another UID.
security.bsd.see_other_uids=0
```

11.9.2. sysctl(8) Read-only

Contributed by Tom Rhodes.

In some cases it may be desirable to modify read-only sysctl(8) values, which will require a reboot of the system.

For instance, on some laptop models the cardbus(4) device will not probe memory ranges and will fail with errors similar to:

```
cbb0: Could not map register memory
device_probe_and_attach: cbb0 attach returned 12
```

The fix requires the modification of a read-only sysctl(8) setting. Add hw.pci.allow_unsupported_io_range=1 to /boot/loader.conf and reboot. Now cardbus(4) should work properly.

11.10. Tuning Disks

The following section will discuss various tuning mechanisms and options which may be applied to disk devices. In many cases, disks with mechanical parts, such as SCSI drives, will be the bottleneck driving down the overall system performance. While a solution is to install a drive without mechanical parts, such as a solid state drive, mechanical drives are not going away anytime in the near future. When tuning disks, it is advisable to utilize the features of the iostat(8) command to test various changes to the system. This command will allow the user to obtain valuable information on system IO.

11.10.1. Sysctl Variables

11.10.1.1. vfs.vmiodirenable

The vfs.vmiodirenable sysctl(8) variable may be set to either 0 (off) or 1 (on). It is set to 1 by default. This variable controls how directories are cached by the system. Most directories are small, using just a single fragment (typically 1 K) in the file system and typically 512 bytes in the buffer cache. With this variable turned off, the buffer cache will only cache a fixed number of directories, even if the system has a huge amount of memory. When turned on, this sysctl(8) allows the buffer cache to use the VM page cache to cache the directories, making all the memory available for caching directories. However, the minimum in-core memory used to cache a directory is the physical page size (typically 4 K) rather than 512 bytes. Keeping this option enabled is recommended if the system is running any services which manipulate large numbers of files. Such services can include web caches, large mail systems, and news systems. Keeping this option on will generally not reduce performance, even with the wasted memory, but one should experiment to find out.

11.10.1.2. vfs.write_behind

The vfs.write_behind sysctl(8) variable defaults to 1 (on). This tells the file system to issue media writes as full clusters are collected, which typically occurs when writing large sequential files. This avoids saturating the buffer cache with dirty buffers when it would not benefit I/O performance. However, this may stall processes and under certain circumstances should be turned off.

11.10.1.3. vfs.hirunningspace

The vfs.hirunningspace sysctl(8) variable determines how much outstanding write I/O may be queued to disk controllers system-wide at any given instance. The default is usually sufficient, but on machines with many disks, try bumping it up to four or five *megabytes*. Setting too high a value which exceeds the buffer cache's write threshold can lead to bad clustering performance. Do not set this value arbitrarily high as higher write values may add latency to reads occurring at the same time.

There are various other buffer cache and VM page cache related sysctl(8) values. Modifying these values is not recommended as the VM system does a good job of automatically tuning itself.

11.10.1.4. vm.swap_idle_enabled

The vm.swap_idle_enabled sysctl(8) variable is useful in large multi-user systems with many active login users and lots of idle processes. Such systems tend to generate continuous pressure on free memory reserves. Turning this feature on and tweaking the swapout hysteresis (in idle seconds) via vm.swap_idle_threshold1 and vm.swap_idle_threshold2 depresses the priority of memory pages associated with idle processes more quickly then the normal pageout algorithm. This gives a helping hand to the pageout daemon. Only turn this option on if needed, because the tradeoff is essentially pre-page memory sooner rather than later which eats more swap and disk bandwidth. In a small system this option will have a determinable effect, but in a large system that is already doing moderate paging, this option allows the VM system to stage whole processes into and out of memory easily.

11.10.1.5. hw.ata.wc

Turning off IDE write caching reduces write bandwidth to IDE disks, but may sometimes be necessary due to data consistency issues introduced by hard drive vendors. The problem is that some IDE drives lie about when a write completes. With IDE write caching turned on, IDE hard drives write data to disk out of order and will sometimes delay writing some blocks indefinitely when under heavy disk load. A crash or power failure may cause serious file system corruption. Check the default on the system by observing the hw.ata.wc sysctl(8) variable. If IDE write caching is turned off, one can set this read-only variable to 1 in /boot/loader.conf in order to enable it at boot time.

For more information, refer to ata(4).

11.10.1.6. SCSI_DELAY (kern.cam.scsi_delay)

The SCSI_DELAY kernel configuration option may be used to reduce system boot times. The defaults are fairly high and can be responsible for 15 seconds of delay in the boot process. Reducing it to 5 seconds usually works with modern drives. The kern.cam.scsi_delay boot time tunable should be used. The tunable and kernel configuration option accept values in terms of *milliseconds* and *not seconds*.

11.10.2. Soft Updates

To fine-tune a file system, use tunefs(8). This program has many different options. To toggle Soft Updates on and off, use:

```
# tunefs -n enable /filesystem
# tunefs -n disable /filesystem
```

A file system cannot be modified with tunefs(8) while it is mounted. A good time to enable Soft Updates is before any partitions have been mounted, in single-user mode.

Soft Updates is recommended for UFS file systems as it drastically improves meta-data performance, mainly file creation and deletion, through the use of a memory cache. There are two downsides to Soft Updates to be aware of. First, Soft Updates guarantee file system consistency in the case of a crash, but could easily be several seconds or even a minute behind updating the physical disk. If the system crashes, unwritten data may be lost. Secondly, Soft Updates delay the freeing of file system blocks. If the root file system is almost full, performing a major update, such as make installworld, can cause the file system to run out of space and the update to fail.

11.10.2.1. More Details About Soft Updates

Meta-data updates are updates to non-content data like inodes or directories. There are two traditional approaches to writing a file system's meta-data back to disk.

Historically, the default behavior was to write out meta-data updates synchronously. If a directory changed, the system waited until the change was actually written to disk. The file data buffers (file contents) were passed through the buffer cache and backed up to disk later on asynchronously. The advantage of this implementation is that it operates safely. If there is a failure during an update, meta-data is always in a consistent state. A file is either created completely or not at all. If the data blocks of a file did not find their way out of the buffer cache onto the disk by the time of the crash, fsck(8) recognizes this and repairs the file system by setting the file length to 0. Additionally, the implementation is clear and simple. The disadvantage is that meta-data changes are slow. For example, rm -r touches all the files in a directory sequentially, but each directory change will be written synchronously to the disk. This includes updates to the directory itself, to the inode table, and possibly to indirect blocks allocated by the file. Similar considerations apply for unrolling large hierarchies using tar -x.

The second approach is to use asynchronous meta-data updates. This is the default for a UFS file system mounted with mount -o async. Since all meta-data updates are also passed through the buffer cache, they will be intermixed with the updates of the file content data. The advantage of this implementation is there is no need to wait until each meta-data update has been written to disk, so all operations which cause huge amounts of meta-data updates work much faster than in the synchronous case. This implementation is still clear and simple, so there is a low risk for bugs creeping into the code. The disadvantage is that there is no guarantee for a consistent state of the file system. If there is a failure during an operation that updated large amounts of meta-data, like a power failure or someone pressing the reset button, the file system will be left in an unpredictable state. There is no opportunity to examine the state of the file system when the system comes up again as the data blocks of a file could already have been written to the disk while the updates of the inode table or the associated directory were not. It is impossible to implement a fsck(8) which is able to clean up the resulting chaos because the necessary information is not available on the disk. If the file system has been damaged beyond repair, the only choice is to reformat it and restore from backup.

The usual solution for this problem is to implement *dirty region logging*, which is also referred to as *journaling*. Meta-data updates are still written synchronously, but only into a small region of the disk. Later on, they are moved to their proper location. Because the logging area is a small, contiguous region on the disk, there are no long distances for the disk heads to move, even during heavy operations, so these operations are quicker than synchronous updates. Additionally, the complexity of the implementation is limited, so the risk of bugs being present is low. A disadvantage is that all meta-data is written twice, once into the logging region and once to the proper location, so performance "pessimization" might result. On the other hand, in case of a crash, all pending meta-data operations can be either quickly rolled back or completed from the logging area after the system comes up again, resulting in a fast file system startup.

Kirk McKusick, the developer of Berkeley FFS, solved this problem with Soft Updates. All pending meta-data updates are kept in memory and written out to disk in a sorted sequence ("ordered meta-data updates"). This has the effect that, in case of heavy meta-data operations, later updates to an item "catch" the earlier ones which are still in memory and have not already been written to disk. All operations are generally performed in memory before the update is written to disk and the data blocks are sorted according to their position so that they will not be on the disk ahead of their meta-data. If the system crashes, an implicit "log rewind" causes all operations which were not written to the disk appear as if they never happened. A consistent file system state is maintained that appears to be the one of 30 to 60 seconds earlier. The algorithm used guarantees that all resources in use are marked as such in their blocks and inodes. After a crash, the only resource allocation error that occurs is that resources are marked as "used" which are actually "free". fsck(8) recognizes this situation, and frees the resources that are no longer used. It is safe to ignore the dirty state of the file system after a crash by forcibly mounting it with mount -f. In order to free resources that may be unused, fsck(8) needs to be run at a later time. This is the idea behind the *background* fsck(8): at system startup time, only a *snapshot* of the file system is recorded and fsck(8) is run afterwards. All file systems can then be mounted "dirty", so the system startup proceeds in multi-user mode. Then, background fsck(8) is scheduled for all file systems where this is required, to free resources that may be unused. File systems that do not use Soft Updates still need the usual foreground fsck(8).

The advantage is that meta-data operations are nearly as fast as asynchronous updates and are faster than *logging*, which has to write the meta-data twice. The disadvantages are the complexity of the code, a higher memory consumption, and some idiosyncrasies. After a crash, the state of the file system appears to be somewhat "older". In situations where the standard synchronous approach would have caused some zero-length files to remain after the fsck(8), these files do not exist at all with Soft Updates because neither the meta-data nor the file contents have been written to disk. Disk space is not released until the updates have been written to disk, which may take place some time after running rm(1). This may cause problems when installing large amounts of data on a file system that does not have enough free space to hold all the files twice.

11.11. Tuning Kernel Limits

11.11.1. File/Process Limits

11.11.1.1. `kern.maxfiles`

The `kern.maxfiles` sysctl(8) variable can be raised or lowered based upon system requirements. This variable indicates the maximum number of file descriptors on the system. When the file descriptor table is full, file: table is full will show up repeatedly in the system message buffer, which can be viewed using dmesg(8).

Each open file, socket, or fifo uses one file descriptor. A large-scale production server may easily require many thousands of file descriptors, depending on the kind and number of services running concurrently.

In older FreeBSD releases, the default value of `kern.maxfiles` is derived from `maxusers` in the kernel configuration file. `kern.maxfiles` grows proportionally to the value of `maxusers`. When compiling a custom kernel, consider setting this kernel configuration option according to the use of the system. From this number, the kernel is given most of its pre-defined limits. Even though a production machine may not have 256 concurrent users, the resources needed may be similar to a high-scale web server.

The read-only sysctl(8) variable `kern.maxusers` is automatically sized at boot based on the amount of memory available in the system, and may be determined at run-time by inspecting the value of `kern.maxusers`. Some systems require larger or smaller values of `kern.maxusers` and values of 64, 128, and 256 are not uncommon. Going above 256 is not recommended unless a huge number of file descriptors is needed. Many of the tunable values set to their defaults by `kern.maxusers` may be individually overridden at boot-time or run-time in /boot/loader.conf. Refer to loader.conf(5) and /boot/defaults/loader.conf for more details and some hints.

In older releases, the system will auto-tune `maxusers` if it is set to 0.[1] When setting this option, set `maxusers` to at least 4, especially if the system runs Xorg or is used to compile software. The most important table set by `maxusers` is the maximum number of processes, which is set to `20 + 16 * maxusers`. If `maxusers` is set to 1, there can only be 36 simultaneous processes, including the 18 or so that the system starts up at boot time and the 15 or so used by Xorg. Even a simple task like reading a manual page will start up nine processes to filter, decompress, and view it. Setting `maxusers` to 64 allows up to 1044 simultaneous processes, which should be enough for nearly all uses. If, however, the proc table full error is displayed when trying to start another program, or a server is running with a large number of simultaneous users, increase the number and rebuild.

Note

`maxusers` does *not* limit the number of users which can log into the machine. It instead sets various table sizes to reasonable values considering the maximum number of users on the system and how many processes each user will be running.

11.11.1.2. `kern.ipc.soacceptqueue`

The `kern.ipc.soacceptqueue` sysctl(8) variable limits the size of the listen queue for accepting new TCP connections. The default value of 128 is typically too low for robust handling of new connections on a heavily loaded web server. For such environments, it is recommended to increase this value to 1024 or higher. A service such as sendmail(8), or Apache may itself limit the listen queue size, but will often have a directive in its configuration file to adjust the queue size. Large listen queues do a better job of avoiding Denial of Service (DoS) attacks.

---

[1]The auto-tuning algorithm sets `maxusers` equal to the amount of memory in the system, with a minimum of 32, and a maximum of 384.

11.11.2. Network Limits

The `NMBCLUSTERS` kernel configuration option dictates the amount of network Mbufs available to the system. A heavily-trafficked server with a low number of Mbufs will hinder performance. Each cluster represents approximately 2 K of memory, so a value of `1024` represents 2 megabytes of kernel memory reserved for network buffers. A simple calculation can be done to figure out how many are needed. A web server which maxes out at `1000` simultaneous connections where each connection uses a 6 K receive and 16 K send buffer, requires approximately 32 MB worth of network buffers to cover the web server. A good rule of thumb is to multiply by 2, so 2x32 MB / 2 KB = 64 MB / 2 kB = `32768`. Values between `4096` and `32768` are recommended for machines with greater amounts of memory. Never specify an arbitrarily high value for this parameter as it could lead to a boot time crash. To observe network cluster usage, use `-m` with netstat(1).

The `kern.ipc.nmbclusters` loader tunable should be used to tune this at boot time. Only older versions of FreeBSD will require the use of the `NMBCLUSTERS` kernel config(8) option.

For busy servers that make extensive use of the sendfile(2) system call, it may be necessary to increase the number of sendfile(2) buffers via the `NSFBUFS` kernel configuration option or by setting its value in `/boot/loader.conf` (see loader(8) for details). A common indicator that this parameter needs to be adjusted is when processes are seen in the `sfbufa` state. The sysctl(8) variable `kern.ipc.nsfbufs` is read-only. This parameter nominally scales with `kern.maxusers` , however it may be necessary to tune accordingly.

Important

Even though a socket has been marked as non-blocking, calling sendfile(2) on the non-blocking socket may result in the sendfile(2) call blocking until enough `struct sf_buf` 's are made available.

11.11.2.1. `net.inet.ip.portrange.*`

The `net.inet.ip.portrange.*` sysctl(8) variables control the port number ranges automatically bound to TCP and UDP sockets. There are three ranges: a low range, a default range, and a high range. Most network programs use the default range which is controlled by `net.inet.ip.portrange.first` and `net.inet.ip.portrange.last`, which default to `1024` and `5000`, respectively. Bound port ranges are used for outgoing connections and it is possible to run the system out of ports under certain circumstances. This most commonly occurs when running a heavily loaded web proxy. The port range is not an issue when running a server which handles mainly incoming connections, such as a web server, or has a limited number of outgoing connections, such as a mail relay. For situations where there is a shortage of ports, it is recommended to increase `net.inet.ip.portrange.last` modestly. A value of `10000`, `20000` or `30000` may be reasonable. Consider firewall effects when changing the port range. Some firewalls may block large ranges of ports, usually low-numbered ports, and expect systems to use higher ranges of ports for outgoing connections. For this reason, it is not recommended that the value of `net.inet.ip.portrange.first` be lowered.

11.11.2.2. TCP Bandwidth Delay Product

TCP bandwidth delay product limiting can be enabled by setting the `net.inet.tcp.inflight.enable` sysctl(8) variable to 1. This instructs the system to attempt to calculate the bandwidth delay product for each connection and limit the amount of data queued to the network to just the amount required to maintain optimum throughput.

This feature is useful when serving data over modems, Gigabit Ethernet, high speed WAN links, or any other link with a high bandwidth delay product, especially when also using window scaling or when a large send window has been configured. When enabling this option, also set `net.inet.tcp.inflight.debug` to 0 to disable debugging. For production use, setting `net.inet.tcp.inflight.min` to at least `6144` may be beneficial. Setting high minimums may effectively disable bandwidth limiting, depending on the link. The limiting feature reduces the amount of data built up in intermediate route and switch packet queues and reduces the amount of data built up in the local host's interface queue. With fewer queued packets, interactive connections, especially over slow modems, will operate with lower *Round Trip Times.* This feature only effects server side data transmission such as uploading. It has no effect on data reception or downloading.

Adjusting net.inet.tcp.inflight.stab is *not* recommended. This parameter defaults to 20, representing 2 maximal packets added to the bandwidth delay product window calculation. The additional window is required to stabilize the algorithm and improve responsiveness to changing conditions, but it can also result in higher ping(8) times over slow links, though still much lower than without the inflight algorithm. In such cases, try reducing this parameter to 15, 10, or 5 and reducing net.inet.tcp.inflight.min to a value such as 3500 to get the desired effect. Reducing these parameters should be done as a last resort only.

11.11.3. Virtual Memory

11.11.3.1. kern.maxvnodes

A vnode is the internal representation of a file or directory. Increasing the number of vnodes available to the operating system reduces disk I/O. Normally, this is handled by the operating system and does not need to be changed. In some cases where disk I/O is a bottleneck and the system is running out of vnodes, this setting needs to be increased. The amount of inactive and free RAM will need to be taken into account.

To see the current number of vnodes in use:

```
# sysctl vfs.numvnodes
vfs.numvnodes: 91349
```

To see the maximum vnodes:

```
# sysctl kern.maxvnodes
kern.maxvnodes: 100000
```

If the current vnode usage is near the maximum, try increasing kern.maxvnodes by a value of 1000. Keep an eye on the number of vfs.numvnodes. If it climbs up to the maximum again, kern.maxvnodes will need to be increased further. Otherwise, a shift in memory usage as reported by top(1) should be visible and more memory should be active.

11.12. Adding Swap Space

Sometimes a system requires more swap space. This section describes two methods to increase swap space: adding swap to an existing partition or new hard drive, and creating a swap file on an existing partition.

For information on how to encrypt swap space, which options exist, and why it should be done, refer to Section 17.13, "Encrypting Swap".

11.12.1. Swap on a New Hard Drive or Existing Partition

Adding a new hard drive for swap gives better performance than using a partition on an existing drive. Setting up partitions and hard drives is explained in Section 17.2, "Adding Disks" while Section 2.6.1, "Designing the Partition Layout" discusses partition layouts and swap partition size considerations.

Use swapon to add a swap partition to the system. For example:

```
# swapon /dev/ada1s1b
```

Warning

It is possible to use any partition not currently mounted, even if it already contains data. Using swapon on a partition that contains data will overwrite and destroy that data. Make

> sure that the partition to be added as swap is really the intended partition before running `swapon`.

To automatically add this swap partition on boot, add an entry to `/etc/fstab`:

```
/dev/ada1s1b none swap sw 0 0
```

See fstab(5) for an explanation of the entries in `/etc/fstab`. More information about `swapon` can be found in swapon(8).

11.12.2. Creating a Swap File

These examples create a 64M swap file called `/usr/swap0` instead of using a partition.

Using swap files requires that the module needed by md(4) has either been built into the kernel or has been loaded before swap is enabled. See Chapter 8, *Configuring the FreeBSD Kernel* for information about building a custom kernel.

Example 11.2. Creating a Swap File on FreeBSD 10.X and Later

1. Create the swap file:

   ```
   # dd if=/dev/zero of=/usr/swap0 bs=1m count=64
   ```

2. Set the proper permissions on the new file:

   ```
   # chmod 0600 /usr/swap0
   ```

3. Inform the system about the swap file by adding a line to `/etc/fstab`:

   ```
   md99 none swap sw,file=/usr/swap0,late 0 0
   ```

   The md(4) device md99 is used, leaving lower device numbers available for interactive use.

4. Swap space will be added on system startup. To add swap space immediately, use swapon(8):

   ```
   # swapon -aL
   ```

Example 11.3. Creating a Swap File on FreeBSD 9.X and Earlier

1. Create the swap file, `/usr/swap0`:

   ```
   # dd if=/dev/zero of=/usr/swap0 bs=1m count=64
   ```

2. Set the proper permissions on `/usr/swap0`:

   ```
   # chmod 0600 /usr/swap0
   ```

3. Enable the swap file in `/etc/rc.conf`:

   ```
   swapfile="/usr/swap0"   # Set to name of swap file
   ```

4. Swap space will be added on system startup. To enable the swap file immediately, specify a free memory device. Refer to Section 17.9, "Memory Disks" for more information about memory devices.

```
# mdconfig -a -t vnode -f  /usr/swap0  -u 0 && swapon /dev/md 0
```

11.13. Power and Resource Management

Written by Hiten Pandya and Tom Rhodes.

It is important to utilize hardware resources in an efficient manner. Power and resource management allows the operating system to monitor system limits and to possibly provide an alert if the system temperature increases unexpectedly. An early specification for providing power management was the Advanced Power Management (APM) facility. APM controls the power usage of a system based on its activity. However, it was difficult and inflexible for operating systems to manage the power usage and thermal properties of a system. The hardware was managed by the BIOS and the user had limited configurability and visibility into the power management settings. The APM BIOS is supplied by the vendor and is specific to the hardware platform. An APM driver in the operating system mediates access to the APM Software Interface, which allows management of power levels.

There are four major problems in APM. First, power management is done by the vendor-specific BIOS, separate from the operating system. For example, the user can set idle-time values for a hard drive in the APM BIOS so that, when exceeded, the BIOS spins down the hard drive without the consent of the operating system. Second, the APM logic is embedded in the BIOS, and it operates outside the scope of the operating system. This means that users can only fix problems in the APM BIOS by flashing a new one into the ROM, which is a dangerous procedure with the potential to leave the system in an unrecoverable state if it fails. Third, APM is a vendor-specific technology, meaning that there is a lot of duplication of efforts and bugs found in one vendor's BIOS may not be solved in others. Lastly, the APM BIOS did not have enough room to implement a sophisticated power policy or one that can adapt well to the purpose of the machine.

The Plug and Play BIOS (PNPBIOS) was unreliable in many situations. PNPBIOS is 16-bit technology, so the operating system has to use 16-bit emulation in order to interface with PNPBIOS methods. FreeBSD provides an APM driver as APM should still be used for systems manufactured at or before the year 2000. The driver is documented in apm(4).

The successor to APM is the Advanced Configuration and Power Interface (ACPI). ACPI is a standard written by an alliance of vendors to provide an interface for hardware resources and power management. It is a key element in *Operating System-directed configuration and Power Management* as it provides more control and flexibility to the operating system.

This chapter demonstrates how to configure ACPI on FreeBSD. It then offers some tips on how to debug ACPI and how to submit a problem report containing debugging information so that developers can diagnosis and fix ACPI issues.

11.13.1. Configuring ACPI

In FreeBSD the acpi(4) driver is loaded by default at system boot and should *not* be compiled into the kernel. This driver cannot be unloaded after boot because the system bus uses it for various hardware interactions. However, if the system is experiencing problems, ACPI can be disabled altogether by rebooting after setting hint.acpi.0.disabled="1" in /boot/loader.conf or by setting this variable at the loader prompt, as described in Section 12.2.3, "Stage Three".

Note

ACPI and APM cannot coexist and should be used separately. The last one to load will terminate if the driver notices the other is running.

ACPI can be used to put the system into a sleep mode with `acpiconf`, the `-s` flag, and a number from 1 to 5. Most users only need 1 (quick suspend to RAM) or 3 (suspend to RAM). Option 5 performs a soft-off which is the same as running `halt -p`.

Other options are available using `sysctl`. Refer to acpi(4) and acpiconf(8) for more information.

11.13.2. Common Problems

ACPI is present in all modern computers that conform to the ia32 (x86), ia64 (Itanium), and amd64 (AMD) architectures. The full standard has many features including CPU performance management, power planes control, thermal zones, various battery systems, embedded controllers, and bus enumeration. Most systems implement less than the full standard. For instance, a desktop system usually only implements bus enumeration while a laptop might have cooling and battery management support as well. Laptops also have suspend and resume, with their own associated complexity.

An ACPI-compliant system has various components. The BIOS and chipset vendors provide various fixed tables, such as FADT, in memory that specify things like the APIC map (used for SMP), config registers, and simple configuration values. Additionally, a bytecode table, the Differentiated System Description Table DSDT, specifies a tree-like name space of devices and methods.

The ACPI driver must parse the fixed tables, implement an interpreter for the bytecode, and modify device drivers and the kernel to accept information from the ACPI subsystem. For FreeBSD, Intel® has provided an interpreter (ACPI-CA) that is shared with Linux® and NetBSD. The path to the ACPI-CA source code is `src/sys/contrib/dev/acpica`. The glue code that allows ACPI-CA to work on FreeBSD is in `src/sys/dev/acpica/Osd`. Finally, drivers that implement various ACPI devices are found in `src/sys/dev/acpica`.

For ACPI to work correctly, all the parts have to work correctly. Here are some common problems, in order of frequency of appearance, and some possible workarounds or fixes. If a fix does not resolve the issue, refer to Section 11.13.4, "Getting and Submitting Debugging Info" for instructions on how to submit a bug report.

11.13.2.1. Mouse Issues

In some cases, resuming from a suspend operation will cause the mouse to fail. A known work around is to add `hint.psm.0.flags="0x3000"` to `/boot/loader.conf`.

11.13.2.2. Suspend/Resume

ACPI has three suspend to RAM (STR) states, S1-S3, and one suspend to disk state (STD), called S4. STD can be implemented in two separate ways. The S4BIOS is a BIOS-assisted suspend to disk and S4OS is implemented entirely by the operating system. The normal state the system is in when plugged in but not powered up is "soft off" (S5).

Use `sysctl hw.acpi` to check for the suspend-related items. These example results are from a Thinkpad:

```
hw.acpi.supported_sleep_state: S3 S4 S5
hw.acpi.s4bios: 0
```

Use `acpiconf -s` to test S3, S4, and S5. An `s4bios` of one (1) indicates S4BIOS support instead of S4 operating system support.

When testing suspend/resume, start with S1, if supported. This state is most likely to work since it does not require much driver support. No one has implemented S2, which is similar to S1. Next, try S3. This is the deepest STR state and requires a lot of driver support to properly reinitialize the hardware.

A common problem with suspend/resume is that many device drivers do not save, restore, or reinitialize their firmware, registers, or device memory properly. As a first attempt at debugging the problem, try:

```
# sysctl debug.bootverbose=1
# sysctl debug.acpi.suspend_bounce=1
```

```
# acpiconf -s 3
```

This test emulates the suspend/resume cycle of all device drivers without actually going into S3 state. In some cases, problems such as losing firmware state, device watchdog time out, and retrying forever, can be captured with this method. Note that the system will not really enter S3 state, which means devices may not lose power, and many will work fine even if suspend/resume methods are totally missing, unlike real S3 state.

Harder cases require additional hardware, such as a serial port and cable for debugging through a serial console, a Firewire port and cable for using dcons(4), and kernel debugging skills.

To help isolate the problem, unload as many drivers as possible. If it works, narrow down which driver is the problem by loading drivers until it fails again. Typically, binary drivers like nvidia.ko, display drivers, and USB will have the most problems while Ethernet interfaces usually work fine. If drivers can be properly loaded and unloaded, automate this by putting the appropriate commands in /etc/rc.suspend and /etc/rc.resume. Try setting hw.acpi.reset_video to 1 if the display is messed up after resume. Try setting longer or shorter values for hw.acpi.sleep_delay to see if that helps.

Try loading a recent Linux® distribution to see if suspend/resume works on the same hardware. If it works on Linux®, it is likely a FreeBSD driver problem. Narrowing down which driver causes the problem will assist developers in fixing the problem. Since the ACPI maintainers rarely maintain other drivers, such as sound or ATA, any driver problems should also be posted to the freebsd-current list and mailed to the driver maintainer. Advanced users can include debugging printf(3)s in a problematic driver to track down where in its resume function it hangs.

Finally, try disabling ACPI and enabling APM instead. If suspend/resume works with APM, stick with APM, especially on older hardware (pre-2000). It took vendors a while to get ACPI support correct and older hardware is more likely to have BIOS problems with ACPI.

11.13.2.3. System Hangs

Most system hangs are a result of lost interrupts or an interrupt storm. Chipsets may have problems based on boot, how the BIOS configures interrupts before correctness of the APIC (MADT) table, and routing of the System Control Interrupt (SCI).

Interrupt storms can be distinguished from lost interrupts by checking the output of vmstat -i and looking at the line that has acpi0. If the counter is increasing at more than a couple per second, there is an interrupt storm. If the system appears hung, try breaking to DDB (CTRL+ALT+ESC on console) and type show interrupts.

When dealing with interrupt problems, try disabling APIC support with hint.apic.0.disabled="1" in /boot/loader.conf.

11.13.2.4. Panics

Panics are relatively rare for ACPI and are the top priority to be fixed. The first step is to isolate the steps to reproduce the panic, if possible, and get a backtrace. Follow the advice for enabling options DDB and setting up a serial console in Section 25.6.4, "Entering the DDB Debugger from the Serial Line" or setting up a dump partition. To get a backtrace in DDB, use tr. When handwriting the backtrace, get at least the last five and the top five lines in the trace.

Then, try to isolate the problem by booting with ACPI disabled. If that works, isolate the ACPI subsystem by using various values of debug.acpi.disable. See acpi(4) for some examples.

11.13.2.5. System Powers Up After Suspend or Shutdown

First, try setting hw.acpi.disable_on_poweroff="0" in /boot/loader.conf. This keeps ACPI from disabling various events during the shutdown process. Some systems need this value set to 1 (the default) for the same reason. This usually fixes the problem of a system powering up spontaneously after a suspend or poweroff.

11.13.2.6. BIOS Contains Buggy Bytecode

Some BIOS vendors provide incorrect or buggy bytecode. This is usually manifested by kernel console messages like this:

```
ACPI-1287: *** Error: Method execution failed [\\_SB_.PCI0.LPC0.FIGD._STA] \\
(Node 0xc3f6d160), AE_NOT_FOUND
```

Often, these problems may be resolved by updating the BIOS to the latest revision. Most console messages are harmless, but if there are other problems, like the battery status is not working, these messages are a good place to start looking for problems.

11.13.3. Overriding the Default AML

The BIOS bytecode, known as ACPI Machine Language (AML), is compiled from a source language called ACPI Source Language (ASL). The AML is found in the table known as the Differentiated System Description Table (DSDT).

The goal of FreeBSD is for everyone to have working ACPI without any user intervention. Workarounds are still being developed for common mistakes made by BIOS vendors. The Microsoft® interpreter (acpi.sys and acpiec.sys) does not strictly check for adherence to the standard, and thus many BIOS vendors who only test ACPI under Windows® never fix their ASL. FreeBSD developers continue to identify and document which non-standard behavior is allowed by Microsoft®'s interpreter and replicate it so that FreeBSD can work without forcing users to fix the ASL.

To help identify buggy behavior and possibly fix it manually, a copy can be made of the system's ASL. To copy the system's ASL to a specified file name, use acpidump with -t, to show the contents of the fixed tables, and -d, to disassemble the AML:

```
# acpidump -td > my.asl
```

Some AML versions assume the user is running Windows®. To override this, set hw.acpi.osname="Windows 2009" in /boot/loader.conf , using the most recent Windows® version listed in the ASL.

Other workarounds may require my.asl to be customized. If this file is edited, compile the new ASL using the following command. Warnings can usually be ignored, but errors are bugs that will usually prevent ACPI from working correctly.

```
# iasl -f my.asl
```

Including -f forces creation of the AML, even if there are errors during compilation. Some errors, such as missing return statements, are automatically worked around by the FreeBSD interpreter.

The default output filename for iasl is DSDT.aml . Load this file instead of the BIOS's buggy copy, which is still present in flash memory, by editing /boot/loader.conf as follows:

```
acpi_dsdt_load="YES"
acpi_dsdt_name="/boot/DSDT.aml"
```

Be sure to copy DSDT.aml to /boot, then reboot the system. If this fixes the problem, send a diff(1) of the old and new ASL to freebsd-acpi so that developers can work around the buggy behavior in acpica.

11.13.4. Getting and Submitting Debugging Info

Written by Nate Lawson.
With contributions from Peter Schultz and Tom Rhodes.

The ACPI driver has a flexible debugging facility. A set of subsystems and the level of verbosity can be specified. The subsystems to debug are specified as layers and are broken down into components (ACPI_ALL_COMPONENTS) and ACPI hardware support (ACPI_ALL_DRIVERS). The verbosity of debugging output is specified as the level and ranges from just report errors (ACPI_LV_ERROR) to everything (ACPI_LV_VERBOSE). The level is a bitmask so multiple options can be set at once, separated by spaces. In practice, a serial console should be used to log the output so it is not lost as the console message buffer flushes. A full list of the individual layers and levels is found in acpi(4).

Debugging output is not enabled by default. To enable it, add `options ACPI_DEBUG` to the custom kernel configuration file if ACPI is compiled into the kernel. Add `ACPI_DEBUG=1` to `/etc/make.conf` to enable it globally. If a module is used instead of a custom kernel, recompile just the `acpi.ko` module as follows:

```
# cd /sys/modules/acpi/acpi && make clean && make ACPI_DEBUG=1
```

Copy the compiled `acpi.ko` to `/boot/kernel` and add the desired level and layer to `/boot/loader.conf`. The entries in this example enable debug messages for all ACPI components and hardware drivers and output error messages at the least verbose level:

```
debug.acpi.layer="ACPI_ALL_COMPONENTS ACPI_ALL_DRIVERS"
debug.acpi.level="ACPI_LV_ERROR"
```

If the required information is triggered by a specific event, such as a suspend and then resume, do not modify `/boot/loader.conf`. Instead, use `sysctl` to specify the layer and level after booting and preparing the system for the specific event. The variables which can be set using `sysctl` are named the same as the tunables in `/boot/loader.conf`.

Once the debugging information is gathered, it can be sent to freebsd-acpi so that it can be used by the FreeBSD ACPI maintainers to identify the root cause of the problem and to develop a solution.

Note

Before submitting debugging information to this mailing list, ensure the latest BIOS version is installed and, if available, the embedded controller firmware version.

When submitting a problem report, include the following information:

- Description of the buggy behavior, including system type, model, and anything that causes the bug to appear. Note as accurately as possible when the bug began occurring if it is new.

- The output of `dmesg` after running `boot -v`, including any error messages generated by the bug.

- The `dmesg` output from `boot -v` with ACPI disabled, if disabling ACPI helps to fix the problem.

- Output from `sysctl hw.acpi`. This lists which features the system offers.

- The URL to a pasted version of the system's ASL. Do *not* send the ASL directly to the list as it can be very large. Generate a copy of the ASL by running this command:

```
# acpidump -dt > name-system.asl
```

Substitute the login name for *name* and manufacturer/model for *system*. For example, use `njl-FooCo6000.asl`.

Most FreeBSD developers watch the FreeBSD-CURRENT mailing list, but one should submit problems to freebsd-acpi to be sure it is seen. Be patient when waiting for a response. If the bug is not immediately apparent, submit a PR using send-pr(1). When entering a PR, include the same information as requested above. This helps developers to track the problem and resolve it. Do not send a PR without emailing freebsd-acpi first as it is likely that the problem has been reported before.

11.13.5. References

More information about ACPI may be found in the following locations:

- The FreeBSD ACPI Mailing List Archives (`https://lists.freebsd.org/pipermail/freebsd-acpi/`)

- The ACPI 2.0 Specification (`http://acpi.info/spec.htm`)

- acpi(4), acpi_thermal(4), acpidump(8), iasl(8), and acpidb(8)

Chapter 12. The FreeBSD Booting Process

12.1. Synopsis

The process of starting a computer and loading the operating system is referred to as "the bootstrap process", or "booting". FreeBSD's boot process provides a great deal of flexibility in customizing what happens when the system starts, including the ability to select from different operating systems installed on the same computer, different versions of the same operating system, or a different installed kernel.

This chapter details the configuration options that can be set. It demonstrates how to customize the FreeBSD boot process, including everything that happens until the FreeBSD kernel has started, probed for devices, and started init(8). This occurs when the text color of the boot messages changes from bright white to grey.

After reading this chapter, you will recognize:

- The components of the FreeBSD bootstrap system and how they interact.

- The options that can be passed to the components in the FreeBSD bootstrap in order to control the boot process.

- How to configure a customized boot splash screen.

- The basics of setting device hints.

- How to boot into single- and multi-user mode and how to properly shut down a FreeBSD system.

> Note
>
> This chapter only describes the boot process for FreeBSD running on x86 and amd64 systems.

12.2. FreeBSD Boot Process

Turning on a computer and starting the operating system poses an interesting dilemma. By definition, the computer does not know how to do anything until the operating system is started. This includes running programs from the disk. If the computer can not run a program from the disk without the operating system, and the operating system programs are on the disk, how is the operating system started?

This problem parallels one in the book *The Adventures of Baron Munchausen*. A character had fallen part way down a manhole, and pulled himself out by grabbing his bootstraps and lifting. In the early days of computing, the term *bootstrap* was applied to the mechanism used to load the operating system. It has since become shortened to "booting".

On x86 hardware, the Basic Input/Output System (BIOS) is responsible for loading the operating system. The BIOS looks on the hard disk for the Master Boot Record (MBR), which must be located in a specific place on the disk. The BIOS has enough knowledge to load and run the MBR, and assumes that the MBR can then carry out the rest of the tasks involved in loading the operating system, possibly with the help of the BIOS.

> **Note**
>
> FreeBSD provides for booting from both the older MBR standard, and the newer GUID Partition Table (GPT). GPT partitioning is often found on computers with the Unified Extensible Firmware Interface (UEFI). However, FreeBSD can boot from GPT partitions even on machines with only a legacy BIOS with gptboot(8). Work is under way to provide direct UEFI booting.

The code within the MBR is typically referred to as a *boot manager*, especially when it interacts with the user. The boot manager usually has more code in the first track of the disk or within the file system. Examples of boot managers include the standard FreeBSD boot manager boot0, also called Boot Easy, and Grub, which is used by many Linux® distributions.

If only one operating system is installed, the MBR searches for the first bootable (active) slice on the disk, and then runs the code on that slice to load the remainder of the operating system. When multiple operating systems are present, a different boot manager can be installed to display a list of operating systems so the user can select one to boot.

The remainder of the FreeBSD bootstrap system is divided into three stages. The first stage knows just enough to get the computer into a specific state and run the second stage. The second stage can do a little bit more, before running the third stage. The third stage finishes the task of loading the operating system. The work is split into three stages because the MBR puts limits on the size of the programs that can be run at stages one and two. Chaining the tasks together allows FreeBSD to provide a more flexible loader.

The kernel is then started and begins to probe for devices and initialize them for use. Once the kernel boot process is finished, the kernel passes control to the user process init(8), which makes sure the disks are in a usable state, starts the user-level resource configuration which mounts file systems, sets up network cards to communicate on the network, and starts the processes which have been configured to run at startup.

This section describes these stages in more detail and demonstrates how to interact with the FreeBSD boot process.

12.2.1. The Boot Manager

The boot manager code in the MBR is sometimes referred to as *stage zero* of the boot process. By default, FreeBSD uses the boot0 boot manager.

The MBR installed by the FreeBSD installer is based on `/boot/boot0` . The size and capability of boot0 is restricted to 446 bytes due to the slice table and `0x55AA` identifier at the end of the MBR. If boot0 and multiple operating systems are installed, a message similar to this example will be displayed at boot time:

Example 12.1. **boot0** Screenshot

```
F1 Win
F2 FreeBSD

Default: F2
```

Other operating systems will overwrite an existing MBR if they are installed after FreeBSD. If this happens, or to replace the existing MBR with the FreeBSD MBR, use the following command:

```
# fdisk -B -b /boot/boot0  device
```

where *device* is the boot disk, such as ad0 for the first IDE disk, ad2 for the first IDE disk on a second IDE controller, or da0 for the first SCSI disk. To create a custom configuration of the MBR, refer to boot0cfg(8).

12.2.2. Stage One and Stage Two

Conceptually, the first and second stages are part of the same program on the same area of the disk. Because of space constraints, they have been split into two, but are always installed together. They are copied from the combined /boot/boot by the FreeBSD installer or bsdlabel.

These two stages are located outside file systems, in the first track of the boot slice, starting with the first sector. This is where boot0, or any other boot manager, expects to find a program to run which will continue the boot process.

The first stage, boot1, is very simple, since it can only be 512 bytes in size. It knows just enough about the FreeBSD *bsdlabel*, which stores information about the slice, to find and execute boot2.

Stage two, boot2, is slightly more sophisticated, and understands the FreeBSD file system enough to find files. It can provide a simple interface to choose the kernel or loader to run. It runs loader, which is much more sophisticated and provides a boot configuration file. If the boot process is interrupted at stage two, the following interactive screen is displayed:

Example 12.2. **boot2** Screenshot

```
>> FreeBSD/i386 BOOT
Default: 0:ad(0,a)/boot/loader
boot:
```

To replace the installed boot1 and boot2, use bsdlabel, where *diskslice* is the disk and slice to boot from, such as ad0s1 for the first slice on the first IDE disk:

```
# bsdlabel -B diskslice
```

 Warning

If just the disk name is used, such as ad0, bsdlabel will create the disk in "dangerously dedicated mode", without slices. This is probably not the desired action, so double check the *diskslice* before pressing Return.

12.2.3. Stage Three

The loader is the final stage of the three-stage bootstrap process. It is located on the file system, usually as /boot/loader.

The loader is intended as an interactive method for configuration, using a built-in command set, backed up by a more powerful interpreter which has a more complex command set.

During initialization, loader will probe for a console and for disks, and figure out which disk it is booting from. It will set variables accordingly, and an interpreter is started where user commands can be passed from a script or interactively.

The loader will then read /boot/loader.rc , which by default reads in /boot/defaults/loader.conf which sets reasonable defaults for variables and reads /boot/loader.conf for local changes to those variables. loader.rc then acts on these variables, loading whichever modules and kernel are selected.

Finally, by default, loader issues a 10 second wait for key presses, and boots the kernel if it is not interrupted. If interrupted, the user is presented with a prompt which understands the command set, where the user may adjust variables, unload all modules, load modules, and then finally boot or reboot. Table 12.1, "Loader Built-In Commands" lists the most commonly used loader commands. For a complete discussion of all available commands, refer to loader(8).

Table 12.1. Loader Built-In Commands

Variable	Description
autoboot *seconds*	Proceeds to boot the kernel if not interrupted within the time span given, in seconds. It displays a countdown, and the default time span is 10 seconds.
boot [*-options*] [*kernelname*]	Immediately proceeds to boot the kernel, with any specified options or kernel name. Providing a kernel name on the command-line is only applicable after an unload has been issued. Otherwise, the previously-loaded kernel will be used. If *kernelname* is not qualified, it will be searched under /boot/kernel and /boot/modules.
boot-conf	Goes through the same automatic configuration of modules based on specified variables, most commonly kernel. This only makes sense if unload is used first, before changing some variables.
help [*topic*]	Shows help messages read from /boot/loader.help . If the topic given is index, the list of available topics is displayed.
include *filename* ...	Reads the specified file and interprets it line by line. An error immediately stops the include.
load [-t *type*] *filename*	Loads the kernel, kernel module, or file of the type given, with the specified filename. Any arguments after *filename* are passed to the file. If *filename* is not qualified, it will be searched under /boot/kernel and /boot/modules.
ls [-l] [*path*]	Displays a listing of files in the given path, or the root directory, if the path is not specified. If -l is specified, file sizes will also be shown.
lsdev [-v]	Lists all of the devices from which it may be possible to load modules. If -v is specified, more details are printed.
lsmod [-v]	Displays loaded modules. If -v is specified, more details are shown.
more *filename*	Displays the files specified, with a pause at each LINES displayed.
reboot	Immediately reboots the system.
set *variable*, set *variable=value*	Sets the specified environment variables.
unload	Removes all loaded modules.

Here are some practical examples of loader usage. To boot the usual kernel in single-user mode :

```
boot -s
```

216

To unload the usual kernel and modules and then load the previous or another, specified kernel:

```
unload
load kernel.old
```

Use `kernel.GENERIC` to refer to the default kernel that comes with an installation, or `kernel.old`, to refer to the previously installed kernel before a system upgrade or before configuring a custom kernel.

Use the following to load the usual modules with another kernel:

```
unload
set kernel=" kernel.old "
boot-conf
```

To load an automated kernel configuration script:

```
load -t userconfig_script  /boot/kernel.conf
```

12.2.4. Last Stage

Once the kernel is loaded by either loader or by boot2, which bypasses loader, it examines any boot flags and adjusts its behavior as necessary. Table 12.2, "Kernel Interaction During Boot" lists the commonly used boot flags. Refer to boot(8) for more information on the other boot flags.

Table 12.2. Kernel Interaction During Boot

Option	Description
-a	During kernel initialization, ask for the device to mount as the root file system.
-C	Boot the root file system from a CDROM.
-s	Boot into single-user mode.
-v	Be more verbose during kernel startup.

Once the kernel has finished booting, it passes control to the user process init(8), which is located at /sbin/init , or the program path specified in the `init_path` variable in `loader`. This is the last stage of the boot process.

The boot sequence makes sure that the file systems available on the system are consistent. If a UFS file system is not, and `fsck` cannot fix the inconsistencies, init drops the system into single-user mode so that the system administrator can resolve the problem directly. Otherwise, the system boots into multi-user mode.

12.2.4.1. Single-User Mode

A user can specify this mode by booting with `-s` or by setting the `boot_single` variable in loader. It can also be reached by running `shutdown now` from multi-user mode. Single-user mode begins with this message:

```
Enter full pathname of shell or RETURN for /bin/sh:
```

If the user presses Enter, the system will enter the default Bourne shell. To specify a different shell, input the full path to the shell.

Single-user mode is usually used to repair a system that will not boot due to an inconsistent file system or an error in a boot configuration file. It can also be used to reset the `root` password when it is unknown. These actions are possible as the single-user mode prompt gives full, local access to the system and its configuration files. There is no networking in this mode.

While single-user mode is useful for repairing a system, it poses a security risk unless the system is in a physically secure location. By default, any user who can gain physical access to a system will have full control of that system after booting into single-user mode.

If the system console is changed to insecure in /etc/ttys , the system will first prompt for the root password before initiating single-user mode. This adds a measure of security while removing the ability to reset the root password when it is unknown.

Example 12.3. Configuring an Insecure Console in **/etc/ttys**

```
# name  getty                             type    status          comments
#
# If console is marked "insecure", then init will ask for the root password
# when going to single-user mode.
console none                              unknown off  insecure
```

An insecure console means that physical security to the console is considered to be insecure, so only someone who knows the root password may use single-user mode.

12.2.4.2. Multi-User Mode

If init finds the file systems to be in order, or once the user has finished their commands in single-user mode and has typed exit to leave single-user mode, the system enters multi-user mode, in which it starts the resource configuration of the system.

The resource configuration system reads in configuration defaults from /etc/defaults/rc.conf and system-specific details from /etc/rc.conf . It then proceeds to mount the system file systems listed in /etc/fstab . It starts up networking services, miscellaneous system daemons, then the startup scripts of locally installed packages.

To learn more about the resource configuration system, refer to rc(8) and examine the scripts located in /etc/rc.d.

12.3. Configuring Boot Time Splash Screens

Contributed by Joseph J. Barbish.

Typically when a FreeBSD system boots, it displays its progress as a series of messages at the console. A boot splash screen creates an alternate boot screen that hides all of the boot probe and service startup messages. A few boot loader messages, including the boot options menu and a timed wait countdown prompt, are displayed at boot time, even when the splash screen is enabled. The display of the splash screen can be turned off by hitting any key on the keyboard during the boot process.

There are two basic environments available in FreeBSD. The first is the default legacy virtual console command line environment. After the system finishes booting, a console login prompt is presented. The second environment is a configured graphical environment. Refer to Chapter 5, *The X Window System* for more information on how to install and configure a graphical display manager and a graphical login manager.

Once the system has booted, the splash screen defaults to being a screen saver. After a time period of non-use, the splash screen will display and will cycle through steps of changing intensity of the image, from bright to very dark and over again. The configuration of the splash screen saver can be overridden by adding a saver= line to /etc/rc.conf . Several built-in screen savers are available and described in splash(4). The saver= option only applies to virtual consoles and has no effect on graphical display managers.

Sample splash screen files can be downloaded from the gallery at http://artwork.freebsdgr.org. By installing the sysutils/bsd-splash-changer package or port, a random splash image from a collection will display at boot.

The splash screen function supports 256-colors in the bitmap (.bmp), ZSoft PCX (.pcx), or TheDraw (.bin) formats. The .bmp, .pcx, or .bin image has to be placed on the root partition, for example in /boot. The splash image files must have a resolution of 320 by 200 pixels or less in order to work on standard VGA adapters. For the default boot display resolution of 256-colors and 320 by 200 pixels or less, add the following lines to /boot/loader.conf . Replace *splash.bmp* with the name of the bitmap file to use:

```
splash_bmp_load="YES"
bitmap_load="YES"
bitmap_name="/boot/splash.bmp "
```

To use a PCX file instead of a bitmap file:

```
splash_pcx_load="YES"
bitmap_load="YES"
bitmap_name="/boot/splash.pcx "
```

To instead use ASCII art in the https://en.wikipedia.org/wiki/TheDraw format:

```
splash_txt="YES"
bitmap_load="YES"
bitmap_name="/boot/splash.bin "
```

To use larger images that fill the whole display screen, up to the maximum resolution of 1024 by 768 pixels, the VESA module must also be loaded during system boot. If using a custom kernel, ensure that the custom kernel configuration file includes the VESA kernel configuration option. To load the VESA module for the splash screen, add this line to /boot/loader.conf before the three lines mentioned in the above examples:

```
vesa_load="YES"
```

Other interesting loader.conf options include:

beastie_disable="YES"
> This will stop the boot options menu from being displayed, but the timed wait count down prompt will still be present. Even with the display of the boot options menu disabled, entering an option selection at the timed wait count down prompt will enact the corresponding boot option.

loader_logo="beastie"
> This will replace the default words "FreeBSD", which are displayed to the right of the boot options menu, with the colored beastie logo.

For more information, refer to splash(4), loader.conf(5), and vga(4).

12.4. Device Hints

Contributed by Tom Rhodes.

During initial system startup, the boot loader(8) reads device.hints(5). This file stores kernel boot information known as variables, sometimes referred to as "device hints". These "device hints" are used by device drivers for device configuration.

Device hints may also be specified at the Stage 3 boot loader prompt, as demonstrated in Section 12.2.3, "Stage Three". Variables can be added using set, removed with unset, and viewed show. Variables set in /boot/device.hints can also be overridden. Device hints entered at the boot loader are not permanent and will not be applied on the next reboot.

Once the system is booted, kenv(1) can be used to dump all of the variables.

The syntax for /boot/device.hints is one variable per line, using the hash "#" as comment markers. Lines are constructed as follows:

```
hint.driver.unit.keyword=" value"
```

The syntax for the Stage 3 boot loader is:

```
set hint.driver.unit.keyword= value
```

where `driver` is the device driver name, `unit` is the device driver unit number, and `keyword` is the hint keyword. The keyword may consist of the following options:

- `at`: specifies the bus which the device is attached to.

- `port`: specifies the start address of the I/O to be used.

- `irq`: specifies the interrupt request number to be used.

- `drq`: specifies the DMA channel number.

- `maddr`: specifies the physical memory address occupied by the device.

- `flags`: sets various flag bits for the device.

- `disabled`: if set to 1 the device is disabled.

Since device drivers may accept or require more hints not listed here, viewing a driver's manual page is recommended. For more information, refer to device.hints(5), kenv(1), loader.conf(5), and loader(8).

12.5. Shutdown Sequence

Upon controlled shutdown using shutdown(8), init(8) will attempt to run the script `/etc/rc.shutdown`, and then proceed to send all processes the `TERM` signal, and subsequently the `KILL` signal to any that do not terminate in a timely manner.

To power down a FreeBSD machine on architectures and systems that support power management, use `shutdown -p now` to turn the power off immediately. To reboot a FreeBSD system, use `shutdown -r now`. One must be `root` or a member of `operator` in order to run shutdown(8). One can also use halt(8) and reboot(8). Refer to their manual pages and to shutdown(8) for more information.

Modify group membership by referring to Section 3.3, "Users and Basic Account Management".

Note

Power management requires acpi(4) to be loaded as a module or statically compiled into a custom kernel.

Chapter 13. Security

Rewritten by Tom Rhodes.

13.1. Synopsis

Security, whether physical or virtual, is a topic so broad that an entire industry has evolved around it. Hundreds of standard practices have been authored about how to secure systems and networks, and as a user of FreeBSD, understanding how to protect against attacks and intruders is a must.

In this chapter, several fundamentals and techniques will be discussed. The FreeBSD system comes with multiple layers of security, and many more third party utilities may be added to enhance security.

After reading this chapter, you will know:

- Basic FreeBSD system security concepts.

- The various crypt mechanisms available in FreeBSD.

- How to set up one-time password authentication.

- How to configure TCP Wrapper for use with inetd(8).

- How to set up Kerberos on FreeBSD.

- How to configure IPsec and create a VPN.

- How to configure and use OpenSSH on FreeBSD.

- How to use file system ACLs.

- How to use pkg to audit third party software packages installed from the Ports Collection.

- How to utilize FreeBSD security advisories.

- What Process Accounting is and how to enable it on FreeBSD.

- How to control user resources using login classes or the resource limits database.

Before reading this chapter, you should:

- Understand basic FreeBSD and Internet concepts.

Additional security topics are covered elsewhere in this Handbook. For example, Mandatory Access Control is discussed in Chapter 15, *Mandatory Access Control* and Internet firewalls are discussed in Chapter 29, *Firewalls*.

13.2. Introduction

Security is everyone's responsibility. A weak entry point in any system could allow intruders to gain access to critical information and cause havoc on an entire network. One of the core principles of information security is the CIA triad, which stands for the Confidentiality, Integrity, and Availability of information systems.

The CIA triad is a bedrock concept of computer security as customers and users expect their data to be protected. For example, a customer expects that their credit card information is securely stored (confidentiality), that their orders are not changed behind the scenes (integrity), and that they have access to their order information at all times (availablility).

To provide CIA, security professionals apply a defense in depth strategy. The idea of defense in depth is to add several layers of security to prevent one single layer failing and the entire security system collapsing. For example, a system administrator cannot simply turn on a firewall and consider the network or system secure. One must also audit accounts, check the integrity of binaries, and ensure malicious tools are not installed. To implement an effective security strategy, one must understand threats and how to defend against them.

What is a threat as it pertains to computer security? Threats are not limited to remote attackers who attempt to access a system without permission from a remote location. Threats also include employees, malicious software, unauthorized network devices, natural disasters, security vulnerabilities, and even competing corporations.

Systems and networks can be accessed without permission, sometimes by accident, or by remote attackers, and in some cases, via corporate espionage or former employees. As a user, it is important to prepare for and admit when a mistake has led to a security breach and report possible issues to the security team. As an administrator, it is important to know of the threats and be prepared to mitigate them.

When applying security to systems, it is recommended to start by securing the basic accounts and system configuration, and then to secure the network layer so that it adheres to the system policy and the organization's security procedures. Many organizations already have a security policy that covers the configuration of technology devices. The policy should include the security configuration of workstations, desktops, mobile devices, phones, production servers, and development servers. In many cases, standard operating procedures (SOPs) already exist. When in doubt, ask the security team.

The rest of this introduction describes how some of these basic security configurations are performed on a FreeBSD system. The rest of this chapter describes some specific tools which can be used when implementing a security policy on a FreeBSD system.

13.2.1. Preventing Logins

In securing a system, a good starting point is an audit of accounts. Ensure that `root` has a strong password and that this password is not shared. Disable any accounts that do not need login access.

To deny login access to accounts, two methods exist. The first is to lock the account. This example locks the `toor` account:

```
# pw lock toor
```

The second method is to prevent login access by changing the shell to `/sbin/nologin`. Only the superuser can change the shell for other users:

```
# chsh -s /usr/sbin/nologin toor
```

The `/usr/sbin/nologin` shell prevents the system from assigning a shell to the user when they attempt to login.

13.2.2. Permitted Account Escalation

In some cases, system administration needs to be shared with other users. FreeBSD has two methods to handle this. The first one, which is not recommended, is a shared root password used by members of the `wheel` group. With this method, a user types `su` and enters the password for `wheel` whenever superuser access is needed. The user should then type `exit` to leave privileged access after finishing the commands that required administrative access. To add a user to this group, edit `/etc/group` and add the user to the end of the `wheel` entry. The user must be separated by a comma character with no space.

The second, and recommended, method to permit privilege escalation is to install the security/sudo package or port. This software provides additional auditing, more fine-grained user control, and can be configured to lock users into running only the specified privileged commands.

After installation, use `visudo` to edit `/usr/local/etc/sudoers`. This example creates a new `webadmin` group, adds the `trhodes` account to that group, and configures that group access to restart apache24:

```
# pw groupadd webadmin -M trhodes -g 6000
# visudo
%webadmin ALL=(ALL) /usr/sbin/service apache24 *
```

13.2.3. Password Hashes

Passwords are a necessary evil of technology. When they must be used, they should be complex and a powerful hash mechanism should be used to encrypt the version that is stored in the password database. FreeBSD supports the DES, MD5, SHA256, SHA512, and Blowfish hash algorithms in its `crypt()` library. The default of SHA512 should not be changed to a less secure hashing algorithm, but can be changed to the more secure Blowfish algorithm.

> **Note**
>
> Blowfish is not part of AES and is not considered compliant with any Federal Information Processing Standards (FIPS). Its use may not be permitted in some environments.

To determine which hash algorithm is used to encrypt a user's password, the superuser can view the hash for the user in the FreeBSD password database. Each hash starts with a symbol which indicates the type of hash mechanism used to encrypt the password. If DES is used, there is no beginning symbol. For MD5, the symbol is $. For SHA256 and SHA512, the symbol is 6. For Blowfish, the symbol is $2a$. In this example, the password for dru is hashed using the default SHA512 algorithm as the hash starts with 6. Note that the encrypted hash, not the password itself, is stored in the password database:

```
# grep dru /etc/master.passwd
dru:$6$pzIjSvCAn.PBYQBA
$PXpSeWPx3g5kscj3IMiM7tUEUSPmGexxta.8Lt9TGSi2lNQqYGKszsBPuGME0:1001:1001::0:0:dru:/usr/
home/dru:/bin/csh
```

The hash mechanism is set in the user's login class. For this example, the user is in the `default` login class and the hash algorithm is set with this line in `/etc/login.conf`:

```
        :passwd_format=sha512:\
```

To change the algorithm to Blowfish, modify that line to look like this:

```
        :passwd_format=blf:\
```

Then run `cap_mkdb /etc/login.conf` as described in Section 13.13.1, "Configuring Login Classes". Note that this change will not affect any existing password hashes. This means that all passwords should be re-hashed by asking users to run `passwd` in order to change their password.

For remote logins, two-factor authentication should be used. An example of two-factor authentication is "something you have", such as a key, and "something you know", such as the passphrase for that key. Since OpenSSH is part of the FreeBSD base system, all network logins should be over an encrypted connection and use key-based authentication instead of passwords. For more information, refer to Section 13.8, "OpenSSH". Kerberos users may need to make additional changes to implement OpenSSH in their network. These changes are described in Section 13.5, "Kerberos".

13.2.4. Password Policy Enforcement

Enforcing a strong password policy for local accounts is a fundamental aspect of system security. In FreeBSD, password length, password strength, and password complexity can be implemented using built-in Pluggable Authentication Modules (PAM).

This section demonstrates how to configure the minimum and maximum password length and the enforcement of mixed characters using the `pam_passwdqc.so` module. This module is enforced when a user changes their password.

To configure this module, become the superuser and uncomment the line containing pam_passwdqc.so in /etc/pam.d/passwd. Then, edit that line to match the password policy:

```
password        requisite       pam_passwdqc.so
  min=disabled,disabled,disabled,12,10 similar=deny retry=3     enforce=users
```

This example sets several requirements for new passwords. The min setting controls the minimum password length. It has five values because this module defines five different types of passwords based on their complexity. Complexity is defined by the type of characters that must exist in a password, such as letters, numbers, symbols, and case. The types of passwords are described in pam_passwdqc(8). In this example, the first three types of passwords are disabled, meaning that passwords that meet those complexity requirements will not be accepted, regardless of their length. The 12 sets a minimum password policy of at least twelve characters, if the password also contains characters with three types of complexity. The 10 sets the password policy to also allow passwords of at least ten characters, if the password contains characters with four types of complexity.

The similar setting denies passwords that are similar to the user's previous password. The retry setting provides a user with three opportunities to enter a new password.

Once this file is saved, a user changing their password will see a message similar to the following:

```
% passwd
Changing local password for trhodes
Old Password:

You can now choose the new password.
A valid password should be a mix of upper and lower case letters,
digits and other characters.  You can use a 12 character long
password with characters from at least 3 of these 4 classes, or
a 10 character long password containing characters from all the
classes.  Characters that form a common pattern are discarded by
the check.
Alternatively, if noone else can see your terminal now, you can
pick this as your password: "trait-useful&knob".
Enter new password:
```

If a password that does not match the policy is entered, it will be rejected with a warning and the user will have an opportunity to try again, up to the configured number of retries.

Most password policies require passwords to expire after so many days. To set a password age time in FreeBSD, set passwordtime for the user's login class in /etc/login.conf. The default login class contains an example:

```
#        :passwordtime=90d:\
```

So, to set an expiry of 90 days for this login class, remove the comment symbol (#), save the edit, and run cap_mkdb /etc/login.conf.

To set the expiration on individual users, pass an expiration date or the number of days to expiry and a username to pw:

```
# pw usermod -p 30-apr-2015  -n trhodes
```

As seen here, an expiration date is set in the form of day, month, and year. For more information, see pw(8).

13.2.5. Detecting Rootkits

A *rootkit* is any unauthorized software that attempts to gain root access to a system. Once installed, this malicious software will normally open up another avenue of entry for an attacker. Realistically, once a system has been compromised by a rootkit and an investigation has been performed, the system should be reinstalled from scratch. There is tremendous risk that even the most prudent security or systems engineer will miss something an attacker left behind.

A rootkit does do one thing useful for administrators: once detected, it is a sign that a compromise happened at some point. But, these types of applications tend to be very well hidden. This section demonstrates a tool that can be used to detect rootkits, security/rkhunter.

After installation of this package or port, the system may be checked using the following command. It will produce a lot of information and will require some manual pressing of ENTER:

```
# rkhunter -c
```

After the process completes, a status message will be printed to the screen. This message will include the amount of files checked, suspect files, possible rootkits, and more. During the check, some generic security warnings may be produced about hidden files, the OpenSSH protocol selection, and known vulnerable versions of installed software. These can be handled now or after a more detailed analysis has been performed.

Every administrator should know what is running on the systems they are responsible for. Third-party tools like rkhunter and sysutils/lsof, and native commands such as netstat and ps, can show a great deal of information on the system. Take notes on what is normal, ask questions when something seems out of place, and be paranoid. While preventing a compromise is ideal, detecting a compromise is a must.

13.2.6. Binary Verification

Verification of system files and binaries is important because it provides the system administration and security teams information about system changes. A software application that monitors the system for changes is called an Intrusion Detection System (IDS).

FreeBSD provides native support for a basic IDS system. While the nightly security emails will notify an administrator of changes, the information is stored locally and there is a chance that a malicious user could modify this information in order to hide their changes to the system. As such, it is recommended to create a separate set of binary signatures and store them on a read-only, root-owned directory or, preferably, on a removable USB disk or remote rsync server.

The built-in mtree utility can be used to generate a specification of the contents of a directory. A seed, or a numeric constant, is used to generate the specification and is required to check that the specification has not changed. This makes it possible to determine if a file or binary has been modified. Since the seed value is unknown by an attacker, faking or checking the checksum values of files will be difficult to impossible. The following example generates a set of SHA256 hashes, one for each system binary in /bin, and saves those values to a hidden file in root's home directory, /root/.bin_chksum_mtree:

```
# mtree -s 3483151339707503  -c -K cksum,sha256digest -p  /bin > /root/.bin_chksum_mtree
# mtree: /bin checksum: 3427012225
```

The *3483151339707503* represents the seed. This value should be remembered, but not shared.

Viewing /root/.bin_cksum_mtree should yield output similar to the following:

```
#           user: root
#        machine: dreadnaught
#           tree: /bin
#           date: Mon Feb  3 10:19:53 2014

# .
/set type=file uid=0 gid=0 mode=0555 nlink=1 flags=none
.               type=dir mode=0755 nlink=2 size=1024 \
                time=1380277977.000000000
    \133        nlink=2 size=11704 time=1380277977.000000000 \
                cksum=484492447 \
                ʊ
sha256digest=6207490fbdb5ed1904441fbfa941279055c3e24d3a4049aeb45094596400662a
    cat         size=12096 time=1380277975.000000000 cksum=3909216944 \
                ʊ
sha256digest=65ea347b9418760b247ab10244f47a7ca2a569c9836d77f074e7a306900c1e69
```

```
    chflags       size=8168 time=1380277975.000000000 cksum=3949425175 \
              ↻
sha256digest=c99eb6fc1c92cac335c08be004a0a5b4c24a0c0ef3712017b12c89a978b2dac3
    chio          size=18520 time=1380277975.000000000 cksum=2208263309 \
              ↻
sha256digest=ddf7c8cb92a58750a675328345560d8cc7fe14fb3ccd3690c34954cbe69fc964
    chmod         size=8640 time=1380277975.000000000 cksum=2214429708 \
              ↻
sha256digest=a435972263bf814ad8df082c0752aa2a7bdd8b74ff01431ccbd52ed1e490bbe7
```

The machine's hostname, the date and time the specification was created, and the name of the user who created the specification are included in this report. There is a checksum, size, time, and SHA256 digest for each binary in the directory.

To verify that the binary signatures have not changed, compare the current contents of the directory to the previously generated specification, and save the results to a file. This command requires the seed that was used to generate the original specification:

```
# mtree -s 3483151339707503 -p /bin < /root/.bin_chksum_mtree >> /root/.bin_chksum_output
# mtree: /bin checksum: 3427012225
```

This should produce the same checksum for /bin that was produced when the specification was created. If no changes have occurred to the binaries in this directory, the /root/.bin_chksum_output output file will be empty. To simulate a change, change the date on /bin/cat using touch and run the verification command again:

```
# touch /bin/cat
# mtree -s 3483151339707503 -p /bin < /root/.bin_chksum_mtree >> /root/.bin_chksum_output
# more /root/.bin_chksum_output
cat changed
  modification time expected Fri Sep 27 06:32:55 2013 found Mon Feb  3 10:28:43 2014
```

It is recommended to create specifications for the directories which contain binaries and configuration files, as well as any directories containing sensitive data. Typically, specifications are created for /bin, /sbin, /usr/bin, /usr/sbin, /usr/local/bin, /etc, and /usr/local/etc.

More advanced IDS systems exist, such as security/aide. In most cases, mtree provides the functionality administrators need. It is important to keep the seed value and the checksum output hidden from malicious users. More information about mtree can be found in mtree(8).

13.2.7. System Tuning for Security

In FreeBSD, many system features can be tuned using sysctl. A few of the security features which can be tuned to prevent Denial of Service (DoS) attacks will be covered in this section. More information about using sysctl, including how to temporarily change values and how to make the changes permanent after testing, can be found in Section 11.9, "Tuning with sysctl(8)".

> **Note**
>
> Any time a setting is changed with sysctl, the chance to cause undesired harm is increased, affecting the availability of the system. All changes should be monitored and, if possible, tried on a testing system before being used on a production system.

By default, the FreeBSD kernel boots with a security level of -1. This is called "insecure mode" because immutable file flags may be turned off and all devices may be read from or written to. The security level will remain at -1 unless it is altered through sysctl or by a setting in the startup scripts. The security level may be increased during system startup by setting kern_securelevel_enable to YES in /etc/rc.conf, and the value of kern_securelevel to the desired security level. See security(7) and init(8) for more information on these settings and the available security levels.

> **Warning**
>
> Increasing the securelevel can break Xorg and cause other issues. Be prepared to do some debugging.

The net.inet.tcp.blackhole and net.inet.udp.blackhole settings can be used to drop incoming SYN packets on closed ports without sending a return RST response. The default behavior is to return an RST to show a port is closed. Changing the default provides some level of protection against ports scans, which are used to determine which applications are running on a system. Set net.inet.tcp.blackhole to 2 and net.inet.udp.blackhole to 1. Refer to blackhole(4) for more information about these settings.

The net.inet.icmp.drop_redirect and net.inet.ip.redirect settings help prevent against *redirect attacks*. A redirect attack is a type of DoS which sends mass numbers of ICMP type 5 packets. Since these packets are not required, set net.inet.icmp.drop_redirect to 1 and set net.inet.ip.redirect to 0.

Source routing is a method for detecting and accessing non-routable addresses on the internal network. This should be disabled as non-routable addresses are normally not routable on purpose. To disable this feature, set net.inet.ip.sourceroute and net.inet.ip.accept_sourceroute to 0.

When a machine on the network needs to send messages to all hosts on a subnet, an ICMP echo request message is sent to the broadcast address. However, there is no reason for an external host to perform such an action. To reject all external broadcast requests, set net.inet.icmp.bmcastecho to 0.

Some additional settings are documented in security(7).

13.3. One-time Passwords

By default, FreeBSD includes support for One-time Passwords In Everything (OPIE). OPIE is designed to prevent replay attacks, in which an attacker discovers a user's password and uses it to access a system. Since a password is only used once in OPIE, a discovered password is of little use to an attacker. OPIE uses a secure hash and a challenge/response system to manage passwords. The FreeBSD implementation uses the MD5 hash by default.

OPIE uses three different types of passwords. The first is the usual UNIX® or Kerberos password. The second is the one-time password which is generated by opiekey. The third type of password is the "secret password" which is used to generate one-time passwords. The secret password has nothing to do with, and should be different from, the UNIX® password.

There are two other pieces of data that are important to OPIE. One is the "seed" or "key", consisting of two letters and five digits. The other is the "iteration count", a number between 1 and 100. OPIE creates the one-time password by concatenating the seed and the secret password, applying the MD5 hash as many times as specified by the iteration count, and turning the result into six short English words which represent the one-time password. The authentication system keeps track of the last one-time password used, and the user is authenticated if the hash of the user-provided password is equal to the previous password. Because a one-way hash is used, it is impossible to generate future one-time passwords if a successfully used password is captured. The iteration count is decremented after each successful login to keep the user and the login program in sync. When the iteration count gets down to 1, OPIE must be reinitialized.

There are a few programs involved in this process. A one-time password, or a consecutive list of one-time passwords, is generated by passing an iteration count, a seed, and a secret password to opiekey(1). In addition to initializing OPIE, opiepasswd(1) is used to change passwords, iteration counts, or seeds. The relevant credential files in /etc/opiekeys are examined by opieinfo(1) which prints out the invoking user's current iteration count and seed.

This section describes four different sorts of operations. The first is how to set up one-time-passwords for the first time over a secure connection. The second is how to use opiepasswd over an insecure connection. The third is how to log in over an insecure connection. The fourth is how to generate a number of keys which can be written down or printed out to use at insecure locations.

13.3.1. Initializing OPIE

To initialize OPIE for the first time, run this command from a secure location:

```
% opiepasswd -c
Adding unfurl:
Only use this method from the console; NEVER from remote. If you are using
telnet, xterm, or a dial-in, type ^C now or exit with no password.
Then run opiepasswd without the -c parameter.
Using MD5 to compute responses.
Enter new secret pass phrase:
Again new secret pass phrase:

ID unfurl OTP key is 499 to4268
MOS MALL GOAT ARM AVID COED
```

The -c sets console mode which assumes that the command is being run from a secure location, such as a computer under the user's control or a SSH session to a computer under the user's control.

When prompted, enter the secret password which will be used to generate the one-time login keys. This password should be difficult to guess and should be different than the password which is associated with the user's login account. It must be between 10 and 127 characters long. Remember this password.

The ID line lists the login name (unfurl), default iteration count (499), and default seed (to4268). When logging in, the system will remember these parameters and display them, meaning that they do not have to be memorized. The last line lists the generated one-time password which corresponds to those parameters and the secret password. At the next login, use this one-time password.

13.3.2. Insecure Connection Initialization

To initialize or change the secret password on an insecure system, a secure connection is needed to some place where opiekey can be run. This might be a shell prompt on a trusted machine. An iteration count is needed, where 100 is probably a good value, and the seed can either be specified or the randomly-generated one used. On the insecure connection, the machine being initialized, use opiepasswd(1):

```
% opiepasswd

Updating unfurl:
You need the response from an OTP generator.
Old secret pass phrase:
  otp-md5 498 to4268 ext
  Response: GAME GAG WELT OUT DOWN CHAT
New secret pass phrase:
  otp-md5 499 to4269
  Response: LINE PAP MILK NELL BUOY TROY

ID mark OTP key is 499 gr4269
LINE PAP MILK NELL BUOY TROY
```

To accept the default seed, press Return. Before entering an access password, move over to the secure connection and give it the same parameters:

```
% opiekey 498 to4268
Using the MD5 algorithm to compute response.
Reminder: Do not use opiekey from telnet or dial-in sessions.
Enter secret pass phrase:
GAME GAG WELT OUT DOWN CHAT
```

Switch back over to the insecure connection, and copy the generated one-time password over to the relevant program.

13.3.3. Generating a Single One-time Password

After initializing OPIE and logging in, a prompt like this will be displayed:

```
% telnet example.com
Trying 10.0.0.1...
Connected to example.com
Escape character is '^]'.

FreeBSD/i386 (example.com) (ttypa)

login: <username>
otp-md5 498 gr4269 ext
Password:
```

The OPIE prompts provides a useful feature. If Return is pressed at the password prompt, the prompt will turn echo on and display what is typed. This can be useful when attempting to type in a password by hand from a printout.

At this point, generate the one-time password to answer this login prompt. This must be done on a trusted system where it is safe to run opiekey(1). There are versions of this command for Windows®, Mac OS® and FreeBSD. This command needs the iteration count and the seed as command line options. Use cut-and-paste from the login prompt on the machine being logged in to.

On the trusted system:

```
% opiekey 498 to4268
Using the MD5 algorithm to compute response.
Reminder: Do not use opiekey from telnet or dial-in sessions.
Enter secret pass phrase:
GAME GAG WELT OUT DOWN CHAT
```

Once the one-time password is generated, continue to log in.

13.3.4. Generating Multiple One-time Passwords

Sometimes there is no access to a trusted machine or secure connection. In this case, it is possible to use opiekey(1) to generate a number of one-time passwords beforehand. For example:

```
% opiekey -n 5 30 zz99999
Using the MD5 algorithm to compute response.
Reminder: Do not use opiekey from telnet or dial-in sessions.
Enter secret pass phrase: <secret password>
26: JOAN BORE FOSS DES NAY QUIT
27: LATE BIAS SLAY FOLK MUCH TRIG
28: SALT TIN ANTI LOON NEAL USE
29: RIO ODIN GO BYE FURY TIC
30: GREW JIVE SAN GIRD BOIL PHI
```

The -n 5 requests five keys in sequence, and 30 specifies what the last iteration number should be. Note that these are printed out in *reverse* order of use. The really paranoid might want to write the results down by hand; otherwise, print the list. Each line shows both the iteration count and the one-time password. Scratch off the passwords as they are used.

13.3.5. Restricting Use of UNIX® Passwords

OPIE can restrict the use of UNIX® passwords based on the IP address of a login session. The relevant file is / etc/opieaccess, which is present by default. Refer to opieaccess(5) for more information on this file and which security considerations to be aware of when using it.

Here is a sample `opieaccess`:

```
permit 192.168.0.0 255.255.0.0
```

This line allows users whose IP source address (which is vulnerable to spoofing) matches the specified value and mask, to use UNIX® passwords at any time.

If no rules in `opieaccess` are matched, the default is to deny non-OPIE logins.

13.4. TCP Wrapper

Written by Tom Rhodes.

TCP Wrapper is a host-based access control system which extends the abilities of Section 28.2, "The inetd Super-Server". It can be configured to provide logging support, return messages, and connection restrictions for the server daemons under the control of inetd. Refer to tcpd(8) for more information about TCP Wrapper and its features.

TCP Wrapper should not be considered a replacement for a properly configured firewall. Instead, TCP Wrapper should be used in conjunction with a firewall and other security enhancements in order to provide another layer of protection in the implementation of a security policy.

13.4.1. Initial Configuration

To enable TCP Wrapper in FreeBSD, add the following lines to `/etc/rc.conf` :

```
inetd_enable="YES"
inetd_flags="-Ww"
```

Then, properly configure `/etc/hosts.allow`.

> ### Note
>
> Unlike other implementations of TCP Wrapper, the use of `hosts.deny` is deprecated in Free-BSD. All configuration options should be placed in `/etc/hosts.allow`.

In the simplest configuration, daemon connection policies are set to either permit or block, depending on the options in `/etc/hosts.allow`. The default configuration in FreeBSD is to allow all connections to the daemons started with inetd.

Basic configuration usually takes the form of `daemon : address : action`, where `daemon` is the daemon which inetd started, `address` is a valid hostname, IP address, or an IPv6 address enclosed in brackets ([ ]), and `action` is either `allow` or `deny`. TCP Wrapper uses a first rule match semantic, meaning that the configuration file is scanned from the beginning for a matching rule. When a match is found, the rule is applied and the search process stops.

For example, to allow POP3 connections via the mail/qpopper daemon, the following lines should be appended to `hosts.allow`:

```
# This line is required for POP3 connections:
qpopper : ALL : allow
```

Whenever this file is edited, restart inetd:

```
# service inetd restart
```

13.4.2. Advanced Configuration

TCP Wrapper provides advanced options to allow more control over the way connections are handled. In some cases, it may be appropriate to return a comment to certain hosts or daemon connections. In other cases, a log entry should be recorded or an email sent to the administrator. Other situations may require the use of a service for local connections only. This is all possible through the use of configuration options known as wildcards, expansion characters, and external command execution.

Suppose that a situation occurs where a connection should be denied yet a reason should be sent to the host who attempted to establish that connection. That action is possible with `twist`. When a connection attempt is made, `twist` executes a shell command or script. An example exists in `hosts.allow`:

```
# The rest of the daemons are protected.
ALL : ALL \
 : severity auth.info \
 : twist /bin/echo "You are not welcome to use %d from %h."
```

In this example, the message "You are not allowed to use *daemon name* from *hostname*." will be returned for any daemon not configured in `hosts.allow`. This is useful for sending a reply back to the connection initiator right after the established connection is dropped. Any message returned *must* be wrapped in quote (") characters.

Warning

It may be possible to launch a denial of service attack on the server if an attacker floods these daemons with connection requests.

Another possibility is to use `spawn`. Like `twist`, `spawn` implicitly denies the connection and may be used to run external shell commands or scripts. Unlike `twist`, `spawn` will not send a reply back to the host who established the connection. For example, consider the following configuration:

```
# We do not allow connections from example.com:
ALL : .example.com \
 : spawn (/bin/echo %a from %h attempted to access %d >> \
   /var/log/connections.log) \
 : deny
```

This will deny all connection attempts from `*.example.com` and log the hostname, IP address, and the daemon to which access was attempted to `/var/log/connections.log` . This example uses the substitution characters `%a` and `%h`. Refer to hosts_access(5) for the complete list.

To match every instance of a daemon, domain, or IP address, use `ALL`. Another wildcard is `PARANOID` which may be used to match any host which provides an IP address that may be forged because the IP address differs from its resolved hostname. In this example, all connection requests to Sendmail which have an IP address that varies from its hostname will be denied:

```
# Block possibly spoofed requests to sendmail:
sendmail : PARANOID : deny
```

Caution

Using the `PARANOID` wildcard will result in denied connections if the client or server has a broken DNS setup.

To learn more about wildcards and their associated functionality, refer to hosts_access(5).

Note

When adding new configuration lines, make sure that any unneeded entries for that daemon are commented out in hosts.allow.

13.5. Kerberos

Contributed by Tillman Hodgson.
Based on a contribution by Mark Murray.

Kerberos is a network authentication protocol which was originally created by the Massachusetts Institute of Technology (MIT) as a way to securely provide authentication across a potentially hostile network. The Kerberos protocol uses strong cryptography so that both a client and server can prove their identity without sending any unencrypted secrets over the network. Kerberos can be described as an identity-verifying proxy system and as a trusted third-party authentication system. After a user authenticates with Kerberos, their communications can be encrypted to assure privacy and data integrity.

The only function of Kerberos is to provide the secure authentication of users and servers on the network. It does not provide authorization or auditing functions. It is recommended that Kerberos be used with other security methods which provide authorization and audit services.

The current version of the protocol is version 5, described in RFC 4120. Several free implementations of this protocol are available, covering a wide range of operating systems. MIT continues to develop their Kerberos package. It is commonly used in the US as a cryptography product, and has historically been subject to US export regulations. In FreeBSD, MIT Kerberos is available as the security/krb5 package or port. The Heimdal Kerberos implementation was explicitly developed outside of the US to avoid export regulations. The Heimdal Kerberos distribution is included in the base FreeBSD installation, and another distribution with more configurable options is available as security/heimdal in the Ports Collection.

In Kerberos users and services are identified as "principals" which are contained within an administrative grouping, called a "realm". A typical user principal would be of the form *user@REALM* (realms are traditionally uppercase).

This section provides a guide on how to set up Kerberos using the Heimdal distribution included in FreeBSD.

For purposes of demonstrating a Kerberos installation, the name spaces will be as follows:

- The DNS domain (zone) will be example.org.

- The Kerberos realm will be EXAMPLE.ORG.

Note

Use real domain names when setting up Kerberos, even if it will run internally. This avoids DNS problems and assures inter-operation with other Kerberos realms.

13.5.1. Setting up a Heimdal KDC

The Key Distribution Center (KDC) is the centralized authentication service that Kerberos provides, the "trusted third party" of the system. It is the computer that issues Kerberos tickets, which are used for clients to authenticate to servers. Because the KDC is considered trusted by all other computers in the Kerberos realm, it has heightened security concerns. Direct access to the KDC should be limited.

While running a KDC requires few computing resources, a dedicated machine acting only as a KDC is recommended for security reasons.

To begin setting up a KDC, add these lines to /etc/rc.conf :

```
kdc_enable="YES"
kadmind_enable="YES"
```

Next, edit /etc/krb5.conf as follows:

```
[libdefaults]
    default_realm = EXAMPLE.ORG
[realms]
    EXAMPLE.ORG  = {
 kdc = kerberos.example.org
 admin_server = kerberos.example.org
    }
[domain_realm]
    .example.org  = EXAMPLE.ORG
```

In this example, the KDC will use the fully-qualified hostname kerberos.example.org. The hostname of the KDC must be resolvable in the DNS.

Kerberos can also use the DNS to locate KDCs, instead of a [realms] section in /etc/krb5.conf . For large organizations that have their own DNS servers, the above example could be trimmed to:

```
[libdefaults]
        default_realm = EXAMPLE.ORG
[domain_realm]
    .example.org  = EXAMPLE.ORG
```

With the following lines being included in the example.org zone file:

```
_kerberos._udp      IN  SRV     01 00 88 kerberos.example.org  .
_kerberos._tcp      IN  SRV     01 00 88 kerberos.example.org  .
_kpasswd._udp       IN  SRV     01 00 464 kerberos.example.org  .
_kerberos-adm._tcp  IN  SRV     01 00 749 kerberos.example.org  .
_kerberos           IN  TXT     EXAMPLE.ORG
```

Note

In order for clients to be able to find the Kerberos services, they *must* have either a fully configured /etc/krb5.conf or a minimally configured /etc/krb5.conf *and* a properly configured DNS server.

Next, create the Kerberos database which contains the keys of all principals (users and hosts) encrypted with a master password. It is not required to remember this password as it will be stored in /var/heimdal/m-key ; it would be reasonable to use a 45-character random password for this purpose. To create the master key, run kstash and enter a password:

```
# kstash
Master key: xxxxxxxxxxxxxxxxxxxxxx
Verifying password - Master key: xxxxxxxxxxxxxxxxxxxxxx
```

Once the master key has been created, the database should be initialized. The Kerberos administrative tool kadmin(8) can be used on the KDC in a mode that operates directly on the database, without using the kadmind(8) network service, as kadmin -l. This resolves the chicken-and-egg problem of trying to connect to the database before it is created. At the kadmin prompt, use init to create the realm's initial database:

```
# kadmin -l
```

```
kadmin> init EXAMPLE.ORG
Realm max ticket life [unlimited]:
```

Lastly, while still in kadmin, create the first principal using add. Stick to the default options for the principal for now, as these can be changed later with modify. Type ? at the prompt to see the available options.

```
kadmin> add tillman
Max ticket life [unlimited]:
Max renewable life [unlimited]:
Attributes []:
Password: xxxxxxxx
Verifying password - Password: xxxxxxxx
```

Next, start the KDC services by running service kdc start and service kadmind start. While there will not be any kerberized daemons running at this point, it is possible to confirm that the KDC is functioning by obtaining a ticket for the principal that was just created:

```
% kinit tillman
tillman@EXAMPLE.ORG's Password:
```

Confirm that a ticket was successfully obtained using klist:

```
% klist
Credentials cache: FILE:/tmp/krb5cc_1001
 Principal: tillman@EXAMPLE.ORG

  Issued               Expires             Principal
Aug 27 15:37:58 2013  Aug 28 01:37:58 2013  krbtgt/EXAMPLE.ORG@EXAMPLE.ORG
```

The temporary ticket can be destroyed when the test is finished:

```
% kdestroy
```

13.5.2. Configuring a Server to Use Kerberos

The first step in configuring a server to use Kerberos authentication is to ensure that it has the correct configuration in /etc/krb5.conf. The version from the KDC can be used as-is, or it can be regenerated on the new system.

Next, create /etc/krb5.keytab on the server. This is the main part of "Kerberizing" a service — it corresponds to generating a secret shared between the service and the KDC. The secret is a cryptographic key, stored in a "keytab". The keytab contains the server's host key, which allows it and the KDC to verify each others' identity. It must be transmitted to the server in a secure fashion, as the security of the server can be broken if the key is made public. Typically, the keytab is generated on an administrator's trusted machine using kadmin, then securely transferred to the server, e.g., with scp(1); it can also be created directly on the server if that is consistent with the desired security policy. It is very important that the keytab is transmitted to the server in a secure fashion: if the key is known by some other party, that party can impersonate any user to the server! Using kadmin on the server directly is convenient, because the entry for the host principal in the KDC database is also created using kadmin.

Of course, kadmin is a kerberized service; a Kerberos ticket is needed to authenticate to the network service, but to ensure that the user running kadmin is actually present (and their session has not been hijacked), kadmin will prompt for the password to get a fresh ticket. The principal authenticating to the kadmin service must be permitted to use the kadmin interface, as specified in kadmind.acl. See the section titled "Remote administration" in info heimdal for details on designing access control lists. Instead of enabling remote kadmin access, the administrator could securely connect to the KDC via the local console or ssh(1), and perform administration locally using kadmin -l.

After installing /etc/krb5.conf, use add --random-key in kadmin. This adds the server's host principal to the database, but does not extract a copy of the host principal key to a keytab. To generate the keytab, use ext to extract the server's host principal key to its own keytab:

```
# kadmin
```

```
kadmin> add --random-key host/myserver.example.org
Max ticket life [unlimited]:
Max renewable life [unlimited]:
Principal expiration time [never]:
Password expiration time [never]:
Attributes []:
kadmin> ext_keytab host/myserver.example.org
kadmin> exit
```

Note that ext_keytab stores the extracted key in /etc/krb5.keytab by default. This is good when being run on the server being kerberized, but the --keytab *path/to/file* argument should be used when the keytab is being extracted elsewhere:

```
# kadmin
kadmin> ext_keytab --keytab=/tmp/example.keytab    host/myserver.example.org
kadmin> exit
```

The keytab can then be securely copied to the server using scp(1) or a removable media. Be sure to specify a non-default keytab name to avoid inserting unneeded keys into the system's keytab.

At this point, the server can read encrypted messages from the KDC using its shared key, stored in krb5.keytab. It is now ready for the Kerberos-using services to be enabled. One of the most common such services is sshd(8), which supports Kerberos via the GSS-API. In /etc/ssh/sshd_config , add the line:

```
GSSAPIAuthentication yes
```

After making this change, sshd(8) must be restarted for the new configuration to take effect: service sshd restart .

13.5.3. Configuring a Client to Use Kerberos

As it was for the server, the client requires configuration in /etc/krb5.conf . Copy the file in place (securely) or re-enter it as needed.

Test the client by using kinit, klist, and kdestroy from the client to obtain, show, and then delete a ticket for an existing principal. Kerberos applications should also be able to connect to Kerberos enabled servers. If that does not work but obtaining a ticket does, the problem is likely with the server and not with the client or the KDC. In the case of kerberized ssh(1), GSS-API is disabled by default, so test using ssh -o GSSAPIAuthentication=yes *hostname*.

When testing a Kerberized application, try using a packet sniffer such as tcpdump to confirm that no sensitive information is sent in the clear.

Various Kerberos client applications are available. With the advent of a bridge so that applications using SASL for authentication can use GSS-API mechanisms as well, large classes of client applications can use Kerberos for authentication, from Jabber clients to IMAP clients.

Users within a realm typically have their Kerberos principal mapped to a local user account. Occasionally, one needs to grant access to a local user account to someone who does not have a matching Kerberos principal. For example, tillman@EXAMPLE.ORG may need access to the local user account webdevelopers. Other principals may also need access to that local account.

The .k5login and .k5users files, placed in a user's home directory, can be used to solve this problem. For example, if the following .k5login is placed in the home directory of webdevelopers, both principals listed will have access to that account without requiring a shared password:

```
tillman@example.org
jdoe@example.org
```

Refer to ksu(1) for more information about .k5users .

13.5.4. MIT Differences

The major difference between the MIT and Heimdal implementations is that kadmin has a different, but equivalent, set of commands and uses a different protocol. If the KDC is MIT, the Heimdal version of kadmin cannot be used to administer the KDC remotely, and vice versa.

Client applications may also use slightly different command line options to accomplish the same tasks. Following the instructions at http://web.mit.edu/Kerberos/www/ is recommended. Be careful of path issues: the MIT port installs into /usr/local/ by default, and the FreeBSD system applications run instead of the MIT versions if PATH lists the system directories first.

When using MIT Kerberos as a KDC on FreeBSD, the following edits should also be made to rc.conf:

```
kerberos5_server="/usr/local/sbin/krb5kdc"
kadmind5_server="/usr/local/sbin/kadmind"
kerberos5_server_flags=""
kerberos5_server_enable="YES"
kadmind5_server_enable="YES"
```

13.5.5. Kerberos Tips, Tricks, and Troubleshooting

When configuring and troubleshooting Kerberos, keep the following points in mind:

- When using either Heimdal or MIT Kerberos from ports, ensure that the PATH lists the port's versions of the client applications before the system versions.

- If all the computers in the realm do not have synchronized time settings, authentication may fail. Section 28.11, "Clock Synchronization with NTP" describes how to synchronize clocks using NTP.

- If the hostname is changed, the host/ principal must be changed and the keytab updated. This also applies to special keytab entries like the HTTP/ principal used for Apache's www/mod_auth_kerb.

- All hosts in the realm must be both forward and reverse resolvable in DNS or, at a minimum, exist in /etc/hosts . CNAMEs will work, but the A and PTR records must be correct and in place. The error message for unresolvable hosts is not intuitive: Kerberos5 refuses authentication because Read req failed: Key table entry not found.

- Some operating systems that act as clients to the KDC do not set the permissions for ksu to be setuid root. This means that ksu does not work. This is a permissions problem, not a KDC error.

- With MIT Kerberos, to allow a principal to have a ticket life longer than the default lifetime of ten hours, use modify_principal at the kadmin(8) prompt to change the maxlife of both the principal in question and the krbtgt principal. The principal can then use kinit -l to request a ticket with a longer lifetime.

- When running a packet sniffer on the KDC to aid in troubleshooting while running kinit from a workstation, the Ticket Granting Ticket (TGT) is sent immediately, even before the password is typed. This is because the Kerberos server freely transmits a TGT to any unauthorized request. However, every TGT is encrypted in a key derived from the user's password. When a user types their password, it is not sent to the KDC, it is instead used to decrypt the TGT that kinit already obtained. If the decryption process results in a valid ticket with a valid time stamp, the user has valid Kerberos credentials. These credentials include a session key for establishing secure communications with the Kerberos server in the future, as well as the actual TGT, which is encrypted with the Kerberos server's own key. This second layer of encryption allows the Kerberos server to verify the authenticity of each TGT.

- Host principals can have a longer ticket lifetime. If the user principal has a lifetime of a week but the host being connected to has a lifetime of nine hours, the user cache will have an expired host principal and the ticket cache will not work as expected.

- When setting up krb5.dict to prevent specific bad passwords from being used as described in kadmind(8), remember that it only applies to principals that have a password policy assigned to them. The format used in krb5.dict is one string per line. Creating a symbolic link to /usr/share/dict/words   might be useful.

13.5.6. Mitigating Kerberos Limitations

Since Kerberos is an all or nothing approach, every service enabled on the network must either be modified to work with Kerberos or be otherwise secured against network attacks. This is to prevent user credentials from being stolen and re-used. An example is when Kerberos is enabled on all remote shells but the non-Kerberized POP3 mail server sends passwords in plain text.

The KDC is a single point of failure. By design, the KDC must be as secure as its master password database. The KDC should have absolutely no other services running on it and should be physically secure. The danger is high because Kerberos stores all passwords encrypted with the same master key which is stored as a file on the KDC.

A compromised master key is not quite as bad as one might fear. The master key is only used to encrypt the Kerberos database and as a seed for the random number generator. As long as access to the KDC is secure, an attacker cannot do much with the master key.

If the KDC is unavailable, network services are unusable as authentication cannot be performed. This can be alleviated with a single master KDC and one or more slaves, and with careful implementation of secondary or fall-back authentication using PAM.

Kerberos allows users, hosts and services to authenticate between themselves. It does not have a mechanism to authenticate the KDC to the users, hosts, or services. This means that a trojanned kinit could record all user names and passwords. File system integrity checking tools like security/tripwire can alleviate this.

13.5.7. Resources and Further Information

- The Kerberos FAQ

- Designing an Authentication System: a Dialog in Four Scenes

- RFC 4120, The Kerberos Network Authentication Service (V5)

- MIT Kerberos home page

- Heimdal Kerberos home page

13.6. OpenSSL

Written by Tom Rhodes.

OpenSSL is an open source implementation of the SSL and TLS protocols. It provides an encryption transport layer on top of the normal communications layer, allowing it to be intertwined with many network applications and services.

The version of OpenSSL included in FreeBSD supports the Secure Sockets Layer v2/v3 (SSLv2/SSLv3) and Transport Layer Security v1 (TLSv1) network security protocols and can be used as a general cryptographic library.

OpenSSL is often used to encrypt authentication of mail clients and to secure web based transactions such as credit card payments. Some ports, such as www/apache24 and databases/postgresql91-server, include a compile option for building with OpenSSL.

FreeBSD provides two versions of OpenSSL: one in the base system and one in the Ports Collection. Users can choose which version to use by default for other ports using the following knobs:

- WITH_OPENSSL_PORT: when set, the port will use OpenSSL from the security/openssl port, even if the version in the base system is up to date or newer.

- WITH_OPENSSL_BASE: when set, the port will compile against OpenSSL provided by the base system.

Another common use of OpenSSL is to provide certificates for use with software applications. Certificates can be used to verify the credentials of a company or individual. If a certificate has not been signed by an external *Certificate Authority* (CA), such as http://www.verisign.com, the application that uses the certificate will produce a warning. There is a cost associated with obtaining a signed certificate and using a signed certificate is not mandatory as certificates can be self-signed. However, using an external authority will prevent warnings and can put users at ease.

This section demonstrates how to create and use certificates on a FreeBSD system. Refer to Section 28.5.2, "Configuring an LDAP Server" for an example of how to create a CA for signing one's own certificates.

For more information about SSL, read the free OpenSSL Cookbook.

13.6.1. Generating Certificates

To generate a certificate that will be signed by an external CA, issue the following command and input the information requested at the prompts. This input information will be written to the certificate. At the Common Name prompt, input the fully qualified name for the system that will use the certificate. If this name does not match the server, the application verifying the certificate will issue a warning to the user, rendering the verification provided by the certificate as useless.

```
# openssl req -new -nodes -out req.pem -keyout cert.key -sha256 -newkey rsa:2048
Generating a 2048 bit RSA private key
..................+++
.........................................................+++
writing new private key to 'cert.key'
-----
You are about to be asked to enter information that will be incorporated
into your certificate request.
What you are about to enter is what is called a Distinguished Name or a DN.
There are quite a few fields but you can leave some blank
For some fields there will be a default value,
If you enter '.', the field will be left blank.
-----
Country Name (2 letter code) [AU]:US
State or Province Name (full name) [Some-State]:PA
Locality Name (eg, city) []:Pittsburgh
Organization Name (eg, company) [Internet Widgits Pty Ltd]:My Company
Organizational Unit Name (eg, section) []:Systems Administrator
Common Name (eg, YOUR name) []:localhost.example.org
Email Address []:trhodes@FreeBSD.org

Please enter the following 'extra' attributes
to be sent with your certificate request
A challenge password []:
An optional company name []:Another Name
```

Other options, such as the expire time and alternate encryption algorithms, are available when creating a certificate. A complete list of options is described in openssl(1).

This command will create two files in the current directory. The certificate request, req.pem, can be sent to a CA who will validate the entered credentials, sign the request, and return the signed certificate. The second file, cert.key , is the private key for the certificate and should be stored in a secure location. If this falls in the hands of others, it can be used to impersonate the user or the server.

Alternately, if a signature from a CA is not required, a self-signed certificate can be created. First, generate the RSA key:

```
# openssl genrsa -rand -genkey -out cert.key 2048
0 semi-random bytes loaded
Generating RSA private key, 2048 bit long modulus
..............................................+++
```

```
. . . . . . . . . . . . . . . . . . . . . . . . . . . . . . . . . . . . . . . . . . . . . . . . . . . . . . . . . . . . . . . . . . . . . . . . . . . . . . . . . . . . . . . . . .
+++
e is 65537 (0x10001)
```

Use this key to create a self-signed certificate. Follow the usual prompts for creating a certificate:

```
# openssl req -new -x509 -days 365 -key cert.key -out cert.crt -sha256
You are about to be asked to enter information that will be incorporated
into your certificate request.
What you are about to enter is what is called a Distinguished Name or a DN.
There are quite a few fields but you can leave some blank
For some fields there will be a default value,
If you enter '.', the field will be left blank.
-----
Country Name (2 letter code) [AU]:US
State or Province Name (full name) [Some-State]:PA
Locality Name (eg, city) []:Pittsburgh
Organization Name (eg, company) [Internet Widgits Pty Ltd]:My Company
Organizational Unit Name (eg, section) []:Systems Administrator
Common Name (e.g. server FQDN or YOUR name) []:localhost.example.org
Email Address []:trhodes@FreeBSD.org
```

This will create two new files in the current directory: a private key file cert.key , and the certificate itself, cert.crt . These should be placed in a directory, preferably under /etc/ssl/ , which is readable only by root. Permissions of 0700 are appropriate for these files and can be set using chmod.

13.6.2. Using Certificates

One use for a certificate is to encrypt connections to the Sendmail mail server in order to prevent the use of clear text authentication.

> **Note**
>
> Some mail clients will display an error if the user has not installed a local copy of the certificate. Refer to the documentation included with the software for more information on certificate installation.

In FreeBSD 10.0-RELEASE and above, it is possible to create a self-signed certificate for Sendmail automatically. To enable this, add the following lines to /etc/rc.conf :

```
sendmail_enable="YES"
sendmail_cert_create="YES"
sendmail_cert_cn="localhost.example.org "
```

This will automatically create a self-signed certificate, /etc/mail/certs/host.cert , a signing key, /etc/mail/certs/host.key , and a CA certificate, /etc/mail/certs/cacert.pem . The certificate will use the Common Name specified in sendmail_cert_cn. After saving the edits, restart Sendmail:

```
# service sendmail restart
```

If all went well, there will be no error messages in /var/log/maillog . For a simple test, connect to the mail server's listening port using telnet:

```
# telnet example.com 25
Trying 192.0.34.166...
Connected to example.com.
Escape character is '^]'.
220 example.com ESMTP Sendmail 8.14.7/8.14.7; Fri, 18 Apr 2014 11:50:32 -0400 (EDT)
ehlo example.com
250-example.com Hello example.com [192.0.34.166], pleased to meet you
```

```
250-ENHANCEDSTATUSCODES
250-PIPELINING
250-8BITMIME
250-SIZE
250-DSN
250-ETRN
250-AUTH LOGIN PLAIN
250-STARTTLS
250-DELIVERBY
250 HELP
quit
221 2.0.0 example.com closing connection
Connection closed by foreign host.
```

If the STARTTLS line appears in the output, everything is working correctly.

13.7. VPN over IPsec

Written by Nik Clayton.
Written by Hiten M. Pandya.

Internet Protocol Security (IPsec) is a set of protocols which sit on top of the Internet Protocol (IP) layer. It allows two or more hosts to communicate in a secure manner by authenticating and encrypting each IP packet of a communication session. The FreeBSD IPsec network stack is based on the http://www.kame.net/ implementation and supports both IPv4 and IPv6 sessions.

IPsec is comprised of the following sub-protocols:

* *Encapsulated Security Payload (ESP)*: this protocol protects the IP packet data from third party interference by encrypting the contents using symmetric cryptography algorithms such as Blowfish and 3DES.

* *Authentication Header (AH)*: this protocol protects the IP packet header from third party interference and spoofing by computing a cryptographic checksum and hashing the IP packet header fields with a secure hashing function. This is then followed by an additional header that contains the hash, to allow the information in the packet to be authenticated.

* *IP Payload Compression Protocol (IPComp)*: this protocol tries to increase communication performance by compressing the IP payload in order to reduce the amount of data sent.

These protocols can either be used together or separately, depending on the environment.

IPsec supports two modes of operation. The first mode, *Transport Mode*, protects communications between two hosts. The second mode, *Tunnel Mode*, is used to build virtual tunnels, commonly known as Virtual Private Networks (VPNs). Consult ipsec(4) for detailed information on the IPsec subsystem in FreeBSD.

IPsec support is enabled by default on FreeBSD 11 and later. For previous versions of FreeBSD, add these options to a custom kernel configuration file and rebuild the kernel using the instructions in Chapter 8, *Configuring the FreeBSD Kernel*:

```
options    IPSEC       #IP security
device     crypto
```

If IPsec debugging support is desired, the following kernel option should also be added:

```
options   IPSEC_DEBUG #debug for IP security
```

This rest of this chapter demonstrates the process of setting up an IPsec VPN between a home network and a corporate network. In the example scenario:

* Both sites are connected to the Internet through a gateway that is running FreeBSD.

- The gateway on each network has at least one external IP address. In this example, the corporate LAN's external IP address is `172.16.5.4` and the home LAN's external IP address is `192.168.1.12`.

- The internal addresses of the two networks can be either public or private IP addresses. However, the address space must not collide. For example, both networks cannot use `192.168.1.x`. In this example, the corporate LAN's internal IP address is `10.246.38.1` and the home LAN's internal IP address is `10.0.0.5`.

13.7.1. Configuring a VPN on FreeBSD

Written by Tom Rhodes.

To begin, security/ipsec-tools must be installed from the Ports Collection. This software provides a number of applications which support the configuration.

The next requirement is to create two gif(4) pseudo-devices which will be used to tunnel packets and allow both networks to communicate properly. As root, run the following commands, replacing *internal* and *external* with the real IP addresses of the internal and external interfaces of the two gateways:

```
# ifconfig gif0 create
# ifconfig gif0 internal1 internal2
# ifconfig gif0 tunnel  external1 external2
```

Verify the setup on each gateway, using `ifconfig`. Here is the output from Gateway 1:

```
gif0: flags=8051 mtu 1280
tunnel inet 172.16.5.4 --> 192.168.1.12
inet6 fe80::2e0:81ff:fe02:5881%gif0 prefixlen 64 scopeid 0x6
inet 10.246.38.1 --> 10.0.0.5 netmask 0xffffff00
```

Here is the output from Gateway 2:

```
gif0: flags=8051 mtu 1280
tunnel inet 192.168.1.12 --> 172.16.5.4
inet 10.0.0.5 --> 10.246.38.1 netmask 0xffffff00
inet6 fe80::250:bfff:fe3a:c1f%gif0 prefixlen 64 scopeid 0x4
```

Once complete, both internal IP addresses should be reachable using ping(8):

```
priv-net# ping 10.0.0.5
PING 10.0.0.5 (10.0.0.5): 56 data bytes
64 bytes from 10.0.0.5: icmp_seq=0 ttl=64 time=42.786 ms
64 bytes from 10.0.0.5: icmp_seq=1 ttl=64 time=19.255 ms
64 bytes from 10.0.0.5: icmp_seq=2 ttl=64 time=20.440 ms
64 bytes from 10.0.0.5: icmp_seq=3 ttl=64 time=21.036 ms
--- 10.0.0.5 ping statistics ---
4 packets transmitted, 4 packets received, 0% packet loss
round-trip min/avg/max/stddev = 19.255/25.879/42.786/9.782 ms

corp-net# ping 10.246.38.1
PING 10.246.38.1 (10.246.38.1): 56 data bytes
64 bytes from 10.246.38.1: icmp_seq=0 ttl=64 time=28.106 ms
64 bytes from 10.246.38.1: icmp_seq=1 ttl=64 time=42.917 ms
64 bytes from 10.246.38.1: icmp_seq=2 ttl=64 time=127.525 ms
64 bytes from 10.246.38.1: icmp_seq=3 ttl=64 time=119.896 ms
64 bytes from 10.246.38.1: icmp_seq=4 ttl=64 time=154.524 ms
--- 10.246.38.1 ping statistics ---
5 packets transmitted, 5 packets received, 0% packet loss
round-trip min/avg/max/stddev = 28.106/94.594/154.524/49.814 ms
```

As expected, both sides have the ability to send and receive ICMP packets from the privately configured addresses. Next, both gateways must be told how to route packets in order to correctly send traffic from either network. The following commands will achieve this goal:

```
corp-net# route add 10.0.0.0 10.0.0.5 255.255.255.0
```

```
corp-net# route add net 10.0.0.0: gateway 10.0.0.5
priv-net# route add 10.246.38.0 10.246.38.1 255.255.255.0
priv-net# route add host 10.246.38.0: gateway 10.246.38.1
```

At this point, internal machines should be reachable from each gateway as well as from machines behind the gateways. Again, use ping(8) to confirm:

```
corp-net# ping 10.0.0.8
PING 10.0.0.8 (10.0.0.8): 56 data bytes
64 bytes from 10.0.0.8: icmp_seq=0 ttl=63 time=92.391 ms
64 bytes from 10.0.0.8: icmp_seq=1 ttl=63 time=21.870 ms
64 bytes from 10.0.0.8: icmp_seq=2 ttl=63 time=198.022 ms
64 bytes from 10.0.0.8: icmp_seq=3 ttl=63 time=22.241 ms
64 bytes from 10.0.0.8: icmp_seq=4 ttl=63 time=174.705 ms
--- 10.0.0.8 ping statistics ---
5 packets transmitted, 5 packets received, 0% packet loss
round-trip min/avg/max/stddev = 21.870/101.846/198.022/74.001 ms

priv-net# ping 10.246.38.107
PING 10.246.38.1 (10.246.38.107): 56 data bytes
64 bytes from 10.246.38.107: icmp_seq=0 ttl=64 time=53.491 ms
64 bytes from 10.246.38.107: icmp_seq=1 ttl=64 time=23.395 ms
64 bytes from 10.246.38.107: icmp_seq=2 ttl=64 time=23.865 ms
64 bytes from 10.246.38.107: icmp_seq=3 ttl=64 time=21.145 ms
64 bytes from 10.246.38.107: icmp_seq=4 ttl=64 time=36.708 ms
--- 10.246.38.107 ping statistics ---
5 packets transmitted, 5 packets received, 0% packet loss
round-trip min/avg/max/stddev = 21.145/31.721/53.491/12.179 ms
```

Setting up the tunnels is the easy part. Configuring a secure link is a more in depth process. The following configuration uses pre-shared (PSK) RSA keys. Other than the IP addresses, the /usr/local/etc/racoon/racoon.conf on both gateways will be identical and look similar to:

```
path    pre_shared_key  "/usr/local/etc/racoon/psk.txt"; #location of pre-shared key file
log     debug; #log verbosity setting: set to 'notify' when testing and debugging is ↵
complete

padding # options are not to be changed
{
        maximum_length  20;
        randomize       off;
        strict_check    off;
        exclusive_tail  off;
}

timer # timing options. change as needed
{
        counter         5;
        interval        20 sec;
        persend         1;
#       natt_keepalive  15 sec;
        phase1          30 sec;
        phase2          15 sec;
}

listen # address [port] that racoon will listen on
{
        isakmp          172.16.5.4 [500];
        isakmp_natt     172.16.5.4 [4500];
}

remote  192.168.1.12 [500]
{
        exchange_mode   main,aggressive;
        doi             ipsec_doi;
        situation       identity_only;
```

```
        my_identifier    address 172.16.5.4;
        peers_identifier         address 192.168.1.12;
        lifetime         time 8 hour;
        passive          off;
        proposal_check   obey;
#       nat_traversal    off;
        generate_policy off;

                        proposal {
                                encryption_algorithm      blowfish;
                                hash_algorithm            md5;
                                authentication_method     pre_shared_key;
                                lifetime time             30 sec;
                                dh_group                  1;
                        }
}

sainfo  (address 10.246.38.0/24 any address 10.0.0.0/24 any) # address $network/
$netmask $type address $network/$netmask $type ( $type being any or esp)
{       # $network must be the two internal networks you are joining.
        pfs_group        1;
        lifetime         time    36000 sec;
        encryption_algorithm     blowfish,3des;
        authentication_algorithm         hmac_md5,hmac_sha1;
        compression_algorithm    deflate;
}
```

For descriptions of each available option, refer to the manual page for racoon.conf .

The Security Policy Database (SPD) needs to be configured so that FreeBSD and racoon are able to encrypt and decrypt network traffic between the hosts.

This can be achieved with a shell script, similar to the following, on the corporate gateway. This file will be used during system initialization and should be saved as /usr/local/etc/racoon/setkey.conf .

```
flush;
spdflush;
# To the home network
spdadd 10.246.38.0/24 10.0.0.0/24 any -P out ipsec esp/tunnel/172.16.5.4-192.168.1.12/
use;
spdadd 10.0.0.0/24 10.246.38.0/24 any -P in ipsec esp/tunnel/192.168.1.12-172.16.5.4/use;
```

Once in place, racoon may be started on both gateways using the following command:

 # /usr/local/sbin/racoon -F -f /usr/local/etc/racoon/racoon.conf -l /var/log/racoon.log

The output should be similar to the following:

```
corp-net# /usr/local/sbin/racoon -F -f /usr/local/etc/racoon/racoon.conf
Foreground mode.
2006-01-30 01:35:47: INFO: begin Identity Protection mode.
2006-01-30 01:35:48: INFO: received Vendor ID: KAME/racoon
2006-01-30 01:35:55: INFO: received Vendor ID: KAME/racoon
2006-01-30 01:36:04: INFO: ISAKMP-SA established 172.16.5.4[500]-192.168.1.12[500] ↵
spi:623b9b3bd2492452:7deab82d54ff704a
2006-01-30 01:36:05: INFO: initiate new phase 2 negotiation: 172.16.5.4[0]192.168.1.12[0]
2006-01-30 01:36:09: INFO: IPsec-SA established: ESP/Tunnel 192.168.1.12[0]-
>172.16.5.4[0] spi=28496098(0x1b2d0e2)
2006-01-30 01:36:09: INFO: IPsec-SA established: ESP/Tunnel 172.16.5.4[0]-
>192.168.1.12[0] spi=47784998(0x2d92426)
2006-01-30 01:36:13: INFO: respond new phase 2 negotiation: 172.16.5.4[0]192.168.1.12[0]
2006-01-30 01:36:18: INFO: IPsec-SA established: ESP/Tunnel 192.168.1.12[0]-
>172.16.5.4[0] spi=124397467(0x76a279b)
2006-01-30 01:36:18: INFO: IPsec-SA established: ESP/Tunnel 172.16.5.4[0]-
>192.168.1.12[0] spi=175852902(0xa7b4d66)
```

To ensure the tunnel is working properly, switch to another console and use tcpdump(1) to view network traffic using the following command. Replace em0 with the network interface card as required:

```
# tcpdump -i em0 host  172.16.5.4 and dst 192.168.1.12
```

Data similar to the following should appear on the console. If not, there is an issue and debugging the returned data will be required.

```
01:47:32.021683 IP corporatenetwork.com > 192.168.1.12.privatenetwork.com: ESPↄ
(spi=0x02acbf9f,seq=0xa)
01:47:33.022442 IP corporatenetwork.com > 192.168.1.12.privatenetwork.com: ESPↄ
(spi=0x02acbf9f,seq=0xb)
01:47:34.024218 IP corporatenetwork.com > 192.168.1.12.privatenetwork.com: ESPↄ
(spi=0x02acbf9f,seq=0xc)
```

At this point, both networks should be available and seem to be part of the same network. Most likely both networks are protected by a firewall. To allow traffic to flow between them, rules need to be added to pass packets. For the ipfw(8) firewall, add the following lines to the firewall configuration file:

```
ipfw add 00201 allow log esp from any to any
ipfw add 00202 allow log ah from any to any
ipfw add 00203 allow log ipencap from any to any
ipfw add 00204 allow log udp from any 500 to any
```

> ## Note
>
> The rule numbers may need to be altered depending on the current host configuration.

For users of pf(4) or ipf(8), the following rules should do the trick:

```
pass in quick proto esp from any to any
pass in quick proto ah from any to any
pass in quick proto ipencap from any to any
pass in quick proto udp from any port = 500 to any port = 500
pass in quick on gif0 from any to any
pass out quick proto esp from any to any
pass out quick proto ah from any to any
pass out quick proto ipencap from any to any
pass out quick proto udp from any port = 500 to any port = 500
pass out quick on gif0 from any to any
```

Finally, to allow the machine to start support for the VPN during system initialization, add the following lines to /etc/rc.conf :

```
ipsec_enable="YES"
ipsec_program="/usr/local/sbin/setkey"
ipsec_file="/usr/local/etc/racoon/setkey.conf" # allows setting up spd policies on boot
racoon_enable="yes"
```

13.8. OpenSSH

Contributed by Chern Lee.

OpenSSH is a set of network connectivity tools used to provide secure access to remote machines. Additionally, TCP/IP connections can be tunneled or forwarded securely through SSH connections. OpenSSH encrypts all traffic to effectively eliminate eavesdropping, connection hijacking, and other network-level attacks.

OpenSSH is maintained by the OpenBSD project and is installed by default in FreeBSD. It is compatible with both SSH version 1 and 2 protocols.

When data is sent over the network in an unencrypted form, network sniffers anywhere in between the client and server can steal user/password information or data transferred during the session. OpenSSH offers a variety of authentication and encryption methods to prevent this from happening. More information about OpenSSH is available from http://www.openssh.com/.

This section provides an overview of the built-in client utilities to securely access other systems and securely transfer files from a FreeBSD system. It then describes how to configure a SSH server on a FreeBSD system. More information is available in the man pages mentioned in this chapter.

13.8.1. Using the SSH Client Utilities

To log into a SSH server, use ssh and specify a username that exists on that server and the IP address or hostname of the server. If this is the first time a connection has been made to the specified server, the user will be prompted to first verify the server's fingerprint:

```
# ssh user@example.com
The authenticity of host 'example.com (10.0.0.1)' can't be established.
ECDSA key fingerprint is 25:cc:73:b5:b3:96:75:3d:56:19:49:d2:5c:1f:91:3b.
Are you sure you want to continue connecting (yes/no)? yes
Permanently added 'example.com' (ECDSA) to the list of known hosts.
Password for user@example.com: user_password
```

SSH utilizes a key fingerprint system to verify the authenticity of the server when the client connects. When the user accepts the key's fingerprint by typing yes when connecting for the first time, a copy of the key is saved to .ssh/known_hosts in the user's home directory. Future attempts to login are verified against the saved key and ssh will display an alert if the server's key does not match the saved key. If this occurs, the user should first verify why the key has changed before continuing with the connection.

By default, recent versions of OpenSSH only accept SSHv2 connections. By default, the client will use version 2 if possible and will fall back to version 1 if the server does not support version 2. To force ssh to only use the specified protocol, include -1 or -2. Additional options are described in ssh(1).

Use scp(1) to securely copy a file to or from a remote machine. This example copies COPYRIGHT on the remote system to a file of the same name in the current directory of the local system:

```
# scp user@example.com:/COPYRIGHT COPYRIGHT
Password for user@example.com: *******
COPYRIGHT                100% |*****************************|  4735
00:00
#
```

Since the fingerprint was already verified for this host, the server's key is automatically checked before prompting for the user's password.

The arguments passed to scp are similar to cp. The file or files to copy is the first argument and the destination to copy to is the second. Since the file is fetched over the network, one or more of the file arguments takes the form user@host:<path_to_remote_file>. Be aware when copying directories recursively that scp uses -r, whereas cp uses -R.

To open an interactive session for copying files, use sftp. Refer to sftp(1) for a list of available commands while in an sftp session.

13.8.1.1. Key-based Authentication

Instead of using passwords, a client can be configured to connect to the remote machine using keys. To generate RSA authentication keys, use ssh-keygen. To generate a public and private key pair, specify the type of key and follow the prompts. It is recommended to protect the keys with a memorable, but hard to guess passphrase.

```
% ssh-keygen -t rsa
Generating public/private rsa key pair.
```

```
Enter file in which to save the key (/home/user/.ssh/id_rsa):
Enter passphrase (empty for no passphrase):  ❶
Enter same passphrase again:                 ❷
Your identification has been saved in /home/user/.ssh/id_rsa.
Your public key has been saved in /home/user/.ssh/id_rsa.pub.
The key fingerprint is:
SHA256:54Xm9Uvtv6H4NOo6yjP/YCfODryvUU7yWHzMqeXwhq8 user@host.example.com
The key's randomart image is:
+---[RSA 2048]----+
|                 |
|                 |
|                 |
|      . o..      |
|      .S*+*o     |
|     . O=Oo . .  |
|      = Oo= oo.. |
|     .oB.* +.oo. |
|      =0E**.o..=|
+----[SHA256]-----+
```

❶   Type a passphrase here. It can contain spaces and symbols.
❷   Retype the passphrase to verify it.

The private key is stored in ~/.ssh/id_rsa and the public key is stored in ~/.ssh/id_rsa.pub. The *public* key must be copied to ~/.ssh/authorized_keys on the remote machine for key-based authentication to work.

Warning

Many users believe that keys are secure by design and will use a key without a passphrase. This is *dangerous* behavior. An administrator can verify that a key pair is protected by a passphrase by viewing the private key manually. If the private key file contains the word ENCRYPTED, the key owner is using a passphrase. In addition, to better secure end users, from may be placed in the public key file. For example, adding from="192.168.10.5" in front of the ssh-rsa prefix will only allow that specific user to log in from that IP address.

The options and files vary with different versions of OpenSSH. To avoid problems, consult ssh-keygen(1).

If a passphrase is used, the user is prompted for the passphrase each time a connection is made to the server. To load SSH keys into memory and remove the need to type the passphrase each time, use ssh-agent(1) and ssh-add(1).

Authentication is handled by ssh-agent, using the private keys that are loaded into it. ssh-agent can be used to launch another application like a shell or a window manager.

To use ssh-agent in a shell, start it with a shell as an argument. Add the identity by running ssh-add and entering the passphrase for the private key. The user will then be able to ssh to any host that has the corresponding public key installed. For example:

```
% ssh-agent csh
% ssh-add
Enter passphrase for key '/usr/home/user/.ssh/id_rsa':  ❶
Identity added: /usr/home/user/.ssh/id_rsa (/usr/home/user/.ssh/id_rsa)
%
```

❶   Enter the passphrase for the key.

To use ssh-agent in Xorg, add an entry for it in ~/.xinitrc. This provides the ssh-agent services to all programs launched in Xorg. An example ~/.xinitrc might look like this:

```
exec ssh-agent startxfce4
```

This launches `ssh-agent` , which in turn launches XFCE, every time Xorg starts. Once Xorg has been restarted so that the changes can take effect, run `ssh-add` to load all of the SSH keys.

13.8.1.2. SSH Tunneling

OpenSSH has the ability to create a tunnel to encapsulate another protocol in an encrypted session.

The following command tells `ssh` to create a tunnel for telnet:

```
% ssh -2 -N -f -L 5023:localhost:23 user@foo.example.com
%
```

This example uses the following options:

-2

> Forces `ssh` to use version 2 to connect to the server.

-N

> Indicates no command, or tunnel only. If omitted, `ssh` initiates a normal session.

-f

> Forces `ssh` to run in the background.

-L

> Indicates a local tunnel in *localport:remotehost:remoteport* format.

user@foo.example.com
> The login name to use on the specified remote SSH server.

An SSH tunnel works by creating a listen socket on `localhost` on the specified `localport`. It then forwards any connections received on `localport` via the SSH connection to the specified `remotehost:remoteport`. In the example, port `5023` on the client is forwarded to port `23` on the remote machine. Since port `23` is used by telnet, this creates an encrypted telnet session through an SSH tunnel.

This method can be used to wrap any number of insecure TCP protocols such as SMTP, POP3, and FTP, as seen in the following examples.

Example 13.1. Create a Secure Tunnel for SMTP

```
% ssh -2 -N -f -L 5025:localhost:25 user@mailserver.example.com
user@mailserver.example.com's password: *****
% telnet localhost 5025
Trying 127.0.0.1...
Connected to localhost.
Escape character is '^]'.
220 mailserver.example.com ESMTP
```

This can be used in conjunction with `ssh-keygen` and additional user accounts to create a more seamless SSH tunneling environment. Keys can be used in place of typing a password, and the tunnels can be run as a separate user.

Example 13.2. Secure Access of a POP3 Server

In this example, there is an SSH server that accepts connections from the outside. On the same network resides a mail server running a POP3 server. To check email in a secure manner, create an SSH connection to the SSH server and tunnel through to the mail server:

```
% ssh -2 -N -f -L 2110:mail.example.com:110 user@ssh-server.example.com
user@ssh-server.example.com's password: ******
```

Once the tunnel is up and running, point the email client to send POP3 requests to localhost on port 2110. This connection will be forwarded securely across the tunnel to mail.example.com.

Example 13.3. Bypassing a Firewall

Some firewalls filter both incoming and outgoing connections. For example, a firewall might limit access from remote machines to ports 22 and 80 to only allow SSH and web surfing. This prevents access to any other service which uses a port other than 22 or 80.

The solution is to create an SSH connection to a machine outside of the network's firewall and use it to tunnel to the desired service:

```
% ssh -2 -N -f -L 8888:music.example.com:8000 user@unfirewalled-system.example.org
user@unfirewalled-system.example.org's password: *******
```

In this example, a streaming Ogg Vorbis client can now be pointed to localhost port 8888, which will be forwarded over to music.example.com on port 8000, successfully bypassing the firewall.

13.8.2. Enabling the SSH Server

In addition to providing built-in SSH client utilities, a FreeBSD system can be configured as an SSH server, accepting connections from other SSH clients.

To see if sshd is operating, use the service(8) command:

```
# service sshd status
```

If the service is not running, add the following line to /etc/rc.conf .

```
sshd_enable="YES"
```

This will start sshd, the daemon program for OpenSSH, the next time the system boots. To start it now:

```
# service sshd start
```

The first time sshd starts on a FreeBSD system, the system's host keys will be automatically created and the fingerprint will be displayed on the console. Provide users with the fingerprint so that they can verify it the first time they connect to the server.

Refer to sshd(8) for the list of available options when starting sshd and a more complete discussion about authentication, the login process, and the various configuration files.

At this point, the sshd should be available to all users with a username and password on the system.

13.8.3. SSH Server Security

While sshd is the most widely used remote administration facility for FreeBSD, brute force and drive by attacks are common to any system exposed to public networks. Several additional parameters are available to prevent the success of these attacks and will be described in this section.

It is a good idea to limit which users can log into the SSH server and from where using the AllowUsers keyword in the OpenSSH server configuration file. For example, to only allow root to log in from 192.168.1.32 , add this line to /etc/ssh/sshd_config :

```
AllowUsers root@192.168.1.32
```

To allow `admin` to log in from anywhere, list that user without specifying an IP address:

```
AllowUsers admin
```

Multiple users should be listed on the same line, like so:

```
AllowUsers root@192.168.1.32 admin
```

After making changes to `/etc/ssh/sshd_config`, tell sshd to reload its configuration file by running:

```
# service sshd reload
```

Note

When this keyword is used, it is important to list each user that needs to log into this machine. Any user that is not specified in that line will be locked out. Also, the keywords used in the OpenSSH server configuration file are case-sensitive. If the keyword is not spelled correctly, including its case, it will be ignored. Always test changes to this file to make sure that the edits are working as expected. Refer to sshd_config(5) to verify the spelling and use of the available keywords.

In addition, users may be forced to use two factor authentication via the use of a public and private key. When required, the user may generate a key pair through the use of ssh-keygen(1) and send the administrator the public key. This key file will be placed in the `authorized_keys` as described above in the client section. To force the users to use keys only, the following option may be configured:

```
AuthenticationMethods publickey
```

Tip

Do not confuse `/etc/ssh/sshd_config` with `/etc/ssh/ssh_config` (note the extra d in the first filename). The first file configures the server and the second file configures the client. Refer to ssh_config(5) for a listing of the available client settings.

13.9. Access Control Lists

Contributed by Tom Rhodes.

Access Control Lists (ACLs) extend the standard UNIX® permission model in a POSIX®.1e compatible way. This permits an administrator to take advantage of a more fine-grained permissions model.

The FreeBSD **GENERIC** kernel provides ACL support for UFS file systems. Users who prefer to compile a custom kernel must include the following option in their custom kernel configuration file:

```
options UFS_ACL
```

If this option is not compiled in, a warning message will be displayed when attempting to mount a file system with ACL support. ACLs rely on extended attributes which are natively supported in UFS2.

This chapter describes how to enable ACL support and provides some usage examples.

13.9.1. Enabling ACL Support

ACLs are enabled by the mount-time administrative flag, `acls`, which may be added to `/etc/fstab`. The mount-time flag can also be automatically set in a persistent manner using tunefs(8) to modify a superblock ACLs flag in the file system header. In general, it is preferred to use the superblock flag for several reasons:

- The superblock flag cannot be changed by a remount using `mount -u` as it requires a complete `umount` and fresh `mount`. This means that ACLs cannot be enabled on the root file system after boot. It also means that ACL support on a file system cannot be changed while the system is in use.

- Setting the superblock flag causes the file system to always be mounted with ACLs enabled, even if there is not an `fstab` entry or if the devices re-order. This prevents accidental mounting of the file system without ACL support.

Note

It is desirable to discourage accidental mounting without ACLs enabled because nasty things can happen if ACLs are enabled, then disabled, then re-enabled without flushing the extended attributes. In general, once ACLs are enabled on a file system, they should not be disabled, as the resulting file protections may not be compatible with those intended by the users of the system, and re-enabling ACLs may re-attach the previous ACLs to files that have since had their permissions changed, resulting in unpredictable behavior.

File systems with ACLs enabled will show a plus (+) sign in their permission settings:

```
drwx------  2 robert   robert   512 Dec 27 11:54 private
drwxrwx---+ 2 robert   robert   512 Dec 23 10:57 directory1
drwxrwx---+ 2 robert   robert   512 Dec 22 10:20 directory2
drwxrwx---+ 2 robert   robert   512 Dec 27 11:57 directory3
drwxr-xr-x  2 robert   robert   512 Nov 10 11:54 public_html
```

In this example, `directory1`, `directory2`, and `directory3` are all taking advantage of ACLs, whereas `public_html` is not.

13.9.2. Using ACLs

File system ACLs can be viewed using `getfacl`. For instance, to view the ACL settings on `test`:

```
% getfacl test
#file:test
#owner:1001
#group:1001
user::rw-
group::r--
other::r--
```

To change the ACL settings on this file, use `setfacl`. To remove all of the currently defined ACLs from a file or file system, include `-k`. However, the preferred method is to use `-b` as it leaves the basic fields required for ACLs to work.

```
% setfacl -k test
```

To modify the default ACL entries, use `-m`:

```
% setfacl -m u:trhodes:rwx,group:web:r--,o::--- test
```

In this example, there were no pre-defined entries, as they were removed by the previous command. This command restores the default options and assigns the options listed. If a user or group is added which does not exist on the system, an Invalid argument error will be displayed.

Refer to getfacl(1) and setfacl(1) for more information about the options available for these commands.

13.10. Monitoring Third Party Security Issues

Contributed by Tom Rhodes.

In recent years, the security world has made many improvements to how vulnerability assessment is handled. The threat of system intrusion increases as third party utilities are installed and configured for virtually any operating system available today.

Vulnerability assessment is a key factor in security. While FreeBSD releases advisories for the base system, doing so for every third party utility is beyond the FreeBSD Project's capability. There is a way to mitigate third party vulnerabilities and warn administrators of known security issues. A FreeBSD add on utility known as pkg includes options explicitly for this purpose.

pkg polls a database for security issues. The database is updated and maintained by the FreeBSD Security Team and ports developers.

Please refer to instructions for installing pkg.

Installation provides periodic(8) configuration files for maintaining the pkg audit database, and provides a programmatic method of keeping it updated. This functionality is enabled if daily_status_security_pkgaudit_enable is set to YES in periodic.conf(5). Ensure that daily security run emails, which are sent to root's email account, are being read.

After installation, and to audit third party utilities as part of the Ports Collection at any time, an administrator may choose to update the database and view known vulnerabilities of installed packages by invoking:

```
# pkg audit -F
```

pkg displays messages any published vulnerabilities in installed packages:

```
Affected package: cups-base-1.1.22.0_1
Type of problem: cups-base -- HPGL buffer overflow vulnerability.
Reference: <https://www.FreeBSD.org/ports/portaudit/40a3bca2-6809-11d9-
a9e7-0001020eed82.html>

1 problem(s) in your installed packages found.

You are advised to update or deinstall the affected package(s) immediately.
```

By pointing a web browser to the displayed URL, an administrator may obtain more information about the vulnerability. This will include the versions affected, by FreeBSD port version, along with other web sites which may contain security advisories.

pkg is a powerful utility and is extremely useful when coupled with ports-mgmt/portmaster.

13.11. FreeBSD Security Advisories

Contributed by Tom Rhodes.

Like many producers of quality operating systems, the FreeBSD Project has a security team which is responsible for determining the End-of-Life (EoL) date for each FreeBSD release and to provide security updates for supported releases which have not yet reached their EoL. More information about the FreeBSD security team and the supported releases is available on the FreeBSD security page.

One task of the security team is to respond to reported security vulnerabilities in the FreeBSD operating system. Once a vulnerability is confirmed, the security team verifies the steps necessary to fix the vulnerability and updates the source code with the fix. It then publishes the details as a "Security Advisory". Security advisories are published on the FreeBSD website and mailed to the freebsd-security-notifications, freebsd-security, and freebsd-announce mailing lists.

This section describes the format of a FreeBSD security advisory.

13.11.1. Format of a Security Advisory

Here is an example of a FreeBSD security advisory:

```
================================================================
-----BEGIN PGP SIGNED MESSAGE-----
Hash: SHA512


================================================================
FreeBSD-SA-14:04.bind                              Security Advisory
                                                  The FreeBSD Project

Topic:          BIND remote denial of service vulnerability

Category:       contrib
Module:         bind
Announced:      2014-01-14
Credits:        ISC
Affects:        FreeBSD 8.x and FreeBSD 9.x
Corrected:      2014-01-14 19:38:37 UTC (stable/9, 9.2-STABLE)
                2014-01-14 19:42:28 UTC (releng/9.2, 9.2-RELEASE-p3)
                2014-01-14 19:42:28 UTC (releng/9.1, 9.1-RELEASE-p10)
                2014-01-14 19:38:37 UTC (stable/8, 8.4-STABLE)
                2014-01-14 19:42:28 UTC (releng/8.4, 8.4-RELEASE-p7)
                2014-01-14 19:42:28 UTC (releng/8.3, 8.3-RELEASE-p14)
CVE Name:       CVE-2014-0591

For general information regarding FreeBSD Security Advisories,
including descriptions of the fields above, security branches, and the
following sections, please visit <URL:http://security.FreeBSD.org/>.

I.   Background

BIND 9 is an implementation of the Domain Name System (DNS) protocols.
The named(8) daemon is an Internet Domain Name Server.

II.  Problem Description

Because of a defect in handling queries for NSEC3-signed zones, BIND can
crash with an "INSIST" failure in name.c when processing queries possessing
certain properties.  This issue only affects authoritative nameservers with
at least one NSEC3-signed zone.  Recursive-only servers are not at risk.

III. Impact

An attacker who can send a specially crafted query could cause named(8)
to crash, resulting in a denial of service.

IV.  Workaround

No workaround is available, but systems not running authoritative DNS service
with at least one NSEC3-signed zone using named(8) are not vulnerable.

V.   Solution

Perform one of the following:

1) Upgrade your vulnerable system to a supported FreeBSD stable or
release / security branch (releng) dated after the correction date.

2) To update your vulnerable system via a source code patch:

The following patches have been verified to apply to the applicable
FreeBSD release branches.
```

a) Download the relevant patch from the location below, and verify the detached PGP signature using your PGP utility.

```
[FreeBSD 8.3, 8.4, 9.1, 9.2-RELEASE and 8.4-STABLE]
# fetch http://security.FreeBSD.org/patches/SA-14:04/bind-release.patch
# fetch http://security.FreeBSD.org/patches/SA-14:04/bind-release.patch.asc
# gpg --verify bind-release.patch.asc

[FreeBSD 9.2-STABLE]
# fetch http://security.FreeBSD.org/patches/SA-14:04/bind-stable-9.patch
# fetch http://security.FreeBSD.org/patches/SA-14:04/bind-stable-9.patch.asc
# gpg --verify bind-stable-9.patch.asc
```

b) Execute the following commands as root:

```
# cd /usr/src
# patch < /path/to/patch
```

Recompile the operating system using buildworld and installworld as described in <URL:https://www.FreeBSD.org/handbook/makeworld.html>.

Restart the applicable daemons, or reboot the system.

3) To update your vulnerable system via a binary patch:

Systems running a RELEASE version of FreeBSD on the i386 or amd64 platforms can be updated via the freebsd-update(8) utility:

```
# freebsd-update fetch
# freebsd-update install
```

VI. Correction details

The following list contains the correction revision numbers for each affected branch.

Branch/path	Revision
stable/8/	r260646
releng/8.3/	r260647
releng/8.4/	r260647
stable/9/	r260646
releng/9.1/	r260647
releng/9.2/	r260647

To see which files were modified by a particular revision, run the following command, replacing NNNNNN with the revision number, on a machine with Subversion installed:

```
# svn diff -cNNNNNN --summarize svn://svn.freebsd.org/base
```

Or visit the following URL, replacing NNNNNN with the revision number:

<URL:https://svnweb.freebsd.org/base?view=revision&revision=NNNNNN>

VII. References

<URL:https://kb.isc.org/article/AA-01078>

<URL:http://cve.mitre.org/cgi-bin/cvename.cgi?name=CVE-2014-0591>

The latest revision of this advisory is available at
<URL:http://security.FreeBSD.org/advisories/FreeBSD-SA-14:04.bind.asc>
-----BEGIN PGP SIGNATURE-----

```
iQIcBAEBCgAGBQJS1ZTYAAoJEO1n7NZdz2rnOvQP/2/68/s9Cu35PmqNtSZVVxVG
ZSQP5EGWx/lramNf9566iKxOrLRMq/h3XWcC4goVd+gZFrvITJSVOWSa7ntDQ7TO
XcinfRZ/iyiJbs/Rg2wLHc/t5oVSyeouyccqODYFbOwOlk35JjOTMUG1YcX+Zasg
ax8RV+7Zt1QSBkMlOz/myBLXUjlTZ3Xg2FXVsfFQW5/g2CjuHpRSFx1bVNX6ysoG
9DT58EQcYxIS8WfkHRbbXKh9I1nSfZ7/Hky/kTafRdRMrjAgbqFgHkYTYsBZeav5
fYWKGQRJulYfeZQ90yMTvlpF42DjCC3uJYamJnwDIu8OhS1WRBI8fQfr9DRzmRua
OK3BK9hUiScDZOJB6OqeVzUTfe7MAA4/UwrDtTYQ+PqAenv1PK8DZqwXyxA9ThHb
zKO3OwuKOVHJnKvpOcr+eNwo7jbnHlis0oBksj/mrq2P9m2ueF9gzCiq5Ri5Syag
Wssb1HUoMGwqU0roS8+pRpNC8YgsWpsttvUWSZ8u6Vj/FLeHpiV3mYXPVMaKRhVm
067BA2uj4Th1JKtGleox+Em0R7OFbCc/9aWC67wiqI6KRyit9pYiF3npph+7D5Eq
7zPsUdDd+qc+UTiLp3liCRp5w6484wWdhZO6wRtmUgxGjNkxFoNnX8CitzF8AaqO
UWWemqWuz3lAZuORQ9KX
=OQzQ
-----END PGP SIGNATURE-----
```

Every security advisory uses the following format:

- Each security advisory is signed by the PGP key of the Security Officer. The public key for the Security Officer can be verified at Appendix D, *OpenPGP Keys*.

- The name of the security advisory always begins with FreeBSD-SA- (for FreeBSD Security Advisory), followed by the year in two digit format (14:), followed by the advisory number for that year (04.), followed by the name of the affected application or subsystem (bind). The advisory shown here is the fourth advisory for 2014 and it affects BIND.

- The Topic field summarizes the vulnerability.

- The Category refers to the affected part of the system which may be one of core, contrib, or ports. The core category means that the vulnerability affects a core component of the FreeBSD operating system. The contrib category means that the vulnerability affects software included with FreeBSD, such as BIND. The ports category indicates that the vulnerability affects software available through the Ports Collection.

- The Module field refers to the component location. In this example, the bind module is affected; therefore, this vulnerability affects an application installed with the operating system.

- The Announced field reflects the date the security advisory was published. This means that the security team has verified that the problem exists and that a patch has been committed to the FreeBSD source code repository.

- The Credits field gives credit to the individual or organization who noticed the vulnerability and reported it.

- The Affects field explains which releases of FreeBSD are affected by this vulnerability.

- The Corrected field indicates the date, time, time offset, and releases that were corrected. The section in parentheses shows each branch for which the fix has been merged, and the version number of the corresponding release from that branch. The release identifier itself includes the version number and, if appropriate, the patch level. The patch level is the letter p followed by a number, indicating the sequence number of the patch, allowing users to track which patches have already been applied to the system.

- The CVE Name field lists the advisory number, if one exists, in the public cve.mitre.org security vulnerabilities database.

- The Background field provides a description of the affected module.

- The Problem Description field explains the vulnerability. This can include information about the flawed code and how the utility could be maliciously used.

- The Impact field describes what type of impact the problem could have on a system.

- The Workaround field indicates if a workaround is available to system administrators who cannot immediately patch the system .

- The Solution field provides the instructions for patching the affected system. This is a step by step tested and verified method for getting a system patched and working securely.

- The Correction Details field displays each affected Subversion branch with the revision number that contains the corrected code.

- The References field offers sources of additional information regarding the vulnerability.

13.12. Process Accounting

Contributed by Tom Rhodes.

Process accounting is a security method in which an administrator may keep track of system resources used and their allocation among users, provide for system monitoring, and minimally track a user's commands.

Process accounting has both positive and negative points. One of the positives is that an intrusion may be narrowed down to the point of entry. A negative is the amount of logs generated by process accounting, and the disk space they may require. This section walks an administrator through the basics of process accounting.

 Note

If more fine-grained accounting is needed, refer to Chapter 16, *Security Event Auditing*.

13.12.1. Enabling and Utilizing Process Accounting

Before using process accounting, it must be enabled using the following commands:

```
# touch /var/account/acct
# chmod 600 /var/account/acct
# accton /var/account/acct
# echo 'accounting_enable="YES"' >> /etc/rc.conf
```

Once enabled, accounting will begin to track information such as CPU statistics and executed commands. All accounting logs are in a non-human readable format which can be viewed using sa. If issued without any options, sa prints information relating to the number of per-user calls, the total elapsed time in minutes, total CPU and user time in minutes, and the average number of I/O operations. Refer to sa(8) for the list of available options which control the output.

To display the commands issued by users, use lastcomm. For example, this command prints out all usage of ls by trhodes on the ttyp1 terminal:

```
# lastcomm ls trhodes ttyp1
```

Many other useful options exist and are explained in lastcomm(1), acct(5), and sa(8).

13.13. Resource Limits

Contributed by Tom Rhodes.

FreeBSD provides several methods for an administrator to limit the amount of system resources an individual may use. Disk quotas limit the amount of disk space available to users. Quotas are discussed in Section 17.11, "Disk Quotas".

Limits to other resources, such as CPU and memory, can be set using either a flat file or a command to configure a resource limits database. The traditional method defines login classes by editing /etc/login.conf. While this method is still supported, any changes require a multi-step process of editing this file, rebuilding the resource database, making necessary changes to /etc/master.passwd, and rebuilding the password database. This can become time consuming, depending upon the number of users to configure.

Beginning with FreeBSD 9.0-RELEASE, rctl can be used to provide a more fine-grained method for controlling resource limits. This command supports more than user limits as it can also be used to set resource constraints on processes and jails.

This section demonstrates both methods for controlling resources, beginning with the traditional method.

13.13.1. Configuring Login Classes

In the traditional method, login classes and the resource limits to apply to a login class are defined in /etc/login.conf. Each user account can be assigned to a login class, where default is the default login class. Each login class has a set of login capabilities associated with it. A login capability is a *name=value* pair, where *name* is a well-known identifier and *value* is an arbitrary string which is processed accordingly depending on the *name*.

Note

Whenever /etc/login.conf is edited, the /etc/login.conf.db must be updated by executing the following command:

```
# cap_mkdb /etc/login.conf
```

Resource limits differ from the default login capabilities in two ways. First, for every limit, there is a *soft* and *hard* limit. A soft limit may be adjusted by the user or application, but may not be set higher than the hard limit. The hard limit may be lowered by the user, but can only be raised by the superuser. Second, most resource limits apply per process to a specific user.

Table 13.1, "Login Class Resource Limits" lists the most commonly used resource limits. All of the available resource limits and capabilities are described in detail in login.conf(5).

Table 13.1. Login Class Resource Limits

Resource Limit	Description
coredumpsize	The limit on the size of a core file generated by a program is subordinate to other limits on disk usage, such as filesize or disk quotas. This limit is often used as a less severe method of controlling disk space consumption. Since users do not generate core files and often do not delete them, this setting may save them from running out of disk space should a large program crash.
cputime	The maximum amount of CPU time a user's process may consume. Offending processes will be killed by the kernel. This is a limit on CPU *time* consumed, not the percentage of the CPU as displayed in some of the fields generated by top and ps.
filesize	The maximum size of a file the user may own. Unlike disk quotas (Section 17.11, "Disk Quotas"), this limit is enforced on individual files, not the set of all files a user owns.
maxproc	The maximum number of foreground and background processes a user can run. This limit may not be larger

Resource Limit	Description
	than the system limit specified by `kern.maxproc`. Setting this limit too small may hinder a user's productivity as some tasks, such as compiling a large program, start lots of processes.
memorylocked	The maximum amount of memory a process may request to be locked into main memory using mlock(2). Some system-critical programs, such as amd(8), lock into main memory so that if the system begins to swap, they do not contribute to disk thrashing.
memoryuse	The maximum amount of memory a process may consume at any given time. It includes both core memory and swap usage. This is not a catch-all limit for restricting memory consumption, but is a good start.
openfiles	The maximum number of files a process may have open. In FreeBSD, files are used to represent sockets and IPC channels, so be careful not to set this too low. The system-wide limit for this is defined by `kern.maxfiles`.
sbsize	The limit on the amount of network memory a user may consume. This can be generally used to limit network communications.
stacksize	The maximum size of a process stack. This alone is not sufficient to limit the amount of memory a program may use, so it should be used in conjunction with other limits.

There are a few other things to remember when setting resource limits:

- Processes started at system startup by /etc/rc are assigned to the daemon login class.

- Although the default /etc/login.conf is a good source of reasonable values for most limits, they may not be appropriate for every system. Setting a limit too high may open the system up to abuse, while setting it too low may put a strain on productivity.

- Xorg takes a lot of resources and encourages users to run more programs simultaneously.

- Many limits apply to individual processes, not the user as a whole. For example, setting openfiles to 50 means that each process the user runs may open up to 50 files. The total amount of files a user may open is the value of openfiles multiplied by the value of maxproc. This also applies to memory consumption.

For further information on resource limits and login classes and capabilities in general, refer to cap_mkdb(1), getrlimit(2), and login.conf(5).

13.13.2. Enabling and Configuring Resource Limits

As of FreeBSD 10.2, rctl support is built into the kernel. Previous supported releases will need to be recompiled using the instructions in Chapter 8, *Configuring the FreeBSD Kernel*. Add these lines to either GENERIC or a custom kernel configuration file, then rebuild the kernel:

```
options        RACCT
options        RCTL
```

Once the system has rebooted into the new kernel, rctl may be used to set rules for the system.

Rule syntax is controlled through the use of a subject, subject-id, resource, and action, as seen in this example rule:

```
user:trhodes:maxproc:deny=10/user
```

In this rule, the subject is user, the subject-id is trhodes, the resource, maxproc, is the maximum number of processes, and the action is deny, which blocks any new processes from being created. This means that the user, trhodes, will be constrained to no greater than 10 processes. Other possible actions include logging to the console, passing a notification to devd(8), or sending a sigterm to the process.

Some care must be taken when adding rules. Since this user is constrained to 10 processes, this example will prevent the user from performing other tasks after logging in and executing a screen session. Once a resource limit has been hit, an error will be printed, as in this example:

```
% man test
    /usr/bin/man: Cannot fork: Resource temporarily unavailable
eval: Cannot fork: Resource temporarily unavailable
```

As another example, a jail can be prevented from exceeding a memory limit. This rule could be written as:

```
# rctl -a jail:httpd:memoryuse:deny=2G/jail
```

Rules will persist across reboots if they have been added to /etc/rctl.conf . The format is a rule, without the preceding command. For example, the previous rule could be added as:

```
# Block jail from using more than 2G memory:
jail:httpd:memoryuse:deny=2G/jail
```

To remove a rule, use rctl to remove it from the list:

```
# rctl -r user:trhodes:maxproc:deny=10/user
```

A method for removing all rules is documented in rctl(8). However, if removing all rules for a single user is required, this command may be issued:

```
# rctl -r user:trhodes
```

Many other resources exist which can be used to exert additional control over various subjects. See rctl(8) to learn about them.

13.14. Shared Administration with Sudo

Contributed by Tom Rhodes.

System administrators often need the ability to grant enhanced permissions to users so they may perform privileged tasks. The idea that team members are provided access to a FreeBSD system to perform their specific tasks opens up unique challenges to every administrator. These team members only need a subset of access beyond normal end user levels; however, they almost always tell management they are unable to perform their tasks without superuser access. Thankfully, there is no reason to provide such access to end users because tools exist to manage this exact requirement.

Up to this point, the security chapter has covered permitting access to authorized users and attempting to prevent unauthorized access. Another problem arises once authorized users have access to the system resources. In many cases, some users may need access to application startup scripts, or a team of administrators need to maintain the system. Traditionally, the standard users and groups, file permissions, and even the su(1) command would manage this access. And as applications required more access, as more users needed to use system resources, a better solution was required. The most used application is currently Sudo.

Sudo allows administrators to configure more rigid access to system commands and provide for some advanced logging features. As a tool, it is available from the Ports Collection as security/sudo or by use of the pkg(8) utility. To use the pkg(8) tool:

```
# pkg install sudo
```

After the installation is complete, the installed `visudo` will open the configuration file with a text editor. Using `visudo` is highly recommended as it comes with a built in syntax checker to verify there are no errors before the file is saved.

The configuration file is made up of several small sections which allow for extensive configuration. In the following example, web application maintainer, user1, needs to start, stop, and restart the web application known as *webservice*. To grant this user permission to perform these tasks, add this line to the end of `/usr/local/etc/sudoers` :

```
user1   ALL=(ALL)        /usr/sbin/service webservice *
```

The user may now start *webservice* using this command:

```
% sudo /usr/sbin/service  webservice start
```

While this configuration allows a single user access to the webservice service; however, in most organizations, there is an entire web team in charge of managing the service. A single line can also give access to an entire group. These steps will create a web group, add a user to this group, and allow all members of the group to manage the service:

```
# pw groupadd -g 6001 -n webteam
```

Using the same pw(8) command, the user is added to the webteam group:

```
# pw groupmod -m user1 -n webteam
```

Finally, this line in `/usr/local/etc/sudoers` allows any member of the webteam group to manage *webservice*:

```
%webteam   ALL=(ALL)        /usr/sbin/service webservice *
```

Unlike su(1), Sudo only requires the end user password. This adds an advantage where users will not need shared passwords, a finding in most security audits and just bad all the way around.

Users permitted to run applications with Sudo only enter their own passwords. This is more secure and gives better control than su(1), where the root password is entered and the user acquires all root permissions.

Tip

Most organizations are moving or have moved toward a two factor authentication model. In these cases, the user may not have a password to enter. Sudo provides for these cases with the NOPASSWD variable. Adding it to the configuration above will allow all members of the webteam group to manage the service without the password requirement:

```
%webteam   ALL=(ALL)        NOPASSWD: /usr/sbin/service webservice *
```

13.14.1. Logging Output

An advantage to implementing Sudo is the ability to enable session logging. Using the built in log mechanisms and the included sudoreplay command, all commands initiated through Sudo are logged for later verification. To enable this feature, add a default log directory entry, this example uses a user variable. Several other log filename conventions exist, consult the manual page for sudoreplay for additional information.

```
Defaults iolog_dir=/var/log/sudo-io/%{user}
```

Tip

This directory will be created automatically after the logging is configured. It is best to let the system create directory with default permissions just to be safe. In addition, this entry will also log administrators who use the sudoreplay command. To change this behavior, read and uncomment the logging options inside sudoers.

Once this directive has been added to the sudoers file, any user configuration can be updated with the request to log access. In the example shown, the updated *webteam* entry would have the following additional changes:

```
%webteam ALL=(ALL) NOPASSWD: LOG_INPUT: LOG_OUTPUT: /usr/sbin/service webservice *
```

From this point on, all *webteam* members altering the status of the *webservice* application will be logged. The list of previous and current sessions can be displayed with:

```
# sudoreplay -l
```

In the output, to replay a specific session, search for the TSID= entry, and pass that to sudoreplay with no other options to replay the session at normal speed. For example:

```
# sudoreplay user1/00/00/02
```

Warning

While sessions are logged, any administrator is able to remove sessions and leave only a question of why they had done so. It is worthwhile to add a daily check through an intrusion detection system (IDS) or similar software so that other administrators are alerted to manual alterations.

The sudoreplay is extremely extendable. Consult the documentation for more information.

Chapter 14. Jails

Contributed by Matteo Riondato.

14.1. Synopsis

Since system administration is a difficult task, many tools have been developed to make life easier for the administrator. These tools often enhance the way systems are installed, configured, and maintained. One of the tools which can be used to enhance the security of a FreeBSD system is *jails*. Jails have been available since FreeBSD 4.X and continue to be enhanced in their usefulness, performance, reliability, and security.

Jails build upon the chroot(2) concept, which is used to change the root directory of a set of processes. This creates a safe environment, separate from the rest of the system. Processes created in the chrooted environment can not access files or resources outside of it. For that reason, compromising a service running in a chrooted environment should not allow the attacker to compromise the entire system. However, a chroot has several limitations. It is suited to easy tasks which do not require much flexibility or complex, advanced features. Over time, many ways have been found to escape from a chrooted environment, making it a less than ideal solution for securing services.

Jails improve on the concept of the traditional chroot environment in several ways. In a traditional chroot environment, processes are only limited in the part of the file system they can access. The rest of the system resources, system users, running processes, and the networking subsystem are shared by the chrooted processes and the processes of the host system. Jails expand this model by virtualizing access to the file system, the set of users, and the networking subsystem. More fine-grained controls are available for tuning the access of a jailed environment. Jails can be considered as a type of operating system-level virtualization.

A jail is characterized by four elements:

- A directory subtree: the starting point from which a jail is entered. Once inside the jail, a process is not permitted to escape outside of this subtree.

- A hostname: which will be used by the jail.

- An IP address: which is assigned to the jail. The IP address of a jail is often an alias address for an existing network interface.

- A command: the path name of an executable to run inside the jail. The path is relative to the root directory of the jail environment.

Jails have their own set of users and their own root account which are limited to the jail environment. The root account of a jail is not allowed to perform operations to the system outside of the associated jail environment.

This chapter provides an overview of the terminology and commands for managing FreeBSD jails. Jails are a powerful tool for both system administrators, and advanced users.

After reading this chapter, you will know:

- What a jail is and what purpose it may serve in FreeBSD installations.

- How to build, start, and stop a jail.

- The basics of jail administration, both from inside and outside the jail.

 Important

Jails are a powerful tool, but they are not a security panacea. While it is not possible for a jailed process to break out on its own, there are several ways in which an unprivileged user outside the jail can cooperate with a privileged user inside the jail to obtain elevated privileges in the host environment.

Most of these attacks can be mitigated by ensuring that the jail root is not accessible to unprivileged users in the host environment. As a general rule, untrusted users with privileged access to a jail should not be given access to the host environment.

14.2. Terms Related to Jails

To facilitate better understanding of parts of the FreeBSD system related to jails, their internals and the way they interact with the rest of FreeBSD, the following terms are used further in this chapter:

chroot(8) (command)

Utility, which uses chroot(2) FreeBSD system call to change the root directory of a process and all its descendants.

chroot(2) (environment)

The environment of processes running in a "chroot". This includes resources such as the part of the file system which is visible, user and group IDs which are available, network interfaces and other IPC mechanisms, etc.

jail(8) (command)

The system administration utility which allows launching of processes within a jail environment.

host (system, process, user, etc.)

The controlling system of a jail environment. The host system has access to all the hardware resources available, and can control processes both outside of and inside a jail environment. One of the important differences of the host system from a jail is that the limitations which apply to superuser processes inside a jail are not enforced for processes of the host system.

hosted (system, process, user, etc.)

A process, user or other entity, whose access to resources is restricted by a FreeBSD jail.

14.3. Creating and Controlling Jails

Some administrators divide jails into the following two types: "complete" jails, which resemble a real FreeBSD system, and "service" jails, dedicated to one application or service, possibly running with privileges. This is only a conceptual division and the process of building a jail is not affected by it. When creating a "complete" jail there are two options for the source of the userland: use prebuilt binaries (such as those supplied on an install media) or build from source.

To install the userland from installation media, first create the root directory for the jail. This can be done by setting the DESTDIR variable to the proper location.

Start a shell and define DESTDIR:

```
# sh
# export DESTDIR=/here/is/the/jail
```

Mount the install media as covered in mdconfig(8) when using the install ISO:

```
# mount -t cd9660 /dev/`mdconfig -f cdimage.iso` /mnt
```

Extract the binaries from the tarballs on the install media into the declared destination. Minimally, only the base set needs to be extracted, but a complete install can be performed when preferred.

To install just the base system:

```
# tar -xf /mnt/usr/freebsd-dist/base.txz -C $DESTDIR
```

To install everything except the kernel:

```
# for sets in BASE PORTS; do tar -xf /mnt/FREEBSD_INSTALL/USR/FREEBSD_DIST/$    sets.TXZ -C ↺
$DESTDIR -; done
```

The jail(8) manual page explains the procedure for building a jail:

```
# setenv D /here/is/the/jail
# mkdir -p $D        ❶
# cd /usr/src
# make buildworld    ❷
# make installworld DESTDIR=$D   ❸
# make distribution DESTDIR=$D   ❹
# mount -t devfs devfs $D/dev    ❺
```

❶ Selecting a location for a jail is the best starting point. This is where the jail will physically reside within the file system of the jail's host. A good choice can be /usr/jail/ jailname, where jailname is the hostname identifying the jail. Usually, /usr/ has enough space for the jail file system, which for "complete" jails is, essentially, a replication of every file present in a default installation of the FreeBSD base system.

❷ If you have already rebuilt your userland using make world or make buildworld, you can skip this step and install your existing userland into the new jail.

❸ This command will populate the directory subtree chosen as jail's physical location on the file system with the necessary binaries, libraries, manual pages and so on.

❹ The distribution target for make installs every needed configuration file. In simple words, it installs every installable file of /usr/src/etc/ to the /etc directory of the jail environment: $D/etc/.

❺ Mounting the devfs(8) file system inside a jail is not required. On the other hand, any, or almost any application requires access to at least one device, depending on the purpose of the given application. It is very important to control access to devices from inside a jail, as improper settings could permit an attacker to do nasty things in the jail. Control over devfs(8) is managed through rulesets which are described in the devfs(8) and devfs.conf(5) manual pages.

Once a jail is installed, it can be started by using the jail(8) utility. The jail(8) utility takes four mandatory arguments which are described in the Section 14.1, "Synopsis". Other arguments may be specified too, e.g., to run the jailed process with the credentials of a specific user. The *command* argument depends on the type of the jail; for a *virtual system*, /etc/rc is a good choice, since it will replicate the startup sequence of a real FreeBSD system. For a *service* jail, it depends on the service or application that will run within the jail.

Jails are often started at boot time and the FreeBSD rc mechanism provides an easy way to do this.

1. A list of the jails which are enabled to start at boot time should be added to the rc.conf(5) file:

```
jail_enable="YES"    # Set to NO to disable starting of any jails
jail_list="www"      # Space separated list of names of jails
```

> Note
>
> Jail names in jail_list should contain alphanumeric characters only.

2. For each jail listed in jail_list , a group of rc.conf(5) settings, which describe the particular jail, should be added:

```
jail_www_rootdir="/usr/jail/www"       # jail's root directory
jail_www_hostname="www.example.org"    # jail's hostname
jail_www_ip="192.168.0.10"             # jail's IP address
```

```
jail_www_devfs_enable="YES"          # mount devfs in the jail
```

The default startup of jails configured in rc.conf(5), will run the /etc/rc script of the jail, which assumes the jail is a complete virtual system. For service jails, the default startup command of the jail should be changed, by setting the jail_*jailname*_exec_start option appropriately.

> ## Note
>
> For a full list of available options, please see the rc.conf(5) manual page.

service(8) can be used to start or stop a jail by hand, if an entry for it exists in rc.conf:

```
# service jail start www
# service jail stop www
```

Jails can be shut down with jexec(8). Use jls(8) to identify the jail's JID, then use jexec(8) to run the shutdown script in that jail.

```
# jls
   JID  IP Address      Hostname                 Path
     3  192.168.0.10    www                      /usr/jail/www
# jexec 3 /etc/rc.shutdown
```

More information about this can be found in the jail(8) manual page.

14.4. Fine Tuning and Administration

There are several options which can be set for any jail, and various ways of combining a host FreeBSD system with jails, to produce higher level applications. This section presents:

- Some of the options available for tuning the behavior and security restrictions implemented by a jail installation.

- Some of the high-level applications for jail management, which are available through the FreeBSD Ports Collection, and can be used to implement overall jail-based solutions.

14.4.1. System Tools for Jail Tuning in FreeBSD

Fine tuning of a jail's configuration is mostly done by setting sysctl(8) variables. A special subtree of sysctl exists as a basis for organizing all the relevant options: the security.jail.* hierarchy of FreeBSD kernel options. Here is a list of the main jail-related sysctls, complete with their default value. Names should be self-explanatory, but for more information about them, please refer to the jail(8) and sysctl(8) manual pages.

- security.jail.set_hostname_allowed: 1

- security.jail.socket_unixiproute_only: 1

- security.jail.sysvipc_allowed: 0

- security.jail.enforce_statfs: 2

- security.jail.allow_raw_sockets: 0

- security.jail.chflags_allowed: 0

- security.jail.jailed: 0

These variables can be used by the system administrator of the *host system* to add or remove some of the limitations imposed by default on the root user. Note that there are some limitations which cannot be removed. The root user is not allowed to mount or unmount file systems from within a jail(8). The root inside a jail may not load or unload devfs(8) rulesets, set firewall rules, or do many other administrative tasks which require modifications of in-kernel data, such as setting the securelevel of the kernel.

The base system of FreeBSD contains a basic set of tools for viewing information about the active jails, and attaching to a jail to run administrative commands. The jls(8) and jexec(8) commands are part of the base FreeBSD system, and can be used to perform the following simple tasks:

- Print a list of active jails and their corresponding jail identifier (JID), IP address, hostname and path.

- Attach to a running jail, from its host system, and run a command inside the jail or perform administrative tasks inside the jail itself. This is especially useful when the root user wants to cleanly shut down a jail. The jexec(8) utility can also be used to start a shell in a jail to do administration in it; for example:

```
# jexec 1 tcsh
```

14.4.2. High-Level Administrative Tools in the FreeBSD Ports Collection

Among the many third-party utilities for jail administration, one of the most complete and useful is sysutils/ezjail. It is a set of scripts that contribute to jail(8) management. Please refer to the handbook section on ezjail for more information.

14.4.3. Keeping Jails Patched and up to Date

Jails should be kept up to date from the host operating system as attempting to patch userland from within the jail may likely fail as the default behavior in FreeBSD is to disallow the use of chflags(1) in a jail which prevents the replacement of some files. It is possible to change this behavior but it is recommended to use freebsd-update(8) to maintain jails instead. Use -b to specify the path of the jail to be updated.

```
# freebsd-update -b  /here/is/the/jail  fetch
# freebsd-update -b  /here/is/the/jail  install
```

14.5. Updating Multiple Jails

Contributed by Daniel Gerzo.
Based upon an idea presented by Simon L. B. Nielsen.
And an article written by Ken Tom.

The management of multiple jails can become problematic because every jail has to be rebuilt from scratch whenever it is upgraded. This can be time consuming and tedious if a lot of jails are created and manually updated.

This section demonstrates one method to resolve this issue by safely sharing as much as is possible between jails using read-only mount_nullfs(8) mounts, so that updating is simpler. This makes it more attractive to put single services, such as HTTP, DNS, and SMTP, into individual jails. Additionally, it provides a simple way to add, remove, and upgrade jails.

Note

Simpler solutions exist, such as ezjail, which provides an easier method of administering FreeBSD jails but is less versatile than this setup. ezjail is covered in more detail in Section 14.6, "Managing Jails with ezjail".

The goals of the setup described in this section are:

- Create a simple and easy to understand jail structure that does not require running a full installworld on each and every jail.

- Make it easy to add new jails or remove existing ones.

- Make it easy to update or upgrade existing jails.

- Make it possible to run a customized FreeBSD branch.

- Be paranoid about security, reducing as much as possible the possibility of compromise.

- Save space and inodes, as much as possible.

This design relies on a single, read-only master template which is mounted into each jail and one read-write device per jail. A device can be a separate physical disc, a partition, or a vnode backed memory device. This example uses read-write nullfs mounts.

The file system layout is as follows:

- The jails are based under the /home partition.

- Each jail will be mounted under the /home/j directory.

- The template for each jail and the read-only partition for all of the jails is /home/j/mroot .

- A blank directory will be created for each jail under the /home/j directory.

- Each jail will have a /s directory that will be linked to the read-write portion of the system.

- Each jail will have its own read-write system that is based upon /home/j/skel .

- The read-write portion of each jail will be created in /home/js .

14.5.1. Creating the Template

This section describes the steps needed to create the master template.

It is recommended to first update the host FreeBSD system to the latest -RELEASE branch using the instructions in Section 23.5, "Updating FreeBSD from Source". Additionally, this template uses the sysutils/cpdup package or port and portsnap will be used to download the FreeBSD Ports Collection.

1. First, create a directory structure for the read-only file system which will contain the FreeBSD binaries for the jails. Then, change directory to the FreeBSD source tree and install the read-only file system to the jail template:

```
# mkdir /home/j /home/j/mroot
# cd /usr/src
# make installworld DESTDIR=/home/j/mroot
```

2. Next, prepare a FreeBSD Ports Collection for the jails as well as a FreeBSD source tree, which is required for mergemaster:

```
# cd /home/j/mroot
# mkdir usr/ports
# portsnap -p /home/j/mroot/usr/ports fetch extract
# cpdup /usr/src /home/j/mroot/usr/src
```

3. Create a skeleton for the read-write portion of the system:

```
# mkdir /home/j/skel /home/j/skel/home /home/j/skel/usr-X11R6 /home/j/skel/distfiles
# mv etc /home/j/skel
# mv usr/local /home/j/skel/usr-local
# mv tmp /home/j/skel
# mv var /home/j/skel
# mv root /home/j/skel
```

4. Use mergemaster to install missing configuration files. Then, remove the extra directories that mergemaster creates:

```
# mergemaster -t /home/j/skel/var/tmp/temproot -D /home/j/skel -i
# cd /home/j/skel
# rm -R bin boot lib libexec mnt proc rescue sbin sys usr dev
```

5. Now, symlink the read-write file system to the read-only file system. Ensure that the symlinks are created in the correct s/ locations as the creation of directories in the wrong locations will cause the installation to fail.

```
# cd /home/j/mroot
# mkdir s
# ln -s s/etc etc
# ln -s s/home home
# ln -s s/root root
# ln -s ../s/usr-local usr/local
# ln -s ../s/usr-X11R6 usr/X11R6
# ln -s ../../s/distfiles usr/ports/distfiles
# ln -s s/tmp tmp
# ln -s s/var var
```

6. As a last step, create a generic /home/j/skel/etc/make.conf containing this line:

```
WRKDIRPREFIX?=  /s/portbuild
```

This makes it possible to compile FreeBSD ports inside each jail. Remember that the ports directory is part of the read-only system. The custom path for WRKDIRPREFIX allows builds to be done in the read-write portion of every jail.

14.5.2. Creating Jails

The jail template can now be used to setup and configure the jails in /etc/rc.conf . This example demonstrates the creation of 3 jails: NS, MAIL and WWW.

1. Add the following lines to /etc/fstab , so that the read-only template for the jails and the read-write space will be available in the respective jails:

```
/home/j/mroot    /home/j/ns      nullfs  ro  0   0
/home/j/mroot    /home/j/mail    nullfs  ro  0   0
/home/j/mroot    /home/j/www     nullfs  ro  0   0
/home/js/ns      /home/j/ns/s    nullfs  rw  0   0
/home/js/mail    /home/j/mail/s  nullfs  rw  0   0
/home/js/www     /home/j/www/s   nullfs  rw  0   0
```

To prevent fsck from checking nullfs mounts during boot and dump from backing up the read-only nullfs mounts of the jails, the last two columns are both set to 0.

2. Configure the jails in /etc/rc.conf :

```
jail_enable="YES"
jail_set_hostname_allow="NO"
jail_list="ns mail www"
jail_ns_hostname="ns.example.org"
jail_ns_ip="192.168.3.17"
jail_ns_rootdir="/usr/home/j/ns"
jail_ns_devfs_enable="YES"
jail_mail_hostname="mail.example.org"
jail_mail_ip="192.168.3.18"
jail_mail_rootdir="/usr/home/j/mail"
jail_mail_devfs_enable="YES"
jail_www_hostname="www.example.org"
jail_www_ip="62.123.43.14"
jail_www_rootdir="/usr/home/j/www"
jail_www_devfs_enable="YES"
```

The jail_*name*_rootdir variable is set to /usr/home instead of /home because the physical path of /home on a default FreeBSD installation is /usr/home . The jail_*name*_rootdir variable must *not* be set to a path which includes a symbolic link, otherwise the jails will refuse to start.

3. Create the required mount points for the read-only file system of each jail:

```
# mkdir /home/j/ns /home/j/mail /home/j/www
```

4. Install the read-write template into each jail using sysutils/cpdup:

```
# mkdir /home/js
# cpdup /home/j/skel /home/js/ns
# cpdup /home/j/skel /home/js/mail
# cpdup /home/j/skel /home/js/www
```

5. In this phase, the jails are built and prepared to run. First, mount the required file systems for each jail, and then start them:

```
# mount -a
# service jail start
```

The jails should be running now. To check if they have started correctly, use jls. Its output should be similar to the following:

```
# jls
   JID  IP Address      Hostname              Path
     3  192.168.3.17    ns.example.org        /home/j/ns
     2  192.168.3.18    mail.example.org      /home/j/mail
     1  62.123.43.14    www.example.org       /home/j/www
```

At this point, it should be possible to log onto each jail, add new users, or configure daemons. The JID column indicates the jail identification number of each running jail. Use the following command to perform administrative tasks in the jail whose JID is 3:

```
# jexec 3 tcsh
```

14.5.3. Upgrading

The design of this setup provides an easy way to upgrade existing jails while minimizing their downtime. Also, it provides a way to roll back to the older version should a problem occur.

1. The first step is to upgrade the host system. Then, create a new temporary read-only template in /home/j/mroot2.

```
# mkdir /home/j/mroot2
# cd /usr/src
# make installworld DESTDIR=/home/j/mroot2
# cd /home/j/mroot2
# cpdup /usr/src usr/src
# mkdir s
```

The installworld creates a few unnecessary directories, which should be removed:

```
# chflags -R 0 var
# rm -R etc var root usr/local tmp
```

2. Recreate the read-write symlinks for the master file system:

```
# ln -s s/etc etc
# ln -s s/root root
# ln -s s/home home
# ln -s ../s/usr-local usr/local
# ln -s ../s/usr-X11R6 usr/X11R6
```

```
# ln -s s/tmp tmp
# ln -s s/var var
```

3. Next, stop the jails:

```
# service jail stop
```

4. Unmount the original file systems as the read-write systems are attached to the read-only system (/s):

```
# umount /home/j/ns/s
# umount /home/j/ns
# umount /home/j/mail/s
# umount /home/j/mail
# umount /home/j/www/s
# umount /home/j/www
```

5. Move the old read-only file system and replace it with the new one. This will serve as a backup and archive of the old read-only file system should something go wrong. The naming convention used here corresponds to when a new read-only file system has been created. Move the original FreeBSD Ports Collection over to the new file system to save some space and inodes:

```
# cd /home/j
# mv mroot mroot.20060601
# mv mroot2 mroot
# mv mroot.20060601/usr/ports mroot/usr
```

6. At this point the new read-only template is ready, so the only remaining task is to remount the file systems and start the jails:

```
# mount -a
# service jail start
```

Use `jls` to check if the jails started correctly. Run `mergemaster` in each jail to update the configuration files.

14.6. Managing Jails with ezjail

Originally contributed by Warren Block.

Creating and managing multiple jails can quickly become tedious and error-prone. Dirk Engling's ezjail automates and greatly simplifies many jail tasks. A *basejail* is created as a template. Additional jails use mount_nullfs(8) to share many of the basejail directories without using additional disk space. Each additional jail takes only a few megabytes of disk space before applications are installed. Upgrading the copy of the userland in the basejail automatically upgrades all of the other jails.

Additional benefits and features are described in detail on the ezjail web site, https://erdgeist.org/arts/software/ezjail/.

14.6.1. Installing ezjail

Installing ezjail consists of adding a loopback interface for use in jails, installing the port or package, and enabling the service.

1. To keep jail loopback traffic off the host's loopback network interface lo0, a second loopback interface is created by adding an entry to /etc/rc.conf :

```
cloned_interfaces="lo1"
```

The second loopback interface lo1 will be created when the system starts. It can also be created manually without a restart:

```
# service netif cloneup
```

```
Created clone interfaces: lo1.
```

Jails can be allowed to use aliases of this secondary loopback interface without interfering with the host.

Inside a jail, access to the loopback address `127.0.0.1` is redirected to the first IP address assigned to the jail. To make the jail loopback correspond with the new `lo1` interface, that interface must be specified first in the list of interfaces and IP addresses given when creating a new jail.

Give each jail a unique loopback address in the `127.0.0.0/8` netblock.

2. Install sysutils/ezjail:

```
# cd /usr/ports/sysutils/ezjail
# make install clean
```

3. Enable ezjail by adding this line to `/etc/rc.conf` :

```
ezjail_enable="YES"
```

4. The service will automatically start on system boot. It can be started immediately for the current session:

```
# service ezjail start
```

14.6.2. Initial Setup

With ezjail installed, the basejail directory structure can be created and populated. This step is only needed once on the jail host computer.

In both of these examples, -p causes the ports tree to be retrieved with portsnap(8) into the basejail. That single copy of the ports directory will be shared by all the jails. Using a separate copy of the ports directory for jails isolates them from the host. The ezjail FAQ explains in more detail: http://erdgeist.org/arts/software/ezjail/#FAQ.

• • To Populate the Jail with FreeBSD-RELEASE

For a basejail based on the FreeBSD RELEASE matching that of the host computer, use `install`. For example, on a host computer running FreeBSD 10-STABLE, the latest RELEASE version of FreeBSD -10 will be installed in the jail):

```
# ezjail-admin install -p
```

• To Populate the Jail with `installworld`

The basejail can be installed from binaries created by `buildworld` on the host with `ezjail-admin update`.

In this example, FreeBSD 10-STABLE has been built from source. The jail directories are created. Then `installworld` is executed, installing the host's `/usr/obj` into the basejail.

```
# ezjail-admin update -i -p
```

The host's `/usr/src` is used by default. A different source directory on the host can be specified with `-s` and a path, or set with `ezjail_sourcetree` in `/usr/local/etc/ezjail.conf` .

Tip

The basejail's ports tree is shared by other jails. However, downloaded distfiles are stored in the jail that downloaded them. By default, these files are stored in `/var/ports/distfiles` within each jail. `/var/ports` inside each jail is also used as a work directory when building ports.

Tip

The FTP protocol is used by default to download packages for the installation of the basejail. Firewall or proxy configurations can prevent or interfere with FTP transfers. The HTTP protocol works differently and avoids these problems. It can be chosen by specifying a full URL for a particular download mirror in /usr/local/etc/ezjail.conf :

```
ezjail_ftphost=http://ftp.FreeBSD.org
```

See Section A.2, "FTP Sites" for a list of sites.

14.6.3. Creating and Starting a New Jail

New jails are created with ezjail-admin create. In these examples, the lo1 loopback interface is used as described above.

Procedure 14.1. Create and Start a New Jail

1. Create the jail, specifying a name and the loopback and network interfaces to use, along with their IP addresses. In this example, the jail is named dnsjail.

```
# ezjail-admin create  dnsjail 'lo1|127.0.1.1 ,em0|192.168.1.50 '
```

Tip

Most network services run in jails without problems. A few network services, most notably ping(8), use *raw network sockets*. In jails, raw network sockets are disabled by default for security. Services that require them will not work.

Occasionally, a jail genuinely needs raw sockets. For example, network monitoring applications often use ping(8) to check the availability of other computers. When raw network sockets are actually needed in a jail, they can be enabled by editing the ezjail configuration file for the individual jail, /usr/local/etc/ezjail/ *jailname*. Modify the parameters entry:

```
export jail_jailname_parameters="allow.raw_sockets=1"
```

Do not enable raw network sockets unless services in the jail actually require them.

2. Start the jail:

```
# ezjail-admin start  dnsjail
```

3. Use a console on the jail:

```
# ezjail-admin console  dnsjail
```

The jail is operating and additional configuration can be completed. Typical settings added at this point include:

1. Set the **root** Password

Connect to the jail and set the root user's password:

```
# ezjail-admin console  dnsjail
# passwd
Changing local password for root
New Password:
Retype New Password:
```

2. Time Zone Configuration

    The jail's time zone can be set with tzsetup(8). To avoid spurious error messages, the adjkerntz(8) entry in /etc/crontab can be commented or removed. This job attempts to update the computer's hardware clock with time zone changes, but jails are not allowed to access that hardware.

3. DNS Servers

    Enter domain name server lines in /etc/resolv.conf so DNS works in the jail.

4. Edit **/etc/hosts**

    Change the address and add the jail name to the localhost entries in /etc/hosts .

5. Configure **/etc/rc.conf**

    Enter configuration settings in /etc/rc.conf . This is much like configuring a full computer. The host name and IP address are not set here. Those values are already provided by the jail configuration.

With the jail configured, the applications for which the jail was created can be installed.

Tip

Some ports must be built with special options to be used in a jail. For example, both of the network monitoring plugin packages net-mgmt/nagios-plugins and net-mgmt/monitoring-plugins have a JAIL option which must be enabled for them to work correctly inside a jail.

14.6.4. Updating Jails

14.6.4.1. Updating the Operating System

Because the basejail's copy of the userland is shared by the other jails, updating the basejail automatically updates all of the other jails. Either source or binary updates can be used.

To build the world from source on the host, then install it in the basejail, use:

```
# ezjail-admin update -b
```

If the world has already been compiled on the host, install it in the basejail with:

```
# ezjail-admin update -i
```

Binary updates use freebsd-update(8). These updates have the same limitations as if freebsd-update(8) were being run directly. The most important one is that only -RELEASE versions of FreeBSD are available with this method.

Update the basejail to the latest patched release of the version of FreeBSD on the host. For example, updating from RELEASE-p1 to RELEASE-p2.

```
# ezjail-admin update -u
```

To upgrade the basejail to a new version, first upgrade the host system as described in Section 23.2.3, "Performing Major and Minor Version Upgrades". Once the host has been upgraded and rebooted, the basejail can then be upgraded. freebsd-update(8) has no way of determining which version is currently installed in the basejail, so the original version must be specified. Use file(1) to determine the original version in the basejail:

```
# file /usr/jails/basejail/bin/sh
/usr/jails/basejail/bin/sh: ELF 64-bit LSB executable, x86-64, version 1 (FreeBSD), ↺
dynamically linked (uses shared libs), for FreeBSD 9.3, stripped
```

Now use this information to perform the upgrade from 9.3-RELEASE to the current version of the host system:

```
# ezjail-admin update -U -s  9.3-RELEASE
```

After updating the basejail, mergemaster(8) must be run to update each jail's configuration files.

How to use mergemaster(8) depends on the purpose and trustworthiness of a jail. If a jail's services or users are not trusted, then mergemaster(8) should only be run from within that jail:

Example 14.1. mergemaster(8) on Untrusted Jail

Delete the link from the jail's /usr/src into the basejail and create a new /usr/src in the jail as a mount-point. Mount the host computer's /usr/src read-only on the jail's new /usr/src mountpoint:

```
# rm /usr/jails/ jailname /usr/src
# mkdir /usr/jails/ jailname /usr/src
# mount -t nullfs -o ro /usr/src /usr/jails/  jailname /usr/src
```

Get a console in the jail:

```
# ezjail-admin console  jailname
```

Inside the jail, run mergemaster. Then exit the jail console:

```
# cd /usr/src
# mergemaster -U
# exit
```

Finally, unmount the jail's /usr/src :

```
# umount /usr/jails/ jailname /usr/src
```

Example 14.2. mergemaster(8) on Trusted Jail

If the users and services in a jail are trusted, mergemaster(8) can be run from the host:

```
# mergemaster -U -D /usr/jails/  jailname
```

14.6.4.2. Updating Ports

The ports tree in the basejail is shared by the other jails. Updating that copy of the ports tree gives the other jails the updated version also.

The basejail ports tree is updated with portsnap(8):

```
# ezjail-admin update -P
```

14.6.5. Controlling Jails

14.6.5.1. Stopping and Starting Jails

ezjail automatically starts jails when the computer is started. Jails can be manually stopped and restarted with stop and start:

```
# ezjail-admin stop  sambajail
Stopping jails: sambajail.
```

By default, jails are started automatically when the host computer starts. Autostarting can be disabled with config:

```
# ezjail-admin config -r norun  seldomjail
```

This takes effect the next time the host computer is started. A jail that is already running will not be stopped.

Enabling autostart is very similar:

```
# ezjail-admin config -r run  oftenjail
```

14.6.5.2. Archiving and Restoring Jails

Use archive to create a .tar.gz archive of a jail. The file name is composed from the name of the jail and the current date. Archive files are written to the archive directory, /usr/jails/ezjail_archives . A different archive directory can be chosen by setting ezjail_archivedir in the configuration file.

The archive file can be copied elsewhere as a backup, or an existing jail can be restored from it with restore. A new jail can be created from the archive, providing a convenient way to clone existing jails.

Stop and archive a jail named wwwserver:

```
# ezjail-admin stop  wwwserver
Stopping jails: wwwserver.
# ezjail-admin archive  wwwserver
# ls /usr/jails/ezjail-archives/
wwwserver-201407271153.13.tar.gz
```

Create a new jail named wwwserver-clone from the archive created in the previous step. Use the em1 interface and assign a new IP address to avoid conflict with the original:

```
# ezjail-admin create -a /usr/jails/ezjail_archives/wwwserver-201407271153.13.tar.␒
gz wwwserver-clone  'lo1|127.0.3.1,em1|192.168.1.51'
```

14.6.6. Full Example: BIND in a Jail

Putting the BIND DNS server in a jail improves security by isolating it. This example creates a simple caching-only name server.

- The jail will be called dns1.

- The jail will use IP address 192.168.1.240 on the host's re0 interface.

- The upstream ISP's DNS servers are at 10.0.0.62 and 10.0.0.61 .

- The basejail has already been created and a ports tree installed as shown in Section 14.6.2, "Initial Setup".

> ## Example 14.3. Running BIND in a Jail
>
> Create a cloned loopback interface by adding a line to /etc/rc.conf :

```
cloned_interfaces="lo1"
```

Immediately create the new loopback interface:

```
# service netif cloneup
Created clone interfaces: lo1.
```

Create the jail:

```
# ezjail-admin create dns1 'lo1|127.0.2.1,re0|192.168.1.240'
```

Start the jail, connect to a console running on it, and perform some basic configuration:

```
# ezjail-admin start dns1
# ezjail-admin console dns1
# passwd
Changing local password for root
New Password:
Retype New Password:
# tzsetup
# sed -i .bak -e '/adjkerntz/ s/^/#/' /etc/crontab
# sed -i .bak -e 's/127.0.0.1/127.0.2.1/g; s/localhost.my.domain/dns1.my.domain ↵
dns1/' /etc/hosts
```

Temporarily set the upstream DNS servers in /etc/resolv.conf so ports can be downloaded:

```
nameserver 10.0.0.62
nameserver 10.0.0.61
```

Still using the jail console, install dns/bind99.

```
# make -C /usr/ports/dns/bind99 install clean
```

Configure the name server by editing /usr/local/etc/namedb/named.conf .

Create an Access Control List (ACL) of addresses and networks that are permitted to send DNS queries to this name server. This section is added just before the options section already in the file:

```
...
// or cause huge amounts of useless Internet traffic.

acl "trusted" {
 192.168.1.0/24;
 localhost;
 localnets;
};

options {
...
```

Use the jail IP address in the listen-on setting to accept DNS queries from other computers on the network:

```
 listen-on { 192.168.1.240; };
```

A simple caching-only DNS name server is created by changing the forwarders section. The original file contains:

```
/*
 forwarders {
  127.0.0.1;
 };
*/
```

Uncomment the section by removing the /* and */ lines. Enter the IP addresses of the upstream DNS servers. Immediately after the forwarders section, add references to the trusted ACL defined earlier:

```
forwarders {
  10.0.0.62;
  10.0.0.61;
};

allow-query        { any; };
allow-recursion    { trusted; };
allow-query-cache { trusted; };
```

Enable the service in /etc/rc.conf :

```
named_enable="YES"
```

Start and test the name server:

```
# service named start
wrote key file "/usr/local/etc/namedb/rndc.key"
Starting named.
# /usr/local/bin/dig @192.168.1.240 freebsd.org
```

A response that includes

```
;; Got answer;
```

shows that the new DNS server is working. A long delay followed by a response including

```
;; connection timed out; no servers could be reached
```

shows a problem. Check the configuration settings and make sure any local firewalls allow the new DNS access to the upstream DNS servers.

The new DNS server can use itself for local name resolution, just like other local computers. Set the address of the DNS server in the client computer's /etc/resolv.conf :

```
nameserver 192.168.1.240
```

A local DHCP server can be configured to provide this address for a local DNS server, providing automatic configuration on DHCP clients.

Chapter 15. Mandatory Access Control

Written by Tom Rhodes.

15.1. Synopsis

FreeBSD supports security extensions based on the POSIX®.1e draft. These security mechanisms include file system Access Control Lists (Section 13.9, "Access Control Lists") and Mandatory Access Control (MAC). MAC allows access control modules to be loaded in order to implement security policies. Some modules provide protections for a narrow subset of the system, hardening a particular service. Others provide comprehensive labeled security across all subjects and objects. The mandatory part of the definition indicates that enforcement of controls is performed by administrators and the operating system. This is in contrast to the default security mechanism of Discretionary Access Control (DAC) where enforcement is left to the discretion of users.

This chapter focuses on the MAC framework and the set of pluggable security policy modules FreeBSD provides for enabling various security mechanisms.

After reading this chapter, you will know:

- The terminology associated with the MAC framework.

- The capabilities of MAC security policy modules as well as the difference between a labeled and non-labeled policy.

- The considerations to take into account before configuring a system to use the MAC framework.

- Which MAC security policy modules are included in FreeBSD and how to configure them.

- How to implement a more secure environment using the MAC framework.

- How to test the MAC configuration to ensure the framework has been properly implemented.

Before reading this chapter, you should:

- Understand UNIX® and FreeBSD basics (Chapter 3, *FreeBSD Basics*).

- Have some familiarity with security and how it pertains to FreeBSD (Chapter 13, *Security*).

 Warning

Improper MAC configuration may cause loss of system access, aggravation of users, or inability to access the features provided by Xorg. More importantly, MAC should not be relied upon to completely secure a system. The MAC framework only augments an existing security policy. Without sound security practices and regular security checks, the system will never be completely secure.

The examples contained within this chapter are for demonstration purposes and the example settings should *not* be implemented on a production system. Implementing any security policy takes a good deal of understanding, proper design, and thorough testing.

While this chapter covers a broad range of security issues relating to the MAC framework, the development of new MAC security policy modules will not be covered. A number of security policy modules included with the MAC framework have specific characteristics which are provided for both testing and new module development.

Refer to mac_test(4), mac_stub(4) and mac_none(4) for more information on these security policy modules and the various mechanisms they provide.

15.2. Key Terms

The following key terms are used when referring to the MAC framework:

- *compartment*: a set of programs and data to be partitioned or separated, where users are given explicit access to specific component of a system. A compartment represents a grouping, such as a work group, department, project, or topic. Compartments make it possible to implement a need-to-know-basis security policy.

- *integrity*: the level of trust which can be placed on data. As the integrity of the data is elevated, so does the ability to trust that data.

- *level*: the increased or decreased setting of a security attribute. As the level increases, its security is considered to elevate as well.

- *label*: a security attribute which can be applied to files, directories, or other items in the system. It could be considered a confidentiality stamp. When a label is placed on a file, it describes the security properties of that file and will only permit access by files, users, and resources with a similar security setting. The meaning and interpretation of label values depends on the policy configuration. Some policies treat a label as representing the integrity or secrecy of an object while other policies might use labels to hold rules for access.

- *multilabel*: this property is a file system option which can be set in single-user mode using tunefs(8), during boot using fstab(5), or during the creation of a new file system. This option permits an administrator to apply different MAC labels on different objects. This option only applies to security policy modules which support labeling.

- *single label*: a policy where the entire file system uses one label to enforce access control over the flow of data. Whenever multilabel is not set, all files will conform to the same label setting.

- *object*: an entity through which information flows under the direction of a *subject*. This includes directories, files, fields, screens, keyboards, memory, magnetic storage, printers or any other data storage or moving device. An object is a data container or a system resource. Access to an object effectively means access to its data.

- *subject*: any active entity that causes information to flow between *objects* such as a user, user process, or system process. On FreeBSD, this is almost always a thread acting in a process on behalf of a user.

- *policy*: a collection of rules which defines how objectives are to be achieved. A policy usually documents how certain items are to be handled. This chapter considers a policy to be a collection of rules which controls the flow of data and information and defines who has access to that data and information.

- *high-watermark*: this type of policy permits the raising of security levels for the purpose of accessing higher level information. In most cases, the original level is restored after the process is complete. Currently, the FreeBSD MAC framework does not include this type of policy.

- *low-watermark*: this type of policy permits lowering security levels for the purpose of accessing information which is less secure. In most cases, the original security level of the user is restored after the process is complete. The only security policy module in FreeBSD to use this is mac_lomac(4).

- *sensitivity*: usually used when discussing Multilevel Security (MLS). A sensitivity level describes how important or secret the data should be. As the sensitivity level increases, so does the importance of the secrecy, or confidentiality, of the data.

15.3. Understanding MAC Labels

A MAC label is a security attribute which may be applied to subjects and objects throughout the system. When setting a label, the administrator must understand its implications in order to prevent unexpected or undesired behavior of the system. The attributes available on an object depend on the loaded policy module, as policy modules interpret their attributes in different ways.

The security label on an object is used as a part of a security access control decision by a policy. With some policies, the label contains all of the information necessary to make a decision. In other policies, the labels may be processed as part of a larger rule set.

There are two types of label policies: single label and multi label. By default, the system will use single label. The administrator should be aware of the pros and cons of each in order to implement policies which meet the requirements of the system's security model.

A single label security policy only permits one label to be used for every subject or object. Since a single label policy enforces one set of access permissions across the entire system, it provides lower administration overhead, but decreases the flexibility of policies which support labeling. However, in many environments, a single label policy may be all that is required.

A single label policy is somewhat similar to DAC as `root` configures the policies so that users are placed in the appropriate categories and access levels. A notable difference is that many policy modules can also restrict `root`. Basic control over objects will then be released to the group, but `root` may revoke or modify the settings at any time.

When appropriate, a multi label policy can be set on a UFS file system by passing `multilabel` to tunefs(8). A multi label policy permits each subject or object to have its own independent MAC label. The decision to use a multi label or single label policy is only required for policies which implement the labeling feature, such as `biba`, `lomac`, and `mls`. Some policies, such as `seeotheruids` , `portacl` and `partition`, do not use labels at all.

Using a multi label policy on a partition and establishing a multi label security model can increase administrative overhead as everything in that file system has a label. This includes directories, files, and even device nodes.

The following command will set `multilabel` on the specified UFS file system. This may only be done in single-user mode and is not a requirement for the swap file system:

```
# tunefs -l enable /
```

> **Note**
>
> Some users have experienced problems with setting the `multilabel` flag on the root partition. If this is the case, please review Section 15.8, "Troubleshooting the MAC Framework".

Since the multi label policy is set on a per-file system basis, a multi label policy may not be needed if the file system layout is well designed. Consider an example security MAC model for a FreeBSD web server. This machine uses the single label, `biba/high`, for everything in the default file systems. If the web server needs to run at `biba/low` to prevent write up capabilities, it could be installed to a separate UFS /usr/local file system set at `biba/low`.

15.3.1. Label Configuration

Virtually all aspects of label policy module configuration will be performed using the base system utilities. These commands provide a simple interface for object or subject configuration or the manipulation and verification of the configuration.

All configuration may be done using `setfmac`, which is used to set MAC labels on system objects, and `setpmac`, which is used to set the labels on system subjects. For example, to set the biba MAC label to `high` on `test`:

```
# setfmac biba/high test
```

If the configuration is successful, the prompt will be returned without error. A common error is Permission denied which usually occurs when the label is being set or modified on a restricted object. Other conditions may produce different failures. For instance, the file may not be owned by the user attempting to relabel the object, the object may not exist, or the object may be read-only. A mandatory policy will not allow the process to relabel the file, maybe because of a property of the file, a property of the process, or a property of the proposed new label value. For example, if a user running at low integrity tries to change the label of a high integrity file, or a user running at low integrity tries to change the label of a low integrity file to a high integrity label, these operations will fail.

The system administrator may use `setpmac` to override the policy module's settings by assigning a different label to the invoked process:

```
# setfmac biba/high test
Permission denied
# setpmac biba/low setfmac biba/high test
# getfmac test
test: biba/high
```

For currently running processes, such as sendmail, `getpmac` is usually used instead. This command takes a process ID (PID) in place of a command name. If users attempt to manipulate a file not in their access, subject to the rules of the loaded policy modules, the Operation not permitted error will be displayed.

15.3.2. Predefined Labels

A few FreeBSD policy modules which support the labeling feature offer three predefined labels: `low`, `equal`, and `high`, where:

- `low` is considered the lowest label setting an object or subject may have. Setting this on objects or subjects blocks their access to objects or subjects marked high.

- `equal` sets the subject or object to be disabled or unaffected and should only be placed on objects considered to be exempt from the policy.

- `high` grants an object or subject the highest setting available in the Biba and MLS policy modules.

Such policy modules include mac_biba(4), mac_mls(4) and mac_lomac(4). Each of the predefined labels establishes a different information flow directive. Refer to the manual page of the module to determine the traits of the generic label configurations.

15.3.3. Numeric Labels

The Biba and MLS policy modules support a numeric label which may be set to indicate the precise level of hierarchical control. This numeric level is used to partition or sort information into different groups of classification, only permitting access to that group or a higher group level. For example:

```
biba/10:2+3+6(5:2+3-20:2+3+4+5+6)
```

may be interpreted as "Biba Policy Label/Grade 10:Compartments 2, 3 and 6: (grade 5 ...)"

In this example, the first grade would be considered the effective grade with effective compartments, the second grade is the low grade, and the last one is the high grade. In most configurations, such fine-grained settings are not needed as they are considered to be advanced configurations.

System objects only have a current grade and compartment. System subjects reflect the range of available rights in the system, and network interfaces, where they are used for access control.

The grade and compartments in a subject and object pair are used to construct a relationship known as *dominance*, in which a subject dominates an object, the object dominates the subject, neither dominates the other, or both dominate each other. The "both dominate" case occurs when the two labels are equal. Due to the information flow nature of Biba, a user has rights to a set of compartments that might correspond to projects, but objects also have a set of compartments. Users may have to subset their rights using `su` or `setpmac` in order to access objects in a compartment from which they are not restricted.

15.3.4. User Labels

Users are required to have labels so that their files and processes properly interact with the security policy defined on the system. This is configured in /etc/login.conf using login classes. Every policy module that uses labels will implement the user class setting.

To set the user class default label which will be enforced by MAC, add a label entry. An example label entry containing every policy module is displayed below. Note that in a real configuration, the administrator would never enable every policy module. It is recommended that the rest of this chapter be reviewed before any configuration is implemented.

```
default:\
 :copyright=/etc/COPYRIGHT:\
 :welcome=/etc/motd:\
 :setenv=MAIL=/var/mail/$,BLOCKSIZE=K:\
 :path=~/bin:/sbin:/bin:/usr/sbin:/usr/bin:/usr/local/sbin:/usr/local/bin:\
 :manpath=/usr/share/man /usr/local/man:\
 :nologin=/usr/sbin/nologin:\
 :cputime=1h30m:\
 :datasize=8M:\
 :vmemoryuse=100M:\
 :stacksize=2M:\
 :memorylocked=4M:\
 :memoryuse=8M:\
 :filesize=8M:\
 :coredumpsize=8M:\
 :openfiles=24:\
 :maxproc=32:\
 :priority=0:\
 :requirehome:\
 :passwordtime=91d:\
 :umask=022:\
 :ignoretime@:\
 :label=partition/13,mls/5,biba/10(5-15),lomac/10[2]:
```

While users can not modify the default value, they may change their label after they login, subject to the constraints of the policy. The example above tells the Biba policy that a process's minimum integrity is 5, its maximum is 15, and the default effective label is 10. The process will run at 10 until it chooses to change label, perhaps due to the user using setpmac, which will be constrained by Biba to the configured range.

After any change to login.conf, the login class capability database must be rebuilt using cap_mkdb.

Many sites have a large number of users requiring several different user classes. In depth planning is required as this can become difficult to manage.

15.3.5. Network Interface Labels

Labels may be set on network interfaces to help control the flow of data across the network. Policies using network interface labels function in the same way that policies function with respect to objects. Users at high settings in Biba, for example, will not be permitted to access network interfaces with a label of low.

When setting the MAC label on network interfaces, maclabel may be passed to ifconfig:

```
# ifconfig bge0 maclabel biba/equal
```

This example will set the MAC label of biba/equal on the bge0 interface. When using a setting similar to biba/high(low-high), the entire label should be quoted to prevent an error from being returned.

Each policy module which supports labeling has a tunable which may be used to disable the MAC label on network interfaces. Setting the label to equal will have a similar effect. Review the output of sysctl, the policy manual pages, and the information in the rest of this chapter for more information on those tunables.

15.4. Planning the Security Configuration

Before implementing any MAC policies, a planning phase is recommended. During the planning stages, an administrator should consider the implementation requirements and goals, such as:

- How to classify information and resources available on the target systems.

- Which information or resources to restrict access to along with the type of restrictions that should be applied.

- Which MAC modules will be required to achieve this goal.

A trial run of the trusted system and its configuration should occur *before* a MAC implementation is used on production systems. Since different environments have different needs and requirements, establishing a complete security profile will decrease the need of changes once the system goes live.

Consider how the MAC framework augments the security of the system as a whole. The various security policy modules provided by the MAC framework could be used to protect the network and file systems or to block users from accessing certain ports and sockets. Perhaps the best use of the policy modules is to load several security policy modules at a time in order to provide a MLS environment. This approach differs from a hardening policy, which typically hardens elements of a system which are used only for specific purposes. The downside to MLS is increased administrative overhead.

The overhead is minimal when compared to the lasting effect of a framework which provides the ability to pick and choose which policies are required for a specific configuration and which keeps performance overhead down. The reduction of support for unneeded policies can increase the overall performance of the system as well as offer flexibility of choice. A good implementation would consider the overall security requirements and effectively implement the various security policy modules offered by the framework.

A system utilizing MAC guarantees that a user will not be permitted to change security attributes at will. All user utilities, programs, and scripts must work within the constraints of the access rules provided by the selected security policy modules and control of the MAC access rules is in the hands of the system administrator.

It is the duty of the system administrator to carefully select the correct security policy modules. For an environment that needs to limit access control over the network, the mac_portacl(4), mac_ifoff(4), and mac_biba(4) policy modules make good starting points. For an environment where strict confidentiality of file system objects is required, consider the mac_bsdextended(4) and mac_mls(4) policy modules.

Policy decisions could be made based on network configuration. If only certain users should be permitted access to ssh(1), the mac_portacl(4) policy module is a good choice. In the case of file systems, access to objects might be considered confidential to some users, but not to others. As an example, a large development team might be broken off into smaller projects where developers in project A might not be permitted to access objects written by developers in project B. Yet both projects might need to access objects created by developers in project C. Using the different security policy modules provided by the MAC framework, users could be divided into these groups and then given access to the appropriate objects.

Each security policy module has a unique way of dealing with the overall security of a system. Module selection should be based on a well thought out security policy which may require revision and reimplementation. Understanding the different security policy modules offered by the MAC framework will help administrators choose the best policies for their situations.

The rest of this chapter covers the available modules, describes their use and configuration, and in some cases, provides insight on applicable situations.

 Caution

Implementing MAC is much like implementing a firewall since care must be taken to prevent being completely locked out of the system. The ability to revert back to a previous configura-

> tion should be considered and the implementation of MAC over a remote connection should be done with extreme caution.

15.5. Available MAC Policies

The default FreeBSD kernel includes options MAC. This means that every module included with the MAC framework can be loaded with kldload as a run-time kernel module. After testing the module, add the module name to /boot/loader.conf so that it will load during boot. Each module also provides a kernel option for those administrators who choose to compile their own custom kernel.

FreeBSD includes a group of policies that will cover most security requirements. Each policy is summarized below. The last three policies support integer settings in place of the three default labels.

15.5.1. The MAC See Other UIDs Policy

Module name: mac_seeotheruids.ko

Kernel configuration line: options MAC_SEEOTHERUIDS

Boot option: mac_seeotheruids_load="YES"

The mac_seeotheruids(4) module extends the security.bsd.see_other_uids and security.bsd.see_other_gids sysctl tunables. This option does not require any labels to be set before configuration and can operate transparently with other modules.

After loading the module, the following sysctl tunables may be used to control its features:

- security.mac.seeotheruids.enabled enables the module and implements the default settings which deny users the ability to view processes and sockets owned by other users.

- security.mac.seeotheruids.specificgid_enabled allows specified groups to be exempt from this policy. To exempt specific groups, use the security.mac.seeotheruids.specificgid=XXX sysctl tunable, replacing XXX with the numeric group ID to be exempted.

- security.mac.seeotheruids.primarygroup_enabled is used to exempt specific primary groups from this policy. When using this tunable, security.mac.seeotheruids.specificgid_enabled may not be set.

15.5.2. The MAC BSD Extended Policy

Module name: mac_bsdextended.ko

Kernel configuration line: options MAC_BSDEXTENDED

Boot option: mac_bsdextended_load="YES"

The mac_bsdextended(4) module enforces a file system firewall. It provides an extension to the standard file system permissions model, permitting an administrator to create a firewall-like ruleset to protect files, utilities, and directories in the file system hierarchy. When access to a file system object is attempted, the list of rules is iterated until either a matching rule is located or the end is reached. This behavior may be changed using security.mac.bsdextended.firstmatch_enabled. Similar to other firewall modules in FreeBSD, a file containing the access control rules can be created and read by the system at boot time using an rc.conf(5) variable.

The rule list may be entered using ugidfw(8) which has a syntax similar to ipfw(8). More tools can be written by using the functions in the libugidfw(3) library.

After the mac_bsdextended(4) module has been loaded, the following command may be used to list the current rule configuration:

```
# ugidfw list
0 slots, 0 rules
```

By default, no rules are defined and everything is completely accessible. To create a rule which blocks all access by users but leaves root unaffected:

```
# ugidfw add subject not uid root new object not uid root mode n
```

While this rule is simple to implement, it is a very bad idea as it blocks all users from issuing any commands. A more realistic example blocks user1 all access, including directory listings, to *user2*'s home directory:

```
# ugidfw set 2 subject uid  user1 object uid user2 mode n
# ugidfw set 3 subject uid  user1 object gid user2 mode n
```

Instead of user1, not uid *user2* could be used in order to enforce the same access restrictions for all users. However, the root user is unaffected by these rules.

> ## Note
>
> Extreme caution should be taken when working with this module as incorrect use could block access to certain parts of the file system.

15.5.3. The MAC Interface Silencing Policy

Module name: mac_ifoff.ko

Kernel configuration line: options MAC_IFOFF

Boot option: mac_ifoff_load="YES"

The mac_ifoff(4) module is used to disable network interfaces on the fly and to keep network interfaces from being brought up during system boot. It does not use labels and does not depend on any other MAC modules.

Most of this module's control is performed through these sysctl tunables:

* security.mac.ifoff.lo_enabled enables or disables all traffic on the loopback, lo(4), interface.

* security.mac.ifoff.bpfrecv_enabled enables or disables all traffic on the Berkeley Packet Filter interface, bpf(4).

* security.mac.ifoff.other_enabled enables or disables traffic on all other interfaces.

One of the most common uses of mac_ifoff(4) is network monitoring in an environment where network traffic should not be permitted during the boot sequence. Another use would be to write a script which uses an application such as security/aide to automatically block network traffic if it finds new or altered files in protected directories.

15.5.4. The MAC Port Access Control List Policy

Module name: mac_portacl.ko

Kernel configuration line: MAC_PORTACL

Boot option: mac_portacl_load="YES"

The mac_portacl(4) module is used to limit binding to local TCP and UDP ports, making it possible to allow non-root users to bind to specified privileged ports below 1024.

Once loaded, this module enables the MAC policy on all sockets. The following tunables are available:

- `security.mac.portacl.enabled` enables or disables the policy completely.

- `security.mac.portacl.port_high` sets the highest port number that mac_portacl(4) protects.

- `security.mac.portacl.suser_exempt`, when set to a non-zero value, exempts the `root` user from this policy.

- `security.mac.portacl.rules` specifies the policy as a text string of the form `rule[,rule,...]`, with as many rules as needed, and where each rule is of the form `idtype:id:protocol:port`. The *idtype* is either `uid` or `gid`. The *protocol* parameter can be `tcp` or `udp`. The *port* parameter is the port number to allow the specified user or group to bind to. Only numeric values can be used for the user ID, group ID, and port parameters.

By default, ports below 1024 can only be used by privileged processes which run as `root`. For mac_portacl(4) to allow non-privileged processes to bind to ports below 1024, set the following tunables as follows:

```
# sysctl security.mac.portacl.port_high=1023
# sysctl net.inet.ip.portrange.reservedlow=0
# sysctl net.inet.ip.portrange.reservedhigh=0
```

To prevent the `root` user from being affected by this policy, set `security.mac.portacl.suser_exempt` to a non-zero value.

```
# sysctl security.mac.portacl.suser_exempt=1
```

To allow the `www` user with UID 80 to bind to port 80 without ever needing `root` privilege:

```
# sysctl security.mac.portacl.rules=uid:80:tcp:80
```

This next example permits the user with the UID of 1001 to bind to TCP ports 110 (POP3) and 995 (POP3s):

```
# sysctl security.mac.portacl.rules=uid:1001:tcp:110,uid:1001:tcp:995
```

15.5.5. The MAC Partition Policy

Module name: `mac_partition.ko`

Kernel configuration line: `options MAC_PARTITION`

Boot option: `mac_partition_load="YES"`

The mac_partition(4) policy drops processes into specific "partitions" based on their MAC label. Most configuration for this policy is done using setpmac(8). One `sysctl` tunable is available for this policy:

- `security.mac.partition.enabled` enables the enforcement of MAC process partitions.

When this policy is enabled, users will only be permitted to see their processes, and any others within their partition, but will not be permitted to work with utilities outside the scope of this partition. For instance, a user in the `insecure` class will not be permitted to access `top` as well as many other commands that must spawn a process.

This example adds `top` to the label set on users in the `insecure` class. All processes spawned by users in the insecure class will stay in the `partition/13` label.

```
# setpmac partition/13 top
```

This command displays the partition label and the process list:

```
# ps Zax
```

285

This command displays another user's process partition label and that user's currently running processes:

```
# ps -ZU trhodes
```

> **Note**
>
> Users can see processes in root's label unless the mac_seeotheruids(4) policy is loaded.

15.5.6. The MAC Multi-Level Security Module

Module name: mac_mls.ko

Kernel configuration line: options MAC_MLS

Boot option: mac_mls_load="YES"

The mac_mls(4) policy controls access between subjects and objects in the system by enforcing a strict information flow policy.

In MLS environments, a "clearance" level is set in the label of each subject or object, along with compartments. Since these clearance levels can reach numbers greater than several thousand, it would be a daunting task to thoroughly configure every subject or object. To ease this administrative overhead, three labels are included in this policy: mls/low, mls/equal, and mls/high, where:

- Anything labeled with mls/low will have a low clearance level and not be permitted to access information of a higher level. This label also prevents objects of a higher clearance level from writing or passing information to a lower level.

- mls/equal should be placed on objects which should be exempt from the policy.

- mls/high is the highest level of clearance possible. Objects assigned this label will hold dominance over all other objects in the system; however, they will not permit the leaking of information to objects of a lower class.

MLS provides:

- A hierarchical security level with a set of non-hierarchical categories.

- Fixed rules of no read up, no write down . This means that a subject can have read access to objects on its own level or below, but not above. Similarly, a subject can have write access to objects on its own level or above, but not beneath.

- Secrecy, or the prevention of inappropriate disclosure of data.

- A basis for the design of systems that concurrently handle data at multiple sensitivity levels without leaking information between secret and confidential.

The following sysctl tunables are available:

- security.mac.mls.enabled is used to enable or disable the MLS policy.

- security.mac.mls.ptys_equal labels all pty(4) devices as mls/equal during creation.

- security.mac.mls.revocation_enabled revokes access to objects after their label changes to a label of a lower grade.

- security.mac.mls.max_compartments sets the maximum number of compartment levels allowed on a system.

To manipulate MLS labels, use setfmac(8). To assign a label to an object:

```
# setfmac mls/5 test
```

To get the MLS label for the file `test`:

```
# getfmac test
```

Another approach is to create a master policy file in `/etc/` which specifies the MLS policy information and to feed that file to `setfmac`.

When using the MLS policy module, an administrator plans to control the flow of sensitive information. The default `block read up block write down` sets everything to a low state. Everything is accessible and an administrator slowly augments the confidentiality of the information.

Beyond the three basic label options, an administrator may group users and groups as required to block the information flow between them. It might be easier to look at the information in clearance levels using descriptive words, such as classifications of `Confidential`, `Secret`, and `Top Secret`. Some administrators instead create different groups based on project levels. Regardless of the classification method, a well thought out plan must exist before implementing a restrictive policy.

Some example situations for the MLS policy module include an e-commerce web server, a file server holding critical company information, and financial institution environments.

15.5.7. The MAC Biba Module

Module name: `mac_biba.ko`

Kernel configuration line: `options MAC_BIBA`

Boot option: `mac_biba_load="YES"`

The mac_biba(4) module loads the MAC Biba policy. This policy is similar to the MLS policy with the exception that the rules for information flow are slightly reversed. This is to prevent the downward flow of sensitive information whereas the MLS policy prevents the upward flow of sensitive information.

In Biba environments, an "integrity" label is set on each subject or object. These labels are made up of hierarchical grades and non-hierarchical components. As a grade ascends, so does its integrity.

Supported labels are `biba/low`, `biba/equal`, and `biba/high`, where:

- `biba/low` is considered the lowest integrity an object or subject may have. Setting this on objects or subjects blocks their write access to objects or subjects marked as `biba/high`, but will not prevent read access.

- `biba/equal` should only be placed on objects considered to be exempt from the policy.

- `biba/high` permits writing to objects set at a lower label, but does not permit reading that object. It is recommended that this label be placed on objects that affect the integrity of the entire system.

Biba provides:

- Hierarchical integrity levels with a set of non-hierarchical integrity categories.

- Fixed rules are `no write up, no read down`, the opposite of MLS. A subject can have write access to objects on its own level or below, but not above. Similarly, a subject can have read access to objects on its own level or above, but not below.

- Integrity by preventing inappropriate modification of data.

- Integrity levels instead of MLS sensitivity levels.

The following tunables can be used to manipulate the Biba policy:

- `security.mac.biba.enabled` is used to enable or disable enforcement of the Biba policy on the target machine.

- `security.mac.biba.ptys_equal` is used to disable the Biba policy on pty(4) devices.

- `security.mac.biba.revocation_enabled` forces the revocation of access to objects if the label is changed to dominate the subject.

To access the Biba policy setting on system objects, use `setfmac` and `getfmac`:

```
# setfmac biba/low test
# getfmac test
test: biba/low
```

Integrity, which is different from sensitivity, is used to guarantee that information is not manipulated by untrusted parties. This includes information passed between subjects and objects. It ensures that users will only be able to modify or access information they have been given explicit access to. The mac_biba(4) security policy module permits an administrator to configure which files and programs a user may see and invoke while assuring that the programs and files are trusted by the system for that user.

During the initial planning phase, an administrator must be prepared to partition users into grades, levels, and areas. The system will default to a high label once this policy module is enabled, and it is up to the administrator to configure the different grades and levels for users. Instead of using clearance levels, a good planning method could include topics. For instance, only allow developers modification access to the source code repository, source code compiler, and other development utilities. Other users would be grouped into other categories such as testers, designers, or end users and would only be permitted read access.

A lower integrity subject is unable to write to a higher integrity subject and a higher integrity subject cannot list or read a lower integrity object. Setting a label at the lowest possible grade could make it inaccessible to subjects. Some prospective environments for this security policy module would include a constrained web server, a development and test machine, and a source code repository. A less useful implementation would be a personal workstation, a machine used as a router, or a network firewall.

15.5.8. The MAC Low-watermark Module

Module name: `mac_lomac.ko`

Kernel configuration line: `options MAC_LOMAC`

Boot option: `mac_lomac_load="YES"`

Unlike the MAC Biba policy, the mac_lomac(4) policy permits access to lower integrity objects only after decreasing the integrity level to not disrupt any integrity rules.

The Low-watermark integrity policy works almost identically to Biba, with the exception of using floating labels to support subject demotion via an auxiliary grade compartment. This secondary compartment takes the form `[auxgrade]`. When assigning a policy with an auxiliary grade, use the syntax `lomac/10[2]`, where 2 is the auxiliary grade.

This policy relies on the ubiquitous labeling of all system objects with integrity labels, permitting subjects to read from low integrity objects and then downgrading the label on the subject to prevent future writes to high integrity objects using `[auxgrade]`. The policy may provide greater compatibility and require less initial configuration than Biba.

Like the Biba and MLS policies, `setfmac` and `setpmac` are used to place labels on system objects:

```
# setfmac /usr/home/trhodes lomac/high[low]
# getfmac /usr/home/trhodes lomac/high[low]
```

The auxiliary grade `low` is a feature provided only by the MAC LOMAC policy.

15.6. User Lock Down

This example considers a relatively small storage system with fewer than fifty users. Users will have login capabilities and are permitted to store data and access resources.

For this scenario, the mac_bsdextended(4) and mac_seeotheruids(4) policy modules could co-exist and block access to system objects while hiding user processes.

Begin by adding the following line to `/boot/loader.conf` :

```
mac_seeotheruids_load="YES"
```

The mac_bsdextended(4) security policy module may be activated by adding this line to `/etc/rc.conf` :

```
ugidfw_enable="YES"
```

Default rules stored in `/etc/rc.bsdextended` will be loaded at system initialization. However, the default entries may need modification. Since this machine is expected only to service users, everything may be left commented out except the last two lines in order to force the loading of user owned system objects by default.

Add the required users to this machine and reboot. For testing purposes, try logging in as a different user across two consoles. Run `ps aux` to see if processes of other users are visible. Verify that running ls(1) on another user's home directory fails.

Do not try to test with the `root` user unless the specific `sysctl`s have been modified to block super user access.

Note

When a new user is added, their mac_bsdextended(4) rule will not be in the ruleset list. To update the ruleset quickly, unload the security policy module and reload it again using kldunload(8) and kldload(8).

15.7. Nagios in a MAC Jail

This section demonstrates the steps that are needed to implement the Nagios network monitoring system in a MAC environment. This is meant as an example which still requires the administrator to test that the implemented policy meets the security requirements of the network before using in a production environment.

This example requires `multilabel` to be set on each file system. It also assumes that net-mgmt/nagios-plugins, net-mgmt/nagios, and www/apache22 are all installed, configured, and working correctly before attempting the integration into the MAC framework.

15.7.1. Create an Insecure User Class

Begin the procedure by adding the following user class to `/etc/login.conf`:

```
insecure:\
:copyright=/etc/COPYRIGHT:\
:welcome=/etc/motd:\
:setenv=MAIL=/var/mail/$,BLOCKSIZE=K:\
:path=~/bin:/sbin:/bin:/usr/sbin:/usr/bin:/usr/local/sbin:/usr/local/bin
:manpath=/usr/share/man /usr/local/man:\
```

```
:nologin=/usr/sbin/nologin:\
:cputime=1h30m:\
:datasize=8M:\
:vmemoryuse=100M:\
:stacksize=2M:\
:memorylocked=4M:\
:memoryuse=8M:\
:filesize=8M:\
:coredumpsize=8M:\
:openfiles=24:\
:maxproc=32:\
:priority=0:\
:requirehome:\
:passwordtime=91d:\
:umask=022:\
:ignoretime@:\
:label=biba/10(10-10):
```

Then, add the following line to the default user class section:

```
:label=biba/high:
```

Save the edits and issue the following command to rebuild the database:

```
# cap_mkdb /etc/login.conf
```

15.7.2. Configure Users

Set the root user to the default class using:

```
# pw usermod root -L default
```

All user accounts that are not root will now require a login class. The login class is required, otherwise users will be refused access to common commands. The following sh script should do the trick:

```
# for x in `awk -F: '($3 >= 1001) && ($3 != 65534) { print $1 }' \
 /etc/passwd`; do pw usermod $x -L default; done;
```

Next, drop the nagios and www accounts into the insecure class:

```
# pw usermod nagios -L insecure
# pw usermod www -L insecure
```

15.7.3. Create the Contexts File

A contexts file should now be created as /etc/policy.contexts:

```
# This is the default BIBA policy for this system.

# System:
/var/run(/.*)?   biba/equal

/dev/(/.*)?   biba/equal

/var    biba/equal
/var/spool(/.*)?  biba/equal

/var/log(/.*)?   biba/equal

/tmp(/.*)?   biba/equal
/var/tmp(/.*)?   biba/equal

/var/spool/mqueue  biba/equal
/var/spool/clientmqueue   biba/equal
```

```
# For Nagios:
/usr/local/etc/nagios(/.*)? biba/10

/var/spool/nagios(/.*)?  biba/10

# For apache
/usr/local/etc/apache(/.*)? biba/10
```

This policy enforces security by setting restrictions on the flow of information. In this specific configuration, users, including root, should never be allowed to access Nagios. Configuration files and processes that are a part of Nagios will be completely self contained or jailed.

This file will be read after running setfsmac on every file system. This example sets the policy on the root file system:

 # setfsmac -ef /etc/policy.contexts /

Next, add these edits to the main section of /etc/mac.conf :

```
default_labels file ?biba
default_labels ifnet ?biba
default_labels process ?biba
default_labels socket ?biba
```

15.7.4. Loader Configuration

To finish the configuration, add the following lines to /boot/loader.conf :

```
mac_biba_load="YES"
mac_seeotheruids_load="YES"
security.mac.biba.trust_all_interfaces=1
```

And the following line to the network card configuration stored in /etc/rc.conf . If the primary network configuration is done via DHCP, this may need to be configured manually after every system boot:

```
maclabel biba/equal
```

15.7.5. Testing the Configuration

First, ensure that the web server and Nagios will not be started on system initialization and reboot. Ensure that root cannot access any of the files in the Nagios configuration directory. If root can list the contents of /var/spool/nagios , something is wrong. Instead, a "permission denied" error should be returned.

If all seems well, Nagios, Apache, and Sendmail can now be started:

```
# cd /etc/mail && make stop && \
setpmac biba/equal make start && setpmac biba/10\(10-10\) apachectl start && \
setpmac biba/10\(10-10\) /usr/local/etc/rc.d/nagios.sh forcestart
```

Double check to ensure that everything is working properly. If not, check the log files for error messages. If needed, use sysctl(8) to disable the mac_biba(4) security policy module and try starting everything again as usual.

Note

The root user can still change the security enforcement and edit its configuration files. The following command will permit the degradation of the security policy to a lower grade for a newly spawned shell:

 # setpmac biba/10 csh

> To block this from happening, force the user into a range using login.conf(5). If setpmac(8) attempts to run a command outside of the compartment's range, an error will be returned and the command will not be executed. In this case, set root to `biba/high(high-high)` .

15.8. Troubleshooting the MAC Framework

This section discusses common configuration errors and how to resolve them.

The `multilabel` flag does not stay enabled on the root (/) partition:
　The following steps may resolve this transient error:

1. Edit `/etc/fstab` and set the root partition to `ro` for read-only.

2. Reboot into single user mode.

3. Run `tunefs -l enable` on `/`.

4. Reboot the system.

5. Run `mount -urw /` and change the `ro` back to `rw` in `/etc/fstab` and reboot the system again.

6. Double-check the output from `mount` to ensure that `multilabel` has been properly set on the root file system.

After establishing a secure environment with MAC, Xorg no longer starts:
　This could be caused by the MAC `partition` policy or by a mislabeling in one of the MAC labeling policies. To debug, try the following:

1. Check the error message. If the user is in the `insecure` class, the `partition` policy may be the culprit. Try setting the user's class back to the `default` class and rebuild the database with `cap_mkdb` . If this does not alleviate the problem, go to step two.

2. Double-check that the label policies are set correctly for the user, Xorg, and the `/dev` entries.

3. If neither of these resolve the problem, send the error message and a description of the environment to the FreeBSD general questions mailing list.

The _secure_path: unable to stat .login_conf error appears:
　This error can appear when a user attempts to switch from the `root` user to another user in the system. This message usually occurs when the user has a higher label setting than that of the user they are attempting to become. For instance, if `joe` has a default label of `biba/low` and `root` has a label of `biba/high`, `root` cannot view `joe`'s home directory. This will happen whether or not `root` has used `su` to become `joe` as the Biba integrity model will not permit `root` to view objects set at a lower integrity level.

The system no longer recognizes `root`:
　When this occurs, `whoami` returns `0` and `su` returns who are you?.

　This can happen if a labeling policy has been disabled by sysctl(8) or the policy module was unloaded. If the policy is disabled, the login capabilities database needs to be reconfigured. Double check `/etc/login.conf` to ensure that all `label` options have been removed and rebuild the database with `cap_mkdb` .

　This may also happen if a policy restricts access to `master.passwd`. This is usually caused by an administrator altering the file under a label which conflicts with the general policy being used by the system. In these cases, the user information would be read by the system and access would be blocked as the file has inherited the new label. Disable the policy using sysctl(8) and everything should return to normal.

Chapter 16. Security Event Auditing

Written by Tom Rhodes and Robert Watson.

16.1. Synopsis

The FreeBSD operating system includes support for security event auditing. Event auditing supports reliable, fine-grained, and configurable logging of a variety of security-relevant system events, including logins, configuration changes, and file and network access. These log records can be invaluable for live system monitoring, intrusion detection, and postmortem analysis. FreeBSD implements Sun™'s published Basic Security Module (BSM) Application Programming Interface (API) and file format, and is interoperable with the Solaris™ and Mac OS® X audit implementations.

This chapter focuses on the installation and configuration of event auditing. It explains audit policies and provides an example audit configuration.

After reading this chapter, you will know:

- What event auditing is and how it works.

- How to configure event auditing on FreeBSD for users and processes.

- How to review the audit trail using the audit reduction and review tools.

Before reading this chapter, you should:

- Understand UNIX® and FreeBSD basics (Chapter 3, *FreeBSD Basics*).

- Be familiar with the basics of kernel configuration/compilation (Chapter 8, *Configuring the FreeBSD Kernel*).

- Have some familiarity with security and how it pertains to FreeBSD (Chapter 13, *Security*).

 Warning

The audit facility has some known limitations. Not all security-relevant system events are auditable and some login mechanisms, such as Xorg-based display managers and third-party daemons, do not properly configure auditing for user login sessions.

The security event auditing facility is able to generate very detailed logs of system activity. On a busy system, trail file data can be very large when configured for high detail, exceeding gigabytes a week in some configurations. Administrators should take into account the disk space requirements associated with high volume audit configurations. For example, it may be desirable to dedicate a file system to /var/audit so that other file systems are not affected if the audit file system becomes full.

16.2. Key Terms

The following terms are related to security event auditing:

- *event*: an auditable event is any event that can be logged using the audit subsystem. Examples of security-relevant events include the creation of a file, the building of a network connection, or a user logging in. Events are either "attributable", meaning that they can be traced to an authenticated user, or "non-attributable". Examples of non-attributable events are any events that occur before authentication in the login process, such as bad password attempts.

- *class*: a named set of related events which are used in selection expressions. Commonly used classes of events include "file creation" (fc), "exec" (ex), and "login_logout" (lo).

- *record*: an audit log entry describing a security event. Records contain a record event type, information on the subject (user) performing the action, date and time information, information on any objects or arguments, and a success or failure condition.

- *trail*: a log file consisting of a series of audit records describing security events. Trails are in roughly chronological order with respect to the time events completed. Only authorized processes are allowed to commit records to the audit trail.

- *selection expression*: a string containing a list of prefixes and audit event class names used to match events.

- *preselection*: the process by which the system identifies which events are of interest to the administrator. The preselection configuration uses a series of selection expressions to identify which classes of events to audit for which users, as well as global settings that apply to both authenticated and unauthenticated processes.

- *reduction*: the process by which records from existing audit trails are selected for preservation, printing, or analysis. Likewise, the process by which undesired audit records are removed from the audit trail. Using reduction, administrators can implement policies for the preservation of audit data. For example, detailed audit trails might be kept for one month, but after that, trails might be reduced in order to preserve only login information for archival purposes.

16.3. Audit Configuration

User space support for event auditing is installed as part of the base FreeBSD operating system. Kernel support is available in the GENERIC kernel by default, and auditd(8) can be enabled by adding the following line to /etc/rc.conf:

```
auditd_enable="YES"
```

Then, start the audit daemon:

```
# service auditd start
```

Users who prefer to compile a custom kernel must include the following line in their custom kernel configuration file:

```
options AUDIT
```

16.3.1. Event Selection Expressions

Selection expressions are used in a number of places in the audit configuration to determine which events should be audited. Expressions contain a list of event classes to match. Selection expressions are evaluated from left to right, and two expressions are combined by appending one onto the other.

Table 16.1, "Default Audit Event Classes" summarizes the default audit event classes:

Table 16.1. Default Audit Event Classes

Class Name	Description	Action
all	all	Match all event classes.
aa	authentication and authorization	

Class Name	Description	Action
ad	administrative	Administrative actions performed on the system as a whole.
ap	application	Application defined action.
cl	file close	Audit calls to the close system call.
ex	exec	Audit program execution. Auditing of command line arguments and environmental variables is controlled via audit_control(5) using the argv and envv parameters to the policy setting.
fa	file attribute access	Audit the access of object attributes such as stat(1) and pathconf(2).
fc	file create	Audit events where a file is created as a result.
fd	file delete	Audit events where file deletion occurs.
fm	file attribute modify	Audit events where file attribute modification occurs, such as by chown(8), chflags(1), and flock(2).
fr	file read	Audit events in which data is read or files are opened for reading.
fw	file write	Audit events in which data is written or files are written or modified.
io	ioctl	Audit use of the ioctl system call.
ip	ipc	Audit various forms of Inter-Process Communication, including POSIX pipes and System V IPC operations.
lo	login_logout	Audit login(1) and logout(1) events.
na	non attributable	Audit non-attributable events.
no	invalid class	Match no audit events.
nt	network	Audit events related to network actions such as connect(2) and accept(2).
ot	other	Audit miscellaneous events.
pc	process	Audit process operations such as exec(3) and exit(3).

These audit event classes may be customized by modifying the audit_class and audit_event configuration files.

Each audit event class may be combined with a prefix indicating whether successful/failed operations are matched, and whether the entry is adding or removing matching for the class and type. Table 16.2, "Prefixes for Audit Event Classes" summarizes the available prefixes:

Table 16.2. Prefixes for Audit Event Classes

Prefix	Action
+	Audit successful events in this class.
-	Audit failed events in this class.

Prefix	Action
^	Audit neither successful nor failed events in this class.
^+	Do not audit successful events in this class.
^-	Do not audit failed events in this class.

If no prefix is present, both successful and failed instances of the event will be audited.

The following example selection string selects both successful and failed login/logout events, but only successful execution events:

```
lo,+ex
```

16.3.2. Configuration Files

The following configuration files for security event auditing are found in /etc/security :

- audit_class: contains the definitions of the audit classes.

- audit_control: controls aspects of the audit subsystem, such as default audit classes, minimum disk space to leave on the audit log volume, and maximum audit trail size.

- audit_event: textual names and descriptions of system audit events and a list of which classes each event is in.

- audit_user: user-specific audit requirements to be combined with the global defaults at login.

- audit_warn: a customizable shell script used by auditd(8) to generate warning messages in exceptional situations, such as when space for audit records is running low or when the audit trail file has been rotated.

 Warning

Audit configuration files should be edited and maintained carefully, as errors in configuration may result in improper logging of events.

In most cases, administrators will only need to modify audit_control and audit_user. The first file controls system-wide audit properties and policies and the second file may be used to fine-tune auditing by user.

16.3.2.1. The audit_control File

A number of defaults for the audit subsystem are specified in audit_control:

```
dir:/var/audit
dist:off
flags:lo,aa
minfree:5
naflags:lo,aa
policy:cnt,argv
filesz:2M
expire-after:10M
```

The dir entry is used to set one or more directories where audit logs will be stored. If more than one directory entry appears, they will be used in order as they fill. It is common to configure audit so that audit logs are stored on a dedicated file system, in order to prevent interference between the audit subsystem and other subsystems if the file system fills.

If the dist field is set to on or yes, hard links will be created to all trail files in /var/audit/dist .

The flags field sets the system-wide default preselection mask for attributable events. In the example above, successful and failed login/logout events as well as authentication and authorization are audited for all users.

The minfree entry defines the minimum percentage of free space for the file system where the audit trail is stored.

The naflags entry specifies audit classes to be audited for non-attributed events, such as the login/logout process and authentication and authorization.

The policy entry specifies a comma-separated list of policy flags controlling various aspects of audit behavior. The cnt indicates that the system should continue running despite an auditing failure (this flag is highly recommended). The other flag, argv, causes command line arguments to the execve(2) system call to be audited as part of command execution.

The filesz entry specifies the maximum size for an audit trail before automatically terminating and rotating the trail file. A value of 0 disables automatic log rotation. If the requested file size is below the minimum of 512k, it will be ignored and a log message will be generated.

The expire-after field specifies when audit log files will expire and be removed.

16.3.2.2. The audit_user File

The administrator can specify further audit requirements for specific users in audit_user. Each line configures auditing for a user via two fields: the alwaysaudit field specifies a set of events that should always be audited for the user, and the neveraudit field specifies a set of events that should never be audited for the user.

The following example entries audit login/logout events and successful command execution for root and file creation and successful command execution for www. If used with the default audit_control, the lo entry for root is redundant, and login/logout events will also be audited for www.

```
root:lo,+ex:no
www:fc,+ex:no
```

16.4. Working with Audit Trails

Since audit trails are stored in the BSM binary format, several built-in tools are available to modify or convert these trails to text. To convert trail files to a simple text format, use praudit. To reduce the audit trail file for analysis, archiving, or printing purposes, use auditreduce. This utility supports a variety of selection parameters, including event type, event class, user, date or time of the event, and the file path or object acted on.

For example, to dump the entire contents of a specified audit log in plain text:

```
# praudit /var/audit/ AUDITFILE
```

Where *AUDITFILE* is the audit log to dump.

Audit trails consist of a series of audit records made up of tokens, which praudit prints sequentially, one per line. Each token is of a specific type, such as header (an audit record header) or path (a file path from a name lookup). The following is an example of an execve event:

```
header,133,10,execve(2),0,Mon Sep 25 15:58:03 2006, + 384 msec
exec arg,finger,doug
path,/usr/bin/finger
attribute,555,root,wheel,90,24918,104944
subject,robert,root,wheel,root,wheel,38439,38032,42086,128.232.9.100
return,success,0
trailer,133
```

This audit represents a successful execve call, in which the command finger doug has been run. The exec arg token contains the processed command line presented by the shell to the kernel. The path token holds the path to the executable as looked up by the kernel. The attribute token describes the binary and includes the file mode.

The subject token stores the audit user ID, effective user ID and group ID, real user ID and group ID, process ID, session ID, port ID, and login address. Notice that the audit user ID and real user ID differ as the user robert switched to the root account before running this command, but it is audited using the original authenticated user. The return token indicates the successful execution and the trailer concludes the record.

XML output format is also supported and can be selected by including -x.

Since audit logs may be very large, a subset of records can be selected using auditreduce. This example selects all audit records produced for the user trhodes stored in AUDITFILE:

```
# auditreduce -u trhodes /var/audit/AUDITFILE | praudit
```

Members of the audit group have permission to read audit trails in /var/audit. By default, this group is empty, so only the root user can read audit trails. Users may be added to the audit group in order to delegate audit review rights. As the ability to track audit log contents provides significant insight into the behavior of users and processes, it is recommended that the delegation of audit review rights be performed with caution.

16.4.1. Live Monitoring Using Audit Pipes

Audit pipes are cloning pseudo-devices which allow applications to tap the live audit record stream. This is primarily of interest to authors of intrusion detection and system monitoring applications. However, the audit pipe device is a convenient way for the administrator to allow live monitoring without running into problems with audit trail file ownership or log rotation interrupting the event stream. To track the live audit event stream:

```
# praudit /dev/auditpipe
```

By default, audit pipe device nodes are accessible only to the root user. To make them accessible to the members of the audit group, add a devfs rule to /etc/devfs.rules:

```
add path 'auditpipe*' mode 0440 group audit
```

See devfs.rules(5) for more information on configuring the devfs file system.

> **Warning**
>
> It is easy to produce audit event feedback cycles, in which the viewing of each audit event results in the generation of more audit events. For example, if all network I/O is audited, and praudit is run from an SSH session, a continuous stream of audit events will be generated at a high rate, as each event being printed will generate another event. For this reason, it is advisable to run praudit on an audit pipe device from sessions without fine-grained I/O auditing.

16.4.2. Rotating and Compressing Audit Trail Files

Audit trails are written to by the kernel and managed by the audit daemon, auditd(8). Administrators should not attempt to use newsyslog.conf(5) or other tools to directly rotate audit logs. Instead, audit should be used to shut down auditing, reconfigure the audit system, and perform log rotation. The following command causes the audit daemon to create a new audit log and signal the kernel to switch to using the new log. The old log will be terminated and renamed, at which point it may then be manipulated by the administrator:

```
# audit -n
```

If auditd(8) is not currently running, this command will fail and an error message will be produced.

Adding the following line to /etc/crontab will schedule this rotation every twelve hours:

```
0    */12    *    *    *    root    /usr/sbin/audit -n
```

The change will take effect once /etc/crontab is saved.

Automatic rotation of the audit trail file based on file size is possible using filesz in audit_control as described in Section 16.3.2.1, "The audit_control File".

As audit trail files can become very large, it is often desirable to compress or otherwise archive trails once they have been closed by the audit daemon. The audit_warn script can be used to perform customized operations for a variety of audit-related events, including the clean termination of audit trails when they are rotated. For example, the following may be added to /etc/security/audit_warn to compress audit trails on close:

```
#
# Compress audit trail files on close.
#
if [ "$1" = closefile -]; then
        gzip -9 $2
fi
```

Other archiving activities might include copying trail files to a centralized server, deleting old trail files, or reducing the audit trail to remove unneeded records. This script will be run only when audit trail files are cleanly terminated, so will not be run on trails left unterminated following an improper shutdown.

Chapter 17. Storage

17.1. Synopsis

This chapter covers the use of disks and storage media in FreeBSD. This includes SCSI and IDE disks, CD and DVD media, memory-backed disks, and USB storage devices.

After reading this chapter, you will know:

- How to add additional hard disks to a FreeBSD system.

- How to grow the size of a disk's partition on FreeBSD.

- How to configure FreeBSD to use USB storage devices.

- How to use CD and DVD media on a FreeBSD system.

- How to use the backup programs available under FreeBSD.

- How to set up memory disks.

- What file system snapshots are and how to use them efficiently.

- How to use quotas to limit disk space usage.

- How to encrypt disks and swap to secure them against attackers.

- How to configure a highly available storage network.

Before reading this chapter, you should:

- Know how to configure and install a new FreeBSD kernel.

17.2. Adding Disks

Originally contributed by David O'Brien.

This section describes how to add a new SATA disk to a machine that currently only has a single drive. First, turn off the computer and install the drive in the computer following the instructions of the computer, controller, and drive manufacturers. Reboot the system and become `root`.

Inspect `/var/run/dmesg.boot` to ensure the new disk was found. In this example, the newly added SATA drive will appear as `ada1`.

For this example, a single large partition will be created on the new disk. The GPT partitioning scheme will be used in preference to the older and less versatile MBR scheme.

Note

If the disk to be added is not blank, old partition information can be removed with `gpart delete`. See gpart(8) for details.

The partition scheme is created, and then a single partition is added. To improve performance on newer disks with larger hardware block sizes, the partition is aligned to one megabyte boundaries:

```
# gpart create -s GPT ada1
```

```
# gpart add -t freebsd-ufs -a 1M ada1
```

Depending on use, several smaller partitions may be desired. See gpart(8) for options to create partitions smaller than a whole disk.

The disk partition information can be viewed with gpart show:

```
% gpart show ada1
=>          34   1465146988   ada1   GPT   (699G)
            34         2014          - free -   (1.0M)
          2048   1465143296      1   freebsd-ufs   (699G)
     1465145344         1678          - free -   (839K)
```

A file system is created in the new partition on the new disk:

```
# newfs -U /dev/ada1p1
```

An empty directory is created as a *mountpoint*, a location for mounting the new disk in the original disk's file system:

```
# mkdir /newdisk
```

Finally, an entry is added to /etc/fstab so the new disk will be mounted automatically at startup:

```
/dev/ada1p1 /newdisk ufs rw 2 2
```

The new disk can be mounted manually, without restarting the system:

```
# mount /newdisk
```

17.3. Resizing and Growing Disks

Originally contributed by Allan Jude.

A disk's capacity can increase without any changes to the data already present. This happens commonly with virtual machines, when the virtual disk turns out to be too small and is enlarged. Sometimes a disk image is written to a USB memory stick, but does not use the full capacity. Here we describe how to resize or *grow* disk contents to take advantage of increased capacity.

Determine the device name of the disk to be resized by inspecting /var/run/dmesg.boot . In this example, there is only one SATA disk in the system, so the drive will appear as ada0.

List the partitions on the disk to see the current configuration:

```
# gpart show ada0
=>       34   83886013   ada0   GPT   (48G) [CORRUPT]
         34        128      1   freebsd-boot   (64k)
        162   79691648      2   freebsd-ufs   (38G)
   79691810    4194236      3   freebsd-swap   (2G)
   83886046          1          - free -   (512B)
```

Note

If the disk was formatted with the GPT partitioning scheme, it may show as "corrupted" because the GPT backup partition table is no longer at the end of the drive. Fix the backup partition table with gpart:

```
# gpart recover ada0
ada0 recovered
```

Now the additional space on the disk is available for use by a new partition, or an existing partition can be expanded:

```
# gpart show ada0
=>        34  102399933  ada0  GPT  (48G)
          34        128     1  freebsd-boot  (64k)
         162   79691648     2  freebsd-ufs   (38G)
    79691810    4194236     3  freebsd-swap  (2G)
    83886046   18513921     -  free -  (8.8G)
```

Partitions can only be resized into contiguous free space. Here, the last partition on the disk is the swap partition, but the second partition is the one that needs to be resized. Swap partitions only contain temporary data, so it can safely be unmounted, deleted, and then recreated after resizing other partitions.

```
# swapoff  /dev/ada0p3
# gpart delete -i  3 ada0
ada0p3 deleted
# gpart show ada0
=>        34  102399933  ada0  GPT  (48G)
          34        128     1  freebsd-boot  (64k)
         162   79691648     2  freebsd-ufs   (38G)
    79691810   22708157     -  free -  (10G)
```

Warning

There is risk of data loss when modifying the partition table of a mounted file system. It is best to perform the following steps on an unmounted file system while running from a live CD-ROM or USB device. However, if absolutely necessary, a mounted file system can be resized after disabling GEOM safety features:

```
# sysctl kern.geom.debugflags=16
```

Resize the partition, leaving room to recreate a swap partition of the desired size. This only modifies the size of the partition. The file system in the partition will be expanded in a separate step.

```
# gpart resize -i  2 -a 4k -s 47G ada0
ada0p2 resized
# gpart show ada0
=>        34  102399933  ada0  GPT  (48G)
          34        128     1  freebsd-boot  (64k)
         162   98566144     2  freebsd-ufs   (47G)
    98566306    3833661     -  free -  (1.8G)
```

Recreate the swap partition:

```
# gpart add -t freebsd-swap -a 4k  ada0
ada0p3 added
# gpart show ada0
=>        34  102399933  ada0  GPT  (48G)
          34        128     1  freebsd-boot  (64k)
         162   98566144     2  freebsd-ufs   (47G)
    98566306    3833661     3  freebsd-swap  (1.8G)
# swapon  /dev/ada0p3
```

Grow the UFS file system to use the new capacity of the resized partition:

Note

Growing a live UFS file system is only possible in FreeBSD 10.0-RELEASE and later. For earlier versions, the file system must not be mounted.

```
# growfs /dev/ada0p2
Device is mounted read-write; resizing will result in temporary write suspension for /.
It's strongly recommended to make a backup before growing the file system.
OK to grow file system on /dev/ada0p2, mounted on /, from 38GB to 47GB? [Yes/No] Yes
super-block backups (for fsck -b #) at:
 80781312, 82063552, 83345792, 84628032, 85910272, 87192512, 88474752,
 89756992, 91039232, 92321472, 93603712, 94885952, 96168192, 97450432
```

Both the partition and the file system on it have now been resized to use the newly-available disk space.

17.4. USB Storage Devices

Contributed by Marc Fonvieille.

Many external storage solutions, such as hard drives, USB thumbdrives, and CD and DVD burners, use the Universal Serial Bus (USB). FreeBSD provides support for USB 1.x, 2.0, and 3.0 devices.

> Note
>
> USB 3.0 support is not compatible with some hardware, including Haswell (Lynx point) chipsets. If FreeBSD boots with a failed with error 19 message, disable xHCI/USB3 in the system BIOS.

Support for USB storage devices is built into the GENERIC kernel. For a custom kernel, be sure that the following lines are present in the kernel configuration file:

```
device scbus # SCSI bus (required for ATA/SCSI)
device da # Direct Access (disks)
device pass # Passthrough device (direct ATA/SCSI access)
device uhci # provides USB 1.x support
device ohci # provides USB 1.x support
device ehci # provides USB 2.0 support
device xhci # provides USB 3.0 support
device usb # USB Bus (required)
device umass # Disks/Mass storage - Requires scbus and da
device cd # needed for CD and DVD burners
```

FreeBSD uses the umass(4) driver which uses the SCSI subsystem to access USB storage devices. Since any USB device will be seen as a SCSI device by the system, if the USB device is a CD or DVD burner, do *not* include device atapicam in a custom kernel configuration file.

The rest of this section demonstrates how to verify that a USB storage device is recognized by FreeBSD and how to configure the device so that it can be used.

17.4.1. Device Configuration

To test the USB configuration, plug in the USB device. Use dmesg to confirm that the drive appears in the system message buffer. It should look something like this:

```
umass0: <STECH Simple Drive, class 0/0, rev 2.00/1.04, addr 3> on usbus0
umass0:  SCSI over Bulk-Only; quirks = 0x0100
umass0:4:0:-1: Attached to scbus4
da0 at umass-sim0 bus 0 scbus4 target 0 lun 0
da0: <STECH Simple Drive 1.04> Fixed Direct Access SCSI-4 device
da0: Serial Number WD-WXE508CAN263
da0: 40.000MB/s transfers
da0: 152627MB (312581808 512 byte sectors: 255H 63S/T 19457C)
```

```
da0: quirks=0x2<NO_6_BYTE>
```

The brand, device node (da0), speed, and size will differ according to the device.

Since the USB device is seen as a SCSI one, camcontrol can be used to list the USB storage devices attached to the system:

```
# camcontrol devlist
<STECH Simple Drive 1.04>          at scbus4 target 0 lun 0 (pass3,da0)
```

Alternately, usbconfig can be used to list the device. Refer to usbconfig(8) for more information about this command.

```
# usbconfig
ugen0.3: <Simple Drive STECH> at usbus0, cfg=0 md=HOST spd=HIGH (480Mbps) pwr=ON (2mA)
```

If the device has not been formatted, refer to Section 17.2, "Adding Disks" for instructions on how to format and create partitions on the USB drive. If the drive comes with a file system, it can be mounted by root using the instructions in Section 3.7, "Mounting and Unmounting File Systems".

Warning

Allowing untrusted users to mount arbitrary media, by enabling vfs.usermount as described below, should not be considered safe from a security point of view. Most file systems were not built to safeguard against malicious devices.

To make the device mountable as a normal user, one solution is to make all users of the device a member of the operator group using pw(8). Next, ensure that operator is able to read and write the device by adding these lines to /etc/devfs.rules:

```
[localrules=5]
add path 'da*' mode 0660 group operator
```

Note

If internal SCSI disks are also installed in the system, change the second line as follows:

```
add path 'da[3-9]*' mode 0660 group operator
```

This will exclude the first three SCSI disks (da0 to da2)from belonging to the operator group. Replace 3 with the number of internal SCSI disks. Refer to devfs.rules(5) for more information about this file.

Next, enable the ruleset in /etc/rc.conf :

```
devfs_system_ruleset="localrules"
```

Then, instruct the system to allow regular users to mount file systems by adding the following line to /etc/sysctl.conf :

```
vfs.usermount=1
```

Since this only takes effect after the next reboot, use sysctl to set this variable now:

```
# sysctl vfs.usermount=1
vfs.usermount: 0 -> 1
```

The final step is to create a directory where the file system is to be mounted. This directory needs to be owned by the user that is to mount the file system. One way to do that is for root to create a subdirectory owned by that user as /mnt/*username*. In the following example, replace *username* with the login name of the user and *usergroup* with the user's primary group:

```
# mkdir /mnt/username
# chown username:usergroup /mnt/username
```

Suppose a USB thumbdrive is plugged in, and a device /dev/da0s1 appears. If the device is formatted with a FAT file system, the user can mount it using:

```
% mount -t msdosfs -o -m=644,-M=755 /dev/da0s1 /mnt/username
```

Before the device can be unplugged, it *must* be unmounted first:

```
% umount /mnt/username
```

After device removal, the system message buffer will show messages similar to the following:

```
umass0: at uhub3, port 2, addr 3 (disconnected)
da0 at umass-sim0 bus 0 scbus4 target 0 lun 0
da0: <STECH Simple Drive 1.04> s/n WD-WXE508CAN263          detached
(da0:umass-sim0:0:0:0): Periph destroyed
```

17.4.2. Automounting Removable Media

> Note
>
> autofs(5) supports automatic mounting of removable media starting with FreeBSD 10.2-RE-LEASE.

USB devices can be automatically mounted by uncommenting this line in /etc/auto_master:

```
/media  -media  -nosuid
```

Then add these lines to /etc/devd.conf:

```
notify 100 {
 match "system" "GEOM";
 match "subsystem" "DEV";
 action "/usr/sbin/automount -c";
};
```

Reload the configuration if autofs(5) and devd(8) are already running:

```
# service automount reload
# service devd restart
```

autofs(5) can be set to start at boot by adding this line to /etc/rc.conf:

```
autofs_enable="YES"
```

autofs(5) requires devd(8) to be enabled, as it is by default.

Start the services immediately with:

```
# service automount start
# service automountd start
# service autounmountd start
# service devd start
```

Each file system that can be automatically mounted appears as a directory in /media/. The directory is named after the file system label. If the label is missing, the directory is named after the device node.

The file system is transparently mounted on the first access, and unmounted after a period of inactivity. Auto-mounted drives can also be unmounted manually:

```
# automount -fu
```

This mechanism is typically used for memory cards and USB memory sticks. It can be used with any block device, including optical drives or iSCSI LUNs.

17.4.3. USB Mass Storage Target

> **Note**
>
> The cfumass(4) driver is a USB device mode driver first available in FreeBSD 12.0.

When running on USB OTG-compliant hardware like that built into many embedded boards, the FreeBSD USB stack can run in *device mode*. Device mode makes it possible for the computer to present itself as different kinds of USB device classes, including serial ports, network adapters, and mass storage. A USB host like a laptop or desktop computer is able to access them just like physical USB devices.

The usb_template(4) kernel module allows the USB stack to switch between host-side and device-side automatically, depending on what is connected to the USB port. Connecting a USB device like a memory stick to the USB OTG port causes FreeBSD to switch to host mode. Connecting a USB host like a computer causes FreeBSD to switch to device mode.

What FreeBSD presents to the USB host depends on the hw.usb.template sysctl. See usb_template(4) for the list of available values. Note that for the host to notice the configuration change, it must be either physically disconnected and reconnected, or forced to rescan the USB bus in a system-specific way. When FreeBSD is running on the host, usbconfig(8) reset can be used. This also must be done after loading usb_template.ko if the USB host was already connected to the USB OTG socket.

The hw.usb.template sysctl is set to 0 by default, making FreeBSD work as a USB Mass Storage target. Both usb_template(4) and cfumass(4) kernel modules must be loaded. cfumass(4) interfaces to the CTL subsystem, the same one that is used for iSCSI or Fibre Channel targets. On the host side, USB Mass Storage initiators can only access a single LUN, LUN 0.

USB Mass Storage does not require the ctld(8) daemon to be running, although it can be used if desired. This is different from iSCSI. Thus, there are two ways to configure the target: ctladm(8), or ctld(8). Both require the cfumass.ko kernel module to be loaded. The module can be loaded manually:

```
# kldload cfumass
```

If cfumass.ko has not been built into the kernel, /boot/loader.conf can be set to load the module at boot:

```
cfumass_load="YES"
```

A LUN can be created without the ctld(8) daemon:

```
# ctladm create -b block -o file=/data/target0
```

This presents the contents of the image file /data/target0 as a LUN to the USB host. The file must exist before executing the command. To configure the LUN at system startup, add the command to /etc/rc.local.

ctld(8) can also be used to manage LUNs. Create /etc/ctl.conf, add a line to /etc/rc.conf to make sure ctld(8) is automatically started at boot, and then start the daemon.

This is an example of a simple `/etc/ctl.conf` configuration file. Refer to ctl.conf(5) for a more complete description of the options.

```
target naa.50015178f369f092 {
 lun 0 {
  path /data/target0
  size 4G
 }
}
```

The example creates a single target with a single LUN. The `naa.50015178f369f092` is a device identifier composed of 32 random hexadecimal digits. The `path` line defines the full path to a file or zvol backing the LUN. That file must exist before starting ctld(8). The second line is optional and specifies the size of the LUN.

To make sure the ctld(8) daemon is started at boot, add this line to `/etc/rc.conf`:

```
ctld_enable="YES"
```

To start ctld(8) now, run this command:

```
# service ctld start
```

As the ctld(8) daemon is started, it reads `/etc/ctl.conf`. If this file is edited after the daemon starts, reload the changes so they take effect immediately:

```
# service ctld reload
```

17.5. Creating and Using CD Media

Contributed by Mike Meyer.

Compact Disc (CD) media provide a number of features that differentiate them from conventional disks. They are designed so that they can be read continuously without delays to move the head between tracks. While CD media do have tracks, these refer to a section of data to be read continuously, and not a physical property of the disk. The ISO 9660 file system was designed to deal with these differences.

The FreeBSD Ports Collection provides several utilities for burning and duplicating audio and data CDs. This chapter demonstrates the use of several command line utilities. For CD burning software with a graphical utility, consider installing the sysutils/xcdroast or sysutils/k3b packages or ports.

17.5.1. Supported Devices

Contributed by Marc Fonvieille.

The GENERIC kernel provides support for SCSI, USB, and ATAPI CD readers and burners. If a custom kernel is used, the options that need to be present in the kernel configuration file vary by the type of device.

For a SCSI burner, make sure these options are present:

```
device scbus # SCSI bus (required for ATA/SCSI)
device da # Direct Access (disks)
device pass # Passthrough device (direct ATA/SCSI access)
device cd # needed for CD and DVD burners
```

For a USB burner, make sure these options are present:

```
device scbus # SCSI bus (required for ATA/SCSI)
device da # Direct Access (disks)
device pass # Passthrough device (direct ATA/SCSI access)
device cd # needed for CD and DVD burners
device uhci # provides USB 1.x support
```

```
device ohci # provides USB 1.x support
device ehci # provides USB 2.0 support
device xhci # provides USB 3.0 support
device usb # USB Bus (required)
device umass # Disks/Mass storage - Requires scbus and da
```

For an ATAPI burner, make sure these options are present:

```
device ata # Legacy ATA/SATA controllers
device scbus # SCSI bus (required for ATA/SCSI)
device pass # Passthrough device (direct ATA/SCSI access)
device cd # needed for CD and DVD burners
```

Note

On FreeBSD versions prior to 10.x, this line is also needed in the kernel configuration file if the burner is an ATAPI device:

```
device atapicam
```

Alternately, this driver can be loaded at boot time by adding the following line to /boot/loader.conf :

```
atapicam_load="YES"
```

This will require a reboot of the system as this driver can only be loaded at boot time.

To verify that FreeBSD recognizes the device, run dmesg and look for an entry for the device. On systems prior to 10.x, the device name in the first line of the output will be acd0 instead of cd0.

```
% dmesg | grep cd
cd0 at ahcich1 bus 0 scbus1 target 0 lun 0
cd0: <HL-DT-ST DVDRAM GU70N LT20> Removable CD-ROM SCSI-0 device
cd0: Serial Number M30D3S34152
cd0: 150.000MB/s transfers (SATA 1.x, UDMA6, ATAPI 12bytes, PIO 8192bytes)
cd0: Attempt to query device size failed: NOT READY, Medium not present - tray closed
```

17.5.2. Burning a CD

In FreeBSD, cdrecord can be used to burn CDs. This command is installed with the sysutils/cdrtools package or port.

While cdrecord has many options, basic usage is simple. Specify the name of the ISO file to burn and, if the system has multiple burner devices, specify the name of the device to use:

```
# cdrecord dev=device imagefile.iso
```

To determine the device name of the burner, use -scanbus which might produce results like this:

```
# cdrecord -scanbus
ProDVD-ProBD-Clone 3.00 (amd64-unknown-freebsd10.0) Copyright (C) 1995-2010 Jörg ↵
Schilling
Using libscg version 'schily-0.9'
scsibus0:
        0,0,0     0) 'SEAGATE ' 'ST39236LW       ' '0004' Disk
        0,1,0     1) 'SEAGATE ' 'ST39173W        ' '5958' Disk
        0,2,0     2) *
        0,3,0     3) 'iomega  ' 'jaz 1GB         ' 'J.86' Removable Disk
        0,4,0     4) 'NEC     ' 'CD-ROM DRIVE:466' '1.26' Removable CD-ROM
        0,5,0     5) *
        0,6,0     6) *
```

```
        0,7,0      7) *
scsibus1:
        1,0,0    100) *
        1,1,0    101) *
        1,2,0    102) *
        1,3,0    103) *
        1,4,0    104) *
        1,5,0    105) 'YAMAHA   ' 'CRW4260          ' '1.0q' Removable CD-ROM
        1,6,0    106) 'ARTEC    ' 'AM12S            ' '1.06' Scanner
        1,7,0    107) *
```

Locate the entry for the CD burner and use the three numbers separated by commas as the value for dev. In this case, the Yamaha burner device is 1,5,0, so the appropriate input to specify that device is dev=1,5,0. Refer to the manual page for cdrecord for other ways to specify this value and for information on writing audio tracks and controlling the write speed.

Alternately, run the following command to get the device address of the burner:

```
# camcontrol devlist
<MATSHITA CDRW/DVD UJDA740 1.00>   at scbus1 target 0 lun 0 (cd0,pass0)
```

Use the numeric values for scbus, target, and lun. For this example, 1,0,0 is the device name to use.

17.5.3. Writing Data to an ISO File System

In order to produce a data CD, the data files that are going to make up the tracks on the CD must be prepared before they can be burned to the CD. In FreeBSD, sysutils/cdrtools installs mkisofs, which can be used to produce an ISO 9660 file system that is an image of a directory tree within a UNIX® file system. The simplest usage is to specify the name of the ISO file to create and the path to the files to place into the ISO 9660 file system:

```
# mkisofs -o imagefile.iso /path/to/tree
```

This command maps the file names in the specified path to names that fit the limitations of the standard ISO 9660 file system, and will exclude files that do not meet the standard for ISO file systems.

A number of options are available to overcome the restrictions imposed by the standard. In particular, -R enables the Rock Ridge extensions common to UNIX® systems and -J enables Joliet extensions used by Microsoft® systems.

For CDs that are going to be used only on FreeBSD systems, -U can be used to disable all filename restrictions. When used with -R, it produces a file system image that is identical to the specified FreeBSD tree, even if it violates the ISO 9660 standard.

The last option of general use is -b. This is used to specify the location of a boot image for use in producing an "El Torito" bootable CD. This option takes an argument which is the path to a boot image from the top of the tree being written to the CD. By default, mkisofs creates an ISO image in "floppy disk emulation" mode, and thus expects the boot image to be exactly 1200, 1440 or 2880 KB in size. Some boot loaders, like the one used by the FreeBSD distribution media, do not use emulation mode. In this case, -no-emul-boot should be used. So, if /tmp/myboot holds a bootable FreeBSD system with the boot image in /tmp/myboot/boot/cdboot, this command would produce /tmp/bootable.iso:

```
# mkisofs -R -no-emul-boot -b boot/cdboot -o /tmp/bootable.iso /tmp/myboot
```

The resulting ISO image can be mounted as a memory disk with:

```
# mdconfig -a -t vnode -f /tmp/bootable.iso -u 0
# mount -t cd9660 /dev/md0 /mnt
```

One can then verify that /mnt and /tmp/myboot are identical.

There are many other options available for mkisofs to fine-tune its behavior. Refer to mkisofs(8) for details.

Note

It is possible to copy a data CD to an image file that is functionally equivalent to the image file created with mkisofs. To do so, use dd with the device name as the input file and the name of the ISO to create as the output file:

```
# dd if=/dev/ cd0 of=file.iso bs=2048
```

The resulting image file can be burned to CD as described in Section 17.5.2, "Burning a CD".

17.5.4. Using Data CDs

Once an ISO has been burned to a CD, it can be mounted by specifying the file system type, the name of the device containing the CD, and an existing mount point:

```
# mount -t cd9660 /dev/cd0 /mnt
```

Since mount assumes that a file system is of type ufs, a Incorrect super block error will occur if -t cd9660 is not included when mounting a data CD.

While any data CD can be mounted this way, disks with certain ISO 9660 extensions might behave oddly. For example, Joliet disks store all filenames in two-byte Unicode characters. If some non-English characters show up as question marks, specify the local charset with -C. For more information, refer to mount_cd9660(8).

Note

In order to do this character conversion with the help of -C, the kernel requires the cd9660_iconv.ko module to be loaded. This can be done either by adding this line to loader.conf :

```
cd9660_iconv_load="YES"
```

and then rebooting the machine, or by directly loading the module with kldload.

Occasionally, Device not configured will be displayed when trying to mount a data CD. This usually means that the CD drive has not detected a disk in the tray, or that the drive is not visible on the bus. It can take a couple of seconds for a CD drive to detect media, so be patient.

Sometimes, a SCSI CD drive may be missed because it did not have enough time to answer the bus reset. To resolve this, a custom kernel can be created which increases the default SCSI delay. Add the following option to the custom kernel configuration file and rebuild the kernel using the instructions in Section 8.5, "Building and Installing a Custom Kernel":

```
options SCSI_DELAY=15000
```

This tells the SCSI bus to pause 15 seconds during boot, to give the CD drive every possible chance to answer the bus reset.

Note

It is possible to burn a file directly to CD, without creating an ISO 9660 file system. This is known as burning a raw data CD and some people do this for backup purposes.

This type of disk can not be mounted as a normal data CD. In order to retrieve the data burned to such a CD, the data must be read from the raw device node. For example, this command will extract a compressed tar file located on the second CD device into the current working directory:

```
# tar xzvf /dev/ cd1
```

In order to mount a data CD, the data must be written using mkisofs.

17.5.5. Duplicating Audio CDs

To duplicate an audio CD, extract the audio data from the CD to a series of files, then write these files to a blank CD.

Procedure 17.1, "Duplicating an Audio CD" describes how to duplicate and burn an audio CD. If the FreeBSD version is less than 10.0 and the device is ATAPI, the atapicam module must be first loaded using the instructions in Section 17.5.1, "Supported Devices".

Procedure 17.1. Duplicating an Audio CD

1. The sysutils/cdrtools package or port installs cdda2wav. This command can be used to extract all of the audio tracks, with each track written to a separate WAV file in the current working directory:

```
% cdda2wav -vall -B -Owav
```

A device name does not need to be specified if there is only one CD device on the system. Refer to the cdda2wav manual page for instructions on how to specify a device and to learn more about the other options available for this command.

2. Use cdrecord to write the .wav files:

```
% cdrecord -v dev= 2,0 -dao -useinfo *.wav
```

Make sure that 2,0 is set appropriately, as described in Section 17.5.2, "Burning a CD".

17.6. Creating and Using DVD Media

Contributed by Marc Fonvieille.
With inputs from Andy Polyakov.

Compared to the CD, the DVD is the next generation of optical media storage technology. The DVD can hold more data than any CD and is the standard for video publishing.

Five physical recordable formats can be defined for a recordable DVD:

- DVD-R: This was the first DVD recordable format available. The DVD-R standard is defined by the DVD Forum. This format is write once.

- DVD-RW: This is the rewritable version of the DVD-R standard. A DVD-RW can be rewritten about 1000 times.

- DVD-RAM: This is a rewritable format which can be seen as a removable hard drive. However, this media is not compatible with most DVD-ROM drives and DVD-Video players as only a few DVD writers support the DVD-RAM format. Refer to Section 17.6.8, "Using a DVD-RAM" for more information on DVD-RAM use.

- DVD+RW: This is a rewritable format defined by the DVD+RW Alliance. A DVD+RW can be rewritten about 1000 times.

- DVD+R: This format is the write once variation of the DVD+RW format.

A single layer recordable DVD can hold up to 4,700,000,000 bytes which is actually 4.38 GB or 4485 MB as 1 kilobyte is 1024 bytes.

Note

A distinction must be made between the physical media and the application. For example, a DVD-Video is a specific file layout that can be written on any recordable DVD physical media such as DVD-R, DVD+R, or DVD-RW. Before choosing the type of media, ensure that both the burner and the DVD-Video player are compatible with the media under consideration.

17.6.1. Configuration

To perform DVD recording, use growisofs(1). This command is part of the sysutils/dvd+rw-tools utilities which support all DVD media types.

These tools use the SCSI subsystem to access the devices, therefore ATAPI/CAM support must be loaded or statically compiled into the kernel. This support is not needed if the burner uses the USB interface. Refer to Section 17.4, "USB Storage Devices" for more details on USB device configuration.

DMA access must also be enabled for ATAPI devices, by adding the following line to /boot/loader.conf :

```
hw.ata.atapi_dma="1"
```

Before attempting to use dvd+rw-tools, consult the Hardware Compatibility Notes.

Note

For a graphical user interface, consider using sysutils/k3b which provides a user friendly interface to growisofs(1) and many other burning tools.

17.6.2. Burning Data DVDs

Since growisofs(1) is a front-end to mkisofs, it will invoke mkisofs(8) to create the file system layout and perform the write on the DVD. This means that an image of the data does not need to be created before the burning process.

To burn to a DVD+R or a DVD-R the data in /path/to/data , use the following command:

```
# growisofs -dvd-compat -Z /dev/cd0 -J -R /path/to/data
```

In this example, -J -R is passed to mkisofs(8) to create an ISO 9660 file system with Joliet and Rock Ridge extensions. Refer to mkisofs(8) for more details.

For the initial session recording, -Z is used for both single and multiple sessions. Replace /dev/cd0 , with the name of the DVD device. Using -dvd-compat indicates that the disk will be closed and that the recording will be unappendable. This should also provide better media compatibility with DVD-ROM drives.

To burn a pre-mastered image, such as *imagefile.iso*, use:

```
# growisofs -dvd-compat -Z /dev/cd0 =imagefile.iso
```

The write speed should be detected and automatically set according to the media and the drive being used. To force the write speed, use -speed= . Refer to growisofs(1) for example usage.

Note

In order to support working files larger than 4.38GB, an UDF/ISO-9660 hybrid file system must be created by passing -udf -iso-level 3 to mkisofs(8) and all related programs, such as growisofs(1). This is required only when creating an ISO image file or when writing files directly to a disk. Since a disk created this way must be mounted as an UDF file system with mount_udf(8), it will be usable only on an UDF aware operating system. Otherwise it will look as if it contains corrupted files.

To create this type of ISO file:

```
% mkisofs -R -J -udf -iso-level 3 -o  imagefile.iso  /path/to/data
```

To burn files directly to a disk:

```
# growisofs -dvd-compat -udf -iso-level 3 -Z   /dev/cd0  -J -R /path/to/data
```

When an ISO image already contains large files, no additional options are required for growisofs(1) to burn that image on a disk.

Be sure to use an up-to-date version of sysutils/cdrtools, which contains mkisofs(8), as an older version may not contain large files support. If the latest version does not work, install sysutils/cdrtools-devel and read its mkisofs(8).

17.6.3. Burning a DVD-Video

A DVD-Video is a specific file layout based on the ISO 9660 and micro-UDF (M-UDF) specifications. Since DVD-Video presents a specific data structure hierarchy, a particular program such as multimedia/dvdauthor is needed to author the DVD.

If an image of the DVD-Video file system already exists, it can be burned in the same way as any other image. If dvdauthor was used to make the DVD and the result is in /path/to/video , the following command should be used to burn the DVD-Video:

```
# growisofs -Z /dev/cd0 -dvd-video /path/to/video
```

-dvd-video is passed to mkisofs(8) to instruct it to create a DVD-Video file system layout. This option implies the -dvd-compat growisofs(1) option.

17.6.4. Using a DVD+RW

Unlike CD-RW, a virgin DVD+RW needs to be formatted before first use. It is *recommended* to let growisofs(1) take care of this automatically whenever appropriate. However, it is possible to use dvd+rw-format to format the DVD +RW:

```
# dvd+rw-format /dev/cd0
```

Only perform this operation once and keep in mind that only virgin DVD+RW medias need to be formatted. Once formatted, the DVD+RW can be burned as usual.

To burn a totally new file system and not just append some data onto a DVD+RW, the media does not need to be blanked first. Instead, write over the previous recording like this:

```
# growisofs -Z /dev/cd0 -J -R /path/to/newdata
```

The DVD+RW format supports appending data to a previous recording. This operation consists of merging a new session to the existing one as it is not considered to be multi-session writing. growisofs(1) will *grow* the ISO 9660 file system present on the media.

For example, to append data to a DVD+RW, use the following:

```
# growisofs -M /dev/cd0 -J -R /path/to/nextdata
```

The same mkisofs(8) options used to burn the initial session should be used during next writes.

Note

Use -dvd-compat for better media compatibility with DVD-ROM drives. When using DVD +RW, this option will not prevent the addition of data.

To blank the media, use:

```
# growisofs -Z /dev/cd0 =/dev/zero
```

17.6.5. Using a DVD-RW

A DVD-RW accepts two disc formats: incremental sequential and restricted overwrite. By default, DVD-RW discs are in sequential format.

A virgin DVD-RW can be directly written without being formatted. However, a non-virgin DVD-RW in sequential format needs to be blanked before writing a new initial session.

To blank a DVD-RW in sequential mode:

```
# dvd+rw-format -blank=full /dev/cd0
```

Note

A full blanking using -blank=full will take about one hour on a 1x media. A fast blanking can be performed using -blank, if the DVD-RW will be recorded in Disk-At-Once (DAO) mode. To burn the DVD-RW in DAO mode, use the command:

```
# growisofs -use-the-force-luke=dao -Z /dev/cd0 =imagefile.iso
```

Since growisofs(1) automatically attempts to detect fast blanked media and engage DAO write, -use-the-force-luke=dao should not be required.

One should instead use restricted overwrite mode with any DVD-RW as this format is more flexible than the default of incremental sequential.

To write data on a sequential DVD-RW, use the same instructions as for the other DVD formats:

```
# growisofs -Z /dev/cd0 -J -R /path/to/data
```

To append some data to a previous recording, use -M with growisofs(1). However, if data is appended on a DVD-RW in incremental sequential mode, a new session will be created on the disc and the result will be a multi-session disc.

A DVD-RW in restricted overwrite format does not need to be blanked before a new initial session. Instead, over-write the disc with -Z. It is also possible to grow an existing ISO 9660 file system written on the disc with -M. The result will be a one-session DVD.

To put a DVD-RW in restricted overwrite format, the following command must be used:

```
# dvd+rw-format  /dev/cd0
```

To change back to sequential format, use:

```
# dvd+rw-format -blank=full  /dev/cd0
```

17.6.6. Multi-Session

Few DVD-ROM drives support multi-session DVDs and most of the time only read the first session. DVD+R, DVD-R and DVD-RW in sequential format can accept multiple sessions. The notion of multiple sessions does not exist for the DVD+RW and the DVD-RW restricted overwrite formats.

Using the following command after an initial non-closed session on a DVD+R, DVD-R, or DVD-RW in sequential format, will add a new session to the disc:

```
# growisofs -M  /dev/cd0  -J -R /path/to/nextdata
```

Using this command with a DVD+RW or a DVD-RW in restricted overwrite mode will append data while merging the new session to the existing one. The result will be a single-session disc. Use this method to add data after an initial write on these types of media.

> ### Note
>
> Since some space on the media is used between each session to mark the end and start of sessions, one should add sessions with a large amount of data to optimize media space. The number of sessions is limited to 154 for a DVD+R, about 2000 for a DVD-R, and 127 for a DVD +R Double Layer.

17.6.7. For More Information

To obtain more information about a DVD, use dvd+rw-mediainfo /dev/cd0 while the disc in the specified drive.

More information about dvd+rw-tools can be found in growisofs(1), on the dvd+rw-tools web site, and in the cdwrite mailing list archives.

> ### Note
>
> When creating a problem report related to the use of dvd+rw-tools, always include the output of dvd+rw-mediainfo .

17.6.8. Using a DVD-RAM

DVD-RAM writers can use either a SCSI or ATAPI interface. For ATAPI devices, DMA access has to be enabled by adding the following line to /boot/loader.conf :

```
hw.ata.atapi_dma="1"
```

A DVD-RAM can be seen as a removable hard drive. Like any other hard drive, the DVD-RAM must be formatted before it can be used. In this example, the whole disk space will be formatted with a standard UFS2 file system:

```
# dd if=/dev/zero of= /dev/acd0  bs=2k count=1
# bsdlabel -Bw  acd0
```

```
# newfs /dev/acd0
```

The DVD device, acd0, must be changed according to the configuration.

Once the DVD-RAM has been formatted, it can be mounted as a normal hard drive:

```
# mount /dev/acd0 /mnt
```

Once mounted, the DVD-RAM will be both readable and writeable.

17.7. Creating and Using Floppy Disks

This section explains how to format a 3.5 inch floppy disk in FreeBSD.

Procedure 17.2. Steps to Format a Floppy

A floppy disk needs to be low-level formatted before it can be used. This is usually done by the vendor, but formatting is a good way to check media integrity. To low-level format the floppy disk on FreeBSD, use fdformat(1). When using this utility, make note of any error messages, as these can help determine if the disk is good or bad.

1. To format the floppy, insert a new 3.5 inch floppy disk into the first floppy drive and issue:

    ```
    # /usr/sbin/fdformat -f 1440 /dev/fd0
    ```

2. After low-level formatting the disk, create a disk label as it is needed by the system to determine the size of the disk and its geometry. The supported geometry values are listed in /etc/disktab.

    To write the disk label, use bsdlabel(8):

    ```
    # /sbin/bsdlabel -B -w /dev/fd0 fd1440
    ```

3. The floppy is now ready to be high-level formatted with a file system. The floppy's file system can be either UFS or FAT, where FAT is generally a better choice for floppies.

    To format the floppy with FAT, issue:

    ```
    # /sbin/newfs_msdos /dev/fd0
    ```

The disk is now ready for use. To use the floppy, mount it with mount_msdosfs(8). One can also install and use emulators/mtools from the Ports Collection.

17.8. Backup Basics

Implementing a backup plan is essential in order to have the ability to recover from disk failure, accidental file deletion, random file corruption, or complete machine destruction, including destruction of on-site backups.

The backup type and schedule will vary, depending upon the importance of the data, the granularity needed for file restores, and the amount of acceptable downtime. Some possible backup techniques include:

• Archives of the whole system, backed up onto permanent, off-site media. This provides protection against all of the problems listed above, but is slow and inconvenient to restore from, especially for non-privileged users.

• File system snapshots, which are useful for restoring deleted files or previous versions of files.

• Copies of whole file systems or disks which are synchronized with another system on the network using a scheduled net/rsync.

• Hardware or software RAID, which minimizes or avoids downtime when a disk fails.

Typically, a mix of backup techniques is used. For example, one could create a schedule to automate a weekly, full system backup that is stored off-site and to supplement this backup with hourly ZFS snapshots. In addition, one could make a manual backup of individual directories or files before making file edits or deletions.

This section describes some of the utilities which can be used to create and manage backups on a FreeBSD system.

17.8.1. File System Backups

The traditional UNIX® programs for backing up a file system are dump(8), which creates the backup, and restore(8), which restores the backup. These utilities work at the disk block level, below the abstractions of the files, links, and directories that are created by file systems. Unlike other backup software, dump backs up an entire file system and is unable to backup only part of a file system or a directory tree that spans multiple file systems. Instead of writing files and directories, dump writes the raw data blocks that comprise files and directories.

> ### Note
>
> If dump is used on the root directory, it will not back up /home, /usr or many other directories since these are typically mount points for other file systems or symbolic links into those file systems.

When used to restore data, restore stores temporary files in /tmp/ by default. When using a recovery disk with a small /tmp, set TMPDIR to a directory with more free space in order for the restore to succeed.

When using dump, be aware that some quirks remain from its early days in Version 6 of AT&T UNIX®,circa 1975. The default parameters assume a backup to a 9-track tape, rather than to another type of media or to the high-density tapes available today. These defaults must be overridden on the command line.

It is possible to backup a file system across the network to a another system or to a tape drive attached to another computer. While the rdump(8) and rrestore(8) utilities can be used for this purpose, they are not considered to be secure.

Instead, one can use dump and restore in a more secure fashion over an SSH connection. This example creates a full, compressed backup of /usr and sends the backup file to the specified host over a SSH connection.

Example 17.1. Using dump over ssh

```
# /sbin/dump -0uan -f - /usr | gzip -2 | ssh -c blowfish \
        targetuser@targetmachine.example.com dd of=/mybigfiles/dump-usr-l0.gz
```

This example sets RSH in order to write the backup to a tape drive on a remote system over a SSH connection:

Example 17.2. Using dump over ssh with RSH Set

```
# env RSH=/usr/bin/ssh /sbin/dump -0uan -f targetuser@targetmachine.example.com:/
dev/sa0 /usr
```

17.8.2. Directory Backups

Several built-in utilities are available for backing up and restoring specified files and directories as needed.

A good choice for making a backup of all of the files in a directory is tar(1). This utility dates back to Version 6 of AT&T UNIX® and by default assumes a recursive backup to a local tape device. Switches can be used to instead specify the name of a backup file.

This example creates a compressed backup of the current directory and saves it to /tmp/mybackup.tgz. When creating a backup file, make sure that the backup is not saved to the same directory that is being backed up.

Example 17.3. Backing Up the Current Directory with tar

```
# tar czvf /tmp/mybackup.tgz  .
```

To restore the entire backup, cd into the directory to restore into and specify the name of the backup. Note that this will overwrite any newer versions of files in the restore directory. When in doubt, restore to a temporary directory or specify the name of the file within the backup to restore.

Example 17.4. Restoring Up the Current Directory with tar

```
# tar xzvf /tmp/mybackup.tgz
```

There are dozens of available switches which are described in tar(1). This utility also supports the use of exclude patterns to specify which files should not be included when backing up the specified directory or restoring files from a backup.

To create a backup using a specified list of files and directories, cpio(1) is a good choice. Unlike tar, cpio does not know how to walk the directory tree and it must be provided the list of files to backup.

For example, a list of files can be created using ls or find. This example creates a recursive listing of the current directory which is then piped to cpio in order to create an output backup file named /tmp/mybackup.cpio.

Example 17.5. Using ls and cpio to Make a Recursive Backup of the Current Directory

```
# ls -R | cpio -ovF /tmp/mybackup.cpio
```

A backup utility which tries to bridge the features provided by tar and cpio is pax(1). Over the years, the various versions of tar and cpio became slightly incompatible. POSIX® created pax which attempts to read and write many of the various cpio and tar formats, plus new formats of its own.

The pax equivalent to the previous examples would be:

Example 17.6. Backing Up the Current Directory with pax

```
# pax -wf /tmp/mybackup.pax  .
```

17.8.3. Using Data Tapes for Backups

While tape technology has continued to evolve, modern backup systems tend to combine off-site backups with local removable media. FreeBSD supports any tape drive that uses SCSI, such as LTO or DAT. There is limited support for SATA and USB tape drives.

For SCSI tape devices, FreeBSD uses the sa(4) driver and the /dev/sa0 , /dev/nsa0 , and /dev/esa0 devices. The physical device name is /dev/sa0 . When /dev/nsa0 is used, the backup application will not rewind the tape after writing a file, which allows writing more than one file to a tape. Using /dev/esa0 ejects the tape after the device is closed.

In FreeBSD, mt is used to control operations of the tape drive, such as seeking through files on a tape or writing tape control marks to the tape. For example, the first three files on a tape can be preserved by skipping past them before writing a new file:

```
# mt -f /dev/nsa0 fsf 3
```

This utility supports many operations. Refer to mt(1) for details.

To write a single file to tape using tar, specify the name of the tape device and the file to backup:

```
# tar cvf /dev/sa0  file
```

To recover files from a tar archive on tape into the current directory:

```
# tar xvf /dev/sa0
```

To backup a UFS file system, use dump. This examples backs up /usr without rewinding the tape when finished:

```
# dump -0aL -b64 -f /dev/nsa0 /usr
```

To interactively restore files from a dump file on tape into the current directory:

```
# restore -i -f /dev/nsa0
```

17.8.4. Third-Party Backup Utilities

The FreeBSD Ports Collection provides many third-party utilities which can be used to schedule the creation of backups, simplify tape backup, and make backups easier and more convenient. Many of these applications are client/server based and can be used to automate the backups of a single system or all of the computers in a network.

Popular utilities include Amanda, Bacula, rsync, and duplicity.

17.8.5. Emergency Recovery

In addition to regular backups, it is recommended to perform the following steps as part of an emergency preparedness plan.

Create a print copy of the output of the following commands:

- gpart show

- more /etc/fstab

- dmesg

Store this printout and a copy of the installation media in a secure location. Should an emergency restore be needed, boot into the installation media and select Live CD to access a rescue shell. This rescue mode can be used to view the current state of the system, and if needed, to reformat disks and restore data from backups.

Note

The installation media for FreeBSD/i386 10.4-RELEASE does not include a rescue shell. For this version, instead download and burn a Livefs CD image from `ftp://ftp.FreeBSD.org/pub/FreeBSD/releases/i386/ISO-IMAGES/10.4/` `FreeBSD-10.4-RELEASE-i386-livefs.iso` .

Next, test the rescue shell and the backups. Make notes of the procedure. Store these notes with the media, the printouts, and the backups. These notes may prevent the inadvertent destruction of the backups while under the stress of performing an emergency recovery.

For an added measure of security, store the latest backup at a remote location which is physically separated from the computers and disk drives by a significant distance.

17.9. Memory Disks

Reorganized and enhanced by Marc Fonvieille.

In addition to physical disks, FreeBSD also supports the creation and use of memory disks. One possible use for a memory disk is to access the contents of an ISO file system without the overhead of first burning it to a CD or DVD, then mounting the CD/DVD media.

In FreeBSD, the md(4) driver is used to provide support for memory disks. The GENERIC kernel includes this driver. When using a custom kernel configuration file, ensure it includes this line:

```
device md
```

17.9.1. Attaching and Detaching Existing Images

To mount an existing file system image, use mdconfig to specify the name of the ISO file and a free unit number. Then, refer to that unit number to mount it on an existing mount point. Once mounted, the files in the ISO will appear in the mount point. This example attaches *diskimage.iso* to the memory device /dev/md0 then mounts that memory device on /mnt:

```
# mdconfig -f diskimage.iso -u 0
# mount /dev/md 0 /mnt
```

If a unit number is not specified with -u, mdconfig will automatically allocate an unused memory device and output the name of the allocated unit, such as md4. Refer to mdconfig(8) for more details about this command and its options.

When a memory disk is no longer in use, its resources should be released back to the system. First, unmount the file system, then use mdconfig to detach the disk from the system and release its resources. To continue this example:

```
# umount /mnt
# mdconfig -d -u 0
```

To determine if any memory disks are still attached to the system, type mdconfig -l.

17.9.2. Creating a File- or Memory-Backed Memory Disk

FreeBSD also supports memory disks where the storage to use is allocated from either a hard disk or an area of memory. The first method is commonly referred to as a file-backed file system and the second method as a memory-backed file system. Both types can be created using mdconfig.

To create a new memory-backed file system, specify a type of swap and the size of the memory disk to create. Then, format the memory disk with a file system and mount as usual. This example creates a 5M memory disk on unit 1. That memory disk is then formatted with the UFS file system before it is mounted:

```
# mdconfig -a -t swap -s 5m -u 1
# newfs -U md1
/dev/md1: 5.0MB (10240 sectors) block size 16384, fragment size 2048
        using 4 cylinder groups of 1.27MB, 81 blks, 192 inodes.
        with soft updates
super-block backups (for fsck -b #) at:
 160, 2752, 5344, 7936
# mount /dev/md1 /mnt
# df /mnt
Filesystem 1K-blocks Used Avail Capacity  Mounted on
/dev/md1        4718    4  4338     0%    /mnt
```

To create a new file-backed memory disk, first allocate an area of disk to use. This example creates an empty 5K file named newimage:

```
# dd if=/dev/zero of= newimage bs=1k count= 5k
5120+0 records in
5120+0 records out
```

Next, attach that file to a memory disk, label the memory disk and format it with the UFS file system, mount the memory disk, and verify the size of the file-backed disk:

```
# mdconfig -f newimage -u 0
# bsdlabel -w md 0 auto
# newfs md0a
/dev/md0a: 5.0MB (10224 sectors) block size 16384, fragment size 2048
        using 4 cylinder groups of 1.25MB, 80 blks, 192 inodes.
super-block backups (for fsck -b #) at:
 160, 2720, 5280, 7840
# mount /dev/md 0a /mnt
# df /mnt
Filesystem 1K-blocks Used Avail Capacity  Mounted on
/dev/md0a       4710    4  4330     0%    /mnt
```

It takes several commands to create a file- or memory-backed file system using mdconfig. FreeBSD also comes with mdmfs which automatically configures a memory disk, formats it with the UFS file system, and mounts it. For example, after creating newimage with dd, this one command is equivalent to running the bsdlabel, newfs, and mount commands shown above:

```
# mdmfs -F newimage -s 5m md0 /mnt
```

To instead create a new memory-based memory disk with mdmfs, use this one command:

```
# mdmfs -s 5m md1 /mnt
```

If the unit number is not specified, mdmfs will automatically select an unused memory device. For more details about mdmfs, refer to mdmfs(8).

17.10. File System Snapshots

Contributed by Tom Rhodes.

FreeBSD offers a feature in conjunction with Soft Updates: file system snapshots.

UFS snapshots allow a user to create images of specified file systems, and treat them as a file. Snapshot files must be created in the file system that the action is performed on, and a user may create no more than 20 snapshots per file system. Active snapshots are recorded in the superblock so they are persistent across unmount and remount operations along with system reboots. When a snapshot is no longer required, it can be removed using rm(1). While snapshots may be removed in any order, all the used space may not be acquired because another snapshot will possibly claim some of the released blocks.

The un-alterable **snapshot** file flag is set by mksnap_ffs(8) after initial creation of a snapshot file. unlink(1) makes an exception for snapshot files since it allows them to be removed.

Snapshots are created using mount(8). To place a snapshot of /var in the file /var/snapshot/snap , use the following command:

```
# mount -u -o snapshot /var/snapshot/snap /var
```

Alternatively, use mksnap_ffs(8) to create the snapshot:

```
# mksnap_ffs /var /var/snapshot/snap
```

One can find snapshot files on a file system, such as /var, using find(1):

```
# find /var -flags snapshot
```

Once a snapshot has been created, it has several uses:

- Some administrators will use a snapshot file for backup purposes, because the snapshot can be transferred to CDs or tape.

- The file system integrity checker, fsck(8), may be run on the snapshot. Assuming that the file system was clean when it was mounted, this should always provide a clean and unchanging result.

- Running dump(8) on the snapshot will produce a dump file that is consistent with the file system and the timestamp of the snapshot. dump(8) can also take a snapshot, create a dump image, and then remove the snapshot in one command by using -L.

- The snapshot can be mounted as a frozen image of the file system. To mount(8) the snapshot /var/snapshot/snap run:

  ```
  # mdconfig -a -t vnode -o readonly -f /var/snapshot/snap -u 4
  # mount -r /dev/md4 /mnt
  ```

The frozen /var is now available through /mnt. Everything will initially be in the same state it was during the snapshot creation time. The only exception is that any earlier snapshots will appear as zero length files. To unmount the snapshot, use:

```
# umount /mnt
# mdconfig -d -u 4
```

For more information about **softupdates** and file system snapshots, including technical papers, visit Marshall Kirk McKusick's website at http://www.mckusick.com/ .

17.11. Disk Quotas

Disk quotas can be used to limit the amount of disk space or the number of files a user or members of a group may allocate on a per-file system basis. This prevents one user or group of users from consuming all of the available disk space.

This section describes how to configure disk quotas for the UFS file system. To configure quotas on the ZFS file system, refer to Section 19.4.8, "Dataset, User, and Group Quotas"

17.11.1. Enabling Disk Quotas

To determine if the FreeBSD kernel provides support for disk quotas:

```
% sysctl kern.features.ufs_quota
kern.features.ufs_quota: 1
```

In this example, the 1 indicates quota support. If the value is instead 0, add the following line to a custom kernel configuration file and rebuild the kernel using the instructions in Chapter 8, *Configuring the FreeBSD Kernel*:

```
options QUOTA
```

Next, enable disk quotas in /etc/rc.conf :

```
quota_enable="YES"
```

Normally on bootup, the quota integrity of each file system is checked by quotacheck(8). This program insures that the data in the quota database properly reflects the data on the file system. This is a time consuming process that will significantly affect the time the system takes to boot. To skip this step, add this variable to /etc/rc.conf :

```
check_quotas="NO"
```

Finally, edit /etc/fstab to enable disk quotas on a per-file system basis. To enable per-user quotas on a file system, add userquota to the options field in the /etc/fstab entry for the file system to enable quotas on. For example:

```
/dev/da1s2g   /home    ufs rw,userquota 1 2
```

To enable group quotas, use groupquota instead. To enable both user and group quotas, separate the options with a comma:

```
/dev/da1s2g    /home    ufs rw,userquota,groupquota 1 2
```

By default, quota files are stored in the root directory of the file system as quota.user and quota.group. Refer to fstab(5) for more information. Specifying an alternate location for the quota files is not recommended.

Once the configuration is complete, reboot the system and /etc/rc will automatically run the appropriate commands to create the initial quota files for all of the quotas enabled in /etc/fstab .

In the normal course of operations, there should be no need to manually run quotacheck(8), quotaon(8), or quotaoff(8). However, one should read these manual pages to be familiar with their operation.

17.11.2. Setting Quota Limits

To verify that quotas are enabled, run:

```
# quota -v
```

There should be a one line summary of disk usage and current quota limits for each file system that quotas are enabled on.

The system is now ready to be assigned quota limits with edquota.

Several options are available to enforce limits on the amount of disk space a user or group may allocate, and how many files they may create. Allocations can be limited based on disk space (block quotas), number of files (inode quotas), or a combination of both. Each limit is further broken down into two categories: hard and soft limits.

A hard limit may not be exceeded. Once a user reaches a hard limit, no further allocations can be made on that file system by that user. For example, if the user has a hard limit of 500 kbytes on a file system and is currently using 490 kbytes, the user can only allocate an additional 10 kbytes. Attempting to allocate an additional 11 kbytes will fail.

Soft limits can be exceeded for a limited amount of time, known as the grace period, which is one week by default. If a user stays over their limit longer than the grace period, the soft limit turns into a hard limit and no further allocations are allowed. When the user drops back below the soft limit, the grace period is reset.

In the following example, the quota for the `test` account is being edited. When `edquota` is invoked, the editor specified by `EDITOR` is opened in order to edit the quota limits. The default editor is set to vi.

```
# edquota -u test
Quotas for user test:
/usr: kbytes in use: 65, limits (soft = 50, hard = 75)
        inodes in use: 7, limits (soft = 50, hard = 60)
/usr/var: kbytes in use: 0, limits (soft = 50, hard = 75)
        inodes in use: 0, limits (soft = 50, hard = 60)
```

There are normally two lines for each file system that has quotas enabled. One line represents the block limits and the other represents the inode limits. Change the value to modify the quota limit. For example, to raise the block limit on `/usr` to a soft limit of `500` and a hard limit of `600`, change the values in that line as follows:

```
/usr: kbytes in use: 65, limits (soft = 500, hard = 600)
```

The new quota limits take effect upon exiting the editor.

Sometimes it is desirable to set quota limits on a range of users. This can be done by first assigning the desired quota limit to a user. Then, use -p to duplicate that quota to a specified range of user IDs (UIDs). The following command will duplicate those quota limits for UIDs `10,000` through `19,999`:

```
# edquota -p test 10000-19999
```

For more information, refer to edquota(8).

17.11.3. Checking Quota Limits and Disk Usage

To check individual user or group quotas and disk usage, use quota(1). A user may only examine their own quota and the quota of a group they are a member of. Only the superuser may view all user and group quotas. To get a summary of all quotas and disk usage for file systems with quotas enabled, use repquota(8).

Normally, file systems that the user is not using any disk space on will not show in the output of quota, even if the user has a quota limit assigned for that file system. Use -v to display those file systems. The following is sample output from quota -v for a user that has quota limits on two file systems.

```
Disk quotas for user test (uid 1002):
     Filesystem  usage   quota   limit   grace   files   quota   limit   grace
          /usr     65*      50      75   5days       7      50      60
      /usr/var       0      50      75               0      50      60
```

In this example, the user is currently 15 kbytes over the soft limit of 50 kbytes on `/usr` and has 5 days of grace period left. The asterisk * indicates that the user is currently over the quota limit.

17.11.4. Quotas over NFS

Quotas are enforced by the quota subsystem on the NFS server. The rpc.rquotad(8) daemon makes quota information available to quota on NFS clients, allowing users on those machines to see their quota statistics.

On the NFS server, enable rpc.rquotad by removing the # from this line in /etc/inetd.conf:

```
rquotad/1       dgram rpc/udp wait root /usr/libexec/rpc.rquotad rpc.rquotad
```

Then, restart inetd:

```
# service inetd restart
```

17.12. Encrypting Disk Partitions

Contributed by Lucky Green.

FreeBSD offers excellent online protections against unauthorized data access. File permissions and Mandatory Access Control (MAC) help prevent unauthorized users from accessing data while the operating system is active and the computer is powered up. However, the permissions enforced by the operating system are irrelevant if an attacker has physical access to a computer and can move the computer's hard drive to another system to copy and analyze the data.

Regardless of how an attacker may have come into possession of a hard drive or powered-down computer, the GEOM-based cryptographic subsystems built into FreeBSD are able to protect the data on the computer's file systems against even highly-motivated attackers with significant resources. Unlike encryption methods that encrypt individual files, the built-in gbde and geli utilities can be used to transparently encrypt entire file systems. No cleartext ever touches the hard drive's platter.

This chapter demonstrates how to create an encrypted file system on FreeBSD. It first demonstrates the process using gbde and then demonstrates the same example using geli.

17.12.1. Disk Encryption with gbde

The objective of the gbde(4) facility is to provide a formidable challenge for an attacker to gain access to the contents of a *cold* storage device. However, if the computer is compromised while up and running and the storage device is actively attached, or the attacker has access to a valid passphrase, it offers no protection to the contents of the storage device. Thus, it is important to provide physical security while the system is running and to protect the passphrase used by the encryption mechanism.

This facility provides several barriers to protect the data stored in each disk sector. It encrypts the contents of a disk sector using 128-bit AES in CBC mode. Each sector on the disk is encrypted with a different AES key. For more information on the cryptographic design, including how the sector keys are derived from the user-supplied passphrase, refer to gbde(4).

FreeBSD provides a kernel module for gbde which can be loaded with this command:

```
# kldload geom_bde
```

If using a custom kernel configuration file, ensure it contains this line:

```
options GEOM_BDE
```

The following example demonstrates adding a new hard drive to a system that will hold a single encrypted partition that will be mounted as /private.

Procedure 17.3. Encrypting a Partition with gbde

1. Add the New Hard Drive

    Install the new drive to the system as explained in Section 17.2, "Adding Disks". For the purposes of this example, a new hard drive partition has been added as /dev/ad4s1c and /dev/ad0s1 * represents the existing standard FreeBSD partitions.

```
# ls /dev/ad*
/dev/ad0        /dev/ad0s1b     /dev/ad0s1e     /dev/ad4s1
/dev/ad0s1      /dev/ad0s1c     /dev/ad0s1f     /dev/ad4s1c
/dev/ad0s1a     /dev/ad0s1d     /dev/ad4
```

2. Create a Directory to Hold **gbde** Lock Files

```
# mkdir /etc/gbde
```

The gbde lock file contains information that gbde requires to access encrypted partitions. Without access to the lock file, gbde will not be able to decrypt the data contained in the encrypted partition without significant manual intervention which is not supported by the software. Each encrypted partition uses a separate lock file.

3. Initialize the **gbde** Partition

A gbde partition must be initialized before it can be used. This initialization needs to be performed only once. This command will open the default editor, in order to set various configuration options in a template. For use with the UFS file system, set the sector_size to 2048:

```
# gbde init /dev/ad4s1c -i -L /etc/gbde/ad4s1c.lock
# $FreeBSD: src/sbin/gbde/template.txt,v 1.1.36.1 2009/08/03 08:13:06 kensmith Exp $
#
# Sector size is the smallest unit of data which can be read or written.
# Making it too small decreases performance and decreases available space.
# Making it too large may prevent filesystems from working.  512 is the
# minimum and always safe.  For UFS, use the fragment size
#
sector_size = 2048
[...-]
```

Once the edit is saved, the user will be asked twice to type the passphrase used to secure the data. The passphrase must be the same both times. The ability of gbde to protect data depends entirely on the quality of the passphrase. For tips on how to select a secure passphrase that is easy to remember, see http://world.std.com/~reinhold/diceware.htm.

This initialization creates a lock file for the gbde partition. In this example, it is stored as /etc/gbde/ad4s1c.lock . Lock files must end in ".lock" in order to be correctly detected by the /etc/rc.d/gbde start up script.

 Caution

Lock files *must* be backed up together with the contents of any encrypted partitions. Without the lock file, the legitimate owner will be unable to access the data on the encrypted partition.

4. Attach the Encrypted Partition to the Kernel

```
# gbde attach /dev/ad4s1c -l /etc/gbde/ad4s1c.lock
```

This command will prompt to input the passphrase that was selected during the initialization of the encrypted partition. The new encrypted device will appear in /dev as /dev/device_name.bde :

```
# ls /dev/ad*
/dev/ad0        /dev/ad0s1b     /dev/ad0s1e     /dev/ad4s1
/dev/ad0s1      /dev/ad0s1c     /dev/ad0s1f     /dev/ad4s1c
/dev/ad0s1a     /dev/ad0s1d     /dev/ad4        /dev/ad4s1c.bde
```

5. Create a File System on the Encrypted Device

    Once the encrypted device has been attached to the kernel, a file system can be created on the device. This example creates a UFS file system with soft updates enabled. Be sure to specify the partition which has a `*.bde` extension:

    ```
    # newfs -U /dev/ad4s1c.bde
    ```

6. Mount the Encrypted Partition

    Create a mount point and mount the encrypted file system:

    ```
    # mkdir /private
    # mount /dev/ad4s1c.bde /private
    ```

7. Verify That the Encrypted File System is Available

    The encrypted file system should now be visible and available for use:

    ```
    % df -H
    Filesystem        Size   Used   Avail  Capacity   Mounted on
    /dev/ad0s1a       1037M   72M   883M      8%      /
    /devfs            1.0K   1.0K    0B      100%     /dev
    /dev/ad0s1f       8.1G    55K   7.5G      0%      /home
    /dev/ad0s1e       1037M  1.1M   953M      0%      /tmp
    /dev/ad0s1d       6.1G   1.9G   3.7G     35%      /usr
    /dev/ad4s1c.bde   150G   4.1K   138G      0%      /private
    ```

After each boot, any encrypted file systems must be manually re-attached to the kernel, checked for errors, and mounted, before the file systems can be used. To configure these steps, add the following lines to `/etc/rc.conf` :

```
gbde_autoattach_all="YES"
gbde_devices="ad4s1c"
gbde_lockdir="/etc/gbde"
```

This requires that the passphrase be entered at the console at boot time. After typing the correct passphrase, the encrypted partition will be mounted automatically. Additional gbde boot options are available and listed in rc.conf(5).

Note

sysinstall is incompatible with gbde-encrypted devices. All `*.bde` devices must be detached from the kernel before starting sysinstall or it will crash during its initial probing for devices. To detach the encrypted device used in the example, use the following command:

```
# gbde detach /dev/ ad4s1c
```

17.12.2. Disk Encryption with `geli`

Contributed by Daniel Gerzo.

An alternative cryptographic GEOM class is available using `geli`. This control utility adds some features and uses a different scheme for doing cryptographic work. It provides the following features:

*   Utilizes the crypto(9) framework and automatically uses cryptographic hardware when it is available.

*   Supports multiple cryptographic algorithms such as AES, Blowfish, and 3DES.

*   Allows the root partition to be encrypted. The passphrase used to access the encrypted root partition will be requested during system boot.

- Allows the use of two independent keys.

- It is fast as it performs simple sector-to-sector encryption.

- Allows backup and restore of master keys. If a user destroys their keys, it is still possible to get access to the data by restoring keys from the backup.

- Allows a disk to attach with a random, one-time key which is useful for swap partitions and temporary file systems.

More features and usage examples can be found in geli(8).

The following example describes how to generate a key file which will be used as part of the master key for the encrypted provider mounted under /private. The key file will provide some random data used to encrypt the master key. The master key will also be protected by a passphrase. The provider's sector size will be 4kB. The example describes how to attach to the geli provider, create a file system on it, mount it, work with it, and finally, how to detach it.

Procedure 17.4. Encrypting a Partition with geli

1. Load **geli** Support

   Support for geli is available as a loadable kernel module. To configure the system to automatically load the module at boot time, add the following line to /boot/loader.conf :

   ```
   geom_eli_load="YES"
   ```

   To load the kernel module now:

   ```
   # kldload geom_eli
   ```

   For a custom kernel, ensure the kernel configuration file contains these lines:

   ```
   options GEOM_ELI
   device crypto
   ```

2. Generate the Master Key

   The following commands generate a master key (/root/da2.key) that is protected with a passphrase. The data source for the key file is /dev/random and the sector size of the provider (/dev/da2.eli) is 4kB as a bigger sector size provides better performance:

   ```
   # dd if=/dev/random of=/root/da2.key bs=64 count=1
   # geli init -s 4096 -K /root/da2.key /dev/da2
   Enter new passphrase:
   Reenter new passphrase:
   ```

   It is not mandatory to use both a passphrase and a key file as either method of securing the master key can be used in isolation.

   If the key file is given as "-", standard input will be used. For example, this command generates three key files:

   ```
   # cat keyfile1 keyfile2 keyfile3 | geli init -K - /dev/da2
   ```

3. Attach the Provider with the Generated Key

   To attach the provider, specify the key file, the name of the disk, and the passphrase:

   ```
   # geli attach -k /root/da2.key /dev/da2
   Enter passphrase:
   ```

   This creates a new device with an .eli extension:

```
# ls /dev/da2*
/dev/da2   /dev/da2.eli
```

4. Create the New File System

Next, format the device with the UFS file system and mount it on an existing mount point:

```
# dd if=/dev/random of=/dev/da2.eli bs=1m
# newfs /dev/da2.eli
# mount /dev/da2.eli  /private
```

The encrypted file system should now be available for use:

```
# df -H
Filesystem      Size  Used  Avail Capacity  Mounted on
/dev/ad0s1a     248M   89M   139M    38%     /
/devfs          1.0K  1.0K    0B    100%     /dev
/dev/ad0s1f     7.7G  2.3G   4.9G    32%     /usr
/dev/ad0s1d     989M  1.5M   909M     0%     /tmp
/dev/ad0s1e     3.9G  1.3G   2.3G    35%     /var
/dev/da2.eli    150G  4.1K   138G     0%     /private
```

Once the work on the encrypted partition is done, and the /private partition is no longer needed, it is prudent to put the device into cold storage by unmounting and detaching the geli encrypted partition from the kernel:

```
# umount /private
# geli detach da2.eli
```

A rc.d script is provided to simplify the mounting of geli-encrypted devices at boot time. For this example, add these lines to /etc/rc.conf :

```
geli_devices="da2"
geli_da2_flags="-k /root/da2.key"
```

This configures /dev/da2 as a geli provider with a master key of /root/da2.key . The system will automatically detach the provider from the kernel before the system shuts down. During the startup process, the script will prompt for the passphrase before attaching the provider. Other kernel messages might be shown before and after the password prompt. If the boot process seems to stall, look carefully for the password prompt among the other messages. Once the correct passphrase is entered, the provider is attached. The file system is then mounted, typically by an entry in /etc/fstab . Refer to Section 3.7, "Mounting and Unmounting File Systems" for instructions on how to configure a file system to mount at boot time.

17.13. Encrypting Swap

Written by Christian Brueffer.

Like the encryption of disk partitions, encryption of swap space is used to protect sensitive information. Consider an application that deals with passwords. As long as these passwords stay in physical memory, they are not written to disk and will be cleared after a reboot. However, if FreeBSD starts swapping out memory pages to free space, the passwords may be written to the disk unencrypted. Encrypting swap space can be a solution for this scenario.

This section demonstrates how to configure an encrypted swap partition using gbde(8) or geli(8) encryption. It assumes that /dev/ada0s1b is the swap partition.

17.13.1. Configuring Encrypted Swap

Swap partitions are not encrypted by default and should be cleared of any sensitive data before continuing. To overwrite the current swap partition with random garbage, execute the following command:

```
# dd if=/dev/random of=/dev/ ada0s1b bs=1m
```

To encrypt the swap partition using gbde(8), add the `.bde` suffix to the swap line in `/etc/fstab` :

```
# Device  Mountpoint FStype Options  Dump Pass#
/dev/ada0s1b.bde none  swap sw  0 0
```

To instead encrypt the swap partition using geli(8), use the `.eli` suffix:

```
# Device  Mountpoint FStype Options  Dump Pass#
/dev/ada0s1b.eli none  swap sw  0 0
```

By default, geli(8) uses the AES algorithm with a key length of 128 bits. Normally the default settings will suffice. If desired, these defaults can be altered in the options field in `/etc/fstab` . The possible flags are:

aalgo

> Data integrity verification algorithm used to ensure that the encrypted data has not been tampered with. See geli(8) for a list of supported algorithms.

ealgo

> Encryption algorithm used to protect the data. See geli(8) for a list of supported algorithms.

keylen

> The length of the key used for the encryption algorithm. See geli(8) for the key lengths that are supported by each encryption algorithm.

sectorsize

> The size of the blocks data is broken into before it is encrypted. Larger sector sizes increase performance at the cost of higher storage overhead. The recommended size is 4096 bytes.

This example configures an encrypted swap partition using the Blowfish algorithm with a key length of 128 bits and a sectorsize of 4 kilobytes:

```
# Device  Mountpoint FStype Options    Dump Pass#
/dev/ada0s1b.eli none  swap sw,ealgo=blowfish,keylen=128,sectorsize=4096 0 0
```

17.13.2. Encrypted Swap Verification

Once the system has rebooted, proper operation of the encrypted swap can be verified using swapinfo.

If gbde(8) is being used:

```
% swapinfo
Device          1K-blocks     Used    Avail Capacity
/dev/ada0s1b.bde   542720        0   542720     0%
```

If geli(8) is being used:

```
% swapinfo
Device          1K-blocks     Used    Avail Capacity
/dev/ada0s1b.eli   542720        0   542720     0%
```

17.14. Highly Available Storage (HAST)

Contributed by Daniel Gerzo.
With inputs from Freddie Cash, Pawel Jakub Dawidek, Michael W. Lucas and Viktor Petersson.

High availability is one of the main requirements in serious business applications and highly-available storage is a key component in such environments. In FreeBSD, the Highly Available STorage (HAST) framework allows transparent storage of the same data across several physically separated machines connected by a TCP/IP network. HAST can be understood as a network-based RAID1 (mirror), and is similar to the DRBD® storage system used in the

GNU/Linux® platform. In combination with other high-availability features of FreeBSD like CARP, HAST makes it possible to build a highly-available storage cluster that is resistant to hardware failures.

The following are the main features of HAST:

- Can be used to mask I/O errors on local hard drives.

- File system agnostic as it works with any file system supported by FreeBSD.

- Efficient and quick resynchronization as only the blocks that were modified during the downtime of a node are synchronized.

- Can be used in an already deployed environment to add additional redundancy.

- Together with CARP, Heartbeat, or other tools, it can be used to build a robust and durable storage system.

After reading this section, you will know:

- What HAST is, how it works, and which features it provides.

- How to set up and use HAST on FreeBSD.

- How to integrate CARP and devd(8) to build a robust storage system.

Before reading this section, you should:

- Understand UNIX® and FreeBSD basics (Chapter 3, *FreeBSD Basics*).

- Know how to configure network interfaces and other core FreeBSD subsystems (Chapter 11, *Configuration and Tuning*).

- Have a good understanding of FreeBSD networking (Part IV, "Network Communication").

The HAST project was sponsored by The FreeBSD Foundation with support from http://www.omc.net/ and http://www.transip.nl/.

17.14.1. HAST Operation

HAST provides synchronous block-level replication between two physical machines: the *primary*, also known as the *master* node, and the *secondary*, or *slave* node. These two machines together are referred to as a cluster.

Since HAST works in a primary-secondary configuration, it allows only one of the cluster nodes to be active at any given time. The primary node, also called *active*, is the one which will handle all the I/O requests to HAST-managed devices. The secondary node is automatically synchronized from the primary node.

The physical components of the HAST system are the local disk on primary node, and the disk on the remote, secondary node.

HAST operates synchronously on a block level, making it transparent to file systems and applications. HAST provides regular GEOM providers in /dev/hast/ for use by other tools or applications. There is no difference between using HAST-provided devices and raw disks or partitions.

Each write, delete, or flush operation is sent to both the local disk and to the remote disk over TCP/IP. Each read operation is served from the local disk, unless the local disk is not up-to-date or an I/O error occurs. In such cases, the read operation is sent to the secondary node.

HAST tries to provide fast failure recovery. For this reason, it is important to reduce synchronization time after a node's outage. To provide fast synchronization, HAST manages an on-disk bitmap of dirty extents and only synchronizes those during a regular synchronization, with an exception of the initial sync.

There are many ways to handle synchronization. HAST implements several replication modes to handle different synchronization methods:

- *memsync*: This mode reports a write operation as completed when the local write operation is finished and when the remote node acknowledges data arrival, but before actually storing the data. The data on the remote node will be stored directly after sending the acknowledgement. This mode is intended to reduce latency, but still provides good reliability. This mode is the default.

- *fullsync*: This mode reports a write operation as completed when both the local write and the remote write complete. This is the safest and the slowest replication mode.

- *async*: This mode reports a write operation as completed when the local write completes. This is the fastest and the most dangerous replication mode. It should only be used when replicating to a distant node where latency is too high for other modes.

17.14.2. HAST Configuration

The HAST framework consists of several components:

- The hastd(8) daemon which provides data synchronization. When this daemon is started, it will automatically load geom_gate.ko.

- The userland management utility, hastctl(8).

- The hast.conf(5) configuration file. This file must exist before starting hastd.

Users who prefer to statically build GEOM_GATE support into the kernel should add this line to the custom kernel configuration file, then rebuild the kernel using the instructions in Chapter 8, *Configuring the FreeBSD Kernel*:

```
options GEOM_GATE
```

The following example describes how to configure two nodes in master-slave/primary-secondary operation using HAST to replicate the data between the two. The nodes will be called hasta, with an IP address of 172.16.0.1, and hastb, with an IP address of 172.16.0.2. Both nodes will have a dedicated hard drive /dev/ad6 of the same size for HAST operation. The HAST pool, sometimes referred to as a resource or the GEOM provider in /dev/hast/, will be called test.

Configuration of HAST is done using /etc/hast.conf. This file should be identical on both nodes. The simplest configuration is:

```
resource test {
 on hasta {
  local /dev/ad6
  remote 172.16.0.2
 }
 on hastb {
  local /dev/ad6
  remote 172.16.0.1
 }
}
```

For more advanced configuration, refer to hast.conf(5).

Tip

It is also possible to use host names in the remote statements if the hosts are resolvable and defined either in /etc/hosts or in the local DNS.

Once the configuration exists on both nodes, the HAST pool can be created. Run these commands on both nodes to place the initial metadata onto the local disk and to start hastd(8):

```
# hastctl create  test
# service hastd onestart
```

Note

It is *not* possible to use GEOM providers with an existing file system or to convert an existing storage to a HAST-managed pool. This procedure needs to store some metadata on the provider and there will not be enough required space available on an existing provider.

A HAST node's primary or secondary role is selected by an administrator, or software like Heartbeat, using hastctl(8). On the primary node, hasta, issue this command:

```
# hastctl role primary  test
```

Run this command on the secondary node, hastb:

```
# hastctl role secondary  test
```

Verify the result by running hastctl on each node:

```
# hastctl status  test
```

Check the status line in the output. If it says degraded, something is wrong with the configuration file. It should say complete on each node, meaning that the synchronization between the nodes has started. The synchronization completes when hastctl status reports 0 bytes of dirty extents.

The next step is to create a file system on the GEOM provider and mount it. This must be done on the primary node. Creating the file system can take a few minutes, depending on the size of the hard drive. This example creates a UFS file system on /dev/hast/test :

```
# newfs -U /dev/hast/ test
# mkdir /hast/ test
# mount /dev/hast/ test /hast/test
```

Once the HAST framework is configured properly, the final step is to make sure that HAST is started automatically during system boot. Add this line to /etc/rc.conf :

```
hastd_enable="YES"
```

17.14.2.1. Failover Configuration

The goal of this example is to build a robust storage system which is resistant to the failure of any given node. If the primary node fails, the secondary node is there to take over seamlessly, check and mount the file system, and continue to work without missing a single bit of data.

To accomplish this task, the Common Address Redundancy Protocol (CARP) is used to provide for automatic failover at the IP layer. CARP allows multiple hosts on the same network segment to share an IP address. Set up CARP on both nodes of the cluster according to the documentation available in Section 30.10, "Common Address Redundancy Protocol (CARP)". In this example, each node will have its own management IP address and a shared IP address of 172.16.0.254 . The primary HAST node of the cluster must be the master CARP node.

The HAST pool created in the previous section is now ready to be exported to the other hosts on the network. This can be accomplished by exporting it through NFS or Samba, using the shared IP address 172.16.0.254 . The only problem which remains unresolved is an automatic failover should the primary node fail.

In the event of CARP interfaces going up or down, the FreeBSD operating system generates a devd(8) event, making it possible to watch for state changes on the CARP interfaces. A state change on the CARP interface is an indication that one of the nodes failed or came back online. These state change events make it possible to run a script which will automatically handle the HAST failover.

To catch state changes on the CARP interfaces, add this configuration to /etc/devd.conf on each node:

```
notify 30 {
 match "system" "IFNET";
 match "subsystem" "carp0";
 match "type" "LINK_UP";
 action "/usr/local/sbin/carp-hast-switch master";
};

notify 30 {
 match "system" "IFNET";
 match "subsystem" "carp0";
 match "type" "LINK_DOWN";
 action "/usr/local/sbin/carp-hast-switch slave";
};
```

> **Note**
>
> If the systems are running FreeBSD 10 or higher, replace carp0 with the name of the CARP-configured interface.

Restart devd(8) on both nodes to put the new configuration into effect:

service devd restart

When the specified interface state changes by going up or down , the system generates a notification, allowing the devd(8) subsystem to run the specified automatic failover script, /usr/local/sbin/carp-hast-switch . For further clarification about this configuration, refer to devd.conf(5).

Here is an example of an automated failover script:

```
#!/bin/sh

# Original script by Freddie Cash <fjwcash@gmail.com>
# Modified by Michael W. Lucas <mwlucas@BlackHelicopters.org>
# and Viktor Petersson <vpetersson@wireload.net>

# The names of the HAST resources, as listed in /etc/hast.conf
resources="test"

# delay in mounting HAST resource after becoming master
# make your best guess
delay=3

# logging
log="local0.debug"
name="carp-hast"

# end of user configurable stuff

case "$1" in
 master)
  logger -p $log -t $name "Switching to primary provider for ${resources}."
  sleep ${delay}

  # Wait for any "hastd secondary" processes to stop
```

```
for disk in ${resources}; do
  while $( pgrep -lf "hastd: ${disk} \(secondary\)" > /dev/null 2>&1 ); do
    sleep 1
  done

  # Switch role for each disk
  hastctl role primary ${disk}
  if [ $? -ne 0 -]; then
   logger -p $log -t $name "Unable to change role to primary for resource ${disk}."
   exit 1
  fi
done

# Wait for the /dev/hast/* devices to appear
for disk in ${resources}; do
  for I in $( jot 60 ); do
   [ -c "/dev/hast/${disk}" -] && break
   sleep 0.5
  done

  if [ ! -c "/dev/hast/${disk}" -]; then
   logger -p $log -t $name "GEOM provider /dev/hast/${disk} did not appear."
   exit 1
  fi
done

logger -p $log -t $name "Role for HAST resources ${resources} switched to primary."


logger -p $log -t $name "Mounting disks."
for disk in ${resources}; do
 mkdir -p /hast/${disk}
 fsck -p -y -t ufs /dev/hast/${disk}
 mount /dev/hast/${disk} /hast/${disk}
done

;;

slave)
  logger -p $log -t $name "Switching to secondary provider for ${resources}."

  # Switch roles for the HAST resources
  for disk in ${resources}; do
   if ! mount | grep -q "^/dev/hast/${disk} on "
   then
   else
    umount -f /hast/${disk}
   fi
   sleep $delay
   hastctl role secondary ${disk} 2>&1
   if [ $? -ne 0 -]; then
    logger -p $log -t $name "Unable to switch role to secondary for resource ${disk}."
    exit 1
   fi
   logger -p $log -t $name "Role switched to secondary for resource ${disk}."
  done
 ;;
esac
```

In a nutshell, the script takes these actions when a node becomes master:

• Promotes the HAST pool to primary on the other node.

• Checks the file system under the HAST pool.

• Mounts the pool.

When a node becomes secondary:

- Unmounts the HAST pool.

- Degrades the HAST pool to secondary.

Caution

This is just an example script which serves as a proof of concept. It does not handle all the possible scenarios and can be extended or altered in any way, for example, to start or stop required services.

Tip

For this example, a standard UFS file system was used. To reduce the time needed for recovery, a journal-enabled UFS or ZFS file system can be used instead.

More detailed information with additional examples can be found at http://wiki.FreeBSD.org/HAST.

17.14.3. Troubleshooting

HAST should generally work without issues. However, as with any other software product, there may be times when it does not work as supposed. The sources of the problems may be different, but the rule of thumb is to ensure that the time is synchronized between the nodes of the cluster.

When troubleshooting HAST, the debugging level of hastd(8) should be increased by starting hastd with -d. This argument may be specified multiple times to further increase the debugging level. Consider also using -F, which starts hastd in the foreground.

17.14.3.1. Recovering from the Split-brain Condition

Split-brain occurs when the nodes of the cluster are unable to communicate with each other, and both are configured as primary. This is a dangerous condition because it allows both nodes to make incompatible changes to the data. This problem must be corrected manually by the system administrator.

The administrator must either decide which node has more important changes, or perform the merge manually. Then, let HAST perform full synchronization of the node which has the broken data. To do this, issue these commands on the node which needs to be resynchronized:

```
# hastctl role init  test
# hastctl create  test
# hastctl role secondary  test
```

Chapter 18. GEOM: Modular Disk Transformation Framework

Written by Tom Rhodes.

18.1. Synopsis

In FreeBSD, the GEOM framework permits access and control to classes, such as Master Boot Records and BSD labels, through the use of providers, or the disk devices in /dev. By supporting various software RAID configurations, GEOM transparently provides access to the operating system and operating system utilities.

This chapter covers the use of disks under the GEOM framework in FreeBSD. This includes the major RAID control utilities which use the framework for configuration. This chapter is not a definitive guide to RAID configurations and only GEOM-supported RAID classifications are discussed.

After reading this chapter, you will know:

- What type of RAID support is available through GEOM.

- How to use the base utilities to configure, maintain, and manipulate the various RAID levels.

- How to mirror, stripe, encrypt, and remotely connect disk devices through GEOM.

- How to troubleshoot disks attached to the GEOM framework.

Before reading this chapter, you should:

- Understand how FreeBSD treats disk devices (Chapter 17, *Storage*).

- Know how to configure and install a new kernel (Chapter 8, *Configuring the FreeBSD Kernel*).

18.2. RAID0 - Striping

Written by Tom Rhodes and Murray Stokely.

Striping combines several disk drives into a single volume. Striping can be performed through the use of hardware RAID controllers. The GEOM disk subsystem provides software support for disk striping, also known as RAID0, without the need for a RAID disk controller.

In RAID0, data is split into blocks that are written across all the drives in the array. As seen in the following illustration, instead of having to wait on the system to write 256k to one disk, RAID0 can simultaneously write 64k to each of the four disks in the array, offering superior I/O performance. This performance can be enhanced further by using multiple disk controllers.

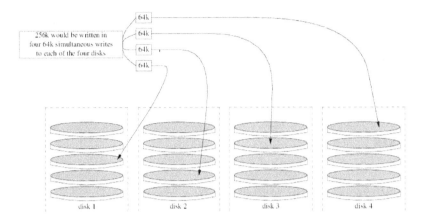

Each disk in a RAID0 stripe must be of the same size, since I/O requests are interleaved to read or write to multiple disks in parallel.

Note

RAID0 does *not* provide any redundancy. This means that if one disk in the array fails, all of the data on the disks is lost. If the data is important, implement a backup strategy that regularly saves backups to a remote system or device.

The process for creating a software, GEOM-based RAID0 on a FreeBSD system using commodity disks is as follows. Once the stripe is created, refer to gstripe(8) for more information on how to control an existing stripe.

Procedure 18.1. Creating a Stripe of Unformatted ATA Disks

1. Load the geom_stripe.ko module:

    ```
    # kldload geom_stripe
    ```

2. Ensure that a suitable mount point exists. If this volume will become a root partition, then temporarily use another mount point such as /mnt.

3. Determine the device names for the disks which will be striped, and create the new stripe device. For example, to stripe two unused and unpartitioned ATA disks with device names of /dev/ad2 and /dev/ad3:

    ```
    # gstripe label -v st0 /dev/ad2 /dev/ad3
    Metadata value stored on /dev/ad2.
    Metadata value stored on /dev/ad3.
    Done.
    ```

4. Write a standard label, also known as a partition table, on the new volume and install the default bootstrap code:

    ```
    # bsdlabel -wB /dev/stripe/st0
    ```

5. This process should create two other devices in /dev/stripe in addition to st0. Those include st0a and st0c. At this point, a UFS file system can be created on st0a using newfs:

    ```
    # newfs -U /dev/stripe/st0a
    ```

    Many numbers will glide across the screen, and after a few seconds, the process will be complete. The volume has been created and is ready to be mounted.

6. To manually mount the created disk stripe:

```
# mount /dev/stripe/st0a /mnt
```

7. To mount this striped file system automatically during the boot process, place the volume information in /
   etc/fstab . In this example, a permanent mount point, named stripe, is created:

```
# mkdir /stripe
# echo "/dev/stripe/st0a /stripe ufs rw 2 2" \
>> /etc/fstab
```

8. The geom_stripe.ko module must also be automatically loaded during system initialization, by adding a line
   to /boot/loader.conf :

```
# echo 'geom_stripe_load="YES"' >> /boot/loader.conf
```

18.3. RAID1 - Mirroring

RAID1, or *mirroring*, is the technique of writing the same data to more than one disk drive. Mirrors are usually used
to guard against data loss due to drive failure. Each drive in a mirror contains an identical copy of the data. When
an individual drive fails, the mirror continues to work, providing data from the drives that are still functioning.
The computer keeps running, and the administrator has time to replace the failed drive without user interruption.

Two common situations are illustrated in these examples. The first creates a mirror out of two new drives and
uses it as a replacement for an existing single drive. The second example creates a mirror on a single new drive,
copies the old drive's data to it, then inserts the old drive into the mirror. While this procedure is slightly more
complicated, it only requires one new drive.

Traditionally, the two drives in a mirror are identical in model and capacity, but gmirror(8) does not require that.
Mirrors created with dissimilar drives will have a capacity equal to that of the smallest drive in the mirror. Extra
space on larger drives will be unused. Drives inserted into the mirror later must have at least as much capacity as
the smallest drive already in the mirror.

Warning

The mirroring procedures shown here are non-destructive, but as with any major disk operation, make a full backup first.

Warning

While dump(8) is used in these procedures to copy file systems, it does not work on file systems with soft updates journaling. See tunefs(8) for information on detecting and disabling
soft updates journaling.

18.3.1. Metadata Issues

Many disk systems store metadata at the end of each disk. Old metadata should be erased before reusing the disk
for a mirror. Most problems are caused by two particular types of leftover metadata: GPT partition tables and old
metadata from a previous mirror.

GPT metadata can be erased with gpart(8). This example erases both primary and backup GPT partition tables from
disk ada8:

```
# gpart destroy -F ada8
```

A disk can be removed from an active mirror and the metadata erased in one step using gmirror(8). Here, the example disk ada8 is removed from the active mirror gm4:

```
# gmirror remove gm4 ada8
```

If the mirror is not running, but old mirror metadata is still on the disk, use gmirror clear to remove it:

```
# gmirror clear ada8
```

gmirror(8) stores one block of metadata at the end of the disk. Because GPT partition schemes also store metadata at the end of the disk, mirroring entire GPT disks with gmirror(8) is not recommended. MBR partitioning is used here because it only stores a partition table at the start of the disk and does not conflict with the mirror metadata.

18.3.2. Creating a Mirror with Two New Disks

In this example, FreeBSD has already been installed on a single disk, ada0. Two new disks, ada1 and ada2, have been connected to the system. A new mirror will be created on these two disks and used to replace the old single disk.

The geom_mirror.ko kernel module must either be built into the kernel or loaded at boot- or run-time. Manually load the kernel module now:

```
# gmirror load
```

Create the mirror with the two new drives:

```
# gmirror label -v gm0 /dev/ada1 /dev/ada2
```

gm0 is a user-chosen device name assigned to the new mirror. After the mirror has been started, this device name appears in /dev/mirror/.

MBR and bsdlabel partition tables can now be created on the mirror with gpart(8). This example uses a traditional file system layout, with partitions for /, swap, /var, /tmp, and /usr. A single / and a swap partition will also work.

Partitions on the mirror do not have to be the same size as those on the existing disk, but they must be large enough to hold all the data already present on ada0.

```
# gpart create -s MBR mirror/gm0
# gpart add -t freebsd -a 4k mirror/gm0
# gpart show mirror/gm0
=>        63  156301423  mirror/gm0  MBR  (74G)
          63         63                 - free -  (31k)
         126  156301299              1  freebsd  (74G)
   156301425         61                 - free -  (30k)

# gpart create -s BSD mirror/gm0s1
# gpart add -t freebsd-ufs  -a 4k -s 2g mirror/gm0s1
# gpart add -t freebsd-swap -a 4k -s 4g mirror/gm0s1
# gpart add -t freebsd-ufs  -a 4k -s 2g mirror/gm0s1
# gpart add -t freebsd-ufs  -a 4k -s 1g mirror/gm0s1
# gpart add -t freebsd-ufs  -a 4k       mirror/gm0s1
# gpart show mirror/gm0s1
=>         0  156301299  mirror/gm0s1  BSD  (74G)
           0          2                  - free -  (1.0k)
           2    4194304               1  freebsd-ufs   (2.0G)
     4194306    8388608               2  freebsd-swap  (4.0G)
    12582914    4194304               4  freebsd-ufs   (2.0G)
    16777218    2097152               5  freebsd-ufs   (1.0G)
    18874370  137426928               6  freebsd-ufs   (65G)
   156301298          1                  - free -  (512B)
```

Make the mirror bootable by installing bootcode in the MBR and bsdlabel and setting the active slice:

```
# gpart bootcode -b /boot/mbr mirror/gm0
```

```
# gpart set -a active -i 1 mirror/gm0
# gpart bootcode -b /boot/boot mirror/gm0s1
```

Format the file systems on the new mirror, enabling soft-updates.

```
# newfs -U /dev/mirror/gm0s1a
# newfs -U /dev/mirror/gm0s1d
# newfs -U /dev/mirror/gm0s1e
# newfs -U /dev/mirror/gm0s1f
```

File systems from the original ada0 disk can now be copied onto the mirror with dump(8) and restore(8).

```
# mount /dev/mirror/gm0s1a /mnt
# dump -C16 -b64 -0aL -f - / | (cd /mnt && restore -rf -)
# mount /dev/mirror/gm0s1d /mnt/var
# mount /dev/mirror/gm0s1e /mnt/tmp
# mount /dev/mirror/gm0s1f /mnt/usr
# dump -C16 -b64 -0aL -f - /var | (cd /mnt/var && restore -rf -)
# dump -C16 -b64 -0aL -f - /tmp | (cd /mnt/tmp && restore -rf -)
# dump -C16 -b64 -0aL -f - /usr | (cd /mnt/usr && restore -rf -)
```

Edit /mnt/etc/fstab to point to the new mirror file systems:

```
# Device  Mountpoint FStype Options Dump Pass#
/dev/mirror/gm0s1a /  ufs rw 1 1
/dev/mirror/gm0s1b none  swap sw 0 0
/dev/mirror/gm0s1d /var  ufs rw 2 2
/dev/mirror/gm0s1e /tmp  ufs rw 2 2
/dev/mirror/gm0s1f /usr  ufs rw 2 2
```

If the geom_mirror.ko kernel module has not been built into the kernel, /mnt/boot/loader.conf is edited to load the module at boot:

```
geom_mirror_load="YES"
```

Reboot the system to test the new mirror and verify that all data has been copied. The BIOS will see the mirror as two individual drives rather than a mirror. Because the drives are identical, it does not matter which is selected to boot.

See Section 18.3.4, "Troubleshooting" if there are problems booting. Powering down and disconnecting the original ada0 disk will allow it to be kept as an offline backup.

In use, the mirror will behave just like the original single drive.

18.3.3. Creating a Mirror with an Existing Drive

In this example, FreeBSD has already been installed on a single disk, ada0. A new disk, ada1, has been connected to the system. A one-disk mirror will be created on the new disk, the existing system copied onto it, and then the old disk will be inserted into the mirror. This slightly complex procedure is required because gmirror needs to put a 512-byte block of metadata at the end of each disk, and the existing ada0 has usually had all of its space already allocated.

Load the geom_mirror.ko kernel module:

```
# gmirror load
```

Check the media size of the original disk with diskinfo:

```
# diskinfo -v ada0 | head -n3
/dev/ada0
 512              # sectorsize
 1000204821504    # mediasize in bytes (931G)
```

Create a mirror on the new disk. To make certain that the mirror capacity is not any larger than the original ada0 drive, gnop(8) is used to create a fake drive of the exact same size. This drive does not store any data, but is used only to limit the size of the mirror. When gmirror(8) creates the mirror, it will restrict the capacity to the size of gzero.nop, even if the new ada1 drive has more space. Note that the *1000204821504* in the second line is equal to ada0's media size as shown by diskinfo above.

```
# geom zero load
# gnop create -s 1000204821504 gzero
# gmirror label -v gm0 gzero.nop ada1
# gmirror forget gm0
```

Since gzero.nop does not store any data, the mirror does not see it as connected. The mirror is told to "forget" unconnected components, removing references to gzero.nop. The result is a mirror device containing only a single disk, ada1.

After creating gm0, view the partition table on ada0. This output is from a 1 TB drive. If there is some unallocated space at the end of the drive, the contents may be copied directly from ada0 to the new mirror.

However, if the output shows that all of the space on the disk is allocated, as in the following listing, there is no space available for the 512-byte mirror metadata at the end of the disk.

```
# gpart show ada0
=>        63  1953525105        ada0  MBR  (931G)
          63  1953525105           1  freebsd  [active]  (931G)
```

In this case, the partition table must be edited to reduce the capacity by one sector on mirror/gm0. The procedure will be explained later.

In either case, partition tables on the primary disk should be first copied using gpart backup and gpart restore.

```
# gpart backup ada0 > table.ada0
# gpart backup ada0s1 > table.ada0s1
```

These commands create two files, table.ada0 and table.ada0s1. This example is from a 1 TB drive:

```
# cat table.ada0
MBR 4
1 freebsd          63 1953525105   [active]
```

```
# cat table.ada0s1
BSD 8
1   freebsd-ufs            0     4194304
2 freebsd-swap      4194304    33554432
4   freebsd-ufs     37748736    50331648
5   freebsd-ufs     88080384    41943040
6   freebsd-ufs    130023424   838860800
7   freebsd-ufs    968884224   984640881
```

If no free space is shown at the end of the disk, the size of both the slice and the last partition must be reduced by one sector. Edit the two files, reducing the size of both the slice and last partition by one. These are the last numbers in each listing.

```
# cat table.ada0
MBR 4
1 freebsd          63 1953525104   [active]
```

```
# cat table.ada0s1
BSD 8
1   freebsd-ufs            0     4194304
2 freebsd-swap      4194304    33554432
4   freebsd-ufs     37748736    50331648
5   freebsd-ufs     88080384    41943040
6   freebsd-ufs    130023424   838860800
```

```
7  freebsd-ufs  968884224  984640880
```

If at least one sector was unallocated at the end of the disk, these two files can be used without modification.

Now restore the partition table into mirror/gm0:

```
# gpart restore mirror/gm0 < table.ada0
# gpart restore mirror/gm0s1 < table.ada0s1
```

Check the partition table with gpart show. This example has gm0s1a for /, gm0s1d for /var, gm0s1e for /usr, gm0s1f for /data1, and gm0s1g for /data2.

```
# gpart show mirror/gm0
=>         63  1953525104  mirror/gm0  MBR  (931G)
           63  1953525042            1  freebsd [active]  (931G)
   1953525105          62               - free -  (31k)

# gpart show mirror/gm0s1
=>          0  1953525042  mirror/gm0s1  BSD  (931G)
            0     2097152              1  freebsd-ufs  (1.0G)
      2097152    16777216              2  freebsd-swap  (8.0G)
     18874368    41943040              4  freebsd-ufs  (20G)
     60817408    20971520              5  freebsd-ufs  (10G)
     81788928   629145600              6  freebsd-ufs  (300G)
    710934528  1242590514              7  freebsd-ufs  (592G)
   1953525042          63               - free -  (31k)
```

Both the slice and the last partition must have at least one free block at the end of the disk.

Create file systems on these new partitions. The number of partitions will vary to match the original disk, ada0.

```
# newfs -U /dev/mirror/gm0s1a
# newfs -U /dev/mirror/gm0s1d
# newfs -U /dev/mirror/gm0s1e
# newfs -U /dev/mirror/gm0s1f
# newfs -U /dev/mirror/gm0s1g
```

Make the mirror bootable by installing bootcode in the MBR and bsdlabel and setting the active slice:

```
# gpart bootcode -b /boot/mbr mirror/gm0
# gpart set -a active -i 1 mirror/gm0
# gpart bootcode -b /boot/boot mirror/gm0s1
```

Adjust /etc/fstab to use the new partitions on the mirror. Back up this file first by copying it to /etc/fstab.orig.

```
# cp /etc/fstab /etc/fstab.orig
```

Edit /etc/fstab, replacing /dev/ada0 with mirror/gm0.

```
# Device  Mountpoint FStype Options Dump Pass#
/dev/mirror/gm0s1a /  ufs rw 1 1
/dev/mirror/gm0s1b none  swap sw 0 0
/dev/mirror/gm0s1d /var  ufs rw 2 2
/dev/mirror/gm0s1e /usr  ufs rw 2 2
/dev/mirror/gm0s1f /data1  ufs rw 2 2
/dev/mirror/gm0s1g /data2  ufs rw 2 2
```

If the geom_mirror.ko kernel module has not been built into the kernel, edit /boot/loader.conf to load it at boot:

```
geom_mirror_load="YES"
```

File systems from the original disk can now be copied onto the mirror with dump(8) and restore(8). Each file system dumped with dump -L will create a snapshot first, which can take some time.

```
# mount /dev/mirror/gm0s1a /mnt
# dump -C16 -b64 -0aL -f - /    | (cd /mnt && restore -rf -)
# mount /dev/mirror/gm0s1d /mnt/var
# mount /dev/mirror/gm0s1e /mnt/usr
# mount /dev/mirror/gm0s1f /mnt/data1
# mount /dev/mirror/gm0s1g /mnt/data2
# dump -C16 -b64 -0aL -f - /usr | (cd /mnt/usr && restore -rf -)
# dump -C16 -b64 -0aL -f - /var | (cd /mnt/var && restore -rf -)
# dump -C16 -b64 -0aL -f - /data1 | (cd /mnt/data1 && restore -rf -)
# dump -C16 -b64 -0aL -f - /data2 | (cd /mnt/data2 && restore -rf -)
```

Restart the system, booting from ada1. If everything is working, the system will boot from mirror/gm0, which now contains the same data as ada0 had previously. See Section 18.3.4, "Troubleshooting" if there are problems booting.

At this point, the mirror still consists of only the single ada1 disk.

After booting from mirror/gm0 successfully, the final step is inserting ada0 into the mirror.

Important

When ada0 is inserted into the mirror, its former contents will be overwritten by data from the mirror. Make certain that mirror/gm0 has the same contents as ada0 before adding ada0 to the mirror. If the contents previously copied by dump(8) and restore(8) are not identical to what was on ada0, revert /etc/fstab to mount the file systems on ada0, reboot, and start the whole procedure again.

```
# gmirror insert gm0 ada0
GEOM_MIRROR: Device gm0: rebuilding provider ada0
```

Synchronization between the two disks will start immediately. Use gmirror status to view the progress.

```
# gmirror status
      Name     Status  Components
mirror/gm0  DEGRADED  ada1 (ACTIVE)
                      ada0 (SYNCHRONIZING, 64%)
```

After a while, synchronization will finish.

```
GEOM_MIRROR: Device gm0: rebuilding provider ada0 finished.
# gmirror status
      Name     Status  Components
mirror/gm0  COMPLETE  ada1 (ACTIVE)
                      ada0 (ACTIVE)
```

mirror/gm0 now consists of the two disks ada0 and ada1, and the contents are automatically synchronized with each other. In use, mirror/gm0 will behave just like the original single drive.

18.3.4. Troubleshooting

If the system no longer boots, BIOS settings may have to be changed to boot from one of the new mirrored drives. Either mirror drive can be used for booting, as they contain identical data.

If the boot stops with this message, something is wrong with the mirror device:

```
Mounting from ufs:/dev/mirror/gm0s1a failed with error 19.

Loader variables:
  vfs.root.mountfrom=ufs:/dev/mirror/gm0s1a
  vfs.root.mountfrom.options=rw
```

```
Manual root filesystem specification:
  <fstype>:<device> [options]
      Mount <device> using filesystem <fstype>
      and with the specified (optional) option list.

    eg. ufs:/dev/da0s1a
        zfs:tank
        cd9660:/dev/acd0 ro
          (which is equivalent to: mount -t cd9660 -o ro /dev/acd0 /)

    ?               List valid disk boot devices
    .               Yield 1 second (for background tasks)
    <empty line>    Abort manual input

mountroot>
```

Forgetting to load the geom_mirror.ko module in /boot/loader.conf can cause this problem. To fix it, boot from a FreeBSD installation media and choose Shell at the first prompt. Then load the mirror module and mount the mirror device:

```
# gmirror load
# mount /dev/mirror/gm0s1a /mnt
```

Edit /mnt/boot/loader.conf , adding a line to load the mirror module:

```
geom_mirror_load="YES"
```

Save the file and reboot.

Other problems that cause error 19 require more effort to fix. Although the system should boot from ada0, another prompt to select a shell will appear if /etc/fstab is incorrect. Enter ufs:/dev/ada0s1a at the boot loader prompt and press Enter. Undo the edits in /etc/fstab then mount the file systems from the original disk (ada0) instead of the mirror. Reboot the system and try the procedure again.

```
Enter full pathname of shell or RETURN for /bin/sh:
# cp /etc/fstab.orig /etc/fstab
# reboot
```

18.3.5. Recovering from Disk Failure

The benefit of disk mirroring is that an individual disk can fail without causing the mirror to lose any data. In the above example, if ada0 fails, the mirror will continue to work, providing data from the remaining working drive, ada1.

To replace the failed drive, shut down the system and physically replace the failed drive with a new drive of equal or greater capacity. Manufacturers use somewhat arbitrary values when rating drives in gigabytes, and the only way to really be sure is to compare the total count of sectors shown by diskinfo -v. A drive with larger capacity than the mirror will work, although the extra space on the new drive will not be used.

After the computer is powered back up, the mirror will be running in a "degraded" mode with only one drive. The mirror is told to forget drives that are not currently connected:

```
# gmirror forget gm0
```

Any old metadata should be cleared from the replacement disk using the instructions in Section 18.3.1, "Metadata Issues". Then the replacement disk, ada4 for this example, is inserted into the mirror:

```
# gmirror insert gm0 /dev/ada4
```

Resynchronization begins when the new drive is inserted into the mirror. This process of copying mirror data to a new drive can take a while. Performance of the mirror will be greatly reduced during the copy, so inserting new drives is best done when there is low demand on the computer.

Progress can be monitored with `gmirror status`, which shows drives that are being synchronized and the percentage of completion. During resynchronization, the status will be DEGRADED, changing to COMPLETE when the process is finished.

18.4. RAID3 - Byte-level Striping with Dedicated Parity

Written by Mark Gladman and Daniel Gerzo.
Based on documentation by Tom Rhodes and Murray Stokely.

RAID3 is a method used to combine several disk drives into a single volume with a dedicated parity disk. In a RAID3 system, data is split up into a number of bytes that are written across all the drives in the array except for one disk which acts as a dedicated parity disk. This means that disk reads from a RAID3 implementation access all disks in the array. Performance can be enhanced by using multiple disk controllers. The RAID3 array provides a fault tolerance of 1 drive, while providing a capacity of 1 - 1/n times the total capacity of all drives in the array, where n is the number of hard drives in the array. Such a configuration is mostly suitable for storing data of larger sizes such as multimedia files.

At least 3 physical hard drives are required to build a RAID3 array. Each disk must be of the same size, since I/O requests are interleaved to read or write to multiple disks in parallel. Also, due to the nature of RAID3, the number of drives must be equal to 3, 5, 9, 17, and so on, or $2^n + 1$.

This section demonstrates how to create a software RAID3 on a FreeBSD system.

> **Note**
>
> While it is theoretically possible to boot from a RAID3 array on FreeBSD, that configuration is uncommon and is not advised.

18.4.1. Creating a Dedicated RAID3 Array

In FreeBSD, support for RAID3 is implemented by the graid3(8) GEOM class. Creating a dedicated RAID3 array on FreeBSD requires the following steps.

1. First, load the `geom_raid3.ko` kernel module by issuing one of the following commands:

    ```
    # graid3 load
    ```

    or:

    ```
    # kldload geom_raid3
    ```

2. Ensure that a suitable mount point exists. This command creates a new directory to use as the mount point:

    ```
    # mkdir /multimedia
    ```

3. Determine the device names for the disks which will be added to the array, and create the new RAID3 device. The final device listed will act as the dedicated parity disk. This example uses three unpartitioned ATA drives: *ada1* and *ada2* for data, and *ada3* for parity.

    ```
    # graid3 label -v gr0 /dev/ada1 /dev/ada2 /dev/ada3
    Metadata value stored on /dev/ada1.
    Metadata value stored on /dev/ada2.
    Metadata value stored on /dev/ada3.
    Done.
    ```

4. Partition the newly created gr0 device and put a UFS file system on it:

```
# gpart create -s GPT /dev/raid3/gr0
# gpart add -t freebsd-ufs /dev/raid3/gr0
# newfs -j /dev/raid3/gr0p1
```

Many numbers will glide across the screen, and after a bit of time, the process will be complete. The volume has been created and is ready to be mounted:

```
# mount /dev/raid3/gr0p1 /multimedia/
```

The RAID3 array is now ready to use.

Additional configuration is needed to retain this setup across system reboots.

1. The geom_raid3.ko module must be loaded before the array can be mounted. To automatically load the kernel module during system initialization, add the following line to /boot/loader.conf :

```
geom_raid3_load="YES"
```

2. The following volume information must be added to /etc/fstab in order to automatically mount the array's file system during the system boot process:

```
/dev/raid3/gr0p1 /multimedia ufs rw 2 2
```

18.5. Software RAID Devices

Originally contributed by Warren Block.

Some motherboards and expansion cards add some simple hardware, usually just a ROM, that allows the computer to boot from a RAID array. After booting, access to the RAID array is handled by software running on the computer's main processor. This "hardware-assisted software RAID" gives RAID arrays that are not dependent on any particular operating system, and which are functional even before an operating system is loaded.

Several levels of RAID are supported, depending on the hardware in use. See graid(8) for a complete list.

graid(8) requires the geom_raid.ko kernel module, which is included in the GENERIC kernel starting with FreeBSD 9.1. If needed, it can be loaded manually with graid load .

18.5.1. Creating an Array

Software RAID devices often have a menu that can be entered by pressing special keys when the computer is booting. The menu can be used to create and delete RAID arrays. graid(8) can also create arrays directly from the command line.

graid label is used to create a new array. The motherboard used for this example has an Intel software RAID chipset, so the Intel metadata format is specified. The new array is given a label of gm0, it is a mirror (RAID1), and uses drives ada0 and ada1.

 Caution

Some space on the drives will be overwritten when they are made into a new array. Back up existing data first!

```
# graid label Intel gm0 RAID1 ada0 ada1
GEOM_RAID: Intel-a29ea104: Array Intel-a29ea104 created.
GEOM_RAID: Intel-a29ea104: Disk ada0 state changed from NONE to ACTIVE.
```

```
GEOM_RAID: Intel-a29ea104: Subdisk gm0:0-ada0 state changed from NONE to ACTIVE.
GEOM_RAID: Intel-a29ea104: Disk ada1 state changed from NONE to ACTIVE.
GEOM_RAID: Intel-a29ea104: Subdisk gm0:1-ada1 state changed from NONE to ACTIVE.
GEOM_RAID: Intel-a29ea104: Array started.
GEOM_RAID: Intel-a29ea104: Volume gm0 state changed from STARTING to OPTIMAL.
Intel-a29ea104 created
GEOM_RAID: Intel-a29ea104: Provider raid/r0 for volume gm0 created.
```

A status check shows the new mirror is ready for use:

```
# graid status
   Name   Status  Components
raid/r0  OPTIMAL  ada0 (ACTIVE (ACTIVE))
                  ada1 (ACTIVE (ACTIVE))
```

The array device appears in /dev/raid/ . The first array is called r0. Additional arrays, if present, will be r1, r2, and so on.

The BIOS menu on some of these devices can create arrays with special characters in their names. To avoid problems with those special characters, arrays are given simple numbered names like r0. To show the actual labels, like gm0 in the example above, use sysctl(8):

```
# sysctl kern.geom.raid.name_format=1
```

18.5.2. Multiple Volumes

Some software RAID devices support more than one *volume* on an array. Volumes work like partitions, allowing space on the physical drives to be split and used in different ways. For example, Intel software RAID devices support two volumes. This example creates a 40 G mirror for safely storing the operating system, followed by a 20 G RAID0 (stripe) volume for fast temporary storage:

```
# graid label -S 40G Intel gm0 RAID1 ada0 ada1
# graid add -S 20G gm0 RAID0
```

Volumes appear as additional r*X* entries in /dev/raid/ . An array with two volumes will show r0 and r1.

See graid(8) for the number of volumes supported by different software RAID devices.

18.5.3. Converting a Single Drive to a Mirror

Under certain specific conditions, it is possible to convert an existing single drive to a graid(8) array without reformatting. To avoid data loss during the conversion, the existing drive must meet these minimum requirements:

- The drive must be partitioned with the MBR partitioning scheme. GPT or other partitioning schemes with metadata at the end of the drive will be overwritten and corrupted by the graid(8) metadata.

- There must be enough unpartitioned and unused space at the end of the drive to hold the graid(8) metadata. This metadata varies in size, but the largest occupies 64 M, so at least that much free space is recommended.

If the drive meets these requirements, start by making a full backup. Then create a single-drive mirror with that drive:

```
# graid label Intel gm0 RAID1 ada0 NONE
```

graid(8) metadata was written to the end of the drive in the unused space. A second drive can now be inserted into the mirror:

```
# graid insert raid/r0 ada1
```

Data from the original drive will immediately begin to be copied to the second drive. The mirror will operate in degraded status until the copy is complete.

18.5.4. Inserting New Drives into the Array

Drives can be inserted into an array as replacements for drives that have failed or are missing. If there are no failed or missing drives, the new drive becomes a spare. For example, inserting a new drive into a working two-drive mirror results in a two-drive mirror with one spare drive, not a three-drive mirror.

In the example mirror array, data immediately begins to be copied to the newly-inserted drive. Any existing information on the new drive will be overwritten.

```
# graid insert raid/r0 ada1
GEOM_RAID: Intel-a29ea104: Disk ada1 state changed from NONE to ACTIVE.
GEOM_RAID: Intel-a29ea104: Subdisk gm0:1-ada1 state changed from NONE to NEW.
GEOM_RAID: Intel-a29ea104: Subdisk gm0:1-ada1 state changed from NEW to REBUILD.
GEOM_RAID: Intel-a29ea104: Subdisk gm0:1-ada1 rebuild start at 0.
```

18.5.5. Removing Drives from the Array

Individual drives can be permanently removed from a from an array and their metadata erased:

```
# graid remove raid/r0 ada1
GEOM_RAID: Intel-a29ea104: Disk ada1 state changed from ACTIVE to OFFLINE.
GEOM_RAID: Intel-a29ea104: Subdisk gm0:1-[unknown] state changed from ACTIVE to NONE.
GEOM_RAID: Intel-a29ea104: Volume gm0 state changed from OPTIMAL to DEGRADED.
```

18.5.6. Stopping the Array

An array can be stopped without removing metadata from the drives. The array will be restarted when the system is booted.

```
# graid stop raid/r0
```

18.5.7. Checking Array Status

Array status can be checked at any time. After a drive was added to the mirror in the example above, data is being copied from the original drive to the new drive:

```
# graid status
   Name     Status  Components
raid/r0  DEGRADED  ada0 (ACTIVE (ACTIVE))
                   ada1 (ACTIVE (REBUILD 28%))
```

Some types of arrays, like RAID0 or CONCAT, may not be shown in the status report if disks have failed. To see these partially-failed arrays, add -ga:

```
# graid status -ga
         Name  Status  Components
Intel-e2d07d9a  BROKEN  ada6 (ACTIVE (ACTIVE))
```

18.5.8. Deleting Arrays

Arrays are destroyed by deleting all of the volumes from them. When the last volume present is deleted, the array is stopped and metadata is removed from the drives:

```
# graid delete raid/r0
```

18.5.9. Deleting Unexpected Arrays

Drives may unexpectedly contain graid(8) metadata, either from previous use or manufacturer testing. graid(8) will detect these drives and create an array, interfering with access to the individual drive. To remove the unwanted metadata:

1.   Boot the system. At the boot menu, select 2 for the loader prompt. Enter:

```
OK set kern.geom.raid.enable=0
OK boot
```

The system will boot with graid(8) disabled.

2. Back up all data on the affected drive.

3. As a workaround, graid(8) array detection can be disabled by adding

    ```
    kern.geom.raid.enable=0
    ```

    to /boot/loader.conf .

    To permanently remove the graid(8) metadata from the affected drive, boot a FreeBSD installation CD-ROM or memory stick, and select Shell. Use status to find the name of the array, typically raid/r0 :

    ```
    # graid status
       Name    Status   Components
    raid/r0  OPTIMAL   ada0 (ACTIVE (ACTIVE))
                        ada1 (ACTIVE (ACTIVE))
    ```

    Delete the volume by name:

    ```
    # graid delete raid/r0
    ```

    If there is more than one volume shown, repeat the process for each volume. After the last array has been deleted, the volume will be destroyed.

    Reboot and verify data, restoring from backup if necessary. After the metadata has been removed, the kern.geom.raid.enable=0 entry in /boot/loader.conf can also be removed.

18.6. GEOM Gate Network

GEOM provides a simple mechanism for providing remote access to devices such as disks, CDs, and file systems through the use of the GEOM Gate network daemon, ggated. The system with the device runs the server daemon which handles requests made by clients using ggatec. The devices should not contain any sensitive data as the connection between the client and the server is not encrypted.

Similar to NFS, which is discussed in Section 28.3, "Network File System (NFS)", ggated is configured using an exports file. This file specifies which systems are permitted to access the exported resources and what level of access they are offered. For example, to give the client 192.168.1.5 read and write access to the fourth slice on the first SCSI disk, create /etc/gg.exports with this line:

```
192.168.1.5 RW /dev/da0s4d
```

Before exporting the device, ensure it is not currently mounted. Then, start ggated:

```
# ggated
```

Several options are available for specifying an alternate listening port or changing the default location of the exports file. Refer to ggated(8) for details.

To access the exported device on the client machine, first use ggatec to specify the IP address of the server and the device name of the exported device. If successful, this command will display a ggate device name to mount. Mount that specified device name on a free mount point. This example connects to the /dev/da0s4d partition on 192.168.1.1 , then mounts /dev/ggate0 on /mnt:

```
# ggatec create -o rw 192.168.1.1 /dev/da0s4d
ggate0
```

```
# mount /dev/ggate0 /mnt
```

The device on the server may now be accessed through /mnt on the client. For more details about ggatec and a few usage examples, refer to ggatec(8).

Note

The mount will fail if the device is currently mounted on either the server or any other client on the network. If simultaneous access is needed to network resources, use NFS instead.

When the device is no longer needed, unmount it with umount so that the resource is available to other clients.

18.7. Labeling Disk Devices

During system initialization, the FreeBSD kernel creates device nodes as devices are found. This method of probing for devices raises some issues. For instance, what if a new disk device is added via USB? It is likely that a flash device may be handed the device name of da0 and the original da0 shifted to da1. This will cause issues mounting file systems if they are listed in /etc/fstab which may also prevent the system from booting.

One solution is to chain SCSI devices in order so a new device added to the SCSI card will be issued unused device numbers. But what about USB devices which may replace the primary SCSI disk? This happens because USB devices are usually probed before the SCSI card. One solution is to only insert these devices after the system has been booted. Another method is to use only a single ATA drive and never list the SCSI devices in /etc/fstab .

A better solution is to use glabel to label the disk devices and use the labels in /etc/fstab . Because glabel stores the label in the last sector of a given provider, the label will remain persistent across reboots. By using this label as a device, the file system may always be mounted regardless of what device node it is accessed through.

Note

glabel can create both transient and permanent labels. Only permanent labels are consistent across reboots. Refer to glabel(8) for more information on the differences between labels.

18.7.1. Label Types and Examples

Permanent labels can be a generic or a file system label. Permanent file system labels can be created with tunefs(8) or newfs(8). These types of labels are created in a sub-directory of /dev, and will be named according to the file system type. For example, UFS2 file system labels will be created in /dev/ufs . Generic permanent labels can be created with glabel label . These are not file system specific and will be created in /dev/label .

Temporary labels are destroyed at the next reboot. These labels are created in /dev/label and are suited to experimentation. A temporary label can be created using glabel create .

To create a permanent label for a UFS2 file system without destroying any data, issue the following command:

```
# tunefs -L home /dev/da3
```

A label should now exist in /dev/ufs which may be added to /etc/fstab :

```
/dev/ufs/home   /home              ufs      rw           2         2
```

Note

The file system must not be mounted while attempting to run `tunefs`.

Now the file system may be mounted:

```
# mount /home
```

From this point on, so long as the `geom_label.ko` kernel module is loaded at boot with `/boot/loader.conf` or the `GEOM_LABEL` kernel option is present, the device node may change without any ill effect on the system.

File systems may also be created with a default label by using the `-L` flag with `newfs`. Refer to newfs(8) for more information.

The following command can be used to destroy the label:

```
# glabel destroy home
```

The following example shows how to label the partitions of a boot disk.

Example 18.1. Labeling Partitions on the Boot Disk

By permanently labeling the partitions on the boot disk, the system should be able to continue to boot normally, even if the disk is moved to another controller or transferred to a different system. For this example, it is assumed that a single ATA disk is used, which is currently recognized by the system as `ad0`. It is also assumed that the standard FreeBSD partition scheme is used, with `/`, `/var`, `/usr` and `/tmp`, as well as a swap partition.

Reboot the system, and at the loader(8) prompt, press 4 to boot into single user mode. Then enter the following commands:

```
# glabel label rootfs /dev/ad0s1a
GEOM_LABEL: Label for provider /dev/ad0s1a is label/rootfs
# glabel label var /dev/ad0s1d
GEOM_LABEL: Label for provider /dev/ad0s1d is label/var
# glabel label usr /dev/ad0s1f
GEOM_LABEL: Label for provider /dev/ad0s1f is label/usr
# glabel label tmp /dev/ad0s1e
GEOM_LABEL: Label for provider /dev/ad0s1e is label/tmp
# glabel label swap /dev/ad0s1b
GEOM_LABEL: Label for provider /dev/ad0s1b is label/swap
# exit
```

The system will continue with multi-user boot. After the boot completes, edit `/etc/fstab` and replace the conventional device names, with their respective labels. The final `/etc/fstab` will look like this:

```
# Device            Mountpoint      FStype  Options     Dump    Pass#
/dev/label/swap     none            swap    sw          0       0
/dev/label/rootfs   /               ufs     rw          1       1
/dev/label/tmp      /tmp            ufs     rw          2       2
/dev/label/usr      /usr            ufs     rw          2       2
/dev/label/var      /var            ufs     rw          2       2
```

The system can now be rebooted. If everything went well, it will come up normally and `mount` will show:

```
# mount
```

```
/dev/label/rootfs on / (ufs, local)
devfs on /dev (devfs, local)
/dev/label/tmp on /tmp (ufs, local, soft-updates)
/dev/label/usr on /usr (ufs, local, soft-updates)
/dev/label/var on /var (ufs, local, soft-updates)
```

The glabel(8) class supports a label type for UFS file systems, based on the unique file system id, ufsid. These labels may be found in /dev/ufsid and are created automatically during system startup. It is possible to use ufsid labels to mount partitions using /etc/fstab . Use glabel status to receive a list of file systems and their corresponding ufsid labels:

```
% glabel status
                   Name   Status   Components
ufsid/486b6fc38d330916      N/A    ad4s1d
ufsid/486b6fc16926168e      N/A    ad4s1f
```

In the above example, ad4s1d represents /var, while ad4s1f represents /usr. Using the ufsid values shown, these partitions may now be mounted with the following entries in /etc/fstab :

```
/dev/ufsid/486b6fc38d330916        /var        ufs        rw        2        2
/dev/ufsid/486b6fc16926168e        /usr        ufs        rw        2        2
```

Any partitions with ufsid labels can be mounted in this way, eliminating the need to manually create permanent labels, while still enjoying the benefits of device name independent mounting.

18.8. UFS Journaling Through GEOM

Support for journals on UFS file systems is available on FreeBSD. The implementation is provided through the GEOM subsystem and is configured using gjournal. Unlike other file system journaling implementations, the gjournal method is block based and not implemented as part of the file system. It is a GEOM extension.

Journaling stores a log of file system transactions, such as changes that make up a complete disk write operation, before meta-data and file writes are committed to the disk. This transaction log can later be replayed to redo file system transactions, preventing file system inconsistencies.

This method provides another mechanism to protect against data loss and inconsistencies of the file system. Unlike Soft Updates, which tracks and enforces meta-data updates, and snapshots, which create an image of the file system, a log is stored in disk space specifically for this task. For better performance, the journal may be stored on another disk. In this configuration, the journal provider or storage device should be listed after the device to enable journaling on.

The GENERIC kernel provides support for gjournal. To automatically load the geom_journal.ko kernel module at boot time, add the following line to /boot/loader.conf :

```
geom_journal_load="YES"
```

If a custom kernel is used, ensure the following line is in the kernel configuration file:

```
options GEOM_JOURNAL
```

Once the module is loaded, a journal can be created on a new file system using the following steps. In this example, da4 is a new SCSI disk:

```
# gjournal load
# gjournal label /dev/ da4
```

This will load the module and create a /dev/da4.journal device node on /dev/da4 .

A UFS file system may now be created on the journaled device, then mounted on an existing mount point:

```
# newfs -O 2 -J /dev/ da4 .journal
# mount /dev/ da4 .journal /mnt
```

> ## Note
>
> In the case of several slices, a journal will be created for each individual slice. For instance, if ad4s1 and ad4s2 are both slices, then gjournal will create ad4s1.journal and ad4s2.journal.

Journaling may also be enabled on current file systems by using tunefs. However, *always* make a backup before attempting to alter an existing file system. In most cases, gjournal will fail if it is unable to create the journal, but this does not protect against data loss incurred as a result of misusing tunefs. Refer to gjournal(8) and tunefs(8) for more information about these commands.

It is possible to journal the boot disk of a FreeBSD system. Refer to the article Implementing UFS Journaling on a Desktop PC for detailed instructions.

Chapter 19. The Z File System (ZFS)

Written by Tom Rhodes, Allan Jude, Benedict Reuschling and Warren Block.

The *Z File System*, or ZFS, is an advanced file system designed to overcome many of the major problems found in previous designs.

Originally developed at Sun™ , ongoing open source ZFS development has moved to the OpenZFS Project.

ZFS has three major design goals:

- Data integrity: All data includes a checksum of the data. When data is written, the checksum is calculated and written along with it. When that data is later read back, the checksum is calculated again. If the checksums do not match, a data error has been detected. ZFS will attempt to automatically correct errors when data redundancy is available.

- Pooled storage: physical storage devices are added to a pool, and storage space is allocated from that shared pool. Space is available to all file systems, and can be increased by adding new storage devices to the pool.

- Performance: multiple caching mechanisms provide increased performance. ARC is an advanced memory-based read cache. A second level of disk-based read cache can be added with L2ARC, and disk-based synchronous write cache is available with ZIL.

A complete list of features and terminology is shown in Section 19.8, "ZFS Features and Terminology".

19.1. What Makes ZFS Different

ZFS is significantly different from any previous file system because it is more than just a file system. Combining the traditionally separate roles of volume manager and file system provides ZFS with unique advantages. The file system is now aware of the underlying structure of the disks. Traditional file systems could only be created on a single disk at a time. If there were two disks then two separate file systems would have to be created. In a traditional hardware RAID configuration, this problem was avoided by presenting the operating system with a single logical disk made up of the space provided by a number of physical disks, on top of which the operating system placed a file system. Even in the case of software RAID solutions like those provided by GEOM, the UFS file system living on top of the RAID transform believed that it was dealing with a single device. ZFS's combination of the volume manager and the file system solves this and allows the creation of many file systems all sharing a pool of available storage. One of the biggest advantages to ZFS's awareness of the physical layout of the disks is that existing file systems can be grown automatically when additional disks are added to the pool. This new space is then made available to all of the file systems. ZFS also has a number of different properties that can be applied to each file system, giving many advantages to creating a number of different file systems and datasets rather than a single monolithic file system.

19.2. Quick Start Guide

There is a startup mechanism that allows FreeBSD to mount ZFS pools during system initialization. To enable it, add this line to /etc/rc.conf :

```
zfs_enable="YES"
```

Then start the service:

```
# service zfs start
```

The examples in this section assume three SCSI disks with the device names *da0*, *da1*, and *da2*. Users of SATA hardware should instead use *ada* device names.

19.2.1. Single Disk Pool

To create a simple, non-redundant pool using a single disk device:

```
# zpool create example /dev/da0
```

To view the new pool, review the output of df:

```
# df
Filesystem    1K-blocks      Used    Avail Capacity  Mounted on
/dev/ad0s1a    2026030    235230  1628718    13%     /
devfs                1         1        0   100%     /dev
/dev/ad0s1d   54098308   1032846 48737598     2%     /usr
example       17547136         0 17547136     0%     /example
```

This output shows that the example pool has been created and mounted. It is now accessible as a file system. Files can be created on it and users can browse it:

```
# cd /example
# ls
# touch testfile
# ls -al
total 4
drwxr-xr-x   2 root  wheel    3 Aug 29 23:15 .
drwxr-xr-x  21 root  wheel  512 Aug 29 23:12 ..
-rw-r--r--   1 root  wheel    0 Aug 29 23:15 testfile
```

However, this pool is not taking advantage of any ZFS features. To create a dataset on this pool with compression enabled:

```
# zfs create example/compressed
# zfs set compression=gzip example/compressed
```

The example/compressed dataset is now a ZFS compressed file system. Try copying some large files to /example/compressed.

Compression can be disabled with:

```
# zfs set compression=off example/compressed
```

To unmount a file system, use zfs umount and then verify with df:

```
# zfs umount example/compressed
# df
Filesystem    1K-blocks      Used    Avail Capacity  Mounted on
/dev/ad0s1a    2026030    235232  1628716    13%     /
devfs                1         1        0   100%     /dev
/dev/ad0s1d   54098308   1032864 48737580     2%     /usr
example       17547008         0 17547008     0%     /example
```

To re-mount the file system to make it accessible again, use zfs mount and verify with df:

```
# zfs mount example/compressed
# df
Filesystem           1K-blocks      Used    Avail Capacity  Mounted on
/dev/ad0s1a           2026030    235234  1628714    13%     /
devfs                       1         1        0   100%     /dev
/dev/ad0s1d          54098308   1032864 48737580     2%     /usr
example              17547008         0 17547008     0%     /example
example/compressed   17547008         0 17547008     0%     /example/compressed
```

The pool and file system may also be observed by viewing the output from mount:

```
# mount
/dev/ad0s1a on / (ufs, local)
devfs on /dev (devfs, local)
/dev/ad0s1d on /usr (ufs, local, soft-updates)
example on /example (zfs, local)
example/compressed on /example/compressed (zfs, local)
```

After creation, ZFS datasets can be used like any file systems. However, many other features are available which can be set on a per-dataset basis. In the example below, a new file system called `data` is created. Important files will be stored here, so it is configured to keep two copies of each data block:

```
# zfs create example/data
# zfs set copies=2 example/data
```

It is now possible to see the data and space utilization by issuing `df`:

```
# df
Filesystem         1K-blocks      Used    Avail Capacity  Mounted on
/dev/ad0s1a         2026030    235234  1628714    13%    /
devfs                     1         1        0   100%    /dev
/dev/ad0s1d        54098308 1032864 48737580     2%    /usr
example            17547008         0 17547008     0%    /example
example/compressed 17547008         0 17547008     0%    /example/compressed
example/data       17547008         0 17547008     0%    /example/data
```

Notice that each file system on the pool has the same amount of available space. This is the reason for using `df` in these examples, to show that the file systems use only the amount of space they need and all draw from the same pool. ZFS eliminates concepts such as volumes and partitions, and allows multiple file systems to occupy the same pool.

To destroy the file systems and then destroy the pool as it is no longer needed:

```
# zfs destroy example/compressed
# zfs destroy example/data
# zpool destroy example
```

19.2.2. RAID-Z

Disks fail. One method of avoiding data loss from disk failure is to implement RAID. ZFS supports this feature in its pool design. RAID-Z pools require three or more disks but provide more usable space than mirrored pools.

This example creates a RAID-Z pool, specifying the disks to add to the pool:

```
# zpool create storage raidz da0 da1 da2
```

Note

Sun™ recommends that the number of devices used in a RAID-Z configuration be between three and nine. For environments requiring a single pool consisting of 10 disks or more, consider breaking it up into smaller RAID-Z groups. If only two disks are available and redundancy is a requirement, consider using a ZFS mirror. Refer to zpool(8) for more details.

The previous example created the `storage` zpool. This example makes a new file system called `home` in that pool:

```
# zfs create storage/home
```

Compression and keeping extra copies of directories and files can be enabled:

```
# zfs set copies=2 storage/home
# zfs set compression=gzip storage/home
```

To make this the new home directory for users, copy the user data to this directory and create the appropriate symbolic links:

```
# cp -rp /home/* /storage/home
# rm -rf /home /usr/home
```

```
# ln -s /storage/home /home
# ln -s /storage/home /usr/home
```

Users data is now stored on the freshly-created /storage/home. Test by adding a new user and logging in as that user.

Try creating a file system snapshot which can be rolled back later:

```
# zfs snapshot storage/home@08-30-08
```

Snapshots can only be made of a full file system, not a single directory or file.

The @ character is a delimiter between the file system name or the volume name. If an important directory has been accidentally deleted, the file system can be backed up, then rolled back to an earlier snapshot when the directory still existed:

```
# zfs rollback storage/home@08-30-08
```

To list all available snapshots, run ls in the file system's .zfs/snapshot directory. For example, to see the previously taken snapshot:

```
# ls /storage/home/.zfs/snapshot
```

It is possible to write a script to perform regular snapshots on user data. However, over time, snapshots can consume a great deal of disk space. The previous snapshot can be removed using the command:

```
# zfs destroy storage/home@08-30-08
```

After testing, /storage/home can be made the real /home using this command:

```
# zfs set mountpoint=/home storage/home
```

Run df and mount to confirm that the system now treats the file system as the real /home:

```
# mount
/dev/ad0s1a on / (ufs, local)
devfs on /dev (devfs, local)
/dev/ad0s1d on /usr (ufs, local, soft-updates)
storage on /storage (zfs, local)
storage/home on /home (zfs, local)
# df
Filesystem     1K-blocks     Used    Avail Capacity  Mounted on
/dev/ad0s1a     2026030   235240  1628708    13%     /
devfs                 1        1        0   100%     /dev
/dev/ad0s1d    54098308  1032826 48737618     2%     /usr
storage        26320512        0 26320512     0%     /storage
storage/home   26320512        0 26320512     0%     /home
```

This completes the RAID-Z configuration. Daily status updates about the file systems created can be generated as part of the nightly periodic(8) runs. Add this line to /etc/periodic.conf:

```
daily_status_zfs_enable="YES"
```

19.2.3. Recovering RAID-Z

Every software RAID has a method of monitoring its state. The status of RAID-Z devices may be viewed with this command:

```
# zpool status -x
```

If all pools are Online and everything is normal, the message shows:

```
all pools are healthy
```

If there is an issue, perhaps a disk is in the Offline state, the pool state will look similar to:

```
  pool: storage
 state: DEGRADED
status: One or more devices has been taken offline by the administrator.
 Sufficient replicas exist for the pool to continue functioning in a
 degraded state.
action: Online the device using 'zpool online' or replace the device with
 'zpool replace'.
 scrub: none requested
config:

    NAME        STATE     READ WRITE CKSUM
    storage     DEGRADED     0     0     0
      raidz1    DEGRADED     0     0     0
        da0     ONLINE       0     0     0
        da1     OFFLINE      0     0     0
        da2     ONLINE       0     0     0

errors: No known data errors
```

This indicates that the device was previously taken offline by the administrator with this command:

 # zpool offline storage da1

Now the system can be powered down to replace da1. When the system is back online, the failed disk can replaced in the pool:

 # zpool replace storage da1

From here, the status may be checked again, this time without -x so that all pools are shown:

```
# zpool status storage
  pool: storage
 state: ONLINE
 scrub: resilver completed with 0 errors on Sat Aug 30 19:44:11 2008
config:

    NAME        STATE     READ WRITE CKSUM
    storage     ONLINE       0     0     0
      raidz1    ONLINE       0     0     0
        da0     ONLINE       0     0     0
        da1     ONLINE       0     0     0
        da2     ONLINE       0     0     0

errors: No known data errors
```

In this example, everything is normal.

19.2.4. Data Verification

ZFS uses checksums to verify the integrity of stored data. These are enabled automatically upon creation of file systems.

Warning

Checksums can be disabled, but it is *not* recommended! Checksums take very little storage space and provide data integrity. Many ZFS features will not work properly with checksums disabled. There is no noticeable performance gain from disabling these checksums.

Checksum verification is known as *scrubbing*. Verify the data integrity of the storage pool with this command:

```
# zpool scrub storage
```

The duration of a scrub depends on the amount of data stored. Larger amounts of data will take proportionally longer to verify. Scrubs are very I/O intensive, and only one scrub is allowed to run at a time. After the scrub completes, the status can be viewed with status:

```
# zpool status storage
  pool: storage
 state: ONLINE
 scrub: scrub completed with 0 errors on Sat Jan 26 19:57:37 2013
config:

  NAME        STATE     READ WRITE CKSUM
  storage     ONLINE       0     0     0
    raidz1    ONLINE       0     0     0
      da0     ONLINE       0     0     0
      da1     ONLINE       0     0     0
      da2     ONLINE       0     0     0

errors: No known data errors
```

The completion date of the last scrub operation is displayed to help track when another scrub is required. Routine scrubs help protect data from silent corruption and ensure the integrity of the pool.

Refer to zfs(8) and zpool(8) for other ZFS options.

19.3. zpool Administration

ZFS administration is divided between two main utilities. The zpool utility controls the operation of the pool and deals with adding, removing, replacing, and managing disks. The zfs utility deals with creating, destroying, and managing datasets, both file systems and volumes.

19.3.1. Creating and Destroying Storage Pools

Creating a ZFS storage pool (*zpool*) involves making a number of decisions that are relatively permanent because the structure of the pool cannot be changed after the pool has been created. The most important decision is what types of vdevs into which to group the physical disks. See the list of vdev types for details about the possible options. After the pool has been created, most vdev types do not allow additional disks to be added to the vdev. The exceptions are mirrors, which allow additional disks to be added to the vdev, and stripes, which can be upgraded to mirrors by attaching an additional disk to the vdev. Although additional vdevs can be added to expand a pool, the layout of the pool cannot be changed after pool creation. Instead, the data must be backed up and the pool destroyed and recreated.

Create a simple mirror pool:

```
# zpool create mypool mirror /dev/ada1 /dev/ada2
# zpool status
  pool: mypool
 state: ONLINE
  scan: none requested
config:

        NAME        STATE     READ WRITE CKSUM
        mypool      ONLINE       0     0     0
          mirror-0  ONLINE       0     0     0
            ada1    ONLINE       0     0     0
            ada2    ONLINE       0     0     0

errors: No known data errors
```

Multiple vdevs can be created at once. Specify multiple groups of disks separated by the vdev type keyword, `mirror` in this example:

```
# zpool create mypool mirror /dev/ada1 /dev/ada2 mirror /dev/ada3 /dev/ada4
  pool: mypool
 state: ONLINE
  scan: none requested
config:

        NAME        STATE    READ WRITE CKSUM
        mypool      ONLINE      0     0     0
          mirror-0  ONLINE      0     0     0
            ada1    ONLINE      0     0     0
            ada2    ONLINE      0     0     0
          mirror-1  ONLINE      0     0     0
            ada3    ONLINE      0     0     0
            ada4    ONLINE      0     0     0

errors: No known data errors
```

Pools can also be constructed using partitions rather than whole disks. Putting ZFS in a separate partition allows the same disk to have other partitions for other purposes. In particular, partitions with bootcode and file systems needed for booting can be added. This allows booting from disks that are also members of a pool. There is no performance penalty on FreeBSD when using a partition rather than a whole disk. Using partitions also allows the administrator to *under-provision* the disks, using less than the full capacity. If a future replacement disk of the same nominal size as the original actually has a slightly smaller capacity, the smaller partition will still fit, and the replacement disk can still be used.

Create a RAID-Z2 [395] pool using partitions:

```
# zpool create mypool raidz2 /dev/ada0p3 /dev/ada1p3 /dev/ada2p3 /dev/ada3p3 /dev/ada4p3 /
dev/ada5p3
# zpool status
  pool: mypool
 state: ONLINE
  scan: none requested
config:

        NAME        STATE    READ WRITE CKSUM
        mypool      ONLINE      0     0     0
          raidz2-0  ONLINE      0     0     0
            ada0p3  ONLINE      0     0     0
            ada1p3  ONLINE      0     0     0
            ada2p3  ONLINE      0     0     0
            ada3p3  ONLINE      0     0     0
            ada4p3  ONLINE      0     0     0
            ada5p3  ONLINE      0     0     0

errors: No known data errors
```

A pool that is no longer needed can be destroyed so that the disks can be reused. Destroying a pool involves first unmounting all of the datasets in that pool. If the datasets are in use, the unmount operation will fail and the pool will not be destroyed. The destruction of the pool can be forced with `-f`, but this can cause undefined behavior in applications which had open files on those datasets.

19.3.2. Adding and Removing Devices

There are two cases for adding disks to a zpool: attaching a disk to an existing vdev with `zpool attach`, or adding vdevs to the pool with `zpool add`. Only some vdev types allow disks to be added to the vdev after creation.

A pool created with a single disk lacks redundancy. Corruption can be detected but not repaired, because there is no other copy of the data. The copies property may be able to recover from a small failure such as a bad sector, but does not provide the same level of protection as mirroring or RAID-Z. Starting with a pool consisting of a single disk vdev, `zpool attach` can be used to add an additional disk to the vdev, creating a mirror. `zpool attach` can also be used to add additional disks to a mirror group, increasing redundancy and read performance. If the disks being used for the pool are partitioned, replicate the layout of the first disk on to the second, `gpart backup` and `gpart restore` can be used to make this process easier.

Upgrade the single disk (stripe) vdev *ada0p3* to a mirror by attaching *ada1p3*:

```
# zpool status
  pool: mypool
 state: ONLINE
  scan: none requested
config:

        NAME          STATE     READ WRITE CKSUM
        mypool        ONLINE       0     0     0
          ada0p3      ONLINE       0     0     0

errors: No known data errors
# zpool attach mypool ada0p3 ada1p3
Make sure to wait until resilver is done before rebooting.

If you boot from pool 'mypool', you may need to update
boot code on newly attached disk 'ada1p3'.

Assuming you use GPT partitioning and 'da0' is your new boot disk
you may use the following command:

        gpart bootcode -b /boot/pmbr -p /boot/gptzfsboot -i 1 da0
# gpart bootcode -b /boot/pmbr -p /boot/gptzfsboot -i 1   ada1
bootcode written to ada1
# zpool status
  pool: mypool
 state: ONLINE
status: One or more devices is currently being resilvered.  The pool will
        continue to function, possibly in a degraded state.
action: Wait for the resilver to complete.
  scan: resilver in progress since Fri May 30 08:19:19 2014
        527M scanned out of 781M at 47.9M/s, 0h0m to go
        527M resilvered, 67.53% done
config:

        NAME          STATE     READ WRITE CKSUM
        mypool        ONLINE       0     0     0
          mirror-0    ONLINE       0     0     0
            ada0p3    ONLINE       0     0     0
            ada1p3    ONLINE       0     0     0  (resilvering)

errors: No known data errors
# zpool status
  pool: mypool
 state: ONLINE
  scan: resilvered 781M in 0h0m with 0 errors on Fri May 30 08:15:58 2014
config:

        NAME          STATE     READ WRITE CKSUM
        mypool        ONLINE       0     0     0
          mirror-0    ONLINE       0     0     0
            ada0p3    ONLINE       0     0     0
            ada1p3    ONLINE       0     0     0

errors: No known data errors
```

When adding disks to the existing vdev is not an option, as for RAID-Z, an alternative method is to add another vdev to the pool. Additional vdevs provide higher performance, distributing writes across the vdevs. Each vdev is responsible for providing its own redundancy. It is possible, but discouraged, to mix vdev types, like `mirror` and

RAID-Z. Adding a non-redundant vdev to a pool containing mirror or RAID-Z vdevs risks the data on the entire pool. Writes are distributed, so the failure of the non-redundant disk will result in the loss of a fraction of every block that has been written to the pool.

Data is striped across each of the vdevs. For example, with two mirror vdevs, this is effectively a RAID 10 that stripes writes across two sets of mirrors. Space is allocated so that each vdev reaches 100% full at the same time. There is a performance penalty if the vdevs have different amounts of free space, as a disproportionate amount of the data is written to the less full vdev.

When attaching additional devices to a boot pool, remember to update the bootcode.

Attach a second mirror group (ada2p3 and ada3p3) to the existing mirror:

```
# zpool status
  pool: mypool
 state: ONLINE
  scan: resilvered 781M in 0h0m with 0 errors on Fri May 30 08:19:35 2014
config:

        NAME        STATE     READ WRITE CKSUM
        mypool      ONLINE       0     0     0
          mirror-0  ONLINE       0     0     0
            ada0p3  ONLINE       0     0     0
            ada1p3  ONLINE       0     0     0

errors: No known data errors
# zpool add mypool mirror ada2p3 ada3p3
# gpart bootcode -b /boot/pmbr -p /boot/gptzfsboot -i 1    ada2
bootcode written to ada2
# gpart bootcode -b /boot/pmbr -p /boot/gptzfsboot -i 1    ada3
bootcode written to ada3
# zpool status
  pool: mypool
 state: ONLINE
  scan: scrub repaired 0 in 0h0m with 0 errors on Fri May 30 08:29:51 2014
config:

        NAME        STATE     READ WRITE CKSUM
        mypool      ONLINE       0     0     0
          mirror-0  ONLINE       0     0     0
            ada0p3  ONLINE       0     0     0
            ada1p3  ONLINE       0     0     0
          mirror-1  ONLINE       0     0     0
            ada2p3  ONLINE       0     0     0
            ada3p3  ONLINE       0     0     0

errors: No known data errors
```

Currently, vdevs cannot be removed from a pool, and disks can only be removed from a mirror if there is enough remaining redundancy. If only one disk in a mirror group remains, it ceases to be a mirror and reverts to being a stripe, risking the entire pool if that remaining disk fails.

Remove a disk from a three-way mirror group:

```
# zpool status
  pool: mypool
 state: ONLINE
  scan: scrub repaired 0 in 0h0m with 0 errors on Fri May 30 08:29:51 2014
config:

        NAME        STATE     READ WRITE CKSUM
        mypool      ONLINE       0     0     0
          mirror-0  ONLINE       0     0     0
            ada0p3  ONLINE       0     0     0
            ada1p3  ONLINE       0     0     0
```

```
            ada2p3  ONLINE       0     0     0

errors: No known data errors
# zpool detach mypool ada2p3
# zpool status
  pool: mypool
 state: ONLINE
  scan: scrub repaired 0 in 0h0m with 0 errors on Fri May 30 08:29:51 2014
config:

        NAME        STATE    READ WRITE CKSUM
        mypool      ONLINE      0     0     0
          mirror-0  ONLINE      0     0     0
            ada0p3  ONLINE      0     0     0
            ada1p3  ONLINE      0     0     0

errors: No known data errors
```

19.3.3. Checking the Status of a Pool

Pool status is important. If a drive goes offline or a read, write, or checksum error is detected, the corresponding error count increases. The status output shows the configuration and status of each device in the pool and the status of the entire pool. Actions that need to be taken and details about the last scrub are also shown.

```
# zpool status
  pool: mypool
 state: ONLINE
  scan: scrub repaired 0 in 2h25m with 0 errors on Sat Sep 14 04:25:50 2013
config:

        NAME        STATE    READ WRITE CKSUM
        mypool      ONLINE      0     0     0
          raidz2-0  ONLINE      0     0     0
            ada0p3  ONLINE      0     0     0
            ada1p3  ONLINE      0     0     0
            ada2p3  ONLINE      0     0     0
            ada3p3  ONLINE      0     0     0
            ada4p3  ONLINE      0     0     0
            ada5p3  ONLINE      0     0     0

errors: No known data errors
```

19.3.4. Clearing Errors

When an error is detected, the read, write, or checksum counts are incremented. The error message can be cleared and the counts reset with zpool clear mypool. Clearing the error state can be important for automated scripts that alert the administrator when the pool encounters an error. Further errors may not be reported if the old errors are not cleared.

19.3.5. Replacing a Functioning Device

There are a number of situations where it may be desirable to replace one disk with a different disk. When replacing a working disk, the process keeps the old disk online during the replacement. The pool never enters a degraded state, reducing the risk of data loss. zpool replace copies all of the data from the old disk to the new one. After the operation completes, the old disk is disconnected from the vdev. If the new disk is larger than the old disk, it may be possible to grow the zpool, using the new space. See Growing a Pool.

Replace a functioning device in the pool:

```
# zpool status
  pool: mypool
 state: ONLINE
  scan: none requested
```

```
config:

        NAME          STATE     READ WRITE CKSUM
        mypool        ONLINE       0     0     0
          mirror-0    ONLINE       0     0     0
            ada0p3    ONLINE       0     0     0
            ada1p3    ONLINE       0     0     0

errors: No known data errors
# zpool replace mypool ada1p3 ada2p3
Make sure to wait until resilver is done before rebooting.

If you boot from pool 'zroot', you may need to update
boot code on newly attached disk 'ada2p3'.

Assuming you use GPT partitioning and 'da0' is your new boot disk
you may use the following command:

        gpart bootcode -b /boot/pmbr -p /boot/gptzfsboot -i 1 da0
# gpart bootcode -b /boot/pmbr -p /boot/gptzfsboot -i 1    ada2
# zpool status
  pool: mypool
 state: ONLINE
status: One or more devices is currently being resilvered.  The pool will
        continue to function, possibly in a degraded state.
action: Wait for the resilver to complete.
  scan: resilver in progress since Mon Jun  2 14:21:35 2014
        604M scanned out of 781M at 46.5M/s, 0h0m to go
        604M resilvered, 77.39% done
config:

        NAME            STATE     READ WRITE CKSUM
        mypool          ONLINE       0     0     0
          mirror-0      ONLINE       0     0     0
            ada0p3      ONLINE       0     0     0
            replacing-1 ONLINE       0     0     0
              ada1p3    ONLINE       0     0     0
              ada2p3    ONLINE       0     0     0  (resilvering)

errors: No known data errors
# zpool status
  pool: mypool
 state: ONLINE
  scan: resilvered 781M in 0h0m with 0 errors on Mon Jun  2 14:21:52 2014
config:

        NAME          STATE     READ WRITE CKSUM
        mypool        ONLINE       0     0     0
          mirror-0    ONLINE       0     0     0
            ada0p3    ONLINE       0     0     0
            ada2p3    ONLINE       0     0     0

errors: No known data errors
```

19.3.6. Dealing with Failed Devices

When a disk in a pool fails, the vdev to which the disk belongs enters the degraded state. All of the data is still available, but performance may be reduced because missing data must be calculated from the available redundancy. To restore the vdev to a fully functional state, the failed physical device must be replaced. ZFS is then instructed to begin the resilver operation. Data that was on the failed device is recalculated from available redundancy and written to the replacement device. After completion, the vdev returns to online status.

If the vdev does not have any redundancy, or if multiple devices have failed and there is not enough redundancy to compensate, the pool enters the faulted state. If a sufficient number of devices cannot be reconnected to the pool, the pool becomes inoperative and data must be restored from backups.

When replacing a failed disk, the name of the failed disk is replaced with the GUID of the device. A new device name parameter for zpool replace is not required if the replacement device has the same device name.

Replace a failed disk using zpool replace:

```
# zpool status
  pool: mypool
 state: DEGRADED
status: One or more devices could not be opened.  Sufficient replicas exist for
        the pool to continue functioning in a degraded state.
action: Attach the missing device and online it using 'zpool online'.
   see: http://illumos.org/msg/ZFS-8000-2Q
  scan: none requested
config:

        NAME                      STATE     READ WRITE CKSUM
        mypool                    DEGRADED     0     0     0
          mirror-0                DEGRADED     0     0     0
            ada0p3                ONLINE       0     0     0
            316502962686821739    UNAVAIL      0     0     0  was /dev/ada1p3

errors: No known data errors
# zpool replace mypool 316502962686821739  ada2p3
# zpool status
  pool: mypool
 state: DEGRADED
status: One or more devices is currently being resilvered.  The pool will
        continue to function, possibly in a degraded state.
action: Wait for the resilver to complete.
  scan: resilver in progress since Mon Jun  2 14:52:21 2014
        641M scanned out of 781M at 49.3M/s, 0h0m to go
        640M resilvered, 82.04% done
config:

        NAME                        STATE     READ WRITE CKSUM
        mypool                      DEGRADED     0     0     0
          mirror-0                  DEGRADED     0     0     0
            ada0p3                  ONLINE       0     0     0
            replacing-1             UNAVAIL      0     0     0
              15732067398082357289  UNAVAIL      0     0     0  was /dev/ada1p3/old
              ada2p3                ONLINE       0     0     0  (resilvering)

errors: No known data errors
# zpool status
  pool: mypool
 state: ONLINE
  scan: resilvered 781M in 0h0m with 0 errors on Mon Jun  2 14:52:38 2014
config:

        NAME         STATE     READ WRITE CKSUM
        mypool       ONLINE       0     0     0
          mirror-0   ONLINE       0     0     0
            ada0p3   ONLINE       0     0     0
            ada2p3   ONLINE       0     0     0

errors: No known data errors
```

19.3.7. Scrubbing a Pool

It is recommended that pools be scrubbed regularly, ideally at least once every month. The scrub operation is very disk-intensive and will reduce performance while running. Avoid high-demand periods when scheduling scrub or use vfs.zfs.scrub_delay [392] to adjust the relative priority of the scrub to prevent it interfering with other workloads.

```
# zpool scrub mypool
```

```
# zpool status
  pool: mypool
 state: ONLINE
  scan: scrub in progress since Wed Feb 19 20:52:54 2014
        116G scanned out of 8.60T at 649M/s, 3h48m to go
        0 repaired, 1.32% done
config:

        NAME          STATE     READ WRITE CKSUM
        mypool        ONLINE       0     0     0
          raidz2-0    ONLINE       0     0     0
            ada0p3    ONLINE       0     0     0
            ada1p3    ONLINE       0     0     0
            ada2p3    ONLINE       0     0     0
            ada3p3    ONLINE       0     0     0
            ada4p3    ONLINE       0     0     0
            ada5p3    ONLINE       0     0     0

errors: No known data errors
```

In the event that a scrub operation needs to be cancelled, issue zpool scrub -s *mypool*.

19.3.8. Self-Healing

The checksums stored with data blocks enable the file system to *self-heal*. This feature will automatically repair data whose checksum does not match the one recorded on another device that is part of the storage pool. For example, a mirror with two disks where one drive is starting to malfunction and cannot properly store the data any more. This is even worse when the data has not been accessed for a long time, as with long term archive storage. Traditional file systems need to run algorithms that check and repair the data like fsck(8). These commands take time, and in severe cases, an administrator has to manually decide which repair operation must be performed. When ZFS detects a data block with a checksum that does not match, it tries to read the data from the mirror disk. If that disk can provide the correct data, it will not only give that data to the application requesting it, but also correct the wrong data on the disk that had the bad checksum. This happens without any interaction from a system administrator during normal pool operation.

The next example demonstrates this self-healing behavior. A mirrored pool of disks /dev/ada0 and /dev/ada1 is created.

```
# zpool create healer mirror /dev/ada0 /dev/ada1
# zpool status healer
  pool: healer
 state: ONLINE
  scan: none requested
config:

    NAME        STATE     READ WRITE CKSUM
    healer      ONLINE       0     0     0
      mirror-0  ONLINE       0     0     0
        ada0    ONLINE       0     0     0
        ada1    ONLINE       0     0     0

errors: No known data errors
# zpool list
NAME     SIZE   ALLOC   FREE    CAP   DEDUP   HEALTH   ALTROOT
healer   960M   92.5K   960M    0%    1.00x   ONLINE   -
```

Some important data that to be protected from data errors using the self-healing feature is copied to the pool. A checksum of the pool is created for later comparison.

```
# cp /some/important/data /healer
# zfs list
NAME     SIZE   ALLOC   FREE    CAP   DEDUP   HEALTH   ALTROOT
healer   960M   67.7M   892M    7%    1.00x   ONLINE   -
```

```
# sha1 /healer > checksum.txt
# cat checksum.txt
SHA1 (/healer) = 2753eff56d77d9a536ece6694bf0a82740344d1f
```

Data corruption is simulated by writing random data to the beginning of one of the disks in the mirror. To prevent ZFS from healing the data as soon as it is detected, the pool is exported before the corruption and imported again afterwards.

Warning

This is a dangerous operation that can destroy vital data. It is shown here for demonstrational purposes only and should not be attempted during normal operation of a storage pool. Nor should this intentional corruption example be run on any disk with a different file system on it. Do not use any other disk device names other than the ones that are part of the pool. Make certain that proper backups of the pool are created before running the command!

```
# zpool export healer
# dd if=/dev/random of=/dev/ada1 bs=1m count=200
200+0 records in
200+0 records out
209715200 bytes transferred in 62.992162 secs (3329227 bytes/sec)
# zpool import healer
```

The pool status shows that one device has experienced an error. Note that applications reading data from the pool did not receive any incorrect data. ZFS provided data from the ada0 device with the correct checksums. The device with the wrong checksum can be found easily as the CKSUM column contains a nonzero value.

```
# zpool status healer
    pool: healer
   state: ONLINE
  status: One or more devices has experienced an unrecoverable error.  An
          attempt was made to correct the error.  Applications are unaffected.
  action: Determine if the device needs to be replaced, and clear the errors
          using 'zpool clear' or replace the device with 'zpool replace'.
     see: http://www.sun.com/msg/ZFS-8000-9P
    scan: none requested
  config:

        NAME        STATE     READ WRITE CKSUM
        healer      ONLINE       0     0     0
          mirror-0  ONLINE       0     0     0
            ada0    ONLINE       0     0     0
            ada1    ONLINE       0     0     1

errors: No known data errors
```

The error was detected and handled by using the redundancy present in the unaffected ada0 mirror disk. A checksum comparison with the original one will reveal whether the pool is consistent again.

```
# sha1 /healer >> checksum.txt
# cat checksum.txt
SHA1 (/healer) = 2753eff56d77d9a536ece6694bf0a82740344d1f
SHA1 (/healer) = 2753eff56d77d9a536ece6694bf0a82740344d1f
```

The two checksums that were generated before and after the intentional tampering with the pool data still match. This shows how ZFS is capable of detecting and correcting any errors automatically when the checksums differ. Note that this is only possible when there is enough redundancy present in the pool. A pool consisting of a single device has no self-healing capabilities. That is also the reason why checksums are so important in ZFS and should not be disabled for any reason. No fsck(8) or similar file system consistency check program is required to detect and correct this and the pool was still available during the time there was a problem. A scrub operation is now required to overwrite the corrupted data on ada1.

```
# zpool scrub healer
# zpool status healer
  pool: healer
 state: ONLINE
status: One or more devices has experienced an unrecoverable error.  An
          attempt was made to correct the error.  Applications are unaffected.
action: Determine if the device needs to be replaced, and clear the errors
          using 'zpool clear' or replace the device with 'zpool replace'.
   see: http://www.sun.com/msg/ZFS-8000-9P
  scan: scrub in progress since Mon Dec 10 12:23:30 2012
        10.4M scanned out of 67.0M at 267K/s, 0h3m to go
        9.63M repaired, 15.56% done
config:

    NAME          STATE     READ WRITE CKSUM
    healer        ONLINE       0     0     0
      mirror-0    ONLINE       0     0     0
        ada0      ONLINE       0     0     0
        ada1      ONLINE       0     0   627  (repairing)

errors: No known data errors
```

The scrub operation reads data from ada0 and rewrites any data with an incorrect checksum on ada1. This is indicated by the (repairing) output from zpool status. After the operation is complete, the pool status changes to:

```
# zpool status healer
  pool: healer
 state: ONLINE
status: One or more devices has experienced an unrecoverable error.  An
          attempt was made to correct the error.  Applications are unaffected.
action: Determine if the device needs to be replaced, and clear the errors
          using 'zpool clear' or replace the device with 'zpool replace'.
   see: http://www.sun.com/msg/ZFS-8000-9P
  scan: scrub repaired 66.5M in 0h2m with 0 errors on Mon Dec 10 12:26:25 2012
config:

    NAME          STATE     READ WRITE CKSUM
    healer        ONLINE       0     0     0
      mirror-0    ONLINE       0     0     0
        ada0      ONLINE       0     0     0
        ada1      ONLINE       0     0 2.72K

errors: No known data errors
```

After the scrub operation completes and all the data has been synchronized from ada0 to ada1, the error messages can be cleared from the pool status by running zpool clear.

```
# zpool clear healer
# zpool status healer
  pool: healer
 state: ONLINE
  scan: scrub repaired 66.5M in 0h2m with 0 errors on Mon Dec 10 12:26:25 2012
config:

    NAME          STATE     READ WRITE CKSUM
    healer        ONLINE       0     0     0
      mirror-0    ONLINE       0     0     0
        ada0      ONLINE       0     0     0
        ada1      ONLINE       0     0     0

errors: No known data errors
```

The pool is now back to a fully working state and all the errors have been cleared.

19.3.9. Growing a Pool

The usable size of a redundant pool is limited by the capacity of the smallest device in each vdev. The smallest device can be replaced with a larger device. After completing a replace or resilver operation, the pool can grow to use the capacity of the new device. For example, consider a mirror of a 1 TB drive and a 2 TB drive. The usable space is 1 TB. When the 1 TB drive is replaced with another 2 TB drive, the resilvering process copies the existing data onto the new drive. Because both of the devices now have 2 TB capacity, the mirror's available space can be grown to 2 TB.

Expansion is triggered by using `zpool online -e` on each device. After expansion of all devices, the additional space becomes available to the pool.

19.3.10. Importing and Exporting Pools

Pools are *exported* before moving them to another system. All datasets are unmounted, and each device is marked as exported but still locked so it cannot be used by other disk subsystems. This allows pools to be *imported* on other machines, other operating systems that support ZFS, and even different hardware architectures (with some caveats, see zpool(8)). When a dataset has open files, `zpool export -f` can be used to force the export of a pool. Use this with caution. The datasets are forcibly unmounted, potentially resulting in unexpected behavior by the applications which had open files on those datasets.

Export a pool that is not in use:

```
# zpool export mypool
```

Importing a pool automatically mounts the datasets. This may not be the desired behavior, and can be prevented with `zpool import -N`. `zpool import -o` sets temporary properties for this import only. `zpool import altroot=` allows importing a pool with a base mount point instead of the root of the file system. If the pool was last used on a different system and was not properly exported, an import might have to be forced with `zpool import -f`. `zpool import -a` imports all pools that do not appear to be in use by another system.

List all available pools for import:

```
# zpool import
   pool: mypool
     id: 9930174748043525076
  state: ONLINE
 action: The pool can be imported using its name or numeric identifier.
 config:

        mypool       ONLINE
          ada2p3     ONLINE
```

Import the pool with an alternative root directory:

```
# zpool import -o altroot= /mnt mypool
# zfs list
zfs list
NAME                USED  AVAIL  REFER  MOUNTPOINT
mypool              110K  47.0G    31K  /mnt/mypool
```

19.3.11. Upgrading a Storage Pool

After upgrading FreeBSD, or if a pool has been imported from a system using an older version of ZFS, the pool can be manually upgraded to the latest version of ZFS to support newer features. Consider whether the pool may ever need to be imported on an older system before upgrading. Upgrading is a one-way process. Older pools can be upgraded, but pools with newer features cannot be downgraded.

Upgrade a v28 pool to support Feature Flags:

```
# zpool status
  pool: mypool
 state: ONLINE
status: The pool is formatted using a legacy on-disk format.  The pool can
        still be used, but some features are unavailable.
action: Upgrade the pool using 'zpool upgrade'.  Once this is done, the
        pool will no longer be accessible on software that does not support feat
        flags.
  scan: none requested
config:

        NAME          STATE      READ WRITE CKSUM
        mypool        ONLINE        0     0     0
          mirror-0    ONLINE        0     0     0
    ada0    ONLINE        0     0     0
    ada1    ONLINE        0     0     0

errors: No known data errors
# zpool upgrade
This system supports ZFS pool feature flags.

The following pools are formatted with legacy version numbers and can
be upgraded to use feature flags.  After being upgraded, these pools
will no longer be accessible by software that does not support feature
flags.

VER  POOL
---  ------------
28   mypool

Use 'zpool upgrade -v' for a list of available legacy versions.
Every feature flags pool has all supported features enabled.
# zpool upgrade mypool
This system supports ZFS pool feature flags.

Successfully upgraded 'mypool' from version 28 to feature flags.
Enabled the following features on 'mypool':
  async_destroy
  empty_bpobj
  lz4_compress
  multi_vdev_crash_dump
```

The newer features of ZFS will not be available until zpool upgrade has completed. zpool upgrade -v can be used to see what new features will be provided by upgrading, as well as which features are already supported.

Upgrade a pool to support additional feature flags:

```
# zpool status
  pool: mypool
 state: ONLINE
status: Some supported features are not enabled on the pool. The pool can
        still be used, but some features are unavailable.
action: Enable all features using 'zpool upgrade'. Once this is done,
        the pool may no longer be accessible by software that does not support
        the features. See zpool-features(7) for details.
  scan: none requested
config:

        NAME          STATE      READ WRITE CKSUM
        mypool        ONLINE        0     0     0
          mirror-0    ONLINE        0     0     0
    ada0    ONLINE        0     0     0
    ada1    ONLINE        0     0     0
```

```
errors: No known data errors
# zpool upgrade
This system supports ZFS pool feature flags.

All pools are formatted using feature flags.


Some supported features are not enabled on the following pools. Once a
feature is enabled the pool may become incompatible with software
that does not support the feature. See zpool-features(7) for details.

POOL  FEATURE
---------------
zstore
      multi_vdev_crash_dump
      spacemap_histogram
      enabled_txg
      hole_birth
      extensible_dataset
      bookmarks
      filesystem_limits
# zpool upgrade mypool
This system supports ZFS pool feature flags.

Enabled the following features on 'mypool':
  spacemap_histogram
  enabled_txg
  hole_birth
  extensible_dataset
  bookmarks
  filesystem_limits
```

Warning

The boot code on systems that boot from a pool must be updated to support the new pool version. Use gpart bootcode on the partition that contains the boot code. See gpart(8) for more information.

19.3.12. Displaying Recorded Pool History

Commands that modify the pool are recorded. Recorded actions include the creation of datasets, changing properties, or replacement of a disk. This history is useful for reviewing how a pool was created and which user performed a specific action and when. History is not kept in a log file, but is part of the pool itself. The command to review this history is aptly named zpool history:

```
# zpool history
History for 'tank':
2013-02-26.23:02:35 zpool create tank mirror /dev/ada0 /dev/ada1
2013-02-27.18:50:58 zfs set atime=off tank
2013-02-27.18:51:09 zfs set checksum=fletcher4 tank
2013-02-27.18:51:18 zfs create tank/backup
```

The output shows zpool and zfs commands that were executed on the pool along with a timestamp. Only commands that alter the pool in some way are recorded. Commands like zfs list are not included. When no pool name is specified, the history of all pools is displayed.

zpool history can show even more information when the options -i or -l are provided. -i displays user-initiated events as well as internally logged ZFS events.

```
# zpool history -i
```

```
History for 'tank':
2013-02-26.23:02:35 [internal pool create txg:5] pool spa 28; zfs spa 28; zpl 5;uts  9.1-
RELEASE 901000 amd64
2013-02-27.18:50:53 [internal property set txg:50] atime=0 dataset = 21
2013-02-27.18:50:58 zfs set atime=off tank
2013-02-27.18:51:04 [internal property set txg:53] checksum=7 dataset = 21
2013-02-27.18:51:09 zfs set checksum=fletcher4 tank
2013-02-27.18:51:13 [internal create txg:55] dataset = 39
2013-02-27.18:51:18 zfs create tank/backup
```

More details can be shown by adding -l. History records are shown in a long format, including information like the name of the user who issued the command and the hostname on which the change was made.

```
# zpool history -l
History for 'tank':
2013-02-26.23:02:35 zpool create tank mirror /dev/ada0 /dev/ada1 [user 0 (root) ↺
on :global]
2013-02-27.18:50:58 zfs set atime=off tank [user 0 (root) on myzfsbox:global]
2013-02-27.18:51:09 zfs set checksum=fletcher4 tank [user 0 (root) on myzfsbox:global]
2013-02-27.18:51:18 zfs create tank/backup [user 0 (root) on myzfsbox:global]
```

The output shows that the root user created the mirrored pool with disks /dev/ada0 and /dev/ada1. The hostname myzfsbox is also shown in the commands after the pool's creation. The hostname display becomes important when the pool is exported from one system and imported on another. The commands that are issued on the other system can clearly be distinguished by the hostname that is recorded for each command.

Both options to zpool history can be combined to give the most detailed information possible for any given pool. Pool history provides valuable information when tracking down the actions that were performed or when more detailed output is needed for debugging.

19.3.13. Performance Monitoring

A built-in monitoring system can display pool I/O statistics in real time. It shows the amount of free and used space on the pool, how many read and write operations are being performed per second, and how much I/O bandwidth is currently being utilized. By default, all pools in the system are monitored and displayed. A pool name can be provided to limit monitoring to just that pool. A basic example:

```
# zpool iostat
            capacity     operations    bandwidth
pool      alloc   free   read  write   read  write
----------  -----  -----  -----  -----  -----  -----
data       288G  1.53T      2     11  11.3K  57.1K
```

To continuously monitor I/O activity, a number can be specified as the last parameter, indicating a interval in seconds to wait between updates. The next statistic line is printed after each interval. Press Ctrl+C to stop this continuous monitoring. Alternatively, give a second number on the command line after the interval to specify the total number of statistics to display.

Even more detailed I/O statistics can be displayed with -v. Each device in the pool is shown with a statistics line. This is useful in seeing how many read and write operations are being performed on each device, and can help determine if any individual device is slowing down the pool. This example shows a mirrored pool with two devices:

```
# zpool iostat -v
                       capacity     operations    bandwidth
pool                 alloc   free   read  write   read  write
--------------------  -----  -----  -----  -----  -----  -----
data                  288G  1.53T      2     12  9.23K  61.5K
  mirror              288G  1.53T      2     12  9.23K  61.5K
    ada1                -      -       0      4  5.61K  61.7K
    ada2                -      -       1      4  5.04K  61.7K
--------------------  -----  -----  -----  -----  -----  -----
```

19.3.14. Splitting a Storage Pool

A pool consisting of one or more mirror vdevs can be split into two pools. Unless otherwise specified, the last member of each mirror is detached and used to create a new pool containing the same data. The operation should first be attempted with -n. The details of the proposed operation are displayed without it actually being performed. This helps confirm that the operation will do what the user intends.

19.4. zfs Administration

The zfs utility is responsible for creating, destroying, and managing all ZFS datasets that exist within a pool. The pool is managed using zpool.

19.4.1. Creating and Destroying Datasets

Unlike traditional disks and volume managers, space in ZFS is *not* preallocated. With traditional file systems, after all of the space is partitioned and assigned, there is no way to add an additional file system without adding a new disk. With ZFS, new file systems can be created at any time. Each *dataset* has properties including features like compression, deduplication, caching, and quotas, as well as other useful properties like readonly, case sensitivity, network file sharing, and a mount point. Datasets can be nested inside each other, and child datasets will inherit properties from their parents. Each dataset can be administered, delegated, replicated, snapshotted, jailed, and destroyed as a unit. There are many advantages to creating a separate dataset for each different type or set of files. The only drawbacks to having an extremely large number of datasets is that some commands like zfs list will be slower, and the mounting of hundreds or even thousands of datasets can slow the FreeBSD boot process.

Create a new dataset and enable LZ4 compression on it:

```
# zfs list
NAME                   USED   AVAIL  REFER  MOUNTPOINT
mypool                 781M   93.2G  144K   none
mypool/ROOT            777M   93.2G  144K   none
mypool/ROOT/default    777M   93.2G  777M   /
mypool/tmp             176K   93.2G  176K   /tmp
mypool/usr             616K   93.2G  144K   /usr
mypool/usr/home        184K   93.2G  184K   /usr/home
mypool/usr/ports       144K   93.2G  144K   /usr/ports
mypool/usr/src         144K   93.2G  144K   /usr/src
mypool/var             1.20M  93.2G  608K   /var
mypool/var/crash       148K   93.2G  148K   /var/crash
mypool/var/log         178K   93.2G  178K   /var/log
mypool/var/mail        144K   93.2G  144K   /var/mail
mypool/var/tmp         152K   93.2G  152K   /var/tmp
# zfs create -o compress=lz4  mypool/usr/mydataset
# zfs list
NAME                   USED   AVAIL  REFER  MOUNTPOINT
mypool                 781M   93.2G  144K   none
mypool/ROOT            777M   93.2G  144K   none
mypool/ROOT/default    777M   93.2G  777M   /
mypool/tmp             176K   93.2G  176K   /tmp
mypool/usr             704K   93.2G  144K   /usr
mypool/usr/home        184K   93.2G  184K   /usr/home
mypool/usr/mydataset   87.5K  93.2G  87.5K  /usr/mydataset
mypool/usr/ports       144K   93.2G  144K   /usr/ports
mypool/usr/src         144K   93.2G  144K   /usr/src
mypool/var             1.20M  93.2G  610K   /var
mypool/var/crash       148K   93.2G  148K   /var/crash
mypool/var/log         178K   93.2G  178K   /var/log
mypool/var/mail        144K   93.2G  144K   /var/mail
mypool/var/tmp         152K   93.2G  152K   /var/tmp
```

Destroying a dataset is much quicker than deleting all of the files that reside on the dataset, as it does not involve scanning all of the files and updating all of the corresponding metadata.

Destroy the previously-created dataset:

```
# zfs list
NAME                   USED  AVAIL  REFER  MOUNTPOINT
mypool                 880M  93.1G   144K  none
mypool/ROOT            777M  93.1G   144K  none
mypool/ROOT/default    777M  93.1G   777M  /
mypool/tmp             176K  93.1G   176K  /tmp
mypool/usr             101M  93.1G   144K  /usr
mypool/usr/home        184K  93.1G   184K  /usr/home
mypool/usr/mydataset   100M  93.1G   100M  /usr/mydataset
mypool/usr/ports       144K  93.1G   144K  /usr/ports
mypool/usr/src         144K  93.1G   144K  /usr/src
mypool/var            1.20M  93.1G   610K  /var
mypool/var/crash       148K  93.1G   148K  /var/crash
mypool/var/log         178K  93.1G   178K  /var/log
mypool/var/mail        144K  93.1G   144K  /var/mail
mypool/var/tmp         152K  93.1G   152K  /var/tmp
# zfs destroy mypool/usr/mydataset
# zfs list
NAME                   USED  AVAIL  REFER  MOUNTPOINT
mypool                 781M  93.2G   144K  none
mypool/ROOT            777M  93.2G   144K  none
mypool/ROOT/default    777M  93.2G   777M  /
mypool/tmp             176K  93.2G   176K  /tmp
mypool/usr             616K  93.2G   144K  /usr
mypool/usr/home        184K  93.2G   184K  /usr/home
mypool/usr/ports       144K  93.2G   144K  /usr/ports
mypool/usr/src         144K  93.2G   144K  /usr/src
mypool/var            1.21M  93.2G   612K  /var
mypool/var/crash       148K  93.2G   148K  /var/crash
mypool/var/log         178K  93.2G   178K  /var/log
mypool/var/mail        144K  93.2G   144K  /var/mail
mypool/var/tmp         152K  93.2G   152K  /var/tmp
```

In modern versions of ZFS, zfs destroy is asynchronous, and the free space might take several minutes to appear in the pool. Use zpool get freeing *poolname* to see the freeing property, indicating how many datasets are having their blocks freed in the background. If there are child datasets, like snapshots or other datasets, then the parent cannot be destroyed. To destroy a dataset and all of its children, use -r to recursively destroy the dataset and all of its children. Use -n -v to list datasets and snapshots that would be destroyed by this operation, but do not actually destroy anything. Space that would be reclaimed by destruction of snapshots is also shown.

19.4.2. Creating and Destroying Volumes

A volume is a special type of dataset. Rather than being mounted as a file system, it is exposed as a block device under /dev/zvol/ *poolname*/*dataset* . This allows the volume to be used for other file systems, to back the disks of a virtual machine, or to be exported using protocols like iSCSI or HAST.

A volume can be formatted with any file system, or used without a file system to store raw data. To the user, a volume appears to be a regular disk. Putting ordinary file systems on these *zvols* provides features that ordinary disks or file systems do not normally have. For example, using the compression property on a 250 MB volume allows creation of a compressed FAT file system.

```
# zfs create -V 250m -o compression=on tank/fat32
# zfs list tank
NAME USED AVAIL REFER MOUNTPOINT
tank 258M  670M   31K /tank
# newfs_msdos -F32 /dev/zvol/tank/fat32
# mount -t msdosfs /dev/zvol/tank/fat32 /mnt
# df -h /mnt | grep fat32
Filesystem             Size Used Avail Capacity Mounted on
/dev/zvol/tank/fat32 249M  24k  249M      0%   /mnt
# mount | grep fat32
/dev/zvol/tank/fat32 on /mnt (msdosfs, local)
```

Destroying a volume is much the same as destroying a regular file system dataset. The operation is nearly instantaneous, but it may take several minutes for the free space to be reclaimed in the background.

19.4.3. Renaming a Dataset

The name of a dataset can be changed with zfs rename. The parent of a dataset can also be changed with this command. Renaming a dataset to be under a different parent dataset will change the value of those properties that are inherited from the parent dataset. When a dataset is renamed, it is unmounted and then remounted in the new location (which is inherited from the new parent dataset). This behavior can be prevented with -u.

Rename a dataset and move it to be under a different parent dataset:

```
# zfs list
NAME                    USED   AVAIL  REFER  MOUNTPOINT
mypool                  780M   93.2G  144K   none
mypool/ROOT             777M   93.2G  144K   none
mypool/ROOT/default     777M   93.2G  777M   /
mypool/tmp              176K   93.2G  176K   /tmp
mypool/usr              704K   93.2G  144K   /usr
mypool/usr/home         184K   93.2G  184K   /usr/home
mypool/usr/mydataset    87.5K  93.2G  87.5K  /usr/mydataset
mypool/usr/ports        144K   93.2G  144K   /usr/ports
mypool/usr/src          144K   93.2G  144K   /usr/src
mypool/var              1.21M  93.2G  614K   /var
mypool/var/crash        148K   93.2G  148K   /var/crash
mypool/var/log          178K   93.2G  178K   /var/log
mypool/var/mail         144K   93.2G  144K   /var/mail
mypool/var/tmp          152K   93.2G  152K   /var/tmp
# zfs rename mypool/usr/mydataset  mypool/var/newname
# zfs list
NAME                    USED   AVAIL  REFER  MOUNTPOINT
mypool                  780M   93.2G  144K   none
mypool/ROOT             777M   93.2G  144K   none
mypool/ROOT/default     777M   93.2G  777M   /
mypool/tmp              176K   93.2G  176K   /tmp
mypool/usr              616K   93.2G  144K   /usr
mypool/usr/home         184K   93.2G  184K   /usr/home
mypool/usr/ports        144K   93.2G  144K   /usr/ports
mypool/usr/src          144K   93.2G  144K   /usr/src
mypool/var              1.29M  93.2G  614K   /var
mypool/var/crash        148K   93.2G  148K   /var/crash
mypool/var/log          178K   93.2G  178K   /var/log
mypool/var/mail         144K   93.2G  144K   /var/mail
mypool/var/newname      87.5K  93.2G  87.5K  /var/newname
mypool/var/tmp          152K   93.2G  152K   /var/tmp
```

Snapshots can also be renamed like this. Due to the nature of snapshots, they cannot be renamed into a different parent dataset. To rename a recursive snapshot, specify -r, and all snapshots with the same name in child datasets with also be renamed.

```
# zfs list -t snapshot
NAME                                     USED  AVAIL  REFER  MOUNTPOINT
mypool/var/newname@first_snapshot         0     -     87.5K  -
# zfs rename mypool/var/newname@first_snapshot  new_snapshot_name
# zfs list -t snapshot
NAME                                     USED  AVAIL  REFER  MOUNTPOINT
mypool/var/newname@new_snapshot_name      0     -     87.5K  -
```

19.4.4. Setting Dataset Properties

Each ZFS dataset has a number of properties that control its behavior. Most properties are automatically inherited from the parent dataset, but can be overridden locally. Set a property on a dataset with zfs set property=value dataset. Most properties have a limited set of valid values, zfs get will display each possible property and valid values. Most properties can be reverted to their inherited values using zfs inherit.

User-defined properties can also be set. They become part of the dataset configuration and can be used to provide additional information about the dataset or its contents. To distinguish these custom properties from the ones supplied as part of ZFS, a colon (:) is used to create a custom namespace for the property.

```
# zfs set custom:costcenter=1234 tank
# zfs get custom:costcenter tank
NAME PROPERTY           VALUE SOURCE
tank custom:costcenter  1234  local
```

To remove a custom property, use `zfs inherit` with `-r`. If the custom property is not defined in any of the parent datasets, it will be removed completely (although the changes are still recorded in the pool's history).

```
# zfs inherit -r custom:costcenter tank            -
# zfs get custom:costcenter tank
NAME     PROPERTY            VALUE              SOURCE
tank     custom:costcenter   -                  -
# zfs get all tank | grep custom:costcenter
#
```

19.4.4.1. Getting and Setting Share Properties

Two commonly used and useful dataset properties are the NFS and SMB share options. Setting these define if and how ZFS datasets may be shared on the network. At present, only setting sharing via NFS is supported on FreeBSD. To get the current status of a share, enter:

```
# zfs get sharenfs mypool/usr/home
NAME                PROPERTY  VALUE   SOURCE
mypool/usr/home     sharenfs  on      local
# zfs get sharesmb mypool/usr/home
NAME                PROPERTY  VALUE   SOURCE
mypool/usr/home     sharesmb  off     local
```

To enable sharing of a dataset, enter:

```
#  zfs set sharenfs=on  mypool/usr/home
```

It is also possible to set additional options for sharing datasets through NFS, such as `-alldirs`, `-maproot` and `-network`. To set additional options to a dataset shared through NFS, enter:

```
#  zfs set sharenfs="-alldirs,-maproot= root,-network= 192.168.1.0/24 " mypool/usr/home
```

19.4.5. Managing Snapshots

Snapshots are one of the most powerful features of ZFS. A snapshot provides a read-only, point-in-time copy of the dataset. With Copy-On-Write (COW), snapshots can be created quickly by preserving the older version of the data on disk. If no snapshots exist, space is reclaimed for future use when data is rewritten or deleted. Snapshots preserve disk space by recording only the differences between the current dataset and a previous version. Snapshots are allowed only on whole datasets, not on individual files or directories. When a snapshot is created from a dataset, everything contained in it is duplicated. This includes the file system properties, files, directories, permissions, and so on. Snapshots use no additional space when they are first created, only consuming space as the blocks they reference are changed. Recursive snapshots taken with `-r` create a snapshot with the same name on the dataset and all of its children, providing a consistent moment-in-time snapshot of all of the file systems. This can be important when an application has files on multiple datasets that are related or dependent upon each other. Without snapshots, a backup would have copies of the files from different points in time.

Snapshots in ZFS provide a variety of features that even other file systems with snapshot functionality lack. A typical example of snapshot use is to have a quick way of backing up the current state of the file system when a risky action like a software installation or a system upgrade is performed. If the action fails, the snapshot can be rolled back and the system has the same state as when the snapshot was created. If the upgrade was successful, the snapshot can be deleted to free up space. Without snapshots, a failed upgrade often requires a restore from backup, which is tedious, time consuming, and may require downtime during which the system cannot be used. Snapshots can be rolled back quickly, even while the system is running in normal operation, with little or no downtime. The time savings are enormous with multi-terabyte storage systems and the time required to copy the data from backup. Snapshots are not a replacement for a complete backup of a pool, but can be used as a quick and easy way to store a copy of the dataset at a specific point in time.

19.4.5.1. Creating Snapshots

Snapshots are created with `zfs snapshot` *dataset @snapshotname*. Adding `-r` creates a snapshot recursively, with the same name on all child datasets.

Create a recursive snapshot of the entire pool:

```
# zfs list -t all
NAME                                    USED   AVAIL  REFER  MOUNTPOINT
mypool                                  780M   93.2G  144K   none
mypool/ROOT                             777M   93.2G  144K   none
mypool/ROOT/default                     777M   93.2G  777M   /
mypool/tmp                              176K   93.2G  176K   /tmp
mypool/usr                              616K   93.2G  144K   /usr
mypool/usr/home                         184K   93.2G  184K   /usr/home
mypool/usr/ports                        144K   93.2G  144K   /usr/ports
mypool/usr/src                          144K   93.2G  144K   /usr/src
mypool/var                              1.29M  93.2G  616K   /var
mypool/var/crash                        148K   93.2G  148K   /var/crash
mypool/var/log                          178K   93.2G  178K   /var/log
mypool/var/mail                         144K   93.2G  144K   /var/mail
mypool/var/newname                      87.5K  93.2G  87.5K  /var/newname
mypool/var/newname@new_snapshot_name    0      -      87.5K  -
mypool/var/tmp                          152K   93.2G  152K   /var/tmp
# zfs snapshot -r mypool@my_recursive_snapshot
# zfs list -t snapshot
NAME                                        USED  AVAIL  REFER  MOUNTPOINT
mypool@my_recursive_snapshot                0     -      144K   -
mypool/ROOT@my_recursive_snapshot           0     -      144K   -
mypool/ROOT/default@my_recursive_snapshot   0     -      777M   -
mypool/tmp@my_recursive_snapshot            0     -      176K   -
mypool/usr@my_recursive_snapshot            0     -      144K   -
mypool/usr/home@my_recursive_snapshot       0     -      184K   -
mypool/usr/ports@my_recursive_snapshot      0     -      144K   -
mypool/usr/src@my_recursive_snapshot        0     -      144K   -
mypool/var@my_recursive_snapshot            0     -      616K   -
mypool/var/crash@my_recursive_snapshot      0     -      148K   -
mypool/var/log@my_recursive_snapshot        0     -      178K   -
mypool/var/mail@my_recursive_snapshot       0     -      144K   -
mypool/var/newname@new_snapshot_name        0     -      87.5K  -
mypool/var/newname@my_recursive_snapshot    0     -      87.5K  -
mypool/var/tmp@my_recursive_snapshot        0     -      152K   -
```

Snapshots are not shown by a normal `zfs list` operation. To list snapshots, `-t snapshot` is appended to `zfs list`. `-t all` displays both file systems and snapshots.

Snapshots are not mounted directly, so path is shown in the MOUNTPOINT column. There is no mention of available disk space in the AVAIL column, as snapshots cannot be written to after they are created. Compare the snapshot to the original dataset from which it was created:

```
# zfs list -rt all mypool/usr/home
NAME                                   USED   AVAIL  REFER  MOUNTPOINT
mypool/usr/home                        184K   93.2G  184K   /usr/home
mypool/usr/home@my_recursive_snapshot  0      -      184K   -
```

Displaying both the dataset and the snapshot together reveals how snapshots work in COW fashion. They save only the changes (*delta*) that were made and not the complete file system contents all over again. This means that snapshots take little space when few changes are made. Space usage can be made even more apparent by copying a file to the dataset, then making a second snapshot:

```
# cp /etc/passwd /var/tmp
# zfs snapshot mypool/var/tmp @after_cp
# zfs list -rt all mypool/var/tmp
NAME                                   USED  AVAIL  REFER  MOUNTPOINT
mypool/var/tmp                         206K  93.2G  118K   /var/tmp
mypool/var/tmp@my_recursive_snapshot    88K      -  152K   -
mypool/var/tmp@after_cp                   0      -  118K   -
```

The second snapshot contains only the changes to the dataset after the copy operation. This yields enormous space savings. Notice that the size of the snapshot *mypool/var/tmp@my_recursive_snapshot* also changed in the USED column to indicate the changes between itself and the snapshot taken afterwards.

19.4.5.2. Comparing Snapshots

ZFS provides a built-in command to compare the differences in content between two snapshots. This is helpful when many snapshots were taken over time and the user wants to see how the file system has changed over time. For example, `zfs diff` lets a user find the latest snapshot that still contains a file that was accidentally deleted. Doing this for the two snapshots that were created in the previous section yields this output:

```
# zfs list -rt all mypool/var/tmp
NAME                                   USED  AVAIL  REFER  MOUNTPOINT
mypool/var/tmp                         206K  93.2G  118K   /var/tmp
mypool/var/tmp@my_recursive_snapshot    88K      -  152K   -
mypool/var/tmp@after_cp                   0      -  118K   -
# zfs diff mypool/var/tmp@my_recursive_snapshot
M       /var/tmp/
+          /var/tmp/passwd
```

The command lists the changes between the specified snapshot (in this case *mypool/var/tmp@my_recursive_snapshot*) and the live file system. The first column shows the type of change:

+	The path or file was added.
-	The path or file was deleted.
M	The path or file was modified.
R	The path or file was renamed.

Comparing the output with the table, it becomes clear that *passwd* was added after the snapshot *mypool/var/tmp@my_recursive_snapshot* was created. This also resulted in a modification to the parent directory mounted at */var/tmp*.

Comparing two snapshots is helpful when using the ZFS replication feature to transfer a dataset to a different host for backup purposes.

Compare two snapshots by providing the full dataset name and snapshot name of both datasets:

```
# cp /var/tmp/passwd /var/tmp/passwd.copy
# zfs snapshot mypool/var/tmp@diff_snapshot
# zfs diff mypool/var/tmp@my_recursive_snapshot    mypool/var/tmp@diff_snapshot
M       /var/tmp/
+          /var/tmp/passwd
+          /var/tmp/passwd.copy
# zfs diff mypool/var/tmp@my_recursive_snapshot    mypool/var/tmp@after_cp
M       /var/tmp/
+          /var/tmp/passwd
```

A backup administrator can compare two snapshots received from the sending host and determine the actual changes in the dataset. See the Replication section for more information.

19.4.5.3. Snapshot Rollback

When at least one snapshot is available, it can be rolled back to at any time. Most of the time this is the case when the current state of the dataset is no longer required and an older version is preferred. Scenarios such as local development tests have gone wrong, botched system updates hampering the system's overall functionality, or the requirement to restore accidentally deleted files or directories are all too common occurrences. Luckily, rolling back a snapshot is just as easy as typing zfs rollback *snapshotname*. Depending on how many changes are involved, the operation will finish in a certain amount of time. During that time, the dataset always remains in a consistent state, much like a database that conforms to ACID principles is performing a rollback. This is happening while the dataset is live and accessible without requiring a downtime. Once the snapshot has been rolled back, the dataset has the same state as it had when the snapshot was originally taken. All other data in that dataset that was not part of the snapshot is discarded. Taking a snapshot of the current state of the dataset before rolling back to a previous one is a good idea when some data is required later. This way, the user can roll back and forth between snapshots without losing data that is still valuable.

In the first example, a snapshot is rolled back because of a careless rm operation that removes too much data than was intended.

```
# zfs list -rt all mypool/var/tmp
NAME                                      USED   AVAIL  REFER  MOUNTPOINT
mypool/var/tmp                            262K   93.2G  120K   /var/tmp
mypool/var/tmp@my_recursive_snapshot      88K    -      152K   -
mypool/var/tmp@after_cp                   53.5K  -      118K   -
mypool/var/tmp@diff_snapshot              0      -      120K   -
# ls /var/tmp
passwd          passwd.copy     vi.recover
# rm /var/tmp/passwd*
# ls /var/tmp
vi.recover
```

At this point, the user realized that too many files were deleted and wants them back. ZFS provides an easy way to get them back using rollbacks, but only when snapshots of important data are performed on a regular basis. To get the files back and start over from the last snapshot, issue the command:

```
# zfs rollback mypool/var/tmp@diff_snapshot
# ls /var/tmp
passwd          passwd.copy     vi.recover
```

The rollback operation restored the dataset to the state of the last snapshot. It is also possible to roll back to a snapshot that was taken much earlier and has other snapshots that were created after it. When trying to do this, ZFS will issue this warning:

```
# zfs list -rt snapshot mypool/var/tmp
AME                                    USED   AVAIL  REFER  MOUNTPOINT
mypool/var/tmp@my_recursive_snapshot   88K    -      152K   -
mypool/var/tmp@after_cp                53.5K  -      118K   -
mypool/var/tmp@diff_snapshot           0      -      120K   -
# zfs rollback mypool/var/tmp@my_recursive_snapshot
cannot rollback to 'mypool/var/tmp@my_recursive_snapshot': more recent snapshots exist
use '-r' to force deletion of the following snapshots:
mypool/var/tmp@after_cp
mypool/var/tmp@diff_snapshot
```

This warning means that snapshots exist between the current state of the dataset and the snapshot to which the user wants to roll back. To complete the rollback, these snapshots must be deleted. ZFS cannot track all the changes between different states of the dataset, because snapshots are read-only. ZFS will not delete the affected snapshots unless the user specifies -r to indicate that this is the desired action. If that is the intention, and the consequences of losing all intermediate snapshots is understood, the command can be issued:

```
# zfs rollback -r mypool/var/tmp@my_recursive_snapshot
# zfs list -rt snapshot mypool/var/tmp
NAME                                    USED   AVAIL  REFER  MOUNTPOINT
```

```
mypool/var/tmp@my_recursive_snapshot      8K        -    152K  -
# ls /var/tmp
vi.recover
```

The output from `zfs list -t snapshot` confirms that the intermediate snapshots were removed as a result of `zfs rollback -r`.

19.4.5.4. Restoring Individual Files from Snapshots

Snapshots are mounted in a hidden directory under the parent dataset: `.zfs/snapshots/` *snapshotname*. By default, these directories will not be displayed even when a standard `ls -a` is issued. Although the directory is not displayed, it is there nevertheless and can be accessed like any normal directory. The property named `snapdir` controls whether these hidden directories show up in a directory listing. Setting the property to `visible` allows them to appear in the output of `ls` and other commands that deal with directory contents.

```
# zfs get snapdir mypool/var/tmp
NAME             PROPERTY  VALUE     SOURCE
mypool/var/tmp   snapdir   hidden    default
# ls -a /var/tmp
.                ..                  passwd          vi.recover
# zfs set snapdir=visible mypool/var/tmp
# ls -a /var/tmp
.                ..                  .zfs       passwd       vi.recover
```

Individual files can easily be restored to a previous state by copying them from the snapshot back to the parent dataset. The directory structure below `.zfs/snapshot` has a directory named exactly like the snapshots taken earlier to make it easier to identify them. In the next example, it is assumed that a file is to be restored from the hidden `.zfs` directory by copying it from the snapshot that contained the latest version of the file:

```
# rm /var/tmp/passwd
# ls -a /var/tmp
.                ..                  .zfs            vi.recover
# ls /var/tmp/.zfs/snapshot
after_cp                my_recursive_snapshot
# ls /var/tmp/.zfs/snapshot/ after_cp
passwd          vi.recover
# cp /var/tmp/.zfs/snapshot/ after_cp/passwd /var/tmp
```

When `ls .zfs/snapshot` was issued, the `snapdir` property might have been set to hidden, but it would still be possible to list the contents of that directory. It is up to the administrator to decide whether these directories will be displayed. It is possible to display these for certain datasets and prevent it for others. Copying files or directories from this hidden `.zfs/snapshot` is simple enough. Trying it the other way around results in this error:

```
# cp /etc/rc.conf /var/tmp/.zfs/snapshot/ after_cp/
cp: /var/tmp/.zfs/snapshot/after_cp/rc.conf: Read-only file system
```

The error reminds the user that snapshots are read-only and cannot be changed after creation. Files cannot be copied into or removed from snapshot directories because that would change the state of the dataset they represent.

Snapshots consume space based on how much the parent file system has changed since the time of the snapshot. The `written` property of a snapshot tracks how much space is being used by the snapshot.

Snapshots are destroyed and the space reclaimed with `zfs destroy` *dataset*@*snapshot*. Adding `-r` recursively removes all snapshots with the same name under the parent dataset. Adding `-n -v` to the command displays a list of the snapshots that would be deleted and an estimate of how much space would be reclaimed without performing the actual destroy operation.

19.4.6. Managing Clones

A clone is a copy of a snapshot that is treated more like a regular dataset. Unlike a snapshot, a clone is not read only, is mounted, and can have its own properties. Once a clone has been created using `zfs clone`, the snapshot it was created from cannot be destroyed. The child/parent relationship between the clone and the snapshot can be reversed using `zfs promote`. After a clone has been promoted, the snapshot becomes a child of the clone, rather than of the original parent dataset. This will change how the space is accounted, but not actually change the amount of space consumed. The clone can be mounted at any point within the ZFS file system hierarchy, not just below the original location of the snapshot.

To demonstrate the clone feature, this example dataset is used:

```
# zfs list -rt all camino/home/joe
NAME                      USED   AVAIL   REFER  MOUNTPOINT
camino/home/joe           108K   1.3G     87K  /usr/home/joe
camino/home/joe@plans      21K      -   85.5K  -
camino/home/joe@backup      0K      -     87K  -
```

A typical use for clones is to experiment with a specific dataset while keeping the snapshot around to fall back to in case something goes wrong. Since snapshots cannot be changed, a read/write clone of a snapshot is created. After the desired result is achieved in the clone, the clone can be promoted to a dataset and the old file system removed. This is not strictly necessary, as the clone and dataset can coexist without problems.

```
# zfs clone camino/home/joe @backup camino/home/joenew
# ls /usr/home/joe*
/usr/home/joe:
backup.txz       plans.txt

/usr/home/joenew:
backup.txz       plans.txt
# df -h /usr/home
Filesystem          Size   Used   Avail Capacity   Mounted on
usr/home/joe        1.3G    31k    1.3G       0%    /usr/home/joe
usr/home/joenew     1.3G    31k    1.3G       0%    /usr/home/joenew
```

After a clone is created it is an exact copy of the state the dataset was in when the snapshot was taken. The clone can now be changed independently from its originating dataset. The only connection between the two is the snapshot. ZFS records this connection in the property `origin`. Once the dependency between the snapshot and the clone has been removed by promoting the clone using `zfs promote`, the `origin` of the clone is removed as it is now an independent dataset. This example demonstrates it:

```
# zfs get origin camino/home/joenew
NAME                  PROPERTY  VALUE                     SOURCE
camino/home/joenew    origin    camino/home/joe@backup    -
# zfs promote camino/home/joenew
# zfs get origin camino/home/joenew
NAME                  PROPERTY  VALUE   SOURCE
camino/home/joenew    origin    -       -
```

After making some changes like copying `loader.conf` to the promoted clone, for example, the old directory becomes obsolete in this case. Instead, the promoted clone can replace it. This can be achieved by two consecutive commands: `zfs destroy` on the old dataset and `zfs rename` on the clone to name it like the old dataset (it could also get an entirely different name).

```
# cp /boot/defaults/loader.conf   /usr/home/joenew
# zfs destroy -f camino/home/joe
# zfs rename camino/home/joenew camino/home/joe
# ls /usr/home/joe
backup.txz       loader.conf       plans.txt
# df -h /usr/home
Filesystem          Size   Used   Avail Capacity   Mounted on
usr/home/joe        1.3G   128k    1.3G       0%    /usr/home/joe
```

The cloned snapshot is now handled like an ordinary dataset. It contains all the data from the original snapshot plus the files that were added to it like `loader.conf`. Clones can be used in different scenarios to provide useful features to ZFS users. For example, jails could be provided as snapshots containing different sets of installed applications. Users can clone these snapshots and add their own applications as they see fit. Once they are satisfied with the changes, the clones can be promoted to full datasets and provided to end users to work with like they would with a real dataset. This saves time and administrative overhead when providing these jails.

19.4.7. Replication

Keeping data on a single pool in one location exposes it to risks like theft and natural or human disasters. Making regular backups of the entire pool is vital. ZFS provides a built-in serialization feature that can send a stream representation of the data to standard output. Using this technique, it is possible to not only store the data on another pool connected to the local system, but also to send it over a network to another system. Snapshots are the basis for this replication (see the section on ZFS snapshots). The commands used for replicating data are `zfs send` and `zfs receive`.

These examples demonstrate ZFS replication with these two pools:

```
# zpool list
NAME     SIZE   ALLOC  FREE   CAP  DEDUP  HEALTH  ALTROOT
backup   960M   77K    896M   0%   1.00x  ONLINE  -
mypool   984M   43.7M  940M   4%   1.00x  ONLINE  -
```

The pool named *mypool* is the primary pool where data is written to and read from on a regular basis. A second pool, *backup* is used as a standby in case the primary pool becomes unavailable. Note that this fail-over is not done automatically by ZFS, but must be manually done by a system administrator when needed. A snapshot is used to provide a consistent version of the file system to be replicated. Once a snapshot of *mypool* has been created, it can be copied to the *backup* pool. Only snapshots can be replicated. Changes made since the most recent snapshot will not be included.

```
# zfs snapshot mypool@backup1
# zfs list -t snapshot
NAME             USED  AVAIL  REFER  MOUNTPOINT
mypool@backup1   0     -      43.6M  -
```

Now that a snapshot exists, `zfs send` can be used to create a stream representing the contents of the snapshot. This stream can be stored as a file or received by another pool. The stream is written to standard output, but must be redirected to a file or pipe or an error is produced:

```
# zfs send mypool@backup1
Error: Stream can not be written to a terminal.
You must redirect standard output.
```

To back up a dataset with `zfs send`, redirect to a file located on the mounted backup pool. Ensure that the pool has enough free space to accommodate the size of the snapshot being sent, which means all of the data contained in the snapshot, not just the changes from the previous snapshot.

```
# zfs send mypool@backup1 > /backup/backup1
# zpool list
NAME     SIZE   ALLOC  FREE   CAP  DEDUP  HEALTH  ALTROOT
backup   960M   63.7M  896M   6%   1.00x  ONLINE  -
mypool   984M   43.7M  940M   4%   1.00x  ONLINE  -
```

The `zfs send` transferred all the data in the snapshot called *backup1* to the pool named *backup*. Creating and sending these snapshots can be done automatically with a cron(8) job.

Instead of storing the backups as archive files, ZFS can receive them as a live file system, allowing the backed up data to be accessed directly. To get to the actual data contained in those streams, `zfs receive` is used to transform the streams back into files and directories. The example below combines `zfs send` and `zfs receive` using a pipe to copy the data from one pool to another. The data can be used directly on the receiving pool after the transfer is complete. A dataset can only be replicated to an empty dataset.

```
# zfs snapshot mypool@replica1
# zfs send -v mypool@replica1 | zfs receive backup/mypool
send from @ to mypool@replica1 estimated size is 50.1M
total estimated size is 50.1M
```

```
TIME        SENT    SNAPSHOT

# zpool list
NAME     SIZE   ALLOC   FREE    CAP  DEDUP  HEALTH  ALTROOT
backup   960M   63.7M   896M    6%   1.00x  ONLINE  -
mypool   984M   43.7M   940M    4%   1.00x  ONLINE  -
```

19.4.7.1. Incremental Backups

zfs send can also determine the difference between two snapshots and send only the differences between the two. This saves disk space and transfer time. For example:

```
# zfs snapshot mypool@replica2
# zfs list -t snapshot
NAME                   USED   AVAIL  REFER  MOUNTPOINT
mypool@replica1        5.72M     -   43.6M  -
mypool@replica2           0     -   44.1M  -
# zpool list
NAME     SIZE   ALLOC   FREE    CAP  DEDUP  HEALTH  ALTROOT
backup   960M   61.7M   898M    6%   1.00x  ONLINE  -
mypool   960M   50.2M   910M    5%   1.00x  ONLINE  -
```

A second snapshot called *replica2* was created. This second snapshot contains only the changes that were made to the file system between now and the previous snapshot, *replica1*. Using zfs send -i and indicating the pair of snapshots generates an incremental replica stream containing only the data that has changed. This can only succeed if the initial snapshot already exists on the receiving side.

```
# zfs send -v -i mypool@replica1 mypool@replica2 | zfs receive /backup/mypool
send from @replica1 to mypool@replica2 estimated size is 5.02M
total estimated size is 5.02M
TIME        SENT    SNAPSHOT

# zpool list
NAME     SIZE   ALLOC   FREE    CAP  DEDUP  HEALTH  ALTROOT
backup   960M   80.8M   879M    8%   1.00x  ONLINE  -
mypool   960M   50.2M   910M    5%   1.00x  ONLINE  -

# zfs list
NAME                   USED   AVAIL  REFER  MOUNTPOINT
backup                 55.4M   240G   152K  /backup
backup/mypool          55.3M   240G  55.2M  /backup/mypool
mypool                 55.6M  11.6G  55.0M  /mypool

# zfs list -t snapshot
NAME                            USED   AVAIL  REFER  MOUNTPOINT
backup/mypool@replica1          104K      -   50.2M  -
backup/mypool@replica2             0      -   55.2M  -
mypool@replica1                29.9K      -   50.0M  -
mypool@replica2                    0      -   55.0M  -
```

The incremental stream was successfully transferred. Only the data that had changed was replicated, rather than the entirety of *replica1*. Only the differences were sent, which took much less time to transfer and saved disk space by not copying the complete pool each time. This is useful when having to rely on slow networks or when costs per transferred byte must be considered.

A new file system, *backup/mypool*, is available with all of the files and data from the pool *mypool*. If -P is specified, the properties of the dataset will be copied, including compression settings, quotas, and mount points. When -R is specified, all child datasets of the indicated dataset will be copied, along with all of their properties. Sending and receiving can be automated so that regular backups are created on the second pool.

19.4.7.2. Sending Encrypted Backups over SSH

Sending streams over the network is a good way to keep a remote backup, but it does come with a drawback. Data sent over the network link is not encrypted, allowing anyone to intercept and transform the streams back into data without the knowledge of the sending user. This is undesirable, especially when sending the streams over the internet to a remote host. SSH can be used to securely encrypt data send over a network connection. Since ZFS only requires the stream to be redirected from standard output, it is relatively easy to pipe it through SSH. To keep the contents of the file system encrypted in transit and on the remote system, consider using PEFS.

A few settings and security precautions must be completed first. Only the necessary steps required for the `zfs send` operation are shown here. For more information on SSH, see Section 13.8, "OpenSSH".

This configuration is required:

- Passwordless SSH access between sending and receiving host using SSH keys

- Normally, the privileges of the `root` user are needed to send and receive streams. This requires logging in to the receiving system as `root`. However, logging in as `root` is disabled by default for security reasons. The ZFS Delegation system can be used to allow a non-`root` user on each system to perform the respective send and receive operations.

- On the sending system:

  ```
  # zfs allow -u someuser send,snapshot   mypool
  ```

- To mount the pool, the unprivileged user must own the directory, and regular users must be allowed to mount file systems. On the receiving system:

  ```
  # sysctl vfs.usermount=1
  vfs.usermount: 0 -> 1
  # sysrc -f /etc/sysctl.conf vfs.usermount=1
  # zfs create recvpool/backup
  # zfs allow -u someuser create,mount,receive   recvpool/backup
  # chown someuser /recvpool/backup
  ```

The unprivileged user now has the ability to receive and mount datasets, and the *home* dataset can be replicated to the remote system:

```
% zfs snapshot -r mypool/home @monday
% zfs send -R mypool/home @monday | ssh someuser@backuphost   zfs recv -dvu recvpool/backup
```

A recursive snapshot called *monday* is made of the file system dataset *home* that resides on the pool *mypool*. Then it is sent with `zfs send -R` to include the dataset, all child datasets, snapshots, clones, and settings in the stream. The output is piped to the waiting `zfs receive` on the remote host *backuphost* through SSH. Using a fully qualified domain name or IP address is recommended. The receiving machine writes the data to the *backup* dataset on the *recvpool* pool. Adding -d to `zfs recv` overwrites the name of the pool on the receiving side with the name of the snapshot. -u causes the file systems to not be mounted on the receiving side. When -v is included, more detail about the transfer is shown, including elapsed time and the amount of data transferred.

19.4.8. Dataset, User, and Group Quotas

Dataset quotas are used to restrict the amount of space that can be consumed by a particular dataset. Reference Quotas work in very much the same way, but only count the space used by the dataset itself, excluding snapshots and child datasets. Similarly, user and group quotas can be used to prevent users or groups from using all of the space in the pool or dataset.

To enforce a dataset quota of 10 GB for `storage/home/bob`:

```
# zfs set quota=10G storage/home/bob
```

To enforce a reference quota of 10 GB for `storage/home/bob`:

```
# zfs set refquota=10G storage/home/bob
```

To remove a quota of 10 GB for `storage/home/bob`:

```
# zfs set quota=none storage/home/bob
```

The general format is userquota@*user*=*size*, and the user's name must be in one of these formats:

- POSIX compatible name such as *joe*.

- POSIX numeric ID such as *789*.

- SID name such as *joe.bloggs@example.com*.

- SID numeric ID such as *S-1-123-456-789* .

For example, to enforce a user quota of 50 GB for the user named *joe*:

```
# zfs set userquota@joe=50G
```

To remove any quota:

```
# zfs set userquota@joe=none
```

 Note

User quota properties are not displayed by zfs get all. Non-root users can only see their own quotas unless they have been granted the userquota privilege. Users with this privilege are able to view and set everyone's quota.

The general format for setting a group quota is: groupquota@*group*=*size*.

To set the quota for the group *firstgroup* to 50 GB, use:

```
# zfs set groupquota@firstgroup=50G
```

To remove the quota for the group *firstgroup*, or to make sure that one is not set, instead use:

```
# zfs set groupquota@firstgroup=none
```

As with the user quota property, non-root users can only see the quotas associated with the groups to which they belong. However, root or a user with the groupquota privilege can view and set all quotas for all groups.

To display the amount of space used by each user on a file system or snapshot along with any quotas, use zfs userspace. For group information, use zfs groupspace. For more information about supported options or how to display only specific options, refer to zfs(1).

Users with sufficient privileges, and root, can list the quota for storage/home/bob using:

```
# zfs get quota storage/home/bob
```

19.4.9. Reservations

Reservations guarantee a minimum amount of space will always be available on a dataset. The reserved space will not be available to any other dataset. This feature can be especially useful to ensure that free space is available for an important dataset or log files.

The general format of the reservation property is reservation=*size*, so to set a reservation of 10 GB on storage/home/bob , use:

```
# zfs set reservation=10G storage/home/bob
```

To clear any reservation:

```
# zfs set reservation=none storage/home/bob
```

The same principle can be applied to the `refreservation` property for setting a Reference Reservation, with the general format `refreservation=size`.

This command shows any reservations or refreservations that exist on `storage/home/bob` :

```
# zfs get reservation storage/home/bob
# zfs get refreservation storage/home/bob
```

19.4.10. Compression

ZFS provides transparent compression. Compressing data at the block level as it is written not only saves space, but can also increase disk throughput. If data is compressed by 25%, but the compressed data is written to the disk at the same rate as the uncompressed version, resulting in an effective write speed of 125%. Compression can also be a great alternative to Deduplication because it does not require additional memory.

ZFS offers several different compression algorithms, each with different trade-offs. With the introduction of LZ4 compression in ZFS v5000, it is possible to enable compression for the entire pool without the large performance trade-off of other algorithms. The biggest advantage to LZ4 is the *early abort* feature. If LZ4 does not achieve at least 12.5% compression in the first part of the data, the block is written uncompressed to avoid wasting CPU cycles trying to compress data that is either already compressed or uncompressible. For details about the different compression algorithms available in ZFS, see the Compression entry in the terminology section.

The administrator can monitor the effectiveness of compression using a number of dataset properties.

```
# zfs get used,compressratio,compression,logicalused   mypool/compressed_dataset
NAME              PROPERTY        VALUE      SOURCE
mypool/compressed_dataset   used            449G       -
mypool/compressed_dataset   compressratio   1.11x      -
mypool/compressed_dataset   compression     lz4        local
mypool/compressed_dataset   logicalused     496G       -
```

The dataset is currently using 449 GB of space (the used property). Without compression, it would have taken 496 GB of space (the `logicalused` property). This results in the 1.11:1 compression ratio.

Compression can have an unexpected side effect when combined with User Quotas. User quotas restrict how much space a user can consume on a dataset, but the measurements are based on how much space is used *after compression*. So if a user has a quota of 10 GB, and writes 10 GB of compressible data, they will still be able to store additional data. If they later update a file, say a database, with more or less compressible data, the amount of space available to them will change. This can result in the odd situation where a user did not increase the actual amount of data (the `logicalused` property), but the change in compression caused them to reach their quota limit.

Compression can have a similar unexpected interaction with backups. Quotas are often used to limit how much data can be stored to ensure there is sufficient backup space available. However since quotas do not consider compression, more data may be written than would fit with uncompressed backups.

19.4.11. Deduplication

When enabled, deduplication uses the checksum of each block to detect duplicate blocks. When a new block is a duplicate of an existing block, ZFS writes an additional reference to the existing data instead of the whole duplicate block. Tremendous space savings are possible if the data contains many duplicated files or repeated information. Be warned: deduplication requires an extremely large amount of memory, and most of the space savings can be had without the extra cost by enabling compression instead.

To activate deduplication, set the `dedup` property on the target pool:

```
# zfs set dedup=on  pool
```

Only new data being written to the pool will be deduplicated. Data that has already been written to the pool will not be deduplicated merely by activating this option. A pool with a freshly activated deduplication property will look like this example:

```
# zpool list
NAME  SIZE ALLOC  FREE CAP DEDUP HEALTH ALTROOT
pool 2.84G 2.19M 2.83G  0% 1.00x ONLINE -
```

The DEDUP column shows the actual rate of deduplication for the pool. A value of 1.00x shows that data has not been deduplicated yet. In the next example, the ports tree is copied three times into different directories on the deduplicated pool created above.

```
# for d in dir1 dir2 dir3; do
> mkdir $d && cp -R /usr/ports $d &
> done
```

Redundant data is detected and deduplicated:

```
# zpool list
NAME SIZE  ALLOC FREE CAP DEDUP HEALTH ALTROOT
pool 2.84G 20.9M 2.82G 0% 3.00x ONLINE -
```

The DEDUP column shows a factor of 3.00x. Multiple copies of the ports tree data was detected and deduplicated, using only a third of the space. The potential for space savings can be enormous, but comes at the cost of having enough memory to keep track of the deduplicated blocks.

Deduplication is not always beneficial, especially when the data on a pool is not redundant. ZFS can show potential space savings by simulating deduplication on an existing pool:

```
# zdb -S pool
Simulated DDT histogram:

bucket              allocated                       referenced
------   ------------------------------   ------------------------------
refcnt   blocks   LSIZE   PSIZE   DSIZE   blocks   LSIZE   PSIZE   DSIZE
------   ------   -----   -----   -----   ------   -----   -----   -----
     1   2.58M    289G    264G    264G    2.58M    289G    264G    264G
     2    206K   12.6G   10.4G   10.4G     430K   26.4G   21.6G   21.6G
     4   37.6K    692M    276M    276M     170K   3.04G   1.26G   1.26G
     8   2.18K   45.2M   19.4M   19.4M    20.0K    425M    176M    176M
    16     174   2.83M   1.20M   1.20M    3.33K   48.4M   20.4M   20.4M
    32      40   2.17M    222K    222K    1.70K   97.2M   9.91M   9.91M
    64       9     56K   10.5K   10.5K      865   4.96M    948K    948K
   128       2   9.50K      2K      2K      419   2.11M    438K    438K
   256       5   61.5K     12K     12K    1.90K   23.0M   4.47M   4.47M
    1K       2      1K      1K      1K    2.98K   1.49M   1.49M   1.49M
 Total   2.82M    303G    275G    275G    3.20M    319G    287G    287G

dedup = 1.05, compress = 1.11, copies = 1.00, dedup * compress / copies = 1.16
```

After zdb -S finishes analyzing the pool, it shows the space reduction ratio that would be achieved by activating deduplication. In this case, 1.16 is a very poor space saving ratio that is mostly provided by compression. Activating deduplication on this pool would not save any significant amount of space, and is not worth the amount of memory required to enable deduplication. Using the formula *ratio = dedup * compress / copies*, system administrators can plan the storage allocation, deciding whether the workload will contain enough duplicate blocks to justify the memory requirements. If the data is reasonably compressible, the space savings may be very good. Enabling compression first is recommended, and compression can also provide greatly increased performance. Only enable deduplication in cases where the additional savings will be considerable and there is sufficient memory for the DDT.

19.4.12. ZFS and Jails

zfs jail and the corresponding jailed property are used to delegate a ZFS dataset to a Jail. zfs jail *jailid* attaches a dataset to the specified jail, and zfs unjail detaches it. For the dataset to be controlled from within a jail, the jailed property must be set. Once a dataset is jailed, it can no longer be mounted on the host because it may have mount points that would compromise the security of the host.

19.5. Delegated Administration

A comprehensive permission delegation system allows unprivileged users to perform ZFS administration functions. For example, if each user's home directory is a dataset, users can be given permission to create and destroy snapshots of their home directories. A backup user can be given permission to use replication features. A usage statistics script can be allowed to run with access only to the space utilization data for all users. It is even possible to delegate the ability to delegate permissions. Permission delegation is possible for each subcommand and most properties.

19.5.1. Delegating Dataset Creation

`zfs allow` *someuser* `create` *mydataset* gives the specified user permission to create child datasets under the selected parent dataset. There is a caveat: creating a new dataset involves mounting it. That requires setting the FreeBSD `vfs.usermount` sysctl(8) to 1 to allow non-root users to mount a file system. There is another restriction aimed at preventing abuse: non-root users must own the mountpoint where the file system is to be mounted.

19.5.2. Delegating Permission Delegation

`zfs allow` *someuser* `allow` *mydataset* gives the specified user the ability to assign any permission they have on the target dataset, or its children, to other users. If a user has the `snapshot` permission and the `allow` permission, that user can then grant the `snapshot` permission to other users.

19.6. Advanced Topics

19.6.1. Tuning

There are a number of tunables that can be adjusted to make ZFS perform best for different workloads.

- *vfs.zfs.arc_max* - Maximum size of the ARC. The default is all RAM less 1 GB, or one half of RAM, whichever is more. However, a lower value should be used if the system will be running any other daemons or processes that may require memory. This value can only be adjusted at boot time, and is set in `/boot/loader.conf` .

- *vfs.zfs.arc_meta_limit* - Limit the portion of the ARC that can be used to store metadata. The default is one fourth of `vfs.zfs.arc_max`. Increasing this value will improve performance if the workload involves operations on a large number of files and directories, or frequent metadata operations, at the cost of less file data fitting in the ARC. This value can only be adjusted at boot time, and is set in `/boot/loader.conf` .

- *vfs.zfs.arc_min* - Minimum size of the ARC. The default is one half of `vfs.zfs.arc_meta_limit`. Adjust this value to prevent other applications from pressuring out the entire ARC. This value can only be adjusted at boot time, and is set in `/boot/loader.conf` .

- *vfs.zfs.vdev.cache.size* - A preallocated amount of memory reserved as a cache for each device in the pool. The total amount of memory used will be this value multiplied by the number of devices. This value can only be adjusted at boot time, and is set in `/boot/loader.conf` .

- *vfs.zfs.min_auto_ashift* - Minimum `ashift` (sector size) that will be used automatically at pool creation time. The value is a power of two. The default value of 9 represents $2^9 = 512$, a sector size of 512 bytes. To avoid *write amplification* and get the best performance, set this value to the largest sector size used by a device in the pool.

  Many drives have 4 KB sectors. Using the default `ashift` of 9 with these drives results in write amplification on these devices. Data that could be contained in a single 4 KB write must instead be written in eight 512-byte writes. ZFS tries to read the native sector size from all devices when creating a pool, but many drives with 4 KB sectors report that their sectors are 512 bytes for compatibility. Setting `vfs.zfs.min_auto_ashift` to 12 (2^{12} = 4096) before creating a pool forces ZFS to use 4 KB blocks for best performance on these drives.

  Forcing 4 KB blocks is also useful on pools where disk upgrades are planned. Future disks are likely to use 4 KB sectors, and `ashift` values cannot be changed after a pool is created.

In some specific cases, the smaller 512-byte block size might be preferable. When used with 512-byte disks for databases, or as storage for virtual machines, less data is transferred during small random reads. This can provide better performance, especially when using a smaller ZFS record size.

• *vfs.zfs.prefetch_disable* - Disable prefetch. A value of 0 is enabled and 1 is disabled. The default is 0, unless the system has less than 4 GB of RAM. Prefetch works by reading larger blocks than were requested into the ARC in hopes that the data will be needed soon. If the workload has a large number of random reads, disabling prefetch may actually improve performance by reducing unnecessary reads. This value can be adjusted at any time with sysctl(8).

• *vfs.zfs.vdev.trim_on_init* - Control whether new devices added to the pool have the TRIM command run on them. This ensures the best performance and longevity for SSDs, but takes extra time. If the device has already been secure erased, disabling this setting will make the addition of the new device faster. This value can be adjusted at any time with sysctl(8).

• *vfs.zfs.vdev.max_pending* - Limit the number of pending I/O requests per device. A higher value will keep the device command queue full and may give higher throughput. A lower value will reduce latency. This value can be adjusted at any time with sysctl(8).

• *vfs.zfs.top_maxinflight* - Maxmimum number of outstanding I/Os per top-level vdev. Limits the depth of the command queue to prevent high latency. The limit is per top-level vdev, meaning the limit applies to each mirror [394], RAID-Z [395], or other vdev independently. This value can be adjusted at any time with sysctl(8).

• *vfs.zfs.l2arc_write_max* - Limit the amount of data written to the L2ARC per second. This tunable is designed to extend the longevity of SSDs by limiting the amount of data written to the device. This value can be adjusted at any time with sysctl(8).

• *vfs.zfs.l2arc_write_boost* - The value of this tunable is added to vfs.zfs.l2arc_write_max [392] and increases the write speed to the SSD until the first block is evicted from the L2ARC. This "Turbo Warmup Phase" is designed to reduce the performance loss from an empty L2ARC after a reboot. This value can be adjusted at any time with sysctl(8).

• *vfs.zfs.scrub_delay* - Number of ticks to delay between each I/O during a scrub. To ensure that a scrub does not interfere with the normal operation of the pool, if any other I/O is happening the scrub will delay between each command. This value controls the limit on the total IOPS (I/Os Per Second) generated by the scrub. The granularity of the setting is determined by the value of kern.hz which defaults to 1000 ticks per second. This setting may be changed, resulting in a different effective IOPS limit. The default value is 4, resulting in a limit of: 1000 ticks/sec / 4 = 250 IOPS. Using a value of *20* would give a limit of: 1000 ticks/sec / 20 = 50 IOPS. The speed of scrub is only limited when there has been recent activity on the pool, as determined by vfs.zfs.scan_idle [392]. This value can be adjusted at any time with sysctl(8).

• *vfs.zfs.resilver_delay* - Number of milliseconds of delay inserted between each I/O during a resilver. To ensure that a resilver does not interfere with the normal operation of the pool, if any other I/O is happening the resilver will delay between each command. This value controls the limit of total IOPS (I/Os Per Second) generated by the resilver. The granularity of the setting is determined by the value of kern.hz which defaults to 1000 ticks per second. This setting may be changed, resulting in a different effective IOPS limit. The default value is 2, resulting in a limit of: 1000 ticks/sec / 2 = 500 IOPS. Returning the pool to an Online state may be more important if another device failing could Fault the pool, causing data loss. A value of 0 will give the resilver operation the same priority as other operations, speeding the healing process. The speed of resilver is only limited when there has been other recent activity on the pool, as determined by vfs.zfs.scan_idle [392]. This value can be adjusted at any time with sysctl(8).

• *vfs.zfs.scan_idle* - Number of milliseconds since the last operation before the pool is considered idle. When the pool is idle the rate limiting for scrub and resilver are disabled. This value can be adjusted at any time with sysctl(8).

• *vfs.zfs.txg.timeout* - Maximum number of seconds between transaction groups. The current transaction group will be written to the pool and a fresh transaction group started if this amount of time has elapsed since the previous transaction group. A transaction group my be triggered earlier if enough data is written. The default value is 5 seconds. A larger value may improve read performance by delaying asynchronous writes, but this may cause uneven performance when the transaction group is written. This value can be adjusted at any time with sysctl(8).

19.6.2. ZFS on i386

Some of the features provided by ZFS are memory intensive, and may require tuning for maximum efficiency on systems with limited RAM.

19.6.2.1. Memory

As a bare minimum, the total system memory should be at least one gigabyte. The amount of recommended RAM depends upon the size of the pool and which ZFS features are used. A general rule of thumb is 1 GB of RAM for every 1 TB of storage. If the deduplication feature is used, a general rule of thumb is 5 GB of RAM per TB of storage to be deduplicated. While some users successfully use ZFS with less RAM, systems under heavy load may panic due to memory exhaustion. Further tuning may be required for systems with less than the recommended RAM requirements.

19.6.2.2. Kernel Configuration

Due to the address space limitations of the i386™ platform, ZFS users on the i386™ architecture must add this option to a custom kernel configuration file, rebuild the kernel, and reboot:

```
options         KVA_PAGES=512
```

This expands the kernel address space, allowing the vm.kvm_size tunable to be pushed beyond the currently imposed limit of 1 GB, or the limit of 2 GB for PAE. To find the most suitable value for this option, divide the desired address space in megabytes by four. In this example, it is 512 for 2 GB.

19.6.2.3. Loader Tunables

The kmem address space can be increased on all FreeBSD architectures. On a test system with 1 GB of physical memory, success was achieved with these options added to /boot/loader.conf , and the system restarted:

```
vm.kmem_size="330M"
vm.kmem_size_max="330M"
vfs.zfs.arc_max="40M"
vfs.zfs.vdev.cache.size="5M"
```

For a more detailed list of recommendations for ZFS-related tuning, see https://wiki.freebsd.org/ZFSTuningGuide.

19.7. Additional Resources

- FreeBSD Wiki - ZFS

- FreeBSD Wiki - ZFS Tuning

- Illumos Wiki - ZFS

- Oracle Solaris ZFS Administration Guide

- ZFS Evil Tuning Guide

- ZFS Best Practices Guide

- Calomel Blog - ZFS Raidz Performance, Capacity and Integrity

19.8. ZFS Features and Terminology

ZFS is a fundamentally different file system because it is more than just a file system. ZFS combines the roles of file system and volume manager, enabling additional storage devices to be added to a live system and having the new space available on all of the existing file systems in that pool immediately. By combining the traditionally separate roles, ZFS is able to overcome previous limitations that prevented RAID groups being able to grow. Each top level device in a pool is called a *vdev*, which can be a simple disk or a RAID transformation such as a mirror or RAID-Z array. ZFS file systems (called *datasets*) each have access to the combined free space of the entire pool. As blocks are allocated from the pool, the space available to each file system decreases. This approach avoids the common pitfall with extensive partitioning where free space becomes fragmented across the partitions.

pool	A storage *pool* is the most basic building block of ZFS. A pool is made up of one or more vdevs, the underlying devices that store the data. A pool is then used to create one or more file systems (datasets) or block devices (volumes). These datasets and volumes share the pool of remaining free space. Each pool is uniquely identified by a name and a GUID. The features available are determined by the ZFS version number on the pool.

Note

FreeBSD 9.0 and 9.1 include support for ZFS version 28. Later versions use ZFS version 5000 with feature flags. The new feature flags system allows greater cross-compatibility with other implementations of ZFS.

vdev Types	A pool is made up of one or more vdevs, which themselves can be a single disk or a group of disks, in the case of a RAID transform. When multiple vdevs are used, ZFS spreads data across the vdevs to increase performance and maximize usable space.

- *Disk* - The most basic type of vdev is a standard block device. This can be an entire disk (such as */dev/ada0* or */dev/da0*) or a partition (*/dev/ada0p3*). On FreeBSD, there is no performance penalty for using a partition rather than the entire disk. This differs from recommendations made by the Solaris documentation.

- *File* - In addition to disks, ZFS pools can be backed by regular files, this is especially useful for testing and experimentation. Use the full path to the file as the device path in zpool create. All vdevs must be at least 128 MB in size.

- *Mirror* - When creating a mirror, specify the mirror keyword followed by the list of member devices for the mirror. A mirror consists of two or more devices, all data will be written to all member devices. A mirror vdev will only hold as much data as its smallest member. A mirror vdev can withstand the failure of all but one of its members without losing any data.

Note

A regular single disk vdev can be upgraded to a mirror vdev at any time with **zpool** attach.

- *RAID-Z* - ZFS implements RAID-Z, a variation on standard RAID-5 that offers better distribution of parity and eliminates the "RAID-5 write hole" in which the data and parity information become inconsistent after an unexpected restart. ZFS supports three levels of RAID-Z which provide varying levels of redundancy in exchange for decreasing levels of usable storage. The types are named RAID-Z1 through RAID-Z3 based on the number of parity devices in the array and the number of disks which can fail while the pool remains operational.

  In a RAID-Z1 configuration with four disks, each 1 TB, usable storage is 3 TB and the pool will still be able to operate in degraded mode with one faulted disk. If an additional disk goes offline before the faulted disk is replaced and resilvered, all data in the pool can be lost.

  In a RAID-Z3 configuration with eight disks of 1 TB, the volume will provide 5 TB of usable space and still be able to operate with three faulted disks. Sun™ recommends no more than nine disks in a single vdev. If the configuration has more disks, it is recommended to divide them into separate vdevs and the pool data will be striped across them.

  A configuration of two RAID-Z2 vdevs consisting of 8 disks each would create something similar to a RAID-60 array. A RAID-Z group's storage capacity is approximately the size of the smallest disk multiplied by the number of non-parity disks. Four 1 TB disks in RAID-Z1 has an effective size of approximately 3 TB, and an array of eight 1 TB disks in RAID-Z3 will yield 5 TB of usable space.

- *Spare* - ZFS has a special pseudo-vdev type for keeping track of available hot spares. Note that installed hot spares are not deployed automatically; they must manually be configured to replace the failed device using **zfs** replace.

- *Log* - ZFS Log Devices, also known as ZFS Intent Log (ZIL) move the intent log from the regular pool devices to a dedicated device, typically an SSD. Having a dedicated log device can significantly improve the performance of applications with a high volume of synchronous writes, especially databases. Log devices can be mirrored, but RAID-Z is not supported. If multiple log devices are used, writes will be load balanced across them.

- *Cache* - Adding a cache vdev to a pool will add the storage of the cache to the L2ARC. Cache devices cannot be mirrored. Since a cache device only stores additional copies of existing data, there is no risk of data loss.

Transaction Group (TXG)	Transaction Groups are the way changed blocks are grouped together and eventually written to the pool. Transaction groups are the atomic unit that ZFS uses to assert consistency. Each transaction group is assigned a unique 64-bit consecutive identifier. There can be up to three active transaction groups at a time, one in each of these three states:

- *Open* - When a new transaction group is created, it is in the open state, and accepts new writes. There is always a transaction group in the open state, however the transaction group may refuse new writes if it has reached a limit. Once the open transaction group has reached a limit, or the vfs.zfs.txg.timeout [392] has been reached, the transaction group advances to the next state.

- *Quiescing* - A short state that allows any pending operations to finish while not blocking the creation of a new open transaction group. Once all of the transactions in the group have completed, the transaction group advances to the final state.

- *Syncing* - All of the data in the transaction group is written to stable storage. This process will in turn modify other data, such as metadata and space maps, that will also need to be written to stable storage. The process of syncing involves multiple passes. The first, all of the changed data blocks, is the biggest, followed by the metadata, which may take multiple passes to complete. Since allocating space for the data blocks generates new metadata, the syncing state cannot finish until a pass completes that does not allocate any additional space. The syncing state is also where *synctasks* are completed. Synctasks are administrative operations, such as creating or destroying snapshots and datasets, that modify the uberblock are completed. Once the sync state is complete, the transaction group in the quiescing state is advanced to the syncing state.

	All administrative functions, such as snapshot are written as part of the transaction group. When a synctask is created, it is added to the currently open transaction group, and that group is advanced as quickly as possible to the syncing state to reduce the latency of administrative commands.
Adaptive Replacement Cache (ARC)	ZFS uses an Adaptive Replacement Cache (ARC), rather than a more traditional Least Recently Used (LRU) cache. An LRU cache is a simple list of items in the cache, sorted by when each object was most recently used. New items are added to the top of the list. When the cache is full, items from the bottom of the list are evicted to make room for more active objects. An ARC consists of four lists; the Most Recently Used (MRU) and Most Frequently Used (MFU) objects, plus a ghost list for each. These ghost lists track recently evicted objects to prevent them from being added back to the cache. This increases the cache hit ratio by avoiding objects that have a history of only being used occasionally. Another advantage of using both an MRU and MFU is that scanning an entire file system would normally evict all data from an MRU or LRU cache in favor of this freshly accessed content. With ZFS, there is also an MFU that only tracks the most frequently used objects, and the cache of the most commonly accessed blocks remains.
L2ARC	L2ARC is the second level of the ZFS caching system. The primary ARC is stored in RAM. Since the amount of available RAM is often limited, ZFS can also use cache vdevs [396]. Solid State Disks (SSDs) are often used as these cache devices due to their higher speed and lower latency compared to traditional spinning disks. L2ARC is entirely optional, but having one will significantly increase read speeds for files that are cached on the SSD instead of having to be read from the regular disks. L2ARC can also speed up deduplication because a DDT that does not fit in RAM but does fit in the L2ARC will be much faster than a DDT that must be read from disk. The rate at which data is added to the cache devices is limited to prevent prematurely wearing out SSDs with too many writes. Until the cache is full (the first block has been evicted to make room), writing to the L2ARC is limited to the sum of the write limit and the boost limit, and afterwards limited to the write limit. A pair of sysctl(8) values control these rate limits. vfs.zfs.l2arc_write_max [392] controls how many bytes are written to the cache per second, while vfs.zfs.l2arc_write_boost [392] adds to this limit during the "Turbo Warmup Phase" (Write Boost).
ZIL	ZIL accelerates synchronous transactions by using storage devices like SSDs that are faster than those used in the main storage pool. When an application requests a synchronous write (a guarantee that the data has been safely stored to disk rather than merely cached to be written later), the data is written to the faster ZIL stor-

	age, then later flushed out to the regular disks. This greatly reduces latency and improves performance. Only synchronous workloads like databases will benefit from a ZIL. Regular asynchronous writes such as copying files will not use the ZIL at all.
Copy-On-Write	Unlike a traditional file system, when data is overwritten on ZFS, the new data is written to a different block rather than overwriting the old data in place. Only when this write is complete is the metadata then updated to point to the new location. In the event of a shorn write (a system crash or power loss in the middle of writing a file), the entire original contents of the file are still available and the incomplete write is discarded. This also means that ZFS does not require a fsck(8) after an unexpected shutdown.
Dataset	*Dataset* is the generic term for a ZFS file system, volume, snapshot or clone. Each dataset has a unique name in the format *poolname/path@snapshot*. The root of the pool is technically a dataset as well. Child datasets are named hierarchically like directories. For example, *mypool/home*, the home dataset, is a child of *mypool* and inherits properties from it. This can be expanded further by creating *mypool/home/user*. This grandchild dataset will inherit properties from the parent and grandparent. Properties on a child can be set to override the defaults inherited from the parents and grandparents. Administration of datasets and their children can be delegated.
File system	A ZFS dataset is most often used as a file system. Like most other file systems, a ZFS file system is mounted somewhere in the systems directory hierarchy and contains files and directories of its own with permissions, flags, and other metadata.
Volume	In additional to regular file system datasets, ZFS can also create volumes, which are block devices. Volumes have many of the same features, including copy-on-write, snapshots, clones, and checksumming. Volumes can be useful for running other file system formats on top of ZFS, such as UFS virtualization, or exporting iSCSI extents.
Snapshot	The copy-on-write (COW) design of ZFS allows for nearly instantaneous, consistent snapshots with arbitrary names. After taking a snapshot of a dataset, or a recursive snapshot of a parent dataset that will include all child datasets, new data is written to new blocks, but the old blocks are not reclaimed as free space. The snapshot contains the original version of the file system, and the live file system contains any changes made since the snapshot was taken. No additional space is used. As new data is written to the live file system, new blocks are allocated to store this data. The apparent size of the snapshot will grow as the blocks are no longer used in the live file system, but only in the snapshot. These snapshots can be mounted read only to allow for the recov-

	ery of previous versions of files. It is also possible to roll-back a live file system to a specific snapshot, undoing any changes that took place after the snapshot was taken. Each block in the pool has a reference counter which keeps track of how many snapshots, clones, datasets, or volumes make use of that block. As files and snapshots are deleted, the reference count is decremented. When a block is no longer referenced, it is reclaimed as free space. Snapshots can also be marked with a hold. When a snapshot is held, any attempt to destroy it will return an **EBUSY** error. Each snapshot can have multiple holds, each with a unique name. The release command removes the hold so the snapshot can deleted. Snapshots can be taken on volumes, but they can only be cloned or rolled back, not mounted independently.
Clone	Snapshots can also be cloned. A clone is a writable version of a snapshot, allowing the file system to be forked as a new dataset. As with a snapshot, a clone initially consumes no additional space. As new data is written to a clone and new blocks are allocated, the apparent size of the clone grows. When blocks are overwritten in the cloned file system or volume, the reference count on the previous block is decremented. The snapshot upon which a clone is based cannot be deleted because the clone depends on it. The snapshot is the parent, and the clone is the child. Clones can be *promoted*, reversing this dependency and making the clone the parent and the previous parent the child. This operation requires no additional space. Because the amount of space used by the parent and child is reversed, existing quotas and reservations might be affected.
Checksum	Every block that is allocated is also checksummed. The checksum algorithm used is a per-dataset property, see set. The checksum of each block is transparently validated as it is read, allowing ZFS to detect silent corruption. If the data that is read does not match the expected checksum, ZFS will attempt to recover the data from any available redundancy, like mirrors or RAID-Z). Validation of all checksums can be triggered with scrub. Checksum algorithms include: • fletcher2 • fletcher4 • sha256 The fletcher algorithms are faster, but sha256 is a strong cryptographic hash and has a much lower chance of collisions at the cost of some performance. Checksums can be disabled, but it is not recommended.
Compression	Each dataset has a compression property, which defaults to off. This property can be set to one of a number of compression algorithms. This will cause all new data that is written to the dataset to be compressed. Beyond a

reduction in space used, read and write throughput often increases because fewer blocks are read or written.

- *LZ4* - Added in ZFS pool version 5000 (feature flags), LZ4 is now the recommended compression algorithm. LZ4 compresses approximately 50% faster than LZJB when operating on compressible data, and is over three times faster when operating on uncompressible data. LZ4 also decompresses approximately 80% faster than LZJB. On modern CPUs, LZ4 can often compress at over 500 MB/s, and decompress at over 1.5 GB/s (per single CPU core).

Note

LZ4 compression is only available after FreeBSD 9.2.

- *LZJB* - The default compression algorithm. Created by Jeff Bonwick (one of the original creators of ZFS). LZJB offers good compression with less CPU overhead compared to GZIP. In the future, the default compression algorithm will likely change to LZ4.

- *GZIP* - A popular stream compression algorithm available in ZFS. One of the main advantages of using GZIP is its configurable level of compression. When setting the `compress` property, the administrator can choose the level of compression, ranging from `gzip1`, the lowest level of compression, to `gzip9`, the highest level of compression. This gives the administrator control over how much CPU time to trade for saved disk space.

- *ZLE* - Zero Length Encoding is a special compression algorithm that only compresses continuous runs of zeros. This compression algorithm is only useful when the dataset contains large blocks of zeros.

Copies	When set to a value greater than 1, the `copies` property instructs ZFS to maintain multiple copies of each block in the File System or Volume. Setting this property on important datasets provides additional redundancy from which to recover a block that does not match its checksum. In pools without redundancy, the copies feature is the only form of redundancy. The copies feature can recover from a single bad sector or other forms of minor corruption, but it does not protect the pool from the loss of an entire disk.
Deduplication	Checksums make it possible to detect duplicate blocks of data as they are written. With deduplication, the reference count of an existing, identical block is increased, saving storage space. To detect duplicate blocks, a dedu-

	plication table (DDT) is kept in memory. The table contains a list of unique checksums, the location of those blocks, and a reference count. When new data is written, the checksum is calculated and compared to the list. If a match is found, the existing block is used. The SHA256 checksum algorithm is used with deduplication to provide a secure cryptographic hash. Deduplication is tunable. If dedup is on, then a matching checksum is assumed to mean that the data is identical. If dedup is set to verify, then the data in the two blocks will be checked byte-for-byte to ensure it is actually identical. If the data is not identical, the hash collision will be noted and the two blocks will be stored separately. Because DDT must store the hash of each unique block, it consumes a very large amount of memory. A general rule of thumb is 5-6 GB of ram per 1 TB of deduplicated data). In situations where it is not practical to have enough RAM to keep the entire DDT in memory, performance will suffer greatly as the DDT must be read from disk before each new block is written. Deduplication can use L2ARC to store the DDT, providing a middle ground between fast system memory and slower disks. Consider using compression instead, which often provides nearly as much space savings without the additional memory requirement.
Scrub	Instead of a consistency check like fsck(8), ZFS has scrub. scrub reads all data blocks stored on the pool and verifies their checksums against the known good checksums stored in the metadata. A periodic check of all the data stored on the pool ensures the recovery of any corrupted blocks before they are needed. A scrub is not required after an unclean shutdown, but is recommended at least once every three months. The checksum of each block is verified as blocks are read during normal use, but a scrub makes certain that even infrequently used blocks are checked for silent corruption. Data security is improved, especially in archival storage situations. The relative priority of scrub can be adjusted with vfs.zfs.scrub_delay[392] to prevent the scrub from degrading the performance of other workloads on the pool.
Dataset Quota	ZFS provides very fast and accurate dataset, user, and group space accounting in addition to quotas and space reservations. This gives the administrator fine grained control over how space is allocated and allows space to be reserved for critical file systems.
	ZFS supports different types of quotas: the dataset quota, the reference quota (refquota), the user quota, and the group quota.
	Quotas limit the amount of space that a dataset and all of its descendants, including snapshots of the dataset, child datasets, and the snapshots of those datasets, can consume.

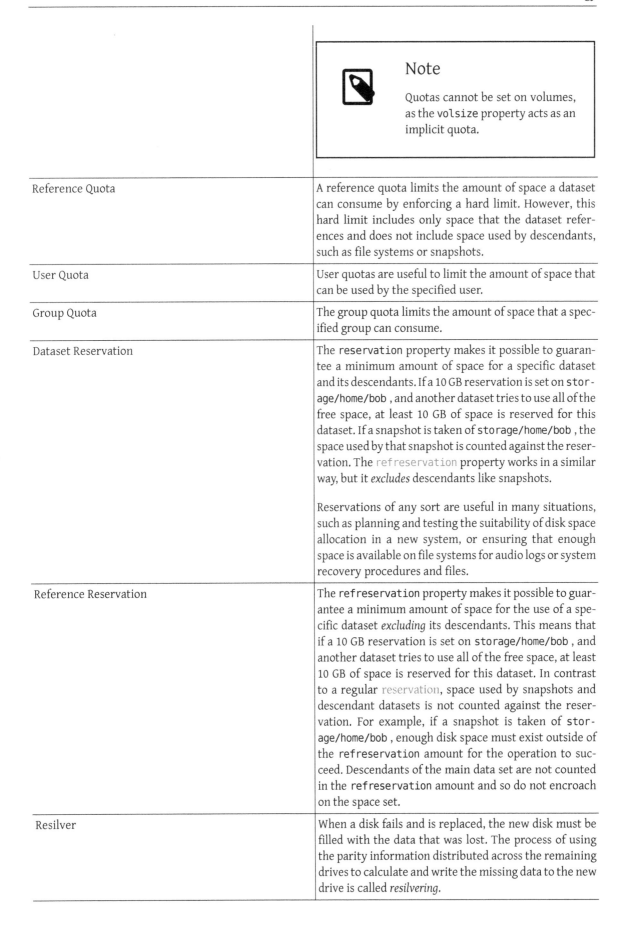

	Note Quotas cannot be set on volumes, as the `volsize` property acts as an implicit quota.
Reference Quota	A reference quota limits the amount of space a dataset can consume by enforcing a hard limit. However, this hard limit includes only space that the dataset references and does not include space used by descendants, such as file systems or snapshots.
User Quota	User quotas are useful to limit the amount of space that can be used by the specified user.
Group Quota	The group quota limits the amount of space that a specified group can consume.
Dataset Reservation	The `reservation` property makes it possible to guarantee a minimum amount of space for a specific dataset and its descendants. If a 10 GB reservation is set on `storage/home/bob`, and another dataset tries to use all of the free space, at least 10 GB of space is reserved for this dataset. If a snapshot is taken of `storage/home/bob`, the space used by that snapshot is counted against the reservation. The `refreservation` property works in a similar way, but it *excludes* descendants like snapshots. Reservations of any sort are useful in many situations, such as planning and testing the suitability of disk space allocation in a new system, or ensuring that enough space is available on file systems for audio logs or system recovery procedures and files.
Reference Reservation	The `refreservation` property makes it possible to guarantee a minimum amount of space for the use of a specific dataset *excluding* its descendants. This means that if a 10 GB reservation is set on `storage/home/bob`, and another dataset tries to use all of the free space, at least 10 GB of space is reserved for this dataset. In contrast to a regular `reservation`, space used by snapshots and descendant datasets is not counted against the reservation. For example, if a snapshot is taken of `storage/home/bob`, enough disk space must exist outside of the `refreservation` amount for the operation to succeed. Descendants of the main data set are not counted in the `refreservation` amount and so do not encroach on the space set.
Resilver	When a disk fails and is replaced, the new disk must be filled with the data that was lost. The process of using the parity information distributed across the remaining drives to calculate and write the missing data to the new drive is called *resilvering*.

Online	A pool or vdev in the Online state has all of its member devices connected and fully operational. Individual devices in the Online state are functioning normally.
Offline	Individual devices can be put in an Offline state by the administrator if there is sufficient redundancy to avoid putting the pool or vdev into a Faulted state. An administrator may choose to offline a disk in preparation for replacing it, or to make it easier to identify.
Degraded	A pool or vdev in the Degraded state has one or more disks that have been disconnected or have failed. The pool is still usable, but if additional devices fail, the pool could become unrecoverable. Reconnecting the missing devices or replacing the failed disks will return the pool to an Online state after the reconnected or new device has completed the Resilver process.
Faulted	A pool or vdev in the Faulted state is no longer operational. The data on it can no longer be accessed. A pool or vdev enters the Faulted state when the number of missing or failed devices exceeds the level of redundancy in the vdev. If missing devices can be reconnected, the pool will return to a Online state. If there is insufficient redundancy to compensate for the number of failed disks, then the contents of the pool are lost and must be restored from backups.

Chapter 20. Other File Systems

Written by Tom Rhodes.

20.1. Synopsis

File systems are an integral part of any operating system. They allow users to upload and store files, provide access to data, and make hard drives useful. Different operating systems differ in their native file system. Traditionally, the native FreeBSD file system has been the Unix File System UFS which has been modernized as UFS2. Since FreeBSD 7.0, the Z File System (ZFS) is also available as a native file system. See Chapter 19, *The Z File System (ZFS)* for more information.

In addition to its native file systems, FreeBSD supports a multitude of other file systems so that data from other operating systems can be accessed locally, such as data stored on locally attached USB storage devices, flash drives, and hard disks. This includes support for the Linux® Extended File System (EXT) and the Reiser file system.

There are different levels of FreeBSD support for the various file systems. Some require a kernel module to be loaded and others may require a toolset to be installed. Some non-native file system support is full read-write while others are read-only.

After reading this chapter, you will know:

- The difference between native and supported file systems.

- Which file systems are supported by FreeBSD.

- How to enable, configure, access, and make use of non-native file systems.

Before reading this chapter, you should:

- Understand UNIX® and FreeBSD basics.

- Be familiar with the basics of kernel configuration and compilation.

- Feel comfortable installing software in FreeBSD.

- Have some familiarity with disks, storage, and device names in FreeBSD.

20.2. Linux® File Systems

FreeBSD provides built-in support for several Linux® file systems. This section demonstrates how to load support for and how to mount the supported Linux® file systems.

20.2.1. ext2

Kernel support for ext2 file systems has been available since FreeBSD 2.2. In FreeBSD 8.x and earlier, the code is licensed under the GPL. Since FreeBSD 9.0, the code has been rewritten and is now BSD licensed.

The ext2fs(5) driver allows the FreeBSD kernel to both read and write to ext2 file systems.

> ### Note
> This driver can also be used to access ext3 and ext4 file systems. However, ext3 journaling and extended attributes are not supported. Support for ext4 is read-only.

To access an ext file system, first load the kernel loadable module:

```
# kldload ext2fs
```

Then, mount the ext volume by specifying its FreeBSD partition name and an existing mount point. This example mounts /dev/ad1s1 on /mnt:

```
# mount -t ext2fs  /dev/ad1s1  /mnt
```

20.2.2. ReiserFS

FreeBSD provides read-only support for The Reiser file system, ReiserFS.

To load the reiserfs(5) driver:

```
# kldload reiserfs
```

Then, to mount a ReiserFS volume located on /dev/ad1s1 :

```
# mount -t reiserfs  /dev/ad1s1  /mnt
```

Chapter 21. Virtualization

Contributed by Murray Stokely.
bhyve section by Allan Jude.
Xen section by Benedict Reuschling.

21.1. Synopsis

Virtualization software allows multiple operating systems to run simultaneously on the same computer. Such software systems for PCs often involve a host operating system which runs the virtualization software and supports any number of guest operating systems.

After reading this chapter, you will know:

- The difference between a host operating system and a guest operating system.

- How to install FreeBSD on an Intel®-based Apple® Mac® computer.

- How to install FreeBSD on Microsoft® Windows® with Virtual PC.

- How to install FreeBSD as a guest in bhyve.

- How to tune a FreeBSD system for best performance under virtualization.

Before reading this chapter, you should:

- Understand the basics of UNIX® and FreeBSD.

- Know how to install FreeBSD.

- Know how to set up a network connection.

- Know how to install additional third-party software.

21.2. FreeBSD as a Guest on Parallels for Mac OS® X

Parallels Desktop for Mac® is a commercial software product available for Intel® based Apple® Mac® computers running Mac OS® 10.4.6 or higher. FreeBSD is a fully supported guest operating system. Once Parallels has been installed on Mac OS® X, the user must configure a virtual machine and then install the desired guest operating system.

21.2.1. Installing FreeBSD on Parallels/Mac OS® X

The first step in installing FreeBSD on Parallels is to create a new virtual machine for installing FreeBSD. Select FreeBSD as the Guest OS Type when prompted:

Choose a reasonable amount of disk and memory depending on the plans for this virtual FreeBSD instance. 4GB of disk space and 512MB of RAM work well for most uses of FreeBSD under Parallels:

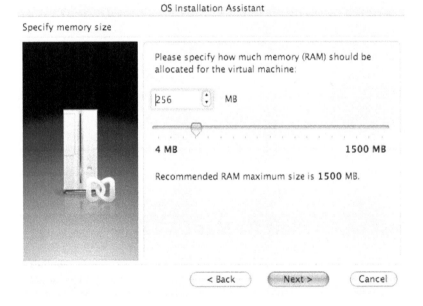

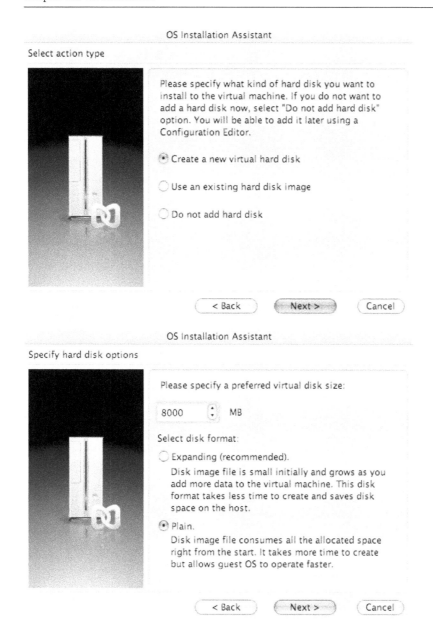

OS Installation Assistant

Select action type

Please specify what kind of hard disk you want to install to the virtual machine. If you do not want to add a hard disk now, select "Do not add hard disk" option. You will be able to add it later using a Configuration Editor.

⦿ Create a new virtual hard disk

◯ Use an existing hard disk image

◯ Do not add hard disk

(< Back)   (Next >)   (Cancel)

OS Installation Assistant

Specify hard disk options

Please specify a preferred virtual disk size:

[8000 ⬍] MB

Select disk format:

◯ Expanding (recommended).
Disk image file is small initially and grows as you add more data to the virtual machine. This disk format takes less time to create and saves disk space on the host.

⦿ Plain.
Disk image file consumes all the allocated space right from the start. It takes more time to create but allows guest OS to operate faster.

(< Back)   (Next >)   (Cancel)

Select an image file

Please specify a location of the hard disk image file:

s/murray/Library/Parallels/otherbsd/otherbsd.hdd ...

< Back   Next >   Cancel

Select the type of networking and a network interface:

OS Installation Assistant

Select a type of networking

Please specify what kind of networking you want to add to the virtual machine:

● Bridged Ethernet.
  Use this option if you need to connect your virtual machine to Local or Wide Area Network.

○ Host-only Networking.
  Use this option if you want to create private network shared with the host.

○ Shared Networking.
  Use this option if you need to provide Network Address Translation feature to your virtual machine.

○ Networking is not required.

< Back   Next >   Cancel

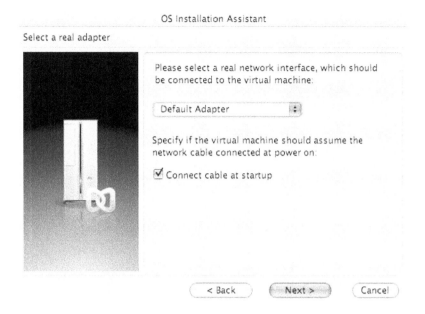

Save and finish the configuration:

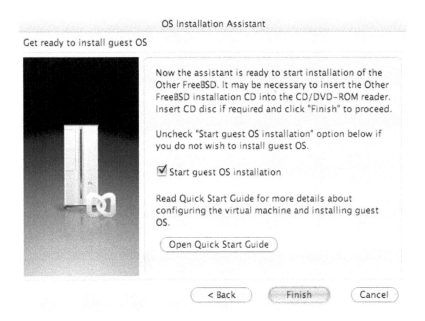

After the FreeBSD virtual machine has been created, FreeBSD can be installed on it. This is best done with an official FreeBSD CD/DVD or with an ISO image downloaded from an official FTP site. Copy the appropriate ISO image to the local Mac® filesystem or insert a CD/DVD in the Mac®'s CD-ROM drive. Click on the disc icon in the bottom right corner of the FreeBSD Parallels window. This will bring up a window that can be used to associate the CD-ROM drive in the virtual machine with the ISO file on disk or with the real CD-ROM drive.

Once this association with the CD-ROM source has been made, reboot the FreeBSD virtual machine by clicking the reboot icon. Parallels will reboot with a special BIOS that first checks if there is a CD-ROM.

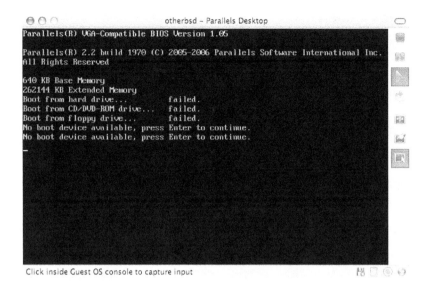

In this case it will find the FreeBSD installation media and begin a normal FreeBSD installation. Perform the installation, but do not attempt to configure Xorg at this time.

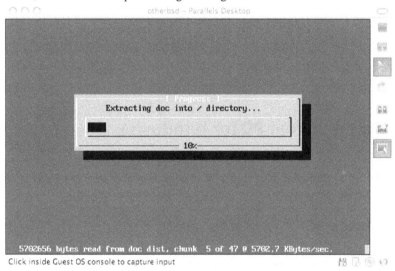

When the installation is finished, reboot into the newly installed FreeBSD virtual machine.

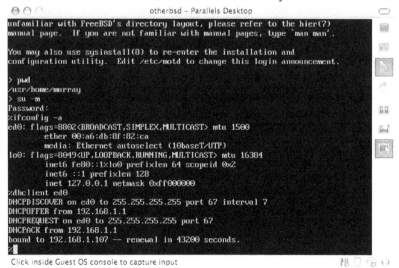

21.2.2. Configuring FreeBSD on Parallels

After FreeBSD has been successfully installed on Mac OS® X with Parallels, there are a number of configuration steps that can be taken to optimize the system for virtualized operation.

1. Set Boot Loader Variables

    The most important step is to reduce the `kern.hz` tunable to reduce the CPU utilization of FreeBSD under the Parallels environment. This is accomplished by adding the following line to `/boot/loader.conf` :

    ```
    kern.hz=100
    ```

    Without this setting, an idle FreeBSD Parallels guest will use roughly 15% of the CPU of a single processor iMac®. After this change the usage will be closer to 5%.

2. Create a New Kernel Configuration File

    All of the SCSI, FireWire, and USB device drivers can be removed from a custom kernel configuration file. Parallels provides a virtual network adapter used by the ed(4) driver, so all network devices except for ed(4) and miibus(4) can be removed from the kernel.

3. Configure Networking

    The most basic networking setup uses DHCP to connect the virtual machine to the same local area network as the host Mac®. This can be accomplished by adding `ifconfig_ed0="DHCP"` to `/etc/rc.conf` . More advanced networking setups are described in Chapter 30, *Advanced Networking*.

21.3. FreeBSD as a Guest on Virtual PC for Windows®

Virtual PC for Windows® is a Microsoft® software product available for free download. See this website for the system requirements. Once Virtual PC has been installed on Microsoft® Windows®, the user can configure a virtual machine and then install the desired guest operating system.

21.3.1. Installing FreeBSD on Virtual PC

The first step in installing FreeBSD on Virtual PC is to create a new virtual machine for installing FreeBSD. Select Create a virtual machine when prompted:

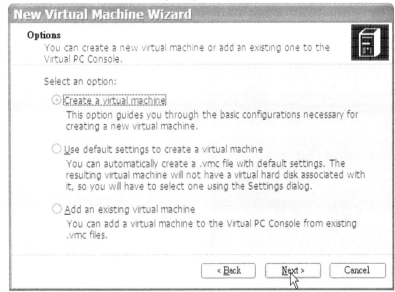

Select Other as the Operating system when prompted:

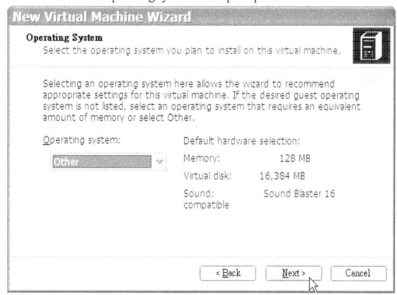

Then, choose a reasonable amount of disk and memory depending on the plans for this virtual FreeBSD instance. 4GB of disk space and 512MB of RAM work well for most uses of FreeBSD under Virtual PC:

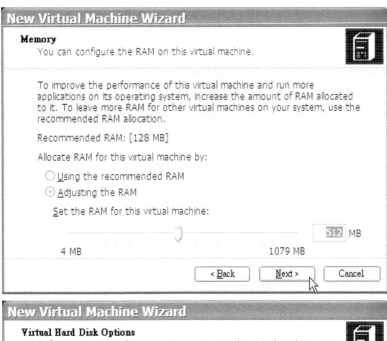

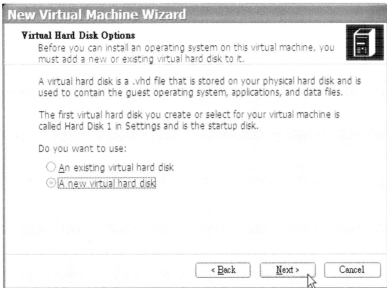

Save and finish the configuration:

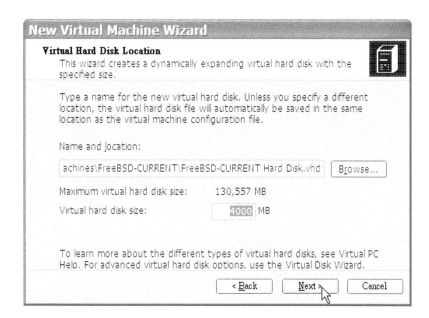

Select the FreeBSD virtual machine and click Settings, then set the type of networking and a network interface:

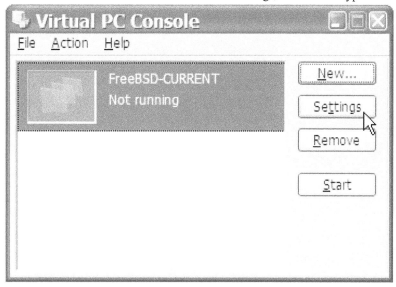

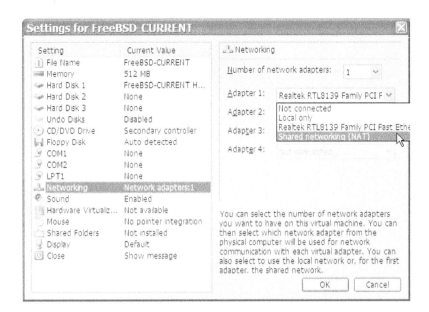

After the FreeBSD virtual machine has been created, FreeBSD can be installed on it. This is best done with an official FreeBSD CD/DVD or with an ISO image downloaded from an official FTP site. Copy the appropriate ISO image to the local Windows® filesystem or insert a CD/DVD in the CD drive, then double click on the FreeBSD virtual machine to boot. Then, click CD and choose Capture ISO Image... on the Virtual PC window. This will bring up a window where the CD-ROM drive in the virtual machine can be associated with an ISO file on disk or with the real CD-ROM drive.

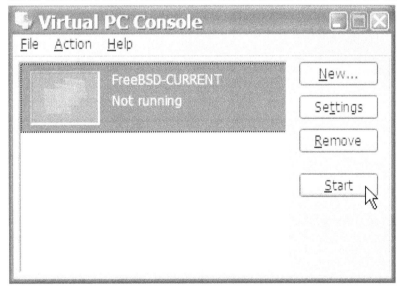

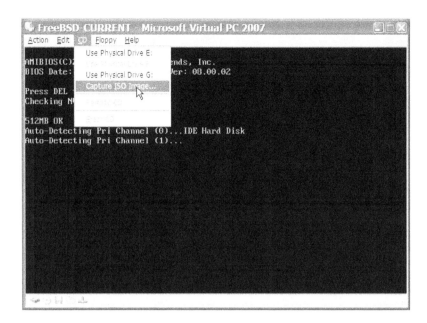

Once this association with the CD-ROM source has been made, reboot the FreeBSD virtual machine by clicking Action and Reset. Virtual PC will reboot with a special BIOS that first checks for a CD-ROM.

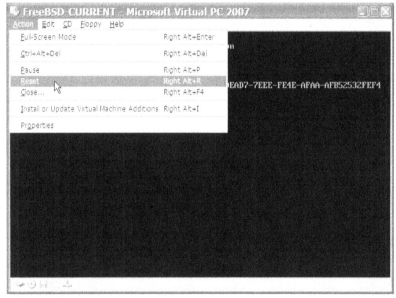

In this case it will find the FreeBSD installation media and begin a normal FreeBSD installation. Continue with the installation, but do not attempt to configure Xorg at this time.

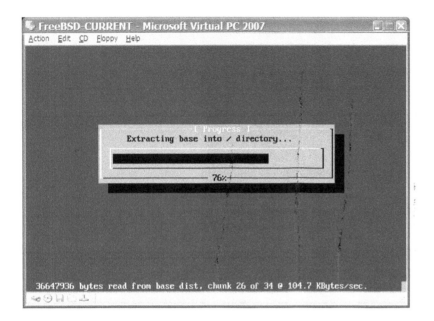

When the installation is finished, remember to eject the CD/DVD or release the ISO image. Finally, reboot into the newly installed FreeBSD virtual machine.

21.3.2. Configuring FreeBSD on Virtual PC

After FreeBSD has been successfully installed on Microsoft® Windows® with Virtual PC, there are a number of configuration steps that can be taken to optimize the system for virtualized operation.

1. Set Boot Loader Variables

   The most important step is to reduce the `kern.hz` tunable to reduce the CPU utilization of FreeBSD under the Virtual PC environment. This is accomplished by adding the following line to `/boot/loader.conf` :

   ```
   kern.hz=100
   ```

   Without this setting, an idle FreeBSD Virtual PC guest OS will use roughly 40% of the CPU of a single processor computer. After this change, the usage will be closer to 3%.

2. Create a New Kernel Configuration File

   All of the SCSI, FireWire, and USB device drivers can be removed from a custom kernel configuration file. Virtual PC provides a virtual network adapter used by the de(4) driver, so all network devices except for de(4) and miibus(4) can be removed from the kernel.

3. Configure Networking

   The most basic networking setup uses DHCP to connect the virtual machine to the same local area network as the Microsoft® Windows® host. This can be accomplished by adding `ifconfig_de0="DHCP"` to `/etc/rc.conf` . More advanced networking setups are described in Chapter 30, *Advanced Networking*.

21.4. FreeBSD as a Guest on VMware Fusion for Mac OS®

VMware Fusion for Mac® is a commercial software product available for Intel® based Apple® Mac® computers running Mac OS® 10.4.9 or higher. FreeBSD is a fully supported guest operating system. Once VMware Fusion has been installed on Mac OS® X, the user can configure a virtual machine and then install the desired guest operating system.

21.4.1. Installing FreeBSD on VMware Fusion

The first step is to start VMware Fusion which will load the Virtual Machine Library. Click New to create the virtual machine:

This will load the New Virtual Machine Assistant. Click Continue to proceed:

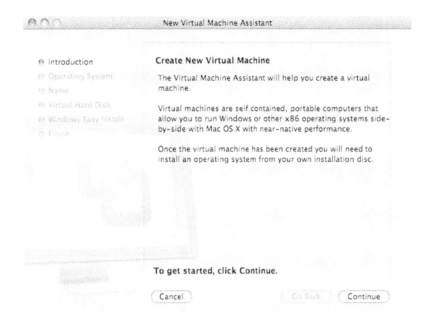

Select Other as the Operating System and either FreeBSD or FreeBSD 64-bit, as the Version when prompted:

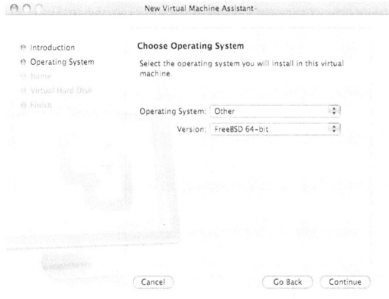

Choose the name of the virtual machine and the directory where it should be saved:

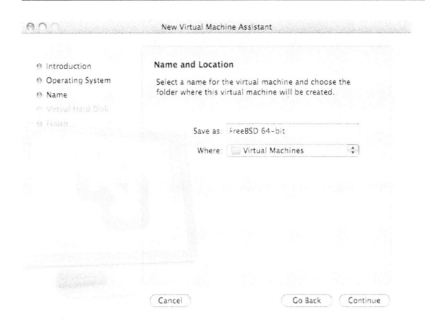

Choose the size of the Virtual Hard Disk for the virtual machine:

Choose the method to install the virtual machine, either from an ISO image or from a CD/DVD:

Click Finish and the virtual machine will boot:

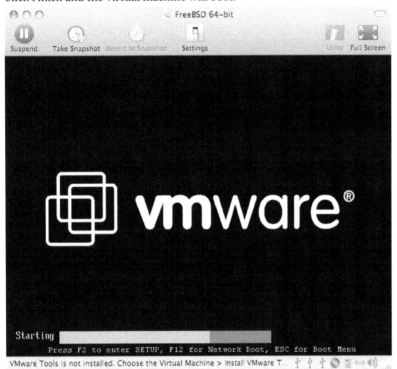

Install FreeBSD as usual:

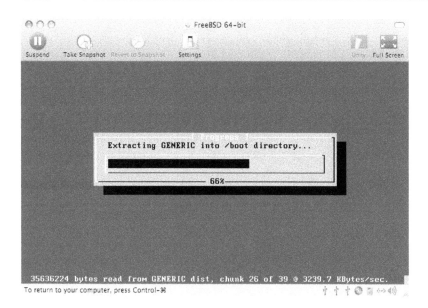

Once the install is complete, the settings of the virtual machine can be modified, such as memory usage:

Note

The System Hardware settings of the virtual machine cannot be modified while the virtual machine is running.

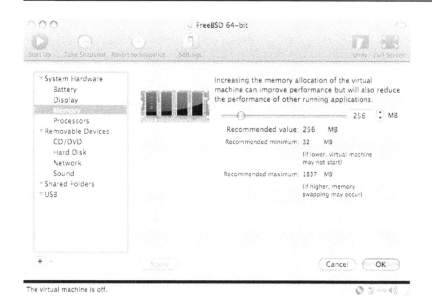

The number of CPUs the virtual machine will have access to:

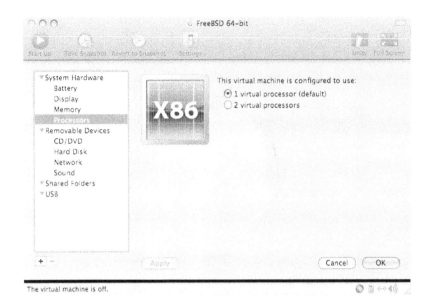

The status of the CD-ROM device. Normally the CD/DVD/ISO is disconnected from the virtual machine when it is no longer needed.

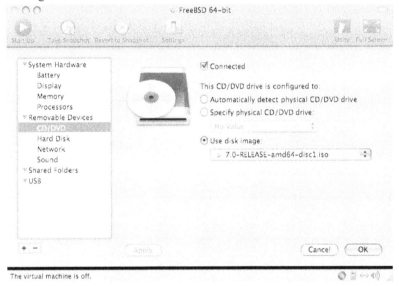

The last thing to change is how the virtual machine will connect to the network. To allow connections to the virtual machine from other machines besides the host, choose Connect directly to the physical network (Bridged). Otherwise, Share the host's internet connection (NAT) is preferred so that the virtual machine can have access to the Internet, but the network cannot access the virtual machine.

After modifying the settings, boot the newly installed FreeBSD virtual machine.

21.4.2. Configuring FreeBSD on VMware Fusion

After FreeBSD has been successfully installed on Mac OS® X with VMware Fusion, there are a number of configuration steps that can be taken to optimize the system for virtualized operation.

1. Set Boot Loader Variables

    The most important step is to reduce the `kern.hz` tunable to reduce the CPU utilization of FreeBSD under the VMware Fusion environment. This is accomplished by adding the following line to `/boot/loader.conf` :

    ```
    kern.hz=100
    ```

    Without this setting, an idle FreeBSD VMware Fusion guest will use roughly 15% of the CPU of a single processor iMac®. After this change, the usage will be closer to 5%.

2. Create a New Kernel Configuration File

    All of the FireWire, and USB device drivers can be removed from a custom kernel configuration file. VMware Fusion provides a virtual network adapter used by the em(4) driver, so all network devices except for em(4) can be removed from the kernel.

3. Configure Networking

    The most basic networking setup uses DHCP to connect the virtual machine to the same local area network as the host Mac®. This can be accomplished by adding `ifconfig_em0="DHCP"` to `/etc/rc.conf` . More advanced networking setups are described in Chapter 30, *Advanced Networking*.

21.5. FreeBSD as a Guest on VirtualBox™

FreeBSD works well as a guest in VirtualBox™ . The virtualization software is available for most common operating systems, including FreeBSD itself.

The VirtualBox™ guest additions provide support for:

• Clipboard sharing.

• Mouse pointer integration.

- Host time synchronization.

- Window scaling.

- Seamless mode.

 Note

These commands are run in the FreeBSD guest.

First, install the emulators/virtualbox-ose-additions package or port in the FreeBSD guest. This will install the port:

```
# cd /usr/ports/emulators/virtualbox-ose-additions && make install clean
```

Add these lines to /etc/rc.conf :

```
vboxguest_enable="YES"
vboxservice_enable="YES"
```

If ntpd(8) or ntpdate(8) is used, disable host time synchronization:

```
vboxservice_flags="--disable-timesync"
```

Xorg will automatically recognize the vboxvideo driver. It can also be manually entered in /etc/X11/xorg.conf :

```
Section "Device"
 Identifier "Card0"
 Driver "vboxvideo"
 VendorName "InnoTek Systemberatung GmbH"
 BoardName "VirtualBox Graphics Adapter"
EndSection
```

To use the vboxmouse driver, adjust the mouse section in /etc/X11/xorg.conf :

```
Section "InputDevice"
 Identifier "Mouse0"
 Driver "vboxmouse"
EndSection
```

HAL users should create the following /usr/local/etc/hal/fdi/policy/90-vboxguest.fdi   or copy it from /usr/local/share/hal/fdi/policy/10osvendor/90-vboxguest.fdi :

```
<?xml version="1.0" encoding="utf-8"?>
<!--
# Sun VirtualBox
# Hal driver description for the vboxmouse driver
# $Id: chapter.xml,v 1.33 2012-03-17 04:53:52 eadler Exp $

 Copyright (C) 2008-2009 Sun Microsystems, Inc.

 This file is part of VirtualBox Open Source Edition (OSE, as
 available from http://www.virtualbox.org. This file is free software;
 you can redistribute it and/or modify it under the terms of the GNU
 General Public License (GPL) as published by the Free Software
 Foundation, in version 2 as it comes in the "COPYING" file of the
 VirtualBox OSE distribution. VirtualBox OSE is distributed in the
 hope that it will be useful, but WITHOUT ANY WARRANTY of any kind.

 Please contact Sun Microsystems, Inc., 4150 Network Circle, Santa
 Clara, CA 95054 USA or visit http://www.sun.com if you need
 additional information or have any questions.
```

```
-->
<deviceinfo version="0.2">
  <device>
    <match key="info.subsystem" string="pci">
      <match key="info.product" string="VirtualBox guest Service">
        <append key="info.capabilities" type="strlist">input</append>
  <append key="info.capabilities" type="strlist">input.mouse</append>
        <merge key="input.x11_driver" type="string">vboxmouse</merge>
  <merge key="input.device" type="string">/dev/vboxguest</merge>
      </match>
    </match>
  </device>
</deviceinfo>
```

21.6. FreeBSD as a Host with VirtualBox

VirtualBox™ is an actively developed, complete virtualization package, that is available for most operating systems including Windows®, Mac OS®, Linux® and FreeBSD. It is equally capable of running Windows® or UNIX®-like guests. It is released as open source software, but with closed-source components available in a separate extension pack. These components include support for USB 2.0 devices. More information may be found on the "Downloads" page of the VirtualBox™ wiki. Currently, these extensions are not available for FreeBSD.

21.6.1. Installing VirtualBox™

VirtualBox™ is available as a FreeBSD package or port in emulators/virtualbox-ose. The port can be installed using these commands:

```
# cd /usr/ports/emulators/virtualbox-ose
# make install clean
```

One useful option in the port's configuration menu is the GuestAdditions suite of programs. These provide a number of useful features in guest operating systems, like mouse pointer integration (allowing the mouse to be shared between host and guest without the need to press a special keyboard shortcut to switch) and faster video rendering, especially in Windows® guests. The guest additions are available in the Devices menu, after the installation of the guest is finished.

A few configuration changes are needed before VirtualBox™ is started for the first time. The port installs a kernel module in /boot/modules which must be loaded into the running kernel:

```
# kldload vboxdrv
```

To ensure the module is always loaded after a reboot, add this line to /boot/loader.conf :

```
vboxdrv_load="YES"
```

To use the kernel modules that allow bridged or host-only networking, add this line to /etc/rc.conf and reboot the computer:

```
vboxnet_enable="YES"
```

The vboxusers group is created during installation of VirtualBox™. All users that need access to VirtualBox™ will have to be added as members of this group. pw can be used to add new members:

```
# pw groupmod vboxusers -m yourusername
```

The default permissions for /dev/vboxnetctl are restrictive and need to be changed for bridged networking:

```
# chown root:vboxusers /dev/vboxnetctl
# chmod 0660 /dev/vboxnetctl
```

To make this permissions change permanent, add these lines to /etc/devfs.conf :

```
own    vboxnetctl root:vboxusers
perm   vboxnetctl 0660
```

To launch VirtualBox™ , type from a Xorg session:

```
% VirtualBox
```

For more information on configuring and using VirtualBox™ , refer to the official website. For FreeBSD-specific information and troubleshooting instructions, refer to the relevant page in the FreeBSD wiki.

21.6.2. VirtualBox™ USB Support

VirtualBox™ can be configured to pass USB devices through to the guest operating system. The host controller of the OSE version is limited to emulating USB 1.1 devices until the extension pack supporting USB 2.0 and 3.0 devices becomes available on FreeBSD.

For VirtualBox™ to be aware of USB devices attached to the machine, the user needs to be a member of the operator group.

```
# pw groupmod operator -m yourusername
```

Restart the login session and VirtualBox™ for these changes to take effect, and create USB filters as necessary.

21.6.3. VirtualBox™ Host DVD/CD Access

Access to the host DVD/CD drives from guests is achieved through the sharing of the physical drives. Within VirtualBox™ , this is set up from the Storage window in the Settings of the virtual machine. If needed, create an empty IDE CD/DVD device first. Then choose the Host Drive from the popup menu for the virtual CD/DVD drive selection. A checkbox labeled Passthrough will appear. This allows the virtual machine to use the hardware directly. For example, audio CDs or the burner will only function if this option is selected.

HAL needs to run for VirtualBox™ DVD/CD functions to work, so enable it in /etc/rc.conf and start it if it is not already running:

```
hald_enable="YES"
```

```
# service hald start
```

In order for users to be able to use VirtualBox™ DVD/CD functions, they need access to /dev/xpt0 , /dev/cdN, and /dev/passN. This is usually achieved by making the user a member of operator. Permissions to these devices have to be corrected by adding these lines to /etc/devfs.conf:

```
perm cd* 0660
perm xpt0 0660
perm pass* 0660
```

```
# service devfs restart
```

21.7. FreeBSD as a Host with bhyve

The bhyve BSD-licensed hypervisor became part of the base system with FreeBSD 10.0-RELEASE. This hypervisor supports a number of guests, including FreeBSD, OpenBSD, and many Linux® distributions. By default, bhyve provides access to serial console and does not emulate a graphical console. Virtualization offload features of newer CPUs are used to avoid the legacy methods of translating instructions and manually managing memory mappings.

The bhyve design requires a processor that supports Intel® Extended Page Tables (EPT) or AMD® Rapid Virtualization Indexing (RVI) or Nested Page Tables (NPT). Hosting Linux® guests or FreeBSD guests with more than one vCPU requires VMX unrestricted mode support (UG). Most newer processors, specifically the Intel® Core™ i3/ i5/i7 and Intel® Xeon™ E3/E5/E7, support these features. UG support was introduced with Intel's Westmere micro-architecture. For a complete list of Intel® processors that support EPT, refer to http://ark.intel.com/search/ advanced?s=t&ExtendedPageTables=true. RVI is found on the third generation and later of the AMD Opteron™ (Barcelona) processors. The easiest way to tell if a processor supports bhyve is to run dmesg or look in /var/run/ dmesg.boot for the POPCNT processor feature flag on the Features2 line for AMD® processors or EPT and UG on the VT-x line for Intel® processors.

21.7.1. Preparing the Host

The first step to creating a virtual machine in bhyve is configuring the host system. First, load the bhyve kernel module:

```
# kldload vmm
```

Then, create a tap interface for the network device in the virtual machine to attach to. In order for the network device to participate in the network, also create a bridge interface containing the tap interface and the physical interface as members. In this example, the physical interface is *igb0*:

```
# ifconfig tap0 create
# sysctl net.link.tap.up_on_open=1
net.link.tap.up_on_open: 0 -> 1
# ifconfig bridge0 create
# ifconfig bridge0 addm igb0 addm tap0
# ifconfig bridge0 up
```

21.7.2. Creating a FreeBSD Guest

Create a file to use as the virtual disk for the guest machine. Specify the size and name of the virtual disk:

```
# truncate -s 16G guest.img
```

Download an installation image of FreeBSD to install:

```
# fetch ftp://ftp.freebsd.org/pub/FreeBSD/releases/ISO-IMAGES/10.3/FreeBSD-10.3-RELEASE-
amd64-bootonly.iso
FreeBSD-10.3-RELEASE-amd64-bootonly.iso          100% of  230 MB  570 kBps 06m17s
```

FreeBSD comes with an example script for running a virtual machine in bhyve. The script will start the virtual machine and run it in a loop, so it will automatically restart if it crashes. The script takes a number of options to control the configuration of the machine: -c controls the number of virtual CPUs, -m limits the amount of memory available to the guest, -t defines which tap device to use, -d indicates which disk image to use, -i tells bhyve to boot from the CD image instead of the disk, and -I defines which CD image to use. The last parameter is the name of the virtual machine, used to track the running machines. This example starts the virtual machine in installation mode:

```
# sh /usr/share/examples/bhyve/vmrun.sh -c  1 -m 1024M -t tap0 -d guest.img -i -
I FreeBSD-10.3-RELEASE-amd64-bootonly.iso    guestname
```

The virtual machine will boot and start the installer. After installing a system in the virtual machine, when the system asks about dropping in to a shell at the end of the installation, choose Yes. A small change needs to be made to make the system start with a serial console. Edit /etc/ttys and replace the existing ttyu0 line with:

```
ttyu0   "/usr/libexec/getty 3wire"   xterm  on secure
```

Note

Beginning with FreeBSD 9.3-RELEASE and 10.1-RELEASE the console is configured automatically.

Reboot the virtual machine. While rebooting the virtual machine causes bhyve to exit, the vmrun.sh script runs bhyve in a loop and will automatically restart it. When this happens, choose the reboot option from the boot loader menu in order to escape the loop. Now the guest can be started from the virtual disk:

```
# sh /usr/share/examples/bhyve/vmrun.sh -c   4 -m 1024M -t tap0 -d guest.img guestname
```

21.7.3. Creating a Linux® Guest

In order to boot operating systems other than FreeBSD, the sysutils/grub2-bhyve port must be first installed.

Next, create a file to use as the virtual disk for the guest machine:

```
# truncate -s 16G linux.img
```

Starting a virtual machine with bhyve is a two step process. First a kernel must be loaded, then the guest can be started. The Linux® kernel is loaded with sysutils/grub2-bhyve. Create a device.map that grub will use to map the virtual devices to the files on the host system:

```
(hd0)  ./linux.img
(cd0)  ./somelinux.iso
```

Use sysutils/grub2-bhyve to load the Linux® kernel from the ISO image:

```
# grub-bhyve -m device.map -r cd0 -M   1024M linuxguest
```

This will start grub. If the installation CD contains a grub.cfg, a menu will be displayed. If not, the vmlinuz and initrd files must be located and loaded manually:

```
grub> ls
(hd0) (cd0) (cd0,msdos1) (host)
grub> ls (cd0)/isolinux
boot.cat boot.msg grub.conf initrd.img isolinux.bin isolinux.cfg memtest
splash.jpg TRANS.TBL vesamenu.c32 vmlinuz
grub> linux (cd0)/isolinux/vmlinuz
grub> initrd (cd0)/isolinux/initrd.img
grub> boot
```

Now that the Linux® kernel is loaded, the guest can be started:

```
# bhyve -A -H -P -s 0:0,hostbridge -s 1:0,lpc -s 2:0,virtio-net,   tap0 -s 3:0,virtio-blk, ./
linux.img \
    -s 4:0,ahci-cd, ./somelinux.iso  -l com1,stdio -c 4 -m 1024M linuxguest
```

The system will boot and start the installer. After installing a system in the virtual machine, reboot the virtual machine. This will cause bhyve to exit. The instance of the virtual machine needs to be destroyed before it can be started again:

```
# bhyvectl --destroy --vm= linuxguest
```

Now the guest can be started directly from the virtual disk. Load the kernel:

```
# grub-bhyve -m device.map -r hd0,msdos1 -M   1024M linuxguest
grub> ls
(hd0) (hd0,msdos2) (hd0,msdos1) (cd0) (cd0,msdos1) (host)
(lvm/VolGroup-lv_swap) (lvm/VolGroup-lv_root)
grub> ls (hd0,msdos1)/
lost+found/ grub/ efi/ System.map-2.6.32-431.el6.x86_64 config-2.6.32-431.el6.x
86_64 symvers-2.6.32-431.el6.x86_64.gz vmlinuz-2.6.32-431.el6.x86_64
initramfs-2.6.32-431.el6.x86_64.img
grub> linux (hd0,msdos1)/vmlinuz-2.6.32-431.el6.x86_64 root=/dev/mapper/VolGroup-lv_root
grub> initrd (hd0,msdos1)/initramfs-2.6.32-431.el6.x86_64.img
grub> boot
```

Boot the virtual machine:

```
# bhyve -A -H -P -s 0:0,hostbridge -s 1:0,lpc -s 2:0,virtio-net,  tap0 \
    -s 3:0,virtio-blk, ./linux.img -l com1,stdio -c  4 -m 1024M linuxguest
```

Linux® will now boot in the virtual machine and eventually present you with the login prompt. Login and use the virtual machine. When you are finished, reboot the virtual machine to exit bhyve. Destroy the virtual machine instance:

```
# bhyvectl --destroy --vm= linuxguest
```

21.7.4. Booting bhyve Virtual Machines with UEFI Firmware

In addition to bhyveload and grub-bhyve, the bhyve hypervisor can also boot virtual machines using the UEFI userspace firmware. This option may support guest operating systems that are not supported by the other loaders.

In order to make use of the UEFI support in bhyve, first obtain the UEFI firmware images. This can be done by installing sysutils/bhyve-firmware port or package.

With the firmware in place, add the flags -l bootrom, /path/to/firmware to your bhyve command line. The actual bhyve command may look like this:

```
# bhyve -AHP -s 0:0,hostbridge -s 1:0,lpc \
-s 2:0,virtio-net, tap1 -s 3:0,virtio-blk, ./disk.img \
-s 4:0,ahci-cd, ./install.iso  -c 4 -m 1024M \
-l bootrom, /usr/local/share/uefi-firmware/BHYVE_UEFI.fd    ↺
\
guest
```

sysutils/bhyve-firmware also contains a CSM-enabled firmware, to boot guests with no UEFI support in legacy BIOS mode:

```
# bhyve -AHP -s 0:0,hostbridge -s 1:0,lpc \
-s 2:0,virtio-net, tap1 -s 3:0,virtio-blk, ./disk.img \
-s 4:0,ahci-cd, ./install.iso  -c 4 -m 1024M \
-l bootrom, /usr/local/share/uefi-firmware/BHYVE_UEFI_CSM.fd    ↺
\
guest
```

21.7.5. Graphical UEFI Framebuffer for bhyve Guests

The UEFI firmware support is particularly useful with predominantly graphical guest operating systems such as Microsoft Windows®.

Support for the UEFI-GOP framebuffer may also be enabled with the -s 29,fbuf,tcp= 0.0.0.0:5900 flags. The framebuffer resolution may be configured with w=800 and h=600, and bhyve can be instructed to wait for a VNC connection before booting the guest by adding wait. The framebuffer may be accessed from the host or over the network via the VNC protocol.

The resulting bhyve command would look like this:

```
# bhyve -AHP -s 0:0,hostbridge -s 31:0,lpc \
-s 2:0,virtio-net, tap1 -s 3:0,virtio-blk, ./disk.img \
-s 4:0,ahci-cd, ./install.iso  -c 4 -m 1024M \
-s 29,fbuf,tcp= 0.0.0.0:5900 ,w=800,h=600,wait \
-l bootrom, /usr/local/share/uefi-firmware/BHYVE_UEFI.fd    ↺
\
guest
```

Note, in BIOS emulation mode, the framebuffer will cease receiving updates once control is passed from firmware to guest operating system.

21.7.6. Using ZFS with bhyve Guests

If ZFS is available on the host machine, using ZFS volumes instead of disk image files can provide significant performance benefits for the guest VMs. A ZFS volume can be created by:

```
# zfs create -V 16G -o volmode=dev zroot/linuxdisk0
```

When starting the VM, specify the ZFS volume as the disk drive:

```
# bhyve -A -H -P -s 0:0,hostbridge -s 1:0,lpc -s 2:0,virtio-net,  tap0 -s3:0,virtio-blk, /dev/
zvol/zroot/linuxdisk0  \
    -l com1,stdio -c 4 -m 1024M linuxguest
```

21.7.7. Virtual Machine Consoles

It is advantageous to wrap the bhyve console in a session management tool such as sysutils/tmux or sysutils/screen in order to detach and reattach to the console. It is also possible to have the console of bhyve be a null modem device that can be accessed with cu. To do this, load the nmdm kernel module and replace -l com1,stdio with -l com1,/dev/nmdm0A. The /dev/nmdm devices are created automatically as needed, where each is a pair, corresponding to the two ends of the null modem cable (/dev/nmdm0A and /dev/nmdm0B). See nmdm(4) for more information.

```
# kldload nmdm
# bhyve -A -H -P -s 0:0,hostbridge -s 1:0,lpc -s 2:0,virtio-net,  tap0 -s 3:0,virtio-blk, ./
linux.img \
    -l com1,/dev/nmdm0A  -c 4 -m 1024M linuxguest
# cu -l /dev/nmdm0B
Connected

Ubuntu 13.10 handbook ttyS0

handbook login:
```

21.7.8. Managing Virtual Machines

A device node is created in /dev/vmm for each virtual machine. This allows the administrator to easily see a list of the running virtual machines:

```
# ls -al /dev/vmm
total 1
dr-xr-xr-x   2 root  wheel    512 Mar 17 12:19 ./
dr-xr-xr-x  14 root  wheel    512 Mar 17 06:38 ../
crw-------   1 root  wheel  0x1a2 Mar 17 12:20 guestname
crw-------   1 root  wheel  0x19f Mar 17 12:19 linuxguest
crw-------   1 root  wheel  0x1a1 Mar 17 12:19 otherguest
```

A specified virtual machine can be destroyed using bhyvectl:

```
# bhyvectl --destroy --vm= guestname
```

21.7.9. Persistent Configuration

In order to configure the system to start bhyve guests at boot time, the following configurations must be made in the specified files:

1. **/etc/sysctl.conf**

   ```
   net.link.tap.up_on_open=1
   ```

2. **/boot/loader.conf**

   ```
   vmm_load="YES"
   nmdm_load="YES"
   if_bridge_load="YES"
   ```

```
if_tap_load="YES"
```

3. **/etc/rc.conf**

```
cloned_interfaces="bridge0 tap0"
ifconfig_bridge0="addm igb0 addm tap0"
```

21.8. FreeBSD as a Xen™-Host

Xen is a GPLv2-licensed type 1 hypervisor for Intel® and ARM® architectures. FreeBSD has included i386™ and AMD® 64-Bit DomU and Amazon EC2 unprivileged domain (virtual machine) support since FreeBSD 8.0 and includes Dom0 control domain (host) support in FreeBSD 11.0. Support for para-virtualized (PV) domains has been removed from FreeBSD 11 in favor of hardware virtualized (HVM) domains, which provides better performance.

Xen™ is a bare-metal hypervisor, which means that it is the first program loaded after the BIOS. A special privileged guest called the Domain-0 (Dom0 for short) is then started. The Dom0 uses its special privileges to directly access the underlying physical hardware, making it a high-performance solution. It is able to access the disk controllers and network adapters directly. The Xen™ management tools to manage and control the Xen™ hypervisor are also used by the Dom0 to create, list, and destroy VMs. Dom0 provides virtual disks and networking for unprivileged domains, often called DomU. Xen™ Dom0 can be compared to the service console of other hypervisor solutions, while the DomU is where individual guest VMs are run.

Xen™ can migrate VMs between different Xen™ servers. When the two xen hosts share the same underlying storage, the migration can be done without having to shut the VM down first. Instead, the migration is performed live while the DomU is running and there is no need to restart it or plan a downtime. This is useful in maintenance scenarios or upgrade windows to ensure that the services provided by the DomU are still provided. Many more features of Xen™ are listed on the Xen Wiki Overview page. Note that not all features are supported on FreeBSD yet.

21.8.1. Hardware Requirements for Xen™ Dom0

To run the Xen™ hypervisor on a host, certain hardware functionality is required. Hardware virtualized domains require Extended Page Table (EPT) and Input/Output Memory Management Unit (IOMMU) support in the host processor.

21.8.2. Xen™ Dom0 Control Domain Setup

The emulators/xen package works with FreeBSD 11 amd64 binary snapshots and equivalent systems built from source. This example assumes VNC output for unprivileged domains which is accessed from a another system using a tool such as net/tightvnc.

Install emulators/xen:

```
# pkg install xen
```

Configuration files must be edited to prepare the host for the Dom0 integration. An entry to /etc/sysctl.conf disables the limit on how many pages of memory are allowed to be wired. Otherwise, DomU VMs with higher memory requirements will not run.

```
# sysrc -f /etc/sysctl.conf vm.max_wired=-1
```

Another memory-related setting involves changing /etc/login.conf, setting the memorylocked option to unlimited. Otherwise, creating DomU domains may fail with Cannot allocate memory errors. After making the change to /etc/login.conf, run cap_mkdb to update the capability database. See Section 13.13, "Resource Limits" for details.

```
# sed -i '' -e 's/memorylocked=64K/memorylocked=unlimited/' /etc/login.conf
# cap_mkdb /etc/login.conf
```

Add an entry for the Xen™ console to /etc/ttys :

```
# echo 'xc0     "/usr/libexec/getty Pc"          xterm   on  secure' >> /etc/ttys
```

Selecting a Xen™ kernel in /boot/loader.conf activates the Dom0. Xen™ also requires resources like CPU and memory from the host machine for itself and other DomU domains. How much CPU and memory depends on the individual requirements and hardware capabilities. In this example, 8 GB of memory and 4 virtual CPUs are made available for the Dom0. The serial console is also activated and logging options are defined.

```
# sysrc -f /boot/loader.conf hw.pci.mcfg=0
# sysrc -f /boot/loader.conf xen_kernel="/boot/xen"
# sysrc -f /boot/loader.conf xen_cmdline="dom0_mem=  8192M dom0_max_vcpus= 4 dom0pvh=1 ↵
console=com1,vga com1=115200,8n1 guest_loglvl=all loglvl=all"
```

Log files that Xen™ creates for the Dom0 and DomU VMs are stored in /var/log/xen . This directory does not exist by default and must be created.

```
# mkdir -p /var/log/xen
# chmod 644 /var/log/xen
```

Xen™ provides a boot menu to activate and de-activate the hypervisor on demand in /boot/menu.rc.local :

```
# echo "try-include /boot/xen.4th" >> /boot/menu.rc.local
```

Activate the xencommons service during system startup:

```
# sysrc xencommons_enable=yes
```

These settings are enough to start a Dom0-enabled system. However, it lacks network functionality for the DomU machines. To fix that, define a bridged interface with the main NIC of the system which the DomU VMs can use to connect to the network. Replace *igb0* with the host network interface name.

```
# sysrc autobridge_interfaces=bridge0
# sysrc autobridge_bridge0= igb0
# sysrc ifconfig_bridge0=SYNCDHCP
```

Restart the host to load the Xen™ kernel and start the Dom0.

```
# reboot
```

After successfully booting the Xen™ kernel and logging into the system again, the Xen™ management tool xl is used to show information about the domains.

```
# xl list
Name                              ID   Mem VCPUs     State   Time(s)
Domain-0                           0  8192     4     r-----    962.0
```

The output confirms that the Dom0 (called Domain-0) has the ID 0 and is running. It also has the memory and virtual CPUs that were defined in /boot/loader.conf earlier. More information can be found in the Xen™ Documentation. DomU guest VMs can now be created.

21.8.3. Xen™ DomU Guest VM Configuration

Unprivileged domains consist of a configuration file and virtual or physical hard disks. Virtual disk storage for the DomU can be files created by truncate(1) or ZFS volumes as described in Section 19.4.2, "Creating and Destroying Volumes". In this example, a 20 GB volume is used. A VM is created with the ZFS volume, a FreeBSD ISO image, 1 GB of RAM and two virtual CPUs. The ISO installation file is retrieved with fetch(1) and saved locally in a file called freebsd.iso.

```
# fetch ftp://ftp.freebsd.org/pub/FreeBSD/releases/ISO-IMAGES/10.3/FreeBSD-10.3-RELEASE-
amd64-bootonly.iso  -o freebsd.iso
```

A ZFS volume of 20 GB called xendisk0 is created to serve as the disk space for the VM.

```
# zfs create -V20G -o volmode=dev zroot/xendisk0
```

The new DomU guest VM is defined in a file. Some specific definitions like name, keymap, and VNC connection details are also defined. The following `freebsd.cfg` contains a minimum DomU configuration for this example:

```
# cat freebsd.cfg
builder = "hvm" ❶
name = "freebsd" ❷
memory = 1024 ❸
vcpus = 2 ❹
vif = [ 'mac=00:16:3E:74:34:32,bridge=bridge0' -] ❺
disk = [
'/dev/zvol/tank/xendisk0,raw,hda,rw', ❻
'/root/freebsd.iso,raw,hdc:cdrom,r' ❼
  -]
vnc = 1 ❽
vnclisten = "0.0.0.0"
serial = "pty"
usbdevice = "tablet"
```

These lines are explained in more detail:

❶   This defines what kind of virtualization to use. hvm refers to hardware-assisted virtualization or hardware virtual machine. Guest operating systems can run unmodified on CPUs with virtualization extensions, providing nearly the same performance as running on physical hardware. generic is the default value and creates a PV domain.

❷   Name of this virtual machine to distinguish it from others running on the same Dom0. Required.

❸   Quantity of RAM in megabytes to make available to the VM. This amount is subtracted from the hypervisor's total available memory, not the memory of the Dom0.

❹   Number of virtual CPUs available to the guest VM. For best performance, do not create guests with more virtual CPUs than the number of physical CPUs on the host.

❺   Virtual network adapter. This is the bridge connected to the network interface of the host. The mac parameter is the MAC address set on the virtual network interface. This parameter is optional, if no MAC is provided Xen™ will generate a random one.

❻   Full path to the disk, file, or ZFS volume of the disk storage for this VM. Options and multiple disk definitions are separated by commas.

❼   Defines the Boot medium from which the initial operating system is installed. In this example, it is the ISO imaged downloaded earlier. Consult the Xen™ documentation for other kinds of devices and options to set.

❽   Options controlling VNC connectivity to the serial console of the DomU. In order, these are: active VNC support, define IP address on which to listen, device node for the serial console, and the input method for precise positioning of the mouse and other input methods. keymap defines which keymap to use, and is english by default.

After the file has been created with all the necessary options, the DomU is created by passing it to xl create as a parameter.

```
# xl create freebsd.cfg
```

Note

Each time the Dom0 is restarted, the configuration file must be passed to xl create again to re-create the DomU. By default, only the Dom0 is created after a reboot, not the individual VMs. The VMs can continue where they left off as they stored the operating system on the virtual disk. The virtual machine configuration can change over time (for example, when adding more memory). The virtual machine configuration files must be properly backed up and kept available to be able to re-create the guest VM when needed.

The output of xl list confirms that the DomU has been created.

```
# xl list
Name                                      ID   Mem VCPUs      State   Time(s)
Domain-0                                   0  8192     4      r-----  1653.4
freebsd                                    1  1024     1      -b----   663.9
```

To begin the installation of the base operating system, start the VNC client, directing it to the main network address of the host or to the IP address defined on the vnclisten line of freebsd.cfg. After the operating system has been installed, shut down the DomU and disconnect the VNC viewer. Edit freebsd.cfg, removing the line with the cdrom definition or commenting it out by inserting a # character at the beginning of the line. To load this new configuration, it is necessary to remove the old DomU with xl destroy, passing either the name or the id as the parameter. Afterwards, recreate it using the modified freebsd.cfg.

```
# xl destroy freebsd
# xl create freebsd.cfg
```

The machine can then be accessed again using the VNC viewer. This time, it will boot from the virtual disk where the operating system has been installed and can be used as a virtual machine.

Chapter 22. Localization - i18n/L10n Usage and Setup

Contributed by Andrey Chernov.
Rewritten by Michael C. Wu.

22.1. Synopsis

FreeBSD is a distributed project with users and contributors located all over the world. As such, FreeBSD supports localization into many languages, allowing users to view, input, or process data in non-English languages. One can choose from most of the major languages, including, but not limited to: Chinese, German, Japanese, Korean, French, Russian, and Vietnamese.

The term internationalization has been shortened to i18n, which represents the number of letters between the first and the last letters of `internationalization`. L10n uses the same naming scheme, but from `localization`. The i18n/L10n methods, protocols, and applications allow users to use languages of their choice.

This chapter discusses the internationalization and localization features of FreeBSD. After reading this chapter, you will know:

- How locale names are constructed.

- How to set the locale for a login shell.

- How to configure the console for non-English languages.

- How to configure Xorg for different languages.

- How to find i18n-compliant applications.

- Where to find more information for configuring specific languages.

Before reading this chapter, you should:

- Know how to install additional third-party applications.

22.2. Using Localization

Localization settings are based on three components: the language code, country code, and encoding. Locale names are constructed from these parts as follows:

LanguageCode _CountryCode .Encoding

The *LanguageCode* and *CountryCode* are used to determine the country and the specific language variation. Table 22.1, "Common Language and Country Codes" provides some examples of *LanguageCode_CountryCode*:

Table 22.1. Common Language and Country Codes

LanguageCode_Country Code	Description
en_US	English, United States
ru_RU	Russian, Russia
zh_TW	Traditional Chinese, Taiwan

A complete listing of available locales can be found by typing:

```
% locale -a | more
```

To determine the current locale setting:

```
% locale
```

Language specific character sets, such as ISO8859-1, ISO8859-15, KOI8-R, and CP437, are described in multibyte(3). The active list of character sets can be found at the IANA Registry.

Some languages, such as Chinese or Japanese, cannot be represented using ASCII characters and require an extended language encoding using either wide or multibyte characters. Examples of wide or multibyte encodings include EUC and Big5. Older applications may mistake these encodings for control characters while newer applications usually recognize these characters. Depending on the implementation, users may be required to compile an application with wide or multibyte character support, or to configure it correctly.

Note

FreeBSD uses Xorg-compatible locale encodings.

The rest of this section describes the various methods for configuring the locale on a FreeBSD system. The next section will discuss the considerations for finding and compiling applications with i18n support.

22.2.1. Setting Locale for Login Shell

Locale settings are configured either in a user's ~/.login_conf or in the startup file of the user's shell: ~/.profile, ~/.bashrc , or ~/.cshrc .

Two environment variables should be set:

- LANG, which sets the locale

- MM_CHARSET , which sets the MIME character set used by applications

In addition to the user's shell configuration, these variables should also be set for specific application configuration and Xorg configuration.

Two methods are available for making the needed variable assignments: the login class method, which is the recommended method, and the startup file method. The next two sections demonstrate how to use both methods.

22.2.1.1. Login Classes Method

This first method is the recommended method as it assigns the required environment variables for locale name and MIME character sets for every possible shell. This setup can either be performed by each user or it can be configured for all users by the superuser.

This minimal example sets both variables for Latin-1 encoding in the .login_conf of an individual user's home directory:

```
me:\
 :charset=ISO-8859-1:\
 :lang=de_DE.ISO8859-1:
```

Here is an example of a user's ~/.login_conf that sets the variables for Traditional Chinese in BIG-5 encoding. More variables are needed because some applications do not correctly respect locale variables for Chinese, Japanese, and Korean:

```
#Users who do not wish to use monetary units or time formats
#of Taiwan can manually change each variable
me:\
  :lang=zh_TW.Big5:\
  :setenv=LC_ALL=zh_TW.Big5,LC_COLLATE=zh_TW.Big5,LC_CTYPE=zh_TW.Big5,LC_MESSAGES=zh_TW.↵
Big5,LC_MONETARY=zh_TW.Big5,LC_NUMERIC=zh_TW.Big5,LC_TIME=zh_TW.Big5:\
  :charset=big5:\
  :xmodifiers="@im=gcin": #Set gcin as the XIM Input Server
```

Alternately, the superuser can configure all users of the system for localization. The following variables in /etc/login.conf are used to set the locale and MIME character set:

```
language_name |Account Type Description :\
  :charset=MIME_charset :\
  :lang=locale_name :\
  :tc=default:
```

So, the previous Latin-1 example would look like this:

```
german|German Users Accounts:\
  :charset=ISO-8859-1:\
  :lang=de_DE.ISO8859-1:\
  :tc=default:
```

See login.conf(5) for more details about these variables.

Whenever /etc/login.conf is edited, remember to execute the following command to update the capability database:

```
# cap_mkdb /etc/login.conf
```

22.2.1.1.1. Utilities Which Change Login Classes

In addition to manually editing /etc/login.conf, several utilities are available for setting the locale for newly created users.

When using vipw to add new users, specify the *language* to set the locale:

```
user:password:1111:11:language :0:0:User Name:/home/user:/bin/sh
```

When using adduser to add new users, the default language can be pre-configured for all new users or specified for an individual user.

If all new users use the same language, set defaultclass=*language* in /etc/adduser.conf.

To override this setting when creating a user, either input the required locale at this prompt:

```
Enter login class: default []:
```

or specify the locale to set when invoking adduser:

```
# adduser -class  language
```

If pw is used to add new users, specify the locale as follows:

```
# pw useradd  user_name  -L language
```

22.2.1.2. Shell Startup File Method

This second method is not recommended as each shell that is used requires manual configuration, where each shell has a different configuration file and differing syntax. As an example, to set the German language for the sh shell, these lines could be added to ~/.profile to set the shell for that user only. These lines could also be added to /etc/profile or /usr/share/skel/dot.profile to set that shell for all users:

```
LANG=de_DE.ISO8859-1; export LANG
MM_CHARSET =ISO-8859-1; export MM_CHARSET
```

However, the name of the configuration file and the syntax used differs for the csh shell. These are the equivalent settings for ~/.csh.login, /etc/csh.login, or /usr/share/skel/dot.login :

```
setenv LANG de_DE.ISO8859-1
setenv MM_CHARSET ISO-8859-1
```

To complicate matters, the syntax needed to configure Xorg in ~/.xinitrc also depends upon the shell. The first example is for the sh shell and the second is for the csh shell:

```
LANG=de_DE.ISO8859-1; export LANG
```

```
setenv LANG de_DE.ISO8859-1
```

22.2.2. Console Setup

Several localized fonts are available for the console. To see a listing of available fonts, type ls /usr/share/syscons/fonts . To configure the console font, specify the *font_name* , without the .fnt suffix, in /etc/rc.conf :

```
font8x16=font_name
font8x14=font_name
font8x8=font_name
```

The keymap and screenmap can be set by adding the following to /etc/rc.conf :

```
scrnmap=screenmap_name
keymap=keymap_name
keychange="fkey_number sequence "
```

To see the list of available screenmaps, type ls /usr/share/syscons/scrnmaps . Do not include the .scm suffix when specifying *screenmap_name*. A screenmap with a corresponding mapped font is usually needed as a workaround for expanding bit 8 to bit 9 on a VGA adapter's font character matrix so that letters are moved out of the pseudographics area if the screen font uses a bit 8 column.

To see the list of available keymaps, type ls /usr/share/syscons/keymaps . When specifying the *keymap_name* , do not include the .kbd suffix. To test keymaps without rebooting, use kbdmap(1).

The keychange entry is usually needed to program function keys to match the selected terminal type because function key sequences cannot be defined in the keymap.

Next, set the correct console terminal type in /etc/ttys for all virtual terminal entries. Table 22.2, "Defined Terminal Types for Character Sets" summarizes the available terminal types.:

Table 22.2. Defined Terminal Types for Character Sets

Character Set	Terminal Type
ISO8859-1 or ISO8859-15	cons25l1
ISO8859-2	cons25l2
ISO8859-7	cons25l7
KOI8-R	cons25r
KOI8-U	cons25u
CP437 (VGA default)	cons25
US-ASCII	cons25w

For languages with wide or multibyte characters, install a console for that language from the FreeBSD Ports Collection. The available ports are summarized in Table 22.3, "Available Console from Ports Collection". Once installed, refer to the port's pkg-message or man pages for configuration and usage instructions.

Table 22.3. Available Console from Ports Collection

Language	Port Location
Traditional Chinese (BIG-5)	chinese/big5con
Chinese/Japanese/Korean	chinese/cce
Chinese/Japanese/Korean	chinese/zhcon
Japanese	chinese/kon2
Japanese	japanese/kon2-14dot
Japanese	japanese/kon2-16dot

If moused is enabled in /etc/rc.conf , additional configuration may be required. By default, the mouse cursor of the syscons(4) driver occupies the 0xd0-0xd3 range in the character set. If the language uses this range, move the cursor's range by adding the following line to /etc/rc.conf :

```
mousechar_start=3
```

22.2.3. Xorg Setup

Chapter 5, *The X Window System* describes how to install and configure Xorg. When configuring Xorg for localization, additional fonts and input methods are available from the FreeBSD Ports Collection. Application specific i18n settings such as fonts and menus can be tuned in ~/.Xresources and should allow users to view their selected language in graphical application menus.

The X Input Method (XIM) protocol is an Xorg standard for inputting non-English characters. Table 22.4, "Available Input Methods" summarizes the input method applications which are available in the FreeBSD Ports Collection. Additional Fcitx and Uim applications are also available.

Table 22.4. Available Input Methods

Language	Input Method
Chinese	chinese/gcin
Chinese	chinese/ibus-chewing
Chinese	chinese/ibus-pinyin
Chinese	chinese/oxim
Chinese	chinese/scim-fcitx
Chinese	chinese/scim-pinyin
Chinese	chinese/scim-tables
Japanese	japanese/ibus-anthy
Japanese	japanese/ibus-mozc
Japanese	japanese/ibus-skk
Japanese	japanese/im-ja
Japanese	japanese/kinput2
Japanese	japanese/scim-anthy
Japanese	japanese/scim-canna
Japanese	japanese/scim-honoka

Language	Input Method
Japanese	japanese/scim-honoka-plugin-romkan
Japanese	japanese/scim-honoka-plugin-wnn
Japanese	japanese/scim-prime
Japanese	japanese/scim-skk
Japanese	japanese/scim-tables
Japanese	japanese/scim-tomoe
Japanese	japanese/scim-uim
Japanese	japanese/skkinput
Japanese	japanese/skkinput3
Japanese	japanese/uim-anthy
Korean	korean/ibus-hangul
Korean	korean/imhangul
Korean	korean/nabi
Korean	korean/scim-hangul
Korean	korean/scim-tables
Vietnamese	vietnamese/xvnkb
Vietnamese	vietnamese/x-unikey

22.3. Finding i18n Applications

i18n applications are programmed using i18n kits under libraries. These allow developers to write a simple file and translate displayed menus and texts to each language.

The FreeBSD Ports Collection contains many applications with built-in support for wide or multibyte characters for several languages. Such applications include i18n in their names for easy identification. However, they do not always support the language needed.

Some applications can be compiled with the specific charset. This is usually done in the port's Makefile or by passing a value to configure. Refer to the i18n documentation in the respective FreeBSD port's source for more information on how to determine the needed configure value or the port's Makefile to determine which compile options to use when building the port.

22.4. Locale Configuration for Specific Languages

This section provides configuration examples for localizing a FreeBSD system for the Russian language. It then provides some additional resources for localizing other languages.

22.4.1. Russian Language (KOI8-R Encoding)

Originally contributed by Andrey Chernov.

This section shows the specific settings needed to localize a FreeBSD system for the Russian language. Refer to Using Localization for a more complete description of each type of setting.

To set this locale for the login shell, add the following lines to each user's ~/.login_conf:

```
me:My Account:\
 :charset=KOI8-R:\
```

```
:lang=ru_RU.KOI8-R:
```

To configure the console, add the following lines to /etc/rc.conf :

```
keymap="ru.koi8-r"
scrnmap="koi8-r2cp866"
font8x16="cp866b-8x16"
font8x14="cp866-8x14"
font8x8="cp866-8x8"
mousechar_start=3
```

For each ttyv entry in /etc/ttys , use cons25r as the terminal type.

To configure printing, a special output filter is needed to convert from KOI8-R to CP866 since most printers with Russian characters come with hardware code page CP866. FreeBSD includes a default filter for this purpose, /usr/libexec/lpr/ru/koi2alt . To use this filter, add this entry to /etc/printcap:

```
lp|Russian local line printer:\
 :sh:of=/usr/libexec/lpr/ru/koi2alt:\
 :lp=/dev/lpt0:sd=/var/spool/output/lpd:lf=/var/log/lpd-errs:
```

Refer to printcap(5) for a more detailed explanation.

To configure support for Russian filenames in mounted MS-DOS® file systems, include -L and the locale name when adding an entry to /etc/fstab :

```
/dev/ad0s2      /dos/c  msdos   rw,-Lru_RU.KOI8-R 0 0
```

Refer to mount_msdosfs(8) for more details.

To configure Russian fonts for Xorg, install the x11-fonts/xorg-fonts-cyrillic package. Then, check the "Files" section in /etc/X11/xorg.conf . The following line must be added *before* any other FontPath entries:

```
FontPath    "/usr/local/lib/X11/fonts/cyrillic"
```

Additional Cyrillic fonts are available in the Ports Collection.

To activate a Russian keyboard, add the following to the "Keyboard" section of /etc/xorg.conf :

```
Option "XkbLayout"   "us,ru"
Option "XkbOptions"  "grp:toggle"
```

Make sure that XkbDisable is commented out in that file.

For grp:toggle use Right Alt, for grp:ctrl_shift_toggle use Ctrl+Shift. For grp:caps_toggle use CapsLock. The old CapsLock function is still available in LAT mode only using Shift+CapsLock. grp:caps_toggle does not work in Xorg for some unknown reason.

If the keyboard has "Windows®" keys, and some non-alphabetical keys are mapped incorrectly, add the following line to /etc/xorg.conf :

```
Option "XkbVariant" ",winkeys"
```

> **Note**
>
> The Russian XKB keyboard may not work with non-localized applications. Minimally local-ized applications should call a XtSetLanguageProc (NULL, NULL, NULL); function early in the program.

See `http://koi8.pp.ru/xwin.html` for more instructions on localizing Xorg applications. For more general information about KOI8-R encoding, refer to `http://koi8.pp.ru/` .

22.4.2. Additional Language-Specific Resources

This section lists some additional resources for configuring other locales.

Traditional Chinese for Taiwan
> The FreeBSD-Taiwan Project has a Chinese HOWTO for FreeBSD at `http://netlab.cse.yzu.edu.tw/~statue/freebsd/zh-tut/` .

Greek Language Localization
> A complete article on Greek support in FreeBSD is available here, in Greek only, as part of the official FreeBSD Greek documentation.

Japanese and Korean Language Localization
> For Japanese, refer to `http://www.jp.FreeBSD.org/` , and for Korean, refer to `http://www.kr.FreeBSD.org/` .

Non-English FreeBSD Documentation
> Some FreeBSD contributors have translated parts of the FreeBSD documentation to other languages. They are available through links on the FreeBSD web site or in `/usr/share/doc` .

Chapter 23. Updating and Upgrading FreeBSD

Restructured, reorganized, and parts updated by Jim Mock.
Original work by Jordan Hubbard, Poul-Henning Kamp, John Polstra and Nik Clayton.

23.1. Synopsis

FreeBSD is under constant development between releases. Some people prefer to use the officially released versions, while others prefer to keep in sync with the latest developments. However, even official releases are often updated with security and other critical fixes. Regardless of the version used, FreeBSD provides all the necessary tools to keep the system updated, and allows for easy upgrades between versions. This chapter describes how to track the development system and the basic tools for keeping a FreeBSD system up-to-date.

After reading this chapter, you will know:

- How to keep a FreeBSD system up-to-date with freebsd-update or Subversion.

- How to compare the state of an installed system against a known pristine copy.

- How to keep the installed documentation up-to-date with Subversion or documentation ports.

- The difference between the two development branches: FreeBSD-STABLE and FreeBSD-CURRENT.

- How to rebuild and reinstall the entire base system.

Before reading this chapter, you should:

- Properly set up the network connection (Chapter 30, *Advanced Networking*).

- Know how to install additional third-party software (Chapter 4, *Installing Applications: Packages and Ports*).

 Note

Throughout this chapter, svn is used to obtain and update FreeBSD sources. To use it, first install the devel/subversion port or package.

23.2. FreeBSD Update

Written by Tom Rhodes.
Based on notes provided by Colin Percival.

Applying security patches in a timely manner and upgrading to a newer release of an operating system are important aspects of ongoing system administration. FreeBSD includes a utility called freebsd-update which can be used to perform both these tasks.

This utility supports binary security and errata updates to FreeBSD, without the need to manually compile and install the patch or a new kernel. Binary updates are available for all architectures and releases currently supported by the security team. The list of supported releases and their estimated end-of-life dates are listed at https://www.FreeBSD.org/security/.

This utility also supports operating system upgrades to minor point releases as well as upgrades to another release branch. Before upgrading to a new release, review its release announcement as it contains important information pertinent to the release. Release announcements are available from `https://www.FreeBSD.org/releases/` .

> **Note**
>
> If a `crontab` utilizing the features of freebsd-update(8) exists, it must be disabled before upgrading the operating system.

This section describes the configuration file used by `freebsd-update`, demonstrates how to apply a security patch and how to upgrade to a minor or major operating system release, and discusses some of the considerations when upgrading the operating system.

23.2.1. The Configuration File

The default configuration file for `freebsd-update` works as-is. Some users may wish to tweak the default configuration in `/etc/freebsd-update.conf` , allowing better control of the process. The comments in this file explain the available options, but the following may require a bit more explanation:

```
# Components of the base system which should be kept updated.
Components world kernel
```

This parameter controls which parts of FreeBSD will be kept up-to-date. The default is to update the entire base system and the kernel. Individual components can instead be specified, such as `src/base` or `src/sys` . However, the best option is to leave this at the default as changing it to include specific items requires every needed item to be listed. Over time, this could have disastrous consequences as source code and binaries may become out of sync.

```
# Paths which start with anything matching an entry in an IgnorePaths
# statement will be ignored.
IgnorePaths /boot/kernel/linker.hints
```

To leave specified directories, such as `/bin` or `/sbin`, untouched during the update process, add their paths to this statement. This option may be used to prevent `freebsd-update` from overwriting local modifications.

```
# Paths which start with anything matching an entry in an UpdateIfUnmodified
# statement will only be updated if the contents of the file have not been
# modified by the user (unless changes are merged; see below).
UpdateIfUnmodified /etc/ /var/ /root/ /.cshrc /.profile
```

This option will only update unmodified configuration files in the specified directories. Any changes made by the user will prevent the automatic updating of these files. There is another option, `KeepModifiedMetadata`, which will instruct `freebsd-update` to save the changes during the merge.

```
# When upgrading to a new FreeBSD release, files which match MergeChanges
# will have any local changes merged into the version from the new release.
MergeChanges /etc/ /var/named/etc/ /boot/device.hints
```

List of directories with configuration files that `freebsd-update` should attempt to merge. The file merge process is a series of diff(1) patches similar to mergemaster(8), but with fewer options. Merges are either accepted, open an editor, or cause `freebsd-update` to abort. When in doubt, backup `/etc` and just accept the merges. See mergemaster(8) for more information about `mergemaster`.

```
# Directory in which to store downloaded updates and temporary
# files used by FreeBSD Update.
# WorkDir /var/db/freebsd-update
```

This directory is where all patches and temporary files are placed. In cases where the user is doing a version upgrade, this location should have at least a gigabyte of disk space available.

```
# When upgrading between releases, should the list of Components be
# read strictly (StrictComponents yes) or merely as a list of components
# which *might* be installed of which FreeBSD Update should figure out
# which actually are installed and upgrade those (StrictComponents no)?
# StrictComponents no
```

When this option is set to `yes`, `freebsd-update` will assume that the `Components` list is complete and will not attempt to make changes outside of the list. Effectively, `freebsd-update` will attempt to update every file which belongs to the `Components` list.

23.2.2. Applying Security Patches

The process of applying FreeBSD security patches has been simplified, allowing an administrator to keep a system fully patched using `freebsd-update`. More information about FreeBSD security advisories can be found in Section 13.11, "FreeBSD Security Advisories".

FreeBSD security patches may be downloaded and installed using the following commands. The first command will determine if any outstanding patches are available, and if so, will list the files that will be modifed if the patches are applied. The second command will apply the patches.

```
# freebsd-update fetch
# freebsd-update install
```

If the update applies any kernel patches, the system will need a reboot in order to boot into the patched kernel. If the patch was applied to any running binaries, the affected applications should be restarted so that the patched version of the binary is used.

The system can be configured to automatically check for updates once every day by adding this entry to /etc/crontab:

```
@daily                                  root    freebsd-update cron
```

If patches exist, they will automatically be downloaded but will not be applied. The `root` user will be sent an email so that the patches may be reviewed and manually installed with `freebsd-update install`.

If anything goes wrong, `freebsd-update` has the ability to roll back the last set of changes with the following command:

```
# freebsd-update rollback
Uninstalling updates... done.
```

Again, the system should be restarted if the kernel or any kernel modules were modified and any affected binaries should be restarted.

Only the `GENERIC` kernel can be automatically updated by `freebsd-update`. If a custom kernel is installed, it will have to be rebuilt and reinstalled after `freebsd-update` finishes installing the updates. However, `freebsd-update` will detect and update the `GENERIC` kernel if /boot/GENERIC exists, even if it is not the current running kernel of the system.

Note

Always keep a copy of the `GENERIC` kernel in /boot/GENERIC . It will be helpful in diagnosing a variety of problems and in performing version upgrades. Refer to Section 23.2.3.1, "Custom Kernels with FreeBSD 9.X and Later" for instructions on how to get a copy of the `GENERIC` kernel.

Unless the default configuration in /etc/freebsd-update.conf has been changed, freebsd-update will install the updated kernel sources along with the rest of the updates. Rebuilding and reinstalling a new custom kernel can then be performed in the usual way.

The updates distributed by freebsd-update do not always involve the kernel. It is not necessary to rebuild a custom kernel if the kernel sources have not been modified by freebsd-update install. However, freebsd-update will always update /usr/src/sys/conf/newvers.sh . The current patch level, as indicated by the -p number reported by uname -r, is obtained from this file. Rebuilding a custom kernel, even if nothing else changed, allows uname to accurately report the current patch level of the system. This is particularly helpful when maintaining multiple systems, as it allows for a quick assessment of the updates installed in each one.

23.2.3. Performing Major and Minor Version Upgrades

Upgrades from one minor version of FreeBSD to another, like from FreeBSD 9.0 to FreeBSD 9.1, are called *minor version* upgrades. *Major version* upgrades occur when FreeBSD is upgraded from one major version to another, like from FreeBSD 9.X to FreeBSD 10.X. Both types of upgrades can be performed by providing freebsd-update with a release version target.

> Note
>
> If the system is running a custom kernel, make sure that a copy of the GENERIC kernel exists in /boot/GENERIC before starting the upgrade. Refer to Section 23.2.3.1, "Custom Kernels with FreeBSD 9.X and Later" for instructions on how to get a copy of the GENERIC kernel.

The following command, when run on a FreeBSD 9.0 system, will upgrade it to FreeBSD 9.1:

```
# freebsd-update -r 9.1-RELEASE upgrade
```

After the command has been received, freebsd-update will evaluate the configuration file and current system in an attempt to gather the information necessary to perform the upgrade. A screen listing will display which components have and have not been detected. For example:

```
Looking up update.FreeBSD.org mirrors... 1 mirrors found.
Fetching metadata signature for 9.0-RELEASE from update1.FreeBSD.org... done.
Fetching metadata index... done.
Inspecting system... done.

The following components of FreeBSD seem to be installed:
kernel/smp src/base src/bin src/contrib src/crypto src/etc src/games
src/gnu src/include src/krb5 src/lib src/libexec src/release src/rescue
src/sbin src/secure src/share src/sys src/tools src/ubin src/usbin
world/base world/info world/lib32 world/manpages

The following components of FreeBSD do not seem to be installed:
kernel/generic world/catpages world/dict world/doc world/games
world/proflibs

Does this look reasonable (y/n)? y
```

At this point, freebsd-update will attempt to download all files required for the upgrade. In some cases, the user may be prompted with questions regarding what to install or how to proceed.

When using a custom kernel, the above step will produce a warning similar to the following:

```
WARNING: This system is running a "MYKERNEL " kernel, which is not a
kernel configuration distributed as part of FreeBSD 9.0-RELEASE.
This kernel will not be updated: you MUST update the kernel manually
before running "/usr/sbin/freebsd-update install"
```

This warning may be safely ignored at this point. The updated GENERIC kernel will be used as an intermediate step in the upgrade process.

Once all the patches have been downloaded to the local system, they will be applied. This process may take a while, depending on the speed and workload of the machine. Configuration files will then be merged. The merging process requires some user intervention as a file may be merged or an editor may appear on screen for a manual merge. The results of every successful merge will be shown to the user as the process continues. A failed or ignored merge will cause the process to abort. Users may wish to make a backup of /etc and manually merge important files, such as master.passwd or group at a later time.

Note

The system is not being altered yet as all patching and merging is happening in another directory. Once all patches have been applied successfully, all configuration files have been merged and it seems the process will go smoothly, the changes can be committed to disk by the user using the following command:

```
# freebsd-update install
```

The kernel and kernel modules will be patched first. If the system is running with a custom kernel, use nextboot(8) to set the kernel for the next boot to the updated /boot/GENERIC :

```
# nextboot -k GENERIC
```

Warning

Before rebooting with the GENERIC kernel, make sure it contains all the drivers required for the system to boot properly and connect to the network, if the machine being updated is accessed remotely. In particular, if the running custom kernel contains built-in functionality usually provided by kernel modules, make sure to temporarily load these modules into the GENERIC kernel using the /boot/loader.conf facility. It is recommended to disable non-essential services as well as any disk and network mounts until the upgrade process is complete.

The machine should now be restarted with the updated kernel:

```
# shutdown -r now
```

Once the system has come back online, restart freebsd-update using the following command. Since the state of the process has been saved, freebsd-update will not start from the beginning, but will instead move on to the next phase and remove all old shared libraries and object files.

```
# freebsd-update install
```

Note

Depending upon whether any library version numbers were bumped, there may only be two install phases instead of three.

The upgrade is now complete. If this was a major version upgrade, reinstall all ports and packages as described in Section 23.2.3.2, "Upgrading Packages After a Major Version Upgrade".

23.2.3.1. Custom Kernels with FreeBSD 9.X and Later

Before using `freebsd-update`, ensure that a copy of the GENERIC kernel exists in `/boot/GENERIC`. If a custom kernel has only been built once, the kernel in `/boot/kernel.old` is the GENERIC kernel. Simply rename this directory to `/boot/kernel`.

If a custom kernel has been built more than once or if it is unknown how many times the custom kernel has been built, obtain a copy of the GENERIC kernel that matches the current version of the operating system. If physical access to the system is available, a copy of the GENERIC kernel can be installed from the installation media:

```
# mount /cdrom
# cd /cdrom/usr/freebsd-dist
# tar -C/ -xvf kernel.txz boot/kernel/kernel
```

Alternately, the GENERIC kernel may be rebuilt and installed from source:

```
# cd /usr/src
# make kernel __MAKE_CONF=/dev/null SRCCONF=/dev/null
```

For this kernel to be identified as the GENERIC kernel by `freebsd-update`, the GENERIC configuration file must not have been modified in any way. It is also suggested that the kernel is built without any other special options.

Rebooting into the GENERIC kernel is not required as `freebsd-update` only needs `/boot/GENERIC` to exist.

23.2.3.2. Upgrading Packages After a Major Version Upgrade

Generally, installed applications will continue to work without problems after minor version upgrades. Major versions use different Application Binary Interfaces (ABIs), which will break most third-party applications. After a major version upgrade, all installed packages and ports need to be upgraded. Packages can be upgraded using `pkg upgrade`. To upgrade installed ports, use a utility such as ports-mgmt/portmaster.

A forced upgrade of all installed packages will replace the packages with fresh versions from the repository even if the version number has not increased. This is required because of the ABI version change when upgrading between major versions of FreeBSD. The forced upgrade can be accomplished by performing:

```
# pkg-static upgrade -f
```

A rebuild of all installed applications can be accomplished with this command:

```
# portmaster -af
```

This command will display the configuration screens for each application that has configurable options and wait for the user to interact with those screens. To prevent this behavior, and use only the default options, include -G in the above command.

Once the software upgrades are complete, finish the upgrade process with a final call to `freebsd-update` in order to tie up all the loose ends in the upgrade process:

```
# freebsd-update install
```

If the GENERIC kernel was temporarily used, this is the time to build and install a new custom kernel using the instructions in Chapter 8, *Configuring the FreeBSD Kernel*.

Reboot the machine into the new FreeBSD version. The upgrade process is now complete.

23.2.4. System State Comparison

The state of the installed FreeBSD version against a known good copy can be tested using `freebsd-update IDS`. This command evaluates the current version of system utilities, libraries, and configuration files and can be used as a built-in Intrusion Detection System (IDS).

Warning

This command is not a replacement for a real IDS such as security/snort. As freebsd-update stores data on disk, the possibility of tampering is evident. While this possibility may be reduced using kern.securelevel and by storing the freebsd-update data on a read-only file system when not in use, a better solution would be to compare the system against a secure disk, such as a DVD or securely stored external USB disk device. An alternative method for providing IDS functionality using a built-in utility is described in Section 13.2.6, "Binary Verification"

To begin the comparison, specify the output file to save the results to:

```
# freebsd-update IDS >> outfile.ids
```

The system will now be inspected and a lengthy listing of files, along with the SHA256 hash values for both the known value in the release and the current installation, will be sent to the specified output file.

The entries in the listing are extremely long, but the output format may be easily parsed. For instance, to obtain a list of all files which differ from those in the release, issue the following command:

```
# cat outfile.ids | awk '{ print $1 }' | more
/etc/master.passwd
/etc/motd
/etc/passwd
/etc/pf.conf
```

This sample output has been truncated as many more files exist. Some files have natural modifications. For example, /etc/passwd will be modified if users have been added to the system. Kernel modules may differ as freebsd-update may have updated them. To exclude specific files or directories, add them to the IDSIgnorePaths option in /etc/freebsd-update.conf .

23.3. Updating the Documentation Set

Documentation is an integral part of the FreeBSD operating system. While an up-to-date version of the FreeBSD documentation is always available on the FreeBSD web site (https://www.freebsd.org/doc/), it can be handy to have an up-to-date, local copy of the FreeBSD website, handbooks, FAQ, and articles.

This section describes how to use either source or the FreeBSD Ports Collection to keep a local copy of the FreeBSD documentation up-to-date.

For information on editing and submitting corrections to the documentation, refer to the FreeBSD Documentation Project Primer for New Contributors (https://www.freebsd.org/doc/en_US.ISO8859-1/books/fdp-primer/).

23.3.1. Updating Documentation from Source

Rebuilding the FreeBSD documentation from source requires a collection of tools which are not part of the FreeBSD base system. The required tools, including svn, can be installed from the textproc/docproj package or port developed by the FreeBSD Documentation Project.

Once installed, use svn to fetch a clean copy of the documentation source:

```
# svn checkout https://svn.FreeBSD.org/doc/head /usr/doc
```

The initial download of the documentation sources may take a while. Let it run until it completes.

Future updates of the documentation sources may be fetched by running:

```
# svn update /usr/doc
```

Once an up-to-date snapshot of the documentation sources has been fetched to /usr/doc , everything is ready for an update of the installed documentation.

A full update of all available languages may be performed by typing:

```
# cd /usr/doc
# make install clean
```

If an update of only a specific language is desired, make can be invoked in a language-specific subdirectory of / usr/doc :

```
# cd /usr/doc/en_US.IS08859-1
# make install clean
```

An alternative way of updating the documentation is to run this command from /usr/doc or the desired language-specific subdirectory:

```
# make update
```

The output formats that will be installed may be specified by setting FORMATS:

```
# cd /usr/doc
# make FORMATS='html html-split' install clean
```

Several options are available to ease the process of updating only parts of the documentation, or the build of specific translations. These options can be set either as system-wide options in /etc/make.conf , or as command-line options passed to make.

The options include:

DOC_LANG
> The list of languages and encodings to build and install, such as en_US.IS08859-1 for English documentation.

FORMATS
> A single format or a list of output formats to be built. Currently, html, html-split , txt, ps, and pdf are supported.

DOCDIR
> Where to install the documentation. It defaults to /usr/share/doc .

For more make variables supported as system-wide options in FreeBSD, refer to make.conf(5).

23.3.2. Updating Documentation from Ports

Based on the work of Marc Fonvieille.

The previous section presented a method for updating the FreeBSD documentation from sources. This section describes an alternative method which uses the Ports Collection and makes it possible to:

- Install pre-built packages of the documentation, without having to locally build anything or install the documentation toolchain.

- Build the documentation sources through the ports framework, making the checkout and build steps a bit easier.

This method of updating the FreeBSD documentation is supported by a set of documentation ports and packages which are updated by the Documentation Engineering Team <doceng@FreeBSD.org> on a monthly basis. These are listed in the FreeBSD Ports Collection, under the docs category (http://www.freshports.org/docs/).

Organization of the documentation ports is as follows:

- The misc/freebsd-doc-en package or port installs all of the English documentation.

- The misc/freebsd-doc-all meta-package or port installs all documentation in all available languages.

- There is a package and port for each translation, such as misc/freebsd-doc-hu for the Hungarian documentation.

When binary packages are used, the FreeBSD documentation will be installed in all available formats for the given language. For example, the following command will install the latest package of the Hungarian documentation:

```
# pkg install hu-freebsd-doc
```

Note

Packages use a format that differs from the corresponding port's name: *lang*-freebsd-doc, where *lang* is the short format of the language code, such as hu for Hungarian, or zh_cn for Simplified Chinese.

To specify the format of the documentation, build the port instead of installing the package. For example, to build and install the English documentation:

```
# cd /usr/ports/misc/freebsd-doc-en
# make install clean
```

The port provides a configuration menu where the format to build and install can be specified. By default, split HTML, similar to the format used on http://www.FreeBSD.org , and PDF are selected.

Alternately, several make options can be specified when building a documentation port, including:

WITH_HTML
Builds the HTML format with a single HTML file per document. The formatted documentation is saved to a file called article.html, or book.html .

WITH_PDF
The formatted documentation is saved to a file called article.pdf or book.pdf .

DOCBASE
Specifies where to install the documentation. It defaults to /usr/local/share/doc/freebsd .

This example uses variables to install the Hungarian documentation as a PDF in the specified directory:

```
# cd /usr/ports/misc/freebsd-doc-hu
# make -DWITH_PDF DOCBASE=share/doc/freebsd/hu install clean
```

Documentation packages or ports can be updated using the instructions in Chapter 4, *Installing Applications: Packages and Ports*. For example, the following command updates the installed Hungarian documentation using ports-mgmt/portmaster by using packages only:

```
# portmaster -PP hu-freebsd-doc
```

23.4. Tracking a Development Branch

FreeBSD has two development branches: FreeBSD-CURRENT and FreeBSD-STABLE.

This section provides an explanation of each branch and its intended audience, as well as how to keep a system up-to-date with each respective branch.

23.4.1. Using FreeBSD-CURRENT

FreeBSD-CURRENT is the "bleeding edge" of FreeBSD development and FreeBSD-CURRENT users are expected to have a high degree of technical skill. Less technical users who wish to track a development branch should track FreeBSD-STABLE instead.

FreeBSD-CURRENT is the very latest source code for FreeBSD and includes works in progress, experimental changes, and transitional mechanisms that might or might not be present in the next official release. While many FreeBSD developers compile the FreeBSD-CURRENT source code daily, there are short periods of time when the source may not be buildable. These problems are resolved as quickly as possible, but whether or not FreeBSD-CURRENT brings disaster or new functionality can be a matter of when the source code was synced.

FreeBSD-CURRENT is made available for three primary interest groups:

1. Members of the FreeBSD community who are actively working on some part of the source tree.

2. Members of the FreeBSD community who are active testers. They are willing to spend time solving problems, making topical suggestions on changes and the general direction of FreeBSD, and submitting patches.

3. Users who wish to keep an eye on things, use the current source for reference purposes, or make the occasional comment or code contribution.

FreeBSD-CURRENT should *not* be considered a fast-track to getting new features before the next release as pre-release features are not yet fully tested and most likely contain bugs. It is not a quick way of getting bug fixes as any given commit is just as likely to introduce new bugs as to fix existing ones. FreeBSD-CURRENT is not in any way "officially supported".

To track FreeBSD-CURRENT:

1. Join the freebsd-current and the svn-src-head lists. This is *essential* in order to see the comments that people are making about the current state of the system and to receive important bulletins about the current state of FreeBSD-CURRENT.

   The svn-src-head list records the commit log entry for each change as it is made, along with any pertinent information on possible side effects.

   To join these lists, go to http://lists.FreeBSD.org/mailman/listinfo, click on the list to subscribe to, and follow the instructions. In order to track changes to the whole source tree, not just the changes to FreeBSD-CURRENT, subscribe to the svn-src-all list.

2. Synchronize with the FreeBSD-CURRENT sources. Typically, svn is used to check out the -CURRENT code from the head branch of one of the Subversion mirror sites listed in Section A.3.6, "Subversion Mirror Sites".

3. Due to the size of the repository, some users choose to only synchronize the sections of source that interest them or which they are contributing patches to. However, users that plan to compile the operating system from source must download *all* of FreeBSD-CURRENT, not just selected portions.

   Before compiling FreeBSD-CURRENT , read /usr/src/Makefile very carefully and follow the instructions in Section 23.5, "Updating FreeBSD from Source". Read the FreeBSD-CURRENT mailing list and /usr/src/UP-DATING to stay up-to-date on other bootstrapping procedures that sometimes become necessary on the road to the next release.

4. Be active! FreeBSD-CURRENT users are encouraged to submit their suggestions for enhancements or bug fixes. Suggestions with accompanying code are always welcome.

23.5. Updating FreeBSD from Source

Updating FreeBSD by compiling from source offers several advantages over binary updates. Code can be built with options to take advantage of specific hardware. Parts of the base system can be built with non-default settings, or left out entirely where they are not needed or desired. The build process takes longer to update a system than just installing binary updates, but allows complete customization to produce a tailored version of FreeBSD.

23.5.1. Quick Start

This is a quick reference for the typical steps used to update FreeBSD by building from source. Later sections describe the process in more detail.

- Update and Build

```
# svn update /usr/src      ❶
check /usr/src/UPDATING     ❷
# cd /usr/src              ❸
# make -j4 buildworld      ❹
# make -j4 kernel          ❺
# shutdown -r now          ❻
# cd /usr/src              ❼
# make installworld        ❽
# mergemaster -Ui          ❾
# shutdown -r now          ❿
```

❶   Get the latest version of the source. See Section 23.5.3, "Updating the Source" for more information on obtaining and updating source.

❷   Check `/usr/src/UPDATING` for any manual steps required before or after building from source.

❸   Go to the source directory.

❹   Compile the world, everything except the kernel.

❺   Compile and install the kernel. This is equivalent to `make buildkernel installkernel`.

❻   Reboot the system to the new kernel.

❼   Go to the source directory.

❽   Install the world.

❾   Update and merge configuration files in `/etc/`.

❿   Restart the system to use the newly-built world and kernel.

23.5.2. Preparing for a Source Update

Read `/usr/src/UPDATING`. Any manual steps that must be performed before or after an update are described in this file.

23.5.3. Updating the Source

FreeBSD source code is located in `/usr/src/`. The preferred method of updating this source is through the Subversion version control system. Verify that the source code is under version control:

```
# svn info /usr/src
Path: /usr/src
Working Copy Root Path: /usr/src
...
```

This indicates that `/usr/src/` is under version control and can be updated with svn(1):

```
# svn update /usr/src
```

The update process can take some time if the directory has not been updated recently. After it finishes, the source code is up to date and the build process described in the next section can begin.

Obtaining the Source

If the output says `'/usr/src' is not a working copy`, the files there are missing or were installed with a different method. A new checkout of the source is required.

Table 23.1. FreeBSD Versions and Repository Paths

uname -r Output	Repository Path	Description
X.Y-RELEASE	base/releng/*X.Y*	The Release version plus only critical security and bug fix patches. This branch is recommended for most users.
X.Y-STABLE	base/stable/*X*	The Release version plus all additional development on that branch. *STABLE* refers to the Applications Binary Interface (ABI) not changing, so software compiled for earlier versions still runs. For example, software compiled to run on FreeBSD 10.1 will still run on FreeBSD 10-STABLE compiled later. STABLE branches occasionally have bugs or incompatibilities which might affect users, although these are typically fixed quickly.
X-CURRENT	base/head/	The latest unreleased development version of FreeBSD. The CURRENT branch can have major bugs or incompatibilities and is recommended only for advanced users.

Determine which version of FreeBSD is being used with uname(1):

```
# uname -r
10.3-RELEASE
```

Based on Table 23.1, "FreeBSD Versions and Repository Paths", the source used to update 10.3-RELEASE has a repository path of base/releng/10.3. That path is used when checking out the source:

```
# mv /usr/src /usr/src.bak       ❶
# svn checkout https://svn.freebsd.org/base/  releng/10.3 /usr/src   ❷
```

❶   Move the old directory out of the way. If there are no local modifications in this directory, it can be deleted.
❷   The path from Table 23.1, "FreeBSD Versions and Repository Paths" is added to the repository URL. The third parameter is the destination directory for the source code on the local system.

23.5.4. Building from Source

The *world*, or all of the operating system except the kernel, is compiled. This is done first to provide up-to-date tools to build the kernel. Then the kernel itself is built:

```
# cd /usr/src
```

```
# make buildworld
# make buildkernel
```

The compiled code is written to /usr/obj .

These are the basic steps. Additional options to control the build are described below.

23.5.4.1. Performing a Clean Build

Some versions of the FreeBSD build system leave previously-compiled code in the temporary object directory, /usr/obj . This can speed up later builds by avoiding recompiling code that has not changed. To force a clean rebuild of everything, use cleanworld before starting a build:

```
# make cleanworld
```

23.5.4.2. Setting the Number of Jobs

Increasing the number of build jobs on multi-core processors can improve build speed. Determine the number of cores with sysctl hw.ncpu . Processors vary, as do the build systems used with different versions of FreeBSD, so testing is the only sure method to tell how a different number of jobs affects the build speed. For a starting point, consider values between half and double the number of cores. The number of jobs is specified with -j.

Example 23.1. Increasing the Number of Build Jobs

Building the world and kernel with four jobs:

```
# make -j4 buildworld buildkernel
```

23.5.4.3. Building Only the Kernel

A buildworld must be completed if the source code has changed. After that, a buildkernel to build a kernel can be run at any time. To build just the kernel:

```
# cd /usr/src
# make buildkernel
```

23.5.4.4. Building a Custom Kernel

The standard FreeBSD kernel is based on a *kernel config file* called GENERIC. The GENERIC kernel includes the most commonly-needed device drivers and options. Sometimes it is useful or necessary to build a custom kernel, adding or removing device drivers or options to fit a specific need.

For example, someone developing a small embedded computer with severely limited RAM could remove unneeded device drivers or options to make the kernel slightly smaller.

Kernel config files are located in /usr/src/sys/ *arch*/conf/ , where *arch* is the output from uname -m. On most computers, that is amd64, giving a config file directory of /usr/src/sys/ *amd64*/conf/ .

Tip

/usr/src can be deleted or recreated, so it is preferable to keep custom kernel config files in a separate directory, like /root. Link the kernel config file into the conf directory. If that directory is deleted or overwritten, the kernel config can be re-linked into the new one.

A custom config file can be created by copying the GENERIC config file. In this example, the new custom kernel is for a storage server, so is named STORAGESERVER:

```
# cp /usr/src/sys/amd64/conf/GENERIC /root/STORAGESERVER
# cd /usr/src/sys/amd64/conf
# ln -s /root/STORAGESERVER .
```

/root/STORAGESERVER is then edited, adding or removing devices or options as shown in config(5).

The custom kernel is built by setting KERNCONF to the kernel config file on the command line:

```
# make buildkernel KERNCONF=STORAGESERVER
```

23.5.5. Installing the Compiled Code

After the buildworld and buildkernel steps have been completed, the new kernel and world are installed:

```
# cd /usr/src
# make installkernel
# shutdown -r now
# cd /usr/src
# make installworld
# shutdown -r now
```

If a custom kernel was built, KERNCONF must also be set to use the new custom kernel:

```
# cd /usr/src
# make installkernel KERNCONF=STORAGESERVER
# shutdown -r now
# cd /usr/src
# make installworld
# shutdown -r now
```

23.5.6. Completing the Update

A few final tasks complete the update. Any modified configuration files are merged with the new versions, outdated libraries are located and removed, then the system is restarted.

23.5.6.1. Merging Configuration Files with mergemaster(8)

mergemaster(8) provides an easy way to merge changes that have been made to system configuration files with new versions of those files.

With -Ui, mergemaster(8) automatically updates files that have not been user-modified and installs new files that are not already present:

```
# mergemaster -Ui
```

If a file must be manually merged, an interactive display allows the user to choose which portions of the files are kept. See mergemaster(8) for more information.

23.5.6.2. Checking for Outdated Files and Libraries

Some obsolete files or directories can remain after an update. These files can be located:

```
# make check-old
```

and deleted:

```
# make delete-old
```

Some obsolete libraries can also remain. These can be detected with:

```
# make check-old-libs
```

and deleted with

```
# make delete-old-libs
```

Programs which were still using those old libraries will stop working when the library has been deleted. These programs must be rebuilt or replaced after deleting the old libraries.

Tip

When all the old files or directories are known to be safe to delete, pressing y and Enter to delete each file can be avoided by setting BATCH_DELETE_OLD_FILES   in the command. For example:

```
# make BATCH_DELETE_OLD_FILES=yes delete-old-libs
```

23.5.6.3. Restarting After the Update

The last step after updating is to restart the computer so all the changes take effect:

```
# shutdown -r now
```

23.6. Tracking for Multiple Machines

Contributed by Mike Meyer.

When multiple machines need to track the same source tree, it is a waste of disk space, network bandwidth, and CPU cycles to have each system download the sources and rebuild everything. The solution is to have one machine do most of the work, while the rest of the machines mount that work via NFS. This section outlines a method of doing so. For more information about using NFS, refer to Section 28.3, "Network File System (NFS)".

First, identify a set of machines which will run the same set of binaries, known as a *build set*. Each machine can have a custom kernel, but will run the same userland binaries. From that set, choose a machine to be the *build machine* that the world and kernel are built on. Ideally, this is a fast machine that has sufficient spare CPU to run make buildworld and make buildkernel.

Select a machine to be the *test machine*, which will test software updates before they are put into production. This *must* be a machine that can afford to be down for an extended period of time. It can be the build machine, but need not be.

All the machines in this build set need to mount /usr/obj and /usr/src from the build machine via NFS. For multiple build sets, /usr/src should be on one build machine, and NFS mounted on the rest.

Ensure that /etc/make.conf and /etc/src.conf on all the machines in the build set agree with the build machine. That means that the build machine must build all the parts of the base system that any machine in the build set is going to install. Also, each build machine should have its kernel name set with KERNCONF in /etc/make.conf , and the build machine should list them all in its KERNCONF, listing its own kernel first. The build machine must have the kernel configuration files for each machine in its /usr/src/sys/ *arch*/conf.

On the build machine, build the kernel and world as described in Section 23.5, "Updating FreeBSD from Source", but do not install anything on the build machine. Instead, install the built kernel on the test machine. On the test machine, mount /usr/src and /usr/obj via NFS. Then, run shutdown now to go to single-user mode in order to install the new kernel and world and run mergemaster as usual. When done, reboot to return to normal multi-user operations.

After verifying that everything on the test machine is working properly, use the same procedure to install the new software on each of the other machines in the build set.

The same methodology can be used for the ports tree. The first step is to share /usr/ports via NFS to all the machines in the build set. To configure /etc/make.conf to share distfiles, set DISTDIR to a common shared directory that is writable by whichever user root is mapped to by the NFS mount. Each machine should set WRKDIRPREFIX to a local build directory, if ports are to be built locally. Alternately, if the build system is to build and distribute packages to the machines in the build set, set PACKAGES on the build system to a directory similar to DISTDIR.

Chapter 24. DTrace

Written by Tom Rhodes.

24.1. Synopsis

DTrace, also known as Dynamic Tracing, was developed by Sun™ as a tool for locating performance bottlenecks in production and pre-production systems. In addition to diagnosing performance problems, DTrace can be used to help investigate and debug unexpected behavior in both the FreeBSD kernel and in userland programs.

DTrace is a remarkable profiling tool, with an impressive array of features for diagnosing system issues. It may also be used to run pre-written scripts to take advantage of its capabilities. Users can author their own utilities using the DTrace D Language, allowing them to customize their profiling based on specific needs.

The FreeBSD implementation provides full support for kernel DTrace and experimental support for userland DTrace. Userland DTrace allows users to perform function boundary tracing for userland programs using the pid provider, and to insert static probes into userland programs for later tracing. Some ports, such as databases/postgres-server and lang/php56 have a DTrace option to enable static probes. FreeBSD 10.0-RELEASE has reasonably good userland DTrace support, but it is not considered production ready. In particular, it is possible to crash traced programs.

The official guide to DTrace is maintained by the Illumos project at DTrace Guide .

After reading this chapter, you will know:

- What DTrace is and what features it provides.

- Differences between the Solaris™ DTrace implementation and the one provided by FreeBSD.

- How to enable and use DTrace on FreeBSD.

Before reading this chapter, you should:

- Understand UNIX® and FreeBSD basics (Chapter 3, *FreeBSD Basics*).

- Have some familiarity with security and how it pertains to FreeBSD (Chapter 13, *Security*).

24.2. Implementation Differences

While the DTrace in FreeBSD is similar to that found in Solaris™ , differences do exist. The primary difference is that in FreeBSD, DTrace is implemented as a set of kernel modules and DTrace can not be used until the modules are loaded. To load all of the necessary modules:

```
# kldload dtraceall
```

Beginning with FreeBSD 10.0-RELEASE, the modules are automatically loaded when dtrace is run.

FreeBSD uses the DDB_CTF kernel option to enable support for loading CTF data from kernel modules and the kernel itself. CTF is the Solaris™ Compact C Type Format which encapsulates a reduced form of debugging information similar to DWARF and the venerable stabs. CTF data is added to binaries by the ctfconvert and ctfmerge build tools. The ctfconvert utility parses DWARF ELF debug sections created by the compiler and ctfmerge merges CTF ELF sections from objects into either executables or shared libraries.

Some different providers exist for FreeBSD than for Solaris™ . Most notable is the dtmalloc provider, which allows tracing malloc() by type in the FreeBSD kernel. Some of the providers found in Solaris™ , such as cpc and mib, are not present in FreeBSD. These may appear in future versions of FreeBSD. Moreover, some of the providers available in both operating systems are not compatible, in the sense that their probes have different argument types. Thus, D scripts written on Solaris™ may or may not work unmodified on FreeBSD, and vice versa.

Due to security differences, only root may use DTrace on FreeBSD. Solaris™ has a few low level security checks which do not yet exist in FreeBSD. As such, the /dev/dtrace/dtrace is strictly limited to root.

DTrace falls under the Common Development and Distribution License (CDDL) license. To view this license on FreeBSD, see /usr/src/cddl/contrib/opensolaris/OPENSOLARIS.LICENSE or view it online at http://open-source.org/licenses/CDDL-1.0. While a FreeBSD kernel with DTrace support is BSD licensed, the CDDL is used when the modules are distributed in binary form or the binaries are loaded.

24.3. Enabling DTrace Support

In FreeBSD 9.2 and 10.0, DTrace support is built into the GENERIC kernel. Users of earlier versions of FreeBSD or who prefer to statically compile in DTrace support should add the following lines to a custom kernel configuration file and recompile the kernel using the instructions in Chapter 8, *Configuring the FreeBSD Kernel*:

```
options         KDTRACE_HOOKS
options         DDB_CTF
makeoptions DEBUG=-g
makeoptions WITH_CTF=1
```

Users of the AMD64 architecture should also add this line:

```
options         KDTRACE_FRAME
```

This option provides support for FBT. While DTrace will work without this option, there will be limited support for function boundary tracing.

Once the FreeBSD system has rebooted into the new kernel, or the DTrace kernel modules have been loaded using kldload dtraceall , the system will need support for the Korn shell as the DTrace Toolkit has several utilities written in ksh. Make sure that the shells/ksh93 package or port is installed. It is also possible to run these tools under shells/pdksh or shells/mksh.

Finally, install the current DTrace Toolkit, a collection of ready-made scripts for collecting system information. There are scripts to check open files, memory, CPU usage, and a lot more. FreeBSD 10 installs a few of these scripts into /usr/share/dtrace . On other FreeBSD versions, or to install the full DTrace Toolkit, use the sysutils/DTrace-Toolkit package or port.

Note

The scripts found in /usr/share/dtrace have been specifically ported to FreeBSD. Not all of the scripts found in the DTrace Toolkit will work as-is on FreeBSD and some scripts may require some effort in order for them to work on FreeBSD.

The DTrace Toolkit includes many scripts in the special language of DTrace. This language is called the D language and it is very similar to C++. An in depth discussion of the language is beyond the scope of this document. It is extensively discussed at http://wikis.oracle.com/display/DTrace/Documentation .

24.4. Using DTrace

DTrace scripts consist of a list of one or more *probes*, or instrumentation points, where each probe is associated with an action. Whenever the condition for a probe is met, the associated action is executed. For example, an action may occur when a file is opened, a process is started, or a line of code is executed. The action might be to log some information or to modify context variables. The reading and writing of context variables allows probes to share information and to cooperatively analyze the correlation of different events.

To view all probes, the administrator can execute the following command:

```
# dtrace -l | more
```

Each probe has an ID, a PROVIDER (dtrace or fbt), a MODULE, and a FUNCTION NAME. Refer to dtrace(1) for more information about this command.

The examples in this section provide an overview of how to use two of the fully supported scripts from the DTrace Toolkit: the hotkernel and procsystime scripts.

The hotkernel script is designed to identify which function is using the most kernel time. It will produce output similar to the following:

```
# cd /usr/share/dtrace/toolkit
# ./hotkernel
Sampling... Hit Ctrl-C to end.
```

As instructed, use the Ctrl+C key combination to stop the process. Upon termination, the script will display a list of kernel functions and timing information, sorting the output in increasing order of time:

```
kernel`_thread_lock_flags                            2    0.0%
0xc1097063                                           2    0.0%
kernel`sched_userret                                 2    0.0%
kernel`kern_select                                   2    0.0%
kernel`generic_copyin                                3    0.0%
kernel`_mtx_assert                                   3    0.0%
kernel`vm_fault                                      3    0.0%
kernel`sopoll_generic                                3    0.0%
kernel`fixup_filename                                4    0.0%
kernel`_isitmyx                                      4    0.0%
kernel`find_instance                                 4    0.0%
kernel`_mtx_unlock_flags                             5    0.0%
kernel`syscall                                       5    0.0%
kernel`DELAY                                         5    0.0%
0xc108a253                                           6    0.0%
kernel`witness_lock                                  7    0.0%
kernel`read_aux_data_no_wait                         7    0.0%
kernel`Xint0x80_syscall                              7    0.0%
kernel`witness_checkorder                            7    0.0%
kernel`sse2_pagezero                                 8    0.0%
kernel`strncmp                                       9    0.0%
kernel`spinlock_exit                                10    0.0%
kernel`_mtx_lock_flags                              11    0.0%
kernel`witness_unlock                               15    0.0%
kernel`sched_idletd                                137    0.3%
0xc10981a5                                        42139   99.3%
```

This script will also work with kernel modules. To use this feature, run the script with -m:

```
# ./hotkernel -m
Sampling... Hit Ctrl-C to end.
^C
MODULE                                            COUNT   PCNT
0xc107882e                                            1    0.0%
0xc10e6aa4                                            1    0.0%
0xc1076983                                            1    0.0%
0xc109708a                                            1    0.0%
0xc1075a5d                                            1    0.0%
0xc1077325                                            1    0.0%
0xc108a245                                            1    0.0%
0xc107730d                                            1    0.0%
0xc1097063                                            2    0.0%
```

```
0xc108a253                                        73    0.0%
kernel                                           874    0.4%
0xc10981a5                                    213781   99.6%
```

The procsystime script captures and prints the system call time usage for a given process ID (PID) or process name. In the following example, a new instance of /bin/csh was spawned. Then, procsystime was executed and remained waiting while a few commands were typed on the other incarnation of csh. These are the results of this test:

```
# ./procsystime -n csh
Tracing... Hit Ctrl-C to end...
^C

Elapsed Times for processes csh,

        SYSCALL        TIME (ns)
         getpid             6131
      sigreturn             8121
          close            19127
          fcntl            19959
            dup            26955
        setpgid            28070
           stat            31899
       setitimer           40938
          wait4            62717
      sigaction            67372
    sigprocmask           119091
   gettimeofday           183710
          write           263242
         execve           492547
          ioctl           770073
          vfork          3258923
      sigsuspend         6985124
           read       3988049784
```

As shown, the read() system call used the most time in nanoseconds while the getpid() system call used the least amount of time.

Part IV. Network Communication

FreeBSD is one of the most widely deployed operating systems for high performance network servers. The chapters in this part cover:

- Serial communication

- PPP and PPP over Ethernet

- Electronic Mail

- Running Network Servers

- Firewalls

- Other Advanced Networking Topics

These chapters are designed to be read when the information is needed. They do not need to be read in any particular order, nor is it necessary to read all of them before using FreeBSD in a network environment.

Table of Contents

Chapter 25. Serial Communications

25.1. Synopsis

UNIX® has always had support for serial communications as the very first UNIX® machines relied on serial lines for user input and output. Things have changed a lot from the days when the average terminal consisted of a 10-character-per-second serial printer and a keyboard. This chapter covers some of the ways serial communications can be used on FreeBSD.

After reading this chapter, you will know:

• How to connect terminals to a FreeBSD system.

• How to use a modem to dial out to remote hosts.

• How to allow remote users to login to a FreeBSD system with a modem.

• How to boot a FreeBSD system from a serial console.

Before reading this chapter, you should:

• Know how to configure and install a custom kernel.

• Understand FreeBSD permissions and processes.

• Have access to the technical manual for the serial hardware to be used with FreeBSD.

25.2. Serial Terminology and Hardware

The following terms are often used in serial communications:

bps
: Bits per Second (bps) is the rate at which data is transmitted.

DTE
: Data Terminal Equipment (DTE) is one of two endpoints in a serial communication. An example would be a computer.

DCE
: Data Communications Equipment (DTE) is the other endpoint in a serial communication. Typically, it is a modem or serial terminal.

RS-232
: The original standard which defined hardware serial communications. It has since been renamed to TIA-232.

When referring to communication data rates, this section does not use the term *baud*. Baud refers to the number of electrical state transitions made in a period of time, while bps is the correct term to use.

To connect a serial terminal to a FreeBSD system, a serial port on the computer and the proper cable to connect to the serial device are needed. Users who are already familiar with serial hardware and cabling can safely skip this section.

25.2.1. Serial Cables and Ports

There are several different kinds of serial cables. The two most common types are null-modem cables and standard RS-232 cables. The documentation for the hardware should describe the type of cable required.

These two types of cables differ in how the wires are connected to the connector. Each wire represents a signal, with the defined signals summarized in Table 25.1, "RS-232C Signal Names". A standard serial cable passes all of the RS-232C signals straight through. For example, the "Transmitted Data" pin on one end of the cable goes to the "Transmitted Data" pin on the other end. This is the type of cable used to connect a modem to the FreeBSD system, and is also appropriate for some terminals.

A null-modem cable switches the "Transmitted Data" pin of the connector on one end with the "Received Data" pin on the other end. The connector can be either a DB-25 or a DB-9.

A null-modem cable can be constructed using the pin connections summarized in Table 25.2, "DB-25 to DB-25 Null-Modem Cable", Table 25.3, "DB-9 to DB-9 Null-Modem Cable", and Table 25.4, "DB-9 to DB-25 Null-Modem Cable". While the standard calls for a straight-through pin 1 to pin 1 "Protective Ground" line, it is often omitted. Some terminals work using only pins 2, 3, and 7, while others require different configurations. When in doubt, refer to the documentation for the hardware.

Table 25.1. RS-232C Signal Names

Acronyms	Names
RD	Received Data
TD	Transmitted Data
DTR	Data Terminal Ready
DSR	Data Set Ready
DCD	Data Carrier Detect
SG	Signal Ground
RTS	Request to Send
CTS	Clear to Send

Table 25.2. DB-25 to DB-25 Null-Modem Cable

Signal	Pin #		Pin #	Signal
SG	7	connects to	7	SG
TD	2	connects to	3	RD
RD	3	connects to	2	TD
RTS	4	connects to	5	CTS
CTS	5	connects to	4	RTS
DTR	20	connects to	6	DSR
DTR	20	connects to	8	DCD
DSR	6	connects to	20	DTR
DCD	8	connects to	20	DTR

Table 25.3. DB-9 to DB-9 Null-Modem Cable

Signal	Pin #		Pin #	Signal
RD	2	connects to	3	TD
TD	3	connects to	2	RD
DTR	4	connects to	6	DSR
DTR	4	connects to	1	DCD
SG	5	connects to	5	SG
DSR	6	connects to	4	DTR

Signal	Pin #		Pin #	Signal
DCD	1	connects to	4	DTR
RTS	7	connects to	8	CTS
CTS	8	connects to	7	RTS

Table 25.4. DB-9 to DB-25 Null-Modem Cable

Signal	Pin #		Pin #	Signal
RD	2	connects to	2	TD
TD	3	connects to	3	RD
DTR	4	connects to	6	DSR
DTR	4	connects to	8	DCD
SG	5	connects to	7	SG
DSR	6	connects to	20	DTR
DCD	1	connects to	20	DTR
RTS	7	connects to	5	CTS
CTS	8	connects to	4	RTS

Note

When one pin at one end connects to a pair of pins at the other end, it is usually implemented with one short wire between the pair of pins in their connector and a long wire to the other single pin.

Serial ports are the devices through which data is transferred between the FreeBSD host computer and the terminal. Several kinds of serial ports exist. Before purchasing or constructing a cable, make sure it will fit the ports on the terminal and on the FreeBSD system.

Most terminals have DB-25 ports. Personal computers may have DB-25 or DB-9 ports. A multiport serial card may have RJ-12 or RJ-45/ ports. See the documentation that accompanied the hardware for specifications on the kind of port or visually verify the type of port.

In FreeBSD, each serial port is accessed through an entry in /dev. There are two different kinds of entries:

• Call-in ports are named /dev/ttyu N where N is the port number, starting from zero. If a terminal is connected to the first serial port (COM1), use /dev/ttyu0 to refer to the terminal. If the terminal is on the second serial port (COM2), use /dev/ttyu1 , and so forth. Generally, the call-in port is used for terminals. Call-in ports require that the serial line assert the "Data Carrier Detect" signal to work correctly.

• Call-out ports are named /dev/cuau N on FreeBSD versions 8.X and higher and /dev/cuad N on FreeBSD versions 7.X and lower. Call-out ports are usually not used for terminals, but are used for modems. The call-out port can be used if the serial cable or the terminal does not support the "Data Carrier Detect" signal.

FreeBSD also provides initialization devices (/dev/ttyu N.init and /dev/cuau N.init or /dev/cuad N.init) and locking devices (/dev/ttyu N.lock and /dev/cuau N.lock or /dev/cuad N.lock). The initialization devices are used to initialize communications port parameters each time a port is opened, such as crtscts for modems which use RTS/CTS signaling for flow control. The locking devices are used to lock flags on ports to prevent users or programs changing certain parameters. Refer to termios(4), sio(4), and stty(1) for information on terminal settings, locking and initializing devices, and setting terminal options, respectively.

25.2.2. Serial Port Configuration

By default, FreeBSD supports four serial ports which are commonly known as COM1, COM2, COM3, and COM4. FreeBSD also supports dumb multi-port serial interface cards, such as the BocaBoard 1008 and 2016, as well as more intelligent multi-port cards such as those made by Digiboard. However, the default kernel only looks for the standard COM ports.

To see if the system recognizes the serial ports, look for system boot messages that start with uart:

```
# grep uart /var/run/dmesg.boot
```

If the system does not recognize all of the needed serial ports, additional entries can be added to /boot/device.hints. This file already contains hint.uart.0.* entries for COM1 and hint.uart.1.* entries for COM2. When adding a port entry for COM3 use 0x3E8, and for COM4 use 0x2E8. Common IRQ addresses are 5 for COM3 and 9 for COM4.

To determine the default set of terminal I/O settings used by the port, specify its device name. This example determines the settings for the call-in port on COM2:

```
# stty -a -f /dev/ ttyu1
```

System-wide initialization of serial devices is controlled by /etc/rc.d/serial . This file affects the default settings of serial devices. To change the settings for a device, use stty. By default, the changed settings are in effect until the device is closed and when the device is reopened, it goes back to the default set. To permanently change the default set, open and adjust the settings of the initialization device. For example, to turn on CLOCAL mode, 8 bit communication, and XON/XOFF flow control for ttyu5, type:

```
# stty -f /dev/ttyu5.init clocal cs8 ixon ixoff
```

To prevent certain settings from being changed by an application, make adjustments to the locking device. For example, to lock the speed of ttyu5 to 57600 bps, type:

```
# stty -f /dev/ttyu5.lock 57600
```

Now, any application that opens ttyu5 and tries to change the speed of the port will be stuck with 57600 bps.

25.3. Terminals

Contributed by Sean Kelly.

Terminals provide a convenient and low-cost way to access a FreeBSD system when not at the computer's console or on a connected network. This section describes how to use terminals with FreeBSD.

The original UNIX® systems did not have consoles. Instead, users logged in and ran programs through terminals that were connected to the computer's serial ports.

The ability to establish a login session on a serial port still exists in nearly every UNIX®-like operating system today, including FreeBSD. By using a terminal attached to an unused serial port, a user can log in and run any text program that can normally be run on the console or in an xterm window.

Many terminals can be attached to a FreeBSD system. An older spare computer can be used as a terminal wired into a more powerful computer running FreeBSD. This can turn what might otherwise be a single-user computer into a powerful multiple-user system.

FreeBSD supports three types of terminals:

Dumb terminals
> Dumb terminals are specialized hardware that connect to computers over serial lines. They are called "dumb" because they have only enough computational power to display, send, and receive text. No programs can be run on these devices. Instead, dumb terminals connect to a computer that runs the needed programs.

There are hundreds of kinds of dumb terminals made by many manufacturers, and just about any kind will work with FreeBSD. Some high-end terminals can even display graphics, but only certain software packages can take advantage of these advanced features.

Dumb terminals are popular in work environments where workers do not need access to graphical applications.

Computers Acting as Terminals

Since a dumb terminal has just enough ability to display, send, and receive text, any spare computer can be a dumb terminal. All that is needed is the proper cable and some *terminal emulation* software to run on the computer.

This configuration can be useful. For example, if one user is busy working at the FreeBSD system's console, another user can do some text-only work at the same time from a less powerful personal computer hooked up as a terminal to the FreeBSD system.

There are at least two utilities in the base-system of FreeBSD that can be used to work through a serial connection: cu(1) and tip(1).

For example, to connect from a client system that runs FreeBSD to the serial connection of another system:

```
# cu -l serial-port-device
```

Replace *serial-port-device* with the device name of the connected serial port. These device files are called /dev/cuau*N* on FreeBSD versions 10.x and higher and /dev/cuad*N* on FreeBSD versions 9.x and lower. In either case, *N* is the serial port number, starting from zero. This means that COM1 is /dev/cuau0 or /dev/cuad0 in FreeBSD.

Additional programs are available through the Ports Collection, such as comms/minicom.

X Terminals

X terminals are the most sophisticated kind of terminal available. Instead of connecting to a serial port, they usually connect to a network like Ethernet. Instead of being relegated to text-only applications, they can display any Xorg application.

This chapter does not cover the setup, configuration, or use of X terminals.

25.3.1. Terminal Configuration

This section describes how to configure a FreeBSD system to enable a login session on a serial terminal. It assumes that the system recognizes the serial port to which the terminal is connected and that the terminal is connected with the correct cable.

In FreeBSD, init reads /etc/ttys and starts a getty process on the available terminals. The getty process is responsible for reading a login name and starting the login program. The ports on the FreeBSD system which allow logins are listed in /etc/ttys . For example, the first virtual console, ttyv0, has an entry in this file, allowing logins on the console. This file also contains entries for the other virtual consoles, serial ports, and pseudo-ttys. For a hardwired terminal, the serial port's /dev entry is listed without the /dev part. For example, /dev/ttyv0 is listed as ttyv0.

The default /etc/ttys configures support for the first four serial ports, ttyu0 through ttyu3:

```
ttyu0   "/usr/libexec/getty std.9600"   dialup  off secure
ttyu1   "/usr/libexec/getty std.9600"   dialup  off secure
ttyu2   "/usr/libexec/getty std.9600"   dialup  off secure
ttyu3   "/usr/libexec/getty std.9600"   dialup  off secure
```

When attaching a terminal to one of those ports, modify the default entry to set the required speed and terminal type, to turn the device on and, if needed, to change the port's secure setting. If the terminal is connected to another port, add an entry for the port.

Example 25.1, "Configuring Terminal Entries" configures two terminals in /etc/ttys . The first entry configures a Wyse-50 connected to COM2. The second entry configures an old computer running Procomm terminal software emulating a VT-100 terminal. The computer is connected to the sixth serial port on a multi-port serial card.

Example 25.1. Configuring Terminal Entries

```
ttyu1❶  "/usr/libexec/getty std.38400"❷  wy50❸  on❹  insecure❺
ttyu5   "/usr/libexec/getty std.19200"  vt100  on  insecure
```

❶   The first field specifies the device name of the serial terminal.

❷   The second field tells getty to initialize and open the line, set the line speed, prompt for a user name, and then execute the login program. The optional *getty type* configures characteristics on the terminal line, like bps rate and parity. The available getty types are listed in /etc/gettytab . In almost all cases, the getty types that start with std will work for hardwired terminals as these entries ignore parity. There is a std entry for each bps rate from 110 to 115200. Refer to gettytab(5) for more information.

When setting the getty type, make sure to match the communications settings used by the terminal. For this example, the Wyse-50 uses no parity and connects at 38400 bps. The computer uses no parity and connects at 19200 bps.

❸   The third field is the type of terminal. For dial-up ports, unknown or dialup is typically used since users may dial up with practically any type of terminal or software. Since the terminal type does not change for hardwired terminals, a real terminal type from /etc/termcap can be specified. For this example, the Wyse-50 uses the real terminal type while the computer running Procomm is set to emulate a VT-100.

❹   The fourth field specifies if the port should be enabled. To enable logins on this port, this field must be set to on.

❺   The final field is used to specify whether the port is secure. Marking a port as secure means that it is trusted enough to allow root to login from that port. Insecure ports do not allow root logins. On an insecure port, users must login from unprivileged accounts and then use su or a similar mechanism to gain superuser privileges, as described in Section 3.3.1.3, "The Superuser Account". For security reasons, it is recommended to change this setting to insecure.

After making any changes to /etc/ttys , send a SIGHUP (hangup) signal to the init process to force it to re-read its configuration file:

```
# kill -HUP 1
```

Since init is always the first process run on a system, it always has a process ID of 1.

If everything is set up correctly, all cables are in place, and the terminals are powered up, a getty process should now be running on each terminal and login prompts should be available on each terminal.

25.3.2. Troubleshooting the Connection

Even with the most meticulous attention to detail, something could still go wrong while setting up a terminal. Here is a list of common symptoms and some suggested fixes.

If no login prompt appears, make sure the terminal is plugged in and powered up. If it is a personal computer acting as a terminal, make sure it is running terminal emulation software on the correct serial port.

Make sure the cable is connected firmly to both the terminal and the FreeBSD computer. Make sure it is the right kind of cable.

Make sure the terminal and FreeBSD agree on the bps rate and parity settings. For a video display terminal, make sure the contrast and brightness controls are turned up. If it is a printing terminal, make sure paper and ink are in good supply.

Use ps to make sure that a getty process is running and serving the terminal. For example, the following listing shows that a getty is running on the second serial port, ttyu1, and is using the std.38400 entry in /etc/gettytab:

```
# ps -axww|grep ttyu
22189  d1  Is+    0:00.03 /usr/libexec/getty std.38400 ttyu1
```

If no getty process is running, make sure the port is enabled in /etc/ttys . Remember to run kill -HUP 1 after modifying /etc/ttys .

If the getty process is running but the terminal still does not display a login prompt, or if it displays a prompt but will not accept typed input, the terminal or cable may not support hardware handshaking. Try changing the entry in /etc/ttys from std.38400 to 3wire.38400 , then run kill -HUP 1 after modifying /etc/ttys . The 3wire entry is similar to std, but ignores hardware handshaking. The baud rate may need to be reduced or software flow control enabled when using 3wire to prevent buffer overflows.

If garbage appears instead of a login prompt, make sure the terminal and FreeBSD agree on the bps rate and parity settings. Check the getty processes to make sure the correct *getty* type is in use. If not, edit /etc/ttys and run kill -HUP 1.

If characters appear doubled and the password appears when typed, switch the terminal, or the terminal emulation software, from "half duplex" or "local echo" to "full duplex."

25.4. Dial-in Service

Contributed by Guy Helmer.
Additions by Sean Kelly.

Configuring a FreeBSD system for dial-in service is similar to configuring terminals, except that modems are used instead of terminal devices. FreeBSD supports both external and internal modems.

External modems are more convenient because they often can be configured via parameters stored in non-volatile RAM and they usually provide lighted indicators that display the state of important RS-232 signals, indicating whether the modem is operating properly.

Internal modems usually lack non-volatile RAM, so their configuration may be limited to setting DIP switches. If the internal modem has any signal indicator lights, they are difficult to view when the system's cover is in place.

When using an external modem, a proper cable is needed. A standard RS-232C serial cable should suffice.

FreeBSD needs the RTS and CTS signals for flow control at speeds above 2400 bps, the CD signal to detect when a call has been answered or the line has been hung up, and the DTR signal to reset the modem after a session is complete. Some cables are wired without all of the needed signals, so if a login session does not go away when the line hangs up, there may be a problem with the cable. Refer to Section 25.2.1, "Serial Cables and Ports" for more information about these signals.

Like other UNIX®-like operating systems, FreeBSD uses the hardware signals to find out when a call has been answered or a line has been hung up and to hangup and reset the modem after a call. FreeBSD avoids sending commands to the modem or watching for status reports from the modem.

FreeBSD supports the NS8250, NS16450, NS16550, and NS16550A-based RS-232C (CCITT V.24) communications interfaces. The 8250 and 16450 devices have single-character buffers. The 16550 device provides a 16-character buffer, which allows for better system performance. Bugs in plain 16550 devices prevent the use of the 16-character buffer, so use 16550A devices if possible. Because single-character-buffer devices require more work by the operating system than the 16-character-buffer devices, 16550A-based serial interface cards are preferred. If the system has many active serial ports or will have a heavy load, 16550A-based cards are better for low-error-rate communications.

The rest of this section demonstrates how to configure a modem to receive incoming connections, how to communicate with the modem, and offers some troubleshooting tips.

25.4.1. Modem Configuration

As with terminals, init spawns a getty process for each configured serial port used for dial-in connections. When a user dials the modem's line and the modems connect, the "Carrier Detect" signal is reported by the modem. The kernel notices that the carrier has been detected and instructs getty to open the port and display a login: prompt at the specified initial line speed. In a typical configuration, if garbage characters are received, usually due to the modem's connection speed being different than the configured speed, getty tries adjusting the line speeds until it receives reasonable characters. After the user enters their login name, getty executes login, which completes the login process by asking for the user's password and then starting the user's shell.

There are two schools of thought regarding dial-up modems. One configuration method is to set the modems and systems so that no matter at what speed a remote user dials in, the dial-in RS-232 interface runs at a locked speed. The benefit of this configuration is that the remote user always sees a system login prompt immediately. The downside is that the system does not know what a user's true data rate is, so full-screen programs like Emacs will not adjust their screen-painting methods to make their response better for slower connections.

The second method is to configure the RS-232 interface to vary its speed based on the remote user's connection speed. Because getty does not understand any particular modem's connection speed reporting, it gives a login: message at an initial speed and watches the characters that come back in response. If the user sees junk, they should press Enter until they see a recognizable prompt. If the data rates do not match, getty sees anything the user types as junk, tries the next speed, and gives the login: prompt again. This procedure normally only takes a keystroke or two before the user sees a good prompt. This login sequence does not look as clean as the locked-speed method, but a user on a low-speed connection should receive better interactive response from full-screen programs.

When locking a modem's data communications rate at a particular speed, no changes to /etc/gettytab should be needed. However, for a matching-speed configuration, additional entries may be required in order to define the speeds to use for the modem. This example configures a 14.4 Kbps modem with a top interface speed of 19.2 Kbps using 8-bit, no parity connections. It configures getty to start the communications rate for a V.32bis connection at 19.2 Kbps, then cycles through 9600 bps, 2400 bps, 1200 bps, 300 bps, and back to 19.2 Kbps. Communications rate cycling is implemented with the nx= (next table) capability. Each line uses a tc= (table continuation) entry to pick up the rest of the settings for a particular data rate.

```
#
# Additions for a V.32bis Modem
#
um|V300|High Speed Modem at 300,8-bit:\
        :nx=V19200:tc=std.300:
un|V1200|High Speed Modem at 1200,8-bit:\
        :nx=V300:tc=std.1200:
uo|V2400|High Speed Modem at 2400,8-bit:\
        :nx=V1200:tc=std.2400:
up|V9600|High Speed Modem at 9600,8-bit:\
        :nx=V2400:tc=std.9600:
uq|V19200|High Speed Modem at 19200,8-bit:\
        :nx=V9600:tc=std.19200:
```

For a 28.8 Kbps modem, or to take advantage of compression on a 14.4 Kbps modem, use a higher communications rate, as seen in this example:

```
#
# Additions for a V.32bis or V.34 Modem
# Starting at 57.6 Kbps
#
vm|VH300|Very High Speed Modem at 300,8-bit:\
```

```
        :nx=VH57600:tc=std.300:
vn|VH1200|Very High Speed Modem at 1200,8-bit:\
        :nx=VH300:tc=std.1200:
vo|VH2400|Very High Speed Modem at 2400,8-bit:\
        :nx=VH1200:tc=std.2400:
vp|VH9600|Very High Speed Modem at 9600,8-bit:\
        :nx=VH2400:tc=std.9600:
vq|VH57600|Very High Speed Modem at 57600,8-bit:\
        :nx=VH9600:tc=std.57600:
```

For a slow CPU or a heavily loaded system without 16550A-based serial ports, this configuration may produce sio "silo" errors at 57.6 Kbps.

The configuration of `/etc/ttys` is similar to Example 25.1, "Configuring Terminal Entries", but a different argument is passed to `getty` and `dialup` is used for the terminal type. Replace *xxx* with the process `init` will run on the device:

```
ttyu0   "/usr/libexec/getty xxx"   dialup on
```

The `dialup` terminal type can be changed. For example, setting `vt102` as the default terminal type allows users to use VT102 emulation on their remote systems.

For a locked-speed configuration, specify the speed with a valid type listed in `/etc/gettytab`. This example is for a modem whose port speed is locked at 19.2 Kbps:

```
ttyu0   "/usr/libexec/getty std.19200"   dialup on
```

In a matching-speed configuration, the entry needs to reference the appropriate beginning "auto-baud" entry in `/etc/gettytab`. To continue the example for a matching-speed modem that starts at 19.2 Kbps, use this entry:

```
ttyu0   "/usr/libexec/getty V19200"   dialup on
```

After editing `/etc/ttys`, wait until the modem is properly configured and connected before signaling `init`:

```
# kill -HUP 1
```

High-speed modems, like V.32, V.32bis, and V.34 modems, use hardware (RTS/CTS) flow control. Use `stty` to set the hardware flow control flag for the modem port. This example sets the `crtscts` flag on COM2's dial-in and dial-out initialization devices:

```
# stty -f /dev/ttyu1.init crtscts
# stty -f /dev/cuau1.init crtscts
```

25.4.2. Troubleshooting

This section provides a few tips for troubleshooting a dial-up modem that will not connect to a FreeBSD system.

Hook up the modem to the FreeBSD system and boot the system. If the modem has status indication lights, watch to see whether the modem's DTR indicator lights when the `login:` prompt appears on the system's console. If it lights up, that should mean that FreeBSD has started a `getty` process on the appropriate communications port and is waiting for the modem to accept a call.

If the DTR indicator does not light, login to the FreeBSD system through the console and type `ps ax` to see if FreeBSD is running a `getty` process on the correct port:

```
 114 ??  I      0:00.10 /usr/libexec/getty V19200 ttyu0
```

If the second column contains a `d0` instead of a `??` and the modem has not accepted a call yet, this means that `getty` has completed its open on the communications port. This could indicate a problem with the cabling or a misconfigured modem because `getty` should not be able to open the communications port until the carrier detect signal has been asserted by the modem.

If no getty processes are waiting to open the port, double-check that the entry for the port is correct in /etc/ttys. Also, check /var/log/messages to see if there are any log messages from init or getty.

Next, try dialing into the system. Be sure to use 8 bits, no parity, and 1 stop bit on the remote system. If a prompt does not appear right away, or the prompt shows garbage, try pressing Enter about once per second. If there is still no login: prompt, try sending a BREAK. When using a high-speed modem, try dialing again after locking the dialing modem's interface speed.

If there is still no login: prompt, check /etc/gettytab again and double-check that:

- The initial capability name specified in the entry in /etc/ttys matches the name of a capability in /etc/gettytab.

- Each nx= entry matches another gettytab capability name.

- Each tc= entry matches another gettytab capability name.

If the modem on the FreeBSD system will not answer, make sure that the modem is configured to answer the phone when DTR is asserted. If the modem seems to be configured correctly, verify that the DTR line is asserted by checking the modem's indicator lights.

If it still does not work, try sending an email to the FreeBSD general questions mailing list describing the modem and the problem.

25.5. Dial-out Service

The following are tips for getting the host to connect over the modem to another computer. This is appropriate for establishing a terminal session with a remote host.

This kind of connection can be helpful to get a file on the Internet if there are problems using PPP. If PPP is not working, use the terminal session to FTP the needed file. Then use zmodem to transfer it to the machine.

25.5.1. Using a Stock Hayes Modem

A generic Hayes dialer is built into tip. Use at=hayes in /etc/remote.

The Hayes driver is not smart enough to recognize some of the advanced features of newer modems messages like BUSY, NO DIALTONE, or CONNECT 115200. Turn those messages off when using tip with ATX0&W.

The dial timeout for tip is 60 seconds. The modem should use something less, or else tip will think there is a communication problem. Try ATS7=45&W.

25.5.2. Using AT Commands

Create a "direct" entry in /etc/remote. For example, if the modem is hooked up to the first serial port, /dev/cuau0, use the following line:

```
cuau0:dv=/dev/cuau0:br#19200:pa=none
```

Use the highest bps rate the modem supports in the br capability. Then, type tip cuau0 to connect to the modem.

Or, use cu as root with the following command:

```
# cu -lline -sspeed
```

line is the serial port, such as /dev/cuau0, and speed is the speed, such as 57600. When finished entering the AT commands, type ~. to exit.

25.5.3. The @ Sign Does Not Work

The @ sign in the phone number capability tells tip to look in /etc/phones for a phone number. But, the @ sign is also a special character in capability files like /etc/remote, so it needs to be escaped with a backslash:

```
pn=\@
```

25.5.4. Dialing from the Command Line

Put a "generic" entry in /etc/remote. For example:

```
tip115200|Dial any phone number at 115200 bps:\
        :dv=/dev/cuau0:br#115200:at=hayes:pa=none:du:
tip57600|Dial any phone number at 57600 bps:\
        :dv=/dev/cuau0:br#57600:at=hayes:pa=none:du:
```

This should now work:

```
# tip -115200 5551234
```

Users who prefer cu over tip, can use a generic cu entry:

```
cu115200|Use cu to dial any number at 115200bps:\
        :dv=/dev/cuau1:br#57600:at=hayes:pa=none:du:
```

and type:

```
# cu 5551234 -s 115200
```

25.5.5. Setting the bps Rate

Put in an entry for tip1200 or cu1200, but go ahead and use whatever bps rate is appropriate with the br capability. tip thinks a good default is 1200 bps which is why it looks for a tip1200 entry. 1200 bps does not have to be used, though.

25.5.6. Accessing a Number of Hosts Through a Terminal Server

Rather than waiting until connected and typing CONNECT *host* each time, use tip's cm capability. For example, these entries in /etc/remote will let you type tip pain or tip muffin to connect to the hosts pain or muffin, and tip deep13 to connect to the terminal server.

```
pain|pain.deep13.com|Forrester's machine:\
        :cm=CONNECT pain\n:tc=deep13:
muffin|muffin.deep13.com|Frank's machine:\
        :cm=CONNECT muffin\n:tc=deep13:
deep13:Gizmonics Institute terminal server:\
        :dv=/dev/cuau2:br#38400:at=hayes:du:pa=none:pn=5551234:
```

25.5.7. Using More Than One Line with tip

This is often a problem where a university has several modem lines and several thousand students trying to use them.

Make an entry in /etc/remote and use @ for the pn capability:

```
big-university:\
        :pn=\@:tc=dialout
dialout:\
        :dv=/dev/cuau3:br#9600:at=courier:du:pa=none:
```

Then, list the phone numbers in /etc/phones :

```
big-university 5551111
```

```
big-university 5551112
big-university 5551113
big-university 5551114
```

tip will try each number in the listed order, then give up. To keep retrying, run tip in a while loop.

25.5.8. Using the Force Character

Ctrl+P is the default "force" character, used to tell tip that the next character is literal data. The force character can be set to any other character with the ~s escape, which means "set a variable."

Type ~sforce=*single-char* followed by a newline. *single-char* is any single character. If *single-char* is left out, then the force character is the null character, which is accessed by typing Ctrl+2 or Ctrl+Space. A pretty good value for *single-char* is Shift+Ctrl+6, which is only used on some terminal servers.

To change the force character, specify the following in ~/.tiprc :

```
force=single-char
```

25.5.9. Upper Case Characters

This happens when Ctrl+A is pressed, which is tip's "raise character", specially designed for people with broken caps-lock keys. Use ~s to set raisechar to something reasonable. It can be set to be the same as the force character, if neither feature is used.

Here is a sample ~/.tiprc for Emacs users who need to type Ctrl+2 and Ctrl+A:

```
force=^^
raisechar=^^
```

The ^^ is Shift+Ctrl+6.

25.5.10. File Transfers with tip

When talking to another UNIX®-like operating system, files can be sent and received using ~p (put) and ~t (take). These commands run cat and echo on the remote system to accept and send files. The syntax is:

~p local-file [remote-file]

~t remote-file [local-file]

There is no error checking, so another protocol, like zmodem, should probably be used.

25.5.11. Using zmodem with tip?

To receive files, start the sending program on the remote end. Then, type ~C rz to begin receiving them locally.

To send files, start the receiving program on the remote end. Then, type ~C sz *files* to send them to the remote system.

25.6. Setting Up the Serial Console

Contributed by Kazutaka YOKOTA.
Based on a document by Bill Paul.

FreeBSD has the ability to boot a system with a dumb terminal on a serial port as a console. This configuration is useful for system administrators who wish to install FreeBSD on machines that have no keyboard or monitor attached, and developers who want to debug the kernel or device drivers.

As described in Chapter 12, *The FreeBSD Booting Process*, FreeBSD employs a three stage bootstrap. The first two stages are in the boot block code which is stored at the beginning of the FreeBSD slice on the boot disk. The boot block then loads and runs the boot loader as the third stage code.

In order to set up booting from a serial console, the boot block code, the boot loader code, and the kernel need to be configured.

25.6.1. Quick Serial Console Configuration

This section provides a fast overview of setting up the serial console. This procedure can be used when the dumb terminal is connected to COM1.

Procedure 25.1. Configuring a Serial Console on COM1

1. Connect the serial cable to COM1 and the controlling terminal.

2. To configure boot messages to display on the serial console, issue the following command as the superuser:

   ```
   # echo 'console="comconsole"' >> /boot/loader.conf
   ```

3. Edit /etc/ttys and change off to on and dialup to vt100 for the ttyu0 entry. Otherwise, a password will not be required to connect via the serial console, resulting in a potential security hole.

4. Reboot the system to see if the changes took effect.

If a different configuration is required, see the next section for a more in-depth configuration explanation.

25.6.2. In-Depth Serial Console Configuration

This section provides a more detailed explanation of the steps needed to setup a serial console in FreeBSD.

Procedure 25.2. Configuring a Serial Console

1. Prepare a serial cable.

   Use either a null-modem cable or a standard serial cable and a null-modem adapter. See Section 25.2.1, "Serial Cables and Ports" for a discussion on serial cables.

2. Unplug the keyboard.

   Many systems probe for the keyboard during the Power-On Self-Test (POST) and will generate an error if the keyboard is not detected. Some machines will refuse to boot until the keyboard is plugged in.

   If the computer complains about the error, but boots anyway, no further configuration is needed.

   If the computer refuses to boot without a keyboard attached, configure the BIOS so that it ignores this error. Consult the motherboard's manual for details on how to do this.

    Tip

   Try setting the keyboard to "Not installed" in the BIOS. This setting tells the BIOS not to probe for a keyboard at power-on so it should not complain if the keyboard is absent. If that option is not present in the BIOS, look for an "Halt on Error" option instead. Setting this to "All but Keyboard" or to "No Errors" will have the same effect.

   If the system has a PS/2® mouse, unplug it as well. PS/2® mice share some hardware with the keyboard and leaving the mouse plugged in can fool the keyboard probe into thinking the keyboard is still there.

Note

While most systems will boot without a keyboard, quite a few will not boot without a graphics adapter. Some systems can be configured to boot with no graphics adapter by changing the "graphics adapter" setting in the BIOS configuration to "Not installed". Other systems do not support this option and will refuse to boot if there is no display hardware in the system. With these machines, leave some kind of graphics card plugged in, even if it is just a junky mono board. A monitor does not need to be attached.

3. Plug a dumb terminal, an old computer with a modem program, or the serial port on another UNIX® box into the serial port.

4. Add the appropriate `hint.sio.*` entries to `/boot/device.hints` for the serial port. Some multi-port cards also require kernel configuration options. Refer to sio(4) for the required options and device hints for each supported serial port.

5. Create `boot.config` in the root directory of the `a` partition on the boot drive.

   This file instructs the boot block code how to boot the system. In order to activate the serial console, one or more of the following options are needed. When using multiple options, include them all on the same line:

   `-h`
   > Toggles between the internal and serial consoles. Use this to switch console devices. For instance, to boot from the internal (video) console, use `-h` to direct the boot loader and the kernel to use the serial port as its console device. Alternatively, to boot from the serial port, use `-h` to tell the boot loader and the kernel to use the video display as the console instead.

   `-D`
   > Toggles between the single and dual console configurations. In the single configuration, the console will be either the internal console (video display) or the serial port, depending on the state of `-h`. In the dual console configuration, both the video display and the serial port will become the console at the same time, regardless of the state of `-h`. However, the dual console configuration takes effect only while the boot block is running. Once the boot loader gets control, the console specified by `-h` becomes the only console.

   `-P`
   > Makes the boot block probe the keyboard. If no keyboard is found, the `-D` and `-h` options are automatically set.

Note

Due to space constraints in the current version of the boot blocks, `-P` is capable of detecting extended keyboards only. Keyboards with less than 101 keys and without F11 and F12 keys may not be detected. Keyboards on some laptops may not be properly found because of this limitation. If this is the case, do not use `-P`.

Use either `-P` to select the console automatically or `-h` to activate the serial console. Refer to boot(8) and boot.config(5) for more details.

The options, except for `-P`, are passed to the boot loader. The boot loader will determine whether the internal video or the serial port should become the console by examining the state of `-h`. This means that if `-D` is specified but -h is not specified in /boot.config, the serial port can be used as the console only during the boot block as the boot loader will use the internal video display as the console.

6. Boot the machine.

    When FreeBSD starts, the boot blocks echo the contents of /boot.config to the console. For example:

    ```
    /boot.config: -P
    Keyboard: no
    ```

    The second line appears only if -P is in /boot.config and indicates the presence or absence of the keyboard. These messages go to either the serial or internal console, or both, depending on the option in /boot.config:

Options	Message goes to
none	internal console
-h	serial console
-D	serial and internal consoles
-Dh	serial and internal consoles
-P, keyboard present	internal console
-P, keyboard absent	serial console

    After the message, there will be a small pause before the boot blocks continue loading the boot loader and before any further messages are printed to the console. Under normal circumstances, there is no need to interrupt the boot blocks, but one can do so in order to make sure things are set up correctly.

    Press any key, other than Enter, at the console to interrupt the boot process. The boot blocks will then prompt for further action:

    ```
    >> FreeBSD/i386 BOOT
    Default: 0:ad(0,a)/boot/loader
    boot:
    ```

    Verify that the above message appears on either the serial or internal console, or both, according to the options in /boot.config. If the message appears in the correct console, press Enter to continue the boot process.

    If there is no prompt on the serial terminal, something is wrong with the settings. Enter -h then Enter or Return to tell the boot block (and then the boot loader and the kernel) to choose the serial port for the console. Once the system is up, go back and check what went wrong.

During the third stage of the boot process, one can still switch between the internal console and the serial console by setting appropriate environment variables in the boot loader. See loader(8) for more information.

Note

This line in /boot/loader.conf or /boot/loader.conf.local configures the boot loader and the kernel to send their boot messages to the serial console, regardless of the options in /boot.config:

```
console="comconsole"
```

That line should be the first line of /boot/loader.conf so that boot messages are displayed on the serial console as early as possible.

If that line does not exist, or if it is set to console="vidconsole", the boot loader and the kernel will use whichever console is indicated by -h in the boot block. See loader.conf(5) for more information.

At the moment, the boot loader has no option equivalent to -P in the boot block, and there is no provision to automatically select the internal console and the serial console based on the presence of the keyboard.

Tip

While it is not required, it is possible to provide a login prompt over the serial line. To configure this, edit the entry for the serial port in /etc/ttys using the instructions in Section 25.3.1, "Terminal Configuration". If the speed of the serial port has been changed, change std.9600 to match the new setting.

25.6.3. Setting a Faster Serial Port Speed

By default, the serial port settings are 9600 baud, 8 bits, no parity, and 1 stop bit. To change the default console speed, use one of the following options:

- Edit /etc/make.conf and set BOOT_COMCONSOLE_SPEED to the new console speed. Then, recompile and install the boot blocks and the boot loader:

```
# cd /sys/boot
# make clean
# make
# make install
```

If the serial console is configured in some other way than by booting with -h, or if the serial console used by the kernel is different from the one used by the boot blocks, add the following option, with the desired speed, to a custom kernel configuration file and compile a new kernel:

```
options CONSPEED=19200
```

- Add the -S19200 boot option to /boot.config, replacing 19200 with the speed to use.

- Add the following options to /boot/loader.conf . Replace 115200 with the speed to use.

```
boot_multicons="YES"
boot_serial="YES"
comconsole_speed="115200"
console="comconsole,vidconsole"
```

25.6.4. Entering the DDB Debugger from the Serial Line

To configure the ability to drop into the kernel debugger from the serial console, add the following options to a custom kernel configuration file and compile the kernel using the instructions in Chapter 8, *Configuring the FreeBSD Kernel*. Note that while this is useful for remote diagnostics, it is also dangerous if a spurious BREAK is generated on the serial port. Refer to ddb(4) and ddb(8) for more information about the kernel debugger.

```
options BREAK_TO_DEBUGGER
options DDB
```

Chapter 26. PPP

26.1. Synopsis

FreeBSD supports the Point-to-Point (PPP) protocol which can be used to establish a network or Internet connection using a dial-up modem. This chapter describes how to configure modem-based communication services in FreeBSD.

After reading this chapter, you will know:

- How to configure, use, and troubleshoot a PPP connection.

- How to set up PPP over Ethernet (PPPoE).

- How to set up PPP over ATM (PPPoA).

Before reading this chapter, you should:

- Be familiar with basic network terminology.

- Understand the basics and purpose of a dial-up connection and PPP.

26.2. Configuring PPP

FreeBSD provides built-in support for managing dial-up PPP connections using ppp(8). The default FreeBSD kernel provides support for tun which is used to interact with a modem hardware. Configuration is performed by editing at least one configuration file, and configuration files containing examples are provided. Finally, ppp is used to start and manage connections.

In order to use a PPP connection, the following items are needed:

- A dial-up account with an Internet Service Provider (ISP).

- A dial-up modem.

- The dial-up number for the ISP.

- The login name and password assigned by the ISP.

- The IP address of one or more DNS servers. Normally, the ISP provides these addresses. If it did not, FreeBSD can be configured to use DNS negotiation.

If any of the required information is missing, contact the ISP.

The following information may be supplied by the ISP, but is not necessary:

- The IP address of the default gateway. If this information is unknown, the ISP will automatically provide the correct value during connection setup. When configuring PPP on FreeBSD, this address is referred to as HISADDR.

- The subnet mask. If the ISP has not provided one, 255.255.255.255 will be used in the ppp(8) configuration file.

-
  If the ISP has assigned a static IP address and hostname, it should be input into the configuration file. Otherwise, this information will be automatically provided during connection setup.

The rest of this section demonstrates how to configure FreeBSD for common PPP connection scenarios. The required configuration file is /etc/ppp/ppp.conf and additional files and examples are available in /usr/share/examples/ppp/.

Note

Throughout this section, many of the file examples display line numbers. These line numbers have been added to make it easier to follow the discussion and are not meant to be placed in the actual file.

When editing a configuration file, proper indentation is important. Lines that end in a : start in the first column (beginning of the line) while all other lines should be indented as shown using spaces or tabs.

26.2.1. Basic Configuration

In order to configure a PPP connection, first edit /etc/ppp/ppp.conf with the dial-in information for the ISP. This file is described as follows:

```
1    default:
2      set log Phase Chat LCP IPCP CCP tun command
3      ident user-ppp VERSION
4      set device /dev/cuau0
5      set speed 115200
6      set dial "ABORT BUSY ABORT NO\\sCARRIER TIMEOUT 5 \
7              \"\" AT OK-AT-OK ATE1Q0 OK \\dATDT\\T TIMEOUT 40 CONNECT"
8      set timeout 180
9      enable dns
10
11   provider:
12      set phone "(123) 456 7890"
13      set authname foo
14      set authkey bar
15      set timeout 300
16      set ifaddr x.x.x.x/0 y.y.y.y/0 255.255.255.255 0.0.0.0
17      add default HISADDR
```

Line 1:
    Identifies the default entry. Commands in this entry (lines 2 through 9) are executed automatically when ppp is run.

Line 2:
    Enables verbose logging parameters for testing the connection. Once the configuration is working satisfactorily, this line should be reduced to:

```
set log phase tun
```

Line 3:
    Displays the version of ppp(8) to the PPP software running on the other side of the connection.

Line 4:
    Identifies the device to which the modem is connected, where COM1 is /dev/cuau0 and COM2 is /dev/cuau1.

Line 5:
    Sets the connection speed. If 115200 does not work on an older modem, try 38400 instead.

Lines 6 & 7:
    The dial string written as an expect-send syntax. Refer to chat(8) for more information.

Note that this command continues onto the next line for readability. Any command in ppp.conf may do this if the last character on the line is \.

Line 8:

Sets the idle timeout for the link in seconds.

Line 9:

Instructs the peer to confirm the DNS settings. If the local network is running its own DNS server, this line should be commented out, by adding a # at the beginning of the line, or removed.

Line 10:

A blank line for readability. Blank lines are ignored by ppp(8).

Line 11:

Identifies an entry called provider. This could be changed to the name of the ISP so that load *ISP* can be used to start the connection.

Line 12:

Use the phone number for the ISP. Multiple phone numbers may be specified using the colon (:) or pipe character (|) as a separator. To rotate through the numbers, use a colon. To always attempt to dial the first number first and only use the other numbers if the first number fails, use the pipe character. Always enclose the entire set of phone numbers between quotation marks (") to prevent dialing failures.

Lines 13 & 14:

Use the user name and password for the ISP.

Line 15:

Sets the default idle timeout in seconds for the connection. In this example, the connection will be closed automatically after 300 seconds of inactivity. To prevent a timeout, set this value to zero.

Line 16:

Sets the interface addresses. The values used depend upon whether a static IP address has been obtained from the ISP or if it instead negotiates a dynamic IP address during connection.

If the ISP has allocated a static IP address and default gateway, replace *x.x.x.x* with the static IP address and replace *y.y.y.y* with the IP address of the default gateway. If the ISP has only provided a static IP address without a gateway address, replace *y.y.y.y* with 10.0.0.2/0.

If the IP address changes whenever a connection is made, change this line to the following value. This tells ppp(8) to use the IP Configuration Protocol (IPCP) to negotiate a dynamic IP address:

```
set ifaddr 10.0.0.1/0 10.0.0.2/0 255.255.255.255 0.0.0.0
```

Line 17:

Keep this line as-is as it adds a default route to the gateway. The HISADDR will automatically be replaced with the gateway address specified on line 16. It is important that this line appears after line 16.

Depending upon whether ppp(8) is started manually or automatically, a /etc/ppp/ppp.linkup may also need to be created which contains the following lines. This file is required when running ppp in -auto mode. This file is used after the connection has been established. At this point, the IP address will have been assigned and it is now be possible to add the routing table entries. When creating this file, make sure that *provider* matches the value demonstrated in line 11 of ppp.conf.

```
provider:
    add default HISADDR
```

This file is also needed when the default gateway address is "guessed" in a static IP address configuration. In this case, remove line 17 from ppp.conf and create /etc/ppp/ppp.linkup with the above two lines. More examples for this file can be found in /usr/share/examples/ppp/.

By default, ppp must be run as root. To change this default, add the account of the user who should run ppp to the network group in /etc/group .

Then, give the user access to one or more entries in /etc/ppp/ppp.conf with allow. For example, to give fred and mary permission to only the provider: entry, add this line to the provider: section:

```
allow users fred mary
```

To give the specified users access to all entries, put that line in the default section instead.

26.2.2. Advanced Configuration

It is possible to configure PPP to supply DNS and NetBIOS nameserver addresses on demand.

To enable these extensions with PPP version 1.x, the following lines might be added to the relevant section of /etc/ppp/ppp.conf .

```
enable msext
set ns 203.14.100.1 203.14.100.2
set nbns 203.14.100.5
```

And for PPP version 2 and above:

```
accept dns
set dns 203.14.100.1 203.14.100.2
set nbns 203.14.100.5
```

This will tell the clients the primary and secondary name server addresses, and a NetBIOS nameserver host.

In version 2 and above, if the set dns line is omitted, PPP will use the values found in /etc/resolv.conf .

26.2.2.1. PAP and CHAP Authentication

Some ISPs set their system up so that the authentication part of the connection is done using either of the PAP or CHAP authentication mechanisms. If this is the case, the ISP will not give a login: prompt at connection, but will start talking PPP immediately.

PAP is less secure than CHAP, but security is not normally an issue here as passwords, although being sent as plain text with PAP, are being transmitted down a serial line only. There is not much room for crackers to "eavesdrop".

The following alterations must be made:

```
13      set authname MyUserName
14  ,   set authkey MyPassword
15      set login
```

Line 13:
> This line specifies the PAP/CHAP user name. Insert the correct value for MyUserName.

Line 14:
> This line specifies the PAP/CHAP password. Insert the correct value for MyPassword. You may want to add an additional line, such as:

```
16      accept PAP
```

or

```
16      accept CHAP
```

to make it obvious that this is the intention, but PAP and CHAP are both accepted by default.

Line 15:

The ISP will not normally require a login to the server when using PAP or CHAP. Therefore, disable the "set login" string.

26.2.2.2. Using PPP Network Address Translation Capability

PPP has ability to use internal NAT without kernel diverting capabilities. This functionality may be enabled by the following line in /etc/ppp/ppp.conf :

```
nat enable yes
```

Alternatively, NAT may be enabled by command-line option -nat. There is also /etc/rc.conf knob named ppp_nat, which is enabled by default.

When using this feature, it may be useful to include the following /etc/ppp/ppp.conf options to enable incoming connections forwarding:

```
nat port tcp 10.0.0.2:ftp ftp
nat port tcp 10.0.0.2:http http
```

or do not trust the outside at all

```
nat deny_incoming yes
```

26.2.3. Final System Configuration

While ppp is now configured, some edits still need to be made to /etc/rc.conf .

Working from the top down in this file, make sure the hostname= line is set:

```
hostname="foo.example.com"
```

If the ISP has supplied a static IP address and name, use this name as the host name.

Look for the network_interfaces variable. To configure the system to dial the ISP on demand, make sure the tun0 device is added to the list, otherwise remove it.

```
network_interfaces="lo0 tun0"
ifconfig_tun0=
```

Note

The ifconfig_tun0 variable should be empty, and a file called /etc/start_if.tun0 should be created. This file should contain the line:

```
ppp -auto mysystem
```

This script is executed at network configuration time, starting the ppp daemon in automatic mode. If this machine acts as a gateway, consider including -alias. Refer to the manual page for further details.

Make sure that the router program is set to NO with the following line in /etc/rc.conf :

```
router_enable="NO"
```

It is important that the routed daemon is not started, as routed tends to delete the default routing table entries created by ppp.

It is probably a good idea to ensure that the `sendmail_flags` line does not include the `-q` option, otherwise `send-mail` will attempt to do a network lookup every now and then, possibly causing your machine to dial out. You may try:

```
sendmail_flags="-bd"
```

The downside is that `sendmail` is forced to re-examine the mail queue whenever the ppp link. To automate this, include `!bg` in `ppp.linkup`:

```
1     provider:
2       delete ALL
3       add 0 0 HISADDR
4       !bg sendmail -bd -q30m
```

An alternative is to set up a "dfilter" to block SMTP traffic. Refer to the sample files for further details.

26.2.4. Using ppp

All that is left is to reboot the machine. After rebooting, either type:

```
# ppp
```

and then `dial provider` to start the PPP session, or, to configure ppp to establish sessions automatically when there is outbound traffic and `start_if.tun0` does not exist, type:

```
# ppp -auto provider
```

It is possible to talk to the ppp program while it is running in the background, but only if a suitable diagnostic port has been set up. To do this, add the following line to the configuration:

```
set server /var/run/ppp-tun%d DiagnosticPassword 0177
```

This will tell PPP to listen to the specified UNIX® domain socket, asking clients for the specified password before allowing access. The `%d` in the name is replaced with the `tun` device number that is in use.

Once a socket has been set up, the pppctl(8) program may be used in scripts that wish to manipulate the running program.

26.2.5. Configuring Dial-in Services

Section 25.4, "Dial-in Service" provides a good description on enabling dial-up services using getty(8).

An alternative to `getty` is comms/mgetty+sendfax port), a smarter version of `getty` designed with dial-up lines in mind.

The advantages of using `mgetty` is that it actively *talks* to modems, meaning if port is turned off in `/etc/ttys` then the modem will not answer the phone.

Later versions of `mgetty` (from 0.99beta onwards) also support the automatic detection of PPP streams, allowing clients scriptless access to the server.

Refer to http://mgetty.greenie.net/doc/mgetty_toc.html for more information on `mgetty`.

By default the comms/mgetty+sendfax port comes with the `AUTO_PPP` option enabled allowing `mgetty` to detect the LCP phase of PPP connections and automatically spawn off a ppp shell. However, since the default login/password sequence does not occur it is necessary to authenticate users using either PAP or CHAP.

This section assumes the user has successfully compiled, and installed the comms/mgetty+sendfax port on his system.

Ensure that /usr/local/etc/mgetty+sendfax/login.config has the following:

```
/AutoPPP/ -        - /etc/ppp/ppp-pap-dialup
```

This tells mgetty to run ppp-pap-dialup for detected PPP connections.

Create an executable file called /etc/ppp/ppp-pap-dialup containing the following:

```
#!/bin/sh
exec /usr/sbin/ppp -direct pap$IDENT
```

For each dial-up line enabled in /etc/ttys , create a corresponding entry in /etc/ppp/ppp.conf . This will happily co-exist with the definitions we created above.

```
pap:
  enable pap
  set ifaddr 203.14.100.1 203.14.100.20-203.14.100.40
  enable proxy
```

Each user logging in with this method will need to have a username/password in /etc/ppp/ppp.secret , or alternatively add the following option to authenticate users via PAP from /etc/passwd .

```
enable passwdauth
```

To assign some users a static IP number, specify the number as the third argument in /etc/ppp/ppp.secret . See /usr/share/examples/ppp/ppp.secret.sample for examples.

26.3. Troubleshooting PPP Connections

This section covers a few issues which may arise when using PPP over a modem connection. Some ISPs present the ssword prompt while others present password. If the ppp script is not written accordingly, the login attempt will fail. The most common way to debug ppp connections is by connecting manually as described in this section.

26.3.1. Check the Device Nodes

When using a custom kernel, make sure to include the following line in the kernel configuration file:

```
device    uart
```

The uart device is already included in the GENERIC kernel, so no additional steps are necessary in this case. Just check the dmesg output for the modem device with:

```
# dmesg | grep uart
```

This should display some pertinent output about the uart devices. These are the COM ports we need. If the modem acts like a standard serial port, it should be listed on uart1, or COM2. If so, a kernel rebuild is not required. When matching up, if the modem is on uart1, the modem device would be /dev/cuau1 .

26.3.2. Connecting Manually

Connecting to the Internet by manually controlling ppp is quick, easy, and a great way to debug a connection or just get information on how the ISP treats ppp client connections. Lets start PPP from the command line. Note that in all of our examples we will use *example* as the hostname of the machine running PPP. To start ppp:

```
# ppp
```

```
ppp ON example> set device /dev/cuau1
```

This second command sets the modem device to cuau1 .

```
ppp ON example> set speed 115200
```

This sets the connection speed to 115,200 kbps.

```
ppp ON example> enable dns
```

This tells ppp to configure the resolver and add the nameserver lines to /etc/resolv.conf. If ppp cannot determine the hostname, it can manually be set later.

```
ppp ON example> term
```

This switches to "terminal" mode in order to manually control the modem.

```
deflink: Entering terminal mode on /dev/cuau1
type '~h' for help
```

```
at
OK
atdt 123456789
```

Use at to initialize the modem, then use atdt and the number for the ISP to begin the dial in process.

```
CONNECT
```

Confirmation of the connection, if we are going to have any connection problems, unrelated to hardware, here is where we will attempt to resolve them.

```
ISP Login:myusername
```

At this prompt, return the prompt with the username that was provided by the ISP.

```
ISP Pass:mypassword
```

At this prompt, reply with the password that was provided by the ISP. Just like logging into FreeBSD, the password will not echo.

```
Shell or PPP:ppp
```

Depending on the ISP, this prompt might not appear. If it does, it is asking whether to use a shell on the provider or to start ppp. In this example, ppp was selected in order to establish an Internet connection.

```
Ppp ON example>
```

Notice that in this example the first p has been capitalized. This shows that we have successfully connected to the ISP.

```
PPp ON example>
```

We have successfully authenticated with our ISP and are waiting for the assigned IP address.

```
PPP ON example>
```

We have made an agreement on an IP address and successfully completed our connection.

```
PPP ON example>add default HISADDR
```

Here we add our default route, we need to do this before we can talk to the outside world as currently the only established connection is with the peer. If this fails due to existing routes, put a bang character ! in front of the add. Alternatively, set this before making the actual connection and it will negotiate a new route accordingly.

If everything went good we should now have an active connection to the Internet, which could be thrown into the background using CTRL+z If PPP returns to ppp then the connection has bee lost. This is good to know because it shows the connection status. Capital P's represent a connection to the ISP and lowercase p's show that the connection has been lost.

26.3.3. Debugging

If a connection cannot be established, turn hardware flow CTS/RTS to off using `set ctsrts off`. This is mainly the case when connected to some PPP-capable terminal servers, where PPP hangs when it tries to write data to the communication link, and waits for a Clear To Send (CTS) signal which may never come. When using this option, include `set accmap` as it may be required to defeat hardware dependent on passing certain characters from end to end, most of the time XON/XOFF. Refer to ppp(8) for more information on this option and how it is used.

An older modem may need `set parity even`. Parity is set at none be default, but is used for error checking with a large increase in traffic, on older modems.

PPP may not return to the command mode, which is usually a negotiation error where the ISP is waiting for negotiating to begin. At this point, using ~p will force ppp to start sending the configuration information.

If a login prompt never appears, PAP or CHAP authentication is most likely required. To use PAP or CHAP, add the following options to PPP before going into terminal mode:

```
ppp ON example> set authname myusername
```

Where *myusername* should be replaced with the username that was assigned by the ISP.

```
ppp ON example> set authkey mypassword
```

Where *mypassword* should be replaced with the password that was assigned by the ISP.

If a connection is established, but cannot seem to find any domain name, try to ping(8) an IP address. If there is 100 percent (100%) packet loss, it is likely that a default route was not assigned. Double check that `add default HISADDR` was set during the connection. If a connection can be made to a remote IP address, it is possible that a resolver address has not been added to `/etc/resolv.conf`. This file should look like:

```
domain example.com
nameserver x.x.x.x
nameserver y.y.y.y
```

Where *x.x.x.x* and *y.y.y.y* should be replaced with the IP address of the ISP's DNS servers.

To configure syslog(3) to provide logging for the PPP connection, make sure this line exists in `/etc/syslog.conf`:

```
!ppp
*.*       /var/log/ppp.log
```

26.4. Using PPP over Ethernet (PPPoE)

This section describes how to set up PPP over Ethernet (PPPoE).

Here is an example of a working `ppp.conf`:

```
default:
  set log Phase tun command # you can add more detailed logging if you wish
  set ifaddr 10.0.0.1/0 10.0.0.2/0

name_of_service_provider:
  set device PPPoE:xl1 # replace xl1 with your Ethernet device
  set authname YOURLOGINNAME
  set authkey YOURPASSWORD
  set dial
  set login
  add default HISADDR
```

As root, run:

```
# ppp -ddial name_of_service_provider
```

Add the following to /etc/rc.conf :

```
ppp_enable="YES"
ppp_mode="ddial"
ppp_nat="YES" # if you want to enable nat for your local network, otherwise NO
ppp_profile="name_of_service_provider"
```

26.4.1. Using a PPPoE Service Tag

Sometimes it will be necessary to use a service tag to establish the connection. Service tags are used to distinguish between different PPPoE servers attached to a given network.

Any required service tag information should be in the documentation provided by the ISP.

As a last resort, one could try installing the net/rr-pppoe package or port. Bear in mind however, this may de-program your modem and render it useless, so think twice before doing it. Simply install the program shipped with the modem. Then, access the System menu from the program. The name of the profile should be listed there. It is usually *ISP*.

The profile name (service tag) will be used in the PPPoE configuration entry in ppp.conf as the provider part for set device. Refer to ppp(8) for full details. It should look like this:

```
set device PPPoE:xl1:ISP
```

Do not forget to change *xl1* to the proper device for the Ethernet card.

Do not forget to change *ISP* to the profile.

For additional information, refer to Cheaper Broadband with FreeBSD on DSL by Renaud Waldura.

26.4.2. PPPoE with a 3Com® HomeConnect® ADSL Modem Dual Link

This modem does not follow the PPPoE specification defined in RFC 2516.

In order to make FreeBSD capable of communicating with this device, a sysctl must be set. This can be done automatically at boot time by updating /etc/sysctl.conf :

```
net.graph.nonstandard_pppoe=1
```

or can be done immediately with the command:

```
# sysctl net.graph.nonstandard_pppoe=1
```

Unfortunately, because this is a system-wide setting, it is not possible to talk to a normal PPPoE client or server and a 3Com® HomeConnect® ADSL Modem at the same time.

26.5. Using PPP over ATM (PPPoA)

The following describes how to set up PPP over ATM (PPPoA). PPPoA is a popular choice among European DSL providers.

26.5.1. Using mpd

The mpd application can be used to connect to a variety of services, in particular PPTP services. It can be installed using the net/mpd5 package or port. Many ADSL modems require that a PPTP tunnel is created between the modem and computer.

Once installed, configure mpd to suit the provider's settings. The port places a set of sample configuration files which are well documented in /usr/local/etc/mpd/ . A complete guide to configure mpd is available in HTML format in /usr/ports/share/doc/mpd/ . Here is a sample configuration for connecting to an ADSL service with mpd. The configuration is spread over two files, first the mpd.conf :

> **Note**
>
> This example mpd.conf only works with mpd 4.x.

```
default:
    load adsl

adsl:
    new -i ng0 adsl adsl
    set bundle authname username ❶
    set bundle password password ❷
    set bundle disable multilink

    set link no pap acfcomp protocomp
    set link disable chap
    set link accept chap
    set link keep-alive 30 10

    set ipcp no vjcomp
    set ipcp ranges 0.0.0.0/0 0.0.0.0/0

    set iface route default
    set iface disable on-demand
    set iface enable proxy-arp
    set iface idle 0

    open
```

❶ The username used to authenticate with your ISP.
❷ The password used to authenticate with your ISP.

Information about the link, or links, to establish is found in mpd.links . An example mpd.links to accompany the above example is given beneath:

```
adsl:
    set link type pptp
    set pptp mode active
    set pptp enable originate outcall
    set pptp self 10.0.0.1 ❶
    set pptp peer 10.0.0.138 ❷
```

❶ The IP address of FreeBSD computer running mpd.
❷ The IP address of the ADSL modem. The Alcatel SpeedTouch™ Home defaults to 10.0.0.138 .

It is possible to initialize the connection easily by issuing the following command as root:

```
# mpd -b adsl
```

To view the status of the connection:

```
% ifconfig ng0
ng0: flags=88d1<UP,POINTOPOINT,RUNNING,NOARP,SIMPLEX,MULTICAST> mtu 1500
        inet 216.136.204.117 --> 204.152.186.171 netmask 0xffffffff
```

Using mpd is the recommended way to connect to an ADSL service with FreeBSD.

26.5.2. Using pptpclient

It is also possible to use FreeBSD to connect to other PPPoA services using net/pptpclient.

To use net/pptpclient to connect to a DSL service, install the port or package, then edit /etc/ppp/ppp.conf . An example section of ppp.conf is given below. For further information on ppp.conf options consult ppp(8).

```
adsl:
 set log phase chat lcp ipcp ccp tun command
 set timeout 0
 enable dns
 set authname username ❶
 set authkey password ❷
 set ifaddr 0 0
 add default HISADDR
```

❶   The username for the DSL provider.
❷   The password for your account.

Warning

Since the account's password is added to ppp.confin plain text form, make sure nobody can read the contents of this file:

```
# chown root:wheel /etc/ppp/ppp.conf
# chmod 600 /etc/ppp/ppp.conf
```

This will open a tunnel for a PPP session to the DSL router. Ethernet DSL modems have a preconfigured LAN IP address to connect to. In the case of the Alcatel SpeedTouch™ Home, this address is 10.0.0.138 . The router's documentation should list the address the device uses. To open the tunnel and start a PPP session:

```
# pptp address adsl
```

Tip

If an ampersand ("&") is added to the end of this command, pptp will return the prompt.

A tun virtual tunnel device will be created for interaction between the pptp and ppp processes. Once the prompt is returned, or the pptp process has confirmed a connection, examine the tunnel:

```
% ifconfig tun0
tun0: flags=8051<UP,POINTOPOINT,RUNNING,MULTICAST> mtu 1500
        inet 216.136.204.21 --> 204.152.186.171 netmask 0xffffff00
 Opened by PID 918
```

If the connection fails, check the configuration of the router, which is usually accessible using a web browser. Also, examine the output of pptp and the contents of the log file, /var/log/ppp.log for clues.

Chapter 27. Electronic Mail

Original work by Bill Lloyd.
Rewritten by Jim Mock.

27.1. Synopsis

"Electronic Mail", better known as email, is one of the most widely used forms of communication today. This chapter provides a basic introduction to running a mail server on FreeBSD, as well as an introduction to sending and receiving email using FreeBSD. For more complete coverage of this subject, refer to the books listed in Appendix B, *Bibliography*.

After reading this chapter, you will know:

- Which software components are involved in sending and receiving electronic mail.

- Where basic Sendmail configuration files are located in FreeBSD.

- The difference between remote and local mailboxes.

- How to block spammers from illegally using a mail server as a relay.

- How to install and configure an alternate Mail Transfer Agent, replacing Sendmail.

- How to troubleshoot common mail server problems.

- How to set up the system to send mail only.

- How to use mail with a dialup connection.

- How to configure SMTP authentication for added security.

- How to install and use a Mail User Agent, such as mutt, to send and receive email.

- How to download mail from a remote POP or IMAP server.

- How to automatically apply filters and rules to incoming email.

Before reading this chapter, you should:

- Properly set up a network connection (Chapter 30, *Advanced Networking*).

- Properly set up the DNS information for a mail host (Chapter 28, *Network Servers*).

- Know how to install additional third-party software (Chapter 4, *Installing Applications: Packages and Ports*).

27.2. Mail Components

There are five major parts involved in an email exchange: the Mail User Agent (MUA), the Mail Transfer Agent (MTA), a mail host, a remote or local mailbox, and DNS. This section provides an overview of these components.

Mail User Agent (MUA)
>   The Mail User Agent (MUA) is an application which is used to compose, send, and receive emails. This application can be a command line program, such as the built-in `mail` utility or a third-party application from the Ports Collection, such as mutt, alpine, or elm. Dozens of graphical programs are also available in the Ports Collection, including Claws Mail, Evolution, and Thunderbird. Some organizations provide a web mail program

which can be accessed through a web browser. More information about installing and using a MUA on FreeBSD can be found in Section 27.10, "Mail User Agents".

Mail Transfer Agent (MTA)

The Mail Transfer Agent (MTA) is responsible for receiving incoming mail and delivering outgoing mail. FreeBSD ships with Sendmail as the default MTA, but it also supports numerous other mail server daemons, including Exim, Postfix, and qmail. Sendmail configuration is described in Section 27.3, "Sendmail Configuration Files". If another MTA is installed using the Ports Collection, refer to its post-installation message for FreeBSD-specific configuration details and the application's website for more general configuration instructions.

Mail Host and Mailboxes

The mail host is a server that is responsible for delivering and receiving mail for a host or a network. The mail host collects all mail sent to the domain and stores it either in the default mbox or the alternative Maildir format, depending on the configuration. Once mail has been stored, it may either be read locally using a MUA or remotely accessed and collected using protocols such as POP or IMAP. If mail is read locally, a POP or IMAP server does not need to be installed.

To access mailboxes remotely, a POP or IMAP server is required as these protocols allow users to connect to their mailboxes from remote locations. IMAP offers several advantages over POP. These include the ability to store a copy of messages on a remote server after they are downloaded and concurrent updates. IMAP can be useful over low-speed links as it allows users to fetch the structure of messages without downloading them. It can also perform tasks such as searching on the server in order to minimize data transfer between clients and servers.

Several POP and IMAP servers are available in the Ports Collection. These include mail/qpopper, mail/imap-uw, mail/courier-imap, and mail/dovecot2.

Warning

It should be noted that both POP and IMAP transmit information, including username and password credentials, in clear-text. To secure the transmission of information across these protocols, consider tunneling sessions over ssh(1) (Section 13.8.1.2, "SSH Tunneling") or using SSL (Section 13.6, "OpenSSL").

Domain Name System (DNS)

The Domain Name System (DNS) and its daemon named play a large role in the delivery of email. In order to deliver mail from one site to another, the MTA will look up the remote site in DNS to determine which host will receive mail for the destination. This process also occurs when mail is sent from a remote host to the MTA.

In addition to mapping hostnames to IP addresses, DNS is responsible for storing information specific to mail delivery, known as Mail eXchanger MX records. The MX record specifies which hosts will receive mail for a particular domain.

To view the MX records for a domain, specify the type of record. Refer to host(1), for more details about this command:

```
% host -t mx FreeBSD.org
FreeBSD.org mail is handled by 10 mx1.FreeBSD.org
```

Refer to Section 28.7, "Domain Name System (DNS)" for more information about DNS and its configuration.

27.3. Sendmail Configuration Files

Contributed by Christopher Shumway.

Sendmail is the default MTA installed with FreeBSD. It accepts mail from MUAs and delivers it to the appropriate mail host, as defined by its configuration. Sendmail can also accept network connections and deliver mail to local mailboxes or to another program.

The configuration files for Sendmail are located in /etc/mail . This section describes these files in more detail.

/etc/mail/access

This access database file defines which hosts or IP addresses have access to the local mail server and what kind of access they have. Hosts listed as OK, which is the default option, are allowed to send mail to this host as long as the mail's final destination is the local machine. Hosts listed as REJECT are rejected for all mail connections. Hosts listed as RELAY are allowed to send mail for any destination using this mail server. Hosts listed as ERROR will have their mail returned with the specified mail error. If a host is listed as SKIP, Sendmail will abort the current search for this entry without accepting or rejecting the mail. Hosts listed as QUARANTINE will have their messages held and will receive the specified text as the reason for the hold.

Examples of using these options for both IPv4 and IPv6 addresses can be found in the FreeBSD sample configuration, /etc/mail/access.sample :

```
# $FreeBSD$
#
# Mail relay access control list.  Default is to reject mail unless the
# destination is local, or listed in /etc/mail/local-host-names
#
## Examples (commented out for safety)
#From:cyberspammer.com            ERROR:"550 We don't accept mail from spammers"
#From:okay.cyberspammer.com       OK
#Connect:sendmail.org             RELAY
#To:sendmail.org                  RELAY
#Connect:128.32                   RELAY
#Connect:128.32.2                 SKIP
#Connect:IPv6:1:2:3:4:5:6:7       RELAY
#Connect:suspicious.example.com QUARANTINE:Mail from suspicious host
#Connect:[127.0.0.3]              OK
#Connect:[IPv6:1:2:3:4:5:6:7:8] OK
```

To configure the access database, use the format shown in the sample to make entries in /etc/mail/access , but do not put a comment symbol (#) in front of the entries. Create an entry for each host or network whose access should be configured. Mail senders that match the left side of the table are affected by the action on the right side of the table.

Whenever this file is updated, update its database and restart Sendmail:

```
# makemap hash /etc/mail/access < /etc/mail/access
# service sendmail restart
```

/etc/mail/aliases

This database file contains a list of virtual mailboxes that are expanded to users, files, programs, or other aliases. Here are a few entries to illustrate the file format:

```
root: localuser
ftp-bugs: joe,eric,paul
bit.bucket:  /dev/null
procmail: "|/usr/local/bin/procmail"
```

The mailbox name on the left side of the colon is expanded to the target(s) on the right. The first entry expands the root mailbox to the localuser mailbox, which is then looked up in the /etc/mail/aliases database. If no match is found, the message is delivered to localuser. The second entry shows a mail list. Mail to ftp-bugs is expanded to the three local mailboxes joe, eric, and paul. A remote mailbox could be specified as *user@example.com*. The third entry shows how to write mail to a file, in this case /dev/null . The last entry demonstrates how to send mail to a program, /usr/local/bin/procmail , through a UNIX® pipe. Refer to aliases(5) for more information about the format of this file.

Whenever this file is updated, run `newaliases` to update and initialize the aliases database.

`/etc/mail/sendmail.cf`

This is the master configuration file for Sendmail. It controls the overall behavior of Sendmail, including everything from rewriting email addresses to printing rejection messages to remote mail servers. Accordingly, this configuration file is quite complex. Fortunately, this file rarely needs to be changed for standard mail servers.

The master Sendmail configuration file can be built from m4(1) macros that define the features and behavior of Sendmail. Refer to `/usr/src/contrib/sendmail/cf/README` for some of the details.

Whenever changes to this file are made, Sendmail needs to be restarted for the changes to take effect.

`/etc/mail/virtusertable`

This database file maps mail addresses for virtual domains and users to real mailboxes. These mailboxes can be local, remote, aliases defined in `/etc/mail/aliases` , or files. This allows multiple virtual domains to be hosted on one machine.

FreeBSD provides a sample configuration file in `/etc/mail/virtusertable.sample` to further demonstrate its format. The following example demonstrates how to create custom entries using that format:

```
root@example.com            root
postmaster@example.com      postmaster@noc.example.net
@example.com                joe
```

This file is processed in a first match order. When an email address matches the address on the left, it is mapped to the local mailbox listed on the right. The format of the first entry in this example maps a specific email address to a local mailbox, whereas the format of the second entry maps a specific email address to a remote mailbox. Finally, any email address from `example.com` which has not matched any of the previous entries will match the last mapping and be sent to the local mailbox `joe`. When creating custom entries, use this format and add them to `/etc/mail/virtusertable` . Whenever this file is edited, update its database and restart Sendmail:

```
# makemap hash /etc/mail/virtusertable < /etc/mail/virtusertable
# service sendmail restart
```

`/etc/mail/relay-domains`

In a default FreeBSD installation, Sendmail is configured to only send mail from the host it is running on. For example, if a POP server is available, users will be able to check mail from remote locations but they will not be able to send outgoing emails from outside locations. Typically, a few moments after the attempt, an email will be sent from `MAILER-DAEMON` with a 5.7 Relaying Denied message.

The most straightforward solution is to add the ISP's FQDN to `/etc/mail/relay-domains` . If multiple addresses are needed, add them one per line:

```
your.isp.example.com
other.isp.example.net
users-isp.example.org
www.example.org
```

After creating or editing this file, restart Sendmail with `service sendmail restart` .

Now any mail sent through the system by any host in this list, provided the user has an account on the system, will succeed. This allows users to send mail from the system remotely without opening the system up to relaying SPAM from the Internet.

27.4. Changing the Mail Transfer Agent

Written by Andrew Boothman.

Information taken from emails written by Gregory Neil Shapiro.

FreeBSD comes with Sendmail already installed as the MTA which is in charge of outgoing and incoming mail. However, the system administrator can change the system's MTA. A wide choice of alternative MTAs is available from the `mail` category of the FreeBSD Ports Collection.

Once a new MTA is installed, configure and test the new software before replacing Sendmail. Refer to the documentation of the new MTA for information on how to configure the software.

Once the new MTA is working, use the instructions in this section to disable Sendmail and configure FreeBSD to use the replacement MTA.

27.4.1. Disable Sendmail

 Warning

If Sendmail's outgoing mail service is disabled, it is important that it is replaced with an alternative mail delivery system. Otherwise, system functions such as periodic(8) will be unable to deliver their results by email. Many parts of the system expect a functional MTA. If applications continue to use Sendmail's binaries to try to send email after they are disabled, mail could go into an inactive Sendmail queue and never be delivered.

In order to completely disable Sendmail, add or edit the following lines in /etc/rc.conf :

```
sendmail_enable="NO"
sendmail_submit_enable="NO"
sendmail_outbound_enable="NO"
sendmail_msp_queue_enable="NO"
```

To only disable Sendmail's incoming mail service, use only this entry in /etc/rc.conf :

```
sendmail_enable="NO"
```

More information on Sendmail's startup options is available in rc.sendmail(8).

27.4.2. Replace the Default MTA

When a new MTA is installed using the Ports Collection, its startup script is also installed and startup instructions are mentioned in its package message. Before starting the new MTA, stop the running Sendmail processes. This example stops all of these services, then starts the Postfix service:

```
# service sendmail stop
# service postfix start
```

To start the replacement MTA at system boot, add its configuration line to /etc/rc.conf . This entry enables the Postfix MTA:

```
postfix_enable="YES"
```

Some extra configuration is needed as Sendmail is so ubiquitous that some software assumes it is already installed and configured. Check /etc/periodic.conf and make sure that these values are set to NO. If this file does not exist, create it with these entries:

```
daily_clean_hoststat_enable="NO"
daily_status_mail_rejects_enable="NO"
daily_status_include_submit_mailq="NO"
```

```
daily_submit_queuerun="NO"
```

Some alternative MTAs provide their own compatible implementations of the Sendmail command-line interface in order to facilitate using them as drop-in replacements for Sendmail. However, some MUAs may try to execute standard Sendmail binaries instead of the new MTA's binaries. FreeBSD uses /etc/mail/mailer.conf to map the expected Sendmail binaries to the location of the new binaries. More information about this mapping can be found in mailwrapper(8).

The default /etc/mail/mailer.conf looks like this:

```
# $FreeBSD$
#
# Execute the "real" sendmail program, named /usr/libexec/sendmail/sendmail
#
sendmail        /usr/libexec/sendmail/sendmail
send-mail       /usr/libexec/sendmail/sendmail
mailq           /usr/libexec/sendmail/sendmail
newaliases      /usr/libexec/sendmail/sendmail
hoststat        /usr/libexec/sendmail/sendmail
purgestat       /usr/libexec/sendmail/sendmail
```

When any of the commands listed on the left are run, the system actually executes the associated command shown on the right. This system makes it easy to change what binaries are executed when these default binaries are invoked.

Some MTAs, when installed using the Ports Collection, will prompt to update this file for the new binaries. For example, Postfix will update the file like this:

```
#
# Execute the Postfix sendmail program, named /usr/local/sbin/sendmail
#
sendmail        /usr/local/sbin/sendmail
send-mail       /usr/local/sbin/sendmail
mailq           /usr/local/sbin/sendmail
newaliases      /usr/local/sbin/sendmail
```

If the installation of the MTA does not automatically update /etc/mail/mailer.conf , edit this file in a text editor so that it points to the new binaries. This example points to the binaries installed by mail/ssmtp:

```
sendmail        /usr/local/sbin/ssmtp
send-mail       /usr/local/sbin/ssmtp
mailq           /usr/local/sbin/ssmtp
newaliases      /usr/local/sbin/ssmtp
hoststat        /usr/bin/true
purgestat       /usr/bin/true
```

Once everything is configured, it is recommended to reboot the system. Rebooting provides the opportunity to ensure that the system is correctly configured to start the new MTA automatically on boot.

27.5. Troubleshooting

Q: Why do I have to use the FQDN for hosts on my site?

A: The host may actually be in a different domain. For example, in order for a host in foo.bar.edu to reach a host called mumble in the bar.edu domain, refer to it by the Fully-Qualified Domain Name FQDN, mumble.bar.edu, instead of just mumble.

This is because the version of BIND which ships with FreeBSD no longer provides default abbreviations for non-FQDNs other than the local domain. An unqualified host such as mumble must either be found as mumble.foo.bar.edu, or it will be searched for in the root domain.

In older versions of BIND, the search continued across `mumble.bar.edu`, and `mumble.edu`. RFC 1535 details why this is considered bad practice or even a security hole.

As a good workaround, place the line:

```
search foo.bar.edu bar.edu
```

instead of the previous:

```
domain foo.bar.edu
```

into `/etc/resolv.conf`. However, make sure that the search order does not go beyond the "boundary between local and public administration", as RFC 1535 calls it.

Q: How can I run a mail server on a dial-up PPP host?

A: Connect to a FreeBSD mail gateway on the LAN. The PPP connection is non-dedicated.

One way to do this is to get a full-time Internet server to provide secondary MX services for the domain. In this example, the domain is `example.com` and the ISP has configured `example.net` to provide secondary MX services to the domain:

```
example.com.           MX      10      example.com.
                       MX      20      example.net.
```

Only one host should be specified as the final recipient. For Sendmail, add `Cw example.com` in `/etc/mail/sendmail.cf` on `example.com`.

When the sending MTA attempts to deliver mail, it will try to connect to the system, `example.com`, over the PPP link. This will time out if the destination is offline. The MTA will automatically deliver it to the secondary MX site at the Internet Service Provider (ISP), `example.net`. The secondary MX site will periodically try to connect to the primary MX host, `example.com`.

Use something like this as a login script:

```
#!/bin/sh
# Put me in /usr/local/bin/pppmyisp
( sleep 60 -; /usr/sbin/sendmail -q ) &
/usr/sbin/ppp -direct pppmyisp
```

When creating a separate login script for users, instead use `sendmail -qRexample.com` in the script above. This will force all mail in the queue for `example.com` to be processed immediately.

A further refinement of the situation can be seen from this example from the FreeBSD Internet service provider's mailing list:

```
> we provide the secondary MX for a customer. The customer connects to
> our services several times a day automatically to get the mails to
> his primary MX (We do not call his site when a mail for his domains
> arrived). Our sendmail sends the mailqueue every 30 minutes. At the
> moment he has to stay 30 minutes online to be sure that all mail is
> gone to the primary MX.
>
> Is there a command that would initiate sendmail to send all the mails
> now? The user has not root-privileges on our machine of course.

In the "privacy flags" section of sendmail.cf, there is a
definition Opgoaway,restrictqrun

Remove restrictqrun to allow non-root users to start the queue processing.
You might also like to rearrange the MXs. We are the 1st MX for our
customers like this, and we have defined:
```

```
# If we are the best MX for a host, try directly instead of generating
# local config error.
OwTrue
```

That way a remote site will deliver straight to you, without trying the customer connection. You then send to your customer. Only works for "hosts", so you need to get your customer to name their mail machine "customer.com" as well as "hostname.customer.com" in the DNS. Just put an A record in the DNS for "customer.com".

27.6. Advanced Topics

This section covers more involved topics such as mail configuration and setting up mail for an entire domain.

27.6.1. Basic Configuration

Out of the box, one can send email to external hosts as long as /etc/resolv.conf is configured or the network has access to a configured DNS server. To have email delivered to the MTA on the FreeBSD host, do one of the following:

- Run a DNS server for the domain.

- Get mail delivered directly to the FQDN for the machine.

In order to have mail delivered directly to a host, it must have a permanent static IP address, not a dynamic IP address. If the system is behind a firewall, it must be configured to allow SMTP traffic. To receive mail directly at a host, one of these two must be configured:

- Make sure that the lowest-numbered MX record in DNS points to the host's static IP address.

- Make sure there is no MX entry in the DNS for the host.

Either of the above will allow mail to be received directly at the host.

Try this:

```
# hostname
example.FreeBSD.org
# host example.FreeBSD.org
example.FreeBSD.org has address 204.216.27.XX
```

In this example, mail sent directly to <yourlogin@example.FreeBSD.org> should work without problems, assuming Sendmail is running correctly on example.FreeBSD.org.

For this example:

```
# host example.FreeBSD.org
example.FreeBSD.org has address 204.216.27.XX
example.FreeBSD.org mail is handled (pri=10) by nevdull.FreeBSD.org
```

All mail sent to example.FreeBSD.org will be collected on hub under the same username instead of being sent directly to your host.

The above information is handled by the DNS server. The DNS record that carries mail routing information is the MX entry. If no MX record exists, mail will be delivered directly to the host by way of its IP address.

The MX entry for freefall.FreeBSD.org at one time looked like this:

```
freefall  MX 30 mail.crl.net
freefall  MX 40 agora.rdrop.com
```

```
freefall  MX 10 freefall.FreeBSD.org
freefall  MX 20 who.cdrom.com
```

`freefall` had many MX entries. The lowest MX number is the host that receives mail directly, if available. If it is not accessible for some reason, the next lower-numbered host will accept messages temporarily, and pass it along when a lower-numbered host becomes available.

Alternate MX sites should have separate Internet connections in order to be most useful. Your ISP can provide this service.

27.6.2. Mail for a Domain

When configuring a MTA for a network, any mail sent to hosts in its domain should be diverted to the MTA so that users can receive their mail on the master mail server.

To make life easiest, a user account with the same *username* should exist on both the MTA and the system with the MUA. Use adduser(8) to create the user accounts.

The MTA must be the designated mail exchanger for each workstation on the network. This is done in theDNS configuration with an MX record:

```
example.FreeBSD.org A 204.216.27.XX  ; Workstation
   MX 10 nevdull.FreeBSD.org ; Mailhost
```

This will redirect mail for the workstation to the MTA no matter where the A record points. The mail is sent to the MX host.

This must be configured on a DNS server. If the network does not run its own DNS server, talk to the ISP or DNS provider.

The following is an example of virtual email hosting. Consider a customer with the domain `customer1.org`, where all the mail for `customer1.org` should be sent to `mail.myhost.com`. The DNS entry should look like this:

```
customer1.org  MX 10 mail.myhost.com
```

An A> record is *not* needed for `customer1.org` in order to only handle email for that domain. However, running ping against `customer1.org` will not work unless an A record exists for it.

Tell the MTA which domains and/or hostnames it should accept mail for. Either of the following will work for Sendmail:

- Add the hosts to `/etc/mail/local-host-names` when using the FEATURE(use_cw_file).

- Add a `Cwyour.host.com` line to `/etc/sendmail.cf`.

27.7. Setting Up to Send Only

Contributed by Bill Moran.

There are many instances where one may only want to send mail through a relay. Some examples are:

- The computer is a desktop machine that needs to use programs such as send-pr(1), using the ISP's mail relay.

- The computer is a server that does not handle mail locally, but needs to pass off all mail to a relay for processing.

While any MTA is capable of filling this particular niche, it can be difficult to properly configure a full-featured MTA just to handle offloading mail. Programs such as Sendmail and Postfix are overkill for this use.

Additionally, a typical Internet access service agreement may forbid one from running a "mail server".

The easiest way to fulfill those needs is to install the mail/ssmtp port:

```
# cd /usr/ports/mail/ssmtp
# make install replace clean
```

Once installed, mail/ssmtp can be configured with /usr/local/etc/ssmtp/ssmtp.conf :

```
root=yourrealemail@example.com
mailhub=mail.example.com
rewriteDomain=example.com
hostname=_HOSTNAME_
```

Use the real email address for root. Enter the ISP's outgoing mail relay in place of mail.example.com. Some ISPs call this the "outgoing mail server" or "SMTP server".

Make sure to disable Sendmail, including the outgoing mail service. See Section 27.4.1, "Disable Sendmail" for details.

mail/ssmtp has some other options available. Refer to the examples in /usr/local/etc/ssmtp or the manual page of ssmtp for more information.

Setting up ssmtp in this manner allows any software on the computer that needs to send mail to function properly, while not violating the ISP's usage policy or allowing the computer to be hijacked for spamming.

27.8. Using Mail with a Dialup Connection

When using a static IP address, one should not need to adjust the default configuration. Set the hostname to the assigned Internet name and Sendmail will do the rest.

When using a dynamically assigned IP address and a dialup PPP connection to the Internet, one usually has a mailbox on the ISP's mail server. In this example, the ISP's domain is example.net, the user name is user, the hostname is bsd.home, and the ISP has allowed relay.example.net as a mail relay.

In order to retrieve mail from the ISP's mailbox, install a retrieval agent from the Ports Collection. mail/fetchmail is a good choice as it supports many different protocols. Usually, the ISP will provide POP. When using user PPP, email can be automatically fetched when an Internet connection is established with the following entry in /etc/ppp/ppp.linkup:

```
MYADDR:
!bg su user -c fetchmail
```

When using Sendmail to deliver mail to non-local accounts, configure Sendmail to process the mail queue as soon as the Internet connection is established. To do this, add this line after the above fetchmail entry in /etc/ppp/ppp.linkup:

```
 !bg su user -c "sendmail -q"
```

In this example, there is an account for user on bsd.home. In the home directory of user on bsd.home, create a .fetchmailrc which contains this line:

```
poll example.net protocol pop3 fetchall pass MySecret
```

This file should not be readable by anyone except user as it contains the password MySecret.

In order to send mail with the correct from: header, configure Sendmail to use <user@example.net> rather than <user@bsd.home> and to send all mail via relay.example.net, allowing quicker mail transmission.

The following .mc should suffice:

```
VERSIONID(`bsd.home.mc version 1.0')
OSTYPE(bsd4.4)dnl
FEATURE(nouucp)dnl
```

```
MAILER(local)dnl
MAILER(smtp)dnl
Cwlocalhost
Cwbsd.home
MASQUERADE_AS(`example.net')dnl
FEATURE(allmasquerade)dnl
FEATURE(masquerade_envelope)dnl
FEATURE(nocanonify)dnl
FEATURE(nodns)dnl
define(`SMART_HOST', `relay.example.net')
Dmbsd.home
define(`confDOMAIN_NAME',`bsd.home')dnl
define(`confDELIVERY_MODE',`deferred')dnl
```

Refer to the previous section for details of how to convert this file into the sendmail.cf format. Do not forget to restart Sendmail after updating sendmail.cf.

27.9. SMTP Authentication

Written by James Gorham.

Configuring SMTP authentication on the MTA provides a number of benefits. SMTP authentication adds a layer of security to Sendmail, and provides mobile users who switch hosts the ability to use the same MTA without the need to reconfigure their mail client's settings each time.

1. Install security/cyrus-sasl2 from the Ports Collection. This port supports a number of compile-time options. For the SMTP authentication method demonstrated in this example, make sure that LOGIN is not disabled.

2. After installing security/cyrus-sasl2, edit /usr/local/lib/sasl2/Sendmail.conf , or create it if it does not exist, and add the following line:

    ```
    pwcheck_method: saslauthd
    ```

3. Next, install security/cyrus-sasl2-saslauthd and add the following line to /etc/rc.conf :

    ```
    saslauthd_enable="YES"
    ```

    Finally, start the saslauthd daemon:

    ```
    # service saslauthd start
    ```

    This daemon serves as a broker for Sendmail to authenticate against the FreeBSD passwd(5) database. This saves the trouble of creating a new set of usernames and passwords for each user that needs to use SMTP authentication, and keeps the login and mail password the same.

4. Next, edit /etc/make.conf and add the following lines:

    ```
    SENDMAIL_CFLAGS=-I/usr/local/include/sasl -DSASL
    SENDMAIL_LDFLAGS=-L/usr/local/lib
    SENDMAIL_LDADD=-lsasl2
    ```

    These lines provide Sendmail the proper configuration options for linking to cyrus-sasl2 at compile time. Make sure that cyrus-sasl2 has been installed before recompiling Sendmail.

5. Recompile Sendmail by executing the following commands:

    ```
    # cd /usr/src/lib/libsmutil
    # make cleandir && make obj && make
    # cd /usr/src/lib/libsm
    # make cleandir && make obj && make
    # cd /usr/src/usr.sbin/sendmail
    # make cleandir && make obj && make && make install
    ```

This compile should not have any problems if /usr/src has not changed extensively and the shared libraries it needs are available.

6. After Sendmail has been compiled and reinstalled, edit /etc/mail/freebsd.mc or the local .mc. Many administrators choose to use the output from hostname(1) as the name of .mc for uniqueness. Add these lines:

```
dnl set SASL options
TRUST_AUTH_MECH(`GSSAPI DIGEST-MD5 CRAM-MD5 LOGIN')dnl
define(`confAUTH_MECHANISMS', `GSSAPI DIGEST-MD5 CRAM-MD5 LOGIN')dnl
```

These options configure the different methods available to Sendmail for authenticating users. To use a method other than pwcheck, refer to the Sendmail documentation.

7. Finally, run make(1) while in /etc/mail . That will run the new .mc and create a .cf named either freebsd.cf or the name used for the local .mc. Then, run make install restart , which will copy the file to sendmail.cf, and properly restart Sendmail. For more information about this process, refer to /etc/mail/Makefile .

To test the configuration, use a MUA to send a test message. For further investigation, set the LogLevel of Sendmail to 13 and watch /var/log/maillog for any errors.

For more information, refer to SMTP authentication.

27.10. Mail User Agents

Contributed by Marc Silver.

A MUA is an application that is used to send and receive email. As email "evolves" and becomes more complex, MUAs are becoming increasingly powerful and provide users increased functionality and flexibility. The mail category of the FreeBSD Ports Collection contains numerous MUAs. These include graphical email clients such as Evolution or Balsa and console based clients such as mutt or alpine.

27.10.1. mail

mail(1) is the default MUA installed with FreeBSD. It is a console based MUA that offers the basic functionality required to send and receive text-based email. It provides limited attachment support and can only access local mailboxes.

Although mail does not natively support interaction with POP or IMAP servers, these mailboxes may be downloaded to a local mbox using an application such as fetchmail.

In order to send and receive email, run mail:

```
% mail
```

The contents of the user's mailbox in /var/mail are automatically read by mail. Should the mailbox be empty, the utility exits with a message indicating that no mail could be found. If mail exists, the application interface starts, and a list of messages will be displayed. Messages are automatically numbered, as can be seen in the following example:

```
Mail version 8.1 6/6/93.  Type ? for help.
"/var/mail/marcs": 3 messages 3 new
>N  1 root@localhost        Mon Mar  8 14:05  14/510   "test"
 N  2 root@localhost        Mon Mar  8 14:05  14/509   "user account"
 N  3 root@localhost        Mon Mar  8 14:05  14/509   "sample"
```

Messages can now be read by typing t followed by the message number. This example reads the first email:

```
& t 1
Message 1:
```

```
From root@localhost  Mon Mar  8 14:05:52 2004
X-Original-To: marcs@localhost
Delivered-To: marcs@localhost
To: marcs@localhost
Subject: test
Date: Mon,  8 Mar 2004 14:05:52 +0200 (SAST)
From: root@localhost (Charlie Root)

This is a test message, please reply if you receive it.
```

As seen in this example, the message will be displayed with full headers. To display the list of messages again, press h.

If the email requires a reply, press either R or r mail keys. R instructs mail to reply only to the sender of the email, while r replies to all other recipients of the message. These commands can be suffixed with the mail number of the message to reply to. After typing the response, the end of the message should be marked by a single . on its own line. An example can be seen below:

```
& R 1
To: root@localhost
Subject: Re: test

Thank you, I did get your email.
.
EOT
```

In order to send a new email, press m, followed by the recipient email address. Multiple recipients may be specified by separating each address with the , delimiter. The subject of the message may then be entered, followed by the message contents. The end of the message should be specified by putting a single . on its own line.

```
& mail root@localhost
Subject: I mastered mail

Now I can send and receive email using mail ... :)
.
EOT
```

While using mail, press ? to display help at any time. Refer to mail(1) for more help on how to use mail.

Note

mail(1) was not designed to handle attachments and thus deals with them poorly. Newer MUAs handle attachments in a more intelligent way. Users who prefer to use mail may find the converters/mpack port to be of considerable use.

27.10.2. mutt

mutt is a powerful MUA, with many features, including:

- The ability to thread messages.

- PGP support for digital signing and encryption of email.

- MIME support.

- Maildir support.

- Highly customizable.

Refer to http://www.mutt.org for more information on mutt.

mutt may be installed using the mail/mutt port. After the port has been installed, mutt can be started by issuing the following command:

```
% mutt
```

mutt will automatically read and display the contents of the user mailbox in /var/mail . If no mails are found, mutt will wait for commands from the user. The example below shows mutt displaying a list of messages:

To read an email, select it using the cursor keys and press Enter. An example of mutt displaying email can be seen below:

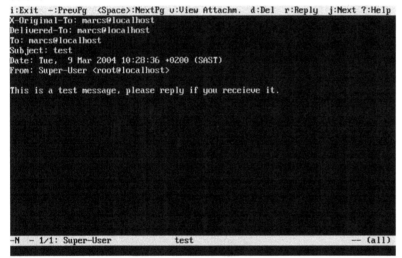

Similar to mail(1), mutt can be used to reply only to the sender of the message as well as to all recipients. To reply only to the sender of the email, press r. To send a group reply to the original sender as well as all the message recipients, press g.

> ## Note
>
> By default, mutt uses the vi(1) editor for creating and replying to emails. Each user can customize this by creating or editing the .muttrc in their home directory and setting the editor variable or by setting the EDITOR environment variable. Refer to http://www.mutt.org/ for more information about configuring mutt.

To compose a new mail message, press m. After a valid subject has been given, mutt will start vi(1) so the email can be written. Once the contents of the email are complete, save and quit from vi. mutt will resume, displaying a summary screen of the mail that is to be delivered. In order to send the mail, press y. An example of the summary screen can be seen below:

```
y:Send  q:Abort  t:To  c:CC  s:Subj  a:Attach file  d:Descrip  ?:Help
      From: Marc Silver <marcs@localhost>
        To: Super-User <root@localhost>
        Cc:
       Bcc:
   Subject: Re: test
  Reply-To:
       Fcc:
  Security: Clear


-- Attachments
- I      1 /tmp/mutt-bsd-c0hobscQ                   [text/plain, 7bit, us-ascii, 1.1K]










-- Mutt: Compose  [Approx. msg size: 1.1K    Atts: 1]-----------------------------
```

mutt contains extensive help which can be accessed from most of the menus by pressing ?. The top line also displays the keyboard shortcuts where appropriate.

27.10.3. alpine

alpine is aimed at a beginner user, but also includes some advanced features.

 Warning

alpine has had several remote vulnerabilities discovered in the past, which allowed remote attackers to execute arbitrary code as users on the local system, by the action of sending a specially-prepared email. While *known* problems have been fixed, alpine code is written in an insecure style and the FreeBSD Security Officer believes there are likely to be other undiscovered vulnerabilities. Users install alpine at their own risk.

The current version of alpine may be installed using the mail/alpine port. Once the port has installed, alpine can be started by issuing the following command:

```
% alpine
```

The first time alpine runs, it displays a greeting page with a brief introduction, as well as a request from the alpine development team to send an anonymous email message allowing them to judge how many users are using their client. To send this anonymous message, press Enter. Alternatively, press E to exit the greeting without sending an anonymous message. An example of the greeting page is shown below:

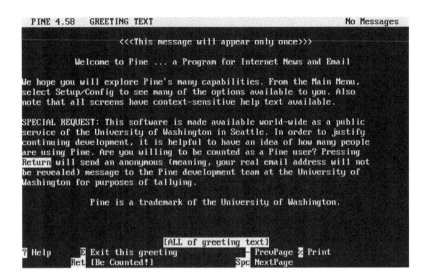

The main menu is then presented, which can be navigated using the cursor keys. This main menu provides short-cuts for the composing new mails, browsing mail directories, and administering address book entries. Below the main menu, relevant keyboard shortcuts to perform functions specific to the task at hand are shown.

The default directory opened by alpine is inbox. To view the message index, press I, or select the MESSAGE INDEX option shown below:

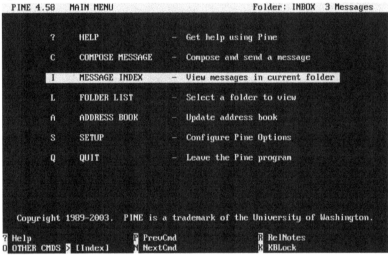

The message index shows messages in the current directory and can be navigated by using the cursor keys. High-lighted messages can be read by pressing Enter.

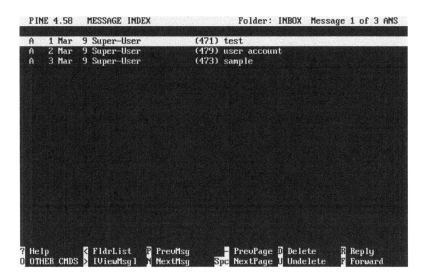

In the screenshot below, a sample message is displayed by alpine. Contextual keyboard shortcuts are displayed at the bottom of the screen. An example of one of a shortcut is r, which tells the MUA to reply to the current message being displayed.

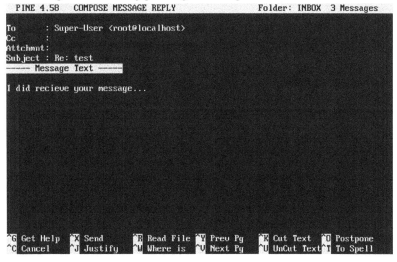

Replying to an email in alpine is done using the pico editor, which is installed by default with alpine. pico makes it easy to navigate the message and is easier for novice users to use than vi(1) or mail(1). Once the reply is complete, the message can be sent by pressing Ctrl+X. alpine will ask for confirmation before sending the message.

```
   PINE 4.58   COMPOSE MESSAGE REPLY            Folder: INBOX  3 Messages

To      : Super-User <root@localhost>
Cc      :
Attchmnt:
Subject : Re: test
------ Message Text ------

I did recieve your message...




^G Get Help  ^X Send      ^R Read File ^Y Prev Pg  ^K Cut Text  ^O Postpone
^C Cancel    ^J Justify   ^W Where is  ^V Next Pg  ^U UnCut Text^T To Spell
```

alpine can be customized using the SETUP option from the main menu. Consult http://www.washington.edu/alpine/ for more information.

27.11. Using fetchmail

Contributed by Marc Silver.

fetchmail is a full-featured IMAP and POP client. It allows users to automatically download mail from remote IMAP and POP servers and save it into local mailboxes where it can be accessed more easily. fetchmail can be installed using the mail/fetchmail port, and offers various features, including:

* Support for the POP3, APOP, KPOP, IMAP, ETRN and ODMR protocols.

* Ability to forward mail using SMTP, which allows filtering, forwarding, and aliasing to function normally.

* May be run in daemon mode to check periodically for new messages.

* Can retrieve multiple mailboxes and forward them, based on configuration, to different local users.

This section explains some of the basic features of fetchmail. This utility requires a .fetchmailrc configuration in the user's home directory in order to run correctly. This file includes server information as well as login credentials. Due to the sensitive nature of the contents of this file, it is advisable to make it readable only by the user, with the following command:

```
% chmod 600 .fetchmailrc
```

The following .fetchmailrc serves as an example for downloading a single user mailbox using POP. It tells fetchmail to connect to example.com using a username of joesoap and a password of XXX. This example assumes that the user joesoap exists on the local system.

```
poll example.com protocol pop3 username "joesoap" password "XXX"
```

The next example connects to multiple POP and IMAP servers and redirects to different local usernames where applicable:

```
poll example.com proto pop3:
user "joesoap", with password "XXX", is "jsoap" here;
user "andrea", with password "XXXX";
poll example2.net proto imap:
user "john", with password "XXXXX", is "myth" here;
```

fetchmail can be run in daemon mode by running it with -d, followed by the interval (in seconds) that fetchmail should poll servers listed in .fetchmailrc. The following example configures fetchmail to poll every 600 seconds:

```
% fetchmail -d 600
```

More information on fetchmail can be found at http://www.fetchmail.info/ .

27.12. Using procmail

Contributed by Marc Silver.

procmail is a powerful application used to filter incoming mail. It allows users to define "rules" which can be matched to incoming mails to perform specific functions or to reroute mail to alternative mailboxes or email addresses. procmail can be installed using the mail/procmail port. Once installed, it can be directly integrated into most MTAs. Consult the MTA documentation for more information. Alternatively, procmail can be integrated by adding the following line to a .forward in the home directory of the user:

```
"|exec /usr/local/bin/procmail || exit 75"
```

The following section displays some basic procmail rules, as well as brief descriptions of what they do. Rules must be inserted into a `.procmailrc`, which must reside in the user's home directory.

The majority of these rules can be found in procmailex(5).

To forward all mail from <user@example.com> to an external address of <goodmail@example2.com>:

```
:0
* ^From.*user@example.com
! goodmail@example2.com
```

To forward all mails shorter than 1000 bytes to an external address of <goodmail@example2.com>:

```
:0
* < 1000
! goodmail@example2.com
```

To send all mail sent to <alternate@example.com> to a mailbox called `alternate`:

```
:0
* ^TOalternate@example.com
alternate
```

To send all mail with a subject of "Spam" to `/dev/null`:

```
:0
^Subject:.*Spam
/dev/null
```

A useful recipe that parses incoming `FreeBSD.org` mailing lists and places each list in its own mailbox:

```
:0
* ^Sender:.owner-freebsd-\/[^@]+@FreeBSD.ORG
{
 LISTNAME=${MATCH}
 :0
 * LISTNAME??^\/[^@]+
 FreeBSD-${MATCH}
}
```

Chapter 28. Network Servers

28.1. Synopsis

This chapter covers some of the more frequently used network services on UNIX® systems. This includes installing, configuring, testing, and maintaining many different types of network services. Example configuration files are included throughout this chapter for reference.

By the end of this chapter, readers will know:

- How to manage the inetd daemon.

- How to set up the Network File System (NFS).

- How to set up the Network Information Server (NIS) for centralizing and sharing user accounts.

- How to set FreeBSD up to act as an LDAP server or client

- How to set up automatic network settings using DHCP.

- How to set up a Domain Name Server (DNS).

- How to set up the Apache HTTP Server.

- How to set up a File Transfer Protocol (FTP) server.

- How to set up a file and print server for Windows® clients using Samba.

- How to synchronize the time and date, and set up a time server using the Network Time Protocol (NTP).

- How to set up iSCSI.

This chapter assumes a basic knowledge of:

- /etc/rc scripts.

- Network terminology.

- Installation of additional third-party software (Chapter 4, *Installing Applications: Packages and Ports*).

28.2. The inetd Super-Server

The inetd(8) daemon is sometimes referred to as a Super-Server because it manages connections for many services. Instead of starting multiple applications, only the inetd service needs to be started. When a connection is received for a service that is managed by inetd, it determines which program the connection is destined for, spawns a process for that program, and delegates the program a socket. Using inetd for services that are not heavily used can reduce system load, when compared to running each daemon individually in stand-alone mode.

Primarily, inetd is used to spawn other daemons, but several trivial protocols are handled internally, such as chargen, auth, time, echo, discard, and daytime.

This section covers the basics of configuring inetd.

28.2.1. Configuration File

Configuration of inetd is done by editing /etc/inetd.conf. Each line of this configuration file represents an application which can be started by inetd. By default, every line starts with a comment (#), meaning that inetd is not listening for any applications. To configure inetd to listen for an application's connections, remove the # at the beginning of the line for that application.

After saving your edits, configure inetd to start at system boot by editing /etc/rc.conf :

```
inetd_enable="YES"
```

To start inetd now, so that it listens for the service you configured, type:

```
# service inetd start
```

Once inetd is started, it needs to be notified whenever a modification is made to /etc/inetd.conf :

Example 28.1. Reloading the inetd Configuration File

```
# service inetd reload
```

Typically, the default entry for an application does not need to be edited beyond removing the #. In some situations, it may be appropriate to edit the default entry.

As an example, this is the default entry for ftpd(8) over IPv4:

```
ftp     stream  tcp     ° nowait  root    /usr/libexec/ftpd       ftpd -l
```

The seven columns in an entry are as follows:

```
service-name
socket-type
protocol
{wait|nowait}[/max-child[/max-connections-per-ip-per-minute[/max-child-per-ip]]]
user[:group][/login-class]
server-program
server-program-arguments
```

where:

service-name

> The service name of the daemon to start. It must correspond to a service listed in /etc/services . This determines which port inetd listens on for incoming connections to that service. When using a custom service, it must first be added to /etc/services .

socket-type

> Either stream, dgram, raw, or seqpacket. Use stream for TCP connections and dgram for UDP services.

protocol

> Use one of the following protocol names:

Protocol Name	Explanation
tcp or tcp4	TCP IPv4
udp or udp4	UDP IPv4
tcp6	TCP IPv6
udp6	UDP IPv6
tcp46	Both TCP IPv4 and IPv6
udp46	Both UDP IPv4 and IPv6

{wait|nowait}[/max-child[/max-connections-per-ip-per-minute[/max-child-per-ip]]]

In this field, `wait` or `nowait` must be specified. `max-child` , `max-connections-per-ip-per-minute` and `max-child-per-ip` are optional.

`wait|nowait` indicates whether or not the service is able to handle its own socket. `dgram` socket types must use `wait` while `stream` daemons, which are usually multi-threaded, should use `nowait`. `wait` usually hands off multiple sockets to a single daemon, while `nowait` spawns a child daemon for each new socket.

The maximum number of child daemons inetd may spawn is set by `max-child` . For example, to limit ten instances of the daemon, place a `/10` after `nowait`. Specifying `/0` allows an unlimited number of children.

`max-connections-per-ip-per-minute` limits the number of connections from any particular IP address per minute. Once the limit is reached, further connections from this IP address will be dropped until the end of the minute. For example, a value of `/10` would limit any particular IP address to ten connection attempts per minute. `max-child-per-ip` limits the number of child processes that can be started on behalf on any single IP address at any moment. These options can limit excessive resource consumption and help to prevent Denial of Service attacks.

An example can be seen in the default settings for fingerd(8):

```
finger stream  tcp     nowait/3/10 nobody /usr/libexec/fingerd fingerd -k -s
```

user

The username the daemon will run as. Daemons typically run as `root`, `daemon`, or `nobody`.

server-program

The full path to the daemon. If the daemon is a service provided by inetd internally, use `internal`.

server-program-arguments

Used to specify any command arguments to be passed to the daemon on invocation. If the daemon is an internal service, use `internal`.

28.2.2. Command-Line Options

Like most server daemons, inetd has a number of options that can be used to modify its behavior. By default, inetd is started with `-wW  -C  60`. These options enable TCP wrappers for all services, including internal services, and prevent any IP address from requesting any service more than 60 times per minute.

To change the default options which are passed to inetd, add an entry for `inetd_flags` in `/etc/rc.conf` . If inetd is already running, restart it with `service inetd restart` .

The available rate limiting options are:

-c maximum

Specify the default maximum number of simultaneous invocations of each service, where the default is unlimited. May be overridden on a per-service basis by using `max-child` in `/etc/inetd.conf` .

-C rate

Specify the default maximum number of times a service can be invoked from a single IP address per minute. May be overridden on a per-service basis by using `max-connections-per-ip-per-minute` in `/etc/inetd.conf`.

-R rate

Specify the maximum number of times a service can be invoked in one minute, where the default is 256. A rate of `0` allows an unlimited number.

-s maximum

Specify the maximum number of times a service can be invoked from a single IP address at any one time, where the default is unlimited. May be overridden on a per-service basis by using `max-child-per-ip` in `/etc/inetd.conf`.

Additional options are available. Refer to inetd(8) for the full list of options.

28.2.3. Security Considerations

Many of the daemons which can be managed by inetd are not security-conscious. Some daemons, such as fingerd, can provide information that may be useful to an attacker. Only enable the services which are needed and monitor the system for excessive connection attempts. `max-connections-per-ip-per-minute` , `max-child` and `max-child-per-ip` can be used to limit such attacks.

By default, TCP wrappers is enabled. Consult hosts_access(5) for more information on placing TCP restrictions on various inetd invoked daemons.

28.3. Network File System (NFS)

Reorganized and enhanced by Tom Rhodes.
Written by Bill Swingle.

FreeBSD supports the Network File System (NFS), which allows a server to share directories and files with clients over a network. With NFS, users and programs can access files on remote systems as if they were stored locally.

NFS has many practical uses. Some of the more common uses include:

- Data that would otherwise be duplicated on each client can be kept in a single location and accessed by clients on the network.

- Several clients may need access to the `/usr/ports/distfiles` directory. Sharing that directory allows for quick access to the source files without having to download them to each client.

- On large networks, it is often more convenient to configure a central NFS server on which all user home directories are stored. Users can log into a client anywhere on the network and have access to their home directories.

- Administration of NFS exports is simplified. For example, there is only one file system where security or backup policies must be set.

- Removable media storage devices can be used by other machines on the network. This reduces the number of devices throughout the network and provides a centralized location to manage their security. It is often more convenient to install software on multiple machines from a centralized installation media.

NFS consists of a server and one or more clients. The client remotely accesses the data that is stored on the server machine. In order for this to function properly, a few processes have to be configured and running.

These daemons must be running on the server:

Daemon	Description
nfsd	The NFS daemon which services requests from NFS clients.
mountd	The NFS mount daemon which carries out requests received from nfsd.
rpcbind	This daemon allows NFS clients to discover which port the NFS server is using.

Running nfsiod(8) on the client can improve performance, but is not required.

28.3.1. Configuring the Server

The file systems which the NFS server will share are specified in `/etc/exports` . Each line in this file specifies a file system to be exported, which clients have access to that file system, and any access options. When adding entries to this file, each exported file system, its properties, and allowed hosts must occur on a single line. If no clients are listed in the entry, then any client on the network can mount that file system.

The following /etc/exports entries demonstrate how to export file systems. The examples can be modified to match the file systems and client names on the reader's network. There are many options that can be used in this file, but only a few will be mentioned here. See exports(5) for the full list of options.

This example shows how to export /cdrom to three hosts named *alpha*, *bravo*, and *charlie*:

```
/cdrom -ro alpha bravo charlie
```

The -ro flag makes the file system read-only, preventing clients from making any changes to the exported file system. This example assumes that the host names are either in DNS or in /etc/hosts . Refer to hosts(5) if the network does not have a DNS server.

The next example exports /home to three clients by IP address. This can be useful for networks without DNS or /etc/hosts entries. The -alldirs flag allows subdirectories to be mount points. In other words, it will not automatically mount the subdirectories, but will permit the client to mount the directories that are required as needed.

```
/usr/home   -alldirs  10.0.0.2 10.0.0.3 10.0.0.4
```

This next example exports /a so that two clients from different domains may access that file system. The -maproot=root allows root on the remote system to write data on the exported file system as root. If -maproot=root is not specified, the client's root user will be mapped to the server's nobody account and will be subject to the access limitations defined for nobody.

```
/a  -maproot=root  host.example.com box.example.org
```

A client can only be specified once per file system. For example, if /usr is a single file system, these entries would be invalid as both entries specify the same host:

```
# Invalid when /usr is one file system
/usr/src   client
/usr/ports client
```

The correct format for this situation is to use one entry:

```
/usr/src /usr/ports   client
```

The following is an example of a valid export list, where /usr and /exports are local file systems:

```
# Export src and ports to client01 and client02, but only
# client01 has root privileges on it
/usr/src /usr/ports -maproot=root    client01
/usr/src /usr/ports               client02
# The client machines have root and can mount anywhere
# on /exports. Anyone in the world can mount /exports/obj read-only
/exports -alldirs -maproot=root      client01 client02
/exports/obj -ro
```

To enable the processes required by the NFS server at boot time, add these options to /etc/rc.conf :

```
rpcbind_enable="YES"
nfs_server_enable="YES"
mountd_flags="-r"
```

The server can be started now by running this command:

```
# service nfsd start
```

Whenever the NFS server is started, mountd also starts automatically. However, mountd only reads /etc/exports when it is started. To make subsequent /etc/exports edits take effect immediately, force mountd to reread it:

```
# service mountd reload
```

28.3.2. Configuring the Client

To enable NFS clients, set this option in each client's /etc/rc.conf :

```
nfs_client_enable="YES"
```

Then, run this command on each NFS client:

```
# service nfsclient start
```

The client now has everything it needs to mount a remote file system. In these examples, the server's name is server and the client's name is client. To mount /home on server to the /mnt mount point on client :

```
# mount server:/home /mnt
```

The files and directories in /home will now be available on client, in the /mnt directory.

To mount a remote file system each time the client boots, add it to /etc/fstab :

```
server:/home /mnt nfs rw 0 0
```

Refer to fstab(5) for a description of all available options.

28.3.3. Locking

Some applications require file locking to operate correctly. To enable locking, add these lines to /etc/rc.conf on both the client and server:

```
rpc_lockd_enable="YES"
rpc_statd_enable="YES"
```

Then start the applications:

```
# service lockd start
# service statd start
```

If locking is not required on the server, the NFS client can be configured to lock locally by including -L when running mount. Refer to mount_nfs(8) for further details.

28.3.4. Automating Mounts with amd(8)

Contributed by Wylie Stilwell.
Rewritten by Chern Lee.

The automatic mounter daemon, amd, automatically mounts a remote file system whenever a file or directory within that file system is accessed. File systems that are inactive for a period of time will be automatically unmounted by amd.

This daemon provides an alternative to modifying /etc/fstab to list every client. It operates by attaching itself as an NFS server to the /host and /net directories. When a file is accessed within one of these directories, amd looks up the corresponding remote mount and automatically mounts it. /net is used to mount an exported file system from an IP address while /host is used to mount an export from a remote hostname. For instance, an attempt to access a file within /host/foobar/usr would tell amd to mount the /usr export on the host foobar.

Example 28.2. Mounting an Export with amd

In this example, showmount -e shows the exported file systems that can be mounted from the NFS server, foobar:

```
% showmount -e foobar
Exports list on foobar:
```

```
/usr                                10.10.10.0
/a                                  10.10.10.0
% cd /host/foobar/usr
```

The output from showmount shows /usr as an export. When changing directories to /host/foobar/usr , amd intercepts the request and attempts to resolve the hostname foobar. If successful, amd automatically mounts the desired export.

To enable amd at boot time, add this line to /etc/rc.conf :

```
amd_enable="YES"
```

To start amd now:

```
# service amd start
```

Custom flags can be passed to amd from the amd_flags environment variable. By default, amd_flags is set to:

```
amd_flags="-a /.amd_mnt -l syslog /host /etc/amd.map /net /etc/amd.map"
```

The default options with which exports are mounted are defined in /etc/amd.map . Some of the more advanced features of amd are defined in /etc/amd.conf .

Consult amd(8) and amd.conf(5) for more information.

28.3.5. Automating Mounts with autofs(5)

> **Note**
>
> The autofs(5) automount facility is supported starting with FreeBSD 10.1-RELEASE. To use the automounter functionality in older versions of FreeBSD, use amd(8) instead. This chapter only describes the autofs(5) automounter.

The autofs(5) facility is a common name for several components that, together, allow for automatic mounting of remote and local filesystems whenever a file or directory within that file system is accessed. It consists of the kernel component, autofs(5), and several userspace applications: automount(8), automountd(8) and autounmountd(8). It serves as an alternative for amd(8) from previous FreeBSD releases. Amd is still provided for backward compatibility purposes, as the two use different map format; the one used by autofs is the same as with other SVR4 automounters, such as the ones in Solaris, MacOS X, and Linux.

The autofs(5) virtual filesystem is mounted on specified mountpoints by automount(8), usually invoked during boot.

Whenever a process attempts to access file within the autofs(5) mountpoint, the kernel will notify automountd(8) daemon and pause the triggering process. The automountd(8) daemon will handle kernel requests by finding the proper map and mounting the filesystem according to it, then signal the kernel to release blocked process. The autounmountd(8) daemon automatically unmounts automounted filesystems after some time, unless they are still being used.

The primary autofs configuration file is /etc/auto_master . It assigns individual maps to top-level mounts. For an explanation of auto_master and the map syntax, refer to auto_master(5).

There is a special automounter map mounted on /net. When a file is accessed within this directory, autofs(5) looks up the corresponding remote mount and automatically mounts it. For instance, an attempt to access a file within /net/foobar/usr would tell automountd(8) to mount the /usr export from the host foobar.

Example 28.3. Mounting an Export with autofs(5)

In this example, showmount -e shows the exported file systems that can be mounted from the NFS server, foobar:

```
% showmount -e foobar
Exports list on foobar:
/usr                          10.10.10.0
/a                            10.10.10.0
% cd /net/foobar/usr
```

The output from showmount shows /usr as an export. When changing directories to /host/foobar/usr, automountd(8) intercepts the request and attempts to resolve the hostname foobar. If successful, automountd(8) automatically mounts the source export.

To enable autofs(5) at boot time, add this line to /etc/rc.conf :

```
autofs_enable="YES"
```

Then autofs(5) can be started by running:

```
# service automount start
# service automountd start
# service autounmountd start
```

The autofs(5) map format is the same as in other operating systems. Information about this format from other sources can be useful, like the Mac OS X document.

Consult the automount(8), automountd(8), autounmountd(8), and auto_master(5) manual pages for more information.

28.4. Network Information System (NIS)

Network Information System (NIS) is designed to centralize administration of UNIX®-like systems such as Solaris™, HP-UX, AIX®, Linux, NetBSD, OpenBSD, and FreeBSD. NIS was originally known as Yellow Pages but the name was changed due to trademark issues. This is the reason why NIS commands begin with yp.

NIS is a Remote Procedure Call (RPC)-based client/server system that allows a group of machines within an NIS domain to share a common set of configuration files. This permits a system administrator to set up NIS client systems with only minimal configuration data and to add, remove, or modify configuration data from a single location.

FreeBSD uses version 2 of the NIS protocol.

28.4.1. NIS Terms and Processes

Table 28.1 summarizes the terms and important processes used by NIS:

Table 28.1. NIS Terminology

Term	Description
NIS domain name	NIS servers and clients share an NIS domain name. Typically, this name does not have anything to do with DNS.

Term	Description
rpcbind(8)	This service enables RPC and must be running in order to run an NIS server or act as an NIS client.
ypbind(8)	This service binds an NIS client to its NIS server. It will take the NIS domain name and use RPC to connect to the server. It is the core of client/server communication in an NIS environment. If this service is not running on a client machine, it will not be able to access the NIS server.
ypserv(8)	This is the process for the NIS server. If this service stops running, the server will no longer be able to respond to NIS requests so hopefully, there is a slave server to take over. Some non-FreeBSD clients will not try to reconnect using a slave server and the ypbind process may need to be restarted on these clients.
rpc.yppasswdd(8)	This process only runs on NIS master servers. This daemon allows NIS clients to change their NIS passwords. If this daemon is not running, users will have to login to the NIS master server and change their passwords there.

28.4.2. Machine Types

There are three types of hosts in an NIS environment:

• NIS master server

This server acts as a central repository for host configuration information and maintains the authoritative copy of the files used by all of the NIS clients. The passwd, group, and other various files used by NIS clients are stored on the master server. While it is possible for one machine to be an NIS master server for more than one NIS domain, this type of configuration will not be covered in this chapter as it assumes a relatively small-scale NIS environment.

• NIS slave servers

NIS slave servers maintain copies of the NIS master's data files in order to provide redundancy. Slave servers also help to balance the load of the master server as NIS clients always attach to the NIS server which responds first.

• NIS clients

NIS clients authenticate against the NIS server during log on.

Information in many files can be shared using NIS. The master.passwd, group, and hosts files are commonly shared via NIS. Whenever a process on a client needs information that would normally be found in these files locally, it makes a query to the NIS server that it is bound to instead.

28.4.3. Planning Considerations

This section describes a sample NIS environment which consists of 15 FreeBSD machines with no centralized point of administration. Each machine has its own /etc/passwd and /etc/master.passwd. These files are kept in sync with each other only through manual intervention. Currently, when a user is added to the lab, the process must be repeated on all 15 machines.

The configuration of the lab will be as follows:

Machine name	IP address	Machine role
ellington	10.0.0.2	NIS master
coltrane	10.0.0.3	NIS slave
basie	10.0.0.4	Faculty workstation

Machine name	IP address	Machine role
bird	10.0.0.5	Client machine
cli[1-11]	10.0.0.[6-17]	Other client machines

If this is the first time an NIS scheme is being developed, it should be thoroughly planned ahead of time. Regardless of network size, several decisions need to be made as part of the planning process.

28.4.3.1. Choosing a NIS Domain Name

When a client broadcasts its requests for info, it includes the name of the NIS domain that it is part of. This is how multiple servers on one network can tell which server should answer which request. Think of the NIS domain name as the name for a group of hosts.

Some organizations choose to use their Internet domain name for their NIS domain name. This is not recommended as it can cause confusion when trying to debug network problems. The NIS domain name should be unique within the network and it is helpful if it describes the group of machines it represents. For example, the Art department at Acme Inc. might be in the "acme-art" NIS domain. This example will use the domain name test-domain.

However, some non-FreeBSD operating systems require the NIS domain name to be the same as the Internet domain name. If one or more machines on the network have this restriction, the Internet domain name *must* be used as the NIS domain name.

28.4.3.2. Physical Server Requirements

There are several things to keep in mind when choosing a machine to use as a NIS server. Since NIS clients depend upon the availability of the server, choose a machine that is not rebooted frequently. The NIS server should ideally be a stand alone machine whose sole purpose is to be an NIS server. If the network is not heavily used, it is acceptable to put the NIS server on a machine running other services. However, if the NIS server becomes unavailable, it will adversely affect all NIS clients.

28.4.4. Configuring the NIS Master Server

The canonical copies of all NIS files are stored on the master server. The databases used to store the information are called NIS maps. In FreeBSD, these maps are stored in /var/yp/[domainname] where [domainname] is the name of the NIS domain. Since multiple domains are supported, it is possible to have several directories, one for each domain. Each domain will have its own independent set of maps.

NIS master and slave servers handle all NIS requests through ypserv(8). This daemon is responsible for receiving incoming requests from NIS clients, translating the requested domain and map name to a path to the corresponding database file, and transmitting data from the database back to the client.

Setting up a master NIS server can be relatively straight forward, depending on environmental needs. Since FreeBSD provides built-in NIS support, it only needs to be enabled by adding the following lines to /etc/rc.conf :

```
nisdomainname="test-domain" ❶
nis_server_enable="YES"  ❷
nis_yppasswdd_enable="YES" ❸
```

❶   This line sets the NIS domain name to test-domain.
❷   This automates the start up of the NIS server processes when the system boots.
❸   This enables the rpc.yppasswdd(8) daemon so that users can change their NIS password from a client machine.

Care must be taken in a multi-server domain where the server machines are also NIS clients. It is generally a good idea to force the servers to bind to themselves rather than allowing them to broadcast bind requests and possibly become bound to each other. Strange failure modes can result if one server goes down and others are dependent upon it. Eventually, all the clients will time out and attempt to bind to other servers, but the delay involved can be considerable and the failure mode is still present since the servers might bind to each other all over again.

A server that is also a client can be forced to bind to a particular server by adding these additional lines to /etc/rc.conf:

```
nis_client_enable="YES" # run client stuff as well
nis_client_flags="-S NIS domain,server"
```

After saving the edits, type /etc/netstart to restart the network and apply the values defined in /etc/rc.conf. Before initializing the NIS maps, start ypserv(8):

```
# service ypserv start
```

28.4.4.1. Initializing the NIS Maps

NIS maps are generated from the configuration files in /etc on the NIS master, with one exception: /etc/master.passwd. This is to prevent the propagation of passwords to all the servers in the NIS domain. Therefore, before the NIS maps are initialized, configure the primary password files:

```
# cp /etc/master.passwd /var/yp/master.passwd
# cd /var/yp
# vi master.passwd
```

It is advisable to remove all entries for system accounts as well as any user accounts that do not need to be propagated to the NIS clients, such as the root and any other administrative accounts.

Note

Ensure that the /var/yp/master.passwd is neither group or world readable by setting its permissions to 600.

After completing this task, initialize the NIS maps. FreeBSD includes the ypinit(8) script to do this. When generating maps for the master server, include -m and specify the NIS domain name:

```
ellington# ypinit -m test-domain
Server Type: MASTER Domain: test-domain
Creating an YP server will require that you answer a few questions.
Questions will all be asked at the beginning of the procedure.
Do you want this procedure to quit on non-fatal errors? [y/n: n] n
Ok, please remember to go back and redo manually whatever fails.
If not, something might not work.
At this point, we have to construct a list of this domains YP servers.
rod.darktech.org is already known as master server.
Please continue to add any slave servers, one per line. When you are
done with the list, type a <control D>.
master server   :  ellington
next host to add:  coltrane
next host to add:  ^D
The current list of NIS servers looks like this:
ellington
coltrane
Is this correct?  [y/n: y] y

[..output from map generation..-]

NIS Map update completed.
ellington has been setup as an YP master server without any errors.
```

This will create /var/yp/Makefile from /var/yp/Makefile.dist. By default, this file assumes that the environment has a single NIS server with only FreeBSD clients. Since test-domain has a slave server, edit this line in /var/yp/Makefile so that it begins with a comment (#):

```
NOPUSH = "True"
```

28.4.4.2. Adding New Users

Every time a new user is created, the user account must be added to the master NIS server and the NIS maps rebuilt. Until this occurs, the new user will not be able to login anywhere except on the NIS master. For example, to add the new user jsmith to the test-domain domain, run these commands on the master server:

```
# pw useradd jsmith
# cd /var/yp
# make test-domain
```

The user could also be added using adduser jsmith instead of pw useradd smith.

28.4.5. Setting up a NIS Slave Server

To set up an NIS slave server, log on to the slave server and edit /etc/rc.conf as for the master server. Do not generate any NIS maps, as these already exist on the master server. When running ypinit on the slave server, use -s (for slave) instead of -m (for master). This option requires the name of the NIS master in addition to the domain name, as seen in this example:

```
coltrane# ypinit -s ellington test-domain

Server Type: SLAVE Domain: test-domain Master: ellington

Creating an YP server will require that you answer a few questions.
Questions will all be asked at the beginning of the procedure.

Do you want this procedure to quit on non-fatal errors? [y/n: n]  n

Ok, please remember to go back and redo manually whatever fails.
If not, something might not work.
There will be no further questions. The remainder of the procedure
should take a few minutes, to copy the databases from ellington.
Transferring netgroup...
ypxfr: Exiting: Map successfully transferred
Transferring netgroup.byuser...
ypxfr: Exiting: Map successfully transferred
Transferring netgroup.byhost...
ypxfr: Exiting: Map successfully transferred
Transferring master.passwd.byuid...
ypxfr: Exiting: Map successfully transferred
Transferring passwd.byuid...
ypxfr: Exiting: Map successfully transferred
Transferring passwd.byname...
ypxfr: Exiting: Map successfully transferred
Transferring group.bygid...
ypxfr: Exiting: Map successfully transferred
Transferring group.byname...
ypxfr: Exiting: Map successfully transferred
Transferring services.byname...
ypxfr: Exiting: Map successfully transferred
Transferring rpc.bynumber...
ypxfr: Exiting: Map successfully transferred
Transferring rpc.byname...
ypxfr: Exiting: Map successfully transferred
Transferring protocols.byname...
ypxfr: Exiting: Map successfully transferred
Transferring master.passwd.byname...
ypxfr: Exiting: Map successfully transferred
Transferring networks.byname...
ypxfr: Exiting: Map successfully transferred
Transferring networks.byaddr...
ypxfr: Exiting: Map successfully transferred
Transferring netid.byname...
ypxfr: Exiting: Map successfully transferred
```

```
Transferring hosts.byaddr...
ypxfr: Exiting: Map successfully transferred
Transferring protocols.bynumber...
ypxfr: Exiting: Map successfully transferred
Transferring ypservers...
ypxfr: Exiting: Map successfully transferred
Transferring hosts.byname...
ypxfr: Exiting: Map successfully transferred

coltrane has been setup as an YP slave server without any errors.
Remember to update map ypservers on ellington.
```

This will generate a directory on the slave server called `/var/yp/test-domain` which contains copies of the NIS master server's maps. Adding these `/etc/crontab` entries on each slave server will force the slaves to sync their maps with the maps on the master server:

```
20      *       *       *       *       root    /usr/libexec/ypxfr passwd.byname
21      *       *       *       *       root    /usr/libexec/ypxfr passwd.byuid
```

These entries are not mandatory because the master server automatically attempts to push any map changes to its slaves. However, since clients may depend upon the slave server to provide correct password information, it is recommended to force frequent password map updates. This is especially important on busy networks where map updates might not always complete.

To finish the configuration, run `/etc/netstart` on the slave server in order to start the NIS services.

28.4.6. Setting Up an NIS Client

An NIS client binds to an NIS server using ypbind(8). This daemon broadcasts RPC requests on the local network. These requests specify the domain name configured on the client. If an NIS server in the same domain receives one of the broadcasts, it will respond to ypbind, which will record the server's address. If there are several servers available, the client will use the address of the first server to respond and will direct all of its NIS requests to that server. The client will automatically ping the server on a regular basis to make sure it is still available. If it fails to receive a reply within a reasonable amount of time, ypbind will mark the domain as unbound and begin broadcasting again in the hopes of locating another server.

To configure a FreeBSD machine to be an NIS client:

1. Edit `/etc/rc.conf` and add the following lines in order to set the NIS domain name and start ypbind(8) during network startup:

    ```
    nisdomainname="test-domain"
    nis_client_enable="YES"
    ```

2. To import all possible password entries from the NIS server, use `vipw` to remove all user accounts except one from `/etc/master.passwd`. When removing the accounts, keep in mind that at least one local account should remain and this account should be a member of `wheel`. If there is a problem with NIS, this local account can be used to log in remotely, become the superuser, and fix the problem. Before saving the edits, add the following line to the end of the file:

    ```
    +:::::::::
    ```

    This line configures the client to provide anyone with a valid account in the NIS server's password maps an account on the client. There are many ways to configure the NIS client by modifying this line. One method is described in Section 28.4.8, "Using Netgroups". For more detailed reading, refer to the book `Managing NFS and NIS`, published by O'Reilly Media.

3. To import all possible group entries from the NIS server, add this line to `/etc/group`:

    ```
    +:*::
    ```

To start the NIS client immediately, execute the following commands as the superuser:

```
# /etc/netstart
# service ypbind start
```

After completing these steps, running `ypcat passwd` on the client should show the server's `passwd` map.

28.4.7. NIS Security

Since RPC is a broadcast-based service, any system running ypbind within the same domain can retrieve the contents of the NIS maps. To prevent unauthorized transactions, ypserv(8) supports a feature called "securenets" which can be used to restrict access to a given set of hosts. By default, this information is stored in /var/yp/securenets, unless ypserv(8) is started with -p and an alternate path. This file contains entries that consist of a network specification and a network mask separated by white space. Lines starting with # are considered to be comments. A sample securenets might look like this:

```
# allow connections from local host -- mandatory
127.0.0.1      255.255.255.255
# allow connections from any host
# on the 192.168.128.0 network
192.168.128.0 255.255.255.0
# allow connections from any host
# between 10.0.0.0 to 10.0.15.255
# this includes the machines in the testlab
10.0.0.0       255.255.240.0
```

If ypserv(8) receives a request from an address that matches one of these rules, it will process the request normally. If the address fails to match a rule, the request will be ignored and a warning message will be logged. If the securenets does not exist, ypserv will allow connections from any host.

Section 13.4, "TCP Wrapper" is an alternate mechanism for providing access control instead of securenets. While either access control mechanism adds some security, they are both vulnerable to "IP spoofing" attacks. All NIS-related traffic should be blocked at the firewall.

Servers using securenets may fail to serve legitimate NIS clients with archaic TCP/IP implementations. Some of these implementations set all host bits to zero when doing broadcasts or fail to observe the subnet mask when calculating the broadcast address. While some of these problems can be fixed by changing the client configuration, other problems may force the retirement of these client systems or the abandonment of securenets.

The use of TCP Wrapper increases the latency of the NIS server. The additional delay may be long enough to cause timeouts in client programs, especially in busy networks with slow NIS servers. If one or more clients suffer from latency, convert those clients into NIS slave servers and force them to bind to themselves.

28.4.7.1. Barring Some Users

In this example, the basie system is a faculty workstation within the NIS domain. The passwd map on the master NIS server contains accounts for both faculty and students. This section demonstrates how to allow faculty logins on this system while refusing student logins.

To prevent specified users from logging on to a system, even if they are present in the NIS database, use vipw to add -*username* with the correct number of colons towards the end of /etc/master.passwd on the client, where *username* is the username of a user to bar from logging in. The line with the blocked user must be before the + line that allows NIS users. In this example, bill is barred from logging on to basie:

```
basie# cat /etc/master.passwd
root:[password]:0:0::0:0:The super-user:/root:/bin/csh
toor:[password]:0:0::0:0:The other super-user:/root:/bin/sh
daemon:*:1:1::0:0:Owner of many system processes:/root:/sbin/nologin
operator:*:2:5::0:0:System &:/:/sbin/nologin
bin:*:3:7::0:0:Binaries Commands and Source,,,:/:/sbin/nologin
tty:*:4:65533::0:0:Tty Sandbox:/:/sbin/nologin
kmem:*:5:65533::0:0:KMem Sandbox:/:/sbin/nologin
games:*:7:13::0:0:Games pseudo-user:/usr/games:/sbin/nologin
news:*:8:8::0:0:News Subsystem:/:/sbin/nologin
```

```
man:*:9:9::0:0:Mister Man Pages:/usr/share/man:/sbin/nologin
bind:*:53:53::0:0:Bind Sandbox:/:/sbin/nologin
uucp:*:66:66::0:0:UUCP pseudo-user:/var/spool/uucppublic:/usr/libexec/uucp/uucico
xten:*:67:67::0:0:X-10 daemon:/usr/local/xten:/sbin/nologin
pop:*:68:6::0:0:Post Office Owner:/nonexistent:/sbin/nologin
nobody:*:65534:65534::0:0:Unprivileged user:/nonexistent:/sbin/nologin
-bill:::::::::
+:::::::::

basie#
```

28.4.8. Using Netgroups

Barring specified users from logging on to individual systems becomes unscaleable on larger networks and quickly loses the main benefit of NIS: *centralized* administration.

Netgroups were developed to handle large, complex networks with hundreds of users and machines. Their use is comparable to UNIX® groups, where the main difference is the lack of a numeric ID and the ability to define a netgroup by including both user accounts and other netgroups.

To expand on the example used in this chapter, the NIS domain will be extended to add the users and systems shown in Tables 28.2 and 28.3:

Table 28.2. Additional Users

User Name(s)	Description
alpha, beta	IT department employees
charlie, delta	IT department apprentices
echo, foxtrott, golf, ...	employees
able, baker, ...	interns

Table 28.3. Additional Systems

Machine Name(s)	Description
war, death, famine, pollution	Only IT employees are allowed to log onto these servers.
pride, greed, envy, wrath, lust, sloth	All members of the IT department are allowed to login onto these servers.
one, two, three, four, ...	Ordinary workstations used by employees.
trashcan	A very old machine without any critical data. Even interns are allowed to use this system.

When using netgroups to configure this scenario, each user is assigned to one or more netgroups and logins are then allowed or forbidden for all members of the netgroup. When adding a new machine, login restrictions must be defined for all netgroups. When a new user is added, the account must be added to one or more netgroups. If the NIS setup is planned carefully, only one central configuration file needs modification to grant or deny access to machines.

The first step is the initialization of the NIS netgroup map. In FreeBSD, this map is not created by default. On the NIS master server, use an editor to create a map named /var/yp/netgroup .

This example creates four netgroups to represent IT employees, IT apprentices, employees, and interns:

```
IT_EMP  (,alpha,test-domain)     (,beta,test-domain)
IT_APP  (,charlie,test-domain)   (,delta,test-domain)
USERS   (,echo,test-domain)      (,foxtrott,test-domain) \
        (,golf,test-domain)
INTERNS (,able,test-domain)      (,baker,test-domain)
```

Each entry configures a netgroup. The first column in an entry is the name of the netgroup. Each set of brackets represents either a group of one or more users or the name of another netgroup. When specifying a user, the three comma-delimited fields inside each group represent:

1. The name of the host(s) where the other fields representing the user are valid. If a hostname is not specified, the entry is valid on all hosts.

2. The name of the account that belongs to this netgroup.

3. The NIS domain for the account. Accounts may be imported from other NIS domains into a netgroup.

If a group contains multiple users, separate each user with whitespace. Additionally, each field may contain wildcards. See netgroup(5) for details.

Netgroup names longer than 8 characters should not be used. The names are case sensitive and using capital letters for netgroup names is an easy way to distinguish between user, machine and netgroup names.

Some non-FreeBSD NIS clients cannot handle netgroups containing more than 15 entries. This limit may be circumvented by creating several sub-netgroups with 15 users or fewer and a real netgroup consisting of the sub-netgroups, as seen in this example:

```
BIGGRP1   (,joe1,domain)   (,joe2,domain)   (,joe3,domain) [...-]
BIGGRP2   (,joe16,domain)  (,joe17,domain) [...-]
BIGGRP3   (,joe31,domain)  (,joe32,domain)
BIGGROUP  BIGGRP1 BIGGRP2 BIGGRP3
```

Repeat this process if more than 225 (15 times 15) users exist within a single netgroup.

To activate and distribute the new NIS map:

```
ellington# cd /var/yp
ellington# make
```

This will generate the three NIS maps netgroup, netgroup.byhost and netgroup.byuser. Use the map key option of ypcat(1) to check if the new NIS maps are available:

```
ellington% ypcat -k netgroup
ellington% ypcat -k netgroup.byhost
ellington% ypcat -k netgroup.byuser
```

The output of the first command should resemble the contents of /var/yp/netgroup . The second command only produces output if host-specific netgroups were created. The third command is used to get the list of netgroups for a user.

To configure a client, use vipw(8) to specify the name of the netgroup. For example, on the server named war, replace this line:

```
+::::::::::
```

with

```
+@IT_EMP:::::::::
```

This specifies that only the users defined in the netgroup IT_EMP will be imported into this system's password database and only those users are allowed to login to this system.

This configuration also applies to the ~ function of the shell and all routines which convert between user names and numerical user IDs. In other words, cd ~user will not work, ls -l will show the numerical ID instead of the username, and find . -user joe -print will fail with the message No such user. To fix this, import all user entries without allowing them to login into the servers. This can be achieved by adding an extra line:

```
+:::::::::/sbin/nologin
```

This line configures the client to import all entries but to replace the shell in those entries with /sbin/nologin .

Make sure that extra line is placed *after* +@IT_EMP:::::::::. Otherwise, all user accounts imported from NIS will have /sbin/nologin as their login shell and no one will be able to login to the system.

To configure the less important servers, replace the old +::::::::: on the servers with these lines:

```
+@IT_EMP:::::::::
+@IT_APP:::::::::
+:::::::::/sbin/nologin
```

The corresponding lines for the workstations would be:

```
+@IT_EMP:::::::::
+@USERS:::::::::
+:::::::::/sbin/nologin
```

NIS supports the creation of netgroups from other netgroups which can be useful if the policy regarding user access changes. One possibility is the creation of role-based netgroups. For example, one might create a netgroup called BIGSRV to define the login restrictions for the important servers, another netgroup called SMALLSRV for the less important servers, and a third netgroup called USERBOX for the workstations. Each of these netgroups contains the netgroups that are allowed to login onto these machines. The new entries for the NIS netgroup map would look like this:

```
BIGSRV     IT_EMP   IT_APP
SMALLSRV   IT_EMP   IT_APP   ITINTERN
USERBOX    IT_EMP   ITINTERN USERS
```

This method of defining login restrictions works reasonably well when it is possible to define groups of machines with identical restrictions. Unfortunately, this is the exception and not the rule. Most of the time, the ability to define login restrictions on a per-machine basis is required.

Machine-specific netgroup definitions are another possibility to deal with the policy changes. In this scenario, the /etc/master.passwd of each system contains two lines starting with "+". The first line adds a netgroup with the accounts allowed to login onto this machine and the second line adds all other accounts with /sbin/nologin as shell. It is recommended to use the "ALL-CAPS" version of the hostname as the name of the netgroup:

```
+@BOXNAME:::::::::
+:::::::::/sbin/nologin
```

Once this task is completed on all the machines, there is no longer a need to modify the local versions of /etc/ master.passwd ever again. All further changes can be handled by modifying the NIS map. Here is an example of a possible netgroup map for this scenario:

```
# Define groups of users first
IT_EMP     (,alpha,test-domain)    (,beta,test-domain)
IT_APP     (,charlie,test-domain)  (,delta,test-domain)
DEPT1      (,echo,test-domain)     (,foxtrott,test-domain)
DEPT2      (,golf,test-domain)     (,hotel,test-domain)
DEPT3      (,india,test-domain)    (,juliet,test-domain)
ITINTERN   (,kilo,test-domain)     (,lima,test-domain)
D_INTERNS  (,able,test-domain)     (,baker,test-domain)
#
# Now, define some groups based on roles
USERS      DEPT1    DEPT2      DEPT3
BIGSRV     IT_EMP   IT_APP
SMALLSRV   IT_EMP   IT_APP     ITINTERN
USERBOX    IT_EMP   ITINTERN   USERS
#
# And a groups for a special tasks
# Allow echo and golf to access our anti-virus-machine
SECURITY   IT_EMP   (,echo,test-domain)   (,golf,test-domain)
#
```

```
# machine-based netgroups
# Our main servers
WAR        BIGSRV
FAMINE     BIGSRV
# User india needs access to this server
POLLUTION  BIGSRV  (,india,test-domain)
#
# This one is really important and needs more access restrictions
DEATH      IT_EMP
#
# The anti-virus-machine mentioned above
ONE        SECURITY
#
# Restrict a machine to a single user
TWO        (,hotel,test-domain)
# [...more groups to follow]
```

It may not always be advisable to use machine-based netgroups. When deploying a couple of dozen or hundreds of systems, role-based netgroups instead of machine-based netgroups may be used to keep the size of the NIS map within reasonable limits.

28.4.9. Password Formats

NIS requires that all hosts within an NIS domain use the same format for encrypting passwords. If users have trouble authenticating on an NIS client, it may be due to a differing password format. In a heterogeneous network, the format must be supported by all operating systems, where DES is the lowest common standard.

To check which format a server or client is using, look at this section of /etc/login.conf:

```
default:\
  :passwd_format=des:\
  :copyright=/etc/COPYRIGHT:\
  [Further entries elided]
```

In this example, the system is using the DES format. Other possible values are blf for Blowfish and md5 for MD5 encrypted passwords.

If the format on a host needs to be edited to match the one being used in the NIS domain, the login capability database must be rebuilt after saving the change:

```
# cap_mkdb /etc/login.conf
```

> **Note**
>
> The format of passwords for existing user accounts will not be updated until each user changes their password *after* the login capability database is rebuilt.

28.5. Lightweight Directory Access Protocol (LDAP)

Written by Tom Rhodes.

The Lightweight Directory Access Protocol (LDAP) is an application layer protocol used to access, modify, and authenticate objects using a distributed directory information service. Think of it as a phone or record book which stores several levels of hierarchical, homogeneous information. It is used in Active Directory and OpenLDAP networks and allows users to access to several levels of internal information utilizing a single account. For example, email authentication, pulling employee contact information, and internal website authentication might all make use of a single user account in the LDAP server's record base.

This section provides a quick start guide for configuring an LDAP server on a FreeBSD system. It assumes that the administrator already has a design plan which includes the type of information to store, what that information will be used for, which users should have access to that information, and how to secure this information from unauthorized access.

28.5.1. LDAP Terminology and Structure

LDAP uses several terms which should be understood before starting the configuration. All directory entries consist of a group of *attributes*. Each of these attribute sets contains a unique identifier known as a *Distinguished Name* (DN) which is normally built from several other attributes such as the common or *Relative Distinguished Name* (RDN). Similar to how directories have absolute and relative paths, consider a DN as an absolute path and the RDN as the relative path.

An example LDAP entry looks like the following. This example searches for the entry for the specified user account (uid), organizational unit (ou), and organization (o):

```
% ldapsearch -xb "uid= trhodes ,ou=users ,o=example.com "
# extended LDIF
#
# LDAPv3
# base <uid=trhodes,ou=users,o=example.com> with scope subtree
# filter: (objectclass=*)
# requesting: ALL
#

# trhodes, users, example.com
dn: uid=trhodes,ou=users,o=example.com
mail: trhodes@example.com
cn: Tom Rhodes
uid: trhodes
telephoneNumber: (123) 456-7890

# search result
search: 2
result: 0 Success

# numResponses: 2
# numEntries: 1
```

This example entry shows the values for the dn, mail, cn, uid, and telephoneNumber attributes. The cn attribute is the RDN.

More information about LDAP and its terminology can be found at http://www.openldap.org/doc/admin24/intro.html.

28.5.2. Configuring an LDAP Server

FreeBSD does not provide a built-in LDAP server. Begin the configuration by installing the net/openldap24-server package or port. Since the port has many configurable options, it is recommended that the default options are reviewed to see if the package is sufficient, and to instead compile the port if any options should be changed. In most cases, the defaults are fine. However, if SQL support is needed, this option must be enabled and the port compiled using the instructions in Section 4.5, "Using the Ports Collection".

Next, create the directories to hold the data and to store the certificates:

```
# mkdir /var/db/openldap-data
# mkdir /usr/local/etc/openldap/private
```

Copy over the database configuration file:

```
# cp /usr/local/etc/openldap/DB_CONFIG.example /var/db/openldap-data/DB_CONFIG
```

The next phase is to configure the certificate authority. The following commands must be executed from /usr/local/etc/openldap/private . This is important as the file permissions need to be restrictive and users should not have access to these files. To create the certificate authority, start with this command and follow the prompts:

```
# openssl req -days  365 -nodes -new -x509 -keyout ca.key -out ../ca.crt
```

The entries for the prompts may be generic *except* for the Common Name. This entry must be *different* than the system hostname. If this will be a self signed certificate, prefix the hostname with CA for certificate authority.

The next task is to create a certificate signing request and a private key. Input this command and follow the prompts:

```
# openssl req -days  365 -nodes -new -keyout server.key -out server.csr
```

During the certificate generation process, be sure to correctly set the Common Name attribute. Once complete, sign the key:

```
# openssl x509 -req -days  365 -in server.csr -out ../server.crt -CA ../ca.crt -CAkey ca.key
  -CAcreateserial
```

The final part of the certificate generation process is to generate and sign the client certificates:

```
# openssl req -days  365 -nodes -new -keyout client.key -out client.csr
# openssl x509 -req -days 3650 -in client.csr -out ../client.crt -CA ../ca.crt -CAkey ca.ɔ
key
```

Remember to use the same Common Name attribute when prompted. When finished, ensure that a total of eight (8) new files have been generated through the proceeding commands. If so, the next step is to edit /usr/local/etc/openldap/slapd.conf and add the following options:

```
TLSCipherSuite HIGH:MEDIUM:+SSLv3
TLSCertificateFile /usr/local/etc/openldap/server.crt
TLSCertificateKeyFile /usr/local/etc/openldap/private/server.key
TLSCACertificateFile /usr/local/etc/openldap/ca.crt
```

Then, edit /usr/local/etc/openldap/ldap.conf   and add the following lines:

```
TLS_CACERT /usr/local/etc/openldap/ca.crt
TLS_CIPHER_SUITE HIGH:MEDIUM:+SSLv3
```

While editing this file, uncomment the following entries and set them to the desired values: BASE, URI, SIZELIMIT and TIMELIMIT . Set the URI to contain ldap:// and ldaps:// . Then, add two entries pointing to the certificate authority. When finished, the entries should look similar to the following:

```
BASE    dc=example,dc=com
URI     ldap:// ldaps://

SIZELIMIT       12
TIMELIMIT       15

TLS_CACERT /usr/local/etc/openldap/ca.crt
TLS_CIPHER_SUITE HIGH:MEDIUM:+SSLv3
```

The default password for the server should then be changed:

```
# slappasswd -h "{SHA}" >> /usr/local/etc/openldap/slapd.conf
```

This command will prompt for the password and, if the process does not fail, a password hash will be added to the end of slapd.conf . Several hashing formats are supported. Refer to the manual page for slappasswd for more information.

Next, edit /usr/local/etc/openldap/slapd.conf   and add the following lines:

```
password-hash {sha}
allow bind_v2
```

The `suffix` in this file must be updated to match the `BASE` used in `/usr/local/etc/openldap/ldap.conf` and `rootdn` should also be set. A recommended value for `rootdn` is something like `cn=Manager`. Before saving this file, place the `rootpw` in front of the password output from `slappasswd` and delete the old `rootpw`. The end result should look similar to this:

```
TLSCipherSuite HIGH:MEDIUM:+SSLv3
TLSCertificateFile /usr/local/etc/openldap/server.crt
TLSCertificateKeyFile /usr/local/etc/openldap/private/server.key
TLSCACertificateFile /usr/local/etc/openldap/ca.crt
rootpw   {SHA}W6ph5Mm5Pz8GgiULbPgzG37mj9g=
```

Finally, enable the OpenLDAP service in `/etc/rc.conf` and set the URI:

```
slapd_enable="YES"
slapd_flags="-4 -h ldaps:///"
```

At this point the server can be started and tested:

```
# service slapd start
```

If everything is configured correctly, a search of the directory should show a successful connection with a single response as in this example:

```
# ldapsearch -Z
# extended LDIF
#
# LDAPv3
# base <dc=example,dc=com> (default) with scope subtree
# filter: (objectclass=*)
# requesting: ALL
#

# search result
search: 3
result: 32 No such object

# numResponses: 1
```

Note

If the command fails and the configuration looks correct, stop the `slapd` service and restart it with debugging options:

```
# service slapd stop
# /usr/local/libexec/slapd -d -1
```

Once the service is responding, the directory can be populated using `ldapadd`. In this example, a file containing this list of users is first created. Each user should use the following format:

```
dn: dc=example,dc=com
objectclass: dcObject
objectclass: organization
o: Example
dc: Example

dn: cn=Manager,dc=example,dc=com
objectclass: organizationalRole
cn: Manager
```

To import this file, specify the file name. The following command will prompt for the password specified earlier and the output should look something like this:

```
# ldapadd -Z -D "cn= Manager ,dc=example ,dc=com" -W -f import.ldif
Enter LDAP Password:
adding new entry "dc=example,dc=com"

adding new entry "cn=Manager,dc=example,dc=com"
```

Verify the data was added by issuing a search on the server using `ldapsearch` :

```
% ldapsearch -Z
# extended LDIF
#
# LDAPv3
# base <dc=example,dc=com> (default) with scope subtree
# filter: (objectclass=*)
# requesting: ALL
#

# example.com
dn: dc=example,dc=com
objectClass: dcObject
objectClass: organization
o: Example
dc: Example

# Manager, example.com
dn: cn=Manager,dc=example,dc=com
objectClass: organizationalRole
cn: Manager

# search result
search: 3
result: 0 Success

# numResponses: 3
# numEntries: 2
```

At this point, the server should be configured and functioning properly.

28.6. Dynamic Host Configuration Protocol (DHCP)

The Dynamic Host Configuration Protocol (DHCP) allows a system to connect to a network in order to be assigned the necessary addressing information for communication on that network. FreeBSD includes the OpenBSD version of `dhclient` which is used by the client to obtain the addressing information. FreeBSD does not install a DHCP server, but several servers are available in the FreeBSD Ports Collection. The DHCP protocol is fully described in RFC 2131. Informational resources are also available at isc.org/downloads/dhcp/.

This section describes how to use the built-in DHCP client. It then describes how to install and configure a DHCP server.

Note

In FreeBSD, the bpf(4) device is needed by both the DHCP server and DHCP client. This device is included in the GENERIC kernel that is installed with FreeBSD. Users who prefer to create a custom kernel need to keep this device if DHCP is used.

It should be noted that bpf also allows privileged users to run network packet sniffers on that system.

28.6.1. Configuring a DHCP Client

DHCP client support is included in the FreeBSD installer, making it easy to configure a newly installed system to automatically receive its networking addressing information from an existing DHCP server. Refer to Section 2.8, "Post-Installation" for examples of network configuration.

When dhclient is executed on the client machine, it begins broadcasting requests for configuration information. By default, these requests use UDP port 68. The server replies on UDP port 67, giving the client an IP address and other relevant network information such as a subnet mask, default gateway, and DNS server addresses. This information is in the form of a DHCP "lease" and is valid for a configurable time. This allows stale IP addresses for clients no longer connected to the network to automatically be reused. DHCP clients can obtain a great deal of information from the server. An exhaustive list may be found in dhcp-options(5).

By default, when a FreeBSD system boots, its DHCP client runs in the background, or *asynchronously*. Other startup scripts continue to run while the DHCP process completes, which speeds up system startup.

Background DHCP works well when the DHCP server responds quickly to the client's requests. However, DHCP may take a long time to complete on some systems. If network services attempt to run before DHCP has assigned the network addressing information, they will fail. Using DHCP in *synchronous* mode prevents this problem as it pauses startup until the DHCP configuration has completed.

This line in /etc/rc.conf is used to configure background or asynchronous mode:

```
ifconfig_fxp0="DHCP"
```

This line may already exist if the system was configured to use DHCP during installation. Replace the *fxp0* shown in these examples with the name of the interface to be dynamically configured, as described in Section 11.5, "Setting Up Network Interface Cards".

To instead configure the system to use synchronous mode, and to pause during startup while DHCP completes, use "SYNCDHCP":

```
ifconfig_fxp0="SYNCDHCP"
```

Additional client options are available. Search for dhclient in rc.conf(5) for details.

The DHCP client uses the following files:

* /etc/dhclient.conf

  The configuration file used by dhclient. Typically, this file contains only comments as the defaults are suitable for most clients. This configuration file is described in dhclient.conf(5).

* /sbin/dhclient

  More information about the command itself can be found in dhclient(8).

* /sbin/dhclient-script

  The FreeBSD-specific DHCP client configuration script. It is described in dhclient-script(8), but should not need any user modification to function properly.

* /var/db/dhclient.leases.*interface*

  The DHCP client keeps a database of valid leases in this file, which is written as a log and is described in dhclient.leases(5).

28.6.2. Installing and Configuring a DHCP Server

This section demonstrates how to configure a FreeBSD system to act as a DHCP server using the Internet Systems Consortium (ISC) implementation of the DHCP server. This implementation and its documentation can be installed using the net/isc-dhcp43-server package or port.

The installation of net/isc-dhcp43-server installs a sample configuration file. Copy /usr/local/etc/dhcpd.con-f.example to /usr/local/etc/dhcpd.conf and make any edits to this new file.

The configuration file is comprised of declarations for subnets and hosts which define the information that is provided to DHCP clients. For example, these lines configure the following:

```
option domain-name "example.org";❶
option domain-name-servers ns1.example.org;❷
option subnet-mask 255.255.255.0;❸

default-lease-time 600;❹
max-lease-time 72400;❺
ddns-update-style none;❻

subnet 10.254.239.0 netmask 255.255.255.224 {
  range 10.254.239.10 10.254.239.20;❼
  option routers rtr-239-0-1.example.org, rtr-239-0-2.example.org;❽
}

host fantasia {
  hardware ethernet 08:00:07:26:c0:a5;❾
  fixed-address fantasia.fugue.com;❿
}
```

❶   This option specifies the default search domain that will be provided to clients. Refer to resolv.conf(5) for more information.

❷   This option specifies a comma separated list of DNS servers that the client should use. They can be listed by their Fully Qualified Domain Names (FQDN), as seen in the example, or by their IP addresses.

❸   The subnet mask that will be provided to clients.

❹   The default lease expiry time in seconds. A client can be configured to override this value.

❺   The maximum allowed length of time, in seconds, for a lease. Should a client request a longer lease, a lease will still be issued, but it will only be valid for max-lease-time .

❻   The default of none disables dynamic DNS updates. Changing this to interim configures the DHCP server to update a DNS server whenever it hands out a lease so that the DNS server knows which IP addresses are associated with which computers in the network. Do not change the default setting unless the DNS server has been configured to support dynamic DNS.

❼   This line creates a pool of available IP addresses which are reserved for allocation to DHCP clients. The range of addresses must be valid for the network or subnet specified in the previous line.

❽   Declares the default gateway that is valid for the network or subnet specified before the opening { bracket.

❾   Specifies the hardware MAC address of a client so that the DHCP server can recognize the client when it makes a request.

❿   Specifies that this host should always be given the same IP address. Using the hostname is correct, since the DHCP server will resolve the hostname before returning the lease information.

This configuration file supports many more options. Refer to dhcpd.conf(5), installed with the server, for details and examples.

Once the configuration of dhcpd.conf is complete, enable the DHCP server in /etc/rc.conf :

```
dhcpd_enable="YES"
dhcpd_ifaces="dc0"
```

Replace the dc0 with the interface (or interfaces, separated by whitespace) that the DHCP server should listen on for DHCP client requests.

Start the server by issuing the following command:

```
# service isc-dhcpd start
```

Any future changes to the configuration of the server will require the dhcpd service to be stopped and then started using service(8).

The DHCP server uses the following files. Note that the manual pages are installed with the server software.

- `/usr/local/sbin/dhcpd`

  More information about the dhcpd server can be found in dhcpd(8).

- `/usr/local/etc/dhcpd.conf`

  The server configuration file needs to contain all the information that should be provided to clients, along with information regarding the operation of the server. This configuration file is described in dhcpd.conf(5).

- `/var/db/dhcpd.leases`

  The DHCP server keeps a database of leases it has issued in this file, which is written as a log. Refer to dhcpd.leases(5), which gives a slightly longer description.

- `/usr/local/sbin/dhcrelay`

  This daemon is used in advanced environments where one DHCP server forwards a request from a client to another DHCP server on a separate network. If this functionality is required, install the net/isc-dhcp43-relay package or port. The installation includes dhcrelay(8) which provides more detail.

28.7. Domain Name System (DNS)

Domain Name System (DNS) is the protocol through which domain names are mapped to IP addresses, and vice versa. DNS is coordinated across the Internet through a somewhat complex system of authoritative root, Top Level Domain (TLD), and other smaller-scale name servers, which host and cache individual domain information. It is not necessary to run a name server to perform DNS lookups on a system.

In FreeBSD 10, the Berkeley Internet Name Domain (BIND) has been removed from the base system and replaced with Unbound. Unbound as configured in the FreeBSD Base is a local caching resolver. BIND is still available from The Ports Collection as dns/bind99 or dns/bind98. In FreeBSD 9 and lower, BIND is included in FreeBSD Base. The FreeBSD version provides enhanced security features, a new file system layout, and automated chroot(8) configuration. BIND is maintained by the Internet Systems Consortium.

The following table describes some of the terms associated with DNS:

Table 28.4. DNS Terminology

Term	Definition
Forward DNS	Mapping of hostnames to IP addresses.
Origin	Refers to the domain covered in a particular zone file.
named, BIND	Common names for the BIND name server package within FreeBSD.
Resolver	A system process through which a machine queries a name server for zone information.
Reverse DNS	Mapping of IP addresses to hostnames.
Root zone	The beginning of the Internet zone hierarchy. All zones fall under the root zone, similar to how all files in a file system fall under the root directory.
Zone	An individual domain, subdomain, or portion of the DNS administered by the same authority.

Examples of zones:

- `.` is how the root zone is usually referred to in documentation.

- `org.` is a Top Level Domain (TLD) under the root zone.

- `example.org.` is a zone under the `org.` TLD.

- `1.168.192.in-addr.arpa` is a zone referencing all IP addresses which fall under the `192.168.1.*` IP address space.

As one can see, the more specific part of a hostname appears to its left. For example, `example.org.` is more specific than `org.`, as `org.` is more specific than the root zone. The layout of each part of a hostname is much like a file system: the `/dev` directory falls within the root, and so on.

28.7.1. Reasons to Run a Name Server

Name servers generally come in two forms: authoritative name servers, and caching (also known as resolving) name servers.

An authoritative name server is needed when:

- One wants to serve DNS information to the world, replying authoritatively to queries.

- A domain, such as `example.org`, is registered and IP addresses need to be assigned to hostnames under it.

- An IP address block requires reverse DNS entries (IP to hostname).

- A backup or second name server, called a slave, will reply to queries.

A caching name server is needed when:

- A local DNS server may cache and respond more quickly than querying an outside name server.

When one queries for `www.FreeBSD.org`, the resolver usually queries the uplink ISP's name server, and retrieves the reply. With a local, caching DNS server, the query only has to be made once to the outside world by the caching DNS server. Additional queries will not have to go outside the local network, since the information is cached locally.

28.7.2. DNS Server Configuration in FreeBSD 10.0 and Later

In FreeBSD 10.0, BIND has been replaced with Unbound. Unbound is a validating caching resolver only. If an authoritative server is needed, many are available from the Ports Collection.

Unbound is provided in the FreeBSD base system. By default, it will provide DNS resolution to the local machine only. While the base system package can be configured to provide resolution services beyond the local machine, it is recommended that such requirements be addressed by installing Unbound from the FreeBSD Ports Collection.

To enable Unbound, add the following to `/etc/rc.conf` :

```
local_unbound_enable="YES"
```

Any existing nameservers in `/etc/resolv.conf` will be configured as forwarders in the new Unbound configuration.

> ### Note
>
> If any of the listed nameservers do not support DNSSEC, local DNS resolution will fail. Be sure to test each nameserver and remove any that fail the test. The following command will show the trust tree or a failure for a nameserver running on `192.168.1.1` :

```
% drill -S FreeBSD.org @ 192.168.1.1
```

Once each nameserver is confirmed to support DNSSEC, start Unbound:

```
# service local_unbound onestart
```

This will take care of updating /etc/resolv.conf so that queries for DNSSEC secured domains will now work. For example, run the following to validate the FreeBSD.org DNSSEC trust tree:

```
% drill -S FreeBSD.org
;; Number of trusted keys: 1
;; Chasing: freebsd.org. A

DNSSEC Trust tree:
freebsd.org. (A)
|---freebsd.org. (DNSKEY keytag: 36786 alg: 8 flags: 256)
    |---freebsd.org. (DNSKEY keytag: 32659 alg: 8 flags: 257)
    |---freebsd.org. (DS keytag: 32659 digest type: 2)
        |---org. (DNSKEY keytag: 49587 alg: 7 flags: 256)
            |---org. (DNSKEY keytag: 9795 alg: 7 flags: 257)
            |---org. (DNSKEY keytag: 21366 alg: 7 flags: 257)
            |---org. (DS keytag: 21366 digest type: 1)
            |    |---. (DNSKEY keytag: 40926 alg: 8 flags: 256)
            |        |---. (DNSKEY keytag: 19036 alg: 8 flags: 257)
            |---org. (DS keytag: 21366 digest type: 2)
                |---. (DNSKEY keytag: 40926 alg: 8 flags: 256)
                |---. (DNSKEY keytag: 19036 alg: 8 flags: 257)
;; Chase successful
```

28.7.3. DNS Server Configuration in FreeBSD 9.X

Important

This chapter is only applicable to FreeBSD 9 and before. BIND9 is no longer part of the base system in FreeBSD 10 and after, where it has been replaced with unbound.

In FreeBSD, the BIND daemon is called named.

File	Description
named(8)	The BIND daemon.
rndc(8)	Name server control utility.
/etc/namedb	Directory where BIND zone information resides.
/etc/namedb/named.conf	Configuration file of the daemon.

Depending on how a given zone is configured on the server, the files related to that zone can be found in the master, slave, or dynamic subdirectories of the /etc/namedb directory. These files contain the DNS information that will be given out by the name server in response to queries.

28.7.3.1. Starting BIND

Since BIND is installed by default, configuring it is relatively simple.

The default named configuration is that of a basic resolving name server, running in a chroot(8) environment, and restricted to listening on the local IPv4 loopback address (127.0.0.1). To start the server one time with this configuration, use the following command:

```
# service named onestart
```

To ensure the named daemon is started at boot each time, put the following line into the /etc/rc.conf :

```
named_enable="YES"
```

There are many configuration options for /etc/namedb/named.conf that are beyond the scope of this document. Other startup options for named on FreeBSD can be found in the named_* flags in /etc/defaults/rc.conf and in rc.conf(5). The Section 11.4, "Managing Services in FreeBSD" section is also a good read.

28.7.3.2. Configuration Files

Configuration files for named currently reside in /etc/namedb directory and will need modification before use unless all that is needed is a simple resolver. This is where most of the configuration will be performed.

28.7.3.2.1. /etc/namedb/named.conf

```
// $FreeBSD$
//
// Refer to the named.conf(5) and named(8) man pages, and the documentation
// in /usr/share/doc/bind9 for more details.
//
// If you are going to set up an authoritative server, make sure you
// understand the hairy details of how DNS works.  Even with
// simple mistakes, you can break connectivity for affected parties,
// or cause huge amounts of useless Internet traffic.

options {
 // All file and path names are relative to the chroot directory,
 // if any, and should be fully qualified.
 directory "/etc/namedb/working";
 pid-file "/var/run/named/pid";
 dump-file "/var/dump/named_dump.db";
 statistics-file "/var/stats/named.stats";

// If named is being used only as a local resolver, this is a safe default.
// For named to be accessible to the network, comment this option, specify
// the proper IP address, or delete this option.
 listen-on { 127.0.0.1; };

// If you have IPv6 enabled on this system, uncomment this option for
// use as a local resolver.  To give access to the network, specify
// an IPv6 address, or the keyword "any".
// listen-on-v6 { ::1; };

// These zones are already covered by the empty zones listed below.
// If you remove the related empty zones below, comment these lines out.
 disable-empty-zone "255.255.255.255.IN-ADDR.ARPA";
 disable-empty-zone "0.0.0.0.0.0.0.0.0.0.0.0.0.0.0.0.0.0.0.0.0.0.0.0.0.0.0.0.0.0.0.0.↺
IP6.ARPA";
 disable-empty-zone "1.0.0.0.0.0.0.0.0.0.0.0.0.0.0.0.0.0.0.0.0.0.0.0.0.0.0.0.0.0.0.0.↺
IP6.ARPA";

// If you have a DNS server around at your upstream provider, enter
// its IP address here, and enable the line below.  This will make you
// benefit from its cache, thus reduce overall DNS traffic in the Internet.
/*
 forwarders {
  127.0.0.1;
 };
*/

// If the 'forwarders' clause is not empty the default is to 'forward first'
// which will fall back to sending a query from your local server if the name
// servers in 'forwarders' do not have the answer.  Alternatively you can
// force your name server to never initiate queries of its own by enabling the
// following line:
// forward only;

// If you wish to have forwarding configured automatically based on
// the entries in /etc/resolv.conf, uncomment the following line and
// set named_auto_forward=yes in /etc/rc.conf.  You can also enable
```

```
// named_auto_forward_only (the effect of which is described above).
// include "/etc/namedb/auto_forward.conf";
```

Just as the comment says, to benefit from an uplink's cache, forwarders can be enabled here. Under normal circumstances, a name server will recursively query the Internet looking at certain name servers until it finds the answer it is looking for. Having this enabled will have it query the uplink's name server (or name server provided) first, taking advantage of its cache. If the uplink name server in question is a heavily trafficked, fast name server, enabling this may be worthwhile.

Warning

127.0.0.1 will *not* work here. Change this IP address to a name server at the uplink.

```
/*
    Modern versions of BIND use a random UDP port for each outgoing
    query by default in order to dramatically reduce the possibility
    of cache poisoning.  All users are strongly encouraged to utilize
    this feature, and to configure their firewalls to accommodate it.

    AS A LAST RESORT in order to get around a restrictive firewall
    policy you can try enabling the option below.  Use of this option
    will significantly reduce your ability to withstand cache poisoning
    attacks, and should be avoided if at all possible.

    Replace NNNNN in the example with a number between 49160 and 65530.
*/
// query-source address * port NNNNN;
};

// If you enable a local name server, do not forget to enter 127.0.0.1
// first in your /etc/resolv.conf so this server will be queried.
// Also, make sure to enable it in /etc/rc.conf.

// The traditional root hints mechanism. Use this, OR the slave zones below.
zone "." { type hint; file "/etc/namedb/named.root"; };

/* Slaving the following zones from the root name servers has some
   significant advantages:
   1. Faster local resolution for your users
   2. No spurious traffic will be sent from your network to the roots
   3. Greater resilience to any potential root server failure/DDoS

   On the other hand, this method requires more monitoring than the
   hints file to be sure that an unexpected failure mode has not
   incapacitated your server.  Name servers that are serving a lot
   of clients will benefit more from this approach than individual
   hosts.  Use with caution.

   To use this mechanism, uncomment the entries below, and comment
   the hint zone above.

   As documented at http://dns.icann.org/services/axfr/ these zones:
   "." (the root), ARPA, IN-ADDR.ARPA, IP6.ARPA, and ROOT-SERVERS.NET
   are available for AXFR from these servers on IPv4 and IPv6:
   xfr.lax.dns.icann.org, xfr.cjr.dns.icann.org
*/
/*
zone "." {
  type slave;
  file "/etc/namedb/slave/root.slave";
  masters {
```

```
  192.5.5.241; // F.ROOT-SERVERS.NET.
 };
 notify no;
};
zone "arpa" {
 type slave;
 file "/etc/namedb/slave/arpa.slave";
 masters {
  192.5.5.241; // F.ROOT-SERVERS.NET.
 };
 notify no;
};
*/

/* Serving the following zones locally will prevent any queries
 for these zones leaving your network and going to the root
 name servers.  This has two significant advantages:
 1. Faster local resolution for your users
 2. No spurious traffic will be sent from your network to the roots
*/
// RFCs 1912 and 5735 (and BCP 32 for localhost)
zone "localhost" { type master; file "/etc/namedb/master/localhost-forward.db"; };
zone "127.in-addr.arpa" { type master; file "/etc/namedb/master/localhost-reverse.db"; };
zone "255.in-addr.arpa" { type master; file "/etc/namedb/master/empty.db"; };

// RFC 1912-style zone for IPv6 localhost address
zone "0.ip6.arpa" { type master; file "/etc/namedb/master/localhost-reverse.db"; };

// "This" Network (RFCs 1912 and 5735)
zone "0.in-addr.arpa" { type master; file "/etc/namedb/master/empty.db"; };

// Private Use Networks (RFCs 1918 and 5735)
zone "10.in-addr.arpa"    { type master; file "/etc/namedb/master/empty.db"; };
zone "16.172.in-addr.arpa" { type master; file "/etc/namedb/master/empty.db"; };
zone "17.172.in-addr.arpa" { type master; file "/etc/namedb/master/empty.db"; };
zone "18.172.in-addr.arpa" { type master; file "/etc/namedb/master/empty.db"; };
zone "19.172.in-addr.arpa" { type master; file "/etc/namedb/master/empty.db"; };
zone "20.172.in-addr.arpa" { type master; file "/etc/namedb/master/empty.db"; };
zone "21.172.in-addr.arpa" { type master; file "/etc/namedb/master/empty.db"; };
zone "22.172.in-addr.arpa" { type master; file "/etc/namedb/master/empty.db"; };
zone "23.172.in-addr.arpa" { type master; file "/etc/namedb/master/empty.db"; };
zone "24.172.in-addr.arpa" { type master; file "/etc/namedb/master/empty.db"; };
zone "25.172.in-addr.arpa" { type master; file "/etc/namedb/master/empty.db"; };
zone "26.172.in-addr.arpa" { type master; file "/etc/namedb/master/empty.db"; };
zone "27.172.in-addr.arpa" { type master; file "/etc/namedb/master/empty.db"; };
zone "28.172.in-addr.arpa" { type master; file "/etc/namedb/master/empty.db"; };
zone "29.172.in-addr.arpa" { type master; file "/etc/namedb/master/empty.db"; };
zone "30.172.in-addr.arpa" { type master; file "/etc/namedb/master/empty.db"; };
zone "31.172.in-addr.arpa" { type master; file "/etc/namedb/master/empty.db"; };
zone "168.192.in-addr.arpa" { type master; file "/etc/namedb/master/empty.db"; };

// Link-local/APIPA (RFCs 3927 and 5735)
zone "254.169.in-addr.arpa" { type master; file "/etc/namedb/master/empty.db"; };

// IETF protocol assignments (RFCs 5735 and 5736)
zone "0.0.192.in-addr.arpa" { type master; file "/etc/namedb/master/empty.db"; };

// TEST-NET-[1-3] for Documentation (RFCs 5735 and 5737)
zone "2.0.192.in-addr.arpa" { type master; file "/etc/namedb/master/empty.db"; };
zone "100.51.198.in-addr.arpa" { type master; file "/etc/namedb/master/empty.db"; };
zone "113.0.203.in-addr.arpa" { type master; file "/etc/namedb/master/empty.db"; };

// IPv6 Range for Documentation (RFC 3849)
zone "8.b.d.0.1.0.0.2.ip6.arpa" { type master; file "/etc/namedb/master/empty.db"; };

// Domain Names for Documentation and Testing (BCP 32)
```

```
zone "test" { type master; file "/etc/namedb/master/empty.db"; };
zone "example" { type master; file "/etc/namedb/master/empty.db"; };
zone "invalid" { type master; file "/etc/namedb/master/empty.db"; };
zone "example.com" { type master; file "/etc/namedb/master/empty.db"; };
zone "example.net" { type master; file "/etc/namedb/master/empty.db"; };
zone "example.org" { type master; file "/etc/namedb/master/empty.db"; };

// Router Benchmark Testing (RFCs 2544 and 5735)
zone "18.198.in-addr.arpa" { type master; file "/etc/namedb/master/empty.db"; };
zone "19.198.in-addr.arpa" { type master; file "/etc/namedb/master/empty.db"; };

// IANA Reserved - Old Class E Space (RFC 5735)
zone "240.in-addr.arpa" { type master; file "/etc/namedb/master/empty.db"; };
zone "241.in-addr.arpa" { type master; file "/etc/namedb/master/empty.db"; };
zone "242.in-addr.arpa" { type master; file "/etc/namedb/master/empty.db"; };
zone "243.in-addr.arpa" { type master; file "/etc/namedb/master/empty.db"; };
zone "244.in-addr.arpa" { type master; file "/etc/namedb/master/empty.db"; };
zone "245.in-addr.arpa" { type master; file "/etc/namedb/master/empty.db"; };
zone "246.in-addr.arpa" { type master; file "/etc/namedb/master/empty.db"; };
zone "247.in-addr.arpa" { type master; file "/etc/namedb/master/empty.db"; };
zone "248.in-addr.arpa" { type master; file "/etc/namedb/master/empty.db"; };
zone "249.in-addr.arpa" { type master; file "/etc/namedb/master/empty.db"; };
zone "250.in-addr.arpa" { type master; file "/etc/namedb/master/empty.db"; };
zone "251.in-addr.arpa" { type master; file "/etc/namedb/master/empty.db"; };
zone "252.in-addr.arpa" { type master; file "/etc/namedb/master/empty.db"; };
zone "253.in-addr.arpa" { type master; file "/etc/namedb/master/empty.db"; };
zone "254.in-addr.arpa" { type master; file "/etc/namedb/master/empty.db"; };

// IPv6 Unassigned Addresses (RFC 4291)
zone "1.ip6.arpa" { type master; file "/etc/namedb/master/empty.db"; };
zone "3.ip6.arpa" { type master; file "/etc/namedb/master/empty.db"; };
zone "4.ip6.arpa" { type master; file "/etc/namedb/master/empty.db"; };
zone "5.ip6.arpa" { type master; file "/etc/namedb/master/empty.db"; };
zone "6.ip6.arpa" { type master; file "/etc/namedb/master/empty.db"; };
zone "7.ip6.arpa" { type master; file "/etc/namedb/master/empty.db"; };
zone "8.ip6.arpa" { type master; file "/etc/namedb/master/empty.db"; };
zone "9.ip6.arpa" { type master; file "/etc/namedb/master/empty.db"; };
zone "a.ip6.arpa" { type master; file "/etc/namedb/master/empty.db"; };
zone "b.ip6.arpa" { type master; file "/etc/namedb/master/empty.db"; };
zone "c.ip6.arpa" { type master; file "/etc/namedb/master/empty.db"; };
zone "d.ip6.arpa" { type master; file "/etc/namedb/master/empty.db"; };
zone "e.ip6.arpa" { type master; file "/etc/namedb/master/empty.db"; };
zone "0.f.ip6.arpa" { type master; file "/etc/namedb/master/empty.db"; };
zone "1.f.ip6.arpa" { type master; file "/etc/namedb/master/empty.db"; };
zone "2.f.ip6.arpa" { type master; file "/etc/namedb/master/empty.db"; };
zone "3.f.ip6.arpa" { type master; file "/etc/namedb/master/empty.db"; };
zone "4.f.ip6.arpa" { type master; file "/etc/namedb/master/empty.db"; };
zone "5.f.ip6.arpa" { type master; file "/etc/namedb/master/empty.db"; };
zone "6.f.ip6.arpa" { type master; file "/etc/namedb/master/empty.db"; };
zone "7.f.ip6.arpa" { type master; file "/etc/namedb/master/empty.db"; };
zone "8.f.ip6.arpa" { type master; file "/etc/namedb/master/empty.db"; };
zone "9.f.ip6.arpa" { type master; file "/etc/namedb/master/empty.db"; };
zone "a.f.ip6.arpa" { type master; file "/etc/namedb/master/empty.db"; };
zone "b.f.ip6.arpa" { type master; file "/etc/namedb/master/empty.db"; };
zone "0.e.f.ip6.arpa" { type master; file "/etc/namedb/master/empty.db"; };
zone "1.e.f.ip6.arpa" { type master; file "/etc/namedb/master/empty.db"; };
zone "2.e.f.ip6.arpa" { type master; file "/etc/namedb/master/empty.db"; };
zone "3.e.f.ip6.arpa" { type master; file "/etc/namedb/master/empty.db"; };
zone "4.e.f.ip6.arpa" { type master; file "/etc/namedb/master/empty.db"; };
zone "5.e.f.ip6.arpa" { type master; file "/etc/namedb/master/empty.db"; };
zone "6.e.f.ip6.arpa" { type master; file "/etc/namedb/master/empty.db"; };
zone "7.e.f.ip6.arpa" { type master; file "/etc/namedb/master/empty.db"; };

// IPv6 ULA (RFC 4193)
zone "c.f.ip6.arpa" { type master; file "/etc/namedb/master/empty.db"; };
zone "d.f.ip6.arpa" { type master; file "/etc/namedb/master/empty.db"; };
```

```
// IPv6 Link Local (RFC 4291)
zone "8.e.f.ip6.arpa" { type master; file "/etc/namedb/master/empty.db"; };
zone "9.e.f.ip6.arpa" { type master; file "/etc/namedb/master/empty.db"; };
zone "a.e.f.ip6.arpa" { type master; file "/etc/namedb/master/empty.db"; };
zone "b.e.f.ip6.arpa" { type master; file "/etc/namedb/master/empty.db"; };

// IPv6 Deprecated Site-Local Addresses (RFC 3879)
zone "c.e.f.ip6.arpa" { type master; file "/etc/namedb/master/empty.db"; };
zone "d.e.f.ip6.arpa" { type master; file "/etc/namedb/master/empty.db"; };
zone "e.e.f.ip6.arpa" { type master; file "/etc/namedb/master/empty.db"; };
zone "f.e.f.ip6.arpa" { type master; file "/etc/namedb/master/empty.db"; };

// IP6.INT is Deprecated (RFC 4159)
zone "ip6.int"  { type master; file "/etc/namedb/master/empty.db"; };

// NB: Do not use the IP addresses below, they are faked, and only
// serve demonstration/documentation purposes!
//
// Example slave zone config entries.  It can be convenient to become
// a slave at least for the zone your own domain is in.  Ask
// your network administrator for the IP address of the responsible
// master name server.
//
// Do not forget to include the reverse lookup zone!
// This is named after the first bytes of the IP address, in reverse
// order, with ".IN-ADDR.ARPA" appended, or ".IP6.ARPA" for IPv6.
//
// Before starting to set up a master zone, make sure you fully
// understand how DNS and BIND work.  There are sometimes
// non-obvious pitfalls.  Setting up a slave zone is usually simpler.
//
// NB: Do not blindly enable the examples below. :-)  Use actual names
// and addresses instead.

/* An example dynamic zone
key "exampleorgkey" {
 algorithm hmac-md5;
 secret "sf87HJqjkqh8ac87a02lla==";
};
zone "example.org" {
 type master;
 allow-update {
  key "exampleorgkey";
 };
 file "/etc/namedb/dynamic/example.org";
};
*/

/* Example of a slave reverse zone
zone "1.168.192.in-addr.arpa" {
 type slave;
 file "/etc/namedb/slave/1.168.192.in-addr.arpa";
 masters {
  192.168.1.1;
 };
};
*/
```

In named.conf , these are examples of slave entries for a forward and reverse zone.

For each new zone served, a new zone entry must be added to named.conf .

For example, the simplest zone entry for example.org can look like:

```
zone "example.org" {
```

```
 type master;
 file "master/example.org";
};
```

The zone is a master, as indicated by the `type` statement, holding its zone information in `/etc/namedb/master/example.org` indicated by the `file` statement.

```
zone "example.org" {
 type slave;
 file "slave/example.org";
};
```

In the slave case, the zone information is transferred from the master name server for the particular zone, and saved in the file specified. If and when the master server dies or is unreachable, the slave name server will have the transferred zone information and will be able to serve it.

28.7.3.2.2. Zone Files

An example master zone file for example.org (existing within /etc/namedb/master/example.org) is as follows:

```
$TTL 3600       -; 1 hour default TTL
example.org.    IN      SOA      ns1.example.org. admin.example.org. (
                                 2006051501      -; Serial
                                 10800           -; Refresh
                                 3600            -; Retry
                                 604800          -; Expire
                                 300             -; Negative Response TTL
                         )

; DNS Servers
                IN      NS       ns1.example.org.
                IN      NS       ns2.example.org.

; MX Records
                IN      MX 10    mx.example.org.
                IN      MX 20    mail.example.org.

                IN      A        192.168.1.1

; Machine Names
localhost       IN      A        127.0.0.1
ns1             IN      A        192.168.1.2
ns2             IN      A        192.168.1.3
mx              IN      A        192.168.1.4
mail            IN      A        192.168.1.5

; Aliases
www             IN      CNAME    example.org.
```

Note that every hostname ending in a "." is an exact hostname, whereas everything without a trailing "." is relative to the origin. For example, ns1 is translated into ns1.*example.org.*

The format of a zone file follows:

```
recordname      IN recordtype   value
```

The most commonly used DNS records:

SOA

    start of zone authority

NS

    an authoritative name server

A
  a host address

CNAME
  the canonical name for an alias

MX
  mail exchanger

PTR
  a domain name pointer (used in reverse DNS)

```
example.org. IN SOA ns1.example.org. admin.example.org. (
                        2006051501      -; Serial
                        10800           -; Refresh after 3 hours
                        3600            -; Retry after 1 hour
                        604800          -; Expire after 1 week
                        300 )           -; Negative Response TTL
```

example.org.
  the domain name, also the origin for this zone file.

ns1.example.org.
  the primary/authoritative name server for this zone.

admin.example.org.
  the responsible person for this zone, email address with "@" replaced. (<admin@example.org> becomes admin.example.org)

2006051501
  the serial number of the file. This must be incremented each time the zone file is modified. Nowadays, many admins prefer a yyyymmddrr format for the serial number. 2006051501 would mean last modified 05/15/2006, the latter 01 being the first time the zone file has been modified this day. The serial number is important as it alerts slave name servers for a zone when it is updated.

```
        IN NS           ns1.example.org.
```

This is an NS entry. Every name server that is going to reply authoritatively for the zone must have one of these entries.

```
localhost       IN      A       127.0.0.1
ns1             IN      A       192.168.1.2
ns2             IN      A       192.168.1.3
mx              IN      A       192.168.1.4
mail            IN      A       192.168.1.5
```

The A record indicates machine names. As seen above, ns1.example.org would resolve to 192.168.1.2.

```
        IN      A       192.168.1.1
```

This line assigns IP address 192.168.1.1 to the current origin, in this case example.org.

```
www             IN CNAME        @
```

The canonical name record is usually used for giving aliases to a machine. In the example, www is aliased to the "master" machine whose name happens to be the same as the domain name example.org (192.168.1.1). CNAMEs can never be used together with another kind of record for the same hostname.

```
        IN MX   10      mail.example.org.
```

The MX record indicates which mail servers are responsible for handling incoming mail for the zone. mail.example.org is the hostname of a mail server, and 10 is the priority of that mail server.

One can have several mail servers, with priorities of 10, 20 and so on. A mail server attempting to deliver to `ex-ample.org` would first try the highest priority MX (the record with the lowest priority number), then the second highest, etc, until the mail can be properly delivered.

For in-addr.arpa zone files (reverse DNS), the same format is used, except with PTR entries instead of A or CNAME.

```
$TTL 3600

1.168.192.in-addr.arpa.  IN SOA ns1.example.org. admin.example.org. (
                            2006051501      -; Serial
                            10800           -; Refresh
                            3600            -; Retry
                            604800          -; Expire
                            300 )           -; Negative Response TTL

        IN      NS      ns1.example.org.
        IN      NS      ns2.example.org.

1       IN      PTR     example.org.
2       IN      PTR     ns1.example.org.
3       IN      PTR     ns2.example.org.
4       IN      PTR     mx.example.org.
5       IN      PTR     mail.example.org.
```

This file gives the proper IP address to hostname mappings for the above fictitious domain.

It is worth noting that all names on the right side of a PTR record need to be fully qualified (i.e., end in a ".").

28.7.3.3. Caching Name Server

A caching name server is a name server whose primary role is to resolve recursive queries. It simply asks queries of its own, and remembers the answers for later use.

28.7.3.4. DNSSEC

Domain Name System Security Extensions, or DNSSEC for short, is a suite of specifications to protect resolving name servers from forged DNS data, such as spoofed DNS records. By using digital signatures, a resolver can verify the integrity of the record. Note that DNSSEC only provides integrity via digitally signing the Resource Records (RRs). It provides neither confidentiality nor protection against false end-user assumptions. This means that it cannot protect against people going to `example.net` instead of `example.com`. The only thing DNSSEC does is authenticate that the data has not been compromised in transit. The security of DNS is an important step in securing the Internet in general. For more in-depth details of how DNSSEC works, the relevant RFCs are a good place to start. See the list in Section 28.7.3.6, "Further Reading".

The following sections will demonstrate how to enable DNSSEC for an authoritative DNS server and a recursive (or caching) DNS server running BIND 9. While all versions of BIND 9 support DNSSEC, it is necessary to have at least version 9.6.2 in order to be able to use the signed root zone when validating DNS queries. This is because earlier versions lack the required algorithms to enable validation using the root zone key. It is strongly recommended to use the latest version of BIND 9.7 or later to take advantage of automatic key updating for the root key, as well as other features to automatically keep zones signed and signatures up to date. Where configurations differ between 9.6.2 and 9.7 and later, differences will be pointed out.

28.7.3.4.1. Recursive DNS Server Configuration

Enabling DNSSEC validation of queries performed by a recursive DNS server requires a few changes to `named.conf`. Before making these changes the root zone key, or trust anchor, must be acquired. Currently the root zone key is not available in a file format BIND understands, so it has to be manually converted into the proper format. The key itself can be obtained by querying the root zone for it using dig. By running

```
% dig +multi +noall +answer DNSKEY . > root.dnskey
```

the key will end up in `root.dnskey` . The contents should look something like this:

```
. 93910 IN DNSKEY 257 3 8 (
AwEAAagAIKlVZrpC6Ia7gEzahOR+9W29euxhJhVVLOyQ
bSEWOO8gcCjFFVQUTf6v58fLjwBd0YI0EzrAcQqBGCzh
/RStIoO8g0NfnfL2MTJRkxoXbfDaUeVPQuYEhg37NZWA
JQ9VnMVDxP/VHL496M/QZxkjf5/Efucp2gaDX6RS6CXp
oY68LsvPVjR0ZSwzz1apAzvN9dlzEheX7ICJBBtuA6G3
LQpzW5hOA2hzCTMjJPJ8LbqF6dsV6DoBQzgul0sGIcGO
Yl7OyQdXfZ57relSQageu+ipAdTTJ25AsRTAoub8ONGc
LmqrAmRLKBP1dfwhYB4N7knNnulqQxA+Uklihz0=
) -; key id = 19036
. 93910 IN DNSKEY 256 3 8 (
AwEAAcaGQEA+OJmOzfzVfoYN249JId7gx+OZMbxy69Hf
UyuGBbRN0+HuTOpBxxBCkNOL+EJB9qJxt+0FEY6ZUVjE
g58sRr4ZQ6Iu6b1xTBKgc193zUARk4mmQ/PPGxn7Cn5V
EGJ/1h6dNaiXuRHwR+7oWh7DnzkIJChcTqlFrXDW3tjt
) -; key id = 34525
```

Do not be alarmed if the obtained keys differ from this example. They might have changed since these instructions were last updated. This output actually contains two keys. The first key in the listing, with the value 257 after the DNSKEY record type, is the one needed. This value indicates that this is a Secure Entry Point (SEP), commonly known as a Key Signing Key (KSK). The second key, with value 256, is a subordinate key, commonly called a Zone Signing Key (ZSK). More on the different key types later in Section 28.7.3.4.2, "Authoritative DNS Server Configuration".

Now the key must be verified and formatted so that BIND can use it. To verify the key, generate a DS RR set. Create a file containing these RRs with

```
% dnssec-dsfromkey -f root.dnskey . > root.ds
```

These records use SHA-1 and SHA-256 respectively, and should look similar to the following example, where the longer is using SHA-256.

```
.    IN DS 19036 8 1
B256BD09DC8DD59F0E0F0D8541B8328DD986DF6E
. IN DS 19036 8 2 49AAC11D7B6F6446702E54A1607371607A1A41855200FD2CE1CDDE32F24E8FB5
```

The SHA-256 RR can now be compared to the digest in https://data.iana.org/root-anchors/root-anchors.xml. To be absolutely sure that the key has not been tampered with the data in the XML file should be verified using a proper PGP signature.

Next, the key must be formatted properly. This differs a little between BIND versions 9.6.2 and 9.7 and later. In version 9.7 support was added to automatically track changes to the key and update it as necessary. This is done using `managed-keys` as seen in the example below. When using the older version, the key is added using a `trusted-keys` statement and updates must be done manually. For BIND 9.6.2 the format should look like:

```
trusted-keys {
 "." 257 3 8
 "AwEAAagAIKlVZrpC6Ia7gEzahOR+9W29euxhJhVVLOyQbSEWOO8gcCjF
 FVQUTf6v58fLjwBd0YI0EzrAcQqBGCzh/RStIoO8g0NfnfL2MTJRkxoX
 bfDaUeVPQuYEhg37NZWAJQ9VnMVDxP/VHL496M/QZxkjf5/Efucp2gaD
 X6RS6CXpoY68LsvPVjR0ZSwzz1apAzvN9dlzEheX7ICJBBtuA6G3LQpz
 W5hOA2hzCTMjJPJ8LbqF6dsV6DoBQzgul0sGIcGOYl7OyQdXfZ57relS
 Qageu+ipAdTTJ25AsRTAoub8ONGcLmqrAmRLKBP1dfwhYB4N7knNnulq
 QxA+Uklihz0=";
};
```

For 9.7 the format will instead be:

```
managed-keys {
 "." initial-key 257 3 8
```

```
 "AwEAAagAIKlVZrpC6Ia7gEzahOR+9W29euxhJhVVLOyQbSEWOO8gcCjF
 FVQUTf6v58fLjwBd0YI0EzrAcQqBGCzh/RStIoO8g0NfnfL2MTJRkxoX
 bfDaUeVPQuYEhg37NZWAJQ9VnMVDxP/VHL496M/QZxkjf5/Efucp2gaD
 X6RS6CXpoY68LsvPVjR0ZSwzz1apAzvN9dlzEheX7ICJBBtuA6G3LQpz
 W5hOA2hzCTMjJPJ8LbqF6dsV6DoBQzgul0sGIcGOYl7OyQdXfZ57relS
 Qageu+ipAdTTJ25AsRTAoub8ONGcLmqrAmRLKBP1dfwhYB4N7knNnulq
 QxA+Uklihz0=";
};
```

The root key can now be added to named.conf either directly or by including a file containing the key. After these steps, configure BIND to do DNSSEC validation on queries by editing named.conf and adding the following to the options directive:

```
dnssec-enable yes;
dnssec-validation yes;
```

To verify that it is actually working use dig to make a query for a signed zone using the resolver just configured. A successful reply will contain the AD flag to indicate the data was authenticated. Running a query such as

```
% dig @resolver +dnssec se ds
```

should return the DS RR for the .se zone. In the flags: section the AD flag should be set, as seen in:

```
...
;; flags: qr rd ra ad; QUERY: 1, ANSWER: 3, AUTHORITY: 0, ADDITIONAL: 1
...
```

The resolver is now capable of authenticating DNS queries.

28.7.3.4.2. Authoritative DNS Server Configuration

In order to get an authoritative name server to serve a DNSSEC signed zone a little more work is required. A zone is signed using cryptographic keys which must be generated. It is possible to use only one key for this. The preferred method however is to have a strong well-protected Key Signing Key (KSK) that is not rotated very often and a Zone Signing Key (ZSK) that is rotated more frequently. Information on recommended operational practices can be found in RFC 4641: DNSSEC Operational Practices. Practices regarding the root zone can be found in DNSSEC Practice Statement for the Root Zone KSK operator and DNSSEC Practice Statement for the Root Zone ZSK operator. The KSK is used to build a chain of authority to the data in need of validation and as such is also called a Secure Entry Point (SEP) key. A message digest of this key, called a Delegation Signer (DS) record, must be published in the parent zone to establish the trust chain. How this is accomplished depends on the parent zone owner. The ZSK is used to sign the zone, and only needs to be published there.

To enable DNSSEC for the example.com zone depicted in previous examples, the first step is to use dnssec-keygen to generate the KSK and ZSK key pair. This key pair can utilize different cryptographic algorithms. It is recommended to use RSA/SHA256 for the keys and 2048 bits key length should be enough. To generate the KSK for example.com, run

```
% dnssec-keygen -f KSK -a RSASHA256 -b 2048 -n ZONE example.com
```

and to generate the ZSK, run

```
% dnssec-keygen -a RSASHA256 -b 2048 -n ZONE example.com
```

dnssec-keygen outputs two files, the public and the private keys in files named similar to Kexample.com.+005+nnnnn.key (public) and Kexample.com.+005+nnnnn.private (private). The nnnnn part of the file name is a five digit key ID. Keep track of which key ID belongs to which key. This is especially important when having more than one key in a zone. It is also possible to rename the keys. For each KSK file do:

```
% mv Kexample.com.+005+nnnnn.key Kexample.com.+005+nnnnn.KSK.key
% mv Kexample.com.+005+nnnnn.private Kexample.com.+005+nnnnn.KSK.private
```

For the ZSK files, substitute KSK for ZSK as necessary. The files can now be included in the zone file, using the `$include` statement. It should look something like this:

```
$include Kexample.com.+005+nnnnn.KSK.key -; KSK
$include Kexample.com.+005+nnnnn.ZSK.key    -; ZSK
```

Finally, sign the zone and tell BIND to use the signed zone file. To sign a zone dnssec-signzone is used. The command to sign the zone example.com, located in example.com.db would look similar to

```
% dnssec-signzone -o example.com -k Kexample.com.+005+nnnnn.KSK example.com.db Kexample.ɔ
com.+005+nnnnn.ZSK.key
```

The key supplied to the `-k` argument is the KSK and the other key file is the ZSK that should be used in the signing. It is possible to supply more than one KSK and ZSK, which will result in the zone being signed with all supplied keys. This can be needed to supply zone data signed using more than one algorithm. The output of dnssec-signzone is a zone file with all RRs signed. This output will end up in a file with the extension `.signed`, such as example.com.db.signed. The DS records will also be written to a separate file `dsset-example.com`. To use this signed zone just modify the zone directive in `named.conf` to use example.com.db.signed. By default, the signatures are only valid 30 days, meaning that the zone needs to be resigned in about 15 days to be sure that resolvers are not caching records with stale signatures. It is possible to make a script and a cron job to do this. See relevant manuals for details.

Be sure to keep private keys confidential, as with all cryptographic keys. When changing a key it is best to include the new key into the zone, while still signing with the old one, and then move over to using the new key to sign. After these steps are done the old key can be removed from the zone. Failure to do this might render the DNS data unavailable for a time, until the new key has propagated through the DNS hierarchy. For more information on key rollovers and other DNSSEC operational issues, see RFC 4641: DNSSEC Operational practices.

28.7.3.4.3. Automation Using BIND 9.7 or Later

Beginning with BIND version 9.7 a new feature called *Smart Signing* was introduced. This feature aims to make the key management and signing process simpler by automating parts of the task. By putting the keys into a directory called a *key repository*, and using the new option `auto-dnssec`, it is possible to create a dynamic zone which will be resigned as needed. To update this zone use nsupdate with the new option `-l`. rndc has also grown the ability to sign zones with keys in the key repository, using the option `sign`. To tell BIND to use this automatic signing and zone updating for example.com, add the following to named.conf :

```
zone example.com {
  type master;
  key-directory "/etc/named/keys";
  update-policy local;
  auto-dnssec maintain;
  file "/etc/named/dynamic/example.com.zone";
};
```

After making these changes, generate keys for the zone as explained in Section 28.7.3.4.2, "Authoritative DNS Server Configuration", put those keys in the key repository given as the argument to the `key-directory` in the zone configuration and the zone will be signed automatically. Updates to a zone configured this way must be done using nsupdate, which will take care of re-signing the zone with the new data added. For further details, see Section 28.7.3.6, "Further Reading" and the BIND documentation.

28.7.3.5. Security

Although BIND is the most common implementation of DNS, there is always the issue of security. Possible and exploitable security holes are sometimes found.

While FreeBSD automatically drops named into a chroot(8) environment; there are several other security mechanisms in place which could help to lure off possible DNS service attacks.

It is always good idea to read CERT's security advisories and to subscribe to the FreeBSD security notifications mailing list to stay up to date with the current Internet and FreeBSD security issues.

> **Tip**
>
> If a problem arises, keeping sources up to date and having a fresh build of named may help.

28.7.3.6. Further Reading

BIND/named manual pages: rndc(8) named(8) named.conf(5) nsupdate(1) dnssec-signzone(8) dnssec-keygen(8)

- Official ISC BIND Page

- Official ISC BIND Forum

- O'Reilly DNS and BIND 5th Edition

- Root DNSSEC

- DNSSEC Trust Anchor Publication for the Root Zone

- RFC1034 - Domain Names - Concepts and Facilities

- RFC1035 - Domain Names - Implementation and Specification

- RFC4033 - DNS Security Introduction and Requirements

- RFC4034 - Resource Records for the DNS Security Extensions

- RFC4035 - Protocol Modifications for the DNS Security Extensions

- RFC4641 - DNSSEC Operational Practices

- RFC 5011 - Automated Updates of DNS Security (DNSSEC Trust Anchors

28.8. Apache HTTP Server

Contributed by Murray Stokely.

The open source Apache HTTP Server is the most widely used web server. FreeBSD does not install this web server by default, but it can be installed from the www/apache24 package or port.

This section summarizes how to configure and start version 2.*x* of the Apache HTTP Server on FreeBSD. For more detailed information about Apache 2.X and its configuration directives, refer to httpd.apache.org.

28.8.1. Configuring and Starting Apache

In FreeBSD, the main Apache HTTP Server configuration file is installed as /usr/local/etc/apache2 *x*/ httpd.conf , where *x* represents the version number. This ASCII text file begins comment lines with a #. The most frequently modified directives are:

ServerRoot "/usr/local"
> Specifies the default directory hierarchy for the Apache installation. Binaries are stored in the bin and sbin subdirectories of the server root and configuration files are stored in the etc/apache2 *x* subdirectory.

ServerAdmin you@example.com
> Change this to the email address to receive problems with the server. This address also appears on some server-generated pages, such as error documents.

ServerName www.example.com:80

Allows an administrator to set a hostname which is sent back to clients for the server. For example, www can be used instead of the actual hostname. If the system does not have a registered DNS name, enter its IP address instead. If the server will listen on an alternate report, change 80 to the alternate port number.

DocumentRoot "/usr/local/www/apache2 *x*/data"

The directory where documents will be served from. By default, all requests are taken from this directory, but symbolic links and aliases may be used to point to other locations.

It is always a good idea to make a backup copy of the default Apache configuration file before making changes. When the configuration of Apache is complete, save the file and verify the configuration using apachectl . Running apachectl configtest should return Syntax OK.

To launch Apache at system startup, add the following line to /etc/rc.conf :

```
apache24_enable="YES"
```

If Apache should be started with non-default options, the following line may be added to /etc/rc.conf to specify the needed flags:

```
apache24_flags=""
```

If apachectl does not report configuration errors, start httpd now:

```
# service apache 24 start
```

The httpd service can be tested by entering http:// *localhost* in a web browser, replacing *localhost* with the fully-qualified domain name of the machine running httpd. The default web page that is displayed is /usr/local/www/apache 24/data/index.html.

The Apache configuration can be tested for errors after making subsequent configuration changes while httpd is running using the following command:

```
# service apache 24 configtest
```

Note

It is important to note that configtest is not an rc(8) standard, and should not be expected to work for all startup scripts.

28.8.2. Virtual Hosting

Virtual hosting allows multiple websites to run on one Apache server. The virtual hosts can be *IP-based* or *name-based*. IP-based virtual hosting uses a different IP address for each website. Name-based virtual hosting uses the clients HTTP/1.1 headers to figure out the hostname, which allows the websites to share the same IP address.

To setup Apache to use name-based virtual hosting, add a VirtualHost block for each website. For example, for the webserver named www.domain.tld with a virtual domain of www.someotherdomain.tld, add the following entries to httpd.conf :

```
<VirtualHost *>
    ServerName www.domain.tld
    DocumentRoot /www/domain.tld
</VirtualHost>

<VirtualHost *>
    ServerName www.someotherdomain.tld
    DocumentRoot /www/someotherdomain.tld
```

```
</VirtualHost>
```

For each virtual host, replace the values for ServerName and DocumentRoot with the values to be used.

For more information about setting up virtual hosts, consult the official Apache documentation at: http://httpd.apache.org/docs/vhosts/ .

28.8.3. Apache Modules

Apache uses modules to augment the functionality provided by the basic server. Refer to http://httpd.apache.org/docs/current/mod/ for a complete listing of and the configuration details for the available modules.

In FreeBSD, some modules can be compiled with the www/apache24 port. Type make config within /usr/ports/www/apache24 to see which modules are available and which are enabled by default. If the module is not compiled with the port, the FreeBSD Ports Collection provides an easy way to install many modules. This section describes three of the most commonly used modules.

28.8.3.1. mod_ssl

The mod_ssl module uses the OpenSSL library to provide strong cryptography via the Secure Sockets Layer (SSLv3) and Transport Layer Security (TLSv1) protocols. This module provides everything necessary to request a signed certificate from a trusted certificate signing authority to run a secure web server on FreeBSD.

In FreeBSD, mod_ssl module is enabled by default in both the package and the port. The available configuration directives are explained at http://httpd.apache.org/docs/current/mod/mod_ssl.html .

28.8.3.2. mod_perl

The mod_perl module makes it possible to write Apache modules in Perl. In addition, the persistent interpreter embedded in the server avoids the overhead of starting an external interpreter and the penalty of Perl start-up time.

The mod_perl can be installed using the www/mod_perl2 package or port. Documentation for using this module can be found at http://perl.apache.org/docs/2.0/index.html .

28.8.3.3. mod_php

Written by Tom Rhodes.

PHP: Hypertext Preprocessor (PHP) is a general-purpose scripting language that is especially suited for web development. Capable of being embedded into HTML, its syntax draws upon C, Java™, and Perl with the intention of allowing web developers to write dynamically generated webpages quickly.

To gain support for PHP5 for the Apache web server, install the www/mod_php56 package or port. This will install and configure the modules required to support dynamic PHP applications. The installation will automatically add this line to /usr/local/etc/apache2 4/httpd.conf :

```
LoadModule php5_module          libexec/apache24/libphp5.so
```

Then, perform a graceful restart to load the PHP module:

```
# apachectl graceful
```

The PHP support provided by www/mod_php56 is limited. Additional support can be installed using the lang/php56-extensions port which provides a menu driven interface to the available PHP extensions.

Alternatively, individual extensions can be installed using the appropriate port. For instance, to add PHP support for the MySQL database server, install databases/php56-mysql.

After installing an extension, the Apache server must be reloaded to pick up the new configuration changes:

```
# apachectl graceful
```

28.8.4. Dynamic Websites

In addition to mod_perl and mod_php, other languages are available for creating dynamic web content. These include Django and Ruby on Rails.

28.8.4.1. Django

Django is a BSD-licensed framework designed to allow developers to write high performance, elegant web applications quickly. It provides an object-relational mapper so that data types are developed as Python objects. A rich dynamic database-access API is provided for those objects without the developer ever having to write SQL. It also provides an extensible template system so that the logic of the application is separated from the HTML presentation.

Django depends on mod_python , and an SQL database engine. In FreeBSD, the www/py-django port automatically installs mod_python and supports the PostgreSQL, MySQL, or SQLite databases, with the default being SQLite. To change the database engine, type make config within /usr/ports/www/py-django , then install the port.

Once Django is installed, the application will need a project directory along with the Apache configuration in order to use the embedded Python interpreter. This interpreter is used to call the application for specific URLs on the site.

To configure Apache to pass requests for certain URLs to the web application, add the following to httpd.conf , specifying the full path to the project directory:

```
<Location "/">
    SetHandler python-program
    PythonPath "['/dir/to/the/django/packages/ '] + sys.path"
    PythonHandler django.core.handlers.modpython
    SetEnv DJANGO_SETTINGS_MODULE mysite.settings
    PythonAutoReload On
    PythonDebug On
</Location>
```

Refer to https://docs.djangoproject.com for more information on how to use Django.

28.8.4.2. Ruby on Rails

Ruby on Rails is another open source web framework that provides a full development stack. It is optimized to make web developers more productive and capable of writing powerful applications quickly. On FreeBSD, it can be installed using the www/rubygem-rails package or port.

Refer to http://guides.rubyonrails.org for more information on how to use Ruby on Rails.

28.9. File Transfer Protocol (FTP)

The File Transfer Protocol (FTP) provides users with a simple way to transfer files to and from an FTP server. FreeBSD includes FTP server software, ftpd, in the base system.

FreeBSD provides several configuration files for controlling access to the FTP server. This section summarizes these files. Refer to ftpd(8) for more details about the built-in FTP server.

28.9.1. Configuration

The most important configuration step is deciding which accounts will be allowed access to the FTP server. A FreeBSD system has a number of system accounts which should not be allowed FTP access. The list of users disallowed any FTP access can be found in `/etc/ftpusers`. By default, it includes system accounts. Additional users that should not be allowed access to FTP can be added.

In some cases it may be desirable to restrict the access of some users without preventing them completely from using FTP. This can be accomplished be creating `/etc/ftpchroot` as described in ftpchroot(5). This file lists users and groups subject to FTP access restrictions.

To enable anonymous FTP access to the server, create a user named `ftp` on the FreeBSD system. Users will then be able to log on to the FTP server with a username of `ftp` or `anonymous`. When prompted for the password, any input will be accepted, but by convention, an email address should be used as the password. The FTP server will call chroot(2) when an anonymous user logs in, to restrict access to only the home directory of the `ftp` user.

There are two text files that can be created to specify welcome messages to be displayed to FTP clients. The contents of `/etc/ftpwelcome` will be displayed to users before they reach the login prompt. After a successful login, the contents of `/etc/ftpmotd` will be displayed. Note that the path to this file is relative to the login environment, so the contents of `~ftp/etc/ftpmotd` would be displayed for anonymous users.

Once the FTP server has been configured, set the appropriate variable in `/etc/rc.conf` to start the service during boot:

```
ftpd_enable="YES"
```

To start the service now:

```
# service ftpd start
```

Test the connection to the FTP server by typing:

```
% ftp localhost
```

The ftpd daemon uses syslog(3) to log messages. By default, the system log daemon will write messages related to FTP in `/var/log/xferlog`. The location of the FTP log can be modified by changing the following line in `/etc/syslog.conf`:

```
ftp.info        /var/log/xferlog
```

Note

Be aware of the potential problems involved with running an anonymous FTP server. In particular, think twice about allowing anonymous users to upload files. It may turn out that the FTP site becomes a forum for the trade of unlicensed commercial software or worse. If anonymous FTP uploads are required, then verify the permissions so that these files cannot be read by other anonymous users until they have been reviewed by an administrator.

28.10. File and Print Services for Microsoft® Windows® Clients (Samba)

Samba is a popular open source software package that provides file and print services using the SMB/CIFS protocol. This protocol is built into Microsoft® Windows® systems. It can be added to non-Microsoft® Windows® systems by installing the Samba client libraries. The protocol allows clients to access shared data and printers. These shares can be mapped as a local disk drive and shared printers can be used as if they were local printers.

On FreeBSD, the Samba client libraries can be installed using the net/samba-smbclient port or package. The client provides the ability for a FreeBSD system to access SMB/CIFS shares in a Microsoft® Windows® network.

A FreeBSD system can also be configured to act as a Samba server by installing the net/samba46 port or package. This allows the administrator to create SMB/CIFS shares on the FreeBSD system which can be accessed by clients running Microsoft® Windows® or the Samba client libraries.

28.10.1. Server Configuration

Samba is configured in /usr/local/etc/smb4.conf . This file must be created before Samba can be used.

A simple smb4.conf to share directories and printers with Windows® clients in a workgroup is shown here. For more complex setups involving LDAP or Active Directory, it is easier to use samba-tool(8) to create the initial smb4.conf.

```
[global]
workgroup = WORKGROUP
server string = Samba Server Version %v
netbios name = ExampleMachine
wins support = Yes
security = user
passdb backend = tdbsam

# Example: share /usr/src accessible only to 'developer' user
[src]
path = /usr/src
valid users = developer
writable  = yes
browsable = yes
read only = no
guest ok = no
public = no
create mask = 0666
directory mask = 0755
```

28.10.1.1. Global Settings

Settings that describe the network are added in /usr/local/etc/smb4.conf :

workgroup
> The name of the workgroup to be served.

netbios name
> The NetBIOS name by which a Samba server is known. By default, it is the same as the first component of the host's DNS name.

server string
> The string that will be displayed in the output of net view and some other networking tools that seek to display descriptive text about the server.

wins support
> Whether Samba will act as a WINS server. Do not enable support for WINS on more than one server on the network.

28.10.1.2. Security Settings

The most important settings in /usr/local/etc/smb4.conf are the security model and the backend password format. These directives control the options:

security
> The most common settings are security = share and security = user. If the clients use usernames that are the same as their usernames on the FreeBSD machine, user level security should be used. This is the default security policy and it requires clients to first log on before they can access shared resources.
>
> In share level security, clients do not need to log onto the server with a valid username and password before attempting to connect to a shared resource. This was the default security model for older versions of Samba.

passdb backend

> Samba has several different backend authentication models. Clients may be authenticated with LDAP, NIS +, an SQL database, or a modified password file. The recommended authentication method, tdbsam, is ideal for simple networks and is covered here. For larger or more complex networks, ldapsam is recommended. smbpasswd was the former default and is now obsolete.

28.10.1.3. Samba Users

FreeBSD user accounts must be mapped to the SambaSAMAccount database for Windows® clients to access the share. Map existing FreeBSD user accounts using pdbedit(8):

```
# pdbedit -a username
```

This section has only mentioned the most commonly used settings. Refer to the Official Samba HOWTO for additional information about the available configuration options.

28.10.2. Starting Samba

To enable Samba at boot time, add the following line to /etc/rc.conf :

```
samba_enable="YES"
```

To enable Samba4, use:

```
samba_server_enable="YES"
```

To start Samba now:

```
# service samba start
Starting SAMBA: removing stale tdbs :
Starting nmbd.
Starting smbd.
```

Samba consists of three separate daemons. Both the nmbd and smbd daemons are started by samba_enable. If winbind name resolution is also required, set:

```
winbindd_enable="YES"
```

Samba can be stopped at any time by typing:

```
# service samba stop
```

Samba is a complex software suite with functionality that allows broad integration with Microsoft® Windows® networks. For more information about functionality beyond the basic configuration described here, refer to http://www.samba.org .

28.11. Clock Synchronization with NTP

Over time, a computer's clock is prone to drift. This is problematic as many network services require the computers on a network to share the same accurate time. Accurate time is also needed to ensure that file timestamps stay consistent. The Network Time Protocol (NTP) is one way to provide clock accuracy in a network.

FreeBSD includes ntpd(8) which can be configured to query other NTP servers in order to synchronize the clock on that machine or to provide time services to other computers in the network. The servers which are queried can be local to the network or provided by an ISP. In addition, an online list of publicly accessible NTP servers is available. When choosing a public NTP server, select one that is geographically close and review its usage policy.

Choosing several NTP servers is recommended in case one of the servers becomes unreachable or its clock proves unreliable. As ntpd receives responses, it favors reliable servers over the less reliable ones.

This section describes how to configure ntpd on FreeBSD. Further documentation can be found in `/usr/share/doc/ntp/` in HTML format.

28.11.1. NTP Configuration

On FreeBSD, the built-in ntpd can be used to synchronize a system's clock. To enable ntpd at boot time, add `ntpd_enable="YES"` to `/etc/rc.conf`. Additional variables can be specified in `/etc/rc.conf`. Refer to rc.conf(5) and ntpd(8) for details.

This application reads `/etc/ntp.conf` to determine which NTP servers to query. Here is a simple example of an `/etc/ntp.conf`:

Example 28.4. Sample `/etc/ntp.conf`

```
server ntplocal.example.com prefer
server timeserver.example.org
server ntp2a.example.net

driftfile /var/db/ntp.drift
```

The format of this file is described in ntp.conf(5). The `server` option specifies which servers to query, with one server listed on each line. If a server entry includes `prefer`, that server is preferred over other servers. A response from a preferred server will be discarded if it differs significantly from other servers' responses; otherwise it will be used. The `prefer` argument should only be used for NTP servers that are known to be highly accurate, such as those with special time monitoring hardware.

The `driftfile` entry specifies which file is used to store the system clock's frequency offset. ntpd uses this to automatically compensate for the clock's natural drift, allowing it to maintain a reasonably correct setting even if it is cut off from all external time sources for a period of time. This file also stores information about previous responses from NTP servers. Since this file contains internal information for NTP, it should not be modified.

By default, an NTP server is accessible to any network host. The `restrict` option in `/etc/ntp.conf` can be used to control which systems can access the server. For example, to deny all machines from accessing the NTP server, add the following line to `/etc/ntp.conf`:

```
restrict default ignore
```

Note

This will also prevent access from other NTP servers. If there is a need to synchronize with an external NTP server, allow only that specific server. Refer to ntp.conf(5) for more information.

To allow machines within the network to synchronize their clocks with the server, but ensure they are not allowed to configure the server or be used as peers to synchronize against, instead use:

```
restrict 192.168.1.0 mask 255.255.255.0 nomodify notrap
```

where `192.168.1.0` is the local network address and `255.255.255.0` is the network's subnet mask.

Multiple `restrict` entries are supported. For more details, refer to the `Access Control Support` subsection of ntp.conf(5).

Once ntpd_enable="YES" has been added to /etc/rc.conf , ntpd can be started now without rebooting the system by typing:

```
# service ntpd start
```

28.11.2. Using NTP with a PPP Connection

ntpd does not need a permanent connection to the Internet to function properly. However, if a PPP connection is configured to dial out on demand, NTP traffic should be prevented from triggering a dial out or keeping the connection alive. This can be configured with filter directives in /etc/ppp/ppp.conf . For example:

```
set filter dial 0 deny udp src eq 123
# Prevent NTP traffic from initiating dial out
set filter dial 1 permit 0 0
set filter alive 0 deny udp src eq 123
# Prevent incoming NTP traffic from keeping the connection open
set filter alive 1 deny udp dst eq 123
# Prevent outgoing NTP traffic from keeping the connection open
set filter alive 2 permit 0/0 0/0
```

For more details, refer to the PACKET FILTERING section in ppp(8) and the examples in /usr/share/examples/ppp/ .

> **Note**
>
> Some Internet access providers block low-numbered ports, preventing NTP from functioning since replies never reach the machine.

28.12. iSCSI Initiator and Target Configuration

iSCSI is a way to share storage over a network. Unlike NFS, which works at the file system level, iSCSI works at the block device level.

In iSCSI terminology, the system that shares the storage is known as the *target*. The storage can be a physical disk, or an area representing multiple disks or a portion of a physical disk. For example, if the disk(s) are formatted with ZFS, a zvol can be created to use as the iSCSI storage.

The clients which access the iSCSI storage are called *initiators*. To initiators, the storage available through iSCSI appears as a raw, unformatted disk known as a LUN. Device nodes for the disk appear in /dev/ and the device must be separately formatted and mounted.

Beginning with 10.0-RELEASE, FreeBSD provides a native, kernel-based iSCSI target and initiator. This section describes how to configure a FreeBSD system as a target or an initiator.

28.12.1. Configuring an iSCSI Target

> **Note**
>
> The native iSCSI target is supported starting with FreeBSD 10.0-RELEASE. To use iSCSI in older versions of FreeBSD, install a userspace target from the Ports Collection, such as net/istgt. This chapter only describes the native target.

To configure an iSCSI target, create the /etc/ctl.conf configuration file, add a line to /etc/rc.conf to make sure the ctld(8) daemon is automatically started at boot, and then start the daemon.

The following is an example of a simple /etc/ctl.conf configuration file. Refer to ctl.conf(5) for a more complete description of this file's available options.

```
portal-group pg0 {
 discovery-auth-group no-authentication
 listen 0.0.0.0
 listen [::]
}

target iqn.2012-06.com.example:target0 {
 auth-group no-authentication
 portal-group pg0

 lun 0 {
  path /data/target0-0
  size 4G
 }
}
```

The first entry defines the pg0 portal group. Portal groups define which network addresses the ctld(8) daemon will listen on. The discovery-auth-group no-authentication entry indicates that any initiator is allowed to perform iSCSI target discovery without authentication. Lines three and four configure ctld(8) to listen on all IPv4 (listen 0.0.0.0) and IPv6 (listen [::]) addresses on the default port of 3260.

It is not necessary to define a portal group as there is a built-in portal group called default. In this case, the difference between default and pg0 is that with default, target discovery is always denied, while with pg0, it is always allowed.

The second entry defines a single target. Target has two possible meanings: a machine serving iSCSI or a named group of LUNs. This example uses the latter meaning, where iqn.2012-06.com.example:target0 is the target name. This target name is suitable for testing purposes. For actual use, change com.example to the real domain name, reversed. The 2012-06 represents the year and month of acquiring control of that domain name, and target0 can be any value. Any number of targets can be defined in this configuration file.

The auth-group no-authentication line allows all initiators to connect to the specified target and portal-group pg0 makes the target reachable through the pg0 portal group.

The next section defines the LUN. To the initiator, each LUN will be visible as a separate disk device. Multiple LUNs can be defined for each target. Each LUN is identified by a number, where LUN 0 is mandatory. The path /data/target0-0 line defines the full path to a file or zvol backing the LUN. That path must exist before starting ctld(8). The second line is optional and specifies the size of the LUN.

Next, to make sure the ctld(8) daemon is started at boot, add this line to /etc/rc.conf :

```
ctld_enable="YES"
```

To start ctld(8) now, run this command:

```
# service ctld start
```

As the ctld(8) daemon is started, it reads /etc/ctl.conf . If this file is edited after the daemon starts, use this command so that the changes take effect immediately:

```
# service ctld reload
```

28.12.1.1. Authentication

The previous example is inherently insecure as it uses no authentication, granting anyone full access to all targets. To require a username and password to access targets, modify the configuration as follows:

```
auth-group ag0 {
 chap username1 secretsecret
 chap username2 anothersecret
}

portal-group pg0 {
 discovery-auth-group no-authentication
 listen 0.0.0.0
 listen [::]
}

target iqn.2012-06.com.example:target0 {
 auth-group ag0
 portal-group pg0
 lun 0 {
  path /data/target0-0
  size 4G
 }
}
```

The `auth-group` section defines username and password pairs. An initiator trying to connect to `iqn.2012-06.com.example:target0` must first specify a defined username and secret. However, target discovery is still permitted without authentication. To require target discovery authentication, set `discovery-auth-group` to a defined `auth-group` name instead of `no-authentication`.

It is common to define a single exported target for every initiator. As a shorthand for the syntax above, the username and password can be specified directly in the target entry:

```
target iqn.2012-06.com.example:target0 {
 portal-group pg0
 chap username1 secretsecret

 lun 0 {
  path /data/target0-0
  size 4G
 }
}
```

28.12.2. Configuring an iSCSI Initiator

Note

The iSCSI initiator described in this section is supported starting with FreeBSD 10.0-RELEASE. To use the iSCSI initiator available in older versions, refer to iscontrol(8).

The iSCSI initiator requires that the iscsid(8) daemon is running. This daemon does not use a configuration file. To start it automatically at boot, add this line to `/etc/rc.conf` :

```
iscsid_enable="YES"
```

To start iscsid(8) now, run this command:

```
# service iscsid start
```

Connecting to a target can be done with or without an `/etc/iscsi.conf` configuration file. This section demonstrates both types of connections.

28.12.2.1. Connecting to a Target Without a Configuration File

To connect an initiator to a single target, specify the IP address of the portal and the name of the target:

```
# iscsictl -A -p 10.10.10.10 -t iqn.2012-06.com.example:target0
```

To verify if the connection succeeded, run `iscsictl` without any arguments. The output should look similar to this:

```
Target name                         Target portal  State
iqn.2012-06.com.example:target0     10.10.10.10    Connected: da0
```

In this example, the iSCSI session was successfully established, with `/dev/da0` representing the attached LUN. If the `iqn.2012-06.com.example:target0` target exports more than one LUN, multiple device nodes will be shown in that section of the output:

```
Connected: da0 da1 da2.
```

Any errors will be reported in the output, as well as the system logs. For example, this message usually means that the iscsid(8) daemon is not running:

```
Target name                         Target portal  State
iqn.2012-06.com.example:target0     10.10.10.10    Waiting for iscsid(8)
```

The following message suggests a networking problem, such as a wrong IP address or port:

```
Target name                         Target portal  State
iqn.2012-06.com.example:target0     10.10.10.11    Connection refused
```

This message means that the specified target name is wrong:

```
Target name                         Target portal  State
iqn.2012-06.com.example:target0     10.10.10.10    Not found
```

This message means that the target requires authentication:

```
Target name                         Target portal  State
iqn.2012-06.com.example:target0     10.10.10.10    Authentication failed
```

To specify a CHAP username and secret, use this syntax:

```
# iscsictl -A -p 10.10.10.10 -t iqn.2012-06.com.example:target0  -u user -s secretsecret
```

28.12.2.2. Connecting to a Target with a Configuration File

To connect using a configuration file, create `/etc/iscsi.conf` with contents like this:

```
t0 {
  TargetAddress    = 10.10.10.10
  TargetName       = iqn.2012-06.com.example:target0
  AuthMethod       = CHAP
  chapIName        = user
  chapSecret       = secretsecret
}
```

The `t0` specifies a nickname for the configuration file section. It will be used by the initiator to specify which configuration to use. The other lines specify the parameters to use during connection. The `TargetAddress` and `TargetName` are mandatory, whereas the other options are optional. In this example, the CHAP username and secret are shown.

To connect to the defined target, specify the nickname:

```
# iscsictl -An t0
```

Alternately, to connect to all targets defined in the configuration file, use:

```
# iscsictl -Aa
```

To make the initiator automatically connect to all targets in `/etc/iscsi.conf`, add the following to `/etc/rc.conf`:

```
iscsictl_enable="YES"
iscsictl_flags="-Aa"
```

Chapter 29. Firewalls

Contributed by Joseph J. Barbish.
Converted to SGML and updated by Brad Davis.

29.1. Synopsis

Firewalls make it possible to filter the incoming and outgoing traffic that flows through a system. A firewall can use one or more sets of "rules" to inspect network packets as they come in or go out of network connections and either allows the traffic through or blocks it. The rules of a firewall can inspect one or more characteristics of the packets such as the protocol type, source or destination host address, and source or destination port.

Firewalls can enhance the security of a host or a network. They can be used to do one or more of the following:

- Protect and insulate the applications, services, and machines of an internal network from unwanted traffic from the public Internet.

- Limit or disable access from hosts of the internal network to services of the public Internet.

- Support network address translation (NAT), which allows an internal network to use private IP addresses and share a single connection to the public Internet using either a single IP address or a shared pool of automatically assigned public addresses.

FreeBSD has three firewalls built into the base system: PF, IPFW, and IPFILTER, also known as IPF. FreeBSD also provides two traffic shapers for controlling bandwidth usage: altq(4) and dummynet(4). ALTQ has traditionally been closely tied with PF and dummynet with IPFW. Each firewall uses rules to control the access of packets to and from a FreeBSD system, although they go about it in different ways and each has a different rule syntax.

FreeBSD provides multiple firewalls in order to meet the different requirements and preferences for a wide variety of users. Each user should evaluate which firewall best meets their needs.

After reading this chapter, you will know:

- How to define packet filtering rules.

- The differences between the firewalls built into FreeBSD.

- How to use and configure the PF firewall.

- How to use and configure the IPFW firewall.

- How to use and configure the IPFILTER firewall.

Before reading this chapter, you should:

- Understand basic FreeBSD and Internet concepts.

 Note

Since all firewalls are based on inspecting the values of selected packet control fields, the creator of the firewall ruleset must have an understanding of how TCP/IP works, what the different values in the packet control fields are, and how these values are used in a normal session conversation. For a good introduction, refer to Daryl's TCP/IP Primer.

29.2. Firewall Concepts

A ruleset contains a group of rules which pass or block packets based on the values contained in the packet. The bi-directional exchange of packets between hosts comprises a session conversation. The firewall ruleset processes both the packets arriving from the public Internet, as well as the packets produced by the system as a response to them. Each TCP/IP service is predefined by its protocol and listening port. Packets destined for a specific service originate from the source address using an unprivileged port and target the specific service port on the destination address. All the above parameters can be used as selection criteria to create rules which will pass or block services.

To lookup unknown port numbers, refer to `/etc/services`. Alternatively, visit `http://en.wikipedia.org/wiki/List_of_TCP_and_UDP_port_numbers` and do a port number lookup to find the purpose of a particular port number.

Check out this link for port numbers used by Trojans `http://www.sans.org/security-resources/idfaq/odd-ports.php`.

FTP has two modes: active mode and passive mode. The difference is in how the data channel is acquired. Passive mode is more secure as the data channel is acquired by the ordinal ftp session requester. For a good explanation of FTP and the different modes, see `http://www.slacksite.com/other/ftp.html`.

A firewall ruleset can be either "exclusive" or "inclusive". An exclusive firewall allows all traffic through except for the traffic matching the ruleset. An inclusive firewall does the reverse as it only allows traffic matching the rules through and blocks everything else.

An inclusive firewall offers better control of the outgoing traffic, making it a better choice for systems that offer services to the public Internet. It also controls the type of traffic originating from the public Internet that can gain access to a private network. All traffic that does not match the rules is blocked and logged. Inclusive firewalls are generally safer than exclusive firewalls because they significantly reduce the risk of allowing unwanted traffic.

> ### Note
>
> Unless noted otherwise, all configuration and example rulesets in this chapter create inclusive firewall rulesets.

Security can be tightened further using a "stateful firewall". This type of firewall keeps track of open connections and only allows traffic which either matches an existing connection or opens a new, allowed connection.

Stateful filtering treats traffic as a bi-directional exchange of packets comprising a session. When state is specified on a matching rule the firewall dynamically generates internal rules for each anticipated packet being exchanged during the session. It has sufficient matching capabilities to determine if a packet is valid for a session. Any packets that do not properly fit the session template are automatically rejected.

When the session completes, it is removed from the dynamic state table.

Stateful filtering allows one to focus on blocking/passing new sessions. If the new session is passed, all its subsequent packets are allowed automatically and any impostor packets are automatically rejected. If a new session is blocked, none of its subsequent packets are allowed. Stateful filtering provides advanced matching abilities capable of defending against the flood of different attack methods employed by attackers.

NAT stands for *Network Address Translation*. NAT function enables the private LAN behind the firewall to share a single ISP-assigned IP address, even if that address is dynamically assigned. NAT allows each computer in the LAN to have Internet access, without having to pay the ISP for multiple Internet accounts or IP addresses.

NAT will automatically translate the private LAN IP address for each system on the LAN to the single public IP address as packets exit the firewall bound for the public Internet. It also performs the reverse translation for returning packets.

According to RFC 1918, the following IP address ranges are reserved for private networks which will never be routed directly to the public Internet, and therefore are available for use with NAT:

- `10.0.0.0/8` .

- `172.16.0.0/12` .

- `192.168.0.0/16` .

Warning

When working with the firewall rules, be *very careful*. Some configurations *can lock the administrator out* of the server. To be on the safe side, consider performing the initial firewall configuration from the local console rather than doing it remotely over ssh.

29.3. PF

Revised and updated by John Ferrell.

Since FreeBSD 5.3, a ported version of OpenBSD's PF firewall has been included as an integrated part of the base system. PF is a complete, full-featured firewall that has optional support for ALTQ (Alternate Queuing), which provides Quality of Service (QoS).

The OpenBSD Project maintains the definitive reference for PF in the PF FAQ. Peter Hansteen maintains a thorough PF tutorial at http://home.nuug.no/~peter/pf/.

Warning

When reading the PF FAQ, keep in mind that FreeBSD uses the same version of PF as Open-BSD 4.5.

The FreeBSD packet filter mailing list is a good place to ask questions about configuring and running the PF firewall. Check the mailing list archives before asking a question as it may have already been answered.

More information about porting PF to FreeBSD can be found at http://pf4freebsd.love2party.net/ .

This section of the Handbook focuses on PF as it pertains to FreeBSD. It demonstrates how to enable PF and ALTQ. It then provides several examples for creating rulesets on a FreeBSD system.

29.3.1. Enabling PF

In order to use PF, its kernel module must be first loaded. This section describes the entries that can be added to `/etc/rc.conf` in order to enable PF.

Start by adding the following line to `/etc/rc.conf` :

```
pf_enable="YES"
```

Additional options, described in pfctl(8), can be passed to PF when it is started. Add this entry to `/etc/rc.conf` and specify any required flags between the two quotes (""):

```
pf_flags=""                    # additional flags for pfctl startup
```

PF will not start if it cannot find its ruleset configuration file. The default ruleset is already created and is named /etc/pf.conf . If a custom ruleset has been saved somewhere else, add a line to /etc/rc.conf which specifies the full path to the file:

```
pf_rules="/path/to/pf.conf "
```

Logging support for PF is provided by pflog(4). To enable logging support, add this line to /etc/rc.conf :

```
pflog_enable="YES"
```

The following lines can also be added in order to change the default location of the log file or to specify any additional flags to pass to pflog(4) when it is started:

```
pflog_logfile="/var/log/pflog"  # where pflogd should store the logfile
pflog_flags=""                  # additional flags for pflogd startup
```

Finally, if there is a LAN behind the firewall and packets need to be forwarded for the computers on the LAN, or NAT is required, add the following option:

```
gateway_enable="YES"            # Enable as LAN gateway
```

After saving the needed edits, PF can be started with logging support by typing:

```
# service pf start
# service pflog start
```

By default, PF reads its configuration rules from /etc/pf.conf and modifies, drops, or passes packets according to the rules or definitions specified in this file. The FreeBSD installation includes several sample files located in /usr/share/examples/pf/ . Refer to the PF FAQ for complete coverage of PF rulesets.

To control PF, use pfctl. Table 29.1, "Useful pfctl Options" summarizes some useful options to this command. Refer to pfctl(8) for a description of all available options:

Table 29.1. Useful pfctl Options

Command	Purpose
pfctl -e	Enable PF.
pfctl -d	Disable PF.
pfctl -F all -f /etc/pf.conf	Flush all NAT, filter, state, and table rules and reload /etc/pf.conf .
pfctl -s [rules | nat | states]	Report on the filter rules, NAT rules, or state table.
pfctl -vnf /etc/pf.conf	Check /etc/pf.conf for errors, but do not load ruleset.

Tip

security/sudo is useful for running commands like pfctl that require elevated privileges. It can be installed from the Ports Collection.

To keep an eye on the traffic that passes through the PF firewall, consider installing the sysutils/pftop package or port. Once installed, pftop can be run to view a running snapshot of traffic in a format which is similar to top(1).

29.3.2. Enabling ALTQ

On FreeBSD, ALTQ can be used with PF to provide Quality of Service (QOS). Once ALTQ is enabled, queues can be defined in the ruleset which determine the processing priority of outbound packets.

Before enabling ALTQ, refer to altq(4) to determine if the drivers for the network cards installed on the system support it.

ALTQ is not available as a loadable kernel module. If the system's interfaces support ALTQ, create a custom kernel using the instructions in Chapter 8, *Configuring the FreeBSD Kernel*. The following kernel options are available. The first is needed to enable ALTQ. At least one of the other options is necessary to specify the queueing scheduler algorithm:

```
options       ALTQ
options       ALTQ_CBQ       # Class Based Queuing (CBQ)
options       ALTQ_RED       # Random Early Detection (RED)
options       ALTQ_RIO       # RED In/Out
options       ALTQ_HFSC      # Hierarchical Packet Scheduler (HFSC)
options       ALTQ_PRIQ      # Priority Queuing (PRIQ)
```

The following scheduler algorithms are available:

CBQ

Class Based Queuing (CBQ) is used to divide a connection's bandwidth into different classes or queues to prioritize traffic based on filter rules.

RED

Random Early Detection (RED) is used to avoid network congestion by measuring the length of the queue and comparing it to the minimum and maximum thresholds for the queue. When the queue is over the maximum, all new packets are randomly dropped.

RIO

In Random Early Detection In and Out (RIO) mode, RED maintains multiple average queue lengths and multiple threshold values, one for each QOS level.

HFSC

Hierarchical Fair Service Curve Packet Scheduler (HFSC) is described in `http://www-2.cs.cmu.edu/~hzhang/HFSC/main.html` .

PRIQ

Priority Queuing (PRIQ) always passes traffic that is in a higher queue first.

More information about the scheduling algorithms and example rulesets are available at `http://www.openbsd.org/faq/pf/queueing.html` .

29.3.3. PF Rulesets

Contributed by Peter N. M. Hansteen.

This section demonstrates how to create a customized ruleset. It starts with the simplest of rulesets and builds upon its concepts using several examples to demonstrate real-world usage of PF's many features.

The simplest possible ruleset is for a single machine that does not run any services and which needs access to one network, which may be the Internet. To create this minimal ruleset, edit `/etc/pf.conf` so it looks like this:

```
block in all
pass out all keep state
```

The first rule denies all incoming traffic by default. The second rule allows connections created by this system to pass out, while retaining state information on those connections. This state information allows return traffic for those connections to pass back and should only be used on machines that can be trusted. The ruleset can be loaded with:

```
# pfctl -e -; pfctl -f /etc/pf.conf
```

In addition to keeping state, PF provides *lists* and *macros* which can be defined for use when creating rules. Macros can include lists and need to be defined before use. As an example, insert these lines at the very top of the ruleset:

```
tcp_services = "{ ssh, smtp, domain, www, pop3, auth, pop3s }"
udp_services = "{ domain }"
```

PF understands port names as well as port numbers, as long as the names are listed in /etc/services . This example creates two macros. The first is a list of seven TCP port names and the second is one UDP port name. Once defined, macros can be used in rules. In this example, all traffic is blocked except for the connections initiated by this system for the seven specified TCP services and the one specified UDP service:

```
tcp_services = "{ ssh, smtp, domain, www, pop3, auth, pop3s }"
udp_services = "{ domain }"
block all
pass out proto tcp to any port $tcp_services keep state
pass proto udp to any port $udp_services keep state
```

Even though UDP is considered to be a stateless protocol, PF is able to track some state information. For example, when a UDP request is passed which asks a name server about a domain name, PF will watch for the response in order to pass it back.

Whenever an edit is made to a ruleset, the new rules must be loaded so they can be used:

```
# pfctl -f /etc/pf.conf
```

If there are no syntax errors, pfctl will not output any messages during the rule load. Rules can also be tested before attempting to load them:

```
# pfctl -nf /etc/pf.conf
```

Including -n causes the rules to be interpreted only, but not loaded. This provides an opportunity to correct any errors. At all times, the last valid ruleset loaded will be enforced until either PF is disabled or a new ruleset is loaded.

> **Tip**
>
> Adding -v to a pfctl ruleset verify or load will display the fully parsed rules exactly the way they will be loaded. This is extremely useful when debugging rules.

29.3.3.1. A Simple Gateway with NAT

This section demonstrates how to configure a FreeBSD system running PF to act as a gateway for at least one other machine. The gateway needs at least two network interfaces, each connected to a separate network. In this example, xl1 is connected to the Internet and xl0 is connected to the internal network.

First, enable the gateway in order to let the machine forward the network traffic it receives on one interface to another interface. This sysctl setting will forward IPv4 packets:

```
# sysctl net.inet.ip.forwarding=1
```

To forward IPv6 traffic, use:

```
# sysctl net.inet6.ip6.forwarding=1
```

To enable these settings at system boot, add the following to /etc/rc.conf :

```
gateway_enable="YES"  #for ipv4
ipv6_gateway_enable="YES" #for ipv6
```

Verify with ifconfig that both of the interfaces are up and running.

Next, create the PF rules to allow the gateway to pass traffic. While the following rule allows stateful traffic to pass from the Internet to hosts on the network, the to keyword does not guarantee passage all the way from source to destination:

```
pass in on xl1 from xl1:network to xl0:network port $ports keep state
```

That rule only lets the traffic pass in to the gateway on the internal interface. To let the packets go further, a matching rule is needed:

```
pass out on xl0 from xl1:network to xl0:network port $ports keep state
```

While these two rules will work, rules this specific are rarely needed. For a busy network admin, a readable ruleset is a safer ruleset. The remainder of this section demonstrates how to keep the rules as simple as possible for readability. For example, those two rules could be replaced with one rule:

```
pass from xl1:network to any port $ports keep state
```

The interface:network notation can be replaced with a macro to make the ruleset even more readable. For example, a $localnet macro could be defined as the network directly attached to the internal interface ($xl1:network). Alternatively, the definition of $localnet could be changed to an *IP address/netmask* notation to denote a network, such as 192.168.100.1/24 for a subnet of private addresses.

If required, $localnet could even be defined as a list of networks. Whatever the specific needs, a sensible $localnet definition could be used in a typical pass rule as follows:

```
pass from $localnet to any port $ports keep state
```

The following sample ruleset allows all traffic initiated by machines on the internal network. It first defines two macros to represent the external and internal 3COM interfaces of the gateway.

Note

For dialup users, the external interface will use tun0. For an ADSL connection, specifically those using PPP over Ethernet (PPPoE), the correct external interface is tun0, not the physical Ethernet interface.

```
ext_if = "xl0" # macro for external interface - use tun0 for PPPoE
int_if = "xl1" # macro for internal interface
localnet = $int_if:network
# ext_if IP address could be dynamic, hence ($ext_if)
nat on $ext_if from $localnet to any -> ($ext_if)
block all
pass from { lo0, $localnet } to any keep state
```

This ruleset introduces the nat rule which is used to handle the network address translation from the non-routable addresses inside the internal network to the IP address assigned to the external interface. The parentheses surrounding the last part of the nat rule ($ext_if) is included when the IP address of the external interface is dynamically assigned. It ensures that network traffic runs without serious interruptions even if the external IP address changes.

Note that this ruleset probably allows more traffic to pass out of the network than is needed. One reasonable setup could create this macro:

```
client_out = "{ ftp-data, ftp, ssh, domain, pop3, auth, nntp, http, \
    https, cvspserver, 2628, 5999, 8000, 8080 }"
```

to use in the main pass rule:

```
pass inet proto tcp from $localnet to any port $client_out \
    flags S/SA keep state
```

A few other pass rules may be needed. This one enables SSH on the external interface::

```
pass in inet proto tcp to $ext_if port ssh
```

This macro definition and rule allows DNS and NTP for internal clients:

```
udp_services = "{ domain, ntp }"
pass quick inet proto { tcp, udp } to any port $udp_services keep state
```

Note the `quick` keyword in this rule. Since the ruleset consists of several rules, it is important to understand the relationships between the rules in a ruleset. Rules are evaluated from top to bottom, in the sequence they are written. For each packet or connection evaluated by PF, *the last matching rule* in the ruleset is the one which is applied. However, when a packet matches a rule which contains the `quick` keyword, the rule processing stops and the packet is treated according to that rule. This is very useful when an exception to the general rules is needed.

29.3.3.2. Creating an FTP Proxy

Configuring working FTP rules can be problematic due to the nature of the FTP protocol. FTP pre-dates firewalls by several decades and is insecure in its design. The most common points against using FTP include:

• Passwords are transferred in the clear.

• The protocol demands the use of at least two TCP connections (control and data) on separate ports.

• When a session is established, data is communicated using randomly selected ports.

All of these points present security challenges, even before considering any potential security weaknesses in client or server software. More secure alternatives for file transfer exist, such as sftp(1) or scp(1), which both feature authentication and data transfer over encrypted connections..

For those situations when FTP is required, PF provides redirection of FTP traffic to a small proxy program called ftp-proxy(8), which is included in the base system of FreeBSD. The role of the proxy is to dynamically insert and delete rules in the ruleset, using a set of anchors, in order to correctly handle FTP traffic.

To enable the FTP proxy, add this line to `/etc/rc.conf` :

```
ftpproxy_enable="YES"
```

Then start the proxy by running `service ftp-proxy start` .

For a basic configuration, three elements need to be added to `/etc/pf.conf` . First, the anchors which the proxy will use to insert the rules it generates for the FTP sessions:

```
nat-anchor "ftp-proxy/*"
rdr-anchor "ftp-proxy/*"
```

Second, a pass rule is needed to allow FTP traffic in to the proxy.

Third, redirection and NAT rules need to be defined before the filtering rules. Insert this `rdr` rule immediately after the `nat` rule:

```
rdr pass on $int_if proto tcp from any to any port ftp -> 127.0.0.1 port 8021
```

Finally, allow the redirected traffic to pass:

```
pass out proto tcp from $proxy to any port ftp
```

where `$proxy` expands to the address the proxy daemon is bound to.

Save `/etc/pf.conf` , load the new rules, and verify from a client that FTP connections are working:

```
# pfctl -f /etc/pf.conf
```

This example covers a basic setup where the clients in the local network need to contact FTP servers elsewhere. This basic configuration should work well with most combinations of FTP clients and servers. As shown in ftp-proxy(8), the proxy's behavior can be changed in various ways by adding options to the `ftpproxy_flags=` line. Some clients or servers may have specific quirks that must be compensated for in the configuration, or there may be a need to integrate the proxy in specific ways such as assigning FTP traffic to a specific queue.

For ways to run an FTP server protected by PF and ftp-proxy(8), configure a separate `ftp-proxy` in reverse mode, using -R, on a separate port with its own redirecting pass rule.

29.3.3.3. Managing ICMP

Many of the tools used for debugging or troubleshooting a TCP/IP network rely on the Internet Control Message Protocol (ICMP), which was designed specifically with debugging in mind.

The ICMP protocol sends and receives *control messages* between hosts and gateways, mainly to provide feedback to a sender about any unusual or difficult conditions enroute to the target host. Routers use ICMP to negotiate packet sizes and other transmission parameters in a process often referred to as *path MTU discovery*.

From a firewall perspective, some ICMP control messages are vulnerable to known attack vectors. Also, letting all diagnostic traffic pass unconditionally makes debugging easier, but it also makes it easier for others to extract information about the network. For these reasons, the following rule may not be optimal:

```
pass inet proto icmp from any to any
```

One solution is to let all ICMP traffic from the local network through while stopping all probes from outside the network:

```
pass inet proto icmp from $localnet to any keep state
pass inet proto icmp from any to $ext_if keep state
```

Additional options are available which demonstrate some of PF's flexibility. For example, rather than allowing all ICMP messages, one can specify the messages used by ping(8) and traceroute(8). Start by defining a macro for that type of message:

```
icmp_types = "echoreq"
```

and a rule which uses the macro:

```
pass inet proto icmp all icmp-type $icmp_types keep state
```

If other types of ICMP packets are needed, expand `icmp_types` to a list of those packet types. Type `more /usr/src/contrib/pf/pfctl/pfctl_parser.c` to see the list of ICMP message types supported by PF. Refer to http://www.iana.org/assignments/icmp-parameters/icmp-parameters.xhtml for an explanation of each message type.

Since Unix `traceroute` uses UDP by default, another rule is needed to allow Unix `traceroute`:

```
# allow out the default range for traceroute(8):
pass out on $ext_if inet proto udp from any to any port 33433 >< 33626 keep state
```

Since TRACERT.EXE on Microsoft Windows systems uses ICMP echo request messages, only the first rule is needed to allow network traces from those systems. Unix `traceroute` can be instructed to use other protocols as well, and will use ICMP echo request messages if -I is used. Check the traceroute(8) man page for details.

29.3.3.3.1. Path MTU Discovery

Internet protocols are designed to be device independent, and one consequence of device independence is that the optimal packet size for a given connection cannot always be predicted reliably. The main constraint on packet size is the *Maximum Transmission Unit* (MTU) which sets the upper limit on the packet size for an interface. Type `ifconfig` to view the MTUs for a system's network interfaces.

TCP/IP uses a process known as path MTU discovery to determine the right packet size for a connection. This process sends packets of varying sizes with the "Do not fragment" flag set, expecting an ICMP return packet of "type 3, code 4" when the upper limit has been reached. Type 3 means "destination unreachable", and code 4 is short for "fragmentation needed, but the do-not-fragment flag is set". To allow path MTU discovery in order to support connections to other MTUs, add the destination unreachable type to the icmp_types macro:

```
icmp_types = "{ echoreq, unreach }"
```

Since the pass rule already uses that macro, it does not need to be modified in order to support the new ICMP type:

```
pass inet proto icmp all icmp-type $icmp_types keep state
```

PF allows filtering on all variations of ICMP types and codes. The list of possible types and codes are documented in icmp(4) and icmp6(4).

29.3.3.4. Using Tables

Some types of data are relevant to filtering and redirection at a given time, but their definition is too long to be included in the ruleset file. PF supports the use of tables, which are defined lists that can be manipulated without needing to reload the entire ruleset, and which can provide fast lookups. Table names are always enclosed within < >, like this:

```
table <clients> { 192.168.2.0/24, !192.168.2.5 }
```

In this example, the 192.168.2.0/24 network is part of the table, except for the address 192.168.2.5, which is excluded using the ! operator. It is also possible to load tables from files where each item is on a separate line, as seen in this example /etc/clients :

```
192.168.2.0/24
!192.168.2.5
```

To refer to the file, define the table like this:

```
table <clients> persist file "/etc/clients"
```

Once the table is defined, it can be referenced by a rule:

```
pass inet proto tcp from <clients> to any port $client_out flags S/SA keep state
```

A table's contents can be manipulated live, using pfctl. This example adds another network to the table:

```
# pfctl -t clients -T add 192.168.1.0/16
```

Note that any changes made this way will take affect now, making them ideal for testing, but will not survive a power failure or reboot. To make the changes permanent, modify the definition of the table in the ruleset or edit the file that the table refers to. One can maintain the on-disk copy of the table using a cron(8) job which dumps the table's contents to disk at regular intervals, using a command such as pfctl -t clients -T show >/etc/clients. Alternatively, /etc/clients can be updated with the in-memory table contents:

```
# pfctl -t clients -T replace -f /etc/clients
```

29.3.3.5. Using Overload Tables to Protect SSH

Those who run SSH on an external interface have probably seen something like this in the authentication logs:

```
Sep 26 03:12:34 skapet sshd[25771]: Failed password for root from 200.72.41.31 port ↺
40992 ssh2
Sep 26 03:12:34 skapet sshd[5279]: Failed password for root from 200.72.41.31 port ↺
40992 ssh2
Sep 26 03:12:35 skapet sshd[5279]: Received disconnect from 200.72.41.31: 11: Bye Bye
Sep 26 03:12:44 skapet sshd[29635]: Invalid user admin from 200.72.41.31
Sep 26 03:12:44 skapet sshd[24703]: input_userauth_request: invalid user admin
Sep 26 03:12:44 skapet sshd[24703]: Failed password for invalid user admin from ↺
200.72.41.31 port 41484 ssh2
```

This is indicative of a brute force attack where somebody or some program is trying to discover the user name and password which will let them into the system.

If external SSH access is needed for legitimate users, changing the default port used by SSH can offer some protection. However, PF provides a more elegant solution. Pass rules can contain limits on what connecting hosts can do and violators can be banished to a table of addresses which are denied some or all access. It is even possible to drop all existing connections from machines which overreach the limits.

To configure this, create this table in the tables section of the ruleset:

```
table <bruteforce> persist
```

Then, somewhere early in the ruleset, add rules to block brute access while allowing legitimate access:

```
block quick from <bruteforce>
pass inet proto tcp from any to $localnet port $tcp_services \
    flags S/SA keep state \
    (max-src-conn 100, max-src-conn-rate 15/5, \
    overload <bruteforce> flush global)
```

The part in parentheses defines the limits and the numbers should be changed to meet local requirements. It can be read as follows:

max-src-conn is the number of simultaneous connections allowed from one host.

max-src-conn-rate is the rate of new connections allowed from any single host (*15*) per number of seconds (*5*).

overload <bruteforce> means that any host which exceeds these limits gets its address added to the bruteforce table. The ruleset blocks all traffic from addresses in the bruteforce table.

Finally, flush global says that when a host reaches the limit, that all (global) of that host's connections will be terminated (flush).

Note

These rules will *not* block slow bruteforcers, as described in http://home.nuug.no/~peter/hailmary2013/.

This example ruleset is intended mainly as an illustration. For example, if a generous number of connections in general are wanted, but the desire is to be more restrictive when it comes to ssh, supplement the rule above with something like the one below, early on in the rule set:

```
pass quick proto { tcp, udp } from any to any port ssh \
    flags S/SA keep state \
    (max-src-conn 15, max-src-conn-rate 5/3, \
    overload <bruteforce> flush global)
```

It May Not be Necessary to Block All Overloaders

It is worth noting that the overload mechanism is a general technique which does not apply exclusively to SSH, and it is not always optimal to entirely block all traffic from offenders.

For example, an overload rule could be used to protect a mail service or a web service, and the overload table could be used in a rule to assign offenders to a queue with a minimal bandwidth allocation or to redirect to a specific web page.

Over time, tables will be filled by overload rules and their size will grow incrementally, taking up more memory. Sometimes an IP address that is blocked is a dynamically assigned one, which has since been assigned to a host who has a legitimate reason to communicate with hosts in the local network.

For situations like these, pfctl provides the ability to expire table entries. For example, this command will remove <bruteforce> table entries which have not been referenced for 86400 seconds:

```
# pfctl -t bruteforce -T expire 86400
```

Similar functionality is provided by security/expiretable, which removes table entries which have not been accessed for a specified period of time.

Once installed, expiretable can be run to remove <bruteforce> table entries older than a specified age. This example removes all entries older than 24 hours:

```
/usr/local/sbin/expiretable -v -d -t 24h bruteforce
```

29.3.3.6. Protecting Against SPAM

Not to be confused with the spamd daemon which comes bundled with spamassassin, mail/spamd can be configured with PF to provide an outer defense against SPAM. This spamd hooks into the PF configuration using a set of redirections.

Spammers tend to send a large number of messages, and SPAM is mainly sent from a few spammer friendly networks and a large number of hijacked machines, both of which are reported to *blacklists* fairly quickly.

When an SMTP connection from an address in a blacklist is received, spamd presents its banner and immediately switches to a mode where it answers SMTP traffic one byte at a time. This technique, which is intended to waste as much time as possible on the spammer's end, is called *tarpitting*. The specific implementation which uses one byte SMTP replies is often referred to as *stuttering*.

This example demonstrates the basic procedure for setting up spamd with automatically updated blacklists. Refer to the man pages which are installed with mail/spamd for more information.

Procedure 29.1. Configuring spamd

1. Install the mail/spamd package or port. In order to use spamd's greylisting features, fdescfs(5) must be mounted at /dev/fd . Add the following line to /etc/fstab :

    ```
    fdescfs /dev/fd fdescfs rw 0 0
    ```

    Then, mount the filesystem:

    ```
    # mount fdescfs
    ```

2. Next, edit the PF ruleset to include:

    ```
    table <spamd> persist
    table <spamd-white> persist
    rdr pass on $ext_if inet proto tcp from <spamd> to \
        { $ext_if, $localnet } port smtp -> 127.0.0.1 port 8025
    rdr pass on $ext_if inet proto tcp from !<spamd-white> to \
        { $ext_if, $localnet } port smtp -> 127.0.0.1 port 8025
    ```

    The two tables <spamd> and <spamd-white> are essential. SMTP traffic from an address listed in <spamd> but not in <spamd-white> is redirected to the spamd daemon listening at port 8025.

3. The next step is to configure spamd in /usr/local/etc/spamd.conf and to add some rc.conf parameters.

    The installation of mail/spamd includes a sample configuration file (/usr/local/etc/spamd.conf.sample) and a man page for spamd.conf . Refer to these for additional configuration options beyond those shown in this example.

One of the first lines in the configuration file that does not begin with a # comment sign contains the block which defines the `all` list, which specifies the lists to use:

```
all:\
    :traplist:whitelist:
```

This entry adds the desired blacklists, separated by colons (:). To use a whitelist to subtract addresses from a blacklist, add the name of the whitelist *immediately* after the name of that blacklist. For example: `:black-list:whitelist:`.

This is followed by the specified blacklist's definition:

```
traplist:\
    :black:\
    :msg="SPAM. Your address %A has sent spam within the last 24 hours":\
    :method=http:\
    :file=www.openbsd.org/spamd/traplist.gz
```

where the first line is the name of the blacklist and the second line specifies the list type. The `msg` field contains the message to display to blacklisted senders during the SMTP dialogue. The `method` field specifies how spamd-setup fetches the list data; supported methods are `http`, `ftp`, from a `file` in a mounted file system, and via `exec` of an external program. Finally, the `file` field specifies the name of the file spamd expects to receive.

The definition of the specified whitelist is similar, but omits the `msg` field since a message is not needed:

```
whitelist:\
    :white:\
    :method=file:\
    :file=/var/mail/whitelist.txt
```

Choose Data Sources with Care

Using all the blacklists in the sample `spamd.conf` will blacklist large blocks of the Internet. Administrators need to edit the file to create an optimal configuration which uses applicable data sources and, when necessary, uses custom lists.

Next, add this entry to `/etc/rc.conf`. Additional flags are described in the man page specified by the comment:

```
spamd_flags="-v" # use "" and see spamd-setup(8) for flags
```

When finished, reload the ruleset, start spamd by typing `service start obspamd`, and complete the configuration using `spamd-setup`. Finally, create a cron(8) job which calls `spamd-setup` to update the tables at reasonable intervals.

On a typical gateway in front of a mail server, hosts will soon start getting trapped within a few seconds to several minutes.

PF also supports *greylisting*, which temporarily rejects messages from unknown hosts with *45n* codes. Messages from greylisted hosts which try again within a reasonable time are let through. Traffic from senders which are set up to behave within the limits set by RFC 1123 and RFC 2821 are immediately let through.

More information about greylisting as a technique can be found at the greylisting.org web site. The most amazing thing about greylisting, apart from its simplicity, is that it still works. Spammers and malware writers have been very slow to adapt in order to bypass this technique.

The basic procedure for configuring greylisting is as follows:

Procedure 29.2. Configuring Greylisting

1. Make sure that fdescfs(5) is mounted as described in Step 1 of the previous Procedure.

2. To run spamd in greylisting mode, add this line to /etc/rc.conf :

    ```
    spamd_grey="YES"  # use spamd greylisting if YES
    ```

    Refer to the spamd man page for descriptions of additional related parameters.

3. To complete the greylisting setup:

    ```
    # service restart obspamd
    # service start spamlogd
    ```

Behind the scenes, the spamdb database tool and the spamlogd whitelist updater perform essential functions for the greylisting feature. spamdb is the administrator's main interface to managing the black, grey, and white lists via the contents of the /var/db/spamdb database.

29.3.3.7. Network Hygiene

This section describes how block-policy , scrub, and antispoof can be used to make the ruleset behave sanely.

The block-policy is an option which can be set in the options part of the ruleset, which precedes the redirection and filtering rules. This option determines which feedback, if any, PF sends to hosts that are blocked by a rule. The option has two possible values: drop drops blocked packets with no feedback, and return returns a status code such as Connection refused.

If not set, the default policy is drop. To change the block-policy , specify the desired value:

```
set block-policy return
```

In PF, scrub is a keyword which enables network packet normalization. This process reassembles fragmented packets and drops TCP packets that have invalid flag combinations. Enabling scrub provides a measure of protection against certain kinds of attacks based on incorrect handling of packet fragments. A number of options are available, but the simplest form is suitable for most configurations:

```
scrub in all
```

Some services, such as NFS, require specific fragment handling options. Refer to https://home.nuug.no/~peter/pf/en/scrub.html for more information.

This example reassembles fragments, clears the "do not fragment" bit, and sets the maximum segment size to 1440 bytes:

```
scrub in all fragment reassemble no-df max-mss 1440
```

The antispoof mechanism protects against activity from spoofed or forged IP addresses, mainly by blocking packets appearing on interfaces and in directions which are logically not possible.

These rules weed out spoofed traffic coming in from the rest of the world as well as any spoofed packets which originate in the local network:

```
antispoof for $ext_if
antispoof for $int_if
```

29.3.3.8. Handling Non-Routable Addresses

Even with a properly configured gateway to handle network address translation, one may have to compensate for other people's misconfigurations. A common misconfiguration is to let traffic with non-routable addresses out to the Internet. Since traffic from non-routeable addresses can play a part in several DoS attack techniques, consider explicitly blocking traffic from non-routeable addresses from entering the network through the external interface.

In this example, a macro containing non-routable addresses is defined, then used in blocking rules. Traffic to and from these addresses is quietly dropped on the gateway's external interface.

```
martians = "{ 127.0.0.0/8, 192.168.0.0/16, 172.16.0.0/12, \
        10.0.0.0/8, 169.254.0.0/16, 192.0.2.0/24, \
        0.0.0.0/8, 240.0.0.0/4 }"

block drop in quick on $ext_if from $martians to any
block drop out quick on $ext_if from any to $martians
```

29.4. IPFW

IPFW is a stateful firewall written for FreeBSD which supports both IPv4 and IPv6. It is comprised of several components: the kernel firewall filter rule processor and its integrated packet accounting facility, the logging facility, NAT, the dummynet(4) traffic shaper, a forward facility, a bridge facility, and an ipstealth facility.

FreeBSD provides a sample ruleset in /etc/rc.firewall which defines several firewall types for common scenarios to assist novice users in generating an appropriate ruleset. IPFW provides a powerful syntax which advanced users can use to craft customized rulesets that meet the security requirements of a given environment.

This section describes how to enable IPFW, provides an overview of its rule syntax, and demonstrates several rulesets for common configuration scenarios.

29.4.1. Enabling IPFW

IPFW is included in the basic FreeBSD install as a kernel loadable module, meaning that a custom kernel is not needed in order to enable IPFW.

For those users who wish to statically compile IPFW support into a custom kernel, refer to the instructions in Chapter 8, *Configuring the FreeBSD Kernel*. The following options are available for the custom kernel configuration file:

```
options     IPFIREWALL   # enables IPFW
options     IPFIREWALL_VERBOSE  # enables logging for rules with log keyword
options     IPFIREWALL_VERBOSE_LIMIT=5 # limits number of logged packets per-entry
options     IPFIREWALL_DEFAULT_TO_ACCEPT # sets default policy to pass what is not ↺
explicitly denied
options     IPDIVERT   # enables NAT
```

To configure the system to enable IPFW at boot time, add the following entry to /etc/rc.conf :

```
firewall_enable="YES"
```

To use one of the default firewall types provided by FreeBSD, add another line which specifies the type:

```
firewall_type="open"
```

The available types are:

- open: passes all traffic.

- client: protects only this machine.

- simple: protects the whole network.

- closed: entirely disables IP traffic except for the loopback interface.

- workstation: protects only this machine using stateful rules.

- UNKNOWN: disables the loading of firewall rules.

- *filename*: full path of the file containing the firewall ruleset.

If `firewall_type` is set to either `client` or `simple`, modify the default rules found in `/etc/rc.firewall` to fit the configuration of the system.

Note that the `filename` type is used to load a custom ruleset.

An alternate way to load a custom ruleset is to set the `firewall_script` variable to the absolute path of an *executable script* that includes IPFW commands. The examples used in this section assume that the `firewall_script` is set to `/etc/ipfw.rules` :

```
firewall_script="/etc/ipfw.rules"
```

To enable logging, include this line:

```
firewall_logging="YES"
```

There is no `/etc/rc.conf` variable to set logging limits. To limit the number of times a rule is logged per connection attempt, specify the number using this line in `/etc/sysctl.conf` :

```
net.inet.ip.fw.verbose_limit=5
```

After saving the needed edits, start the firewall. To enable logging limits now, also set the `sysctl` value specified above:

```
# service ipfw start
# sysctl net.inet.ip.fw.verbose_limit= 5
```

29.4.2. IPFW Rule Syntax

When a packet enters the IPFW firewall, it is compared against the first rule in the ruleset and progresses one rule at a time, moving from top to bottom in sequence. When the packet matches the selection parameters of a rule, the rule's action is executed and the search of the ruleset terminates for that packet. This is referred to as "first match wins". If the packet does not match any of the rules, it gets caught by the mandatory IPFW default rule number 65535, which denies all packets and silently discards them. However, if the packet matches a rule that contains the `count`, `skipto`, or `tee` keywords, the search continues. Refer to ipfw(8) for details on how these keywords affect rule processing.

When creating an IPFW rule, keywords must be written in the following order. Some keywords are mandatory while other keywords are optional. The words shown in uppercase represent a variable and the words shown in lowercase must precede the variable that follows it. The # symbol is used to mark the start of a comment and may appear at the end of a rule or on its own line. Blank lines are ignored.

CMD RULE_NUMBER set SET_NUMBER ACTION log LOG_AMOUNT PROTO from SRC SRC_PORT to DST DST_PORT OPTIONS

This section provides an overview of these keywords and their options. It is not an exhaustive list of every possible option. Refer to ipfw(8) for a complete description of the rule syntax that can be used when creating IPFW rules.

CMD
> Every rule must start with *ipfw add*.

RULE_NUMBER
> Each rule is associated with a number from 1 to 65534. The number is used to indicate the order of rule processing. Multiple rules can have the same number, in which case they are applied according to the order in which they have been added.

SET_NUMBER
> Each rule is associated with a set number from 0 to 31. Sets can be individually disabled or enabled, making it possible to quickly add or delete a set of rules. If a SET_NUMBER is not specified, the rule will be added to set 0.

ACTION

A rule can be associated with one of the following actions. The specified action will be executed when the packet matches the selection criterion of the rule.

allow | *accept* | *pass* | *permit*: these keywords are equivalent and allow packets that match the rule.

check-state : checks the packet against the dynamic state table. If a match is found, execute the action associated with the rule which generated this dynamic rule, otherwise move to the next rule. A check-state rule does not have selection criterion. If no check-state rule is present in the ruleset, the dynamic rules table is checked at the first keep-state or limit rule.

count: updates counters for all packets that match the rule. The search continues with the next rule.

deny | *drop*: either word silently discards packets that match this rule.

Additional actions are available. Refer to ipfw(8) for details.

LOG_AMOUNT

When a packet matches a rule with the log keyword, a message will be logged to syslogd(8) with a facility name of SECURITY. Logging only occurs if the number of packets logged for that particular rule does not exceed a specified LOG_AMOUNT. If no LOG_AMOUNT is specified, the limit is taken from the value of net.inet.ip.fw.verbose_limit. A value of zero removes the logging limit. Once the limit is reached, logging can be re-enabled by clearing the logging counter or the packet counter for that rule, using ipfw resetlog.

Note

Logging is done after all other packet matching conditions have been met, and before performing the final action on the packet. The administrator decides which rules to enable logging on.

PROTO

This optional value can be used to specify any protocol name or number found in /etc/protocols.

SRC

The from keyword must be followed by the source address or a keyword that represents the source address. An address can be represented by any, me (any address configured on an interface on this system), me6, (any IPv6 address configured on an interface on this system), or table followed by the number of a lookup table which contains a list of addresses. When specifying an IP address, it can be optionally followed by its CIDR mask or subnet mask. For example, 1.2.3.4/25 or 1.2.3.4:255.255.255.128 .

SRC_PORT

An optional source port can be specified using the port number or name from /etc/services.

DST

The to keyword must be followed by the destination address or a keyword that represents the destination address. The same keywords and addresses described in the SRC section can be used to describe the destination.

DST_PORT

An optional destination port can be specified using the port number or name from /etc/services.

OPTIONS

Several keywords can follow the source and destination. As the name suggests, OPTIONS are optional. Commonly used options include in or out, which specify the direction of packet flow, icmptypes followed by the type of ICMP message, and keep-state .

When a *keep-state* rule is matched, the firewall will create a dynamic rule which matches bidirectional traffic between the source and destination addresses and ports using the same protocol.

The dynamic rules facility is vulnerable to resource depletion from a SYN-flood attack which would open a huge number of dynamic rules. To counter this type of attack with IPFW, use `limit`. This option limits the number of simultaneous sessions by checking the open dynamic rules, counting the number of times this rule and IP address combination occurred. If this count is greater than the value specified by `limit`, the packet is discarded.

Dozens of OPTIONS are available. Refer to ipfw(8) for a description of each available option.

29.4.3. Example Ruleset

This section demonstrates how to create an example stateful firewall ruleset script named /etc/ipfw.rules . In this example, all connection rules use `in` or `out` to clarify the direction. They also use `via` *interface-name* to specify the interface the packet is traveling over.

> **Note**
>
> When first creating or testing a firewall ruleset, consider temporarily setting this tunable:
>
> ```
> net.inet.ip.fw.default_to_accept="1"
> ```
>
> This sets the default policy of ipfw(8) to be more permissive than the default `deny ip from any to any`, making it slightly more difficult to get locked out of the system right after a reboot.

The firewall script begins by indicating that it is a Bourne shell script and flushes any existing rules. It then creates the cmd variable so that `ipfw add` does not have to be typed at the beginning of every rule. It also defines the `pif` variable which represents the name of the interface that is attached to the Internet.

```
#!/bin/sh
# Flush out the list before we begin.
ipfw -q -f flush

# Set rules command prefix
cmd="ipfw -q add"
pif="dc0"     # interface name of NIC attached to Internet
```

The first two rules allow all traffic on the trusted internal interface and on the loopback interface:

```
# Change xl0 to LAN NIC interface name
$cmd 00005 allow all from any to any via xl0

# No restrictions on Loopback Interface
$cmd 00010 allow all from any to any via lo0
```

The next rule allows the packet through if it matches an existing entry in the dynamic rules table:

```
$cmd 00101 check-state
```

The next set of rules defines which stateful connections internal systems can create to hosts on the Internet:

```
# Allow access to public DNS
# Replace x.x.x.x with the IP address of a public DNS server
# and repeat for each DNS server in /etc/resolv.conf
$cmd 00110 allow tcp from any to x.x.x.x 53 out via $pif setup keep-state
$cmd 00111 allow udp from any to x.x.x.x 53 out via $pif keep-state

# Allow access to ISP's DHCP server for cable/DSL configurations.
# Use the first rule and check log for IP address.
# Then, uncomment the second rule, input the IP address, and delete the first rule
```

```
$cmd 00120 allow log udp from any to any 67 out via $pif keep-state
#$cmd 00120 allow udp from any to x.x.x.x 67 out via $pif keep-state

# Allow outbound HTTP and HTTPS connections
$cmd 00200 allow tcp from any to any 80 out via $pif setup keep-state
$cmd 00220 allow tcp from any to any 443 out via $pif setup keep-state

# Allow outbound email connections
$cmd 00230 allow tcp from any to any 25 out via $pif setup keep-state
$cmd 00231 allow tcp from any to any 110 out via $pif setup keep-state

# Allow outbound ping
$cmd 00250 allow icmp from any to any out via $pif keep-state

# Allow outbound NTP
$cmd 00260 allow udp from any to any 123 out via $pif keep-state

# Allow outbound SSH
$cmd 00280 allow tcp from any to any 22 out via $pif setup keep-state

# deny and log all other outbound connections
$cmd 00299 deny log all from any to any out via $pif
```

The next set of rules controls connections from Internet hosts to the internal network. It starts by denying packets typically associated with attacks and then explicitly allows specific types of connections. All the authorized services that originate from the Internet use limit to prevent flooding.

```
# Deny all inbound traffic from non-routable reserved address spaces
$cmd 00300 deny all from 192.168.0.0/16 to any in via $pif    #RFC 1918 private IP
$cmd 00301 deny all from 172.16.0.0/12 to any in via $pif     #RFC 1918 private IP
$cmd 00302 deny all from 10.0.0.0/8 to any in via $pif        #RFC 1918 private IP
$cmd 00303 deny all from 127.0.0.0/8 to any in via $pif       #loopback
$cmd 00304 deny all from 0.0.0.0/8 to any in via $pif         #loopback
$cmd 00305 deny all from 169.254.0.0/16 to any in via $pif    #DHCP auto-config
$cmd 00306 deny all from 192.0.2.0/24 to any in via $pif      #reserved for docs
$cmd 00307 deny all from 204.152.64.0/23 to any in via $pif   #Sun cluster interconnect
$cmd 00308 deny all from 224.0.0.0/3 to any in via $pif       #Class D & E multicast

# Deny public pings
$cmd 00310 deny icmp from any to any in via $pif

# Deny ident
$cmd 00315 deny tcp from any to any 113 in via $pif

# Deny all Netbios services.
$cmd 00320 deny tcp from any to any 137 in via $pif
$cmd 00321 deny tcp from any to any 138 in via $pif
$cmd 00322 deny tcp from any to any 139 in via $pif
$cmd 00323 deny tcp from any to any 81 in via $pif

# Deny fragments
$cmd 00330 deny all from any to any frag in via $pif

# Deny ACK packets that did not match the dynamic rule table
$cmd 00332 deny tcp from any to any established in via $pif

# Allow traffic from ISP's DHCP server.
# Replace x.x.x.x with the same IP address used in rule 00120.
#$cmd 00360 allow udp from any to x.x.x.x 67 in via $pif keep-state

# Allow HTTP connections to internal web server
$cmd 00400 allow tcp from any to me 80 in via $pif setup limit src-addr 2

# Allow inbound SSH connections
$cmd 00410 allow tcp from any to me 22 in via $pif setup limit src-addr 2
```

```
# Reject and log all other incoming connections
$cmd 00499 deny log all from any to any in via $pif
```

The last rule logs all packets that do not match any of the rules in the ruleset:

```
# Everything else is denied and logged
$cmd 00999 deny log all from any to any
```

29.4.4. Configuring NAT

Contributed by Chern Lee.

FreeBSD's built-in NAT daemon, natd(8), works in conjunction with IPFW to provide network address translation. This can be used to provide an Internet Connection Sharing solution so that several internal computers can connect to the Internet using a single IP address.

To do this, the FreeBSD machine connected to the Internet must act as a gateway. This system must have two NICs, where one is connected to the Internet and the other is connected to the internal LAN. Each machine connected to the LAN should be assigned an IP address in the private network space, as defined by RFC 1918, and have the default gateway set to the natd(8) system's internal IP address.

Some additional configuration is needed in order to activate the NAT function of IPFW. If the system has a custom kernel, the kernel configuration file needs to include option `IPDIVERT` along with the other `IPFIREWALL` options described in Section 29.4.1, "Enabling IPFW".

To enable NAT support at boot time, the following must be in /etc/rc.conf :

```
gateway_enable="YES"  # enables the gateway
natd_enable="YES"  # enables NAT
natd_interface="rl0"  # specify interface name of NIC attached to Internet
natd_flags="-dynamic -m" # -m = preserve port numbers; additional options are listed ↺
in natd(8)
```

> **Note**
>
> It is also possible to specify a configuration file which contains the options to pass to natd(8):
>
> ```
> natd_flags="-f /etc/natd.conf"
> ```
>
> The specified file must contain a list of configuration options, one per line. For example:
>
> ```
> redirect_port tcp 192.168.0.2:6667 6667
> redirect_port tcp 192.168.0.3:80 80
> ```
>
> For more information about this configuration file, consult natd(8).

Next, add the NAT rules to the firewall ruleset. When the rulest contains stateful rules, the positioning of the NAT rules is critical and the `skipto` action is used. The `skipto` action requires a rule number so that it knows which rule to jump to.

The following example builds upon the firewall ruleset shown in the previous section. It adds some additional entries and modifies some existing rules in order to configure the firewall for NAT. It starts by adding some additional variables which represent the rule number to skip to, the `keep-state` option, and a list of TCP ports which will be used to reduce the number of rules:

```
#!/bin/sh
ipfw -q -f flush
cmd="ipfw -q add"
skip="skipto 500"
```

```
pif=dc0
ks="keep-state"
good_tcpo="22,25,37,53,80,443,110"
```

The inbound NAT rule is inserted *after* the two rules which allow all traffic on the trusted internal interface and on the loopback interface and *before* the check-state rule. It is important that the rule number selected for this NAT rule, in this example 100, is higher than the first two rules and lower than the check-state rule:

```
$cmd 005 allow all from any to any via xl0  # exclude LAN traffic
$cmd 010 allow all from any to any via lo0  # exclude loopback traffic
$cmd 100 divert natd ip from any to any in via $pif # NAT any inbound packets
# Allow the packet through if it has an existing entry in the dynamic rules table
$cmd 101 check-state
```

The outbound rules are modified to replace the allow action with the $skip variable, indicating that rule processing will continue at rule 500. The seven tcp rules have been replaced by rule 125 as the $good_tcpo variable contains the seven allowed outbound ports.

```
# Authorized outbound packets
$cmd 120 $skip udp from any to x.x.x.x 53 out via $pif $ks
$cmd 121 $skip udp from any to x.x.x.x 67 out via $pif $ks
$cmd 125 $skip tcp from any to any $good_tcpo out via $pif setup $ks
$cmd 130 $skip icmp from any to any out via $pif $ks
```

The inbound rules remain the same, except for the very last rule which removes the via $pif in order to catch both inbound and outbound rules. The NAT rule must follow this last outbound rule, must have a higher number than that last rule, and the rule number must be referenced by the skipto action. In this ruleset, rule number 500 diverts all packets which match the outbound rules to natd(8) for NAT processing. The next rule allows any packet which has undergone NAT processing to pass.

```
$cmd 499 deny log all from any to any
$cmd 500 divert natd ip from any to any out via $pif # skipto location for outbound ↵
stateful rules
$cmd 510 allow ip from any to any
```

In this example, rules 100, 101, 125, 500, and 510 control the address translation of the outbound and inbound packets so that the entries in the dynamic state table always register the private LAN IP address.

Consider an internal web browser which initializes a new outbound HTTP session over port 80. When the first outbound packet enters the firewall, it does not match rule 100 because it is headed out rather than in. It passes rule 101 because this is the first packet and it has not been posted to the dynamic state table yet. The packet finally matches rule 125 as it is outbound on an allowed port and has a source IP address from the internal LAN. On matching this rule, two actions take place. First, the keep-state action adds an entry to the dynamic state table and the specified action, skipto rule 500, is executed. Next, the packet undergoes NAT and is sent out to the Internet. This packet makes its way to the destination web server, where a response packet is generated and sent back. This new packet enters the top of the ruleset. It matches rule 100 and has its destination IP address mapped back to the original internal address. It then is processed by the check-state rule, is found in the table as an existing session, and is released to the LAN.

On the inbound side, the ruleset has to deny bad packets and allow only authorized services. A packet which matches an inbound rule is posted to the dynamic state table and the packet is released to the LAN. The packet generated as a response is recognized by the check-state rule as belonging to an existing session. It is then sent to rule 500 to undergo NAT before being released to the outbound interface.

29.4.4.1. Port Redirection

The drawback with natd(8) is that the LAN clients are not accessible from the Internet. Clients on the LAN can make outgoing connections to the world but cannot receive incoming ones. This presents a problem if trying to run Internet services on one of the LAN client machines. A simple way around this is to redirect selected Internet ports on the natd(8) machine to a LAN client.

For example, an IRC server runs on client A and a web server runs on client B. For this to work properly, connections received on ports 6667 (IRC) and 80 (HTTP) must be redirected to the respective machines.

The syntax for `-redirect_port` is as follows:

```
-redirect_port proto targetIP:targetPORT[-targetPORT]
            [aliasIP:]aliasPORT[-aliasPORT]
            [remoteIP[:remotePORT[-remotePORT]]]
```

In the above example, the argument should be:

```
-redirect_port tcp 192.168.0.2:6667 6667
-redirect_port tcp 192.168.0.3:80 80
```

This redirects the proper TCP ports to the LAN client machines.

Port ranges over individual ports can be indicated with `-redirect_port`. For example, *tcp 192.168.0.2:2000-3000 2000-3000* would redirect all connections received on ports 2000 to 3000 to ports 2000 to 3000 on client A.

These options can be used when directly running natd(8), placed within the `natd_flags=""` option in `/etc/rc.conf`, or passed via a configuration file.

For further configuration options, consult natd(8)

29.4.4.2. Address Redirection

Address redirection is useful if more than one IP address is available. Each LAN client can be assigned its own external IP address by natd(8), which will then rewrite outgoing packets from the LAN clients with the proper external IP address and redirects all traffic incoming on that particular IP address back to the specific LAN client. This is also known as static NAT. For example, if IP addresses `128.1.1.1`, `128.1.1.2`, and `128.1.1.3` are available, `128.1.1.1` can be used as the natd(8) machine's external IP address, while `128.1.1.2` and `128.1.1.3` are forwarded back to LAN clients A and B.

The `-redirect_address` syntax is as follows:

```
-redirect_address localIP publicIP
```

localIP	The internal IP address of the LAN client.
publicIP	The external IP address corresponding to the LAN client.

In the example, this argument would read:

```
-redirect_address 192.168.0.2 128.1.1.2
-redirect_address 192.168.0.3 128.1.1.3
```

Like `-redirect_port`, these arguments are placed within the `natd_flags=""` option of `/etc/rc.conf`, or passed via a configuration file. With address redirection, there is no need for port redirection since all data received on a particular IP address is redirected.

The external IP addresses on the natd(8) machine must be active and aliased to the external interface. Refer to rc.conf(5) for details.

29.4.5. The IPFW Command

ipfw can be used to make manual, single rule additions or deletions to the active firewall while it is running. The problem with using this method is that all the changes are lost when the system reboots. It is recommended to instead write all the rules in a file and to use that file to load the rules at boot time and to replace the currently running firewall rules whenever that file changes.

`ipfw` is a useful way to display the running firewall rules to the console screen. The IPFW accounting facility dynamically creates a counter for each rule that counts each packet that matches the rule. During the process of testing a rule, listing the rule with its counter is one way to determine if the rule is functioning as expected.

To list all the running rules in sequence:

```
# ipfw list
```

To list all the running rules with a time stamp of when the last time the rule was matched:

```
# ipfw -t list
```

The next example lists accounting information and the packet count for matched rules along with the rules themselves. The first column is the rule number, followed by the number of matched packets and bytes, followed by the rule itself.

```
# ipfw -a list
```

To list dynamic rules in addition to static rules:

```
# ipfw -d list
```

To also show the expired dynamic rules:

```
# ipfw -d -e list
```

To zero the counters:

```
# ipfw zero
```

To zero the counters for just the rule with number *NUM*:

```
# ipfw zero NUM
```

29.4.5.1. Logging Firewall Messages

Even with the logging facility enabled, IPFW will not generate any rule logging on its own. The firewall administrator decides which rules in the ruleset will be logged, and adds the `log` keyword to those rules. Normally only deny rules are logged. It is customary to duplicate the "ipfw default deny everything" rule with the `log` keyword included as the last rule in the ruleset. This way, it is possible to see all the packets that did not match any of the rules in the ruleset.

Logging is a two edged sword. If one is not careful, an over abundance of log data or a DoS attack can fill the disk with log files. Log messages are not only written to syslogd, but also are displayed on the root console screen and soon become annoying.

The `IPFIREWALL_VERBOSE_LIMIT=5` kernel option limits the number of consecutive messages sent to syslogd(8), concerning the packet matching of a given rule. When this option is enabled in the kernel, the number of consecutive messages concerning a particular rule is capped at the number specified. There is nothing to be gained from 200 identical log messages. With this option set to five, five consecutive messages concerning a particular rule would be logged to syslogd and the remainder identical consecutive messages would be counted and posted to syslogd with a phrase like the following:

```
last message repeated 45 times
```

All logged packets messages are written by default to `/var/log/security` , which is defined in `/etc/syslog.conf` .

29.4.5.2. Building a Rule Script

Most experienced IPFW users create a file containing the rules and code them in a manner compatible with running them as a script. The major benefit of doing this is the firewall rules can be refreshed in mass without the need of rebooting the system to activate them. This method is convenient in testing new rules as the procedure can be executed as many times as needed. Being a script, symbolic substitution can be used for frequently used values to be substituted into multiple rules.

This example script is compatible with the syntax used by the sh(1), csh(1), and tcsh(1) shells. Symbolic substitution fields are prefixed with a dollar sign ($). Symbolic fields do not have the $ prefix. The value to populate the symbolic field must be enclosed in double quotes ("").

Start the rules file like this:

```
############## start of example ipfw rules script #############
#
ipfw -q -f flush        # Delete all rules
# Set defaults
oif="tun0"              # out interface
odns="192.0.2.11"       # ISP's DNS server IP address
cmd="ipfw -q add "      # build rule prefix
ks="keep-state"         # just too lazy to key this each time
$cmd 00500 check-state
$cmd 00502 deny all from any to any frag
$cmd 00501 deny tcp from any to any established
$cmd 00600 allow tcp from any to any 80 out via $oif setup $ks
$cmd 00610 allow tcp from any to $odns 53 out via $oif setup $ks
$cmd 00611 allow udp from any to $odns 53 out via $oif $ks
################## End of example ipfw rules script ###########
```

The rules are not important as the focus of this example is how the symbolic substitution fields are populated.

If the above example was in /etc/ipfw.rules , the rules could be reloaded by the following command:

```
# sh /etc/ipfw.rules
```

/etc/ipfw.rules can be located anywhere and the file can have any name.

The same thing could be accomplished by running these commands by hand:

```
# ipfw -q -f flush
# ipfw -q add check-state
# ipfw -q add deny all from any to any frag
# ipfw -q add deny tcp from any to any established
# ipfw -q add allow tcp from any to any 80 out via tun0 setup keep-state
# ipfw -q add allow tcp from any to 192.0.2.11 53 out via tun0 setup keep-state
# ipfw -q add 00611 allow udp from any to 192.0.2.11 53 out via tun0 keep-state
```

29.5. IPFILTER (IPF)

IPFILTER, also known as IPF, is a cross-platform, open source firewall which has been ported to several operating systems, including FreeBSD, NetBSD, OpenBSD, and Solaris™ .

IPFILTER is a kernel-side firewall and NAT mechanism that can be controlled and monitored by userland programs. Firewall rules can be set or deleted using ipf, NAT rules can be set or deleted using ipnat, run-time statistics for the kernel parts of IPFILTER can be printed using ipfstat, and ipmon can be used to log IPFILTER actions to the system log files.

IPF was originally written using a rule processing logic of "the last matching rule wins" and only used stateless rules. Since then, IPF has been enhanced to include the quick and keep state options.

The IPF FAQ is at http://www.phildev.net/ipf/index.html . A searchable archive of the IPFilter mailing list is available at http://marc.info/?l=ipfilter .

This section of the Handbook focuses on IPF as it pertains to FreeBSD. It provides examples of rules that contain the quick and keep state options.

29.5.1. Enabling IPF

IPF is included in the basic FreeBSD install as a kernel loadable module, meaning that a custom kernel is not needed in order to enable IPF.

For users who prefer to statically compile IPF support into a custom kernel, refer to the instructions in Chapter 8, *Configuring the FreeBSD Kernel*. The following kernel options are available:

```
options IPFILTER
options IPFILTER_LOG
options IPFILTER_LOOKUP
options IPFILTER_DEFAULT_BLOCK
```

where `options IPFILTER` enables support for IPFILTER, `options IPFILTER_LOG` enables IPF logging using the `ipl` packet logging pseudo-device for every rule that has the `log` keyword, `IPFILTER_LOOKUP` enables IP pools in order to speed up IP lookups, and `options IPFILTER_DEFAULT_BLOCK` changes the default behavior so that any packet not matching a firewall `pass` rule gets blocked.

To configure the system to enable IPF at boot time, add the following entries to `/etc/rc.conf`. These entries will also enable logging and `default pass all`. To change the default policy to `block all` without compiling a custom kernel, remember to add a `block all` rule at the end of the ruleset.

```
ipfilter_enable="YES"              # Start ipf firewall
ipfilter_rules="/etc/ipf.rules"    # loads rules definition text file
ipmon_enable="YES"                 # Start IP monitor log
ipmon_flags="-Ds"                  # D = start as daemon
                                   # s = log to syslog
                                   # v = log tcp window, ack, seq
                                   # n = map IP & port to names
```

If NAT functionality is needed, also add these lines:

```
gateway_enable="YES"               # Enable as LAN gateway
ipnat_enable="YES"                 # Start ipnat function
ipnat_rules="/etc/ipnat.rules"     # rules definition file for ipnat
```

Then, to start IPF now:

```
# service ipfilter start
```

To load the firewall rules, specify the name of the ruleset file using `ipf`. The following command can be used to replace the currently running firewall rules:

```
# ipf -Fa -f /etc/ipf.rules
```

where `-Fa` flushes all the internal rules tables and `-f` specifies the file containing the rules to load.

This provides the ability to make changes to a custom ruleset and update the running firewall with a fresh copy of the rules without having to reboot the system. This method is convenient for testing new rules as the procedure can be executed as many times as needed.

Refer to ipf(8) for details on the other flags available with this command.

29.5.2. IPF Rule Syntax

This section describes the IPF rule syntax used to create stateful rules. When creating rules, keep in mind that unless the `quick` keyword appears in a rule, every rule is read in order, with the *last matching rule* being the one that is applied. This means that even if the first rule to match a packet is a `pass`, if there is a later matching rule that is a `block`, the packet will be dropped. Sample rulesets can be found in `/usr/share/examples/ipfilter`.

When creating rules, a # character is used to mark the start of a comment and may appear at the end of a rule, to explain that rule's function, or on its own line. Any blank lines are ignored.

The keywords which are used in rules must be written in a specific order, from left to right. Some keywords are mandatory while others are optional. Some keywords have sub-options which may be keywords themselves and also include more sub-options. The keyword order is as follows, where the words shown in uppercase represent a variable and the words shown in lowercase must precede the variable that follows it:

`ACTION DIRECTION OPTIONS proto PROTO_TYPE from SRC_ADDR SRC_PORT to DST_ADDR DST_PORT TCP_FLAG| ICMP_TYPE keep state STATE`

This section describes each of these keywords and their options. It is not an exhaustive list of every possible option. Refer to ipf(5) for a complete description of the rule syntax that can be used when creating IPF rules and examples for using each keyword.

ACTION

The action keyword indicates what to do with the packet if it matches that rule. Every rule *must* have an action. The following actions are recognized:

`block`: drops the packet.

`pass`: allows the packet.

`log`: generates a log record.

`count`: counts the number of packets and bytes which can provide an indication of how often a rule is used.

`auth`: queues the packet for further processing by another program.

`call`: provides access to functions built into IPF that allow more complex actions.

`decapsulate`: removes any headers in order to process the contents of the packet.

DIRECTION

Next, each rule must explicitly state the direction of traffic using one of these keywords:

`in`: the rule is applied against an inbound packet.

`out`: the rule is applied against an outbound packet.

`all`: the rule applies to either direction.

If the system has multiple interfaces, the interface can be specified along with the direction. An example would be `in on fxp0`.

OPTIONS

Options are optional. However, if multiple options are specified, they must be used in the order shown here.

`log`: when performing the specified ACTION, the contents of the packet's headers will be written to the ipl(4) packet log pseudo-device.

`quick`: if a packet matches this rule, the ACTION specified by the rule occurs and no further processing of any following rules will occur for this packet.

`on`: must be followed by the interface name as displayed by ifconfig(8). The rule will only match if the packet is going through the specified interface in the specified direction.

When using the `log` keyword, the following qualifiers may be used in this order:

`body`: indicates that the first 128 bytes of the packet contents will be logged after the headers.

`first`: if the `log` keyword is being used in conjunction with a `keep state` option, this option is recommended so that only the triggering packet is logged and not every packet which matches the stateful connection.

Additional options are available to specify error return messages. Refer to ipf(5) for more details.

PROTO_TYPE

The protocol type is optional. However, it is mandatory if the rule needs to specify a SRC_PORT or a DST_PORT as it defines the type of protocol. When specifying the type of protocol, use the proto keyword followed by either a protocol number or name from /etc/protocols. Example protocol names include tcp, udp, or icmp. If PROTO_TYPE is specified but no SRC_PORT or DST_PORT is specified, all port numbers for that protocol will match that rule.

SRC_ADDR

The from keyword is mandatory and is followed by a keyword which represents the source of the packet. The source can be a hostname, an IP address followed by the CIDR mask, an address pool, or the keyword all. Refer to ipf(5) for examples.

There is no way to match ranges of IP addresses which do not express themselves easily using the dotted numeric form / mask-length notation. The net-mgmt/ipcalc package or port may be used to ease the calculation of the CIDR mask. Additional information is available at the utility's web page: http://jodies.de/ipcalc .

SRC_PORT

The port number of the source is optional. However, if it is used, it requires PROTO_TYPE to be first defined in the rule. The port number must also be preceded by the proto keyword.

A number of different comparison operators are supported: = (equal to), != (not equal to), < (less than), > (greater than), <= (less than or equal to), and >= (greater than or equal to).

To specify port ranges, place the two port numbers between <> (less than and greater than), >< (greater than and less than), or : (greater than or equal to and less than or equal to).

DST_ADDR

The to keyword is mandatory and is followed by a keyword which represents the destination of the packet. Similar to SRC_ADDR, it can be a hostname, an IP address followed by the CIDR mask, an address pool, or the keyword all.

DST_PORT

Similar to SRC_PORT, the port number of the destination is optional. However, if it is used, it requires PROTO_TYPE to be first defined in the rule. The port number must also be preceded by the proto keyword.

TCP_FLAG|ICMP_TYPE

If tcp is specified as the PROTO_TYPE, flags can be specified as letters, where each letter represents one of the possible TCP flags used to determine the state of a connection. Possible values are: S (SYN), A (ACK), P (PSH), F (FIN), U (URG), R (RST), C (CWN), and E (ECN).

If icmp is specified as the PROTO_TYPE, the ICMP type to match can be specified. Refer to ipf(5) for the allowable types.

STATE

If a pass rule contains keep state , IPF will add an entry to its dynamic state table and allow subsequent packets that match the connection. IPF can track state for TCP, UDP, and ICMP sessions. Any packet that IPF can be certain is part of an active session, even if it is a different protocol, will be allowed.

In IPF, packets destined to go out through the interface connected to the public Internet are first checked against the dynamic state table. If the packet matches the next expected packet comprising an active session conversation, it exits the firewall and the state of the session conversation flow is updated in the dynamic state table. Packets that do not belong to an already active session are checked against the outbound ruleset. Packets coming in from the interface connected to the public Internet are first checked against the dynamic state table. If the packet matches the next expected packet comprising an active session, it exits the firewall and the state of the session conversation flow is updated in the dynamic state table. Packets that do not belong to an already active session are checked against the inbound ruleset.

Several keywords can be added after keep state. If used, these keywords set various options that control stateful filtering, such as setting connection limits or connection age. Refer to ipf(5) for the list of available options and their descriptions.

29.5.3. Example Ruleset

This section demonstrates how to create an example ruleset which only allows services matching pass rules and blocks all others.

FreeBSD uses the loopback interface (lo0) and the IP address 127.0.0.1 for internal communication. The firewall ruleset must contain rules to allow free movement of these internally used packets:

```
# no restrictions on loopback interface
pass in quick on lo0 all
pass out quick on lo0 all
```

The public interface connected to the Internet is used to authorize and control access of all outbound and inbound connections. If one or more interfaces are cabled to private networks, those internal interfaces may require rules to allow packets originating from the LAN to flow between the internal networks or to the interface attached to the Internet. The ruleset should be organized into three major sections: any trusted internal interfaces, outbound connections through the public interface, and inbound connections through the public interface.

These two rules allow all traffic to pass through a trusted LAN interface named xl0:

```
# no restrictions on inside LAN interface for private network
pass out quick on xl0 all
pass in quick on xl0 all
```

The rules for the public interface's outbound and inbound sections should have the most frequently matched rules placed before less commonly matched rules, with the last rule in the section blocking and logging all packets for that interface and direction. ⋅

This set of rules defines the outbound section of the public interface named dc0. These rules keep state and identify the specific services that internal systems are authorized for public Internet access. All the rules use quick and specify the appropriate port numbers and, where applicable, destination addresses.

```
# interface facing Internet (outbound)
# Matches session start requests originating from or behind the
# firewall, destined for the Internet.

# Allow outbound access to public DNS servers.
# Replace x.x.x. with address listed in /etc/resolv.conf.
# Repeat for each DNS server.
pass out quick on dc0 proto tcp from any to x.x.x. port = 53 flags S keep state
pass out quick on dc0 proto udp from any to xxx port = 53 keep state

# Allow access to ISP's specified DHCP server for cable or DSL networks.
# Use the first rule, then check log for the IP address of DHCP server.
# Then, uncomment the second rule, replace z.z.z.z with the IP address,
# and comment out the first rule
pass out log quick on dc0 proto udp from any to any port = 67 keep state
#pass out quick on dc0 proto udp from any to z.z.z.z port = 67 keep state

# Allow HTTP and HTTPS
pass out quick on dc0 proto tcp from any to any port = 80 flags S keep state
pass out quick on dc0 proto tcp from any to any port = 443 flags S keep state

# Allow email
pass out quick on dc0 proto tcp from any to any port = 110 flags S keep state
pass out quick on dc0 proto tcp from any to any port = 25 flags S keep state

# Allow NTP
pass out quick on dc0 proto tcp from any to any port = 37 flags S keep state
```

```
# Allow FTP
pass out quick on dc0 proto tcp from any to any port = 21 flags S keep state

# Allow SSH
pass out quick on dc0 proto tcp from any to any port = 22 flags S keep state

# Allow ping
pass out quick on dc0 proto icmp from any to any icmp-type 8 keep state

# Block and log everything else
block out log first quick on dc0 all
```

This example of the rules in the inbound section of the public interface blocks all undesirable packets first. This reduces the number of packets that are logged by the last rule.

```
# interface facing Internet (inbound)
# Block all inbound traffic from non-routable or reserved address spaces
block in quick on dc0 from 192.168.0.0/16 to any     #RFC 1918 private IP
block in quick on dc0 from 172.16.0.0/12 to any      #RFC 1918 private IP
block in quick on dc0 from 10.0.0.0/8 to any         #RFC 1918 private IP
block in quick on dc0 from 127.0.0.0/8 to any        #loopback
block in quick on dc0 from 0.0.0.0/8 to any          #loopback
block in quick on dc0 from 169.254.0.0/16 to any     #DHCP auto-config
block in quick on dc0 from 192.0.2.0/24 to any       #reserved for docs
block in quick on dc0 from 204.152.64.0/23 to any    #Sun cluster interconnect
block in quick on dc0 from 224.0.0.0/3 to any        #Class D & E multicast

# Block fragments and too short tcp packets
block in quick on dc0 all with frags
block in quick on dc0 proto tcp all with short

# block source routed packets
block in quick on dc0 all with opt lsrr
block in quick on dc0 all with opt ssrr

# Block OS fingerprint attempts and log first occurrence
block in log first quick on dc0 proto tcp from any to any flags FUP

# Block anything with special options
block in quick on dc0 all with ipopts

# Block public pings and ident
block in quick on dc0 proto icmp all icmp-type 8
block in quick on dc0 proto tcp from any to any port = 113

# Block incoming Netbios services
block in log first quick on dc0 proto tcp/udp from any to any port = 137
block in log first quick on dc0 proto tcp/udp from any to any port = 138
block in log first quick on dc0 proto tcp/udp from any to any port = 139
block in log first quick on dc0 proto tcp/udp from any to any port = 81
```

Any time there are logged messages on a rule with the log first option, run ipfstat -hio to evaluate how many times the rule has been matched. A large number of matches may indicate that the system is under attack.

The rest of the rules in the inbound section define which connections are allowed to be initiated from the Internet. The last rule denies all connections which were not explicitly allowed by previous rules in this section.

```
# Allow traffic in from ISP's DHCP server. Replace z.z.z.z with
# the same IP address used in the outbound section.
pass in quick on dc0 proto udp from z.z.z.z to any port = 68 keep state

# Allow public connections to specified internal web server
pass in quick on dc0 proto tcp from any to x.x.x.x port = 80 flags S keep state

# Block and log only first occurrence of all remaining traffic.
```

```
block in log first quick on dc0 all
```

29.5.4. Configuring NAT

To enable NAT, add these statements to `/etc/rc.conf` and specify the name of the file containing the NAT rules:

```
gateway_enable="YES"
ipnat_enable="YES"
ipnat_rules="/etc/ipnat.rules"
```

NAT rules are flexible and can accomplish many different things to fit the needs of both commercial and home users. The rule syntax presented here has been simplified to demonstrate common usage. For a complete rule syntax description, refer to ipnat(5).

The basic syntax for a NAT rule is as follows, where `map` starts the rule and *IF* should be replaced with the name of the external interface:

```
map IF LAN_IP_RANGE  -> PUBLIC_ADDRESS
```

The *LAN_IP_RANGE* is the range of IP addresses used by internal clients. Usually, it is a private address range such as `192.168.1.0/24` . The *PUBLIC_ADDRESS* can either be the static external IP address or the keyword `0/32` which represents the IP address assigned to *IF.*

In IPF, when a packet arrives at the firewall from the LAN with a public destination, it first passes through the outbound rules of the firewall ruleset. Then, the packet is passed to the NAT ruleset which is read from the top down, where the first matching rule wins. IPF tests each NAT rule against the packet's interface name and source IP address. When a packet's interface name matches a NAT rule, the packet's source IP address in the private LAN is checked to see if it falls within the IP address range specified in *LAN_IP_RANGE* . On a match, the packet has its source IP address rewritten with the public IP address specified by *PUBLIC_ADDRESS*. IPF posts an entry in its internal NAT table so that when the packet returns from the Internet, it can be mapped back to its original private IP address before being passed to the firewall rules for further processing.

For networks that have large numbers of internal systems or multiple subnets, the process of funneling every private IP address into a single public IP address becomes a resource problem. Two methods are available to relieve this issue.

The first method is to assign a range of ports to use as source ports. By adding the `portmap` keyword, NAT can be directed to only use source ports in the specified range:

```
map dc0 192.168.1.0/24 -> 0/32 portmap tcp/udp 20000:60000
```

Alternately, use the `auto` keyword which tells NAT to determine the ports that are available for use:

```
map dc0 192.168.1.0/24 -> 0/32 portmap tcp/udp auto
```

The second method is to use a pool of public addresses. This is useful when there are too many LAN addresses to fit into a single public address and a block of public IP addresses is available. These public addresses can be used as a pool from which NAT selects an IP address as a packet's address is mapped on its way out.

The range of public IP addresses can be specified using a netmask or CIDR notation. These two rules are equivalent:

```
map dc0 192.168.1.0/24 -> 204.134.75.0/255.255.255.0
map dc0 192.168.1.0/24 -> 204.134.75.0/24
```

A common practice is to have a publically accessible web server or mail server segregated to an internal network segment. The traffic from these servers still has to undergo NAT, but port redirection is needed to direct inbound traffic to the correct server. For example, to map a web server using the internal address `10.0.10.25` to its public IP address of `20.20.20.5` , use this rule:

```
rdr dc0 20.20.20.5/32 port 80 -> 10.0.10.25 port 80
```

If it is the only web server, this rule would also work as it redirects all external HTTP requests to `10.0.10.25` :

```
rdr dc0 0.0.0.0/0 port 80 -> 10.0.10.25 port 80
```

IPF has a built in FTP proxy which can be used with NAT. It monitors all outbound traffic for active or passive FTP connection requests and dynamically creates temporary filter rules containing the port number used by the FTP data channel. This eliminates the need to open large ranges of high order ports for FTP connections.

In this example, the first rule calls the proxy for outbound FTP traffic from the internal LAN. The second rule passes the FTP traffic from the firewall to the Internet, and the third rule handles all non-FTP traffic from the internal LAN:

```
map dc0 10.0.10.0/29 -> 0/32 proxy port 21 ftp/tcp
map dc0 0.0.0.0/0 -> 0/32 proxy port 21 ftp/tcp
map dc0 10.0.10.0/29 -> 0/32
```

The FTP `map` rules go before the NAT rule so that when a packet matches an FTP rule, the FTP proxy creates temporary filter rules to let the FTP session packets pass and undergo NAT. All LAN packets that are not FTP will not match the FTP rules but will undergo NAT if they match the third rule.

Without the FTP proxy, the following firewall rules would instead be needed. Note that without the proxy, all ports above `1024` need to be allowed:

```
# Allow out LAN PC client FTP to public Internet
# Active and passive modes
pass out quick on rl0 proto tcp from any to any port = 21 flags S keep state

# Allow out passive mode data channel high order port numbers
pass out quick on rl0 proto tcp from any to any port > 1024 flags S keep state

# Active mode let data channel in from FTP server
pass in quick on rl0 proto tcp from any to any port = 20 flags S keep state
```

Whenever the file containing the NAT rules is edited, run `ipnat` with `-CF` to delete the current NAT rules and flush the contents of the dynamic translation table. Include `-f` and specify the name of the NAT ruleset to load:

```
# ipnat -CF -f /etc/ipnat.rules
```

To display the NAT statistics:

```
# ipnat -s
```

To list the NAT table's current mappings:

```
# ipnat -l
```

To turn verbose mode on and display information relating to rule processing and active rules and table entries:

```
# ipnat -v
```

29.5.5. Viewing IPF Statistics

IPF includes ipfstat(8) which can be used to retrieve and display statistics which are gathered as packets match rules as they go through the firewall. Statistics are accumulated since the firewall was last started or since the last time they were reset to zero using `ipf -Z`.

The default `ipfstat` output looks like this:

```
input packets: blocked 99286 passed 1255609 nomatch 14686 counted 0
 output packets: blocked 4200 passed 1284345 nomatch 14687 counted 0
 input packets logged: blocked 99286 passed 0
 output packets logged: blocked 0 passed 0
 packets logged: input 0 output 0
```

```
log failures: input 3898 output 0
fragment state(in): kept 0 lost 0
fragment state(out): kept 0 lost 0
packet state(in): kept 169364 lost 0
packet state(out): kept 431395 lost 0
ICMP replies: 0 TCP RSTs sent: 0
Result cache hits(in): 1215208 (out): 1098963
IN Pullups succeeded: 2 failed: 0
OUT Pullups succeeded: 0 failed: 0
Fastroute successes: 0 failures: 0
TCP cksum fails(in): 0 (out): 0
Packet log flags set: (0)
```

Several options are available. When supplied with either -i for inbound or -o for outbound, the command will retrieve and display the appropriate list of filter rules currently installed and in use by the kernel. To also see the rule numbers, include -n. For example, ipfstat -on displays the outbound rules table with rule numbers:

```
@1 pass out on xl0 from any to any
@2 block out on dc0 from any to any
@3 pass out quick on dc0 proto tcp/udp from any to any keep state
```

Include -h to prefix each rule with a count of how many times the rule was matched. For example, ipfstat -oh displays the outbound internal rules table, prefixing each rule with its usage count:

```
2451423 pass out on xl0 from any to any
354727 block out on dc0 from any to any
430918 pass out quick on dc0 proto tcp/udp from any to any keep state
```

To display the state table in a format similar to top(1), use ipfstat -t. When the firewall is under attack, this option provides the ability to identify and see the attacking packets. The optional sub-flags give the ability to select the destination or source IP, port, or protocol to be monitored in real time. Refer to ipfstat(8) for details.

29.5.6. IPF Logging

IPF provides ipmon, which can be used to write the firewall's logging information in a human readable format. It requires that options IPFILTER_LOG be first added to a custom kernel using the instructions in Chapter 8, *Configuring the FreeBSD Kernel*.

This command is typically run in daemon mode in order to provide a continuous system log file so that logging of past events may be reviewed. Since FreeBSD has a built in syslogd(8) facility to automatically rotate system logs, the default rc.conf ipmon_flags statement uses -Ds:

```
ipmon_flags="-Ds" # D = start as daemon
                  # s = log to syslog
                  # v = log tcp window, ack, seq
                  # n = map IP & port to names
```

Logging provides the ability to review, after the fact, information such as which packets were dropped, what addresses they came from, and where they were going. This information is useful in tracking down attackers.

Once the logging facility is enabled in rc.conf and started with service ipmon start, IPF will only log the rules which contain the log keyword. The firewall administrator decides which rules in the ruleset should be logged and normally only deny rules are logged. It is customary to include the log keyword in the last rule in the ruleset. This makes it possible to see all the packets that did not match any of the rules in the ruleset.

By default, ipmon -Ds mode uses local0 as the logging facility. The following logging levels can be used to further segregate the logged data:

```
LOG_INFO - packets logged using the "log" keyword as the action rather than pass or ᴜ
block.
LOG_NOTICE - packets logged which are also passed
LOG_WARNING - packets logged which are also blocked
```

```
LOG_ERR - packets which have been logged and which can be considered short due to an ↵
incomplete header
```

In order to setup IPF to log all data to /var/log/ipfilter.log , first create the empty file:

 # touch /var/log/ipfilter.log

Then, to write all logged messages to the specified file, add the following statement to /etc/syslog.conf :

```
local0.* /var/log/ipfilter.log
```

To activate the changes and instruct syslogd(8) to read the modified /etc/syslog.conf , run service syslogd reload.

Do not forget to edit /etc/newsyslog.conf to rotate the new log file.

Messages generated by ipmon consist of data fields separated by white space. Fields common to all messages are:

1. The date of packet receipt.

2. The time of packet receipt. This is in the form HH:MM:SS.F, for hours, minutes, seconds, and fractions of a second.

3. The name of the interface that processed the packet.

4. The group and rule number of the rule in the format @0:17.

5. The action: p for passed, b for blocked, S for a short packet, n did not match any rules, and L for a log rule.

6. The addresses written as three fields: the source address and port separated by a comma, the -> symbol, and the destination address and port. For example: 209.53.17.22,80 -> 198.73.220.17,1722 .

7. PR followed by the protocol name or number: for example, PR tcp.

8. len followed by the header length and total length of the packet: for example, len 20 40.

If the packet is a TCP packet, there will be an additional field starting with a hyphen followed by letters corresponding to any flags that were set. Refer to ipf(5) for a list of letters and their flags.

If the packet is an ICMP packet, there will be two fields at the end: the first always being "icmp" and the next being the ICMP message and sub-message type, separated by a slash. For example: icmp 3/3 for a port unreachable message.

Chapter 30. Advanced Networking

30.1. Synopsis

This chapter covers a number of advanced networking topics.

After reading this chapter, you will know:

- The basics of gateways and routes.

- How to set up USB tethering.

- How to set up IEEE® 802.11 and Bluetooth® devices.

- How to make FreeBSD act as a bridge.

- How to set up network PXE booting.

- How to set up IPv6 on a FreeBSD machine.

- How to enable and utilize the features of the Common Address Redundancy Protocol (CARP) in FreeBSD.

- How to configure multiple VLANs on FreeBSD.

Before reading this chapter, you should:

- Understand the basics of the /etc/rc scripts.

- Be familiar with basic network terminology.

- Know how to configure and install a new FreeBSD kernel (Chapter 8, *Configuring the FreeBSD Kernel*).

- Know how to install additional third-party software (Chapter 4, *Installing Applications: Packages and Ports*).

30.2. Gateways and Routes

Contributed by Coranth Gryphon.

Routing is the mechanism that allows a system to find the network path to another system. A *route* is a defined pair of addresses which represent the "destination" and a "gateway". The route indicates that when trying to get to the specified destination, send the packets through the specified gateway. There are three types of destinations: individual hosts, subnets, and "default". The "default route" is used if no other routes apply. There are also three types of gateways: individual hosts, interfaces, also called links, and Ethernet hardware (MAC) addresses. Known routes are stored in a routing table.

This section provides an overview of routing basics. It then demonstrates how to configure a FreeBSD system as a router and offers some troubleshooting tips.

30.2.1. Routing Basics

To view the routing table of a FreeBSD system, use netstat(1):

```
% netstat -r
Routing tables

Internet:
Destination      Gateway            Flags    Refs     Use     Netif Expire
default          outside-gw         UGS        37     418       em0
localhost        localhost          UH          0     181       lo0
test0            0:e0:b5:36:cf:4f   UHLW        5   63288       re0     77
```

```
10.20.30.255      link#1            UHLW      1     2421
example.com       link#1            UC        0        0
host1             0:e0:a8:37:8:1e   UHLW      3     4601     lo0
host2             0:e0:a8:37:8:1e   UHLW      0        5     lo0 =>
host2.example.com link#1            UC        0        0
224               link#1            UC        0        0
```

The entries in this example are as follows:

default

> The first route in this table specifies the default route. When the local system needs to make a connection to a remote host, it checks the routing table to determine if a known path exists. If the remote host matches an entry in the table, the system checks to see if it can connect using the interface specified in that entry.

> If the destination does not match an entry, or if all known paths fail, the system uses the entry for the default route. For hosts on a local area network, the Gateway field in the default route is set to the system which has a direct connection to the Internet. When reading this entry, verify that the Flags column indicates that the gateway is usable (UG).

> The default route for a machine which itself is functioning as the gateway to the outside world will be the gateway machine at the Internet Service Provider (ISP).

localhost

> The second route is the localhost route. The interface specified in the Netif column for localhost is lo0, also known as the loopback device. This indicates that all traffic for this destination should be internal, rather than sending it out over the network.

MAC address

> The addresses beginning with 0:e0: are MAC addresses. FreeBSD will automatically identify any hosts, test0 in the example, on the local Ethernet and add a route for that host over the Ethernet interface, re0. This type of route has a timeout, seen in the Expire column, which is used if the host does not respond in a specific amount of time. When this happens, the route to this host will be automatically deleted. These hosts are identified using the Routing Information Protocol (RIP), which calculates routes to local hosts based upon a shortest path determination.

subnet

> FreeBSD will automatically add subnet routes for the local subnet. In this example, 10.20.30.255 is the broadcast address for the subnet 10.20.30 and example.com is the domain name associated with that subnet. The designation link#1 refers to the first Ethernet card in the machine.

> Local network hosts and local subnets have their routes automatically configured by a daemon called routed(8). If it is not running, only routes which are statically defined by the administrator will exist.

host

> The host1 line refers to the host by its Ethernet address. Since it is the sending host, FreeBSD knows to use the loopback interface (lo0) rather than the Ethernet interface.

> The two host2 lines represent aliases which were created using ifconfig(8). The => symbol after the lo0 interface says that an alias has been set in addition to the loopback address. Such routes only show up on the host that supports the alias and all other hosts on the local network will have a link#1 line for such routes.

224

> The final line (destination subnet 224) deals with multicasting.

Various attributes of each route can be seen in the Flags column. Table 30.1, "Commonly Seen Routing Table Flags" summarizes some of these flags and their meanings:

Table 30.1. Commonly Seen Routing Table Flags

Command	Purpose
U	The route is active (up).

Command	Purpose
H	The route destination is a single host.
G	Send anything for this destination on to this gateway, which will figure out from there where to send it.
S	This route was statically configured.
C	Clones a new route based upon this route for machines to connect to. This type of route is normally used for local networks.
W	The route was auto-configured based upon a local area network (clone) route.
L	Route involves references to Ethernet (link) hardware.

On a FreeBSD system, the default route can defined in /etc/rc.conf by specifying the IP address of the default gateway:

```
defaultrouter="10.20.30.1"
```

It is also possible to manually add the route using route:

```
# route add default 10.20.30.1
```

Note that manually added routes will not survive a reboot. For more information on manual manipulation of network routing tables, refer to route(8).

30.2.2. Configuring a Router with Static Routes

Contributed by Al Hoang.

A FreeBSD system can be configured as the default gateway, or router, for a network if it is a dual-homed system. A dual-homed system is a host which resides on at least two different networks. Typically, each network is connected to a separate network interface, though IP aliasing can be used to bind multiple addresses, each on a different subnet, to one physical interface.

In order for the system to forward packets between interfaces, FreeBSD must be configured as a router. Internet standards and good engineering practice prevent the FreeBSD Project from enabling this feature by default, but it can be configured to start at boot by adding this line to /etc/rc.conf :

```
gateway_enable="YES"          # Set to YES if this host will be a gateway
```

To enable routing now, set the sysctl(8) variable net.inet.ip.forwarding to 1. To stop routing, reset this variable to 0.

The routing table of a router needs additional routes so it knows how to reach other networks. Routes can be either added manually using static routes or routes can be automatically learned using a routing protocol. Static routes are appropriate for small networks and this section describes how to add a static routing entry for a small network.

Note

For large networks, static routes quickly become unscalable. FreeBSD comes with the standard BSD routing daemon routed(8), which provides the routing protocols RIP, versions 1 and 2, and IRDP. Support for the BGP and OSPF routing protocols can be installed using the net/zebra package or port.

Consider the following network:

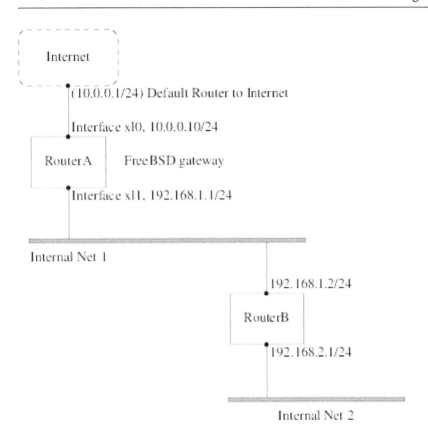

In this scenario, RouterA is a FreeBSD machine that is acting as a router to the rest of the Internet. It has a default route set to 10.0.0.1 which allows it to connect with the outside world. RouterB is already configured to use 192.168.1.1 as its default gateway.

Before adding any static routes, the routing table on RouterA looks like this:

```
% netstat -nr
Routing tables

Internet:
Destination       Gateway           Flags   Refs      Use  Netif  Expire
default           10.0.0.1          UGS        0    49378   xl0
127.0.0.1         127.0.0.1         UH         0        6   lo0
10.0.0.0/24       link#1            UC         0        0   xl0
192.168.1.0/24    link#2            UC         0        0   xl1
```

With the current routing table, RouterA does not have a route to the 192.168.2.0/24 network. The following command adds the Internal Net 2 network to RouterA's routing table using 192.168.1.2 as the next hop:

```
# route add -net 192.168.2.0/24 192.168.1.2
```

Now, RouterA can reach any host on the 192.168.2.0/24 network. However, the routing information will not persist if the FreeBSD system reboots. If a static route needs to be persistent, add it to /etc/rc.conf :

```
# Add Internal Net 2 as a persistent static route
static_routes="internalnet2"
route_internalnet2="-net 192.168.2.0/24 192.168.1.2"
```

The static_routes configuration variable is a list of strings separated by a space, where each string references a route name. The variable route_internalnet2 contains the static route for that route name.

Using more than one string in static_routes creates multiple static routes. The following shows an example of adding static routes for the 192.168.0.0/24 and 192.168.1.0/24 networks:

```
static_routes="net1 net2"
route_net1="-net 192.168.0.0/24 192.168.0.1"
route_net2="-net 192.168.1.0/24 192.168.1.1"
```

30.2.3. Troubleshooting

When an address space is assigned to a network, the service provider configures their routing tables so that all traffic for the network will be sent to the link for the site. But how do external sites know to send their packets to the network's ISP?

There is a system that keeps track of all assigned address spaces and defines their point of connection to the Internet backbone, or the main trunk lines that carry Internet traffic across the country and around the world. Each backbone machine has a copy of a master set of tables, which direct traffic for a particular network to a specific backbone carrier, and from there down the chain of service providers until it reaches a particular network.

It is the task of the service provider to advertise to the backbone sites that they are the point of connection, and thus the path inward, for a site. This is known as route propagation.

Sometimes, there is a problem with route propagation and some sites are unable to connect. Perhaps the most useful command for trying to figure out where routing is breaking down is traceroute. It is useful when ping fails.

When using traceroute, include the address of the remote host to connect to. The output will show the gateway hosts along the path of the attempt, eventually either reaching the target host, or terminating because of a lack of connection. For more information, refer to traceroute(8).

30.2.4. Multicast Considerations

FreeBSD natively supports both multicast applications and multicast routing. Multicast applications do not require any special configuration in order to run on FreeBSD. Support for multicast routing requires that the following option be compiled into a custom kernel:

```
options MROUTING
```

The multicast routing daemon, mrouted can be installed using the net/mrouted package or port. This daemon implements the DVMRP multicast routing protocol and is configured by editing /usr/local/etc/mrouted.conf in order to set up the tunnels and DVMRP. The installation of mrouted also installs map-mbone and mrinfo, as well as their associated man pages. Refer to these for configuration examples.

Note

DVMRP has largely been replaced by the PIM protocol in many multicast installations. Refer to pim(4) for more information.

30.3. Wireless Networking

Loader, Marc Fonvieille and Murray Stokely.

30.3.1. Wireless Networking Basics

Most wireless networks are based on the IEEE® 802.11 standards. A basic wireless network consists of multiple stations communicating with radios that broadcast in either the 2.4GHz or 5GHz band, though this varies according to the locale and is also changing to enable communication in the 2.3GHz and 4.9GHz ranges.

802.11 networks are organized in two ways. In *infrastructure mode*, one station acts as a master with all the other stations associating to it, the network is known as a BSS, and the master station is termed an access point (AP).

In a BSS, all communication passes through the AP; even when one station wants to communicate with another wireless station, messages must go through the AP. In the second form of network, there is no master and stations communicate directly. This form of network is termed an IBSS and is commonly known as an *ad-hoc network*.

802.11 networks were first deployed in the 2.4GHz band using protocols defined by the IEEE® 802.11 and 802.11b standard. These specifications include the operating frequencies and the MAC layer characteristics, including framing and transmission rates, as communication can occur at various rates. Later, the 802.11a standard defined operation in the 5GHz band, including different signaling mechanisms and higher transmission rates. Still later, the 802.11g standard defined the use of 802.11a signaling and transmission mechanisms in the 2.4GHz band in such a way as to be backwards compatible with 802.11b networks.

Separate from the underlying transmission techniques, 802.11 networks have a variety of security mechanisms. The original 802.11 specifications defined a simple security protocol called WEP. This protocol uses a fixed pre-shared key and the RC4 cryptographic cipher to encode data transmitted on a network. Stations must all agree on the fixed key in order to communicate. This scheme was shown to be easily broken and is now rarely used except to discourage transient users from joining networks. Current security practice is given by the IEEE® 802.11i specification that defines new cryptographic ciphers and an additional protocol to authenticate stations to an access point and exchange keys for data communication. Cryptographic keys are periodically refreshed and there are mechanisms for detecting and countering intrusion attempts. Another security protocol specification commonly used in wireless networks is termed WPA, which was a precursor to 802.11i. WPA specifies a subset of the requirements found in 802.11i and is designed for implementation on legacy hardware. Specifically, WPA requires only the TKIP cipher that is derived from the original WEP cipher. 802.11i permits use of TKIP but also requires support for a stronger cipher, AES-CCM, for encrypting data. The AES cipher was not required in WPA because it was deemed too computationally costly to be implemented on legacy hardware.

The other standard to be aware of is 802.11e. It defines protocols for deploying multimedia applications, such as streaming video and voice over IP (VoIP), in an 802.11 network. Like 802.11i, 802.11e also has a precursor specification termed WME (later renamed WMM) that has been defined by an industry group as a subset of 802.11e that can be deployed now to enable multimedia applications while waiting for the final ratification of 802.11e. The most important thing to know about 802.11e and WME/WMM is that it enables prioritized traffic over a wireless network through Quality of Service (QoS) protocols and enhanced media access protocols. Proper implementation of these protocols enables high speed bursting of data and prioritized traffic flow.

FreeBSD supports networks that operate using 802.11a, 802.11b, and 802.11g. The WPA and 802.11i security protocols are likewise supported (in conjunction with any of 11a, 11b, and 11g) and QoS and traffic prioritization required by the WME/WMM protocols are supported for a limited set of wireless devices.

30.3.2. Quick Start

Connecting a computer to an existing wireless network is a very common situation. This procedure shows the steps required.

1. Obtain the SSID (Service Set Identifier) and PSK (Pre-Shared Key) for the wireless network from the network administrator.

2. Identify the wireless adapter. The FreeBSD GENERIC kernel includes drivers for many common wireless adapters. If the wireless adapter is one of those models, it will be shown in the output from ifconfig(8):

    ```
    % ifconfig | grep -B3 -i wireless
    ```

    On FreeBSD 11 or higher, use this command instead:

    ```
    % sysctl net.wlan.devices
    ```

    If a wireless adapter is not listed, an additional kernel module might be required, or it might be a model not supported by FreeBSD.

    This example shows the Atheros ath0 wireless adapter.

3. Add an entry for this network to /etc/wpa_supplicant.conf. If the file does not exist, create it. Replace *myssid* and *mypsk* with the SSID and PSK provided by the network administrator.

```
network={
  ssid="myssid"
  psk="mypsk"
}
```

4. Add entries to /etc/rc.conf to configure the network on startup:

```
wlans_ath0="wlan0"
ifconfig_wlan0="WPA SYNCDHCP"
```

5. Restart the computer, or restart the network service to connect to the network:

```
# service netif restart
```

30.3.3. Basic Setup

30.3.3.1. Kernel Configuration

To use wireless networking, a wireless networking card is needed and the kernel needs to be configured with the appropriate wireless networking support. The kernel is separated into multiple modules so that only the required support needs to be configured.

The most commonly used wireless devices are those that use parts made by Atheros. These devices are supported by ath(4) and require the following line to be added to /boot/loader.conf :

```
if_ath_load="YES"
```

The Atheros driver is split up into three separate pieces: the driver (ath(4)), the hardware support layer that handles chip-specific functions (ath_hal(4)), and an algorithm for selecting the rate for transmitting frames. When this support is loaded as kernel modules, any dependencies are automatically handled. To load support for a different type of wireless device, specify the module for that device. This example is for devices based on the Intersil Prism parts (wi(4)) driver:

```
if_wi_load="YES"
```

Note

The examples in this section use an ath(4) device and the device name in the examples must be changed according to the configuration. A list of available wireless drivers and supported adapters can be found in the FreeBSD Hardware Notes, available on the Release Information page of the FreeBSD website. If a native FreeBSD driver for the wireless device does not exist, it may be possible to use the Windows® driver with the help of the NDIS driver wrapper.

In addition, the modules that implement cryptographic support for the security protocols to use must be loaded. These are intended to be dynamically loaded on demand by the wlan(4) module, but for now they must be manually configured. The following modules are available: wlan_wep(4), wlan_ccmp(4), and wlan_tkip(4). The wlan_ccmp(4) and wlan_tkip(4) drivers are only needed when using the WPA or 802.11i security protocols. If the network does not use encryption, wlan_wep(4) support is not needed. To load these modules at boot time, add the following lines to /boot/loader.conf :

```
wlan_wep_load="YES"
wlan_ccmp_load="YES"
wlan_tkip_load="YES"
```

Once this information has been added to /boot/loader.conf , reboot the FreeBSD box. Alternately, load the modules by hand using kldload(8).

Note

For users who do not want to use modules, it is possible to compile these drivers into the kernel by adding the following lines to a custom kernel configuration file:

```
device wlan            # 802.11 support
device wlan_wep        # 802.11 WEP support
device wlan_ccmp       # 802.11 CCMP support
device wlan_tkip       # 802.11 TKIP support
device wlan_amrr       # AMRR transmit rate control algorithm
device ath             # Atheros pci/cardbus NIC's
device ath_hal         # pci/cardbus chip support
options AH_SUPPORT_AR5416 # enable AR5416 tx/rx descriptors
device ath_rate_sample # SampleRate tx rate control for ath
```

With this information in the kernel configuration file, recompile the kernel and reboot the FreeBSD machine.

Information about the wireless device should appear in the boot messages, like this:

```
ath0: <Atheros 5212> mem 0x88000000-0x8800ffff irq 11 at device 0.0 on cardbus1
ath0: [ITHREAD]
ath0: AR2413 mac 7.9 RF2413 phy 4.5
```

30.3.4. Infrastructure Mode

Infrastructure (BSS) mode is the mode that is typically used. In this mode, a number of wireless access points are connected to a wired network. Each wireless network has its own name, called the SSID. Wireless clients connect to the wireless access points.

30.3.4.1. FreeBSD Clients

30.3.4.1.1. How to Find Access Points

To scan for available networks, use ifconfig(8). This request may take a few moments to complete as it requires the system to switch to each available wireless frequency and probe for available access points. Only the superuser can initiate a scan:

```
# ifconfig wlan0 create wlandev ath0
# ifconfig wlan0 up scan
SSID/MESH ID    BSSID             CHAN RATE   S:N     INT CAPS
dlinkap         00:13:46:49:41:76  11   54M -90:96   100 EPS  WPA WME
freebsdap       00:11:95:c3:0d:ac   1   54M -83:96   100 EPS  WPA
```

Note

The interface must be up before it can scan. Subsequent scan requests do not require the interface to be marked as up again.

The output of a scan request lists each BSS/IBSS network found. Besides listing the name of the network, the SSID, the output also shows the BSSID, which is the MAC address of the access point. The CAPS field identifies the type of each network and the capabilities of the stations operating there:

Table 30.2. Station Capability Codes

Capability Code	Meaning
E	Extended Service Set (ESS). Indicates that the station is part of an infrastructure network rather than an IBSS/ad-hoc network.
I	IBSS/ad-hoc network. Indicates that the station is part of an ad-hoc network rather than an ESS network.
P	Privacy. Encryption is required for all data frames exchanged within the BSS using cryptographic means such as WEP, TKIP or AES-CCMP.
S	Short Preamble. Indicates that the network is using short preambles, defined in 802.11b High Rate/DSSS PHY, and utilizes a 56 bit sync field rather than the 128 bit field used in long preamble mode.
s	Short slot time. Indicates that the 802.11g network is using a short slot time because there are no legacy (802.11b) stations present.

One can also display the current list of known networks with:

```
# ifconfig wlan0 list scan
```

This information may be updated automatically by the adapter or manually with a scan request. Old data is automatically removed from the cache, so over time this list may shrink unless more scans are done.

30.3.4.1.2. Basic Settings

This section provides a simple example of how to make the wireless network adapter work in FreeBSD without encryption. Once familiar with these concepts, it is strongly recommend to use WPA to set up the wireless network.

There are three basic steps to configure a wireless network: select an access point, authenticate the station, and configure an IP address. The following sections discuss each step.

30.3.4.1.2.1. Selecting an Access Point

Most of the time, it is sufficient to let the system choose an access point using the builtin heuristics. This is the default behavior when an interface is marked as up or it is listed in /etc/rc.conf :

```
wlans_ath0="wlan0"
ifconfig_wlan0="DHCP"
```

If there are multiple access points, a specific one can be selected by its SSID:

```
wlans_ath0="wlan0"
ifconfig_wlan0="ssid your_ssid_here DHCP"
```

In an environment where there are multiple access points with the same SSID, which is often done to simplify roaming, it may be necessary to associate to one specific device. In this case, the BSSID of the access point can be specified, with or without the SSID:

```
wlans_ath0="wlan0"
ifconfig_wlan0="ssid your_ssid_here bssid xx:xx:xx:xx:xx:xx DHCP"
```

There are other ways to constrain the choice of an access point, such as limiting the set of frequencies the system will scan on. This may be useful for a multi-band wireless card as scanning all the possible channels can be time-consuming. To limit operation to a specific band, use the mode parameter:

```
wlans_ath0="wlan0"
ifconfig_wlan0="mode 11g ssid your_ssid_here DHCP"
```

This example will force the card to operate in 802.11g, which is defined only for 2.4GHz frequencies so any 5GHz channels will not be considered. This can also be achieved with the `channel` parameter, which locks operation to one specific frequency, and the `chanlist` parameter, to specify a list of channels for scanning. More information about these parameters can be found in ifconfig(8).

30.3.4.1.2.2. Authentication

Once an access point is selected, the station needs to authenticate before it can pass data. Authentication can happen in several ways. The most common scheme, open authentication, allows any station to join the network and communicate. This is the authentication to use for test purposes the first time a wireless network is setup. Other schemes require cryptographic handshakes to be completed before data traffic can flow, either using pre-shared keys or secrets, or more complex schemes that involve backend services such as RADIUS. Open authentication is the default setting. The next most common setup is WPA-PSK, also known as WPA Personal, which is described in Section 30.3.4.1.3.1, "WPA-PSK".

Note

If using an Apple® AirPort® Extreme base station for an access point, shared-key authentication together with a WEP key needs to be configured. This can be configured in `/etc/rc.conf` or by using wpa_supplicant(8). For a single AirPort® base station, access can be configured with:

```
wlans_ath0="wlan0"
ifconfig_wlan0="authmode shared wepmode on weptxkey 1 wepkey 01234567 ↺
DHCP"
```

In general, shared key authentication should be avoided because it uses the WEP key material in a highly-constrained manner, making it even easier to crack the key. If WEP must be used for compatibility with legacy devices, it is better to use WEP with open authentication. More information regarding WEP can be found in Section 30.3.4.1.4, "WEP".

30.3.4.1.2.3. Getting an IP Address with DHCP

Once an access point is selected and the authentication parameters are set, an IP address must be obtained in order to communicate. Most of the time, the IP address is obtained via DHCP. To achieve that, edit `/etc/rc.conf` and add `DHCP` to the configuration for the device:

```
wlans_ath0="wlan0"
ifconfig_wlan0="DHCP"
```

The wireless interface is now ready to bring up:

```
# service netif start
```

Once the interface is running, use ifconfig(8) to see the status of the interface `ath0`:

```
# ifconfig wlan0
wlan0: flags=8843<UP,BROADCAST,RUNNING,SIMPLEX,MULTICAST> mtu 1500
        ether 00:11:95:d5:43:62
        inet 192.168.1.100 netmask 0xffffff00 broadcast 192.168.1.255
        media: IEEE 802.11 Wireless Ethernet OFDM/54Mbps mode 11g
        status: associated
        ssid dlinkap channel 11 (2462 Mhz 11g) bssid 00:13:46:49:41:76
        country US ecm authmode OPEN privacy OFF txpower 21.5 bmiss 7
        scanvalid 60 bgscan bgscanintvl 300 bgscanidle 250 roam:rssi 7
        roam:rate 5 protmode CTS wme burst
```

The `status: associated` line means that it is connected to the wireless network. The `bssid 00:13:46:49:41:76` is the MAC address of the access point and `authmode OPEN` indicates that the communication is not encrypted.

30.3.4.1.2.4. Static IP Address

If an IP address cannot be obtained from a DHCP server, set a fixed IP address. Replace the DHCP keyword shown above with the address information. Be sure to retain any other parameters for selecting the access point:

```
wlans_ath0="wlan0"
ifconfig_wlan0="inet 192.168.1.100 netmask 255.255.255.0 ssid your_ssid_here "
```

30.3.4.1.3. WPA

Wi-Fi Protected Access (WPA) is a security protocol used together with 802.11 networks to address the lack of proper authentication and the weakness of WEP. WPA leverages the 802.1X authentication protocol and uses one of several ciphers instead of WEP for data integrity. The only cipher required by WPA is the Temporary Key Integrity Protocol (TKIP). TKIP is a cipher that extends the basic RC4 cipher used by WEP by adding integrity checking, tamper detection, and measures for responding to detected intrusions. TKIP is designed to work on legacy hardware with only software modification. It represents a compromise that improves security but is still not entirely immune to attack. WPA also specifies the AES-CCMP cipher as an alternative to TKIP, and that is preferred when possible. For this specification, the term WPA2 or RSN is commonly used.

WPA defines authentication and encryption protocols. Authentication is most commonly done using one of two techniques: by 802.1X and a backend authentication service such as RADIUS, or by a minimal handshake between the station and the access point using a pre-shared secret. The former is commonly termed WPA Enterprise and the latter is known as WPA Personal. Since most people will not set up a RADIUS backend server for their wireless network, WPA-PSK is by far the most commonly encountered configuration for WPA.

The control of the wireless connection and the key negotiation or authentication with a server is done using wpa_supplicant(8). This program requires a configuration file, /etc/wpa_supplicant.conf, to run. More information regarding this file can be found in wpa_supplicant.conf(5).

30.3.4.1.3.1. WPA-PSK

WPA-PSK, also known as WPA Personal, is based on a pre-shared key (PSK) which is generated from a given password and used as the master key in the wireless network. This means every wireless user will share the same key. WPA-PSK is intended for small networks where the use of an authentication server is not possible or desired.

Warning

Always use strong passwords that are sufficiently long and made from a rich alphabet so that they will not be easily guessed or attacked.

The first step is the configuration of /etc/wpa_supplicant.conf with the SSID and the pre-shared key of the network:

```
network={
  ssid="freebsdap"
  psk="freebsdmall"
}
```

Then, in /etc/rc.conf, indicate that the wireless device configuration will be done with WPA and the IP address will be obtained with DHCP:

```
wlans_ath0="wlan0"
ifconfig_wlan0="WPA DHCP"
```

Then, bring up the interface:

```
# service netif start
Starting wpa_supplicant.
```

```
DHCPDISCOVER on wlan0 to 255.255.255.255 port 67 interval 5
DHCPDISCOVER on wlan0 to 255.255.255.255 port 67 interval 6
DHCPOFFER from 192.168.0.1
DHCPREQUEST on wlan0 to 255.255.255.255 port 67
DHCPACK from 192.168.0.1
bound to 192.168.0.254 -- renewal in 300 seconds.
wlan0: flags=8843<UP,BROADCAST,RUNNING,SIMPLEX,MULTICAST> mtu 1500
        ether 00:11:95:d5:43:62
        inet 192.168.0.254 netmask 0xffffff00 broadcast 192.168.0.255
        media: IEEE 802.11 Wireless Ethernet OFDM/36Mbps mode 11g
        status: associated
        ssid freebsdap channel 1 (2412 Mhz 11g) bssid 00:11:95:c3:0d:ac
        country US ecm authmode WPA2/802.11i privacy ON deftxkey UNDEF
        AES-CCM 3:128-bit txpower 21.5 bmiss 7 scanvalid 450 bgscan
        bgscanintvl 300 bgscanidle 250 roam:rssi 7 roam:rate 5 protmode CTS
        wme burst roaming MANUAL
```

Or, try to configure the interface manually using the information in /etc/wpa_supplicant.conf:

```
# wpa_supplicant -i wlan0 -c /etc/wpa_supplicant.conf
Trying to associate with 00:11:95:c3:0d:ac (SSID='freebsdap' freq=2412 MHz)
Associated with 00:11:95:c3:0d:ac
WPA: Key negotiation completed with 00:11:95:c3:0d:ac [PTK=CCMP GTK=CCMP]
CTRL-EVENT-CONNECTED - Connection to 00:11:95:c3:0d:ac completed (auth) [id=0 id_str=]
```

The next operation is to launch dhclient(8) to get the IP address from the DHCP server:

```
# dhclient wlan0
DHCPREQUEST on wlan0 to 255.255.255.255 port 67
DHCPACK from 192.168.0.1
bound to 192.168.0.254 -- renewal in 300 seconds.
# ifconfig wlan0
wlan0: flags=8843<UP,BROADCAST,RUNNING,SIMPLEX,MULTICAST> mtu 1500
        ether 00:11:95:d5:43:62
        inet 192.168.0.254 netmask 0xffffff00 broadcast 192.168.0.255
        media: IEEE 802.11 Wireless Ethernet OFDM/36Mbps mode 11g
        status: associated
        ssid freebsdap channel 1 (2412 Mhz 11g) bssid 00:11:95:c3:0d:ac
        country US ecm authmode WPA2/802.11i privacy ON deftxkey UNDEF
        AES-CCM 3:128-bit txpower 21.5 bmiss 7 scanvalid 450 bgscan
        bgscanintvl 300 bgscanidle 250 roam:rssi 7 roam:rate 5 protmode CTS
        wme burst roaming MANUAL
```

Note

If /etc/rc.conf has an ifconfig_wlan0="DHCP" entry, dhclient(8) will be launched automatically after wpa_supplicant(8) associates with the access point.

If DHCP is not possible or desired, set a static IP address after wpa_supplicant(8) has authenticated the station:

```
# ifconfig wlan0 inet 192.168.0.100 netmask 255.255.255.0
# ifconfig wlan0
wlan0: flags=8843<UP,BROADCAST,RUNNING,SIMPLEX,MULTICAST> mtu 1500
        ether 00:11:95:d5:43:62
        inet 192.168.0.100 netmask 0xffffff00 broadcast 192.168.0.255
        media: IEEE 802.11 Wireless Ethernet OFDM/36Mbps mode 11g
        status: associated
        ssid freebsdap channel 1 (2412 Mhz 11g) bssid 00:11:95:c3:0d:ac
        country US ecm authmode WPA2/802.11i privacy ON deftxkey UNDEF
        AES-CCM 3:128-bit txpower 21.5 bmiss 7 scanvalid 450 bgscan
        bgscanintvl 300 bgscanidle 250 roam:rssi 7 roam:rate 5 protmode CTS
        wme burst roaming MANUAL
```

When DHCP is not used, the default gateway and the nameserver also have to be manually set:

```
# route add default your_default_router
# echo "nameserver your_DNS_server " >> /etc/resolv.conf
```

30.3.4.1.3.2. WPA with EAP-TLS

The second way to use WPA is with an 802.1X backend authentication server. In this case, WPA is called WPA Enterprise to differentiate it from the less secure WPA Personal. Authentication in WPA Enterprise is based on the Extensible Authentication Protocol (EAP).

EAP does not come with an encryption method. Instead, EAP is embedded inside an encrypted tunnel. There are many EAP authentication methods, but EAP-TLS, EAP-TTLS, and EAP-PEAP are the most common.

EAP with Transport Layer Security (EAP-TLS) is a well-supported wireless authentication protocol since it was the first EAP method to be certified by the Wi-Fi Alliance. EAP-TLS requires three certificates to run: the certificate of the Certificate Authority (CA) installed on all machines, the server certificate for the authentication server, and one client certificate for each wireless client. In this EAP method, both the authentication server and wireless client authenticate each other by presenting their respective certificates, and then verify that these certificates were signed by the organization's CA.

As previously, the configuration is done via /etc/wpa_supplicant.conf:

```
network={
    ssid="freebsdap"  ❶
    proto=RSN  ❷
    key_mgmt=WPA-EAP  ❸
    eap=TLS  ❹
    identity="loader"  ❺
    ca_cert="/etc/certs/cacert.pem"  ❻
    client_cert="/etc/certs/clientcert.pem"  ❼
    private_key="/etc/certs/clientkey.pem"  ❽
    private_key_passwd="freebsdmallclient"  ❾
}
```

❶   This field indicates the network name (SSID).

❷   This example uses the RSN IEEE® 802.11i protocol, also known as WPA2.

❸   The key_mgmt line refers to the key management protocol to use. In this example, it is WPA using EAP authentication.

❹   This field indicates the EAP method for the connection.

❺   The identity field contains the identity string for EAP.

❻   The ca_cert field indicates the pathname of the CA certificate file. This file is needed to verify the server certificate.

❼   The client_cert line gives the pathname to the client certificate file. This certificate is unique to each wireless client of the network.

❽   The private_key field is the pathname to the client certificate private key file.

❾   The private_key_passwd field contains the passphrase for the private key.

Then, add the following lines to /etc/rc.conf :

```
wlans_ath0="wlan0"
ifconfig_wlan0="WPA DHCP"
```

The next step is to bring up the interface:

```
# service netif start
Starting wpa_supplicant.
DHCPREQUEST on wlan0 to 255.255.255.255 port 67 interval 7
DHCPREQUEST on wlan0 to 255.255.255.255 port 67 interval 15
DHCPACK from 192.168.0.20
bound to 192.168.0.254 -- renewal in 300 seconds.
```

```
wlan0: flags=8843<UP,BROADCAST,RUNNING,SIMPLEX,MULTICAST> mtu 1500
        ether 00:11:95:d5:43:62
        inet 192.168.0.254 netmask 0xffffff00 broadcast 192.168.0.255
        media: IEEE 802.11 Wireless Ethernet DS/11Mbps mode 11g
        status: associated
        ssid freebsdap channel 1 (2412 Mhz 11g) bssid 00:11:95:c3:0d:ac
        country US ecm authmode WPA2/802.11i privacy ON deftxkey UNDEF
        AES-CCM 3:128-bit txpower 21.5 bmiss 7 scanvalid 450 bgscan
        bgscanintvl 300 bgscanidle 250 roam:rssi 7 roam:rate 5 protmode CTS
        wme burst roaming MANUAL
```

It is also possible to bring up the interface manually using wpa_supplicant(8) and ifconfig(8).

30.3.4.1.3.3. WPA with EAP-TTLS

With EAP-TLS, both the authentication server and the client need a certificate. With EAP-TTLS, a client certificate is optional. This method is similar to a web server which creates a secure SSL tunnel even if visitors do not have client-side certificates. EAP-TTLS uses an encrypted TLS tunnel for safe transport of the authentication data.

The required configuration can be added to /etc/wpa_supplicant.conf:

```
network={
  ssid="freebsdap"
  proto=RSN
  key_mgmt=WPA-EAP
  eap=TTLS ❶
  identity="test" ❷
  password="test" ❸
  ca_cert="/etc/certs/cacert.pem" ❹
  phase2="auth=MD5" ❺
}
```

❶   This field specifies the EAP method for the connection.
❷   The identity field contains the identity string for EAP authentication inside the encrypted TLS tunnel.
❸   The password field contains the passphrase for the EAP authentication.
❹   The ca_cert field indicates the pathname of the CA certificate file. This file is needed to verify the server certificate.
❺   This field specifies the authentication method used in the encrypted TLS tunnel. In this example, EAP with MD5-Challenge is used. The "inner authentication" phase is often called "phase2".

Next, add the following lines to /etc/rc.conf :

```
wlans_ath0="wlan0"
ifconfig_wlan0="WPA DHCP"
```

The next step is to bring up the interface:

```
# service netif start
Starting wpa_supplicant.
DHCPREQUEST on wlan0 to 255.255.255.255 port 67 interval 7
DHCPREQUEST on wlan0 to 255.255.255.255 port 67 interval 15
DHCPREQUEST on wlan0 to 255.255.255.255 port 67 interval 21
DHCPACK from 192.168.0.20
bound to 192.168.0.254 -- renewal in 300 seconds.
wlan0: flags=8843<UP,BROADCAST,RUNNING,SIMPLEX,MULTICAST> mtu 1500
        ether 00:11:95:d5:43:62
        inet 192.168.0.254 netmask 0xffffff00 broadcast 192.168.0.255
        media: IEEE 802.11 Wireless Ethernet DS/11Mbps mode 11g
        status: associated
        ssid freebsdap channel 1 (2412 Mhz 11g) bssid 00:11:95:c3:0d:ac
        country US ecm authmode WPA2/802.11i privacy ON deftxkey UNDEF
        AES-CCM 3:128-bit txpower 21.5 bmiss 7 scanvalid 450 bgscan
        bgscanintvl 300 bgscanidle 250 roam:rssi 7 roam:rate 5 protmode CTS
        wme burst roaming MANUAL
```

30.3.4.1.3.4. WPA with EAP-PEAP

Note

PEAPv0/EAP-MSCHAPv2 is the most common PEAP method. In this chapter, the term PEAP is used to refer to that method.

Protected EAP (PEAP) is designed as an alternative to EAP-TTLS and is the most used EAP standard after EAP-TLS. In a network with mixed operating systems, PEAP should be the most supported standard after EAP-TLS.

PEAP is similar to EAP-TTLS as it uses a server-side certificate to authenticate clients by creating an encrypted TLS tunnel between the client and the authentication server, which protects the ensuing exchange of authentication information. PEAP authentication differs from EAP-TTLS as it broadcasts the username in the clear and only the password is sent in the encrypted TLS tunnel. EAP-TTLS will use the TLS tunnel for both the username and password.

Add the following lines to `/etc/wpa_supplicant.conf` to configure the EAP-PEAP related settings:

```
network={
  ssid="freebsdap"
  proto=RSN
  key_mgmt=WPA-EAP
  eap=PEAP ❶
  identity="test" ❷
  password="test" ❸
  ca_cert="/etc/certs/cacert.pem" ❹
  phase1="peaplabel=0" ❺
  phase2="auth=MSCHAPV2" ❻
}
```

❶   This field specifies the EAP method for the connection.
❷   The `identity` field contains the identity string for EAP authentication inside the encrypted TLS tunnel.
❸   The `password` field contains the passphrase for the EAP authentication.
❹   The `ca_cert` field indicates the pathname of the CA certificate file. This file is needed to verify the server certificate.
❺   This field contains the parameters for the first phase of authentication, the TLS tunnel. According to the authentication server used, specify a specific label for authentication. Most of the time, the label will be "client EAP encryption" which is set by using `peaplabel=0`. More information can be found in wpa_supplicant.conf(5).
❻   This field specifies the authentication protocol used in the encrypted TLS tunnel. In the case of PEAP, it is `auth=MSCHAPV2` .

Add the following to `/etc/rc.conf` :

```
wlans_ath0="wlan0"
ifconfig_wlan0="WPA DHCP"
```

Then, bring up the interface:

```
# service netif start
Starting wpa_supplicant.
DHCPREQUEST on wlan0 to 255.255.255.255 port 67 interval 7
DHCPREQUEST on wlan0 to 255.255.255.255 port 67 interval 15
DHCPREQUEST on wlan0 to 255.255.255.255 port 67 interval 21
DHCPACK from 192.168.0.20
bound to 192.168.0.254 -- renewal in 300 seconds.
wlan0: flags=8843<UP,BROADCAST,RUNNING,SIMPLEX,MULTICAST> mtu 1500
      ether 00:11:95:d5:43:62
      inet 192.168.0.254 netmask 0xffffff00 broadcast 192.168.0.255
```

```
media: IEEE 802.11 Wireless Ethernet DS/11Mbps mode 11g
status: associated
ssid freebsdap channel 1 (2412 Mhz 11g) bssid 00:11:95:c3:0d:ac
country US ecm authmode WPA2/802.11i privacy ON deftxkey UNDEF
AES-CCM 3:128-bit txpower 21.5 bmiss 7 scanvalid 450 bgscan
bgscanintvl 300 bgscanidle 250 roam:rssi 7 roam:rate 5 protmode CTS
wme burst roaming MANUAL
```

30.3.4.1.4. WEP

Wired Equivalent Privacy (WEP) is part of the original 802.11 standard. There is no authentication mechanism, only a weak form of access control which is easily cracked.

WEP can be set up using ifconfig(8):

```
# ifconfig wlan0 create wlandev ath0
# ifconfig wlan0 inet 192.168.1.100 netmask 255.255.255.0 \
    ssid my_net wepmode on weptxkey 3 wepkey 3:0x3456789012
```

- The weptxkey specifies which WEP key will be used in the transmission. This example uses the third key. This must match the setting on the access point. When unsure which key is used by the access point, try 1 (the first key) for this value.

- The wepkey selects one of the WEP keys. It should be in the format *index:key*. Key 1 is used by default; the index only needs to be set when using a key other than the first key.

> **Note**
>
> Replace the 0x3456789012 with the key configured for use on the access point.

Refer to ifconfig(8) for further information.

The wpa_supplicant(8) facility can be used to configure a wireless interface with WEP. The example above can be set up by adding the following lines to /etc/wpa_supplicant.conf:

```
network={
  ssid="my_net"
  key_mgmt=NONE
  wep_key3=3456789012
  wep_tx_keyidx=3
}
```

Then:

```
# wpa_supplicant -i wlan0 -c /etc/wpa_supplicant.conf
Trying to associate with 00:13:46:49:41:76 (SSID='dlinkap' freq=2437 MHz)
Associated with 00:13:46:49:41:76
```

30.3.5. Ad-hoc Mode

IBSS mode, also called ad-hoc mode, is designed for point to point connections. For example, to establish an ad-hoc network between the machines A and B, choose two IP addresses and a SSID.

On A:

```
# ifconfig wlan0 create wlandev ath0 wlanmode adhoc
# ifconfig wlan0 inet 192.168.0.1 netmask 255.255.255.0 ssid freebsdap
# ifconfig wlan0
  wlan0: flags=8843<UP,BROADCAST,RUNNING,SIMPLEX,MULTICAST> metric 0 mtu 1500
```

```
ether 00:11:95:c3:0d:ac
inet 192.168.0.1 netmask 0xffffff00 broadcast 192.168.0.255
media: IEEE 802.11 Wireless Ethernet autoselect mode 11g <adhoc>
status: running
ssid freebsdap channel 2 (2417 Mhz 11g) bssid 02:11:95:c3:0d:ac
country US ecm authmode OPEN privacy OFF txpower 21.5 scanvalid 60
protmode CTS wme burst
```

The adhoc parameter indicates that the interface is running in IBSS mode.

B should now be able to detect A:

```
# ifconfig wlan0 create wlandev ath0 wlanmode adhoc
# ifconfig wlan0 up scan
  SSID/MESH ID    BSSID            CHAN RATE   S:N    INT CAPS
  freebsdap       02:11:95:c3:0d:ac  2   54M -64:-96 100 IS   WME
```

The I in the output confirms that A is in ad-hoc mode. Now, configure B with a different IP address:

```
# ifconfig wlan0 inet 192.168.0.2 netmask 255.255.255.0 ssid freebsdap
# ifconfig wlan0
  wlan0: flags=8843<UP,BROADCAST,RUNNING,SIMPLEX,MULTICAST> metric 0 mtu 1500
  ether 00:11:95:d5:43:62
  inet 192.168.0.2 netmask 0xffffff00 broadcast 192.168.0.255
  media: IEEE 802.11 Wireless Ethernet autoselect mode 11g <adhoc>
  status: running
  ssid freebsdap channel 2 (2417 Mhz 11g) bssid 02:11:95:c3:0d:ac
  country US ecm authmode OPEN privacy OFF txpower 21.5 scanvalid 60
  protmode CTS wme burst
```

Both A and B are now ready to exchange information.

30.3.6. FreeBSD Host Access Points

FreeBSD can act as an Access Point (AP) which eliminates the need to buy a hardware AP or run an ad-hoc network. This can be particularly useful when a FreeBSD machine is acting as a gateway to another network such as the Internet.

30.3.6.1. Basic Settings

Before configuring a FreeBSD machine as an AP, the kernel must be configured with the appropriate networking support for the wireless card as well as the security protocols being used. For more details, see Section 30.3.3, "Basic Setup".

Note

The NDIS driver wrapper for Windows® drivers does not currently support AP operation. Only native FreeBSD wireless drivers support AP mode.

Once wireless networking support is loaded, check if the wireless device supports the host-based access point mode, also known as hostap mode:

```
# ifconfig wlan0 create wlandev ath0
# ifconfig wlan0 list caps
drivercaps=6f85edc1<STA,FF,TURBOP,IBSS,HOSTAP,AHDEMO,TXPMGT,SHSLOT,SHPREAMBLE,MONITOR,MBSS,WPA1,WP
cryptocaps=1f<WEP,TKIP,AES,AES_CCM,TKIPMIC>
```

This output displays the card's capabilities. The HOSTAP word confirms that this wireless card can act as an AP. Various supported ciphers are also listed: WEP, TKIP, and AES. This information indicates which security protocols can be used on the AP.

The wireless device can only be put into hostap mode during the creation of the network pseudo-device, so a previously created device must be destroyed first:

```
# ifconfig wlan0 destroy
```

then regenerated with the correct option before setting the other parameters:

```
# ifconfig wlan0 create wlandev ath0 wlanmode hostap
# ifconfig wlan0 inet 192.168.0.1 netmask 255.255.255.0 ssid freebsdap mode 11g channel 1
```

Use ifconfig(8) again to see the status of the wlan0 interface:

```
# ifconfig wlan0
  wlan0: flags=8843<UP,BROADCAST,RUNNING,SIMPLEX,MULTICAST> metric 0 mtu 1500
    ether 00:11:95:c3:0d:ac
    inet 192.168.0.1 netmask 0xffffff00 broadcast 192.168.0.255
    media: IEEE 802.11 Wireless Ethernet autoselect mode 11g <hostap>
    status: running
    ssid freebsdap channel 1 (2412 Mhz 11g) bssid 00:11:95:c3:0d:ac
    country US ecm authmode OPEN privacy OFF txpower 21.5 scanvalid 60
    protmode CTS wme burst dtimperiod 1 -dfs
```

The hostap parameter indicates the interface is running in the host-based access point mode.

The interface configuration can be done automatically at boot time by adding the following lines to /etc/rc.conf :

```
wlans_ath0="wlan0"
create_args_wlan0="wlanmode hostap"
ifconfig_wlan0="inet 192.168.0.1 netmask 255.255.255.0 ssid freebsdap mode 11g channel 1"
```

30.3.6.2. Host-based Access Point Without Authentication or Encryption

Although it is not recommended to run an AP without any authentication or encryption, this is a simple way to check if the AP is working. This configuration is also important for debugging client issues.

Once the AP is configured, initiate a scan from another wireless machine to find the AP:

```
# ifconfig wlan0 create wlandev ath0
# ifconfig wlan0 up scan
SSID/MESH ID    BSSID              CHAN RATE   S:N      INT CAPS
freebsdap       00:11:95:c3:0d:ac   1    54M -66:-96   100 ES    WME
```

The client machine found the AP and can be associated with it:

```
# ifconfig wlan0 inet 192.168.0.2 netmask 255.255.255.0 ssid freebsdap
# ifconfig wlan0
  wlan0: flags=8843<UP,BROADCAST,RUNNING,SIMPLEX,MULTICAST> metric 0 mtu 1500
    ether 00:11:95:d5:43:62
    inet 192.168.0.2 netmask 0xffffff00 broadcast 192.168.0.255
    media: IEEE 802.11 Wireless Ethernet OFDM/54Mbps mode 11g
    status: associated
    ssid freebsdap channel 1 (2412 Mhz 11g) bssid 00:11:95:c3:0d:ac
    country US ecm authmode OPEN privacy OFF txpower 21.5 bmiss 7
    scanvalid 60 bgscan bgscanintvl 300 bgscanidle 250 roam:rssi 7
    roam:rate 5 protmode CTS wme burst
```

30.3.6.3. WPA2 Host-based Access Point

This section focuses on setting up a FreeBSD access point using the WPA2 security protocol. More details regarding WPA and the configuration of WPA-based wireless clients can be found in Section 30.3.4.1.3, "WPA".

The hostapd(8) daemon is used to deal with client authentication and key management on the WPA2-enabled AP.

The following configuration operations are performed on the FreeBSD machine acting as the AP. Once the AP is correctly working, hostapd(8) can be automatically started at boot with this line in /etc/rc.conf :

```
hostapd_enable="YES"
```

Before trying to configure hostapd(8), first configure the basic settings introduced in Section 30.3.6.1, "Basic Settings".

30.3.6.3.1. WPA2-PSK

WPA2-PSK is intended for small networks where the use of a backend authentication server is not possible or desired.

The configuration is done in /etc/hostapd.conf :

```
interface=wlan0              ❶
debug=1                      ❷
ctrl_interface=/var/run/hostapd   ❸
ctrl_interface_group=wheel   ❹
ssid=freebsdap               ❺
wpa=2                        ❻
wpa_passphrase=freebsdmall   ❼
wpa_key_mgmt=WPA-PSK         ❽
wpa_pairwise=CCMP            ❾
```

❶ Wireless interface used for the access point.
❷ Level of verbosity used during the execution of hostapd(8). A value of 1 represents the minimal level.
❸ Pathname of the directory used by hostapd(8) to store domain socket files for communication with external programs such as hostapd_cli(8). The default value is used in this example.
❹ The group allowed to access the control interface files.
❺ The wireless network name, or SSID, that will appear in wireless scans.
❻ Enable WPA and specify which WPA authentication protocol will be required. A value of 2 configures the AP for WPA2 and is recommended. Set to 1 only if the obsolete WPA is required.
❼ ASCII passphrase for WPA authentication.

 Warning

Always use strong passwords that are at least 8 characters long and made from a rich alphabet so that they will not be easily guessed or attacked.

❽ The key management protocol to use. This example sets WPA-PSK.
❾ Encryption algorithms accepted by the access point. In this example, only the CCMP (AES) cipher is accepted. CCMP is an alternative to TKIP and is strongly preferred when possible. TKIP should be allowed only when there are stations incapable of using CCMP.

The next step is to start hostapd(8):

```
# service hostapd forcestart
```

```
# ifconfig wlan0
wlan0: flags=8943<UP,BROADCAST,RUNNING,PROMISC,SIMPLEX,MULTICAST> metric 0 mtu 1500
    ether 04:f0:21:16:8e:10
    inet6 fe80::6f0:21ff:fe16:8e10%wlan0 prefixlen 64 scopeid 0x9
    nd6 options=21<PERFORMNUD,AUTO_LINKLOCAL>
    media: IEEE 802.11 Wireless Ethernet autoselect mode 11na <hostap>
    status: running
    ssid No5ignal channel 36 (5180 MHz 11a ht/40+) bssid 04:f0:21:16:8e:10
    country US ecm authmode WPA2/802.11i privacy MIXED deftxkey 2
    AES-CCM 2:128-bit AES-CCM 3:128-bit txpower 17 mcastrate 6 mgmtrate 6
    scanvalid 60 ampdulimit 64k ampdudensity 8 shortgi wme burst
    dtimperiod 1 -dfs
```

```
groups: wlan
```

Once the AP is running, the clients can associate with it. See Section 30.3.4.1.3, "WPA" for more details. It is possible to see the stations associated with the AP using ifconfig *wlan0* list sta.

30.3.6.4. WEP Host-based Access Point

It is not recommended to use WEP for setting up an AP since there is no authentication mechanism and the encryption is easily cracked. Some legacy wireless cards only support WEP and these cards will only support an AP without authentication or encryption.

The wireless device can now be put into hostap mode and configured with the correct SSID and IP address:

```
# ifconfig wlan0 create wlandev ath0 wlanmode hostap
# ifconfig wlan0 inet 192.168.0.1 netmask 255.255.255.0 \
 ssid freebsdap wepmode on weptxkey 3 wepkey 3:0x3456789012 mode 11g
```

- The weptxkey indicates which WEP key will be used in the transmission. This example uses the third key as key numbering starts with 1. This parameter must be specified in order to encrypt the data.

- The wepkey sets the selected WEP key. It should be in the format *index:key*. If the index is not given, key 1 is set. The index needs to be set when using keys other than the first key.

Use ifconfig(8) to see the status of the wlan0 interface:

```
# ifconfig wlan0
  wlan0: flags=8843<UP,BROADCAST,RUNNING,SIMPLEX,MULTICAST> metric 0 mtu 1500
    ether 00:11:95:c3:0d:ac
    inet 192.168.0.1 netmask 0xffffff00 broadcast 192.168.0.255
    media: IEEE 802.11 Wireless Ethernet autoselect mode 11g <hostap>
    status: running
    ssid freebsdap channel 4 (2427 Mhz 11g) bssid 00:11:95:c3:0d:ac
    country US ecm authmode OPEN privacy ON deftxkey 3 wepkey 3:40-bit
    txpower 21.5 scanvalid 60 protmode CTS wme burst dtimperiod 1 -dfs
```

From another wireless machine, it is now possible to initiate a scan to find the AP:

```
# ifconfig wlan0 create wlandev ath0
# ifconfig wlan0 up scan
SSID            BSSID            CHAN RATE  S:N   INT CAPS
freebsdap       00:11:95:c3:0d:ac  1   54M 22:1  100 EPS
```

In this example, the client machine found the AP and can associate with it using the correct parameters. See Section 30.3.4.1.4, "WEP" for more details.

30.3.7. Using Both Wired and Wireless Connections

A wired connection provides better performance and reliability, while a wireless connection provides flexibility and mobility. Laptop users typically want to roam seamlessly between the two types of connections.

On FreeBSD, it is possible to combine two or even more network interfaces together in a "failover" fashion. This type of configuration uses the most preferred and available connection from a group of network interfaces, and the operating system switches automatically when the link state changes.

Link aggregation and failover is covered in Section 30.7, "Link Aggregation and Failover" and an example for using both wired and wireless connections is provided at Example 30.3, "Failover Mode Between Ethernet and Wireless Interfaces".

30.3.8. Troubleshooting

This section describes a number of steps to help troubleshoot common wireless networking problems.

- If the access point is not listed when scanning, check that the configuration has not limited the wireless device to a limited set of channels.

- If the device cannot associate with an access point, verify that the configuration matches the settings on the access point. This includes the authentication scheme and any security protocols. Simplify the configuration as much as possible. If using a security protocol such as WPA or WEP, configure the access point for open authentication and no security to see if traffic will pass.

  Debugging support is provided by wpa_supplicant(8). Try running this utility manually with -dd and look at the system logs.

- Once the system can associate with the access point, diagnose the network configuration using tools like ping(8).

- There are many lower-level debugging tools. Debugging messages can be enabled in the 802.11 protocol support layer using wlandebug(8). For example, to enable console messages related to scanning for access points and the 802.11 protocol handshakes required to arrange communication:

```
# wlandebug -i wlan0 +scan+auth+debug+assoc
  net.wlan.0.debug: 0 => 0xc80000<assoc,auth,scan>
```

Many useful statistics are maintained by the 802.11 layer and wlanstats , found in /usr/src/tools/tools/net80211 , will dump this information. These statistics should display all errors identified by the 802.11 layer. However, some errors are identified in the device drivers that lie below the 802.11 layer so they may not show up. To diagnose device-specific problems, refer to the drivers' documentation.

If the above information does not help to clarify the problem, submit a problem report and include output from the above tools.

30.4. USB Tethering

Many cellphones provide the option to share their data connection over USB (often called "tethering"). This feature uses either the RNDIS, CDC or a custom Apple® iPhone®/iPad® protocol.

- Android™ devices generally use the urndis(4) driver.

- Apple® devices use the ipheth(4) driver.

- Older devices will often use the cdce(4) driver.

Before attaching a device, load the appropriate driver into the kernel:

```
# kldload if_urndis
# kldload ↺
if_cdce
# kldload if_ipheth
```

Once the device is attached ue0 will be available for use like a normal network device. Be sure that the "USB tethering" option is enabled on the device.

30.5. Bluetooth

Written by Pav Lucistnik.

Bluetooth is a wireless technology for creating personal networks operating in the 2.4 GHz unlicensed band, with a range of 10 meters. Networks are usually formed ad-hoc from portable devices such as cellular phones, handhelds, and laptops. Unlike Wi-Fi wireless technology, Bluetooth offers higher level service profiles, such as FTP-like file servers, file pushing, voice transport, serial line emulation, and more.

This section describes the use of a USB Bluetooth dongle on a FreeBSD system. It then describes the various Bluetooth protocols and utilities.

30.5.1. Loading Bluetooth Support

The Bluetooth stack in FreeBSD is implemented using the netgraph(4) framework. A broad variety of Bluetooth USB dongles is supported by ng_ubt(4). Broadcom BCM2033 based Bluetooth devices are supported by the ubtbcmfw(4) and ng_ubt(4) drivers. The 3Com Bluetooth PC Card 3CRWB60-A is supported by the ng_bt3c(4) driver. Serial and UART based Bluetooth devices are supported by sio(4), ng_h4(4), and hcseriald(8).

Before attaching a device, determine which of the above drivers it uses, then load the driver. For example, if the device uses the ng_ubt(4) driver:

```
# kldload ng_ubt
```

If the Bluetooth device will be attached to the system during system startup, the system can be configured to load the module at boot time by adding the driver to /boot/loader.conf :

```
ng_ubt_load="YES"
```

Once the driver is loaded, plug in the USB dongle. If the driver load was successful, output similar to the following should appear on the console and in /var/log/messages :

```
ubt0: vendor 0x0a12 product 0x0001, rev 1.10/5.25, addr 2
ubt0: Interface 0 endpoints: interrupt=0x81, bulk-in=0x82, bulk-out=0x2
ubt0: Interface 1 (alt.config 5) endpoints: isoc-in=0x83, isoc-out=0x3,
      wMaxPacketSize=49, nframes=6, buffer size=294
```

To start and stop the Bluetooth stack, use its startup script. It is a good idea to stop the stack before unplugging the device. When starting the stack, the output should be similar to the following:

```
# service bluetooth start ubt0
BD_ADDR: 00:02:72:00:d4:1a
Features: 0xff 0xff 0xf 00 00 00 00 00
<3-Slot> <5-Slot> <Encryption> <Slot offset>
<Timing accuracy> <Switch> <Hold mode> <Sniff mode>
<Park mode> <RSSI> <Channel quality> <SCO link>
<HV2 packets> <HV3 packets> <u-law log> <A-law log> <CVSD>
<Paging scheme> <Power control> <Transparent SCO data>
Max. ACL packet size: 192 bytes
Number of ACL packets: 8
Max. SCO packet size: 64 bytes
Number of SCO packets: 8
```

30.5.2. Finding Other Bluetooth Devices

The Host Controller Interface (HCI) provides a uniform method for accessing Bluetooth baseband capabilities. In FreeBSD, a netgraph HCI node is created for each Bluetooth device. For more details, refer to ng_hci(4).

One of the most common tasks is discovery of Bluetooth devices within RF proximity. This operation is called *inquiry*. Inquiry and other HCI related operations are done using hccontrol(8). The example below shows how to find out which Bluetooth devices are in range. The list of devices should be displayed in a few seconds. Note that a remote device will only answer the inquiry if it is set to *discoverable* mode.

```
% hccontrol -n ubt0hci inquiry
Inquiry result, num_responses=1
Inquiry result #0
        BD_ADDR: 00:80:37:29:19:a4
        Page Scan Rep. Mode: 0x1
        Page Scan Period Mode: 00
        Page Scan Mode: 00
        Class: 52:02:04
```

```
      Clock offset: 0x78ef
Inquiry complete. Status: No error [00]
```

The BD_ADDR is the unique address of a Bluetooth device, similar to the MAC address of a network card. This address is needed for further communication with a device and it is possible to assign a human readable name to a BD_ADDR. Information regarding the known Bluetooth hosts is contained in /etc/bluetooth/hosts . The following example shows how to obtain the human readable name that was assigned to the remote device:

```
% hccontrol -n ubt0hci remote_name_request 00:80:37:29:19:a4
BD_ADDR: 00:80:37:29:19:a4
Name: Pav's T39
```

If an inquiry is performed on a remote Bluetooth device, it will find the computer as "your.host.name (ubt0)". The name assigned to the local device can be changed at any time.

The Bluetooth system provides a point-to-point connection between two Bluetooth units, or a point-to-multipoint connection which is shared among several Bluetooth devices. The following example shows how to obtain the list of active baseband connections for the local device:

```
% hccontrol -n ubt0hci read_connection_list
Remote BD_ADDR    Handle Type Mode Role Encrypt Pending Queue State
00:80:37:29:19:a4     41  ACL    0 MAST    NONE       0     0 OPEN
```

A *connection handle* is useful when termination of the baseband connection is required, though it is normally not required to do this by hand. The stack will automatically terminate inactive baseband connections.

```
# hccontrol -n ubt0hci disconnect 41
Connection handle: 41
Reason: Connection terminated by local host [0x16]
```

Type hccontrol help for a complete listing of available HCI commands. Most of the HCI commands do not require superuser privileges.

30.5.3. Device Pairing

By default, Bluetooth communication is not authenticated, and any device can talk to any other device. A Bluetooth device, such as a cellular phone, may choose to require authentication to provide a particular service. Bluetooth authentication is normally done with a *PIN code*, an ASCII string up to 16 characters in length. The user is required to enter the same PIN code on both devices. Once the user has entered the PIN code, both devices will generate a *link key*. After that, the link key can be stored either in the devices or in a persistent storage. Next time, both devices will use the previously generated link key. This procedure is called *pairing*. Note that if the link key is lost by either device, the pairing must be repeated.

The hcsecd(8) daemon is responsible for handling Bluetooth authentication requests. The default configuration file is /etc/bluetooth/hcsecd.conf . An example section for a cellular phone with the PIN code set to 1234 is shown below:

```
device {
        bdaddr  00:80:37:29:19:a4;
        name    "Pav's T39";
        key     nokey;
        pin     "1234";
}
```

The only limitation on PIN codes is length. Some devices, such as Bluetooth headsets, may have a fixed PIN code built in. The -d switch forces hcsecd(8) to stay in the foreground, so it is easy to see what is happening. Set the remote device to receive pairing and initiate the Bluetooth connection to the remote device. The remote device should indicate that pairing was accepted and request the PIN code. Enter the same PIN code listed in hcsecd.conf. Now the computer and the remote device are paired. Alternatively, pairing can be initiated on the remote device.

The following line can be added to /etc/rc.conf to configure hcsecd(8) to start automatically on system start:

```
hcsecd_enable="YES"
```

The following is a sample of the hcsecd(8) daemon output:

```
hcsecd[16484]: Got Link_Key_Request event from 'ubt0hci', remote bdaddr 0:80:37:29:19:a4
hcsecd[16484]: Found matching entry, remote bdaddr 0:80:37:29:19:a4, name 'Pav's T39', ↵
link key doesn't exist
hcsecd[16484]: Sending Link_Key_Negative_Reply to 'ubt0hci' for remote bdaddr ↵
0:80:37:29:19:a4
hcsecd[16484]: Got PIN_Code_Request event from 'ubt0hci', remote bdaddr 0:80:37:29:19:a4
hcsecd[16484]: Found matching entry, remote bdaddr 0:80:37:29:19:a4, name 'Pav's T39', ↵
PIN code exists
hcsecd[16484]: Sending PIN_Code_Reply to 'ubt0hci' for remote bdaddr 0:80:37:29:19:a4
```

30.5.4. Network Access with PPP Profiles

A Dial-Up Networking (DUN) profile can be used to configure a cellular phone as a wireless modem for connecting to a dial-up Internet access server. It can also be used to configure a computer to receive data calls from a cellular phone.

Network access with a PPP profile can be used to provide LAN access for a single Bluetooth device or multiple Bluetooth devices. It can also provide PC to PC connection using PPP networking over serial cable emulation.

In FreeBSD, these profiles are implemented with ppp(8) and the rfcomm_pppd(8) wrapper which converts a Bluetooth connection into something PPP can use. Before a profile can be used, a new PPP label must be created in /etc/ppp/ppp.conf . Consult rfcomm_pppd(8) for examples.

In this example, rfcomm_pppd(8) is used to open a connection to a remote device with a **BD_ADDR** of 00:80:37:29:19:a4 on a DUN RFCOMM channel:

```
# rfcomm_pppd -a 00:80:37:29:19:a4 -c -C dun -l rfcomm-dialup
```

The actual channel number will be obtained from the remote device using the SDP protocol. It is possible to specify the RFCOMM channel by hand, and in this case rfcomm_pppd(8) will not perform the SDP query. Use sdpcontrol(8) to find out the RFCOMM channel on the remote device.

In order to provide network access with the PPP LAN service, sdpd(8) must be running and a new entry for LAN clients must be created in /etc/ppp/ppp.conf . Consult rfcomm_pppd(8) for examples. Finally, start the RFCOMM PPP server on a valid RFCOMM channel number. The RFCOMM PPP server will automatically register the Bluetooth LAN service with the local SDP daemon. The example below shows how to start the RFCOMM PPP server.

```
# rfcomm_pppd -s -C 7 -l rfcomm-server
```

30.5.5. Bluetooth Protocols

This section provides an overview of the various Bluetooth protocols, their function, and associated utilities.

30.5.5.1. Logical Link Control and Adaptation Protocol (L2CAP)

The Logical Link Control and Adaptation Protocol (L2CAP) provides connection-oriented and connectionless data services to upper layer protocols. L2CAP permits higher level protocols and applications to transmit and receive L2CAP data packets up to 64 kilobytes in length.

L2CAP is based around the concept of *channels*. A channel is a logical connection on top of a baseband connection, where each channel is bound to a single protocol in a many-to-one fashion. Multiple channels can be bound to the same protocol, but a channel cannot be bound to multiple protocols. Each L2CAP packet received on a channel is directed to the appropriate higher level protocol. Multiple channels can share the same baseband connection.

In FreeBSD, a netgraph L2CAP node is created for each Bluetooth device. This node is normally connected to the downstream Bluetooth HCI node and upstream Bluetooth socket nodes. The default name for the L2CAP node is "devicel2cap". For more details refer to ng_l2cap(4).

A useful command is l2ping(8), which can be used to ping other devices. Some Bluetooth implementations might not return all of the data sent to them, so 0 bytes in the following example is normal.

```
# l2ping -a 00:80:37:29:19:a4
0 bytes from 0:80:37:29:19:a4 seq_no=0 time=48.633 ms result=0
0 bytes from 0:80:37:29:19:a4 seq_no=1 time=37.551 ms result=0
0 bytes from 0:80:37:29:19:a4 seq_no=2 time=28.324 ms result=0
0 bytes from 0:80:37:29:19:a4 seq_no=3 time=46.150 ms result=0
```

The l2control(8) utility is used to perform various operations on L2CAP nodes. This example shows how to obtain the list of logical connections (channels) and the list of baseband connections for the local device:

```
% l2control -a 00:02:72:00:d4:1a read_channel_list
L2CAP channels:
Remote BD_ADDR     SCID/ DCID   PSM   IMTU/ OMTU State
00:07:e0:00:0b:ca   66/   64     3    132/  672 OPEN
% l2control -a 00:02:72:00:d4:1a read_connection_list
L2CAP connections:
Remote BD_ADDR    Handle Flags Pending State
00:07:e0:00:0b:ca   41 0            0 OPEN
```

Another diagnostic tool is btsockstat(1). It is similar to netstat(1), but for Bluetooth network-related data structures. The example below shows the same logical connection as l2control(8) above.

```
% btsockstat
Active L2CAP sockets
PCB      Recv-Q Send-Q Local address/PSM        Foreign address   CID   State
c2afe900      0      0 00:02:72:00:d4:1a/3       00:07:e0:00:0b:ca 66    OPEN
Active RFCOMM sessions
L2PCB    PCB      Flag MTU   Out-Q DLCs State
c2afe900 c2b53380 1    127   0     Yes  OPEN
Active RFCOMM sockets
PCB      Recv-Q Send-Q Local address     Foreign address   Chan DLCI State
c2e8bc80      0    250 00:02:72:00:d4:1a 00:07:e0:00:0b:ca 3    6    OPEN
```

30.5.5.2. Radio Frequency Communication (RFCOMM)

The RFCOMM protocol provides emulation of serial ports over the L2CAP protocol. RFCOMM is a simple transport protocol, with additional provisions for emulating the 9 circuits of RS-232 (EIATIA-232-E) serial ports. It supports up to 60 simultaneous connections (RFCOMM channels) between two Bluetooth devices.

For the purposes of RFCOMM, a complete communication path involves two applications running on the communication endpoints with a communication segment between them. RFCOMM is intended to cover applications that make use of the serial ports of the devices in which they reside. The communication segment is a direct connect Bluetooth link from one device to another.

RFCOMM is only concerned with the connection between the devices in the direct connect case, or between the device and a modem in the network case. RFCOMM can support other configurations, such as modules that communicate via Bluetooth wireless technology on one side and provide a wired interface on the other side.

In FreeBSD, RFCOMM is implemented at the Bluetooth sockets layer.

30.5.5.3. Service Discovery Protocol (SDP)

The Service Discovery Protocol (SDP) provides the means for client applications to discover the existence of services provided by server applications as well as the attributes of those services. The attributes of a service include the type or class of service offered and the mechanism or protocol information needed to utilize the service.

SDP involves communication between a SDP server and a SDP client. The server maintains a list of service records that describe the characteristics of services associated with the server. Each service record contains information about a single service. A client may retrieve information from a service record maintained by the SDP server by issuing a SDP request. If the client, or an application associated with the client, decides to use a service, it must open a separate connection to the service provider in order to utilize the service. SDP provides a mechanism for discovering services and their attributes, but it does not provide a mechanism for utilizing those services.

Normally, a SDP client searches for services based on some desired characteristics of the services. However, there are times when it is desirable to discover which types of services are described by an SDP server's service records without any prior information about the services. This process of looking for any offered services is called *browsing*.

The Bluetooth SDP server, sdpd(8), and command line client, sdpcontrol(8), are included in the standard FreeBSD installation. The following example shows how to perform a SDP browse query.

```
% sdpcontrol -a 00:01:03:fc:6e:ec browse
Record Handle: 00000000
Service Class ID List:
        Service Discovery Server (0x1000)
Protocol Descriptor List:
        L2CAP (0x0100)
                Protocol specific parameter #1: u/int/uuid16 1
                Protocol specific parameter #2: u/int/uuid16 1

Record Handle: 0x00000001
Service Class ID List:
        Browse Group Descriptor (0x1001)

Record Handle: 0x00000002
Service Class ID List:
        LAN Access Using PPP (0x1102)
Protocol Descriptor List:
        L2CAP (0x0100)
        RFCOMM (0x0003)
                Protocol specific parameter #1: u/int8/bool 1
Bluetooth Profile Descriptor List:
        LAN Access Using PPP (0x1102) ver. 1.0
```

Note that each service has a list of attributes, such as the RFCOMM channel. Depending on the service, the user might need to make note of some of the attributes. Some Bluetooth implementations do not support service browsing and may return an empty list. In this case, it is possible to search for the specific service. The example below shows how to search for the OBEX Object Push (OPUSH) service:

```
% sdpcontrol -a 00:01:03:fc:6e:ec search OPUSH
```

Offering services on FreeBSD to Bluetooth clients is done with the sdpd(8) server. The following line can be added to /etc/rc.conf :

```
sdpd_enable="YES"
```

Then the sdpd(8) daemon can be started with:

```
# service sdpd start
```

The local server application that wants to provide a Bluetooth service to remote clients will register the service with the local SDP daemon. An example of such an application is rfcomm_pppd(8). Once started, it will register the Bluetooth LAN service with the local SDP daemon.

The list of services registered with the local SDP server can be obtained by issuing a SDP browse query via the local control channel:

```
# sdpcontrol -l browse
```

30.5.5.4. OBEX Object Push (OPUSH)

Object Exchange (OBEX) is a widely used protocol for simple file transfers between mobile devices. Its main use is in infrared communication, where it is used for generic file transfers between notebooks or PDAs, and for sending business cards or calendar entries between cellular phones and other devices with Personal Information Manager (PIM) applications.

The OBEX server and client are implemented by obexapp, which can be installed using the comms/obexapp package or port.

The OBEX client is used to push and/or pull objects from the OBEX server. An example object is a business card or an appointment. The OBEX client can obtain the RFCOMM channel number from the remote device via SDP. This can be done by specifying the service name instead of the RFCOMM channel number. Supported service names are: IrMC, FTRN, and OPUSH. It is also possible to specify the RFCOMM channel as a number. Below is an example of an OBEX session where the device information object is pulled from the cellular phone, and a new object, the business card, is pushed into the phone's directory.

```
% obexapp -a 00:80:37:29:19:a4 -C IrMC
obex> get telecom/devinfo.txt devinfo-t39.txt
Success, response: OK, Success (0x20)
obex> put new.vcf
Success, response: OK, Success (0x20)
obex> di
Success, response: OK, Success (0x20)
```

In order to provide the OPUSH service, sdpd(8) must be running and a root folder, where all incoming objects will be stored, must be created. The default path to the root folder is /var/spool/obex . Finally, start the OBEX server on a valid RFCOMM channel number. The OBEX server will automatically register the OPUSH service with the local SDP daemon. The example below shows how to start the OBEX server.

```
# obexapp -s -C 10
```

30.5.5.5. Serial Port Profile (SPP)

The Serial Port Profile (SPP) allows Bluetooth devices to perform serial cable emulation. This profile allows legacy applications to use Bluetooth as a cable replacement, through a virtual serial port abstraction.

In FreeBSD, rfcomm_sppd(1) implements SPP and a pseudo tty is used as a virtual serial port abstraction. The example below shows how to connect to a remote device's serial port service. A RFCOMM channel does not have to be specified as rfcomm_sppd(1) can obtain it from the remote device via SDP. To override this, specify a RFCOMM channel on the command line.

```
# rfcomm_sppd -a 00:07:E0:00:0B:CA -t
rfcomm_sppd[94692]: Starting on /dev/pts/6...
/dev/pts/6
```

Once connected, the pseudo tty can be used as serial port:

```
# cu -l /dev/pts/6
```

The pseudo tty is printed on stdout and can be read by wrapper scripts:

```
PTS=`rfcomm_sppd -a 00:07:E0:00:0B:CA -t`
cu -l $PTS
```

30.5.6. Troubleshooting

By default, when FreeBSD is accepting a new connection, it tries to perform a role switch and become master. Some older Bluetooth devices which do not support role switching will not be able to connect. Since role switching is performed when a new connection is being established, it is not possible to ask the remote device if it supports role switching. However, there is a HCI option to disable role switching on the local side:

```
# hccontrol -n ubt0hci write_node_role_switch 0
```

To display Bluetooth packets, use the third-party package hcidump, which can be installed using the comms/hcidump package or port. This utility is similar to tcpdump(1) and can be used to display the contents of Bluetooth packets on the terminal and to dump the Bluetooth packets to a file.

30.6. Bridging

Written by Andrew Thompson.

It is sometimes useful to divide a network, such as an Ethernet segment, into network segments without having to create IP subnets and use a router to connect the segments together. A device that connects two networks together in this fashion is called a "bridge".

A bridge works by learning the MAC addresses of the devices on each of its network interfaces. It forwards traffic between networks only when the source and destination MAC addresses are on different networks. In many respects, a bridge is like an Ethernet switch with very few ports. A FreeBSD system with multiple network interfaces can be configured to act as a bridge.

Bridging can be useful in the following situations:

Connecting Networks

The basic operation of a bridge is to join two or more network segments. There are many reasons to use a host-based bridge instead of networking equipment, such as cabling constraints or firewalling. A bridge can also connect a wireless interface running in hostap mode to a wired network and act as an access point.

Filtering/Traffic Shaping Firewall

A bridge can be used when firewall functionality is needed without routing or Network Address Translation (NAT).

An example is a small company that is connected via DSL or ISDN to an ISP. There are thirteen public IP addresses from the ISP and ten computers on the network. In this situation, using a router-based firewall is difficult because of subnetting issues. A bridge-based firewall can be configured without any IP addressing issues.

Network Tap

A bridge can join two network segments in order to inspect all Ethernet frames that pass between them using bpf(4) and tcpdump(1) on the bridge interface or by sending a copy of all frames out an additional interface known as a span port.

Layer 2 VPN

Two Ethernet networks can be joined across an IP link by bridging the networks to an EtherIP tunnel or a tap(4) based solution such as OpenVPN.

Layer 2 Redundancy

A network can be connected together with multiple links and use the Spanning Tree Protocol (STP) to block redundant paths.

This section describes how to configure a FreeBSD system as a bridge using if_bridge(4). A netgraph bridging driver is also available, and is described in ng_bridge(4).

Note

Packet filtering can be used with any firewall package that hooks into the pfil(9) framework. The bridge can be used as a traffic shaper with altq(4) or dummynet(4).

30.6.1. Enabling the Bridge

In FreeBSD, if_bridge(4) is a kernel module which is automatically loaded by ifconfig(8) when creating a bridge interface. It is also possible to compile bridge support into a custom kernel by adding `device if_bridge` to the custom kernel configuration file.

The bridge is created using interface cloning. To create the bridge interface:

```
# ifconfig bridge create
bridge0
# ifconfig bridge0
bridge0: flags=8802<BROADCAST,SIMPLEX,MULTICAST> metric 0 mtu 1500
        ether 96:3d:4b:f1:79:7a
        id 00:00:00:00:00:00 priority 32768 hellotime 2 fwddelay 15
        maxage 20 holdcnt 6 proto rstp maxaddr 100 timeout 1200
        root id 00:00:00:00:00:00 priority 0 ifcost 0 port 0
```

When a bridge interface is created, it is automatically assigned a randomly generated Ethernet address. The maxaddr and timeout parameters control how many MAC addresses the bridge will keep in its forwarding table and how many seconds before each entry is removed after it is last seen. The other parameters control how STP operates.

Next, specify which network interfaces to add as members of the bridge. For the bridge to forward packets, all member interfaces and the bridge need to be up:

```
# ifconfig bridge0 addm fxp0 addm fxp1 up
# ifconfig fxp0 up
# ifconfig fxp1 up
```

The bridge can now forward Ethernet frames between fxp0 and fxp1. Add the following lines to /etc/rc.conf so the bridge is created at startup:

```
cloned_interfaces="bridge0"
ifconfig_bridge0="addm fxp0 addm fxp1 up"
ifconfig_fxp0="up"
ifconfig_fxp1="up"
```

If the bridge host needs an IP address, set it on the bridge interface, not on the member interfaces. The address can be set statically or via DHCP. This example sets a static IP address:

```
# ifconfig bridge0 inet 192.168.0.1/24
```

It is also possible to assign an IPv6 address to a bridge interface. To make the changes permanent, add the addressing information to /etc/rc.conf .

Note

When packet filtering is enabled, bridged packets will pass through the filter inbound on the originating interface on the bridge interface, and outbound on the appropriate interfaces. Either stage can be disabled. When direction of the packet flow is important, it is best to firewall on the member interfaces rather than the bridge itself.

The bridge has several configurable settings for passing non-IP and IP packets, and layer2 firewalling with ipfw(8). See if_bridge(4) for more information.

30.6.2. Enabling Spanning Tree

For an Ethernet network to function properly, only one active path can exist between two devices. The STP protocol detects loops and puts redundant links into a blocked state. Should one of the active links fail, STP calculates a different tree and enables one of the blocked paths to restore connectivity to all points in the network.

The Rapid Spanning Tree Protocol (RSTP or 802.1w) provides backwards compatibility with legacy STP. RSTP provides faster convergence and exchanges information with neighboring switches to quickly transition to forwarding mode without creating loops. FreeBSD supports RSTP and STP as operating modes, with RSTP being the default mode.

STP can be enabled on member interfaces using ifconfig(8). For a bridge with fxp0 and fxp1 as the current interfaces, enable STP with:

```
# ifconfig bridge0 stp fxp0 stp fxp1
bridge0: flags=8843<UP,BROADCAST,RUNNING,SIMPLEX,MULTICAST> metric 0 mtu 1500
        ether d6:cf:d5:a0:94:6d
        id 00:01:02:4b:d4:50 priority 32768 hellotime 2 fwddelay 15
        maxage 20 holdcnt 6 proto rstp maxaddr 100 timeout 1200
        root id 00:01:02:4b:d4:50 priority 32768 ifcost 0 port 0
        member: fxp0 flags=1c7<LEARNING,DISCOVER,STP,AUTOEDGE,PTP,AUTOPTP>
                port 3 priority 128 path cost 200000 proto rstp
                role designated state forwarding
        member: fxp1 flags=1c7<LEARNING,DISCOVER,STP,AUTOEDGE,PTP,AUTOPTP>
                port 4 priority 128 path cost 200000 proto rstp
                role designated state forwarding
```

This bridge has a spanning tree ID of 00:01:02:4b:d4:50 and a priority of 32768. As the root id is the same, it indicates that this is the root bridge for the tree.

Another bridge on the network also has STP enabled:

```
bridge0: flags=8843<UP,BROADCAST,RUNNING,SIMPLEX,MULTICAST> metric 0 mtu 1500
        ether 96:3d:4b:f1:79:7a
        id 00:13:d4:9a:06:7a priority 32768 hellotime 2 fwddelay 15
        maxage 20 holdcnt 6 proto rstp maxaddr 100 timeout 1200
        root id 00:01:02:4b:d4:50 priority 32768 ifcost 400000 port 4
        member: fxp0 flags=1c7<LEARNING,DISCOVER,STP,AUTOEDGE,PTP,AUTOPTP>
                port 4 priority 128 path cost 200000 proto rstp
                role root state forwarding
        member: fxp1 flags=1c7<LEARNING,DISCOVER,STP,AUTOEDGE,PTP,AUTOPTP>
                port 5 priority 128 path cost 200000 proto rstp
                role designated state forwarding
```

The line root id 00:01:02:4b:d4:50 priority 32768 ifcost 400000 port 4 shows that the root bridge is 00:01:02:4b:d4:50 and has a path cost of 400000 from this bridge. The path to the root bridge is via port 4 which is fxp0.

30.6.3. Bridge Interface Parameters

Several ifconfig parameters are unique to bridge interfaces. This section summarizes some common uses for these parameters. The complete list of available parameters is described in ifconfig(8).

private
> A private interface does not forward any traffic to any other port that is also designated as a private interface. The traffic is blocked unconditionally so no Ethernet frames will be forwarded, including ARP packets. If traffic needs to be selectively blocked, a firewall should be used instead.

span
> A span port transmits a copy of every Ethernet frame received by the bridge. The number of span ports configured on a bridge is unlimited, but if an interface is designated as a span port, it cannot also be used as a regular bridge port. This is most useful for snooping a bridged network passively on another host connected to one of the span ports of the bridge. For example, to send a copy of all frames out the interface named fxp4:

```
# ifconfig bridge0 span fxp4
```

sticky
> If a bridge member interface is marked as sticky, dynamically learned address entries are treated as static entries in the forwarding cache. Sticky entries are never aged out of the cache or replaced, even if the address is seen on a different interface. This gives the benefit of static address entries without the need to pre-populate the forwarding table. Clients learned on a particular segment of the bridge cannot roam to another segment.

> An example of using sticky addresses is to combine the bridge with VLANs in order to isolate customer networks without wasting IP address space. Consider that CustomerA is on vlan100, CustomerB is on vlan101, and the bridge has the address 192.168.0.1:

```
# ifconfig bridge0 addm vlan100 sticky vlan100 addm vlan101 sticky vlan101
# ifconfig bridge0 inet 192.168.0.1/24
```

In this example, both clients see 192.168.0.1 as their default gateway. Since the bridge cache is sticky, one host cannot spoof the MAC address of the other customer in order to intercept their traffic.

Any communication between the VLANs can be blocked using a firewall or, as seen in this example, private interfaces:

```
# ifconfig bridge0 private vlan100 private vlan101
```

The customers are completely isolated from each other and the full /24 address range can be allocated without subnetting.

The number of unique source MAC addresses behind an interface can be limited. Once the limit is reached, packets with unknown source addresses are dropped until an existing host cache entry expires or is removed.

The following example sets the maximum number of Ethernet devices for CustomerA on vlan100 to 10:

```
# ifconfig bridge0 ifmaxaddr vlan100 10
```

Bridge interfaces also support monitor mode, where the packets are discarded after bpf(4) processing and are not processed or forwarded further. This can be used to multiplex the input of two or more interfaces into a single bpf(4) stream. This is useful for reconstructing the traffic for network taps that transmit the RX/TX signals out through two separate interfaces. For example, to read the input from four network interfaces as one stream:

```
# ifconfig bridge0 addm fxp0 addm fxp1 addm fxp2 addm fxp3 monitor up
# tcpdump -i bridge0
```

30.6.4. SNMP Monitoring

The bridge interface and STP parameters can be monitored via bsnmpd(1) which is included in the FreeBSD base system. The exported bridge MIBs conform to IETF standards so any SNMP client or monitoring package can be used to retrieve the data.

To enable monitoring on the bridge, uncomment this line in /etc/snmpd.config by removing the beginning # symbol:

```
begemotSnmpdModulePath."bridge" = "/usr/lib/snmp_bridge.so"
```

Other configuration settings, such as community names and access lists, may need to be modified in this file. See bsnmpd(1) and snmp_bridge(3) for more information. Once these edits are saved, add this line to /etc/rc.conf :

```
bsnmpd_enable="YES"
```

Then, start bsnmpd(1):

```
# service bsnmpd start
```

The following examples use the Net-SNMP software (net-mgmt/net-snmp) to query a bridge from a client system. The net-mgmt/bsnmptools port can also be used. From the SNMP client which is running Net-SNMP, add the following lines to $HOME/.snmp/snmp.conf in order to import the bridge MIB definitions:

```
mibdirs +/usr/share/snmp/mibs
mibs +BRIDGE-MIB:RSTP-MIB:BEGEMOT-MIB:BEGEMOT-BRIDGE-MIB
```

To monitor a single bridge using the IETF BRIDGE-MIB (RFC4188):

```
% snmpwalk -v 2c -c public bridge1.example.com mib-2.dot1dBridge
BRIDGE-MIB::dot1dBaseBridgeAddress.0 = STRING: 66:fb:9b:6e:5c:44
BRIDGE-MIB::dot1dBaseNumPorts.0 = INTEGER: 1 ports
BRIDGE-MIB::dot1dStpTimeSinceTopologyChange.0 = Timeticks: (189959) 0:31:39.59 centi-
seconds
```

```
BRIDGE-MIB::dot1dStpTopChanges.0 = Counter32: 2
BRIDGE-MIB::dot1dStpDesignatedRoot.0 = Hex-STRING: 80 00 00 01 02 4B D4 50
...
BRIDGE-MIB::dot1dStpPortState.3 = INTEGER: forwarding(5)
BRIDGE-MIB::dot1dStpPortEnable.3 = INTEGER: enabled(1)
BRIDGE-MIB::dot1dStpPortPathCost.3 = INTEGER: 200000
BRIDGE-MIB::dot1dStpPortDesignatedRoot.3 = Hex-STRING: 80 00 00 01 02 4B D4 50
BRIDGE-MIB::dot1dStpPortDesignatedCost.3 = INTEGER: 0
BRIDGE-MIB::dot1dStpPortDesignatedBridge.3 = Hex-STRING: 80 00 00 01 02 4B D4 50
BRIDGE-MIB::dot1dStpPortDesignatedPort.3 = Hex-STRING: 03 80
BRIDGE-MIB::dot1dStpPortForwardTransitions.3 = Counter32: 1
RSTP-MIB::dot1dStpVersion.0 = INTEGER: rstp(2)
```

The `dot1dStpTopChanges.0` value is two, indicating that the STP bridge topology has changed twice. A topology change means that one or more links in the network have changed or failed and a new tree has been calculated. The `dot1dStpTimeSinceTopologyChange.0` value will show when this happened.

To monitor multiple bridge interfaces, the private BEGEMOT-BRIDGE-MIB can be used:

```
% snmpwalk -v 2c -c public bridge1.example.com
enterprises.fokus.begemot.begemotBridge
BEGEMOT-BRIDGE-MIB::begemotBridgeBaseName."bridge0" = STRING: bridge0
BEGEMOT-BRIDGE-MIB::begemotBridgeBaseName."bridge2" = STRING: bridge2
BEGEMOT-BRIDGE-MIB::begemotBridgeBaseAddress."bridge0" = STRING: e:ce:3b:5a:9e:13
BEGEMOT-BRIDGE-MIB::begemotBridgeBaseAddress."bridge2" = STRING: 12:5e:4d:74:d:fc
BEGEMOT-BRIDGE-MIB::begemotBridgeBaseNumPorts."bridge0" = INTEGER: 1
BEGEMOT-BRIDGE-MIB::begemotBridgeBaseNumPorts."bridge2" = INTEGER: 1
...
BEGEMOT-BRIDGE-MIB::begemotBridgeStpTimeSinceTopologyChange."bridge0" = Timeticks: ↺
(116927) 0:19:29.27 centi-seconds
BEGEMOT-BRIDGE-MIB::begemotBridgeStpTimeSinceTopologyChange."bridge2" = Timeticks: ↺
(82773) 0:13:47.73 centi-seconds
BEGEMOT-BRIDGE-MIB::begemotBridgeStpTopChanges."bridge0" = Counter32: 1
BEGEMOT-BRIDGE-MIB::begemotBridgeStpTopChanges."bridge2" = Counter32: 1
BEGEMOT-BRIDGE-MIB::begemotBridgeStpDesignatedRoot."bridge0" = Hex-STRING: 80 00 00 40 ↺
95 30 5E 31
BEGEMOT-BRIDGE-MIB::begemotBridgeStpDesignatedRoot."bridge2" = Hex-STRING: 80 00 00 50 ↺
8B B8 C6 A9
```

To change the bridge interface being monitored via the `mib-2.dot1dBridge` subtree:

```
% snmpset -v 2c -c private bridge1.example.com
BEGEMOT-BRIDGE-MIB::begemotBridgeDefaultBridgeIf.0 s bridge2
```

30.7. Link Aggregation and Failover

Written by Andrew Thompson.

FreeBSD provides the lagg(4) interface which can be used to aggregate multiple network interfaces into one virtual interface in order to provide failover and link aggregation. Failover allows traffic to continue to flow as long as at least one aggregated network interface has an established link. Link aggregation works best on switches which support LACP, as this protocol distributes traffic bi-directionally while responding to the failure of individual links.

The aggregation protocols supported by the lagg interface determine which ports are used for outgoing traffic and whether or not a specific port accepts incoming traffic. The following protocols are supported by lagg(4):

failover

This mode sends and receives traffic only through the master port. If the master port becomes unavailable, the next active port is used. The first interface added to the virtual interface is the master port and all subsequently added interfaces are used as failover devices. If failover to a non-master port occurs, the original port becomes master once it becomes available again.

fec / loadbalance

Cisco® Fast EtherChannel® (FEC) is found on older Cisco® switches. It provides a static setup and does not negotiate aggregation with the peer or exchange frames to monitor the link. If the switch supports LACP, that should be used instead.

lacp

The IEEE® 802.3ad Link Aggregation Control Protocol (LACP) negotiates a set of aggregable links with the peer into one or more Link Aggregated Groups (LAGs). Each LAG is composed of ports of the same speed, set to full-duplex operation, and traffic is balanced across the ports in the LAG with the greatest total speed. Typically, there is only one LAG which contains all the ports. In the event of changes in physical connectivity, LACP will quickly converge to a new configuration.

LACP balances outgoing traffic across the active ports based on hashed protocol header information and accepts incoming traffic from any active port. The hash includes the Ethernet source and destination address and, if available, the VLAN tag, and the IPv4 or IPv6 source and destination address.

roundrobin

This mode distributes outgoing traffic using a round-robin scheduler through all active ports and accepts incoming traffic from any active port. Since this mode violates Ethernet frame ordering, it should be used with caution.

30.7.1. Configuration Examples

This section demonstrates how to configure a Cisco® switch and a FreeBSD system for LACP load balancing. It then shows how to configure two Ethernet interfaces in failover mode as well as how to configure failover mode between an Ethernet and a wireless interface.

Example 30.1. LACP Aggregation with a Cisco® Switch

This example connects two fxp(4) Ethernet interfaces on a FreeBSD machine to the first two Ethernet ports on a Cisco® switch as a single load balanced and fault tolerant link. More interfaces can be added to increase throughput and fault tolerance. Replace the names of the Cisco® ports, Ethernet devices, channel group number, and IP address shown in the example to match the local configuration.

Frame ordering is mandatory on Ethernet links and any traffic between two stations always flows over the same physical link, limiting the maximum speed to that of one interface. The transmit algorithm attempts to use as much information as it can to distinguish different traffic flows and balance the flows across the available interfaces.

On the Cisco® switch, add the *FastEthernet0/1* and *FastEthernet0/2* interfaces to channel group *1*:

```
interface FastEthernet0/1
 channel-group  1 mode active
 channel-protocol lacp
!
interface FastEthernet0/2
 channel-group  1 mode active
 channel-protocol lacp
```

On the FreeBSD system, create the lagg(4) interface using the physical interfaces *fxp0* and *fxp1* and bring the interfaces up with an IP address of *10.0.0.3/24* :

```
# ifconfig  fxp0 up
# ifconfig  fxp1 up
# ifconfig  lagg0 create
# ifconfig  lagg0 up laggproto lacp laggport  fxp0 laggport  fxp1 10.0.0.3/24
```

Next, verify the status of the virtual interface:

```
# ifconfig lagg0
lagg0: flags=8843<UP,BROADCAST,RUNNING,SIMPLEX,MULTICAST> metric 0 mtu 1500
        options=8<VLAN_MTU>
        ether 00:05:5d:71:8d:b8
        inet 10.0.0.3 netmask 0xffffff00 broadcast 10.0.0.255
        media: Ethernet autoselect
        status: active
        laggproto lacp
        laggport: fxp1 flags=1c<ACTIVE,COLLECTING,DISTRIBUTING>
        laggport: fxp0 flags=1c<ACTIVE,COLLECTING,DISTRIBUTING>
```

Ports marked as ACTIVE are part of the LAG that has been negotiated with the remote switch. Traffic will be transmitted and received through these active ports. Add -v to the above command to view the LAG identifiers.

To see the port status on the Cisco® switch:

```
switch# show lacp neighbor
Flags:   S - Device is requesting Slow LACPDUs
         F - Device is requesting Fast LACPDUs
         A - Device is in Active mode          P - Device is in Passive mode

Channel group 1 neighbors

Partner's information:

                        LACP port                     Oper    Port    Port
Port      Flags    Priority   Dev ID        Age       Key     Number  State
Fa0/1     SA       32768      0005.5d71.8db8  29s     0x146   0x3     0x3D
Fa0/2     SA       32768      0005.5d71.8db8  29s     0x146   0x4     0x3D
```

For more detail, type **show lacp neighbor detail**.

To retain this configuration across reboots, add the following entries to /etc/rc.conf on the FreeBSD system:

```
ifconfig_fxp0="up"
ifconfig_fxp1="up"
cloned_interfaces="lagg0"
ifconfig_lagg0="laggproto lacp laggport fxp0 laggport fxp1 10.0.0.3/24 "
```

Example 30.2. Failover Mode

Failover mode can be used to switch over to a secondary interface if the link is lost on the master interface. To configure failover, make sure that the underlying physical interfaces are up, then create the lagg(4) interface. In this example, *fxp0* is the master interface, *fxp1* is the secondary interface, and the virtual interface is assigned an IP address of *10.0.0.15/24* :

```
# ifconfig fxp0 up
# ifconfig fxp1 up
# ifconfig lagg0 create
# ifconfig lagg0 up laggproto failover laggport  fxp0 laggport fxp1 10.0.0.15/24
```

The virtual interface should look something like this:

```
# ifconfig lagg0
lagg0: flags=8843<UP,BROADCAST,RUNNING,SIMPLEX,MULTICAST> metric 0 mtu 1500
        options=8<VLAN_MTU>
        ether 00:05:5d:71:8d:b8
        inet 10.0.0.15 netmask 0xffffff00 broadcast 10.0.0.255
```

```
        media: Ethernet autoselect
        status: active
        laggproto failover
        laggport: fxp1 flags=0<>
        laggport: fxp0 flags=5<MASTER,ACTIVE>
```

Traffic will be transmitted and received on *fxp0*. If the link is lost on *fxp0*, *fxp1* will become the active link. If the link is restored on the master interface, it will once again become the active link.

To retain this configuration across reboots, add the following entries to /etc/rc.conf :

```
ifconfig_fxp0="up"
ifconfig_fxp1="up"
cloned_interfaces="lagg0"
ifconfig_lagg0="laggproto failover laggport fxp0 laggport fxp1 10.0.0.15/24 "
```

Example 30.3. Failover Mode Between Ethernet and Wireless Interfaces

For laptop users, it is usually desirable to configure the wireless device as a secondary which is only used when the Ethernet connection is not available. With lagg(4), it is possible to configure a failover which prefers the Ethernet connection for both performance and security reasons, while maintaining the ability to transfer data over the wireless connection.

This is achieved by overriding the physical wireless interface's MAC address with that of the Ethernet interface.

In this example, the Ethernet interface, *bge0*, is the master and the wireless interface, *wlan0*, is the failover. The *wlan0* device was created from *iwn0* wireless interface, which will be configured with the MAC address of the Ethernet interface. First, determine the MAC address of the Ethernet interface:

```
# ifconfig bge0
bge0: flags=8843<UP,BROADCAST,RUNNING,SIMPLEX,MULTICAST> metric 0 mtu 1500
 options=19b<RXCSUM,TXCSUM,VLAN_MTU,VLAN_HWTAGGING,VLAN_HWCSUM,TSO4>
 ether 00:21:70:da:ae:37
 inet6 fe80::221:70ff:feda:ae37%bge0 prefixlen 64 scopeid 0x2
 nd6 options=29<PERFORMNUD,IFDISABLED,AUTO_LINKLOCAL>
 media: Ethernet autoselect (1000baseT <full-duplex>)
 status: active
```

Replace *bge0* to match the system's Ethernet interface name. The ether line will contain the MAC address of the specified interface. Now, change the MAC address of the underlying wireless interface:

```
# ifconfig iwn0 ether 00:21:70:da:ae:37
```

Bring the wireless interface up, but do not set an IP address:

```
# ifconfig wlan0 create wlandev iwn0 ssid my_router up
```

Make sure the *bge0* interface is up, then create the lagg(4) interface with *bge0* as master with failover to *wlan0*:

```
# ifconfig bge0 up
# ifconfig lagg0 create
# ifconfig lagg0 up laggproto failover laggport  bge0 laggport wlan0
```

The virtual interface should look something like this:

```
# ifconfig lagg0
lagg0: flags=8843<UP,BROADCAST,RUNNING,SIMPLEX,MULTICAST> metric 0 mtu 1500
```

```
                options=8<VLAN_MTU>
                ether 00:21:70:da:ae:37
                media: Ethernet autoselect
                status: active
                laggproto failover
                laggport: wlan0 flags=0<>
                laggport: bge0 flags=5<MASTER,ACTIVE>
```

Then, start the DHCP client to obtain an IP address:

```
# dhclient lagg0
```

To retain this configuration across reboots, add the following entries to /etc/rc.conf :

```
ifconfig_bge0="up"
wlans_iwn0="wlan0"
ifconfig_wlan0="WPA"
create_args_wlan0="wlanaddr 00:21:70:da:ae:37 "
cloned_interfaces="lagg0"
ifconfig_lagg0="up laggproto failover laggport bge0 laggport wlan0 DHCP"
```

30.8. Diskless Operation with PXE

Updated by Jean-François Dockès.
Reorganized and enhanced by Alex Dupre.

The Intel® Preboot eXecution Environment (PXE) allows an operating system to boot over the network. For example, a FreeBSD system can boot over the network and operate without a local disk, using file systems mounted from an NFS server. PXE support is usually available in the BIOS. To use PXE when the machine starts, select the Boot from network option in the BIOS setup or type a function key during system initialization.

In order to provide the files needed for an operating system to boot over the network, a PXE setup also requires properly configured DHCP, TFTP, and NFS servers, where:

- Initial parameters, such as an IP address, executable boot filename and location, server name, and root path are obtained from the DHCP server.

- The operating system loader file is booted using TFTP.

- The file systems are loaded using NFS.

When a computer PXE boots, it receives information over DHCP about where to obtain the initial boot loader file. After the host computer receives this information, it downloads the boot loader via TFTP and then executes the boot loader. In FreeBSD, the boot loader file is /boot/pxeboot . After /boot/pxeboot executes, the FreeBSD kernel is loaded and the rest of the FreeBSD bootup sequence proceeds, as described in Chapter 12, *The FreeBSD Booting Process*.

This section describes how to configure these services on a FreeBSD system so that other systems can PXE boot into FreeBSD. Refer to diskless(8) for more information.

Caution

As described, the system providing these services is insecure. It should live in a protected area of a network and be untrusted by other hosts.

30.8.1. Setting Up the PXE Environment

Written by Craig Rodrigues.

The steps shown in this section configure the built-in NFS and TFTP servers. The next section demonstrates how to install and configure the DHCP server. In this example, the directory which will contain the files used by PXE users is /b/tftpboot/FreeBSD/install. It is important that this directory exists and that the same directory name is set in both /etc/inetd.conf and /usr/local/etc/dhcpd.conf .

1. Create the root directory which will contain a FreeBSD installation to be NFS mounted:

    ```
    # export NFSROOTDIR=/b/tftpboot/FreeBSD/install
    # mkdir -p ${NFSROOTDIR}
    ```

2. Enable the NFS server by adding this line to /etc/rc.conf :

    ```
    nfs_server_enable="YES"
    ```

3. Export the diskless root directory via NFS by adding the following to /etc/exports :

    ```
    /b -ro -alldirs
    ```

4. Start the NFS server:

    ```
    # service nfsd start
    ```

5. Enable inetd(8) by adding the following line to /etc/rc.conf :

    ```
    inetd_enable="YES"
    ```

6. Uncomment the following line in /etc/inetd.conf by making sure it does not start with a # symbol:

    ```
    tftp dgram udp wait root /usr/libexec/tftpd tftpd -l -s /b/tftpboot
    ```

    > **Note**
    >
    > Some PXE versions require the TCP version of TFTP. In this case, uncomment the second tftp line which contains stream tcp.

7. Start inetd(8):

    ```
    # service inetd start
    ```

8. Rebuild the FreeBSD kernel and userland (refer to Section 23.5, "Updating FreeBSD from Source" for more detailed instructions):

    ```
    # cd /usr/src
    # make buildworld
    # make buildkernel
    ```

9. Install FreeBSD into the directory mounted over NFS:

    ```
    # make installworld DESTDIR=${NFSROOTDIR}
    # make installkernel DESTDIR=${NFSROOTDIR}
    # make distribution DESTDIR=${NFSROOTDIR}
    ```

10. Test that the TFTP server works and can download the boot loader which will be obtained via PXE:

    ```
    # tftp localhost
    tftp> get FreeBSD/install/boot/pxeboot
    ```

```
Received 264951 bytes in 0.1 seconds
```

11. Edit ${NFSROOTDIR}/etc/fstab and create an entry to mount the root file system over NFS:

# Device	Mountpoint	FSType	Options	↺
Dump Pass				
myhost.example.com :/b/tftpboot/FreeBSD/install	/	nfs	ro	0
0				

Replace *myhost.example.com* with the hostname or IP address of the NFS server. In this example, the root file system is mounted read-only in order to prevent NFS clients from potentially deleting the contents of the root file system.

12. Set the root password in the PXE environment for client machines which are PXE booting :

```
# chroot ${NFSROOTDIR}
# passwd
```

13. If needed, enable ssh(1) root logins for client machines which are PXE booting by editing ${NFSROOTDIR}/etc/ssh/sshd_config and enabling PermitRootLogin. This option is documented in sshd_config(5).

14. Perform any other needed customizations of the PXE environment in ${NFSROOTDIR}. These customizations could include things like installing packages or editing the password file with vipw(8).

When booting from an NFS root volume, /etc/rc detects the NFS boot and runs /etc/rc.initdiskless. In this case, /etc and /var need to be memory backed file systems so that these directories are writable but the NFS root directory is read-only:

```
# chroot ${NFSROOTDIR}
# mkdir -p conf/base
# tar -c -v -f conf/base/etc.cpio.gz --format cpio --gzip etc
# tar -c -v -f conf/base/var.cpio.gz --format cpio --gzip var
```

When the system boots, memory file systems for /etc and /var will be created and mounted and the contents of the cpio.gz files will be copied into them.

30.8.2. Configuring the DHCP Server

The DHCP server does not need to be the same machine as the TFTP and NFS server, but it needs to be accessible in the network.

DHCP is not part of the FreeBSD base system but can be installed using the net/isc-dhcp43-server port or package.

Once installed, edit the configuration file, /usr/local/etc/dhcpd.conf . Configure the next-server, filename, and root-path settings as seen in this example:

```
subnet 192.168.0.0 netmask 255.255.255.0 {
  range 192.168.0.2 192.168.0.3 -;
  option subnet-mask 255.255.255.0 -;
  option routers 192.168.0.1 -;
  option broadcast-address 192.168.0.255 -;
  option domain-name-servers 192.168.35.35, 192.168.35.36 -;
  option domain-name "example.com";

  # IP address of TFTP server
  next-server 192.168.0.1 -;

  # path of boot loader obtained via tftp
  filename "FreeBSD/install/boot/pxeboot " -;

  # pxeboot boot loader will try to NFS mount this directory for root FS
  option root-path "192.168.0.1:/b/tftpboot/FreeBSD/install/ " -;
```

```
}
```

The next-server directive is used to specify the IP address of the TFTP server.

The filename directive defines the path to /boot/pxeboot . A relative filename is used, meaning that /b/tftpboot is not included in the path.

The root-path option defines the path to the NFS root file system.

Once the edits are saved, enable DHCP at boot time by adding the following line to /etc/rc.conf :

```
dhcpd_enable="YES"
```

Then start the DHCP service:

```
# service isc-dhcpd start
```

30.8.3. Debugging PXE Problems

Once all of the services are configured and started, PXE clients should be able to automatically load FreeBSD over the network. If a particular client is unable to connect, when that client machine boots up, enter the BIOS configuration menu and confirm that it is set to boot from the network.

This section describes some troubleshooting tips for isolating the source of the configuration problem should no clients be able to PXE boot.

1. Use the net/wireshark package or port to debug the network traffic involved during the PXE booting process, which is illustrated in the diagram below.

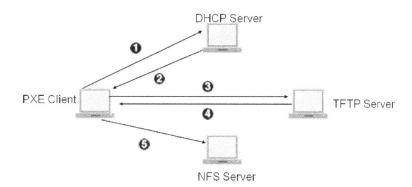

❶   Client broadcasts a DHCPDISCOVER message.
❷   The DHCP server responds with the IP address, next-server , filename, and root-path values.
❸   The client sends a TFTP request to next-server , asking to retrieve filename.
❹   The TFTP server responds and sends filename to client.
❺   The client executes filename, which is pxeboot(8), which then loads the kernel. When the kernel executes, the root file system specified by root-path is mounted over NFS.

Figure 30.1. PXE Booting Process with NFS Root Mount

2. On the TFTP server, read /var/log/xferlog to ensure that pxeboot is being retrieved from the correct location. To test this example configuration:

```
# tftp 192.168.0.1
tftp> get FreeBSD/install/boot/pxeboot
Received 264951 bytes in 0.1 seconds
```

The BUGS sections in tftpd(8) and tftp(1) document some limitations with TFTP.

3. Make sure that the root file system can be mounted via NFS. To test this example configuration:

```
# mount -t nfs 192.168.0.1:/b/tftpboot/FreeBSD/install /mnt
```

30.9. IPv6

Originally Written by Aaron Kaplan.
Restructured and Added by Tom Rhodes.
Extended by Brad Davis.

IPv6 is the new version of the well known IP protocol, also known as IPv4. IPv6 provides several advantages over IPv4 as well as many new features:

* Its 128-bit address space allows for 340,282,366,920,938,463,463,374,607,431,768,211,456 addresses. This addresses the IPv4 address shortage and eventual IPv4 address exhaustion.

* Routers only store network aggregation addresses in their routing tables, thus reducing the average space of a routing table to 8192 entries. This addresses the scalability issues associated with IPv4, which required every allocated block of IPv4 addresses to be exchanged between Internet routers, causing their routing tables to become too large to allow efficient routing.

* Address autoconfiguration (RFC2462).

* Mandatory multicast addresses.

* Built-in IPsec (IP security).

* Simplified header structure.

* Support for mobile IP.

* IPv6-to-IPv4 transition mechanisms.

FreeBSD includes the http://www.kame.net/ IPv6 reference implementation and comes with everything needed to use IPv6. This section focuses on getting IPv6 configured and running.

30.9.1. Background on IPv6 Addresses

There are three different types of IPv6 addresses:

Unicast
> A packet sent to a unicast address arrives at the interface belonging to the address.

Anycast
> These addresses are syntactically indistinguishable from unicast addresses but they address a group of interfaces. The packet destined for an anycast address will arrive at the nearest router interface. Anycast addresses are only used by routers.

Multicast
> These addresses identify a group of interfaces. A packet destined for a multicast address will arrive at all interfaces belonging to the multicast group. The IPv4 broadcast address, usually xxx.xxx.xxx.255 , is expressed by multicast addresses in IPv6.

When reading an IPv6 address, the canonical form is represented as x:x:x:x:x:x:x:x , where each x represents a 16 bit hex value. An example is FEBC:A574:382B:23C1:AA49:4592:4EFE:9982 .

Often, an address will have long substrings of all zeros. A :: (double colon) can be used to replace one substring per address. Also, up to three leading 0s per hex value can be omitted. For example, fe80::1 corresponds to the canonical form fe80:0000:0000:0000:0000:0000:0000:0001 .

A third form is to write the last 32 bits using the well known IPv4 notation. For example, `2002::10.0.0.1` corresponds to the hexadecimal canonical representation `2002:0000:0000:0000:0000:0000:0a00:0001`, which in turn is equivalent to `2002::a00:1`.

To view a FreeBSD system's IPv6 address, use ifconfig(8):

```
# ifconfig
```

```
rl0: flags=8943<UP,BROADCAST,RUNNING,PROMISC,SIMPLEX,MULTICAST> mtu 1500
        inet 10.0.0.10 netmask 0xffffff00 broadcast 10.0.0.255
        inet6 fe80::200:21ff:fe03:8e1%rl0 prefixlen 64 scopeid 0x1
        ether 00:00:21:03:08:e1
        media: Ethernet autoselect (100baseTX )
        status: active
```

In this example, the `rl0` interface is using `fe80::200:21ff:fe03:8e1%rl0`, an auto-configured link-local address which was automatically generated from the MAC address.

Some IPv6 addresses are reserved. A summary of these reserved addresses is seen in Table 30.3, "Reserved IPv6 Addresses":

Table 30.3. Reserved IPv6 Addresses

IPv6 address	Prefixlength (Bits)	Description	Notes
`::`	128 bits	unspecified	Equivalent to `0.0.0.0` in IPv4.
`::1`	128 bits	loopback address	Equivalent to `127.0.0.1` in IPv4.
`::00:xx:xx:xx:xx`	96 bits	embedded IPv4	The lower 32 bits are the compatible IPv4 address.
`::ff:xx:xx:xx:xx`	96 bits	IPv4 mapped IPv6 address	The lower 32 bits are the IPv4 address for hosts which do not support IPv6.
`fe80::/10`	10 bits	link-local	Equivalent to 169.254.0.0/16 in IPv4.
`fc00::/7`	7 bits	unique-local	Unique local addresses are intended for local communication and are only routable within a set of cooperating sites.
`ff00::`	8 bits	multicast	
`2000::-3fff::`	3 bits	global unicast	All global unicast addresses are assigned from this pool. The first 3 bits are `001`.

For further information on the structure of IPv6 addresses, refer to RFC3513.

30.9.2. Configuring IPv6

To configure a FreeBSD system as an IPv6 client, add these two lines to `rc.conf`:

```
ifconfig_rl0_ipv6="inet6 accept_rtadv"
rtsold_enable="YES"
```

The first line enables the specified interface to receive router solicitation messages. The second line enables the router solicitation daemon, rtsol(8).

If the interface needs a statically assigned IPv6 address, add an entry to specify the static address and associated prefix length:

```
ifconfig_rl0_ipv6="inet6 2001:db8:4672:6565:2026:5043:2d42:5344    prefixlen 64"
```

To assign a default router, specify its address:

```
ipv6_defaultrouter="2001:db8:4672:6565::1 "
```

30.9.3. Connecting to a Provider

In order to connect to other IPv6 networks, one must have a provider or a tunnel that supports IPv6:

- Contact an Internet Service Provider to see if they offer IPv6.

- Hurricane Electric offers tunnels with end-points all around the globe.

> **Note**
>
> Install the net/freenet6 package or port for a dial-up connection.

This section demonstrates how to take the directions from a tunnel provider and convert them into /etc/rc.conf settings that will persist through reboots.

The first /etc/rc.conf entry creates the generic tunneling interface gif0:

```
cloned_interfaces="gif0"
```

Next, configure that interface with the IPv4 addresses of the local and remote endpoints. Replace MY_IPv4_ADDR and REMOTE_IPv4_ADDR with the actual IPv4 addresses:

```
create_args_gif0="tunnel MY_IPv4_ADDR REMOTE_IPv4_ADDR "
```

To apply the IPv6 address that has been assigned for use as the IPv6 tunnel endpoint, add this line, replacing MY_ASSIGNED_IPv6_TUNNEL_ENDPOINT_ADDR with the assigned address:

```
ifconfig_gif0_ipv6="inet6 MY_ASSIGNED_IPv6_TUNNEL_ENDPOINT_ADDR  "
```

Then, set the default route for the other side of the IPv6 tunnel. Replace MY_IPv6_REMOTE_TUNNEL_ENDPOINT_ADDR with the default gateway address assigned by the provider:

```
ipv6_defaultrouter="MY_IPv6_REMOTE_TUNNEL_ENDPOINT_ADDR  "
```

If the FreeBSD system will route IPv6 packets between the rest of the network and the world, enable the gateway using this line:

```
ipv6_gateway_enable="YES"
```

30.9.4. Router Advertisement and Host Auto Configuration

This section demonstrates how to setup rtadvd(8) to advertise the IPv6 default route.

To enable rtadvd(8), add the following to /etc/rc.conf :

```
rtadvd_enable="YES"
```

It is important to specify the interface on which to do IPv6 router solicitation. For example, to tell rtadvd(8) to use rl0:

```
rtadvd_interfaces="rl0"
```

Next, create the configuration file, `/etc/rtadvd.conf` as seen in this example:

```
rl0:\
  :addrs#1:addr="2001:db8:1f11:246::":prefixlen#64:tc=ether:
```

Replace `rl0` with the interface to be used and `2001:db8:1f11:246::`   with the prefix of the allocation.

For a dedicated `/64` subnet, nothing else needs to be changed. Otherwise, change the `prefixlen#` to the correct value.

30.9.5. IPv6 and IPv6 Address Mapping

When IPv6 is enabled on a server, there may be a need to enable IPv4 mapped IPv6 address communication. This compatibility option allows for IPv4 addresses to be represented as IPv6 addresses. Permitting IPv6 applications to communicate with IPv4 and vice versa may be a security issue.

This option may not be required in most cases and is available only for compatibility. This option will allow IPv6-only applications to work with IPv4 in a dual stack environment. This is most useful for third party applications which may not support an IPv6-only environment. To enable this feature, add the following to `/etc/rc.conf` :

```
ipv6_ipv4mapping="YES"
```

Reviewing the information in RFC 3493, section 3.6 and 3.7 as well as RFC 4038 section 4.2 may be useful to some administrators.

30.10. Common Address Redundancy Protocol (CARP)

Contributed by Tom Rhodes.
Updated by Allan Jude.

The Common Address Redundancy Protocol (CARP) allows multiple hosts to share the same IP address and Virtual Host ID (VHID) in order to provide *high availability* for one or more services. This means that one or more hosts can fail, and the other hosts will transparently take over so that users do not see a service failure.

In addition to the shared IP address, each host has its own IP address for management and configuration. All of the machines that share an IP address have the same VHID. The VHID for each virtual IP address must be unique across the broadcast domain of the network interface.

High availability using CARP is built into FreeBSD, though the steps to configure it vary slightly depending upon the FreeBSD version. This section provides the same example configuration for versions before and equal to or after FreeBSD 10.

This example configures failover support with three hosts, all with unique IP addresses, but providing the same web content. It has two different masters named `hosta.example.org` and `hostb.example.org`, with a shared backup named `hostc.example.org`.

These machines are load balanced with a Round Robin DNS configuration. The master and backup machines are configured identically except for their hostnames and management IP addresses. These servers must have the same configuration and run the same services. When the failover occurs, requests to the service on the shared IP address can only be answered correctly if the backup server has access to the same content. The backup machine has two additional CARP interfaces, one for each of the master content server's IP addresses. When a failure occurs, the backup server will pick up the failed master machine's IP address.

30.10.1. Using CARP on FreeBSD 10 and Later

Enable boot-time support for CARP by adding an entry for the `carp.ko` kernel module in `/boot/loader.conf` :

```
carp_load="YES"
```

To load the module now without rebooting:

```
# kldload carp
```

For users who prefer to use a custom kernel, include the following line in the custom kernel configuration file and compile the kernel as described in Chapter 8, *Configuring the FreeBSD Kernel*:

```
device carp
```

The hostname, management IP address and subnet mask, shared IP address, and VHID are all set by adding entries to /etc/rc.conf . This example is for hosta.example.org:

```
hostname="hosta.example.org "
ifconfig_em0="inet 192.168.1.3  netmask 255.255.255.0 "
ifconfig_em0_alias0="inet vhid 1 pass testpass alias 192.168.1.50 /32"
```

The next set of entries are for hostb.example.org. Since it represents a second master, it uses a different shared IP address and VHID. However, the passwords specified with pass must be identical as CARP will only listen to and accept advertisements from machines with the correct password.

```
hostname="hostb.example.org "
ifconfig_em0="inet 192.168.1.4  netmask 255.255.255.0 "
ifconfig_em0_alias0="inet vhid 2 pass testpass alias 192.168.1.51 /32"
```

The third machine, hostc.example.org, is configured to handle failover from either master. This machine is configured with two CARP VHIDs, one to handle the virtual IP address for each of the master hosts. The CARP advertising skew, advskew, is set to ensure that the backup host advertises later than the master, since advskew controls the order of precedence when there are multiple backup servers.

```
hostname="hostc.example.org"
ifconfig_em0="inet 192.168.1.5  netmask 255.255.255.0 "
ifconfig_em0_alias0="inet vhid 1 advskew 100 pass testpass  alias 192.168.1.50 /32"
ifconfig_em0_alias1="inet vhid 2 advskew 100 pass testpass  alias 192.168.1.51 /32"
```

Having two CARP VHIDs configured means that hostc.example.org will notice if either of the master servers becomes unavailable. If a master fails to advertise before the backup server, the backup server will pick up the shared IP address until the master becomes available again.

Note

Preemption is disabled by default. If preemption has been enabled, hostc.example.org might not release the virtual IP address back to the original master server. The administrator can force the backup server to return the IP address to the master with the command:

```
# ifconfig em0 vhid 1 state backup
```

Once the configuration is complete, either restart networking or reboot each system. High availability is now enabled.

CARP functionality can be controlled via several sysctl(8) variables documented in the carp(4) manual pages. Other actions can be triggered from CARP events by using devd(8).

30.10.2. Using CARP on FreeBSD 9 and Earlier

The configuration for these versions of FreeBSD is similar to the one described in the previous section, except that a CARP device must first be created and referred to in the configuration.

Enable boot-time support for CARP by loading the if_carp.ko kernel module in /boot/loader.conf :

```
if_carp_load="YES"
```

To load the module now without rebooting:

```
# kldload carp
```

For users who prefer to use a custom kernel, include the following line in the custom kernel configuration file and compile the kernel as described in Chapter 8, *Configuring the FreeBSD Kernel*:

```
device carp
```

Next, on each host, create a CARP device:

```
# ifconfig carp0 create
```

Set the hostname, management IP address, the shared IP address, and VHID by adding the required lines to /etc/ rc.conf. Since a virtual CARP device is used instead of an alias, the actual subnet mask of /24 is used instead of /32. Here are the entries for hosta.example.org:

```
hostname="hosta.example.org "
ifconfig_fxp0="inet 192.168.1.3 netmask 255.255.255.0 "
cloned_interfaces="carp0"
ifconfig_carp0="vhid 1 pass testpass 192.168.1.50/24 "
```

On hostb.example.org:

```
hostname="hostb.example.org "
ifconfig_fxp0="inet 192.168.1.4 netmask 255.255.255.0 "
cloned_interfaces="carp0"
ifconfig_carp0="vhid 2 pass testpass 192.168.1.51/24 "
```

The third machine, hostc.example.org, is configured to handle failover from either of the master hosts:

```
hostname="hostc.example.org "
ifconfig_fxp0="inet 192.168.1.5 netmask 255.255.255.0 "
cloned_interfaces="carp0 carp1"
ifconfig_carp0="vhid 1 advskew 100 pass testpass  192.168.1.50/24 "
ifconfig_carp1="vhid 2 advskew 100 pass testpass  192.168.1.51/24 "
```

Note

Preemption is disabled in the GENERIC FreeBSD kernel. If preemption has been enabled with a custom kernel, hostc.example.org may not release the IP address back to the original content server. The administrator can force the backup server to return the IP address to the master with the command:

```
# ifconfig carp0 down && ifconfig carp0 up
```

This should be done on the carp interface which corresponds to the correct host.

Once the configuration is complete, either restart networking or reboot each system. High availability is now enabled.

30.11. VLANs

VLANs are a way of virtually dividing up a network into many different subnetworks. Each will have its own broadcast domain and be isolated from the rest of the VLANs.

On FreeBSD, VLANs must be supported by the network card driver. To see which drivers support vlans, refer to the vlan(4) manual page.

When configuring a VLAN, a couple pieces of information must be known. First, which network interface? Second, what is the VLAN tag?

To configure VLANs at run time, with a NIC of em0 and a VLAN tag of 5. The command would look like this:

```
# ifconfig em0.5 create vlan 5 vlandev em0 inet 192.168.20.20/24
```

Note

See how the interface name includes the NIC driver name and the VLAN tag, separated by a period? This is a best practice to make maintaining the VLAN configuration easy when many VLANs are present on a machine.

To configure VLANs at boot time, /etc/rc.conf must be updated. To duplicate the configuration above, the following will need to be added:

```
vlans_em0="5"
ifconfig_em0_5="inet 192.168.20.20/24"
```

Additional VLANs may be added, by simply adding the tag to the vlans_em0 field and adding an additional line configuring the network on that VLAN tag's interface.

Part V. Appendices

Table of Contents

Appendix A. Obtaining FreeBSD

A.1. CD and DVD Sets

FreeBSD CD and DVD sets are available from several online retailers:

- FreeBSD Mall, Inc.
  2420 Sand Creek Rd C-1 #347
  Brentwood, CA
  94513
  USA
  Phone: +1 925 240-6652
  Fax: +1 925 674-0821
  Email: <info@freebsdmall.com>
  WWW: https://www.freebsdmall.com

- Getlinux
  78 Rue de la Croix Rochopt
  Épinay-sous-Sénart
  91860
  France
  Email: <contact@getlinux.fr>
  WWW: http://www.getlinux.fr/

- Dr. Hinner EDV
  Kochelseestr. 11
  D-81371 München
  Germany
  Phone: (0177) 428 419 0
  Email: <infow@hinner.de>
  WWW: http://www.hinner.de/linux/freebsd.html

- Linux Center
  Galernaya Street, 55
  Saint-Petersburg
  190000
  Russia
  Phone: +7-812-309-06-86
  Email: <info@linuxcenter.ru>
  WWW: http://linuxcenter.ru/shop/freebsd

A.2. FTP Sites

The official sources for FreeBSD are available via anonymous FTP from a worldwide set of mirror sites. The site `ftp://ftp.FreeBSD.org/pub/FreeBSD/` is available via HTTP and FTP. It is made up of many machines operated by the project cluster administrators and behind GeoDNS to direct users to the closest available mirror.

Additionally, FreeBSD is available via anonymous FTP from the following mirror sites. When obtaining FreeBSD via anonymous FTP, please try to use a nearby site. The mirror sites listed as "Primary Mirror Sites" typically have the entire FreeBSD archive (all the currently available versions for each of the architectures) but faster download speeds are probably available from a site that is in your country or region. The regional sites carry the most recent versions for the most popular architecture(s) but might not carry the entire FreeBSD archive. All sites provide access via anonymous FTP but some sites also provide access via other methods. The access methods available for each site are provided in parentheses after the hostname.

Central Servers, Primary Mirror Sites, Armenia, Australia, Austria, Brazil, China, Czech Republic, Denmark, Estonia, Finland, France, Germany, Greece, Hong Kong, Ireland, Japan, Korea, Latvia, Lithuania, Netherlands, New Zealand, Norway, Poland, Russia, Saudi Arabia, Slovenia, South Africa, Spain, Sweden, Switzerland, Taiwan, Ukraine, United Kingdom, USA.

(as of UTC)

Central Servers

- ftp://ftp.FreeBSD.org/pub/FreeBSD/ (ftp / ftpv6 / http://ftp.FreeBSD.org/pub/FreeBSD/ / http://ftp.FreeBSD.org/pub/FreeBSD/)

Primary Mirror Sites
In case of problems, please contact the hostmaster <mirror-admin@FreeBSD.org> for this domain.

- ftp://ftp1.FreeBSD.org/pub/FreeBSD/ (ftp)

- ftp://ftp2.FreeBSD.org/pub/FreeBSD/ (ftp)

- ftp://ftp3.FreeBSD.org/pub/FreeBSD/ (ftp)

- ftp://ftp4.FreeBSD.org/pub/FreeBSD/ (ftp / ftpv6 / http://ftp4.FreeBSD.org/pub/FreeBSD/ / http://ftp4.FreeBSD.org/pub/FreeBSD/)

- ftp://ftp5.FreeBSD.org/pub/FreeBSD/ (ftp)

- ftp://ftp6.FreeBSD.org/pub/FreeBSD/ (ftp)

- ftp://ftp7.FreeBSD.org/pub/FreeBSD/ (ftp)

- ftp://ftp10.FreeBSD.org/pub/FreeBSD/ (ftp / ftpv6 / http://ftp10.FreeBSD.org/pub/FreeBSD/ / http://ftp10.FreeBSD.org/pub/FreeBSD/)

- ftp://ftp11.FreeBSD.org/pub/FreeBSD/ (ftp)

- ftp://ftp13.FreeBSD.org/pub/FreeBSD/ (ftp)

- ftp://ftp14.FreeBSD.org/pub/FreeBSD/ (ftp / http://ftp14.FreeBSD.org/pub/FreeBSD/)

Armenia
In case of problems, please contact the hostmaster <hostmaster@am.FreeBSD.org> for this domain.

- ftp://ftp1.am.FreeBSD.org/pub/FreeBSD/ (ftp / http://ftp1.am.FreeBSD.org/pub/FreeBSD/ / rsync)

Australia
In case of problems, please contact the hostmaster <hostmaster@au.FreeBSD.org> for this domain.

- ftp://ftp.au.FreeBSD.org/pub/FreeBSD/ (ftp)

- ftp://ftp2.au.FreeBSD.org/pub/FreeBSD/ (ftp)

- ftp://ftp3.au.FreeBSD.org/pub/FreeBSD/ (ftp)

Austria
In case of problems, please contact the hostmaster <hostmaster@at.FreeBSD.org> for this domain.

- ftp://ftp.at.FreeBSD.org/pub/FreeBSD/ (ftp / ftpv6 / http://ftp.at.FreeBSD.org/pub/FreeBSD/ / http://ftp.at.FreeBSD.org/pub/FreeBSD/)

Brazil
In case of problems, please contact the hostmaster <hostmaster@br.FreeBSD.org> for this domain.

- ftp://ftp2.br.FreeBSD.org/FreeBSD/ (ftp / http://ftp2.br.FreeBSD.org/)

- ftp://ftp3.br.FreeBSD.org/pub/FreeBSD/ (ftp / rsync)

- ftp://ftp4.br.FreeBSD.org/pub/FreeBSD/ (ftp)

China
In case of problems, please contact the hostmaster <hostmaster@cn.FreeBSD.org> for this domain.

- ftp://ftp.cn.FreeBSD.org/pub/FreeBSD/ (ftp)

Czech Republic
In case of problems, please contact the hostmaster <hostmaster@cz.FreeBSD.org> for this domain.

- ftp://ftp.cz.FreeBSD.org/pub/FreeBSD/ (ftp / ftp://ftp.cz.FreeBSD.org/pub/FreeBSD/ / http://ftp.cz.FreeBSD.org/pub/FreeBSD/ / http://ftp.cz.FreeBSD.org/pub/FreeBSD/ / rsync / rsyncv6)

- ftp://ftp2.cz.FreeBSD.org/pub/FreeBSD/ (ftp / http://ftp2.cz.FreeBSD.org/pub/FreeBSD/)

Denmark
In case of problems, please contact the hostmaster <hostmaster@dk.FreeBSD.org> for this domain.

- ftp://ftp.dk.FreeBSD.org/pub/FreeBSD/ (ftp / ftpv6 / http://ftp.dk.FreeBSD.org/pub/FreeBSD/ / http://ftp.dk.FreeBSD.org/pub/FreeBSD/)

Estonia
In case of problems, please contact the hostmaster <hostmaster@ee.FreeBSD.org> for this domain.

- ftp://ftp.ee.FreeBSD.org/pub/FreeBSD/ (ftp)

Finland
In case of problems, please contact the hostmaster <hostmaster@fi.FreeBSD.org> for this domain.

- ftp://ftp.fi.FreeBSD.org/pub/FreeBSD/ (ftp)

France
In case of problems, please contact the hostmaster <hostmaster@fr.FreeBSD.org> for this domain.

- ftp://ftp.fr.FreeBSD.org/pub/FreeBSD/ (ftp)

- ftp://ftp1.fr.FreeBSD.org/pub/FreeBSD/ (ftp / http://ftp1.fr.FreeBSD.org/pub/FreeBSD/ / rsync)

- ftp://ftp3.fr.FreeBSD.org/pub/FreeBSD/ (ftp)

- ftp://ftp5.fr.FreeBSD.org/pub/FreeBSD/ (ftp)

- ftp://ftp6.fr.FreeBSD.org/pub/FreeBSD/ (ftp / rsync)

- ftp://ftp7.fr.FreeBSD.org/pub/FreeBSD/ (ftp)

- ftp://ftp8.fr.FreeBSD.org/pub/FreeBSD/ (ftp)

Germany
In case of problems, please contact the hostmaster <de-bsd-hubs@de.FreeBSD.org> for this domain.

- ftp://ftp.de.FreeBSD.org/pub/FreeBSD/ (ftp)

- ftp://ftp1.de.FreeBSD.org/freebsd/ (ftp / http://www1.de.FreeBSD.org/freebsd/ / rsync://rsync3.de.Free-BSD.org/freebsd/)

- ftp://ftp2.de.FreeBSD.org/pub/FreeBSD/ (ftp / http://ftp2.de.FreeBSD.org/pub/FreeBSD/ / rsync)

- ftp://ftp4.de.FreeBSD.org/FreeBSD/ (ftp / http://ftp4.de.FreeBSD.org/pub/FreeBSD/)

- ftp://ftp5.de.FreeBSD.org/pub/FreeBSD/ (ftp)

- ftp://ftp7.de.FreeBSD.org/pub/FreeBSD/ (ftp / http://ftp7.de.FreeBSD.org/pub/FreeBSD/)

- ftp://ftp8.de.FreeBSD.org/pub/FreeBSD/ (ftp)

Greece
In case of problems, please contact the hostmaster <hostmaster@gr.FreeBSD.org> for this domain.

- ftp://ftp.gr.FreeBSD.org/pub/FreeBSD/ (ftp)

- ftp://ftp2.gr.FreeBSD.org/pub/FreeBSD/ (ftp)

Hong Kong

- ftp://ftp.hk.FreeBSD.org/pub/FreeBSD/ (ftp)

Ireland
In case of problems, please contact the hostmaster <hostmaster@ie.FreeBSD.org> for this domain.

- ftp://ftp3.ie.FreeBSD.org/pub/FreeBSD/ (ftp / rsync)

Japan
In case of problems, please contact the hostmaster <hostmaster@jp.FreeBSD.org> for this domain.

- ftp://ftp.jp.FreeBSD.org/pub/FreeBSD/ (ftp)

- ftp://ftp2.jp.FreeBSD.org/pub/FreeBSD/ (ftp)

- ftp://ftp3.jp.FreeBSD.org/pub/FreeBSD/ (ftp)

- ftp://ftp4.jp.FreeBSD.org/pub/FreeBSD/ (ftp)

- ftp://ftp5.jp.FreeBSD.org/pub/FreeBSD/ (ftp)

- ftp://ftp6.jp.FreeBSD.org/pub/FreeBSD/ (ftp)

- ftp://ftp7.jp.FreeBSD.org/pub/FreeBSD/ (ftp)

- ftp://ftp8.jp.FreeBSD.org/pub/FreeBSD/ (ftp)

- ftp://ftp9.jp.FreeBSD.org/pub/FreeBSD/ (ftp)

Korea
In case of problems, please contact the hostmaster <hostmaster@kr.FreeBSD.org> for this domain.

- ftp://ftp.kr.FreeBSD.org/pub/FreeBSD/ (ftp / rsync)

- ftp://ftp2.kr.FreeBSD.org/pub/FreeBSD/ (ftp / http://ftp2.kr.FreeBSD.org/pub/FreeBSD/)

Latvia
In case of problems, please contact the hostmaster <hostmaster@lv.FreeBSD.org> for this domain.

- ftp://ftp.lv.FreeBSD.org/pub/FreeBSD/ (ftp / http://ftp.lv.FreeBSD.org/pub/FreeBSD/)

Lithuania
In case of problems, please contact the hostmaster <hostmaster@lt.FreeBSD.org> for this domain.

- ftp://ftp.lt.FreeBSD.org/pub/FreeBSD/ (ftp / http://ftp.lt.FreeBSD.org/pub/FreeBSD/)

Netherlands
In case of problems, please contact the hostmaster <hostmaster@nl.FreeBSD.org> for this domain.

- ftp://ftp.nl.FreeBSD.org/pub/FreeBSD/ (ftp / http://ftp.nl.FreeBSD.org/os/FreeBSD/ / rsync)

- ftp://ftp2.nl.FreeBSD.org/pub/FreeBSD/ (ftp)

New Zealand

- ftp://ftp.nz.FreeBSD.org/pub/FreeBSD/ (ftp / http://ftp.nz.FreeBSD.org/pub/FreeBSD/)

Norway
In case of problems, please contact the hostmaster <hostmaster@no.FreeBSD.org> for this domain.

- ftp://ftp.no.FreeBSD.org/pub/FreeBSD/ (ftp / rsync)

Poland
In case of problems, please contact the hostmaster <hostmaster@pl.FreeBSD.org> for this domain.

- ftp://ftp.pl.FreeBSD.org/pub/FreeBSD/ (ftp)

- ftp2.pl.FreeBSD.org

Russia
In case of problems, please contact the hostmaster <hostmaster@ru.FreeBSD.org> for this domain.

- ftp://ftp.ru.FreeBSD.org/pub/FreeBSD/ (ftp / http://ftp.ru.FreeBSD.org/FreeBSD/ / rsync)

- ftp://ftp2.ru.FreeBSD.org/pub/FreeBSD/ (ftp / http://ftp2.ru.FreeBSD.org/pub/FreeBSD/ / rsync)

- ftp://ftp4.ru.FreeBSD.org/pub/FreeBSD/ (ftp)

- ftp://ftp5.ru.FreeBSD.org/pub/FreeBSD/ (ftp / http://ftp5.ru.FreeBSD.org/pub/FreeBSD/ / rsync)

- ftp://ftp6.ru.FreeBSD.org/pub/FreeBSD/ (ftp)

Saudi Arabia
In case of problems, please contact the hostmaster <ftpadmin@isu.net.sa> for this domain.

- ftp://ftp.isu.net.sa/pub/ftp.freebsd.org/ (ftp)

Slovenia
In case of problems, please contact the hostmaster <hostmaster@si.FreeBSD.org> for this domain.

- ftp://ftp.si.FreeBSD.org/pub/FreeBSD/ (ftp)

South Africa
In case of problems, please contact the hostmaster <hostmaster@za.FreeBSD.org> for this domain.

- ftp://ftp.za.FreeBSD.org/pub/FreeBSD/ (ftp)

- ftp://ftp2.za.FreeBSD.org/pub/FreeBSD/ (ftp)

- ftp://ftp4.za.FreeBSD.org/pub/FreeBSD/ (ftp)

Spain
In case of problems, please contact the hostmaster <hostmaster@es.FreeBSD.org> for this domain.

- ftp://ftp.es.FreeBSD.org/pub/FreeBSD/ (**ftp** / http://ftp.es.FreeBSD.org/pub/FreeBSD/)

- ftp://ftp3.es.FreeBSD.org/pub/FreeBSD/ (**ftp**)

Sweden

In case of problems, please contact the hostmaster <hostmaster@se.FreeBSD.org> for this domain.

- ftp://ftp.se.FreeBSD.org/pub/FreeBSD/ (**ftp**)

- ftp://ftp2.se.FreeBSD.org/pub/FreeBSD/ (**ftp** / rsync://ftp2.se.FreeBSD.org/)

- ftp://ftp3.se.FreeBSD.org/pub/FreeBSD/ (**ftp**)

- ftp://ftp4.se.FreeBSD.org/pub/FreeBSD/ (**ftp** / ftp://ftp4.se.FreeBSD.org/pub/FreeBSD/ / http://ftp4.se.FreeBSD.org/pub/FreeBSD/ / http://ftp4.se.FreeBSD.org/pub/FreeBSD/ / rsync://ftp4.se.FreeBSD.org/pub/FreeBSD/ / rsync://ftp4.se.FreeBSD.org/pub/FreeBSD/)

- ftp://ftp6.se.FreeBSD.org/pub/FreeBSD/ (**ftp** / http://ftp6.se.FreeBSD.org/pub/FreeBSD/)

Switzerland

In case of problems, please contact the hostmaster <hostmaster@ch.FreeBSD.org> for this domain.

- ftp://ftp.ch.FreeBSD.org/pub/FreeBSD/ (**ftp** / http://ftp.ch.FreeBSD.org/pub/FreeBSD/)

Taiwan

In case of problems, please contact the hostmaster <hostmaster@tw.FreeBSD.org> for this domain.

- ftp://ftp.tw.FreeBSD.org/pub/FreeBSD/ (**ftp** / ftp://ftp.tw.FreeBSD.org/pub/FreeBSD/ / **rsync** / **rsyncv6**)

- ftp://ftp2.tw.FreeBSD.org/pub/FreeBSD/ (**ftp** / ftp://ftp2.tw.FreeBSD.org/pub/FreeBSD/ / http://ftp2.tw.FreeBSD.org/pub/FreeBSD/ / http://ftp2.tw.FreeBSD.org/pub/FreeBSD/ / **rsync** / **rsyncv6**)

- ftp://ftp4.tw.FreeBSD.org/pub/FreeBSD/ (**ftp**)

- ftp://ftp5.tw.FreeBSD.org/pub/FreeBSD/ (**ftp**)

- ftp://ftp6.tw.FreeBSD.org/pub/FreeBSD/ (**ftp** / http://ftp6.tw.FreeBSD.org/ / **rsync**)

- ftp://ftp7.tw.FreeBSD.org/pub/FreeBSD/ (**ftp**)

- ftp://ftp8.tw.FreeBSD.org/pub/FreeBSD/ (**ftp**)

- ftp://ftp11.tw.FreeBSD.org/pub/FreeBSD/ (**ftp** / http://ftp11.tw.FreeBSD.org/FreeBSD/)

- ftp://ftp12.tw.FreeBSD.org/pub/FreeBSD/ (**ftp**)

- ftp://ftp13.tw.FreeBSD.org/pub/FreeBSD/ (**ftp**)

- ftp://ftp14.tw.FreeBSD.org/pub/FreeBSD/ (**ftp**)

- ftp://ftp15.tw.FreeBSD.org/pub/FreeBSD/ (**ftp**)

Ukraine

- ftp://ftp.ua.FreeBSD.org/pub/FreeBSD/ (**ftp** / http://ftp.ua.FreeBSD.org/pub/FreeBSD/)

- ftp://ftp6.ua.FreeBSD.org/pub/FreeBSD/ (**ftp** / http://ftp6.ua.FreeBSD.org/pub/FreeBSD / rsync://ftp6.ua.FreeBSD.org/FreeBSD/)

- ftp://ftp7.ua.FreeBSD.org/pub/FreeBSD/ (**ftp**)

United Kingdom
: In case of problems, please contact the hostmaster <hostmaster@uk.FreeBSD.org> for this domain.

- ftp://ftp.uk.FreeBSD.org/pub/FreeBSD/ (ftp)

- ftp://ftp2.uk.FreeBSD.org/pub/FreeBSD/ (ftp / rsync://ftp2.uk.FreeBSD.org/ftp.freebsd.org/pub/FreeBSD/)

- ftp://ftp3.uk.FreeBSD.org/pub/FreeBSD/ (ftp)

- ftp://ftp4.uk.FreeBSD.org/pub/FreeBSD/ (ftp)

- ftp://ftp5.uk.FreeBSD.org/pub/FreeBSD/ (ftp)

USA
: In case of problems, please contact the hostmaster <hostmaster@us.FreeBSD.org> for this domain.

- ftp://ftp1.us.FreeBSD.org/pub/FreeBSD/ (ftp)

- ftp://ftp2.us.FreeBSD.org/pub/FreeBSD/ (ftp)

- ftp://ftp3.us.FreeBSD.org/pub/FreeBSD/ (ftp)

- ftp://ftp4.us.FreeBSD.org/pub/FreeBSD/ (ftp / ftpv6 / http://ftp4.us.FreeBSD.org/pub/FreeBSD/ / http://ftp4.us.FreeBSD.org/pub/FreeBSD/)

- ftp://ftp5.us.FreeBSD.org/pub/FreeBSD/ (ftp)

- ftp://ftp6.us.FreeBSD.org/pub/FreeBSD/ (ftp)

- ftp://ftp8.us.FreeBSD.org/pub/FreeBSD/ (ftp)

- ftp://ftp10.us.FreeBSD.org/pub/FreeBSD/ (ftp)

- ftp://ftp11.us.FreeBSD.org/pub/FreeBSD/ (ftp)

- ftp://ftp13.us.FreeBSD.org/pub/FreeBSD/ (ftp / http://ftp13.us.FreeBSD.org/pub/FreeBSD/ / rsync)

- ftp://ftp14.us.FreeBSD.org/pub/FreeBSD/ (ftp / http://ftp14.us.FreeBSD.org/pub/FreeBSD/)

- ftp://ftp15.us.FreeBSD.org/pub/FreeBSD/ (ftp)

A.3. Using Subversion

A.3.1. Introduction

As of July 2012, FreeBSD uses Subversion as the only version control system for storing all of FreeBSD's source code, documentation, and the Ports Collection.

> ### Note
>
> Subversion is generally a developer tool. Users may prefer to use freebsd-update (Section 23.2, "FreeBSD Update") to update the FreeBSD base system, and portsnap (Section 4.5, "Using the Ports Collection") to update the FreeBSD Ports Collection.

This section demonstrates how to install Subversion on a FreeBSD system and use it to create a local copy of a FreeBSD repository. Additional information on the use of Subversion is included.

A.3.2. Root SSL Certificates

Installing security/ca_root_nss allows Subversion to verify the identity of HTTPS repository servers. The root SSL certificates can be installed from a port:

```
# cd /usr/ports/security/ca_root_nss
# make install clean
```

or as a package:

```
# pkg install ca_root_nss
```

A.3.3. Svnlite

A lightweight version of Subversion is already installed on FreeBSD as svnlite. The port or package version of Subversion is only needed if the Python or Perl API is needed, or if a later version of Subversion is desired.

The only difference from normal Subversion use is that the command name is svnlite.

A.3.4. Installation

If svnlite is unavailable or the full version of Subversion is needed, then it must be installed.

Subversion can be installed from the Ports Collection:

```
# cd /usr/ports/devel/subversion
# make install clean
```

Subversion can also be installed as a package:

```
# pkg install subversion
```

A.3.5. Running Subversion

To fetch a clean copy of the sources into a local directory, use svn. The files in this directory are called a *local working copy*.

> **Warning**
>
> Move or delete an existing destination directory before using checkout for the first time.
>
> Checkout over an existing non-svn directory can cause conflicts between the existing files and those brought in from the repository.

Subversion uses URLs to designate a repository, taking the form of *protocol://hostname/path*. The first component of the path is the FreeBSD repository to access. There are three different repositories, base for the FreeBSD base system source code, ports for the Ports Collection, and doc for documentation. For example, the URL https://svn.FreeBSD.org/ports/head/ specifies the main branch of the ports repository, using the https protocol.

A checkout from a given repository is performed with a command like this:

```
# svn checkout https://svn.FreeBSD.org/ repository /branch lwcdir
```

where:

- *repository* is one of the Project repositories: `base`, `ports`, or `doc`.

- *branch* depends on the repository used. `ports` and `doc` are mostly updated in the `head` branch, while `base` maintains the latest version of -CURRENT under `head` and the respective latest versions of the -STABLE branches under `stable/9` (9.*x*) and `stable/10` (10.*x*).

- *lwcdir* is the target directory where the contents of the specified branch should be placed. This is usually `/usr/ports` for `ports`, `/usr/src` for `base`, and `/usr/doc` for `doc`.

This example checks out the Ports Collection from the FreeBSD repository using the HTTPS protocol, placing the local working copy in `/usr/ports` . If `/usr/ports` is already present but was not created by `svn`, remember to rename or delete it before the checkout.

```
# svn checkout https://svn.FreeBSD.org/ports/head /usr/ports
```

Because the initial checkout must download the full branch of the remote repository, it can take a while. Please be patient.

After the initial checkout, the local working copy can be updated by running:

```
# svn update lwcdir
```

To update `/usr/ports` created in the example above, use:

```
# svn update /usr/ports
```

The update is much quicker than a checkout, only transferring files that have changed.

An alternate way of updating the local working copy after checkout is provided by the `Makefile` in the `/usr/ports` , `/usr/src` , and `/usr/doc` directories. Set `SVN_UPDATE` and use the `update` target. For example, to update `/usr/src` :

```
# cd /usr/src
# make update SVN_UPDATE=yes
```

A.3.6. Subversion Mirror Sites

The FreeBSD Subversion repository is:

```
svn.FreeBSD.org
```

This is a publicly accessible mirror network that uses GeoDNS to select an appropriate back end server. To view the FreeBSD Subversion repositories through a browser, use https://svnweb.FreeBSD.org/.

HTTPS is the preferred protocol, but the `security/ca_root_nss` package will need to be installed in order to automatically validate certificates.

A.3.7. For More Information

For other information about using Subversion, please see the "Subversion Book", titled Version Control with Subversion, or the Subversion Documentation.

A.4. Using rsync

These sites make FreeBSD available through the rsync protocol. The rsync utility works in much the same way as the rcp(1) command, but has more options and uses the rsync remote-update protocol which transfers only the differences between two sets of files, thus greatly speeding up the synchronization over the network. This is most useful for mirror sites of the FreeBSD FTP server. The rsync suite is available for many operating systems, on FreeBSD, see the net/rsync port or use the package.

Czech Republic
rsync://ftp.cz.FreeBSD.org/

Available collections:

- ftp: A partial mirror of the FreeBSD FTP server.

- FreeBSD: A full mirror of the FreeBSD FTP server.

Netherlands
rsync://ftp.nl.FreeBSD.org/

Available collections:

- FreeBSD: A full mirror of the FreeBSD FTP server.

Russia
rsync://ftp.mtu.ru/

Available collections:

- FreeBSD: A full mirror of the FreeBSD FTP server.

- FreeBSD-Archive: The mirror of FreeBSD Archive FTP server.

Sweden
rsync://ftp4.se.freebsd.org/

Available collections:

- FreeBSD: A full mirror of the FreeBSD FTP server.

Taiwan
rsync://ftp.tw.FreeBSD.org/

rsync://ftp2.tw.FreeBSD.org/

rsync://ftp6.tw.FreeBSD.org/

Available collections:

- FreeBSD: A full mirror of the FreeBSD FTP server.

United Kingdom
rsync://rsync.mirrorservice.org/

Available collections:

- ftp.freebsd.org: A full mirror of the FreeBSD FTP server.

United States of America
rsync://ftp-master.FreeBSD.org/

This server may only be used by FreeBSD primary mirror sites.

Available collections:

- FreeBSD: The master archive of the FreeBSD FTP server.

- acl: The FreeBSD master ACL list.

rsync://ftp13.FreeBSD.org/

Available collections:

- FreeBSD: A full mirror of the FreeBSD FTP server.

Appendix B. Bibliography

While manual pages provide a definitive reference for individual pieces of the FreeBSD operating system, they seldom illustrate how to put the pieces together to make the whole operating system run smoothly. For this, there is no substitute for a good book or users' manual on UNIX® system administration.

B.1. Books Specific to FreeBSD

International books:

- Using FreeBSD (in Traditional Chinese), published by Drmaster, 1997. ISBN 9-578-39435-7.

- FreeBSD Unleashed (Simplified Chinese translation), published by China Machine Press. ISBN 7-111-10201-0.

- FreeBSD From Scratch Second Edition (in Simplified Chinese), published by China Machine Press. ISBN 7-111-10286-X.

- FreeBSD Handbook Second Edition (Simplified Chinese translation), published by Posts & Telecom Press. ISBN 7-115-10541-3.

- FreeBSD & Windows (in Simplified Chinese), published by China Railway Publishing House. ISBN 7-113-03845-X

- FreeBSD Internet Services HOWTO (in Simplified Chinese), published by China Railway Publishing House. ISBN 7-113-03423-3

- FreeBSD (in Japanese), published by CUTT. ISBN 4-906391-22-2 C3055 P2400E.

- Complete Introduction to FreeBSD (in Japanese), published by Shoeisha Co., Ltd. ISBN 4-88135-473-6 P3600E.

- Personal UNIX Starter Kit FreeBSD (in Japanese), published by ASCII. ISBN 4-7561-1733-3 P3000E.

- FreeBSD Handbook (Japanese translation), published by ASCII. ISBN 4-7561-1580-2 P3800E.

- FreeBSD mit Methode (in German), published by Computer und Literatur Verlag/Vertrieb Hanser, 1998. ISBN 3-932311-31-0.

- FreeBSD de Luxe (in German), published by Verlag Modere Industrie, 2003. ISBN 3-8266-1343-0.

- FreeBSD Install and Utilization Manual (in Japanese), published by Mainichi Communications Inc., 1998. ISBN 4-8399-0112-0.

- Onno W Purbo, Dodi Maryanto, Syahrial Hubbany, Widjil Widodo Building Internet Server with FreeBSD (in Indonesia Language), published by Elex Media Komputindo.

- Absolute BSD: The Ultimate Guide to FreeBSD (Traditional Chinese translation), published by GrandTech Press, 2003. ISBN 986-7944-92-5.

- The FreeBSD 6.0 Book (in Traditional Chinese), published by Drmaster, 2006. ISBN 9-575-27878-X.

English language books:

- Absolute FreeBSD, 2nd Edition: The Complete Guide to FreeBSD, published by No Starch Press, 2007. ISBN: 978-1-59327-151-0

- The Complete FreeBSD, published by O'Reilly, 2003. ISBN: 0596005164

- The FreeBSD Corporate Networker's Guide, published by Addison-Wesley, 2000. ISBN: 0201704811

- FreeBSD: An Open-Source Operating System for Your Personal Computer, published by The Bit Tree Press, 2001. ISBN: 0971204500

- Teach Yourself FreeBSD in 24 Hours, published by Sams, 2002. ISBN: 0672324245

- FreeBSD 6 Unleashed, published by Sams, 2006. ISBN: 0672328755

- FreeBSD: The Complete Reference, published by McGrawHill, 2003. ISBN: 0072224096

B.2. Users' Guides

- Ohio State University has written a UNIX Introductory Course which is available online in HTML and PostScript format.

  An Italian translation of this document is available as part of the FreeBSD Italian Documentation Project.

- Jpman Project, Japan FreeBSD Users Group. FreeBSD User's Reference Manual (Japanese translation). Mainichi Communications Inc., 1998. ISBN4-8399-0088-4 P3800E.

- Edinburgh University has written an Online Guide for newcomers to the UNIX environment.

B.3. Administrators' Guides

- Jpman Project, Japan FreeBSD Users Group. FreeBSD System Administrator's Manual (Japanese translation). Mainichi Communications Inc., 1998. ISBN4-8399-0109-0 P3300E.

- Dreyfus, Emmanuel. Cahiers de l'Admin: BSD 2nd Ed. (in French), Eyrolles, 2004. ISBN 2-212-11463-X

B.4. Programmers' Guides

- Computer Systems Research Group, UC Berkeley. *4.4BSD Programmer's Reference Manual*. O'Reilly & Associates, Inc., 1994. ISBN 1-56592-078-3

- Computer Systems Research Group, UC Berkeley. *4.4BSD Programmer's Supplementary Documents*. O'Reilly & Associates, Inc., 1994. ISBN 1-56592-079-1

- Harbison, Samuel P. and Steele, Guy L. Jr. *C: A Reference Manual*. 4th Ed. Prentice Hall, 1995. ISBN 0-13-326224-3

- Kernighan, Brian and Dennis M. Ritchie. *The C Programming Language*. 2nd Ed. PTR Prentice Hall, 1988. ISBN 0-13-110362-8

- Lehey, Greg. *Porting UNIX Software*. O'Reilly & Associates, Inc., 1995. ISBN 1-56592-126-7

- Plauger, P. J. *The Standard C Library*. Prentice Hall, 1992. ISBN 0-13-131509-9

- Spinellis, Diomidis. *Code Reading: The Open Source Perspective*. Addison-Wesley, 2003. ISBN 0-201-79940-5

- Spinellis, Diomidis. *Code Quality: The Open Source Perspective*. Addison-Wesley, 2006. ISBN 0-321-16607-8

- Stevens, W. Richard and Stephen A. Rago. *Advanced Programming in the UNIX Environment*. 2nd Ed. Reading, Mass. : Addison-Wesley, 2005. ISBN 0-201-43307-9

- Stevens, W. Richard. *UNIX Network Programming*. 2nd Ed, PTR Prentice Hall, 1998. ISBN 0-13-490012-X

B.5. Operating System Internals

- Andleigh, Prabhat K. *UNIX System Architecture*. Prentice-Hall, Inc., 1990. ISBN 0-13-949843-5

- Jolitz, William. "Porting UNIX to the 386". *Dr. Dobb's Journal.* January 1991-July 1992.

- Leffler, Samuel J., Marshall Kirk McKusick, Michael J Karels and John Quarterman *The Design and Implementation of the 4.3BSD UNIX Operating System*. Reading, Mass. : Addison-Wesley, 1989. ISBN 0-201-06196-1

- Leffler, Samuel J., Marshall Kirk McKusick, *The Design and Implementation of the 4.3BSD UNIX Operating System: Answer Book*. Reading, Mass. : Addison-Wesley, 1991. ISBN 0-201-54629-9

- McKusick, Marshall Kirk, Keith Bostic, Michael J Karels, and John Quarterman. *The Design and Implementation of the 4.4BSD Operating System*. Reading, Mass. : Addison-Wesley, 1996. ISBN 0-201-54979-4

  (Chapter 2 of this book is available online as part of the FreeBSD Documentation Project.)

- Marshall Kirk McKusick, George V. Neville-Neil *The Design and Implementation of the FreeBSD Operating System*. Boston, Mass. : Addison-Wesley, 2004. ISBN 0-201-70245-2

- Marshall Kirk McKusick, George V. Neville-Neil, Robert N. M. Watson *The Design and Implementation of the FreeBSD Operating System, 2nd Ed.*. Westford, Mass. : Pearson Education, Inc., 2014. ISBN 0-321-96897-2

- Stevens, W. Richard. *TCP/IP Illustrated, Volume 1: The Protocols*. Reading, Mass. : Addison-Wesley, 1996. ISBN 0-201-63346-9

- Schimmel, Curt. *Unix Systems for Modern Architectures*. Reading, Mass. : Addison-Wesley, 1994. ISBN 0-201-63338-8

- Stevens, W. Richard. *TCP/IP Illustrated, Volume 3: TCP for Transactions, HTTP, NNTP and the UNIX Domain Protocols*. Reading, Mass. : Addison-Wesley, 1996. ISBN 0-201-63495-3

- Vahalia, Uresh. *UNIX Internals -- The New Frontiers*. Prentice Hall, 1996. ISBN 0-13-101908-2

- Wright, Gary R. and W. Richard Stevens. *TCP/IP Illustrated, Volume 2: The Implementation*. Reading, Mass. : Addison-Wesley, 1995. ISBN 0-201-63354-X

B.6. Security Reference

- Cheswick, William R. and Steven M. Bellovin. *Firewalls and Internet Security: Repelling the Wily Hacker*. Reading, Mass. : Addison-Wesley, 1995. ISBN 0-201-63357-4

- Garfinkel, Simson. *PGP Pretty Good Privacy* O'Reilly & Associates, Inc., 1995. ISBN 1-56592-098-8

B.7. Hardware Reference

- Anderson, Don and Tom Shanley. *Pentium Processor System Architecture*. 2nd Ed. Reading, Mass. : Addison-Wesley, 1995. ISBN 0-201-40992-5

- Ferraro, Richard F. *Programmer's Guide to the EGA, VGA, and Super VGA Cards*. 3rd ed. Reading, Mass. : Addison-Wesley, 1995. ISBN 0-201-62490-7

- Intel Corporation publishes documentation on their CPUs, chipsets and standards on their developer web site, usually as PDF files.

- Shanley, Tom. *80486 System Architecture*. 3rd Ed. Reading, Mass. : Addison-Wesley, 1995. ISBN 0-201-40994-1

- Shanley, Tom. *ISA System Architecture*. 3rd Ed. Reading, Mass. : Addison-Wesley, 1995. ISBN 0-201-40996-8

- Shanley, Tom. *PCI System Architecture*. 4th Ed. Reading, Mass. : Addison-Wesley, 1999. ISBN 0-201-30974-2

- Van Gilluwe, Frank. *The Undocumented PC*, 2nd Ed. Reading, Mass: Addison-Wesley Pub. Co., 1996. ISBN 0-201-47950-8

- Messmer, Hans-Peter. *The Indispensable PC Hardware Book*, 4th Ed. Reading, Mass : Addison-Wesley Pub. Co., 2002. ISBN 0-201-59616-4

B.8. UNIX® History

- Lion, John *Lion's Commentary on UNIX, 6th Ed. With Source Code*. ITP Media Group, 1996. ISBN 1573980137

- Raymond, Eric S. *The New Hacker's Dictionary, 3rd edition*. MIT Press, 1996. ISBN 0-262-68092-0. Also known as the Jargon File

- Salus, Peter H. *A quarter century of UNIX*. Addison-Wesley Publishing Company, Inc., 1994. ISBN 0-201-54777-5

- Simon Garfinkel, Daniel Weise, Steven Strassmann. *The UNIX-HATERS Handbook*. IDG Books Worldwide, Inc., 1994. ISBN 1-56884-203-1. Out of print, but available online.

- Don Libes, Sandy Ressler *Life with UNIX* — special edition. Prentice-Hall, Inc., 1989. ISBN 0-13-536657-7

- *The BSD family tree.* `https://svnweb.freebsd.org/base/head/share/misc/bsd-family-tree?view=co` or `/usr/share/misc/bsd-family-tree` on a FreeBSD machine.

- *Networked Computer Science Technical Reports Library.* `http://www.ncstrl.org/`

- *Old BSD releases from the Computer Systems Research group (CSRG).* `http://www.mckusick.com/csrg/` : The 4CD set covers all BSD versions from 1BSD to 4.4BSD and 4.4BSD-Lite2 (but not 2.11BSD, unfortunately). The last disk also holds the final sources plus the SCCS files.

B.9. Periodicals, Journals, and Magazines

- Admin Magazin (in German), published by Medialinx AG. ISSN: 2190-1066

- BSD Magazine, published by Software Press Sp. z o.o. SK. ISSN: 1898-9144

- BSD Now — Video Podcast, published by Jupiter Broadcasting LLC

- BSD Talk Podcast, by Will Backman

- FreeBSD Journal, published by S&W Publishing, sponsored by The FreeBSD Foundation. ISBN: 978-0-615-88479-0

Appendix C. Resources on the Internet

The rapid pace of FreeBSD progress makes print media impractical as a means of following the latest developments. Electronic resources are the best, if not often the only, way to stay informed of the latest advances. Since FreeBSD is a volunteer effort, the user community itself also generally serves as a "technical support department" of sorts, with electronic mail, web forums, and USENET news being the most effective way of reaching that community.

The most important points of contact with the FreeBSD user community are outlined below. Please send other resources not mentioned here to the FreeBSD documentation project mailing list so that they may also be included.

C.1. Websites

- The FreeBSD Forums provide a web based discussion forum for FreeBSD questions and technical discussion.

- Planet FreeBSD offers an aggregation feed of dozens of blogs written by FreeBSD developers. Many developers use this to post quick notes about what they are working on, new patches, and other works in progress.

- The BSDConferences YouTube Channel provides a collection of high quality videos from BSD conferences around the world. This is a great way to watch key developers give presentations about new work in FreeBSD.

C.2. Mailing Lists

The mailing lists are the most direct way of addressing questions or opening a technical discussion to a concentrated FreeBSD audience. There are a wide variety of lists on a number of different FreeBSD topics. Sending questions to the most appropriate mailing list will invariably assure a faster and more accurate response.

The charters for the various lists are given at the bottom of this document. *Please read the charter before joining or sending mail to any list.* Most list subscribers receive many hundreds of FreeBSD related messages every day, and the charters and rules for use are meant to keep the signal-to-noise ratio of the lists high. To do less would see the mailing lists ultimately fail as an effective communications medium for the Project.

> ### Note
>
> *To test the ability to send email to FreeBSD lists, send a test message to freebsd-test.* Please do not send test messages to any other list.

When in doubt about what list to post a question to, see How to get best results from the FreeBSD-questions mailing list.

Before posting to any list, please learn about how to best use the mailing lists, such as how to help avoid frequently-repeated discussions, by reading the Mailing List Frequently Asked Questions (FAQ) document.

Archives are kept for all of the mailing lists and can be searched using the FreeBSD World Wide Web server. The keyword searchable archive offers an excellent way of finding answers to frequently asked questions and should be consulted before posting a question. Note that this also means that messages sent to FreeBSD mailing lists are archived in perpetuity. When protecting privacy is a concern, consider using a disposable secondary email address and posting only public information.

C.2.1. List Summary

General lists: The following are general lists which anyone is free (and encouraged) to join:

List	Purpose
freebsd-advocacy	FreeBSD Evangelism
freebsd-announce	Important events and Project milestones (moderated)
freebsd-arch	Architecture and design discussions
freebsd-bugbusters	Discussions pertaining to the maintenance of the FreeBSD problem report database and related tools
freebsd-bugs	Bug reports
freebsd-chat	Non-technical items related to the FreeBSD community
freebsd-chromium	FreeBSD-specific Chromium issues
freebsd-current	Discussion concerning the use of FreeBSD-CURRENT
freebsd-isp	Issues for Internet Service Providers using FreeBSD
freebsd-jobs	FreeBSD employment and consulting opportunities
freebsd-questions	User questions and technical support
freebsd-security-notifications	Security notifications (moderated)
freebsd-stable	Discussion concerning the use of FreeBSD-STABLE
freebsd-test	Where to send test messages instead of to one of the actual lists

Technical lists: The following lists are for technical discussion. Read the charter for each list carefully before joining or sending mail to one as there are firm guidelines for their use and content.

List	Purpose
freebsd-acpi	ACPI and power management development
freebsd-afs	Porting AFS to FreeBSD
freebsd-amd64	Porting FreeBSD to AMD64 systems (moderated)
freebsd-apache	Discussion about Apache related ports
freebsd-arm	Porting FreeBSD to ARM® processors
freebsd-atm	Using ATM networking with FreeBSD
freebsd-bluetooth	Using Bluetooth® technology in FreeBSD
freebsd-cloud	FreeBSD on cloud platforms (EC2, GCE, Azure, etc.)
freebsd-cluster	Using FreeBSD in a clustered environment
freebsd-database	Discussing database use and development under FreeBSD
freebsd-desktop	Using and improving FreeBSD on the desktop
freebsd-doc	Creating FreeBSD related documents
freebsd-drivers	Writing device drivers for FreeBSD
freebsd-dtrace	Using and working on DTrace in FreeBSD
freebsd-eclipse	FreeBSD users of Eclipse IDE, tools, rich client applications and ports.
freebsd-embedded	Using FreeBSD in embedded applications

List	Purpose
freebsd-eol	Peer support of FreeBSD-related software that is no longer supported by the FreeBSD Project.
freebsd-emulation	Emulation of other systems such as Linux/MS-DOS®/Windows®
freebsd-enlightenment	Porting Enlightenment and Enlightenment applications
freebsd-firewire	FreeBSD FireWire® (iLink, IEEE 1394) technical discussion
freebsd-fortran	Fortran on FreeBSD
freebsd-fs	File systems
freebsd-games	Support for Games on FreeBSD
freebsd-gecko	Gecko Rendering Engine issues
freebsd-geom	GEOM-specific discussions and implementations
freebsd-git	Discussion of git use in the FreeBSD project
freebsd-gnome	Porting GNOME and GNOME applications
freebsd-hackers	General technical discussion
freebsd-haskell	FreeBSD-specific Haskell issues and discussions
freebsd-hardware	General discussion of hardware for running FreeBSD
freebsd-i18n	FreeBSD Internationalization
freebsd-ia32	FreeBSD on the IA-32 (Intel® x86) platform
freebsd-ia64	Porting FreeBSD to Intel®'s upcoming IA64 systems
freebsd-infiniband	Infiniband on FreeBSD
freebsd-ipfw	Technical discussion concerning the redesign of the IP firewall code
freebsd-isdn	ISDN developers
freebsd-jail	Discussion about the jail(8) facility
freebsd-java	Java™ developers and people porting JDK™ s to FreeBSD
freebsd-lfs	Porting LFS to FreeBSD
freebsd-mips	Porting FreeBSD to MIPS®
freebsd-mobile	Discussions about mobile computing
freebsd-mono	Mono and C# applications on FreeBSD
freebsd-multimedia	Multimedia applications
freebsd-new-bus	Technical discussions about bus architecture
freebsd-net	Networking discussion and TCP/IP source code
freebsd-numerics	Discussions of high quality implementation of libm functions
freebsd-office	Office applications on FreeBSD
freebsd-performance	Performance tuning questions for high performance/load installations
freebsd-perl	Maintenance of a number of Perl-related ports
freebsd-pf	Discussion and questions about the packet filter firewall system

List	Purpose
freebsd-pkg	Binary package management and package tools discussion
freebsd-pkg-fallout	Fallout logs from package building
freebsd-pkgbase	Packaging the FreeBSD base system
freebsd-platforms	Concerning ports to non Intel® architecture platforms
freebsd-ports	Discussion of the Ports Collection
freebsd-ports-announce	Important news and instructions about the Ports Collection (moderated)
freebsd-ports-bugs	Discussion of the ports bugs/PRs
freebsd-ppc	Porting FreeBSD to the PowerPC®
freebsd-proliant	Technical discussion of FreeBSD on HP ProLiant server platforms
freebsd-python	FreeBSD-specific Python issues
freebsd-rc	Discussion related to the rc.d system and its development
freebsd-realtime	Development of realtime extensions to FreeBSD
freebsd-ruby	FreeBSD-specific Ruby discussions
freebsd-scsi	The SCSI subsystem
freebsd-security	Security issues affecting FreeBSD
freebsd-small	Using FreeBSD in embedded applications (obsolete; use freebsd-embedded instead)
freebsd-snapshots	FreeBSD Development Snapshot Announcements
freebsd-sparc64	Porting FreeBSD to SPARC® based systems
freebsd-standards	FreeBSD's conformance to the C99 and the POSIX® standards
freebsd-sysinstall	sysinstall(8) development
freebsd-tcltk	FreeBSD-specific Tcl/Tk discussions
freebsd-testing	Testing on FreeBSD
freebsd-tex	Porting TeX and its applications to FreeBSD
freebsd-threads	Threading in FreeBSD
freebsd-tilera	Porting FreeBSD to the Tilera family of CPUs
freebsd-tokenring	Support Token Ring in FreeBSD
freebsd-toolchain	Maintenance of FreeBSD's integrated toolchain
freebsd-translators	Translating FreeBSD documents and programs
freebsd-transport	Discussions of transport level network protocols in FreeBSD
freebsd-usb	Discussing FreeBSD support for USB
freebsd-virtualization	Discussion of various virtualization techniques supported by FreeBSD
freebsd-vuxml	Discussion on VuXML infrastructure
freebsd-x11	Maintenance and support of X11 on FreeBSD

List	Purpose
freebsd-xen	Discussion of the FreeBSD port to Xen™ — implementation and usage
freebsd-xfce	XFCE for FreeBSD — porting and maintaining
freebsd-zope	Zope for FreeBSD — porting and maintaining

Limited lists: The following lists are for more specialized (and demanding) audiences and are probably not of interest to the general public. It is also a good idea to establish a presence in the technical lists before joining one of these limited lists in order to understand the communications etiquette involved.

List	Purpose
freebsd-hubs	People running mirror sites (infrastructural support)
freebsd-user-groups	User group coordination
freebsd-wip-status	FreeBSD Work-In-Progress Status
freebsd-wireless	Discussions of 802.11 stack, tools, device driver development

Digest lists: All of the above lists are available in a digest format. Once subscribed to a list, the digest options can be changed in the account options section.

SVN lists: The following lists are for people interested in seeing the log messages for changes to various areas of the source tree. They are *Read-Only* lists and should not have mail sent to them.

List	Source area	Area Description (source for)
svn-doc-all	/usr/doc	All changes to the doc Subversion repository (except for user, projects and translations)
svn-doc-head	/usr/doc	All changes to the "head" branch of the doc Subversion repository
svn-doc-projects	/usr/doc/projects	All changes to the projects area of the doc Subversion repository
svn-doc-svnadmin	/usr/doc	All changes to the administrative scripts, hooks, and other configuration data of the doc Subversion repository
svn-ports-all	/usr/ports	All changes to the ports Subversion repository
svn-ports-head	/usr/ports	All changes to the "head" branch of the ports Subversion repository
svn-ports-svnadmin	/usr/ports	All changes to the administrative scripts, hooks, and other configuration data of the ports Subversion repository
svn-src-all	/usr/src	All changes to the src Subversion repository (except for user and projects)
svn-src-head	/usr/src	All changes to the "head" branch of the src Subversion repository (the FreeBSD-CURRENT branch)

List	Source area	Area Description (source for)
svn-src-projects	/usr/projects	All changes to the projects area of the src Subversion repository
svn-src-release	/usr/src	All changes to the releases area of the src Subversion repository
svn-src-releng	/usr/src	All changes to the releng branches of the src Subversion repository (the security / release engineering branches)
svn-src-stable	/usr/src	All changes to the all stable branches of the src Subversion repository
svn-src-stable-6	/usr/src	All changes to the stable/6 branch of the src Subversion repository
svn-src-stable-7	/usr/src	All changes to the stable/7 branch of the src Subversion repository
svn-src-stable-8	/usr/src	All changes to the stable/8 branch of the src Subversion repository
svn-src-stable-9	/usr/src	All changes to the stable/9 branch of the src Subversion repository
svn-src-stable-10	/usr/src	All changes to the stable/10 branch of the src Subversion repository
svn-src-stable-11	/usr/src	All changes to the stable/11 branch of the src Subversion repository
svn-src-stable-other	/usr/src	All changes to the older stable branches of the src Subversion repository
svn-src-svnadmin	/usr/src	All changes to the administrative scripts, hooks, and other configuration data of the src Subversion repository
svn-src-user	/usr/src	All changes to the experimental user area of the src Subversion repository
svn-src-vendor	/usr/src	All changes to the vendor work area of the src Subversion repository

C.2.2. How to Subscribe

To subscribe to a list, click the list name at http://lists.FreeBSD.org/mailman/listinfo. The page that is displayed should contain all of the necessary subscription instructions for that list.

To actually post to a given list, send mail to <*listname*@FreeBSD.org>. It will then be redistributed to mailing list members world-wide.

To unsubscribe from a list, click on the URL found at the bottom of every email received from the list. It is also possible to send an email to <*listname*-unsubscribe@FreeBSD.org> to unsubscribe.

It is important to keep discussion in the technical mailing lists on a technical track. To only receive important announcements, instead join the FreeBSD announcements mailing list, which is intended for infrequent traffic.

C.2.3. List Charters

All FreeBSD mailing lists have certain basic rules which must be adhered to by anyone using them. Failure to comply with these guidelines will result in two (2) written warnings from the FreeBSD Postmaster <postmaster@Free-BSD.org>, after which, on a third offense, the poster will removed from all FreeBSD mailing lists and filtered from further posting to them. We regret that such rules and measures are necessary at all, but today's Internet is a pretty harsh environment, it would seem, and many fail to appreciate just how fragile some of its mechanisms are.

Rules of the road:

- The topic of any posting should adhere to the basic charter of the list it is posted to. If the list is about technical issues, the posting should contain technical discussion. Ongoing irrelevant chatter or flaming only detracts from the value of the mailing list for everyone on it and will not be tolerated. For free-form discussion on no particular topic, the FreeBSD chat mailing list is freely available and should be used instead.

- No posting should be made to more than 2 mailing lists, and only to 2 when a clear and obvious need to post to both lists exists. For most lists, there is already a great deal of subscriber overlap and except for the most esoteric mixes (say "-stable & -scsi"), there really is no reason to post to more than one list at a time. If a message is received with multiple mailing lists on the Cc line, trim the Cc line before replying. *The person who replies is still responsible for cross-posting, no matter who the originator might have been.*

- Personal attacks and profanity (in the context of an argument) are not allowed, and that includes users and developers alike. Gross breaches of netiquette, like excerpting or reposting private mail when permission to do so was not and would not be forthcoming, are frowned upon but not specifically enforced. *However*, there are also very few cases where such content would fit within the charter of a list and it would therefore probably rate a warning (or ban) on that basis alone.

- Advertising of non-FreeBSD related products or services is strictly prohibited and will result in an immediate ban if it is clear that the offender is advertising by spam.

Individual list charters:

freebsd-acpi
: *ACPI and power management development*

freebsd-afs
: *Andrew File System*

  This list is for discussion on porting and using AFS from CMU/Transarc

freebsd-announce
: *Important events / milestones*

  This is the mailing list for people interested only in occasional announcements of significant FreeBSD events. This includes announcements about snapshots and other releases. It contains announcements of new FreeBSD capabilities. It may contain calls for volunteers etc. This is a low volume, strictly moderated mailing list.

freebsd-arch
: *Architecture and design discussions*

  This list is for discussion of the FreeBSD architecture. Messages will mostly be kept strictly technical in nature. Examples of suitable topics are:

  - How to re-vamp the build system to have several customized builds running at the same time.

  - What needs to be fixed with VFS to make Heidemann layers work.

  - How do we change the device driver interface to be able to use the same drivers cleanly on many buses and architectures.

- How to write a network driver.

freebsd-bluetooth

Bluetooth® in FreeBSD

This is the forum where FreeBSD's Bluetooth® users congregate. Design issues, implementation details, patches, bug reports, status reports, feature requests, and all matters related to Bluetooth® are fair game.

freebsd-bugbusters

Coordination of the Problem Report handling effort

The purpose of this list is to serve as a coordination and discussion forum for the Bugmeister, his Bugbusters, and any other parties who have a genuine interest in the PR database. This list is not for discussions about specific bugs, patches or PRs.

freebsd-bugs

Bug reports

This is the mailing list for reporting bugs in FreeBSD. Whenever possible, bugs should be submitted using the web interface to it.

freebsd-chat

Non technical items related to the FreeBSD community

This list contains the overflow from the other lists about non-technical, social information. It includes discussion about whether Jordan looks like a toon ferret or not, whether or not to type in capitals, who is drinking too much coffee, where the best beer is brewed, who is brewing beer in their basement, and so on. Occasional announcements of important events (such as upcoming parties, weddings, births, new jobs, etc) can be made to the technical lists, but the follow ups should be directed to this -chat list.

freebsd-chromium

FreeBSD-specific Chromium issues

This is a list for the discussion of Chromium support for FreeBSD. This is a technical list to discuss development and installation of Chromium.

freebsd-cloud

Running FreeBSD on various cloud platforms

This list discusses running FreeBSD on Amazon EC2, Google Compute Engine, Microsoft Azure, and other cloud computing platforms.

freebsd-core

FreeBSD core team

This is an internal mailing list for use by the core members. Messages can be sent to it when a serious FreeBSD-related matter requires arbitration or high-level scrutiny.

freebsd-current

Discussions about the use of FreeBSD-CURRENT

This is the mailing list for users of FreeBSD-CURRENT. It includes warnings about new features coming out in -CURRENT that will affect the users, and instructions on steps that must be taken to remain -CURRENT. Anyone running "CURRENT" must subscribe to this list. This is a technical mailing list for which strictly technical content is expected.

freebsd-desktop

Using and improving FreeBSD on the desktop

This is a forum for discussion of FreeBSD on the desktop. It is primarily a place for desktop porters and users to discuss issues and improve FreeBSD's desktop support.

freebsd-doc

Documentation Project

This mailing list is for the discussion of issues and projects related to the creation of documentation for Free-BSD. The members of this mailing list are collectively referred to as "The FreeBSD Documentation Project". It is an open list; feel free to join and contribute!

freebsd-drivers

Writing device drivers for FreeBSD

This is a forum for technical discussions related to device drivers on FreeBSD. It is primarily a place for device driver writers to ask questions about how to write device drivers using the APIs in the FreeBSD kernel.

freebsd-dtrace

Using and working on DTrace in FreeBSD

DTrace is an integrated component of FreeBSD that provides a framework for understanding the kernel as well as user space programs at run time. The mailing list is an archived discussion for developers of the code as well as those using it.

freebsd-eclipse

FreeBSD users of Eclipse IDE, tools, rich client applications and ports.

The intention of this list is to provide mutual support for everything to do with choosing, installing, using, developing and maintaining the Eclipse IDE, tools, rich client applications on the FreeBSD platform and assisting with the porting of Eclipse IDE and plugins to the FreeBSD environment.

The intention is also to facilitate exchange of information between the Eclipse community and the FreeBSD community to the mutual benefit of both.

Although this list is focused primarily on the needs of Eclipse users it will also provide a forum for those who would like to develop FreeBSD specific applications using the Eclipse framework.

freebsd-embedded

Using FreeBSD in embedded applications

This list discusses topics related to using FreeBSD in embedded systems. This is a technical mailing list for which strictly technical content is expected. For the purpose of this list, embedded systems are those computing devices which are not desktops and which usually serve a single purpose as opposed to being general computing environments. Examples include, but are not limited to, all kinds of phone handsets, network equipment such as routers, switches and PBXs, remote measuring equipment, PDAs, Point Of Sale systems, and so on.

freebsd-emulation

Emulation of other systems such as Linux/MS-DOS®/Windows®

This is a forum for technical discussions related to running programs written for other operating systems on FreeBSD.

freebsd-enlightenment

Enlightenment

Discussions concerning the Enlightenment Desktop Environment for FreeBSD systems. This is a technical mailing list for which strictly technical content is expected.

freebsd-eol

Peer support of FreeBSD-related software that is no longer supported by the FreeBSD Project.

This list is for those interested in providing or making use of peer support of FreeBSD-related software for which the FreeBSD Project no longer provides official support in the form of security advisories and patches.

freebsd-firewire

FireWire® (iLink, IEEE 1394)

This is a mailing list for discussion of the design and implementation of a FireWire® (aka IEEE 1394 aka iLink) subsystem for FreeBSD. Relevant topics specifically include the standards, bus devices and their protocols, adapter boards/cards/chips sets, and the architecture and implementation of code for their proper support.

freebsd-fortran

Fortran on FreeBSD

This is the mailing list for discussion of Fortran related ports on FreeBSD: compilers, libraries, scientific and engineering applications from laptops to HPC clusters.

freebsd-fs

File systems

Discussions concerning FreeBSD filesystems. This is a technical mailing list for which strictly technical content is expected.

freebsd-games

Games on FreeBSD

This is a technical list for discussions related to bringing games to FreeBSD. It is for individuals actively working on porting games to FreeBSD, to bring up problems or discuss alternative solutions. Individuals interested in following the technical discussion are also welcome.

freebsd-gecko

Gecko Rendering Engine

This is a forum about Gecko applications using FreeBSD.

Discussion centers around Gecko Ports applications, their installation, their development and their support within FreeBSD.

freebsd-geom

GEOM

Discussions specific to GEOM and related implementations. This is a technical mailing list for which strictly technical content is expected.

freebsd-git

Use of git in the FreeBSD project

Discussions of how to use git in FreeBSD infrastructure including the github mirror and other uses of git for project collaboration. Discussion area for people using git against the FreeBSD github mirror. People wanting to get started with the mirror or git in general on FreeBSD can ask here.

freebsd-gnome

GNOME

Discussions concerning The GNOME Desktop Environment for FreeBSD systems. This is a technical mailing list for which strictly technical content is expected.

freebsd-infiniband

Infiniband on FreeBSD

Technical mailing list discussing Infiniband, OFED, and OpenSM on FreeBSD.

freebsd-ipfw

IP Firewall

This is the forum for technical discussions concerning the redesign of the IP firewall code in FreeBSD. This is a technical mailing list for which strictly technical content is expected.

freebsd-ia64

Porting FreeBSD to IA64

This is a technical mailing list for individuals actively working on porting FreeBSD to the IA-64 platform from Intel®, to bring up problems or discuss alternative solutions. Individuals interested in following the technical discussion are also welcome.

freebsd-isdn

ISDN Communications

This is the mailing list for people discussing the development of ISDN support for FreeBSD.

freebsd-java

Java™ Development

This is the mailing list for people discussing the development of significant Java™ applications for FreeBSD and the porting and maintenance of JDK™ s.

freebsd-jobs

Jobs offered and sought

This is a forum for posting employment notices specifically related to FreeBSD and resumes from those seeking FreeBSD-related employment. This is *not* a mailing list for general employment issues since adequate forums for that already exist elsewhere.

Note that this list, like other `FreeBSD.org` mailing lists, is distributed worldwide. Be clear about the geographic location and the extent to which telecommuting or assistance with relocation is available.

Email should use open formats only — preferably plain text, but basic Portable Document Format (PDF), HTML, and a few others are acceptable to many readers. Closed formats such as Microsoft® Word (`.doc`) will be rejected by the mailing list server.

freebsd-kde

KDE

Discussions concerning KDE on FreeBSD systems. This is a technical mailing list for which strictly technical content is expected.

freebsd-hackers

Technical discussions

This is a forum for technical discussions related to FreeBSD. This is the primary technical mailing list. It is for individuals actively working on FreeBSD, to bring up problems or discuss alternative solutions. Individuals interested in following the technical discussion are also welcome. This is a technical mailing list for which strictly technical content is expected.

freebsd-hardware

General discussion of FreeBSD hardware

General discussion about the types of hardware that FreeBSD runs on, various problems and suggestions concerning what to buy or avoid.

freebsd-hubs

Mirror sites

Announcements and discussion for people who run FreeBSD mirror sites.

freebsd-isp

Issues for Internet Service Providers

This mailing list is for discussing topics relevant to Internet Service Providers (ISPs) using FreeBSD. This is a technical mailing list for which strictly technical content is expected.

freebsd-mono

Mono and C# applications on FreeBSD

This is a list for discussions related to the Mono development framework on FreeBSD. This is a technical mailing list. It is for individuals actively working on porting Mono or C# applications to FreeBSD, to bring up problems or discuss alternative solutions. Individuals interested in following the technical discussion are also welcome.

freebsd-office

Office applications on FreeBSD

Discussion centers around office applications, their installation, their development and their support within FreeBSD.

freebsd-ops-announce

Project Infrastructure Announcements

This is the mailing list for people interested in changes and issues related to the FreeBSD.org Project infrastructure.

This moderated list is strictly for announcements: no replies, requests, discussions, or opinions.

freebsd-performance

Discussions about tuning or speeding up FreeBSD

This mailing list exists to provide a place for hackers, administrators, and/or concerned parties to discuss performance related topics pertaining to FreeBSD. Acceptable topics includes talking about FreeBSD installations that are either under high load, are experiencing performance problems, or are pushing the limits of FreeBSD. Concerned parties that are willing to work toward improving the performance of FreeBSD are highly encouraged to subscribe to this list. This is a highly technical list ideally suited for experienced FreeBSD users, hackers, or administrators interested in keeping FreeBSD fast, robust, and scalable. This list is not a question-and-answer list that replaces reading through documentation, but it is a place to make contributions or inquire about unanswered performance related topics.

freebsd-pf

Discussion and questions about the packet filter firewall system

Discussion concerning the packet filter (pf) firewall system in terms of FreeBSD. Technical discussion and user questions are both welcome. This list is also a place to discuss the ALTQ QoS framework.

freebsd-pkg

Binary package management and package tools discussion

Discussion of all aspects of managing FreeBSD systems by using binary packages to install software, including binary package toolkits and formats, their development and support within FreeBSD, package repository management, and third party packages.

Note that discussion of ports which fail to generate packages correctly should generally be considered as ports problems, and so inappropriate for this list.

freebsd-pkg-fallout

Fallout logs from package building

All packages building failures logs from the package building clusters

freebsd-pkgbase

Packaging the FreeBSD base system.

Discussions surrounding implementation and issues regarding packaging the FreeBSD base system.

freebsd-platforms

Porting to Non Intel® platforms

Cross-platform FreeBSD issues, general discussion and proposals for non Intel® FreeBSD ports. This is a technical mailing list for which strictly technical content is expected.

freebsd-ports

Discussion of "ports"

Discussions concerning FreeBSD's "ports collection" (`/usr/ports`), ports infrastructure, and general ports coordination efforts. This is a technical mailing list for which strictly technical content is expected.

freebsd-ports-announce

Important news and instructions about the FreeBSD "Ports Collection"

Important news for developers, porters, and users of the "Ports Collection" (`/usr/ports`), including architecture/infrastructure changes, new capabilities, critical upgrade instructions, and release engineering information. This is a low-volume mailing list, intended for announcements.

freebsd-ports-bugs

Discussion of "ports" bugs

Discussions concerning problem reports for FreeBSD's "ports collection" (`/usr/ports`), proposed ports, or modifications to ports. This is a technical mailing list for which strictly technical content is expected.

freebsd-proliant

Technical discussion of FreeBSD on HP ProLiant server platforms

This mailing list is to be used for the technical discussion of the usage of FreeBSD on HP ProLiant servers, including the discussion of ProLiant-specific drivers, management software, configuration tools, and BIOS updates. As such, this is the primary place to discuss the hpasmd, hpasmcli, and hpacucli modules.

freebsd-python

Python on FreeBSD

This is a list for discussions related to improving Python-support on FreeBSD. This is a technical mailing list. It is for individuals working on porting Python, its third party modules and Zope stuff to FreeBSD. Individuals interested in following the technical discussion are also welcome.

freebsd-questions

User questions

This is the mailing list for questions about FreeBSD. Do not send "how to" questions to the technical lists unless the question is quite technical.

freebsd-ruby

FreeBSD-specific Ruby discussions

This is a list for discussions related to the Ruby support on FreeBSD. This is a technical mailing list. It is for individuals working on Ruby ports, third party libraries and frameworks.

Individuals interested in the technical discussion are also welcome.

freebsd-scsi

SCSI subsystem

This is the mailing list for people working on the SCSI subsystem for FreeBSD. This is a technical mailing list for which strictly technical content is expected.

freebsd-security

Security issues

FreeBSD computer security issues (DES, Kerberos, known security holes and fixes, etc). This is a technical mailing list for which strictly technical discussion is expected. Note that this is not a question-and-answer list, but that contributions (BOTH question AND answer) to the FAQ are welcome.

freebsd-security-notifications

Security Notifications

Notifications of FreeBSD security problems and fixes. This is not a discussion list. The discussion list is FreeBSD-security.

freebsd-small

Using FreeBSD in embedded applications

This list discusses topics related to unusually small and embedded FreeBSD installations. This is a technical mailing list for which strictly technical content is expected.

Note

This list has been obsoleted by freebsd-embedded.

freebsd-snapshots

FreeBSD Development Snapshot Announcements

This list provides notifications about the availability of new FreeBSD development snapshots for the head/ and stable/ branches.

freebsd-stable

Discussions about the use of FreeBSD-STABLE

This is the mailing list for users of FreeBSD-STABLE. "STABLE" is the branch where development continues after a RELEASE, including bug fixes and new features. The ABI is kept stable for binary compatibility. It includes warnings about new features coming out in -STABLE that will affect the users, and instructions on steps that must be taken to remain -STABLE. Anyone running "STABLE" should subscribe to this list. This is a technical mailing list for which strictly technical content is expected.

freebsd-standards

C99 & POSIX Conformance

This is a forum for technical discussions related to FreeBSD Conformance to the C99 and the POSIX standards.

freebsd-teaching

Teaching with FreeBSD

Non technical mailing list discussing teaching with FreeBSD.

freebsd-testing

Testing on FreeBSD

Technical mailing list discussing testing on FreeBSD, including ATF/Kyua, test build infrastructure, port tests to FreeBSD from other operating systems (NetBSD, ...), etc.

freebsd-tex

Porting TeX and its applications to FreeBSD

This is a technical mailing list for discussions related to TeX and its applications on FreeBSD. It is for individuals actively working on porting TeX to FreeBSD, to bring up problems or discuss alternative solutions. Individuals interested in following the technical discussion are also welcome.

freebsd-toolchain

Maintenance of FreeBSD's integrated toolchain

This is the mailing list for discussions related to the maintenance of the toolchain shipped with FreeBSD. This could include the state of Clang and GCC, but also pieces of software such as assemblers, linkers and debuggers.

freebsd-transport

Discussions of transport level network protocols in FreeBSD

The transport mailing list exists for the discussion of issues and designs around the transport level protocols in the FreeBSD network stack, including TCP, SCTP and UDP. Other networking topics, including driver specific and network protocol issues should be discussed on the FreeBSD networking mailing list.

freebsd-translators

Translating FreeBSD documents and programs

A discussion list where translators of FreeBSD documents from English into other languages can talk about translation methods and tools. New members are asked to introduce themselves and mention the languages they are interested in translating.

freebsd-usb

Discussing FreeBSD support for USB

This is a mailing list for technical discussions related to FreeBSD support for USB.

freebsd-user-groups

User Group Coordination List

This is the mailing list for the coordinators from each of the local area Users Groups to discuss matters with each other and a designated individual from the Core Team. This mail list should be limited to meeting synopsis and coordination of projects that span User Groups.

freebsd-virtualization

Discussion of various virtualization techniques supported by FreeBSD

A list to discuss the various virtualization techniques supported by FreeBSD. On one hand the focus will be on the implementation of the basic functionality as well as adding new features. On the other hand users will have a forum to ask for help in case of problems or to discuss their use cases.

freebsd-wip-status

FreeBSD Work-In-Progress Status

This mailing list can be used by developers to announce the creation and progress of FreeBSD related work. Messages will be moderated. It is suggested to send the message "To:" a more topical FreeBSD list and only "BCC:" this list. This way the WIP can also be discussed on the topical list, as no discussion is allowed on this list.

Look inside the archives for examples of suitable messages.

An editorial digest of the messages to this list might be posted to the FreeBSD website every few months as part of the Status Reports [1]. Past reports are archived.

freebsd-wireless

Discussions of 802.11 stack, tools device driver development

The FreeBSD-wireless list focuses on 802.11 stack (sys/net80211), device driver and tools development. This includes bugs, new features and maintenance.

freebsd-xen

Discussion of the FreeBSD port to Xen™ — implementation and usage

A list that focuses on the FreeBSD Xen™ port. The anticipated traffic level is small enough that it is intended as a forum for both technical discussions of the implementation and design details as well as administrative deployment issues.

freebsd-xfce

XFCE

This is a forum for discussions related to bring the XFCE environment to FreeBSD. This is a technical mailing list. It is for individuals actively working on porting XFCE to FreeBSD, to bring up problems or discuss alternative solutions. Individuals interested in following the technical discussion are also welcome.

freebsd-zope

Zope

This is a forum for discussions related to bring the Zope environment to FreeBSD. This is a technical mailing list. It is for individuals actively working on porting Zope to FreeBSD, to bring up problems or discuss alternative solutions. Individuals interested in following the technical discussion are also welcome.

C.2.4. Filtering on the Mailing Lists

The FreeBSD mailing lists are filtered in multiple ways to avoid the distribution of spam, viruses, and other unwanted emails. The filtering actions described in this section do not include all those used to protect the mailing lists.

Only certain types of attachments are allowed on the mailing lists. All attachments with a MIME content type not found in the list below will be stripped before an email is distributed on the mailing lists.

- application/octet-stream

- application/pdf

- application/pgp-signature

- application/x-pkcs7-signature

- message/rfc822

- multipart/alternative

- multipart/related

- multipart/signed

- text/html

---

[1] https://www.freebsd.org/news/status/

- text/plain

- text/x-diff

- text/x-patch

> **Note**
>
> Some of the mailing lists might allow attachments of other MIME content types, but the above list should be applicable for most of the mailing lists.

If an email contains both an HTML and a plain text version, the HTML version will be removed. If an email contains only an HTML version, it will be converted to plain text.

C.3. Usenet Newsgroups

In addition to two FreeBSD specific newsgroups, there are many others in which FreeBSD is discussed or are otherwise relevant to FreeBSD users.

C.3.1. BSD Specific Newsgroups

- comp.unix.bsd.freebsd.announce

- comp.unix.bsd.freebsd.misc

- de.comp.os.unix.bsd (German)

- fr.comp.os.bsd (French)

- it.comp.os.freebsd (Italian)

C.3.2. Other UNIX® Newsgroups of Interest

- comp.unix

- comp.unix.questions

- comp.unix.admin

- comp.unix.programmer

- comp.unix.shell

- comp.unix.misc

- comp.unix.bsd

C.3.3. X Window System

- comp.windows.x

- comp.windows.x.apps

- comp.windows.x.announce

- comp.emulators.ms-windows.wine

C.4. Official Mirrors

Central Servers, Armenia, Australia, Austria, Czech Republic, Denmark, Finland, France, Germany, Hong Kong, Ireland, Japan, Latvia, Lithuania, Netherlands, Norway, Russia, Slovenia, South Africa, Spain, Sweden, Switzerland, Taiwan, United Kingdom, USA.

(as of UTC)

- Central Servers

    - https://www.FreeBSD.org/

- Armenia

    - http://www1.am.FreeBSD.org/ (IPv6)

- Australia

    - http://www.au.FreeBSD.org/

    - http://www2.au.FreeBSD.org/

- Austria

    - http://www.at.FreeBSD.org/ (IPv6)

- Czech Republic

    - http://www.cz.FreeBSD.org/ (IPv6)

- Denmark

    - http://www.dk.FreeBSD.org/ (IPv6)

- Finland

    - http://www.fi.FreeBSD.org/

- France

    - http://www1.fr.FreeBSD.org/

- Germany

    - http://www.de.FreeBSD.org/

- Hong Kong

    - http://www.hk.FreeBSD.org/

- Ireland

- http://www.ie.FreeBSD.org/

- Japan

  - http://www.jp.FreeBSD.org/www.FreeBSD.org/ (IPv6)

- Latvia

  - http://www.lv.FreeBSD.org/

- Lithuania

  - http://www.lt.FreeBSD.org/

- Netherlands

  - http://www.nl.FreeBSD.org/

- Norway

  - http://www.no.FreeBSD.org/

- Russia

  - http://www.ru.FreeBSD.org/ (IPv6)

- Slovenia

  - http://www.si.FreeBSD.org/

- South Africa

  - http://www.za.FreeBSD.org/

- Spain

  - http://www.es.FreeBSD.org/

  - http://www2.es.FreeBSD.org/

- Sweden

  - http://www.se.FreeBSD.org/

- Switzerland

  - http://www.ch.FreeBSD.org/ (IPv6)

  - http://www2.ch.FreeBSD.org/ (IPv6)

-

Taiwan

- http://www.tw.FreeBSD.org/

- http://www2.tw.FreeBSD.org/

- http://www4.tw.FreeBSD.org/

- http://www5.tw.FreeBSD.org/ **(IPv6)**

•

United Kingdom

- http://www1.uk.FreeBSD.org/

- http://www3.uk.FreeBSD.org/

•

USA

- http://www5.us.FreeBSD.org/ **(IPv6)**

Appendix D. OpenPGP Keys

The OpenPGP keys of the `FreeBSD.org` officers are shown here. These keys can be used to verify a signature or send encrypted email to one of the officers. A full list of FreeBSD OpenPGP keys is available in the PGP Keys article. The complete keyring can be downloaded at https://www.FreeBSD.org/doc/pgpkeyring.txt.

D.1. Officers

D.1.1. Security Officer Team <security-officer@FreeBSD.org>

```
pub    rsa4096/D39792F49EA7E5C2 2017-08-16 [SC] [expires: 2023-01-02]
       Key fingerprint = FC0E 878A E5AF E788 028D  6355 D397 92F4 9EA7 E5C2
uid                            FreeBSD Security Officer <security-officer@FreeBSD.org>
sub    rsa4096/6DD0A349F26ADEFD 2017-08-16 [E] [expires: 2023-01-02]
```

```
-----BEGIN PGP PUBLIC KEY BLOCK-----

mQINBFmT2+ABEACrTVJ7Z/MuDeyKFqoTFnm5FrGG55k66RLeKivzQzq/tT/6RK09
K8DaEvSIqD9b0/xgK02KgLSdp0Bucq8HLDFYUk3McFa6Z3YwjobNCWkxc72ipvVl
uAOGN4H6fuoYOpeg4cLK1H9pktUIrzONTCixaZzc/Bu6X+aX4ywGeCfsuu8g5v03
fLCPBLLgf3Bm5wsyZ6ZaGmsmILrWzd+d/rbr35Mcc5BekdgywUI4R191qo1bdrw9
mEJP1V7Ik3jpExOsNnuhMTvm50QMeCTfUvVEOtBU15QtbT+1LXF5FIOgML0LwS5v
RHZN+5w/xvzSnEULpj24UuMKLDs/u9rj8U/zET8QaE+oG7m/mr4jJWZEmdX8HKdO
WrpnVj6UAppk72qdBIEfLsOW2xB/NOjJpppbCQH3+sw7DRYA2UnKE9Mptj/KKiE4
cs4c8Cupo2WSu93lEZDC5rCrULpT2lFeEXnRYlC/5oIgY5w9sFide9VI4CzHkkWX
Z2NPW/i1w3mFhoXjvnNLGOYMfAMKPxsRC2/Bn3bY0IhKvuIZ4rAeu7FTmKDDqFKQ
YEcrUOW74ZVng17AB29xzjWr4zNJVvp/CybFiUb8JoKkwtVWRqAVZIEgenAjU40d
G5+W4e+ccL0mfTQfEBbXRjnL2BL2tnaoBR42cTfbZGRucPHz7MrlKBEeZQARAQAB
tDdGcmVlQlNEIENIFNlY3VyaXR5IE9mZmljZXIgPHNlY3VyaXR5LW9mZmljZXJARnJl
ZUJTRC5vcmc+iQJUBBMBCgA+FiEE/A6HiuWv54gCjWNV05eS9J6n5cIFAlmT2+AC
GwMFCQoek4AFCwkIBwMFFQoJCAsFFgIDAQACHgECF4AACgkQ05eS9J6n5cKd9A/9
Fz3uGjNy28D0ALT1d/JJGzdQ2R3YwspHk9KHBr1LePkog9wf1WRalwCeNtPmA+g5
cn24psuzOeh1tRElImTZ2eE2ENPZ9XzK/J0ok0nK42MvmIwmMCyz+CaWv9GXW+FK
0oXnFmHi4YaQUVN3p+45TGkD9T+O5biVww7P47n/NnWsTfhLx0bzC7LyjPKXINai
/LgPgtlcOgY65/YhW/qhADCkoU7qMp9is41jMjTu1WB3OBPJkUkNpHfu6r15y8FN
Wqsk7K4W60br/WQ6VKGGXgh/a5mTcaEoFGMO16uHijAY4nXeb2HGZlBKxgmPH9Ur
aT4A9Pz/n+rIRMrK+rs+msFPemQHHNBYxy+x99uBpRBNyT2Su6GouZIxu5J16aIM
V0ZyOy/dy7m/uJ4sMhJPqKkd8a+MoQs/2L1M1y1EAzsO/QZqIrKrCluaftNN9k/B
qU0XClSDqB6sRMF7HFzYqb+f+M6cwSL/3Cp1Yx4rZ/onEE/MdWp64+3R87dETTXd
5tWXQw04qOhfPri5cBTI7r3t/qMO1iNXCGSG5RJbGkas6N6t6Mj83L4ItjI8doLf
aSIWZjj1XP3/me2hFJ6h2G5y5A+khO4ZwhC0ATFSq1fYbVGHw5AtfthIgNn8FoWu
+Sb8h7/RqTr7F6LgWagAoAh0GtVj02SVABZjcNZz/AKJAjcEEAEKACEWIQQc9/9v
rfXKn74bjLLtZ+zWXc9q5wUCWZPcTAMFAngACgkQ7Wfs1l3PauflkRAAgYcaBX0Y
ic4btxKoP/eOVpgUciOPPKEhDCiloQDyf4XQnZFDoMfjgcHpbLTBZ6kiAz2UzDGr
fJ4yUqrD+xfixUfCd5YpwzsaSpCGzDzSxOBcP/SpuAFhe40awSOIf5MruQar9Mlf
33JyslDLULXXeewAq2pcGk0/WrrOragI6Cs2vPGy9XP96VvLxyhjrWjlKmnO+//w
UF8oIO5hhKoqbtoxxlcqJgsWVyHch0mnPzvr6GWwoPhFXocnhloPdbLjX1AwmGm9
ltEYMge4QxONIXlXJR0TvuDuJOaLNvTOC3OI8L97fdBcZS7eNJrG5FAYR5Ft3ISf
KJowIsSLGDt/cYApqpyP2pv7FpCvnwHgXHYar7/q4zhngCFRxQ2DPUx1cIJQ3Bgh
HZolKyK1X7XE5ZVDfZ3s3gcHSVKS89pipgHHZNr4sSmOanA8rXHcyHS4o2zSilie
r4iBwnOk6cCd6UNzEIiq0y/XhP/sc7xeL0mn3wDuV7jDBP9sp65sexL1qtIAfnzL
pLQevm0z41ifrUH5nNeL6RdbXpaoXc8M4PJJeQKJDu04KzLcQpZdUdCJsbS6Q09w
srWR8enQXPEhz2CO4L77bM9TgYO29222jTqEPcbXcmxF/klxO1rpssTTHUnHHi1Z
LUGYCbZPjt+laTJ2YPHTjUtN1Jw85vSKCEuJATMEEAEKAB0WIQS7KNQLNg7uk2rt
FW/l97zLo73d+AUCWjSYRwAKCRDl97zLo73d+JKyB/9N5Ytao12nD5QzMLvceGh5
otCLN99TUryYiDVDLoNkBivq3jHQA/hOX2rwEueFq0+LF8/2DnglJuUICNtCxIzL
WXXf/Hr5iWBUQ0JxYNPQzzjdMSXGE0WMwYVpAbCGxHpIsetKLdHUCwneYhaywe3I
KzmRJSDJGV1IJB0sAfoFtgybZXHgIR61jQjtnNmmyYXliYCd0wmIhXQDFN91tzzG
+EZdJ3Fao9JsMC+x55jO6EOLVySZgRF5E8vCeKUWemQciKFC7EhKcljILPYAA21u
NmHCAgRHKWU9JMdFK0w9lQuN2HQaNfkahjarTNM/Q6LwxY0dLG0vVYifE085WFAf
```

uQINBFmT2+ABEACxi39m5nQZexzY3c9sg/w5mUYCD89ZNSkj427gduQMYYGn7YW6
jSPfVJ/V3+PDK824c0a0XasyDapQFY1CPTZYrReRPoyjb8tJjsSVGXXCTFpJZlFU
br6kS9mgcx58Sypke2PMVk73+W1N1Yco+nahfTECRuM2/T2zHHr0AdKuBPF28U+H
TxyLatKoIgQwHDs4E/f4ZTbAoHvu3PixAl7XHVXCgz0cHaLhRljXizbZDXngOdGm
lqdFlAIpL6/l8E3m1Er0m3IfFo6qSzWRHg/KaBGIL4YKetJ6ACjlkCe5qbatDpmk
gWlg3Ux4RBVjyCK834Xh7eZpEcNf2iwpm28glWh7XMHGUplTHkU3PWQ4vGfNxXB8
HBOd9r02/cHL6MiHwhCAfIzZGVtqR0i9Ira57TMdXTpJWNXUcgsCMsi/Bg2a+hsn
aiYLrZc18uNL5nqOqsqKG3c1TcmeN7nbxVgnrNST4AjteulkhmB9p8tNOXA3u979
OO0T5LPwdqIpobdZOlfw4URnAGw4Wd4Sm9PtRw0RvuAk2M2e5KXNyxPWAuMVkoRR
a7wG6h/R8pki54Gexyc+JkfB4ZcOrzHNLurw6DhxroyfRs8WEgX0wNIGmJvCXSBG
54jb5w9qudYwzIg4YPfvuX8sfeY8MTNhal3rF0tvVloGj3l709wlaWlBYwARAQAB
iQI8BBgBCgAmFiEE/A6HiuWv54gCjWNV05eS9J6n5cIFAlmT2+ACGwwFCQoek4AA
CgkQ05eS9J6n5cKhWw//+PT0R4r2gPAxI8ESEe380BYOmneNAH24MFOgWXqWCj4zX
Uz992BVnW2aL5nH405d822LGeCrYUC7SCpQvlifdHZHjobgtizLTwuu40bc3gSOz
cxWlx2jKfx3Ezn6QQz2mhhK6fZ1AO0ObiQxQq25ldURep95L78E/C8XkCe11YlUR
ng3wQKeHM7awZWRw/QBC92haHuVtU3cx7At+zQL7jTBKSZqd34zzs0uoXIhk2h94
OO7MMDZ8z8MeU337vdL+RKYtD2bljLwpf7/kqg1D/q44RJ4ZpZcha9G0GvtLaQg2
+MAPlLg1vOWZ8wOTLaQHm+uzYRpkqxkIV8OuVd4UikCd8t3VNjNG5rG/YRNIAX0A
UEzs6oMF5YOFE8LmykesbUHAbC07Vcb0AsT5u3XKixDiIpPdnYSwGlkvoOVVLdeh
q/aXLK9V8BpViG5+a8xP2fdF1eMqdnrKAsiO4GEiq193PN/FA049VeIs3fd0izAa
x7+ag1MGtoF5Pij5iTVJm6phH5SUd1P3FY3OmclxWj/MbL4ba/G/6FWcy5NXxdw9
L1bRqaM2KEHJ67aF6NZz7UMldwExAWzFbUon1LUpKysAukxVf0EnntydBeVOQ+JO
HdqEpirrVLMpxPttUB2xxbo947nMj7/Bnme2gvb0vxaC9xSGVxrpW9cg5iCwSdc=
=8rds
-----END PGP PUBLIC KEY BLOCK-----

D.1.2. Security Team Secretary <secteam-secretary@FreeBSD.org>

```
pub    4096R/3CB2EAFCC3D6C666 2013-09-24 [expires: 2018-01-01]
       Key fingerprint = FA97 AA04 4DF9 0969 D5EF  4ADA 3CB2 EAFC C3D6 C666
uid                           FreeBSD Security Team Secretary <secteam-secretary@FreeBSD.org>
sub    4096R/509B26612335EB65 2013-09-24 [expires: 2018-01-01]
```

-----BEGIN PGP PUBLIC KEY BLOCK-----

mQINBFJBjIIBEADadvvpXSkdnBOGV2xcsFwBBcSwAdryWuLk6v2VxjwsPcY6Lwqz
NAZr2Ox1BaSgX7106Psa6v9si8nxoOtMc5BCM/ps/fmedFU48YtqOTGF+utxvACg
Ou6SKintEMUa1eoPcww1jzDZ3mxx49bQaNAJLjVxeiAZoYHe9loTe1fxsprCONnx
Era1hrI+YA2KjMWDORcwa0sSXRCI3V+b4PUnbMUOQa3fFVUriM4QjjUBU6hW0Ub0
GDPcZq45nd7PoPPtb3/EauaYfk/zdx8Xt0OmuKTi9/vMkvB09AEUyShbyzoebaKH
dKtXlzyAPCZoH9dihFM67rhUg4umckFLc8vc5P2tNblwYrnhgL8ymUaOIjZB/fOi
Z2OZLVCiDeHNjjK3VZ6jLAiPyiYTG1Hrk9E8NaZDeUgIb9X/KO6JXVBQIKNSGfX5
LLp/j2wr+Kbg3QtEBkcStlUGBOzfcbhKpE2nySnuIyspfDb/6JbhD/qYqMJerX0T
d5ekkJ1tXtM6aX2iTXgZ8cqv+5gyouEF5akrkLi1ySgZetQfjm+zhy/lx/NjGd0u
35QbUye7sTbfSimwzCXKIIpy06zIO4iNA0P/vgG4v7ydjMvXsW8FRULSecDT19Gq
xOZGfSPVrSRSAhgNxHzwUivxJbr05NNdwhJSbx9m57naXouLfvVPAMeJYwARAQAB
tD9GcmVlQlNEIFNlY3VyaXR5IFRlYW0gU2VjcmV0YXJ5IDxzZWN0ZWFtLXNlY3Jl
dGFyeUBGcmVlQlNELm9yZz6JAj0EEwEKACcFAlJBjIICGwMFCQgH7b8FCwkIBwMF
FQoJCAsFFgIDAQACHgECF4AACgkQPLLq/MPWxmYt8Q/+IfFhPIbqglh4rwFzgR58
8YonMZcq+5Op3qiUBh6tE6yRz6VEqBqTahyCQGIk4xGzrHSIOIj2e6gEk5a4zYtf
0jNJprk3pxu2Og05USJmd8lPSbyBF20FVm5W0dhWMKHagL5dGS8zInlwRYxr6mMi
UuJjj+2Hm3PoUNGAwL1SH2BVOeAeudtzu80vAlbRlujYVmjIDn/dWVjqnWgEBNHT
SD+WpA3yW4mBJyxWil0sAJQbTlt5EM/XPORVZ2tvETxJIrXea/Sda9mFwvJ02pJn
gHi6TGyOYydmbu0ob9Ma9AvUrRlxv8V9eN7eZUtvNa6n+IT8WEJj2+snJlO4SpHL
D3Z+l7zwfYeM8FOdzGZdVFgxeyBU7t3AnPjYfHmoneqgLcCO0nJDKq/98ohz5T9i
FbNR/vtLaEiYFBeX3C9Ee96pP6BU26BXhw+dRSnFeyIhD+4g+/AZ0XJ1CPF19D+5
z0ojanJkh7lZn4JL+V6+mF1eOExiGrydIiiSXDA/p5FhavMMu8Om4S0sn5iaQ2aX
wRUv2SUKHbHDqhIILLeQKlB3X26obx1Vg0nRhy47qNQn/xc9oSWLAQSVOgsShQeC
6DSzrKIBdKB3V8uWOmuM7lWAoCP53bDRW+XIOu9wfpSaXN2VTyqzU7zpTq5BHX1a
+XRw8KNHZGnCSAOCofZWnKyJAhwEEAEKAAYFAlJBjYgACgkQ7Wfsl13PaudFcQ//
UiM7EXsIHLwHxez32TzA/0uNMPWFHQN4Ezzg4PKB6Cc4amva5qbgbhoeCPuP+XPI
2ELfRviAHbmyZ/zIgqplDC4nmyisMoKlpK0Yo1w4qbix9EVVZr2ztL8F43qN3Xe/
NUSMTBgt/Jio7l5lYyhuVS3JQCfDlYGbq6NPk0xfYoYOMOZASoPhEquCxM5D4D0Z

3J3CBeAjyVzdF37HUw9rVQe2IRlxGn1YAyMb5EpR2Ij612GFad8c/5ikzDh5q6JD
tB9ApdvLkr0czTBucDljChSpFJ7ENPjAgZuH9N5Dmx2rRUj2mdBmi7HKqxAN9Kdm
+pg/6vZ3vM18rBlXmw1poQdc3srAL+6MHmIfHHrq49oksLyHwyeL8T6BO4d4nTZU
xObP7PLAeWrdrd1Sb3EWlZJ9HB/m2UL9w9Om1c6cb6X2DoCzQAStVypAE6SQCMBK
pxkWRj90L41BS62snja+BlZTELuuLTHULRkWqS3fFkUxlDSMUn96QksWlwZLcxCv
hKxJXOX+pHAiUuMIImaPQ0TBDBWWf5d8zOQlNPsyhSGFR5Skwzlg+m9ErQ+jy7Uz
UmNCNztlYgRKeckXuvr73seoKoNXHrn7vWQ6qB1IRURj2bfphsqlmYuITmcBhfFS
Dw0fdYXSDXrmG9wad98g49g4HwCJhPAl0j55f93gHLGIRgQQEQoABgUCUkGO5gAK
CRAV1ogEymzfsol4AKCI7rOnptuoXgwYx2Z9HkUKuugSRwCgkyW9pxa5EovDijEF
j1jG/cdxTOaJAhwEEAEKAAYFAlJBkdUACgkQkshDRW2mpm6aLxAAzpWNHMZVFt7e
wQnCJnf/FMLTjduGTEhVFnVCkEtI+YKarveE6pclqKJfSRFDxruZ6PHGG2CDfMig
J6mdDdmXCkN//TbIlRGowVgsxpIRg4jQVh4S3D0Nz50h+Zb7CHbjp6WAPVoWZz7b
Myp+pN7qx/miJJwEiw22Eet4Hjj1QymKwjWyY146V928BV/wDBS/xiwfg3xIVPZr
RqtiOGN/AGpMGeGQKKplkeITY7AXiAd+mL4H/eNf8b+o0Ce2Z9oSxSsGPF3DzMTL
kIX7sWD3rjy3Xe2BM20stIDrJS2a1fbnIwFvqszS3Z3sF5bLc6W0iyPJdtbQ0pt6
nekRl9nboAdUs0R+n/6QNYBkj4AcSh3jpZKe82NwnD/6WyzHWtC0SDRTVkcQWXPW
EaWLmv8VqfzdBiw6aLcxlmXQSAr0cUA6zo6/bMQZosKwiCfGl3tR4Pbwgvbyjoii
pF+ZXfz7rWWUqZ2C79hy3YTytwIlVMOnp3MyOV+9ubOsFhLuRDxAksIMaRTsO7ii
5J4z1d+jzWMW4g1B50CoQ8W+FyAfVp/8qGwzvGN7wxN8P1iR+DZjtpCt7J+Xb9Pt
L+lRKSO/aOgOfDksyt2fEKY4yEWdzq9A3VkRo1HCdUQY6SJ/qt7IyQHumxvL90F6
vbB3edrR/fVGeJsz4vE10hzy7kI1QT65Ag0EUkGMggEQAMTsvyKEdUsgEehymKz9
MRn9wiwfHEX5CLmpJAvnX9MITgcsTX8MKiPyrTBnyY/QzA0rh+yyhzkY/y55yxMP
INdpL5xgJCS1SHyJK85HOdN77uKDCkwHfphlWYGlBPuaXyxkiWYXJTVUggSju04b
jeKwDqFl/4Xc0XeZNgWVjqHtKF91wwgdXXgAzUL1/nwN3IglxiIR31y10GQdOQEG
4T3ufx6gv73+qbFc0RzgZUQiJykQ3tZK1+Gw6aDirgjQYOc90o2Je0RJHjdObyZQ
aQc4PTZ2DC7CElFEt2EHJCXLyP/taeLq+IdpKe6sLPckwakqtbqwunWVoPTbgkxo
Q1eCMzgrkRu23B2TJaY9zbZAFP3cpL65vQAVJVQISqJvDL8K5hvAWJ3vi92qfBcz
jqydAcbhjkzJUI9t44v63cIXTI0+QyqTQhqkvEJhHZkbb8MYoimebDVxFVtQ3I1p
EynOYPfn4IMvaItLFbkgZpR/zjHYau5snErR9NC4AOIfNFpxM+fFFJQ7W88JP3cG
JLl9dcRGERq28PDU/CTDH9rlk1kZ0xzpRDkJijKDnFIxT2ajijVOZx7l2jPL1njx
s4xa1jK0/39kh6XnrCgK49WQsJM5IflVR2JAi8BLi2q/e0NQG2pgn0QL695Sqbbp
NbrrJGRcRJD9sUkQTpMsLlQTABEBAAGJAiUEGAEKAA8FAlJBjIICGwwFCQgH7b8A
CgkQPLLq/MPWxmZAew//et/LToMVR3q6/qP/pf9ob/QwQ3MgejkC0DY3Md7JBRl/
6GWfySYnO0Vm5IoJofcv1hbhc/y3OeZTvK4s+BOQsNokYe34mCxZG4dypNaepkQi
x0mLujeU/n4Y0p0LTLjhGLVdKina2dM9HmllgYr4KumT58g6eGjxs2oZD6z5ty0L
viU5tx3lz3o0c3I9soH2RN2zNHVjXNW0EvWJwFLxFeLJbk/Y3UY1/kXCtcyMzLua
S5L5012eUOEvaZr5iYDKjy+wOxY4SUCNYf0GPmSej8CBbwHOF2XCwXytSzm6hNb3
5TRgCGbOSFTIy9MxfV5lpddQcdzijmuFSl8LySkL2yuJxjlI7uKNDN+NlfODIPMg
rdH0hBSyKci6Uz7Nz/Up3qdE+aISq68k+Hk1fiKJG1UcBRJidheds29FCzj3hoyZ
VDmf6OL60hL0YI1/4GjIkJyetlPzjMp8J7K3GweOUkfHcFihYZlbiMe7z+oIWEc7
0fNScrAGF/+JN3L6mjXKB6Pv+ER5ztzpfuhBJ/j7AV5BaNMmDXAVO4aTphWl7Dje
iecENuGTpkK8Ugv5cMJc4QJaWDkj/9sACc0EFgigPo68KjegvKg5R8jUPwb8E7T6
lIjBtlclVhaUrE2uLx/yTz2Apbm+GAmD8M0dQ7IYsOFlZNBW9zjgLLCtWDW+p1A=
=5gJ7
-----END PGP PUBLIC KEY BLOCK-----

D.1.3. Core Team Secretary <core-secretary@FreeBSD.org>

```
pub    rsa4096/36A7C05FE1ECF9BB 2014-07-09 [SC] [expires: 2018-07-08]
       Key fingerprint = C07B F5E3 10AE 64BF 6120  B0F6 36A7 C05F E1EC F9BB
uid                             FreeBSD Core Team Secretary <core-secretary@freebsd.org>
uid                             Core Secretary <core-secretary@freebsd.org>
sub    rsa4096/7B5150C8D7CE5D02 2014-07-09 [E] [expires: 2018-07-08]
```

-----BEGIN PGP PUBLIC KEY BLOCK-----

mQINBFO9HvEBEADRfuWeoNUwib7ZjNmhg0Kt1kjiGEEosf3O2yMDfYuAXt4De6qK
S4KECe5+vZH2T8g+zmNLl/7JxdqHiWj9cnoZ6T3bqKh7w7pW7QzC/Q2k4mZsZqKGl
xzhStHvaHSPKw5808TME0d3ewAfs0dQkDuA0eari0HipCbOVzqHUMTIROr/syPXs
jHxb2bj0KVzzq7wgy+vF4Cv25VzaAPBVgPv3HAoO/gLOr4SnXqBCw2vgprWx335t
QX1JslWlsUDmwwq40q4+eMnSFPZ0ing1DgfhMb+Dnrl6Rbxhb0pwPhbwubppUKfe
W6owOrTuUbATVoAhsfNySmUWQKc2p9w/8uFV/jJj9HOSgIMKrNONvqekPrjWOQn9
/lcQtGhldWmtPbMogOfaQisBEn1XjMZ3VEOagQxIe/6LDjU7GGoYvSdwf8Z0wXUY

/qDntPwudjJA4wQid1Tzf53gpUjr0tYq7aclpiBGs3F5EOs4HMXq5/xlwRGtBDHY
i9RNAlbRSfSD2s1nGsfsImPowlpjtLa+3PqYs/cRLGDu51DsgV/p/CqtAyebG+9O
WsF0Ydt4Q62jEuU8HY7SOj+AuKJVdUkyAZGk5vkPvsKzjdZUqRslurme7d3LqKai
FjBGj8UyId/IomDCjth3baGc/Y4e+JKyx1XDXgFY2HoQ2KzEoANrizjy5QARAQAB
tDhGcmVlQlNEIENvcmUgVGVhbSBTZWNyZXRhcnkgPGVrcmVttc2VjcmV0YXJ5QGZy
ZWVic2Qub3JnPokCVAQTAQoAPgIbAwULCQgHAwUVCgkICwUWAwIBAAIeAQIXgBYh
BMB79eMQrmS/YSCw9janwF/h7Pm7BQJZYPzzBQkHhRGCAAoJEDanwF/h7Pm7cMcP
/jMsEmlRAdWd8rTUxYD2112aOpI8xqphqEiUh/U1xC0mqdMfEt0INe4QvXs4mk6O
WcbNdTokVHKyHyNqHibpQ+TwOAuh0mW3vUmVrxvT2ueoPnJthfoXUiWGkB3gMlnO
l76bcMBlSGAxvWa6f6pjflrfEb3k4Q+3hnV0xO2nL5sfukya2cFXnGJ2/AG3LgDW
doXIFjTA+15tJkFz4hM+7CSKxlzco/SSVAHoICfTF8AiYz7YOGLi3sAhwyKVFe6r
cDSZGTP39PAgOhG4y9xv2Jjq7fQq1E5Ylcs1XBmKsgcbCgi4ZHoaBd8n/3uq26RI
Aqno4Bo1nFY2oUHMRE7zFlG/R7WBLPISEwJ3d15QV1twsjfPOAMCjEvS5csF7T0T
ARrBSGZYxXpwXKr7gnRXqEOyzEgivgs/cFLd47uOwB3Ul4/eOKH6yDFFcPKaa9u3
S8cVX2bllSU/hktwLWCDnpE3KimZSOGIYhLvYWvQxMR4Uc3Da37Xq1HL9DoU+VdQ
MuCYqRCKjWMuVwL+1so7zbyS/ns95VHUMXquaAdk2z3uHh7fCxUc3yd1T5aaWwFP
mWxun8OkeU2hJ/z4kfTY0gNLvEGGRVXkYJqt1P7eM4rCYt2SPydTlhvU/ko4VzZh
eD8tZA1PG7eTnFCiwuYWmz5b3hn6W2g3CF8NepTOMcxGiQEcBBABAgAGBQJTvTXF
AAoJEE1Y/c0spJd2Y4YIAMTJLPPhDrAqzH+AuIDKFg1slQluK/UyKvGGMhgY/0yo2
nHEjX5DeS6PTUroQsgy4CF6GhA6BTgCywlDG7urvz6HPY7uz5XRLKX6m8Q6XbNQK
ACY5h+V74FDvlkQSIg0G6HpI5cFUuF82n3QVnnkpRJbgR7KhP4DidEYdGAJMR9nl
YeLeUaVotB1n2+It80oD8PGstbDD6OhM8gSFzd5TWaAOtyZ/Gj8v3kSZPJRrkG0T
Ra4vBARpjwcnd4GAD1jXfS5u7PNjiMaXhII150zN4iugfDYGiB3dX4TloW0Z3yBl
SNdevyszrJc+m20/YdzwGJ7ZhcjY19+rBWqkvR3Gje6JAhwEEAECAAYFAlO9NhEA
CgkQwBMwnW1+RFxwzg/9FuDRbqXgo8VS/IpxQTqh1HChcTFEYd0b2pbxV/rG1bl5
dRf8BmgKdcN/fJZa23GDM3V7yI1GHRph+41IV04dwe63/HDoZnXKoBJu4OYZZDq5
NvTIdhBzBDmKhpFplmjlymdKzSplSmetLN1TPJWaUqwP7W63T9nzIzxYZHKGmVZf
R19cqdRTEkbKHgZBzZ1CifW+uyK4NMPaGvcRW56zuV7hZT5yx6BlMY+A+OFNIfpk
0V0Ozhjko+K6eNfH5fpq88o9IkKcL1iU8yQjRFyiRUslb4rf7hCdupTybYyllZVp
o6jmz08LHUjbTwQdDvsDsQAVg0Ws9ma1JXlfcGFTatg2hG7R+mw2okLfg6Lsl1l2
mU+g7sUdEAIDJAnK/wpQbxVXMruboq386SrssFzxG68tClQdK/VnX19C8WBN6Azk
9ymnf9+6X8dAghztdESUznt763yRuyhGk6Voprc6SXcqKxd2SxYHgW7pd1UCtj+M
ghAazp0KlhqOFFlyOSMdQA+9j86oPaYFLCPRjA/RGgxW8Ucw/VyAHeCNoHfsD4Ml
6IoRdNbMZ7V8oLVPEJw5RmytypedTLLbeUpX0JcLvNrd4Hbd08h9bMmcP0GxWBix
6ZFUnHyvdK9AgvnOMpUNEC5Xcz8dsK1I6A7rwwTELRMUSX/ws8gxbyhUJjj6KqWJ
AhwEEAEKAAYFAlO9LQIACgkQA29snufznr8ZNA/+MBCWq4N5zvwfJLPrOw2nb6Zj
WazUhnnkeKkhHmZR9cnt9MQ9RwxPnpCVwve03eJilik620VRFxdctWgQnvLS+QW7
EQ5sMysKb9zqkNa4aMJQCmQ/IXQRMhJ9eXImqEYrBSqVgL/pppmXk5xubGDqPQRd
b9+lq1/vQDr8u8nblXGRN5CzaIr0vvG13uVC4+rjKMqP3gubpKt+X9adagc66ZTH
Pr7O8/DaXO2BT9jkYUf5lYNK2BS5D1XT1d7hZK5G/2dklbtNgSBVhHiaIxARGxTX
84h1GkPGe2XbZGfTiEtWdFrsuuMY4DkVlXE5UXuAMGSlQvAybBbPRpPYJ7D5ny4D
OOqXCmmnOOOcPblEMyi8XQgSiz8TFfyRwUazIIcmoXr8J6bLgTpPpXbAjaoxWngJ
1QJr92LU22dSXaK7qXhWuuSco0KJ+5dScFg+uz+zdMa59YMSfvbhlHh8BgLwxdyE
a+RAiEigFvdjXy2Ljacr+q3v27egPhcWkgPhPD+2fiOBpeZd+3M8/vXImIqYrrMH
g7sXnLTpRJ4dd/lil7lG+vL+mc28Bo5FvMLp2r4QDfX1saqoBVtLSrZqQDhxc5jT
sOVhj3xnSjs3PoOWakbdwkRFR4/7oszSbB832nZE6mLpvpEE2suLUoBh9EtxAIhx
rBMuGGeDP58XSMmpJrCJAhwEEAEKAAYFAlO9R1IACgkQ7Wfs1l3PaudfGw/9HxYe
S7WfGMQup0z0zvYksPxQGVoAjAtK0PKGdO8trQY7p43SvZ4nX60byYoH49ko6823
x5lxI7+SNS9MgEgu3t8C03UGGxamNDOf625VazgzZWg9Cywzg3T0BhTPHyeLhvIAN
jqf2XjOh/Yew+yNe+7D9vNhdy0pNDGCAPeezC0sZjerq6dh7AgKHJobwNK2KEUtx
ciFdvBzoQ6p083dVbA0icb/rTZRM7Yt5egQz61NpeQTnU/mi0AJUffsBbRWqqHUb
GSViUxgusoqf9ggFG8tVLkb73mIqzeAwmGdp4U0Paz12Y5NfIrJ9NR9+v9dMv89U
lIJt2rCK5dlCnwnvsy1jImfXbrYfySjn06U+2q+kE27LByjT8XwE4W9JPDmxLwKZ
TQQe/K6cpqh9LebEIV3YHQPNfz34ChhljsIpTw5i39WqGx+wvQL4Mvj5exyEE5Sh
ODoeuobgXr36B6uQrg+zb3zi855Nd7ciqVg38Gf3ab2sbL08qSmobkLrDlfnwGC9
95ZMCQzhffatkco6bJhIJ1ElDDswZJHbg5pYo+aAq8xofwxBonH2hJoCAXXLXz3b
7KRUj2e0JXDLCSbE2DWV8y5UUzhWH2P4Ls6eCdtBuFi1sUb3TP3N+gyWff3PwpPb
IM/gDseSXDTGaZPq3wp24YPa1+Zpbj6jP1q21PKJAhwEEAEKAAYFAlO9R2QACgkQ
kshdDRW2mpm4s1A/9FrNdO2TWaLGYt+6etJyCH/Ua1vpc9UNM/lIZv/wdV1jVr50M
EKVQgAVsQBQEhwE7j81WVb26fggfKuLF0P+KMT8Kv8EwudIVTkSYcqfzI5zcG/p5
NNFsnwRiu7QKPkx1IgCirwkoXwtvFtqEEXD1lIilEQ8aXGcojdMS4clCt5JlHTv8
Y+TnSy5MrYJfHMSyThVl6xJOfC3/Wb6Gt23I2R7f7DLxHRSx74oqCZPOlD2mFzzC
re6EcXMsnkdsTbVVEeAV3n6ixm5IO4ePDmj/NTmjQGr0MNjdNZc8P2WCopDY+Afk
Mbqh32COmMl29elelyTTwck07ZX67szNbmWye2EOxbf1hUtEPhnBklBrD7TAG4YM
PFX7zHh9iFgmdcPxm1QcJDnoWVwzLMubTRZEs3EFImNG8fXaB6DnErclZnxXoJ75
eG8gB240RqoO5QpCha9MzNhq+KpCF9XXNc023mvEM1P6MyLCcC0N4JNk8x8a/M4/D

2xgHPlFRriWJU+saIRb+ycCFwwH0kMqMwCwoe8nAi8H1CtEL2zPokiASq/6OWx2S
yURVTYAAuVwndC5eVbSP1nbqrSw0a3zkVWqFzgM7Je1mEpHlG7wvJzezBhGLah+7
1GjJyrcvSzBwygac6KRFuPY+65F1CJSjMnuZPomY0XzKeXH/X67OeJWd4SWJAhwE
EgEIAAYFAlQYNz4ACgkQ6rA8WL/cR48SlQ/+LansEu3Ku6MWbCvrDGu7wbYcFbJI
V5FntgLmIfVkiIY8+Lue6KdYS/oVpbp1bx/OvCYnLSJSmy0ozwJR1HXQ9nrpSfoD
3J+P0y5hJYENDDOR3fBInb4c8t5pOxyFvnjkJicgkFpQBbJ+5/Kh4Hb67cM1B3ig
e/lx4jvzUPonSH0xTPVs2BXbDemu5sP2jzJxpS9eoesAOoNmJQDXNuWbX0CZskgl
uB5RpcPyLCTKTaFEdJxV71ovN3YnhNc8hC30OP9WdbdMu9O0w8SWzVIz6lD3FgXc
gHPkFZusy6TejeamwiKOz69+Ml2/vtBR7JPRSvR8nnFrvNbEKzkAykIUN0sZFbWP
MViKkkEGENWTKUiOmvd6gghT9HFULp/l1NpbwZ5qymWXIlPwEp7nhH27+5/tA+Ai
S5d0h1pniptt+0vG/IEmToDaBIz+wtip6ij7NHEqL6Uxn9nDwxRn8437ITVxxAkC
TUYOoCFSzl/vMI9TrEEsV5eHP13psU8EZZnd3LuZloeAAsMapJ3bjSEiiSfDOodp
ZkrmVZObMhVRRA9XVWfryy1xpWy5oV22cYe/8ky8CPUX1mUMNHBo/HQBNNdBsEjo
mW8NDy7a1MohgSzC17P96eSNfV0AsWW1XkU1qu0hYaIdZjGQZVGWH9C0BvQ2wFTj
/m5mRalbMbQa06eJAj0EEwEKACcFAlO9LMcCGwMFCQHhM4AFCwkIBwMFFQoJCAsF
FgMCAQACHgECF4AACgkQNqfAX+Hs+btkeA/+KO0G/4Rc91xUYgS7XLK/r+QktX2I
JFTdl6eNHTk7bfl6Nue/taEA7EujHDV0+10gBTk6xVvlyA/BgZ2OvmaUWM6J7TAi
Xduahh8xgbNmhQP0Tn4Xb6TpIZ4MbGBvPfiDlI0ukkTahvOSK6OniO2S4vLM5xIW
XZR9YxFh4iYRLmzr3HnVktc0h6TmcDSKckFeXdjt/xIQDiUVoMvFZnoHkCxoNM6n
S6/TCn4PPzsDUJcrI67AOTEZ2TGQJupBDt/Nc2IPPkcHvh7bKcy/9XLuDO5OWgcN
JmvJ0oYF06n4F/qcFtswQS/HONqeQ9yYeDnuykNShL8rGSRljuWY0faeCi7uPV9m
JfXLg9yIuvjc/f3FJRBmjJuCPDd46UjR/hgo+5NVmvSljIdmcZlTuQDC/IeIPgO2
k6jWrCqRuFy16XGd/LDsNv4ehtpMJ6wnpdVYgntGeKcXlveW8URKrOqZJMpuls+L
MheTJG2tLsBYVoOcwQDQbXl3zkv1lN3yxFnh172bvbeOL8rz/OKqmXzcwYc/abg1
YpDwGOLomSuAUw5GGWa92DSiCMBEP643CUgymShienbBygUotKBsRWaQhPmDB/2a
qoU0B4F2zCli4Ce8cUWCUv2qb4J03dQ30830SeyE+1wnTC9PkI/Hg+PA8MjLvrgA
Kv9OPIsobv0fET+0K0NvcmUgU2VjcmV0YXJ5IDxjb3JlLXNlY3JldGFyeUBmcmVl
YnNkLm9yZz6JAhwEEAEKAAYFAlO9H0EACgkQA29snufznr9AYBAA1/tCfcC9MHUK
j2gK0qhtu0vE7H8UXDr+Od+6snFDZjXw33NM0nUoLMjylhtqeJxZAWpR8LXC7oWu
dKU0ZC9bjrg2pwRESVsUTjWm+pf5Nvr905fTuYwFlgrzCAsNwcSOXiLs0e6vHUAo
Dauj/m61G98iqaE/FwfCE2I/Ud7gwPU2CTKvGZFa07hUz32aFd2b6mX/xfC4Umt2
Di/fqkTCzq1gmA/ANzzr9euZ4lPoY4JEVER3BefqixK+9VifHg/K2j/FMbkWbixr
tLhvGC+9LOnb8v547gmk4Ze6GIgaF8TAhK1rXJ/XgYpNrhrRB36Cq6aXjJ3UMHJs
2hrTNzP+wk4FQt78IsrNKzki4aR90fSizVYSN2pDsk9y3diLNvsjD+PVh+80acz6
23cQxTUMnW21j35cHqlm+2NIc0CloM99J6LOy2mguV7eS8QIEnIQivm7+EvvZ1gR
m0WJgWUdy9YiroqpYmUgms5ru8buvnzqqy2IbbvS0J5pU59lPmCso1wN/i9gSjEv
7Y0pwdUDSuiBFY8zBJZltYQBoiKUr/oBXNzzGZ59kkQcfEfs+mtw+wfcw+k7CZaN
+F4cEp8h8S7VSpYAP5xFCYT6MTPW9zoPNVR8DhzbuP38ZdP381CwFNqYLqtPdhRk
paUW6UILedxHB/1lMZKyJPmoK5XUQKeJAlQEEwEKAD4CGwMFCwkIBwMFFQoJCAsF
FgMCAQACHgECF4AWIQTAe/XjEK5kv2EgsPY2p8Bf4ez5uwUCWWD88wUJB4URggAK
CRA2p8Bf4ez5uwziEACfqvM+99JXOoqnx2NzZ+BMfTgNBjYPwwobtCiqVOlkdHum
xW07/BW+Wjfufjxv7ZX4gfdf3lD9zOBv+Ev7zyh68N+08v+aoOpGaXXlQ1ORhYBY
xtCdhB8TVioGh4ztsPQ+8yV4pIGiBfMMqpPS7mGoZGNcNwRDyu+XM3a4qAyyOLR7
KctM00WVSfL1UAettQQl/PLPs2+niQWET/7mm8rlAxtnCJSps+c/s9aWSms9mniO
hns6g0yv06G1xHS9gziVCl8JeglYH+KYlrHl6q0KkoJ100S7NFQO2j3usX238bb5
6h2S6q5l32u7fglp0ufH6vRQIqRbchq7ExfD2QdpW5ra1fdqdhJ/5bFBBNP2Joz3
03k/WIwcvAt5OxX2R2ltvqar2rUhEn1/PngjAvW288nwNOuhuyLja9PI+XqRFAkI
VnEDnZogfs3tP1g25S7Kltnj1PLE+utyKHksCeLR0g6PhExESwKCp9iII8eoHcxX
vZum4J8pkSYvrQhvbf7Ecy1GlZ6RNSOMw1SE+Aq0QPi40g6wRS4WpnckmxyGcxbN
c/2MUH49owyCo5Zkf69gu2sDpXLJ1V4teeGxPB6VAR9fiNrOXtRA7ACbxqlsz1Qr
KcxLHDUwCpHOirn1E5aMSJOyMxNfCVYRsiHO5nDyGHehsEXWi0uf0Wvkvk3u4YkC
HAQQAQoABgUCU71HUgAKCRDtZ+zWXc9q51QnD/984eMuzKy51ed+qwdLQzjPpbD9
1GA5nJVmZkxDWfq9BEjOGCcw4yjupbV4YfjHWKg3XWN76i57CkzWLjIyoruo3dBE
8uE4cx8VYXMq4JdclscmkrHYuYDDp8DVQpR3zg+YGjhdI3USZy0yzLngBDN38jc0
lIwThyaZPkXCFd6/7vC7zxVdqsC1mvd+72MHy0SfY2kLq+TJxFTlgc+wgdINRdOi
QHC79ehcloiwjgcV2SXfe+JSlx3dshDJEpRdzn9al+RSOhStx0FPnOniXK1nOePv
s74Fh2UzN0sGPYOa5eels/VaYtdxL+gKyCCBEPT9VYSCuM8lu/KxaDNPY7qh5DeL
lAlrpNH+e1whZKwwP5+mAknwMUmF3NSPjCqQJv+sgWIgTacktyc+RxjtktEBrD7A
XFBxhJjupP2em6CS8GggBsdnUkPOEeA0HhQHdzYwT2m9sUzZYrXDovsZ4nQiWaA1
kKKseXUi8C3jkbMNuYpDlq6FEtYan7Wthw556LuM7sqaaL9EPudCRhSSK4pfLL6FJ
i37kpN11K5cTx4C+e1qeSvDTiFOLvw0rV+FGkbh0PlLvRlfnOq69xeOvjKKKlyEg
MOXJv5AzMLjn00BjqPCfwA1Hy0GumvyZ1hYN4W/64Lf5RycY2ZYjmcvBtPB8gXXT
XygkwWrqhMj2Fkx84IkCHAQQAQoABgUCU71HZAAKCRCSyENFbaambv4NEADFxKvL
Da2hDW98zvMIrHRNFGVzhrkHblw0q8KXtui/Zgkf7rI3lnhqmxvW+pj/nwMF8Zvw
aL3ZBd21oLqNRgs87RB8vmkweL6MSOpRJ8gygfBht5pZFYzQGw41Yv4wmX3uk2ye
sQ4V++t93nrNQJ/Lb4szB0a/s/M0N8ReDDY5cS82sDxO/wLObh2k+kNzYRkxshta

```
BrFZTvKWKfe6dhP3eOJuiJWOVxMztgNnyKvtDeHXMvKJk1/D+HlGRZVHs0W22bTT
/AL++4RElzu/YKZkIq/Xwuf6jAYCTft4gfTvlXAdEni5tE71FrUhVC6hHQ5CgKyz
oGX9BzZ7Lu/629bUfc6kmDfILBdzLxdETR1HW8hIdfPS2U5mqcEsXGqFGD3KDgX8
KNDKjLhLsgpDFkg+dwb7Gkm3LNjlimAKfqJbjNE65y7qd+zthvxG8ZjER2VVcrl+
tKSEA1zuA4y6PbamzOjlDQhvtbShF+wbPRiM1C9psWdO9qhPMdQPnonUs8uU8dpx
Owzrq84orr/BtyTxQ7S5FFbT8fYKssht8Jn04ZDApdY57rWA43raXgvC3COUvZhR
PAVwZGu6hBGNfRiP9SyXHzCPJTJ9ejiE2L+P3MKljzG40jIOiaVgQhXbMUZiFooI
CqHbei357hHIgoXo5PHsE3+v+O8+2lYXQZGGjokCHAQSAQgABgUCVBg3PgAKCRDq
sDxYv9xHjwjNEACha5LdMFvmpvzvGcyHo0gmPobVopRgCGukRJOYL9NJNnSjwln+
azTwF3kEQF+KiLZnd+Yc+3MxJZthFW68pQw/hfbjfMG5AjC3SHvPHGln6I9dpSQA
gHdDYgUsCT4K2o7xEfdn69e9yN9XCk+ocFz+m4I1NyeByAnNYe4eY+4Pv2Enh1Gn
D0omODLlwEGqOntgbRSO+yzsBbyBRXQhDHWQ8KB/u5SBfSPiq5u6IzBeX2rmkiuH
t5C9NvULoCBWJYG+x3gxi5aJwUp+NGFz3p2nwIp9JTRljFlb90ije7cHjZChITFa
FUXq6KY2KUYPpISmjLpsCfW3RpGD/I6uw8Ail8vydq3wlM7MlV+Rmu5Hk/GbZ8uE
TumKhbU68q2okj68Q2UNBrepHNZt7vuL4fd6iZPn6FA0Ui1n1o5l/WkX/u/uM3bG
ATq6bd7Wm+hal61uyHCPqfDwsgVuHP1h5FN2Fq3hG2ttQVxojA6MX4UPTsr0h7eh
vJIDvfpPLEWP+/KBmMUeAGorfP2OeA5h5MmSknsLvekqNPkw5nG5HmrWrQ4a2rG4
30C1sfN+t7Z0L5oVqcP26Vhpg0Ay1Ux5/TnF5XJBlNX4lDO+9tYOLNlHYo0zKcmF
n7C02sTrox8sZMJAQbRldwwmrORKdijzH0joH92FbT0B/SGqLSUsPwOhXYkCPQQT
AQoAJwUCU70e8QIbAwUJAeEzgAULCQgHAwUVCgkICwUWAwIBAAIeAQIXgAAKCRA2
p8Bf4ez5u0LzEAChN6TN3uy6wx+vsbHWn8W/0cZ1cFCOhWqDd3SGUYyCIew8nels
qQ+N/n+HOAHiF/m+/EbgrrvqGTDJB5OP2ODyEb+o8NcLhmuu4h6KRV8vSj2IxEDr
S6bWVAKK6gutgs6FSccG6SD8NQJCgWoOxRSrYspkCm8UgJBJAjk2uuERfhRQyc1K
m0UDyTDISkd+ZSf1t03zUEFYhf58nQ3TZkmPoGAD1PJKoceCuyvWpfQ1MFWvz3S9
JeePQSzh85hXBLcOBUDhjGLeBpJmufujiDCTrqDPwAwFM+6nXFmGHbBZeNh8wu97
uzBi3HxpBJXGSpB/LJ9s7irE07Uyg+a4S3yIrtd9ryu76qDjXSS3e1NV9gcIn/7m
9cHu8eHhqJ2Y4SmoxDaQ96P9WNO9oC8vK5Wda+vyfhkPUxMFATVfDTTnwz79KcUz
+jghTxxBQOLaBtK0QZuziMZkFxVpn8TE9zZ8Aajwrn1pTpttCYWlP6XnzwqhyVXP
AKfpOv23Ld4jbgINW7oIBVQ1oPPbgahfb33RC4ggxd50WJuG0OktXFsb57uWqvTG
XbeA3NVp00jX2Pf84yiVpht5or9Q9XqN30slSTWFX1c0NtyjDj8Ef43a+OxpXvP+
TjN/Mz4Wfrwvlw//y6tP3PIjDt/QeKcENAW/BQIZP+lINHGG2qfpT1pGPrkCDQRT
vR7xARAAsp25exIHESBlj+zuodTupq2FzWdiaSQYGKLKos3Qx8q7tp0EqzX4IsAD
NX3gdjSyQtHKEM0TtbAytiT++9Pnit2YW1kj+QVjdraEhVRBpVaRliwRqHn2nmZ2
QNtiA86TiIyIu4gvdiQbE1xErAaFfIhta8pUNeaXBNNyEBLrg7va+x/ESd70319X
PmvgfDFB5+epJ90JHRtm5VdP94Ixaqmr2XjsWaQJsp/Z/VXN8ggj5GoLTUMJXjcm
Tkji441aQY53BOnQE3Szo/OaYXzlOnjv9GzFwIE6+5mONRCKmKnT0GK2Pd8khoAb
wZMjWh+QJQzWWcCeHXbQzBaD/J1IQaEa3+QKWMh3BJkl2oS31t2tqqz5v8OVSxBi
7ed/+hmbxHraT/k7QSwMV+l2gtklwDq830mRDXWLfxM0hf3UwmettptHluuYlcEo
tbDWQ9oTRT7P9dmtrXpuwwFqg9m4vAZbSkWzvvE+wQEcCJeYVxqufmJzvg4EyH+E
mJErfGoj2MAwBd2EpM6YlJmaAUkbekm/bGd8yMaX567SxZknro84p8glTcxXZ/hy
sWbyPTHN07/y6j67lblh7dQI/nsoB+W0WcOD07DDV9RcTPyvIUWPdQOhcqdxgpG+
Uc6nRBrkjjQbHmmYqwtHfhGGeLJstY8nac8E9TvFY2OMIuQXYMEAEQEAAYkCPAQY
AQoAJgIbDBYhBMB79eMQrmS/YSCw9janwF/h7Pm7BQJZYP0lBQkHhRG0AAoJEDan
wF/h7Pm76ngP/0s33IzGYS/8kylJquBiIdURLj4r7DMNbHWmlc2i7KLYmkHIMtlr
jstme0Hhh4F9SlVue+pyTf9+TeO5DfqY0xHk0Cevu/JQY40/BWTbrG7fNAF5cOpL
RfijilDRqS9I6+FATt7qsONi3ZTwKkxYoPPRJR5v0XF7P1gapaOPJ3tXY/6kbChr
RgHvk4QAfskp/BNYCfaCZjYtdhuMvsBxMONQUoZkiJ6g4R16WdajTr2z7zmtjF1K
XGQMM/t9NYbgraeW+N6aw1GOAyZhPw6Y/sSsEXVcE+rwTFyHkw45j1BYDYb4Vm5m
zHLwS0MZohJLhmAXrIJW5irHyW/I7seVcU1l7KtSP64JoMnmIRfhQZnCQBafLWGt
NWRcP+kbAIwNpod2Lw0+JKAOl9sa7XZohwWZvvIVoIj+qdyBuz2+IsL4341p7ikq
4t3Mr6C60MBzqi5Cx4mQikyxAsMPZ7hEtX1Y88+sqYGRcFPtlZfYFaUKTKmw+vZe
WJgx3WxGJeRpWMeaz3rnWL/JRK0spqGEboWAPQzz2TLy2pOM/RaEnMWykLa8Mvbx
w3U+Uo+bLIVd6lf4PtsTbU3NmDebPM8r0yBf7kMY4HtHjDlqvcrcMTF82R2zLZDr
fF+R3IdOYqfk6hdiQBLK7Xgu/g0sH5IFtx+sUAr+1zksT+ODXkZB1wul
=+zKf
-----END PGP PUBLIC KEY BLOCK-----
```

D.1.4. Ports Management Team Secretary <portmgr-secretary@FreeBSD.org>

```
pub   rsa2048/D8294EC3BBC4D7D5 2012-07-24 [SC]
      Key fingerprint = FB37 45C8 6F15 E8ED AC81  32FC D829 4EC3 BBC4 D7D5
uid                          FreeBSD Ports Management Team Secretary <portmgr-
secretary@FreeBSD.org>
sub   rsa2048/5CC117965F65CFE7 2012-07-24 [E]
```

-----BEGIN PGP PUBLIC KEY BLOCK-----

mQENBFAOzqYBCACYd+KGv0/DduIRpSEKWZG2yfDILStzWfdaQMD+8zdWihB0x7dd
JDBUpV0o0Ixzt9mvu5CHybx+9lOHeFRhZshFXc+bIJOPyi+JrSs100o7Lo6jg6+c
Si2vME0ixG4x9YjCi8DisXIGJ1kZiDXhmVWwCvL+vLInpeXrtJnK8yFkmszCOr4Y
Q3GXuvdU0BF2tL/Wo/eCbSf+3U9syopVS2L2wKcP76bbYU0io035Y503rJEK6R5G
TchwYvYjSXuhv4ec7N1/j3thrMC9GNpoqjVninTynOk2kn+YZuMpO3c6b/pfoNcq
MxoizGlTu8VT4OO/SF1y52OkKjpAsENbFaNTABEBAAG0R0ZyZWVCU0QgUG9ydHMg
TWFuYWdlbWVudCBUZWFtIFNlY3JldGFyeSA8cG9ydG1nci1zZWNyZXRhcnlARnJl
ZUJTRC5vcmc+iQE4BBMBAgAiBQJQDs6mAhsDBgsJCAcDAgYVCAIJCgsEFgIDAQIe
AQIXgAAKCRDYKU7Du8TX1QW2B/0coHe8utbTfGGKpeM4BY9IyC+PFgkE58Hq50o8d
shoB9gfommcUaK9PNwJPxTEJNlwiKPZy+VoKs/+dO8gahovchbRdSyP1ejn3CFy+
H8pol0hDDU4n7Ldc50q54GLuZijdcJZqlgOloZqWOYtXFklKPZjdUvYN8KHAntgf
u361rwM4DZ40HngYY9fdGc4SbXurGA5m+vLAURLzPv+QRQqHfaI1DZF6gzMgY49x
qS1JBF4kPoicpgvs3o6CuX8MD9ewGFSAMM3EdzV6ZdC8pnpXC8+8Q+p6FjNqmtjk
GpW39Zq/p8SJVglRortCH6qWLe7dW7TaFYov7gF1V/DYwDN5iEYEEBECAAYFAlN2
WksACgkQtzkaJjSHbFtuMwCg0MXdQTcGMMOma7LC3L5b4MEoZ+wAn0WyUHpHwHnn
pn2oYDlfAbwTloWIiQEcBBABAgAGBQJQDuVrAAoJENk3EJekc8mQ3KwIAImNDMXA
F8ajPwCZFpM6KDi3F/jpwyBPISGY1oWuYPEi1zN94k5jS90aZb3W8Y8x4JTh35Ew
b6XODi3uGLSLCmnlqu2a80yPfXf5IuWmIQdFNQxvosj9UHrg+icZGFmm+f0hPJxM
TsZREv3AvivQfnb/N3xIICxW4SjKSYXQcq4hr4ObhUx7GKnjayq+ofU2cRlujr87
uOH0fO3xhOJG4+cX5mI1HGK38k0Csc1zqYa/66Qe5dnIZz+sNXpEPMLAHIt1a45U
B967igJdZSDFN33bPl1QWmf3aUXU3d1VttiSyHkpm4kb9KgsDkUk1IJ5nUe9OXyd
WtoqNW5afDa5N0aIRgQQEQIABgUCUA7lwwAKCRB59uBxdBRinNh2AJ41+zfsaQSR
HWvSkqOXGcP/fgOduwCfUJDT+M1eXe2udmKof/9yzGYMirKJASIEEAECAAwFAlAa
IT8FAwASdQAACgkQlxC4m8pXrXwCHAf+J7l+L7AvRpqlQcezjnjFS/zG1098qkDf
lThHZlpVnrBMJZaXdvL6LzVgiIYVWZC5CSSazW9EWFjp9VjM7FBHdWFZNMV7GAuU
t0jzx6gGXOWwi+/v/hs1P11RyDZN5hICHdPNmyZVupciDxe+sIEP9aEbVxcaiccq
zM/pFzIVIMMP5tCiA42q6Mz3h0hy6hntUKptS8Uon6sje5cDVcVlKAUj1wO2cphC
qkYlwMQfZV5J9f/hcW50DriD3cBwK8SocA2Cq5JYF8kYDL1+pXnUutGnvAHUYt87
RWvQdKmfXjzBcMFJ2LlPUB1+IFvwQ13V9R8j9B/EdLmSWQYT9qRA2okCHAQTAQoA
BgUCV1XMpwAKCRCtu/hhCjeJt2CyD/9JLe+Ck23CJkeRSF8oC+4SF0UdSAmejSzn
klPwmEClffABYd/kck01T6um+2FUcXuJZQE1nKKUNvZ8pBWwsm1RDHsyroKi/XB1
0a1Tdx/rvlU88ytbeLfUCLzoCrf6pkMQWoU6/3qS6elV0WwOlDufk+XjD1sja2wu
sshG8y+1WCA5JjP3rZdD9NVdzo5DgkotTRUfuYN1LJIN4zlDgHj7FVP7wW7+R0cZ
FoOiNsLJCA0FN8SiyU98UysjawLiIY9dTJz6XVA0DgB0TZWO3mWiDjITeKrdGcqf
PNiJhmvUKBkn07YpTPNfkoTT/p/q5ChYmu0ubGeyS1ELKjmklJ+DzynfZLzvnXYX
Ngo5ckeuqEqUNxM0J63v8lmfhDRROFveqHWdp0XMxXVmR5bMunSldg5EZsoLyQbN
+ScIPnDTAEPGrCtf0t84RQxNQeET6/WBbZfzeSeAFmpBFCdicsZ6Mjwtwjr4+ol5
n1QMTZco1NaTqf8vXwzl9wM4aYtg1OkF4z8HdHuy50CHCet4mT5eJgwZUfFvXdbM
pHXprEI0Y9OOL4aMinC1egF3dXt/0n57i6CE+E2k3UJPNvMrtp0HaDEnKZ8cfkBU
EBzkUYi5wwqntHV2JRisqoRnHdvJT7ImlHMe7WaJsifBK874PnToaKg8P6K1Tph+
FyLxULaYjYkCHAQSAQgABgUCVBg2zwAKCRDqsDxYv9xHj1klEADXYJdHC3zsdx7w
DsJsttWdykcZoOd/VUKUdN0BAU72nLV0tLn4uFjETA6MhHZVxzwIDTeLB8kqyEpc
fZnoVbqJIUJz1sJXMdOty7CwZzlZlAwmUaIfFiazJY1p398JbyYfSrVKNOpw9wCm
Db7WP9dBritwvjaLzu8HQsiztO0S/5ha/EDfTU3qocBUTjbCtGR9LqAmPE4X8+li
F2EfZMEoJd3rJWsYv2y/k6pSgC/MpQewnyr6f+JQ/781UoZB6PpxCxfu4D6xl0yd
ERBUg+FfDAWYR+KX+DGOalRlUyaSz8Nvxl8/b0Im/AQhx9afqyEZxIDpg52zt8jJ
t3wx23YP8EQGUgwF8pIrj3wFSBSG3a/cskiBNUIhChIR9hQrVPUahN/jx7DGAGxk
/Ka9qsRGYTHfSr9jjTUQ+htfeFBRDR0nkZKMo5+Wk/cAcBKVbPlBpwvnzT3fh+wL
cF3ErBbx5jp+BoFee8D6ATeUvQxMcgVbDPUkgMsy3EtKMVO10jhIoXoVV+Sg9GZ8
zMEy1tORKn0zsd2ZgXC2sRJOm5ttCSdYQ4ddbM1A9jg6tiRx4hES16GDywvkL8P2
M9+qyIfjQxjGU33f/r8zp9DyNT1VlrtwhFxtOoMdmrsbYOCTja4Xg14hKlhRac0k
GB7bj6w97p8uMrQT3PlSMtoyrRyo7bkBDQRQDs6mAQgAzNxJYpf5PrqV8pdRXkn3
6Fe45q671YtbZ2WrT7D0CVZ8Z+AZsxnP/tiY1SrM2MepCeA2xBAhKGsWBWo1aRk5
mfZOksKsiXsi2XeBVhdZlCkrOMKBTVian7I1lH59ZnNIMX0Nl0tlj3L1IjeWWNvf
ej43URV81S9EmSwpjaWboatr2A+1oJku5m7nPD9JIOckE1TzBsyhx7zIUN9w6MKr
7gFw8DCzypwUKyYgKYToVm8QlkT/L3B0fuQHWhT6ROGk4o8SC71ia5tc1TzUzGEZ
1AQO8bbnbmJLBDKveWHCoaeAkRzINzoD9wAn9z4pnilze59QtKC1cOqUksTvBSDh
6wARAQABiQEfBBgBAgAJBQJQDs6mAhsMAAoJENgpTsO7xNfVOHoH/i5VyggVdwpq
PX8YBmN5mXQziYZNQoiON8IhOsxpX4W2nXCj5m6MACV6nJDVV6wyUH8/VvDQC9nH
arCe1oaNsHXJz0HamYt5gHJ0G1bYuBcuJp/FEjLa48XFI7nXQjJHn8rlwZMjK/PW
jllw2WZiekviuzTEDH8c3YStGJSa+gYe8Eyq3XJVAe2VQOhImoWgGDR3tWfgrya/
IdEFb/jmjHSG5XUfbI0vNwqlf832BqSQKPG/Zix4MmBJgvAz4R71PH8WBmbmNFjD
elxVyfz80+iMgEb9aL91MfeBNC2KB1pFmg91mQTsiq7ajwVLVJK8NplHAkdLmkBC

```
O8MgMjzGhlE=
=iw7d
-----END PGP PUBLIC KEY BLOCK-----
```

FreeBSD Glossary

This glossary contains terms and acronyms used within the FreeBSD community and documentation.

A

ACL	See Access Control List.
ACPI	See Advanced Configuration and Power Interface.
AMD	See Automatic Mount Daemon.
AML	See ACPI Machine Language.
API	See Application Programming Interface.
APIC	See Advanced Programmable Interrupt Controller.
APM	See Advanced Power Management.
APOP	See Authenticated Post Office Protocol.
ASL	See ACPI Source Language.
ATA	See Advanced Technology Attachment.
ATM	See Asynchronous Transfer Mode.
ACPI Machine Language	Pseudocode, interpreted by a virtual machine within an ACPI-compliant operating system, providing a layer between the underlying hardware and the documented interface presented to the OS.
ACPI Source Language	The programming language AML is written in.
Access Control List	A list of permissions attached to an object, usually either a file or a network device.
Advanced Configuration and Power Interface	A specification which provides an abstraction of the interface the hardware presents to the operating system, so that the operating system should need to know nothing about the underlying hardware to make the most of it. ACPI evolves and supersedes the functionality provided previously by APM, PNPBIOS and other technologies, and provides facilities for controlling power consumption, machine suspension, device enabling and disabling, etc.
Application Programming Interface	A set of procedures, protocols and tools that specify the canonical interaction of one or more program parts; how, when and why they do work together, and what data they share or operate on.
Advanced Power Management	An API enabling the operating system to work in conjunction with the BIOS in order to achieve power management. APM has been superseded by the much more generic and powerful ACPI specification for most applications.
Advanced Programmable Interrupt Controller	
Advanced Technology Attachment	
Asynchronous Transfer Mode	

Authenticated Post Office Protocol	
Automatic Mount Daemon	A daemon that automatically mounts a filesystem when a file or directory within that filesystem is accessed.

B

BAR	See Base Address Register.
BIND	See Berkeley Internet Name Domain.
BIOS	See Basic Input/Output System.
BSD	See Berkeley Software Distribution.
Base Address Register	The registers that determine which address range a PCI device will respond to.
Basic Input/Output System	The definition of BIOS depends a bit on the context. Some people refer to it as the ROM chip with a basic set of routines to provide an interface between software and hardware. Others refer to it as the set of routines contained in the chip that help in bootstrapping the system. Some might also refer to it as the screen used to configure the bootstrapping process. The BIOS is PC-specific but other systems have something similar.
Berkeley Internet Name Domain	An implementation of the DNS protocols.
Berkeley Software Distribution	This is the name that the Computer Systems Research Group (CSRG) at The University of California at Berkeley gave to their improvements and modifications to AT&T's 32V UNIX®. FreeBSD is a descendant of the CSRG work.
Bikeshed Building	A phenomenon whereby many people will give an opinion on an uncomplicated topic, whilst a complex topic receives little or no discussion. See the FAQ for the origin of the term.

C

CD	See Carrier Detect.
CHAP	See Challenge Handshake Authentication Protocol.
CLIP	See Classical IP over ATM.
COFF	See Common Object File Format.
CPU	See Central Processing Unit.
CTS	See Clear To Send.
Carrier Detect	An RS232C signal indicating that a carrier has been detected.
Central Processing Unit	Also known as the processor. This is the brain of the computer where all calculations take place. There are a number of different architectures with different instruction sets. Among the more well-known are the Intel-x86 and derivatives, Sun SPARC, PowerPC, and Alpha.
Challenge Handshake Authentication Protocol	A method of authenticating a user, based on a secret shared between client and server.

Classical IP over ATM

Clear To Send   An RS232C signal giving the remote system permission to send data.
                                       See Also Request To Send.

Common Object File Format

D

DAC   See Discretionary Access Control.

DDB   See Debugger.

DES   See Data Encryption Standard.

DHCP   See Dynamic Host Configuration Protocol.

DNS   See Domain Name System.

DSDT   See Differentiated System Description Table.

DSR   See Data Set Ready.

DTR   See Data Terminal Ready.

DVMRP   See Distance-Vector Multicast Routing Protocol.

Discretionary Access Control

Data Encryption Standard   A method of encrypting information, traditionally used as the method of en-
                                       cryption for UNIX® passwords and the crypt(3) function.

Data Set Ready   An RS232C signal sent from the modem to the computer or terminal indicat-
                                       ing a readiness to send and receive data.
                                       See Also Data Terminal Ready.

Data Terminal Ready   An RS232C signal sent from the computer or terminal to the modem indicat-
                                       ing a readiness to send and receive data.

Debugger   An interactive in-kernel facility for examining the status of a system, often
                                       used after a system has crashed to establish the events surrounding the fail-
                                       ure.

Differentiated System Descrip-   An ACPI table, supplying basic configuration information about the base sys-
tion Table   tem.

Distance-Vector Multicast Routing Protocol

Domain Name System   The system that converts humanly readable hostnames (i.e., mail.exam-
                                       ple.net) to Internet addresses and vice versa.

Dynamic Host Configuration   A protocol that dynamically assigns IP addresses to a computer (host) when
Protocol   it requests one from the server. The address assignment is called a "lease".

E

ECOFF   See Extended COFF.

ELF   See Executable and Linking Format.

ESP	See Encapsulated Security Payload.
Encapsulated Security Payload	
Executable and Linking Format	
Extended COFF	

F

FADT	See Fixed ACPI Description Table.
FAT	See File Allocation Table.
FAT16	See File Allocation Table (16-bit).
FTP	See File Transfer Protocol.
File Allocation Table	
File Allocation Table (16-bit)	
File Transfer Protocol	A member of the family of high-level protocols implemented on top of TCP which can be used to transfer files over a TCP/IP network.
Fixed ACPI Description Table	

G

GUI	See Graphical User Interface.
Giant	The name of a mutual exclusion mechanism (a sleep mutex) that protects a large set of kernel resources. Although a simple locking mechanism was adequate in the days where a machine might have only a few dozen processes, one networking card, and certainly only one processor, in current times it is an unacceptable performance bottleneck. FreeBSD developers are actively working to replace it with locks that protect individual resources, which will allow a much greater degree of parallelism for both single-processor and multi-processor machines.
Graphical User Interface	A system where the user and computer interact with graphics.

H

HTML	See HyperText Markup Language.
HUP	See HangUp.
HangUp	
HyperText Markup Language	The markup language used to create web pages.

I

I/O	See Input/Output.
IASL	See Intel's ASL compiler.

IMAP	See Internet Message Access Protocol.
IP	See Internet Protocol.
IPFW	See IP Firewall.
IPP	See Internet Printing Protocol.
IPv4	See IP Version 4.
IPv6	See IP Version 6.
ISP	See Internet Service Provider.
IP Firewall	
IP Version 4	The IP protocol version 4, which uses 32 bits for addressing. This version is still the most widely used, but it is slowly being replaced with IPv6. See Also IP Version 6.
IP Version 6	The new IP protocol. Invented because the address space in IPv4 is running out. Uses 128 bits for addressing.
Input/Output	
Intel's ASL compiler	Intel's compiler for converting ASL into AML.
Internet Message Access Protocol	A protocol for accessing email messages on a mail server, characterised by the messages usually being kept on the server as opposed to being downloaded to the mail reader client. See Also Post Office Protocol Version 3.
Internet Printing Protocol	
Internet Protocol	The packet transmitting protocol that is the basic protocol on the Internet. Originally developed at the U.S. Department of Defense and an extremely important part of the TCP/IP stack. Without the Internet Protocol, the Internet would not have become what it is today. For more information, see RFC 791.
Internet Service Provider	A company that provides access to the Internet.

K

KAME	Japanese for "turtle", the term KAME is used in computing circles to refer to the KAME Project, who work on an implementation of IPv6.
KDC	See Key Distribution Center.
KLD	See Kernel ld(1).
KSE	See Kernel Scheduler Entities.
KVA	See Kernel Virtual Address.
Kbps	See Kilo Bits Per Second.
Kernel ld(1)	A method of dynamically loading functionality into a FreeBSD kernel without rebooting the system.
Kernel Scheduler Entities	A kernel-supported threading system. See the project home page for further details.

Kernel Virtual Address

Key Distribution Center

Kilo Bits Per Second	Used to measure bandwidth (how much data can pass a given point at a specified amount of time). Alternates to the Kilo prefix include Mega, Giga, Tera, and so forth.

L

LAN	See Local Area Network.
LOR	See Lock Order Reversal.
LPD	See Line Printer Daemon.
Line Printer Daemon	
Local Area Network	A network used on a local area, e.g. office, home, or so forth.
Lock Order Reversal	The FreeBSD kernel uses a number of resource locks to arbitrate contention for those resources. A run-time lock diagnostic system found in FreeBSD-CURRENT kernels (but removed for releases), called witness(4), detects the potential for deadlocks due to locking errors. (witness(4) is actually slightly conservative, so it is possible to get false positives.) A true positive report indicates that "if you were unlucky, a deadlock would have happened here".
	True positive LORs tend to get fixed quickly, so check http://lists.Free-BSD.org/mailman/listinfo/freebsd-current and the LORs Seen page before posting to the mailing lists.

M

MAC	See Mandatory Access Control.
MADT	See Multiple APIC Description Table.
MFC	See Merge From Current.
MFH	See Merge From Head.
MFP4	See Merge From Perforce.
MFS	See Merge From Stable.
MIT	See Massachusetts Institute of Technology.
MLS	See Multi-Level Security.
MOTD	See Message Of The Day.
MTA	See Mail Transfer Agent.
MUA	See Mail User Agent.
Mail Transfer Agent	An application used to transfer email. An MTA has traditionally been part of the BSD base system. Today Sendmail is included in the base system, but there are many other MTAs, such as postfix, qmail and Exim.
Mail User Agent	An application used by users to display and write email.

Mandatory Access Control

Massachusetts Institute of Technology

Merge From Current

To merge functionality or a patch from the -CURRENT branch to another, most often -STABLE.

Merge From Head

To merge functionality or a patch from a repository HEAD to an earlier branch.

Merge From Perforce

To merge functionality or a patch from the Perforce repository to the -CURRENT branch.
See Also Perforce.

Merge From Stable

In the normal course of FreeBSD development, a change will be committed to the -CURRENT branch for testing before being merged to -STABLE. On rare occasions, a change will go into -STABLE first and then be merged to -CURRENT.

This term is also used when a patch is merged from -STABLE to a security branch.
See Also Merge From Current.

Message Of The Day

A message, usually shown on login, often used to distribute information to users of the system.

Multi-Level Security

Multiple APIC Description Table

N

NAT

See Network Address Translation.

NDISulator

See Project Evil.

NFS

See Network File System.

NTFS

See New Technology File System.

NTP

See Network Time Protocol.

Network Address Translation

A technique where IP packets are rewritten on the way through a gateway, enabling many machines behind the gateway to effectively share a single IP address.

Network File System

New Technology File System

A filesystem developed by Microsoft and available in its "New Technology" operating systems, such as Windows® 2000, Windows NT® and Windows® XP.

Network Time Protocol

A means of synchronizing clocks over a network.

O

OBE

See Overtaken By Events.

ODMR

See On-Demand Mail Relay.

OS	See Operating System.
On-Demand Mail Relay	
Operating System	A set of programs, libraries and tools that provide access to the hardware resources of a computer. Operating systems range today from simplistic designs that support only one program running at a time, accessing only one device to fully multi-user, multi-tasking and multi-process systems that can serve thousands of users simultaneously, each of them running dozens of different applications.
Overtaken By Events	Indicates a suggested change (such as a Problem Report or a feature request) which is no longer relevant or applicable due to such things as later changes to FreeBSD, changes in networking standards, the affected hardware having since become obsolete, and so forth.

P

p4	See Perforce.
PAE	See Physical Address Extensions.
PAM	See Pluggable Authentication Modules.
PAP	See Password Authentication Protocol.
PC	See Personal Computer.
PCNSFD	See Personal Computer Network File System Daemon.
PDF	See Portable Document Format.
PID	See Process ID.
POLA	See Principle Of Least Astonishment.
POP	See Post Office Protocol.
POP3	See Post Office Protocol Version 3.
PPD	See PostScript Printer Description.
PPP	See Point-to-Point Protocol.
PPPoA	See PPP over ATM.
PPPoE	See PPP over Ethernet.
PPP over ATM	
PPP over Ethernet	
PR	See Problem Report.
PXE	See Preboot eXecution Environment.
Password Authentication Protocol	
Perforce	A source code control product made by Perforce Software. Although not open source, its use is free of charge to open-source projects such as FreeBSD.

706

Some FreeBSD developers use a Perforce repository as a staging area for code that is considered too experimental for the -CURRENT branch.

Personal Computer

Personal Computer Network File System Daemon

Physical Address Extensions

A method of enabling access to up to 64 GB of RAM on systems which only physically have a 32-bit wide address space (and would therefore be limited to 4 GB without PAE).

Pluggable Authentication Modules

Point-to-Point Protocol

Pointy Hat

A mythical piece of headgear, much like a dunce cap, awarded to any FreeBSD committer who breaks the build, makes revision numbers go backwards, or creates any other kind of havoc in the source base. Any committer worth his or her salt will soon accumulate a large collection. The usage is (almost always?) humorous.

Portable Document Format

Post Office Protocol

See Also Post Office Protocol Version 3.

Post Office Protocol Version 3

A protocol for accessing email messages on a mail server, characterised by the messages usually being downloaded from the server to the client, as opposed to remaining on the server.
See Also Internet Message Access Protocol.

PostScript Printer Description

Preboot eXecution Environment

Principle Of Least Astonishment

As FreeBSD evolves, changes visible to the user should be kept as unsurprising as possible. For example, arbitrarily rearranging system startup variables in /etc/defaults/rc.conf violates POLA. Developers consider POLA when contemplating user-visible system changes.

Problem Report

A description of some kind of problem that has been found in either the FreeBSD source or documentation. See Writing FreeBSD Problem Reports.

Process ID

A number, unique to a particular process on a system, which identifies it and allows actions to be taken against it.

Project Evil

The working title for the NDISulator, written by Bill Paul, who named it referring to how awful it is (from a philosophical standpoint) to need to have something like this in the first place. The NDISulator is a special compatibility module to allow Microsoft Windows™ NDIS miniport network drivers to be used with FreeBSD/i386. This is usually the only way to use cards where the driver is closed-source. See src/sys/compat/ndis/subr_ndis.c.

R

RA

See Router Advertisement.

RAID

See Redundant Array of Inexpensive Disks.

RAM	See Random Access Memory.
RD	See Received Data.
RFC	See Request For Comments.
RISC	See Reduced Instruction Set Computer.
RPC	See Remote Procedure Call.
RS232C	See Recommended Standard 232C.
RTS	See Request To Send.
Random Access Memory	
Revision Control System	The *Revision Control System* (RCS) is one of the oldest software suites that implement "revision control" for plain files. It allows the storage, retrieval, archival, logging, identification and merging of multiple revisions for each file. RCS consists of many small tools that work together. It lacks some of the features found in more modern revision control systems, like Git, but it is very simple to install, configure, and start using for a small set of files. See Also Subversion.
Received Data	An RS232C pin or wire that data is received on. See Also Transmitted Data.
Recommended Standard 232C	A standard for communications between serial devices.
Reduced Instruction Set Computer	An approach to processor design where the operations the hardware can perform are simplified but made as general purpose as possible. This can lead to lower power consumption, fewer transistors and in some cases, better performance and increased code density. Examples of RISC processors include the Alpha, SPARC®, ARM® and PowerPC®.
Redundant Array of Inexpensive Disks	
Remote Procedure Call	
Request For Comments	A set of documents defining Internet standards, protocols, and so forth. See www.rfc-editor.org.
	Also used as a general term when someone has a suggested change and wants feedback.
Request To Send	An RS232C signal requesting that the remote system commences transmission of data. See Also Clear To Send.
Router Advertisement	

S

SCI	See System Control Interrupt.
SCSI	See Small Computer System Interface.
SG	See Signal Ground.
SMB	See Server Message Block.

SMP	See Symmetric MultiProcessor.
SMTP	See Simple Mail Transfer Protocol.
SMTP AUTH	See SMTP Authentication.
SSH	See Secure Shell.
STR	See Suspend To RAM.
SVN	See Subversion.
SMTP Authentication	
Server Message Block	
Signal Ground	An RS232 pin or wire that is the ground reference for the signal.
Simple Mail Transfer Protocol	
Secure Shell	
Small Computer System Interface	
Subversion	Subversion is a version control system currently used by the FreeBSD project.
Suspend To RAM	
Symmetric MultiProcessor	
System Control Interrupt	

T

TCP	See Transmission Control Protocol.
TCP/IP	See Transmission Control Protocol/Internet Protocol.
TD	See Transmitted Data.
TFTP	See Trivial FTP.
TGT	See Ticket-Granting Ticket.
TSC	See Time Stamp Counter.
Ticket-Granting Ticket	
Time Stamp Counter	A profiling counter internal to modern Pentium® processors that counts core frequency clock ticks.
Transmission Control Protocol	A protocol that sits on top of (e.g.) the IP protocol and guarantees that packets are delivered in a reliable, ordered, fashion.
Transmission Control Protocol/Internet Protocol	The term for the combination of the TCP protocol running over the IP protocol. Much of the Internet runs over TCP/IP.
Transmitted Data	An RS232C pin or wire that data is transmitted on. See Also Received Data.
Trivial FTP	

U

UDP	See User Datagram Protocol.
UFS1	See Unix File System Version 1.
UFS2	See Unix File System Version 2.
UID	See User ID.
URL	See Uniform Resource Locator.
USB	See Universal Serial Bus.
Uniform Resource Locator	A method of locating a resource, such as a document on the Internet and a means to identify that resource.
Unix File System Version 1	The original UNIX® file system, sometimes called the Berkeley Fast File System.
Unix File System Version 2	An extension to UFS1, introduced in FreeBSD 5-CURRENT. UFS2 adds 64 bit block pointers (breaking the 1T barrier), support for extended file storage and other features.
Universal Serial Bus	A hardware standard used to connect a wide variety of computer peripherals to a universal interface.
User ID	A unique number assigned to each user of a computer, by which the resources and permissions assigned to that user can be identified.
User Datagram Protocol	A simple, unreliable datagram protocol which is used for exchanging data on a TCP/IP network. UDP does not provide error checking and correction like TCP.

V

VPN	See Virtual Private Network.
Virtual Private Network	A method of using a public telecommunication such as the Internet, to provide remote access to a localized network, such as a corporate LAN.

Index

Symbols

A

B

Colophon

This book is the combined work of hundreds of contributors to "The FreeBSD Documentation Project". The text is authored in XML according to the DocBook DTD and is formatted from XML into many different presentation formats using XSLT. The printed version of this document would not be possible without Donald Knuth's TeX typesetting language, Leslie Lamport's LaTeX, or Sebastian Rahtz's JadeTeX macro package.